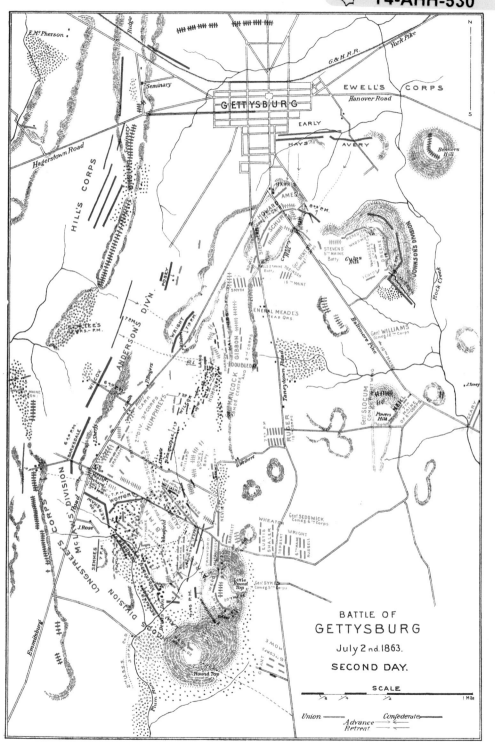

BATTLE OF
GETTYSBURG
July 2nd 1863.

SECOND DAY.

SCALE

⅛   ¼   ½   1 Mile

Union ——————   Confederate ——————
Advance ——→
Retreat ←——

NATIONAL CEMETERY MONUMENT—GETTYSBURG.

MAINE AT GETTYSBURG

REPORT

OF

MAINE COMMISSIONERS

PREPARED BY

THE EXECUTIVE COMMITTEE

STAN CLARK MILITARY BOOKS
Gettysburg, Pennsylvania

MAINE GETTYSBURG COMMISSION

The Governor of Maine, *ex officio.*
Charles Hamlin, Bvt. Brig.-Gen., A. A. G. Vols. 2d Div. 3d Corps.
Moses B. Lakeman, Colonel 3d Regt.
Elijah Walker, Colonel 4th Regt.
Clark S. Edwards, Bvt. Brig.-Gen., Colonel 5th Regt.
†Benjamin F. Harris, Bvt. Brig.-Gen., Lt.-Col. 6th Regt.
Alexander B. Sumner, Lieut.-Colonel 6th Regt.
†Selden Connor, Brig.-Gen., Lt.-Col. 7th Regt.
Thomas W. Hyde, Bvt. Brig.-Gen., Lt.-Col. 7th Regt.
John D. Beardsley, Lt.-Col. U. S. C. T., Capt. 10th Battn.
Charles W. Tilden, Bvt. Brig.-Gen., Col. 16th Regt.
*Charles B. Merrill, Lieut.-Colonel 17th Regt.
George W. Verrill, Captain 17th Regt.
*Francis E. Heath, Bvt. Brig.-Gen., Col. 19th Regt.
Charles E. Nash, Captain 19th Regt.
Joshua L. Chamberlain, Bvt. Maj.-Gen., Col. 20th Regt.
*Jacob McClure, Lt.-Col. Me. S. S., Capt. Co. D 2d U. S. S. S.
†Charles H. Smith, Bvt. Major.-Gen. U. S. A., Col. 1st Cav.
Sidney W. Thaxter, Major 1st Cav. Regt.
*James A. Hall, Bvt. Brig.-Gen., Captain 2d Batty.
Greenlief T. Stevens, Bvt. Major, Captain 5th Batty.
Edwin B. Dow, Bvt. Major, Captain 6th Batty.

EXECUTIVE COMMITTEE.

Charles Hamlin chairman, Greenlief T. Stevens secretary, Charles H. Smith†, Francis E. Heath*, Charles B. Merrill*, Sidney W. Thaxter, George W. Verrill, Charles E. Nash.

*Deceased.   †Resigned.

PREFACE

The Executive Committee of the Maine Gettysburg Commission were charged, among other duties, with preparing and publishing a report of the Commission and its work.

This volume constitutes the report so prepared by the Committee. It will be found to contain principally an account of the monuments erected by the State of Maine on the Gettysburg battlefield "to commemorate and perpetuate the conspicuous valor and heroism of Maine soldiers on that decisive battlefield of the war of the rebellion"; a full description of each monument, accompanied with half-tone pictures; the exercises attending their dedication; a statement of the part taken by each of the fifteen regiments, battalions, batteries, or other commands of Maine troops, illustrated with maps and diagrams; a list of the participants in each command, with the casualties in the same; a list of Maine Generals, and staff and other officers additional to Maine organizations; a historical sketch of each command; and a brief summary of the work of the Committee.

The different features of the report, taken as a whole, are dissimilar to those issued by other States; but the contributions thus made to history will serve to add to its value. To procure all the materials of the report has required more time and labor than was originally contemplated. The time and labor thus spent have, however, aided in setting forth the facts more fully, accurately and reliably, and in a manner justly due to the memory of those who so freely gave their lives to their country on this eventful field.

CHARLES HAMLIN,
GREENLIEF T. STEVENS,
SIDNEY W. THAXTER,
GEORGE W. VERRILL,
CHARLES E. NASH.

CONTENTS

Preface   V.

PART I.

The Battle of Gettysburg, a sketch by Brevet Brig.-Gen. Charles Hamlin   1
Four maps of the battlefield in colors, drawn by G. W. Verrill.

[Concerning each of the following Maine organizations are given the picture, description and location of its monument (and markers, if any), its part in the battle, nominal lists of participants and of casualties, a general historical sketch, and a roster of its officers.—See under GETTYSBURG in Index.]

Hall's Second Maine Battery   14
Historical Sketch, compiled by Charles Hamlin.

Sixteenth Maine Regiment   37
Diagram showing positions, by C. K. Tilden,—Incidents of the battle, by Major A. R. Small,—Historical Sketch, by Lieut. Francis Wiggin.

Stevens' Fifth Maine Battery   80
At Gettysburg, by Brevet Major G. T. Stevens and Brevet Captain E. N. Whittier, —Historical Sketch, by Brevet Major Greenlief T. Stevens.

Third Maine Regiment   126
Itinerary, by Col. Moses B. Lakeman,—Historical Sketch, compiled by the Editors.

Fourth Maine Regiment   158
Dedication of Monument and Historical Address, by Col. Elijah Walker.

Seventeenth Maine Regiment   190
Diagrams showing positions, by G. W. Verrill,—Dedication of Monument: Prayer by Rev. C. G. Holyoke, Address by Brevet Lt.-Col. Edward Moore, Poem by G. W. Verrill, Oration by Brevet Brig.-Gen. William Hobson,—Historical Sketch by Captain George W. Verrill.

Twentieth Maine Regiment   249
Diagram showing positions, by G. W. Verrill,—At Gettysburg, excerpts from Address of Lieut. S. L. Miller and from field notes by Brevet Maj.-Gen. J. L. Chamberlain,—Historical Sketch, by an Officer of the Regiment,—The Last Act, by Editors, from information furnished by Gen. Chamberlain and Gen. Spear.

Nineteenth Maine Regiment   289
Historical Sketch, by Officers of the Regiment (Brevet Brig.-Gen. Francis E. Heath, Major David E. Parsons and Lt.-Col. Joseph W. Spaulding).

Dow's Sixth Maine Battery   325
Historical Sketch, compiled by Brevet Brig.-Gen. Charles Hamlin.

Company D, Second U. S. Sharpshooters   348
Historical Sketch, by the Editors.

Fifth Maine Regiment   364
Dedication of Monument and Historical Address, by Brevet Brig.-Gen. Clark S. Edwards,—Poem by Helen S. Packard.

Sixth Maine Regiment   395
At Gettysburg, letter from Brevet Lt.-Col. Charles A. Clark,—Historical Sketch, compiled by Charles Hamlin.

Seventh Maine Regiment   430
  Historical Sketch, by Brig.-Gen. Selden Connor.
First Maine Cavalry   469
  Dedication of Monument: Address by Brevet Maj.-Gen. C. H. Smith, Poem by
  Edward P. Tobie,—Historical Sketch, by Lieut. Edward P. Tobie.
Tenth Maine Battalion   517
  At Gettysburg, and Historical Sketch of 1-10-29th Regt. by Major John M. Gould.
High Water Mark Monument   537
Additional Participating Officers, compiled by the Editors   540
Gettysburg Summaries, Maine Participants and Casualties   542

PART II.

Dedication of Monuments   545
  Order of the Day and exercises,—Gen. Chamberlain's Address,—Prayer
  by Rev. Theo. Gerrish,—Address by Gen. Charles Hamlin,—Address
  by Hon. Edwin C. Burleigh, Governor of Maine,—Address by Major
  John M. Krauth for the Battlefield Memorial Association,—Oration by
  Gen. Selden Connor,—Prayer and Benediction by Rev. G. R. Palmer.
Soldiers National Cemetery and Monument, by G. W. Verrill   582
Maine Gettysburg Commission and its Work, by Charles Hamlin,
  chairman of the Executive Committee   586
Index   597

PART I

THE BATTLE OF GETTYSBURG.

BY BREVET BRIGADIER-GENERAL CHARLES HAMLIN,

LATE ASSISTANT ADJUTANT GENERAL,

SECOND DIVISION THIRD ARMY CORPS, ARMY OF POTOMAC.

A BRIEF sketch of this battle will enable the reader to understand the operations of both Union and Confederate
troops given in detail, as they appear in the various
accounts of the battle, hereafter in this volume. Such a sketch,
indeed, is necessary for the general reader who desires a connected account, because the main purpose of this volume is to
give a particular account of the various regiments and batteries
of the State of Maine, rather than a single and connected view.

An invasion of the North was determined upon by the Confederate authorities soon after the battle of Chancellorsville in
May, 1863. It seems evident now that the causes which led
to this invasion were, that the term of many of the Union soldiers was expiring; the late defeat at Chancellorsville; and
the hope and expectation to capture Philadelphia, Baltimore,
and Washington, which might end the war through a recognition of the Confederacy by foreign governments, followed by
their intervention.

On the second of June, *Lee* began his movement north
with the withdrawal of his army from Fredericksburg. On
the eighth, *Ewell* and *Longstreet* arrived at Culpeper, to
which place *Stuart* had already advanced his cavalry. General
Hooker, on June 5th, ordered a reconnaissance below Fredericksburg, suspecting some important movement by General
Lee. On the eighth, Pleasonton's cavalry and two brigades
of infantry were ordered across the Rappahannock. On the
morning of the ninth these forces crossed the river and attacked
Stuart's cavalry at Brandy Station. Here occurred the first

successful fight by our cavalry when engaged in a large body. The First Maine Cavalry under Kilpatrick was engaged in this battle in desperate conflict and in which it bore itself with great credit. This struggle at Brandy Station ended in defeating and driving the Confederate cavalry from the field; but on the arrival of *Ewell's* infantry from Culpeper, Pleasonton withdrew his forces and recrossed the river. By the capture of *Stuart's* headquarters *Lee's* orders were found that showed his movement was north beyond the Union lines.

On the tenth, *Ewell's* corps advanced beyond the Blue Ridge, passed north through Chester Gap, and marched rapidly up the Shenandoah Valley. *Stuart's* cavalry was directed east of the Blue Ridge, to guard the passes, mask *Lee's* movements, and delay the advance of Hooker's army. On the fourteenth, *Ewell* attacked General Milroy at Winchester, who was hemmed in without definite information of the movement of *Lee's* army up the valley. Milroy attempted early in the morning of the fifteenth to steal his way out, and although discovered by the Confederates, succeeded in breaking through and retreated in haste, with heavy losses in men and material.

Hill and *Longstreet* hurried northward, the latter covering the mountain gaps in his movements. On the sixteenth, *Jenkins* with two thousand Confederate cavalry penetrated into Pennsylvania as far as Chambersburg.

June 13th, Hooker put the Union army in motion and kept his command between the enemy and Washington. Pleasonton's cavalry encountered that of *Stuart's* on the seventeenth at Aldie; and on the nineteenth at Middleburg and on the twenty-first at Upperville. On each of these fields the First Maine Regiment of Cavalry won new honors. After a severe engagement at Upperville the Confederate cavalry fell back through Ashby's Gap, and Pleasonton rejoined the infantry. *Lee* now seemed convinced that Hooker would not attack him south of the Potomac; and on the twenty-second he ordered *Ewell* to cross the river into Maryland, where he came to the support of *Jenkins*, who being reinforced advanced again to Chambersburg. Here *Rodes'* and *Johnson's* divisions joined him on the twenty-third. *Early's* division, in the meantime, moved via Gettysburg to York with instructions to destroy the railroads and secure the bridge across the Susquehanna, after which he moved north and undertook with *Rodes* and *Johnson* to take possession of Harrisburg. On the twenty-third, *Lee* ordered *Hill* and *Longstreet* across the Potomac to unite at Hagerstown, and follow *Ewell's* corps up the Cumberland valley.

When Hooker learned that *Lee* was concentrating his forces north of the Potomac, he advanced the Union army on a line parallel with that of the enemy. On the twenty-fifth and twenty-sixth, the Union army having crossed the Potomac, was massed between Harper's Ferry and Frederick City. On the twenty-sixth, *Gordon's* brigade of *Early's* division passed through the town of Gettysburg, and on the twenty-eighth *Early's* division reached York and Wrightsville. *Gordon's* brigade was prevented from crossing the Susquehanna by the destruction of the bridge at Wrightsville. On the twenty-eighth, Gen. George G. Meade was appointed to the command of the Union army, to succeed Hooker, who had asked, in the meantime, to be relieved. The immediate cause of Hooker's resignation arose from the refusal of Halleck, General-in-chief, to give Hooker the control of ten thousand men under French at Harper's Ferry. Meade at once ordered the Union forces northward, placed his left wing, consisting of the First, Third, and Eleventh corps, under Reynolds, directing him to Emmitsburg, and advanced his right wing to New Windsor. At this time the cavalry was disposed as follows: Buford on the left, Kilpatrick in front, and Gregg on the right. *Stuart* had separated himself from *Lee's* infantry in Virginia, and set off on a raid around the right of the Union army on the twenty-fourth. He crossed the Potomac on the twenty-seventh, in rear of Hooker, intending to rejoin *Lee* by marching through Maryland. On the thirtieth he encountered Kilpatrick's cavalry at Hanover, where a short and spirited struggle ensued, in which *Stuart* was forced to retreat northward, at the same time abandoning some of his trains containing captured property. On the next day, July 1st, he reached Carlisle, where he learned that *Ewell* had moved south towards

Gettysburg. He bombarded Carlisle with shell, burned the government barracks, and then moved south, via Mount Holly Gap, and did not arrive on the battlefield until the afternoon of July 2d, having been separated seven days from General *Lee*. The absence of *Stuart's* cavalry proved to be disadvantageous to General *Lee*, who did not know until the evening of the twenty-eighth, while at Chambersburg, that Hooker had crossed the Potomac into Maryland. *Lee* still believed that Hooker was in Virginia, held there in check by *Stuart*.

Lee at once began to concentrate his army, sent *Ewell* orders to retire from Carlisle and to recall his troops near Harrisburg. *Rodes'* and *Early's* divisions were ordered to join *Hill's* corps in the vicinity of Gettysburg, while *Johnson's* division with the artillery and trains approached the Chambersburg Pike via Shippensburg and Fayetteville. *Hill's* and *Ewell's* corps, on the thirtieth, advanced towards Gettysburg. *Pettigrew's* brigade, on the same day, was ordered with several wagons to Gettysburg to secure clothing and shoes.

POSITION OF THE UNION ARMY,

ON THE EVENING OF JUNE 30, 1863, TO THE SOUTH AND EAST, AND DISTANT FROM GETTYSBURG.

First Corps, Doubleday (Second and Fifth Maine Batteries and Sixteenth Maine Regiment with this Corps), Marsh Creek, 5 1-2 miles south. Second Corps, Hancock (Nineteenth Maine Regiment with this Corps), Uniontown, 20 miles south. Third Corps, Sickles (Third, Fourth, and Seventeenth Maine Regiments with this Corps), Bridgeport, 12 miles south. Fifth Corps, Sykes (Twentieth Maine Regiment with this Corps), Union Mills, 16 miles southeast. Sixth Corps, Sedgwick (Fifth, Sixth, and Seventh Maine Regiments with this Corps), Manchester, 34 miles southeast. Eleventh Corps, Howard, Emmitsburg, 10 miles south. Twelfth Corps, Slocum (Tenth Maine Battalion at Corps headquarters), Littlestown, 10 miles southeast. Buford's cavalry, two brigades, Gamble's and Devin's, at Gettysburg. Merritt's (Regular) Brigade, Mechanicstown, 18 miles south. Gregg's cavalry (First Maine Regiment with Gregg), Westminster, 34 miles southeast. Kilpatrick's cavalry, Hanover, 14 miles east.

Dow's Sixth Maine Battery was with the Fourth Brigade of the reserve artillery, at Taneytown, 12 miles south. Co. D, 2d U. S. Sharpshooters was with the Third Corps.

General Meade's orders for July 1st were, for the First and Eleventh corps to move to Gettysburg, the Third to Emmitsburg, the Second to Taneytown, the Fifth to Hanover, and the Twelfth to Two Taverns; the Sixth was left at Manchester.

POSITION OF THE CONFEDERATE ARMY,
ON THE EVENING OF JUNE 30, 1863, NORTH AND WEST, AND DISTANT FROM GETTYSBURG.

First Corps, *Longstreet's*, at Chambersburg, 25 miles northwest. Second Corps, *Ewell's:* divisions, *Early's*, near Heidlersburg, 12 miles northeast; *Rodes'*, Heidlersburg, 10 miles northeast; *Johnson's*, vicinity of Fayetteville, 21 miles northwest. Third Corps, *Hill's:* divisions, *Anderson's*, Fayetteville, 18 miles northwest; *Pender's*, near Cashtown, 10 miles northwest; *Heth's*, at Cashtown, 8 miles northwest; *Pettigrew's* brigade, at Marsh Creek, 3 1-2 miles northwest; *Stuart's* cavalry, near Dover, 21 miles northeast.

General *Lee's* orders to *Hill* and *Longstreet*, for July 1st, were, for *Heth's* division with eight batteries to occupy Gettysburg, *Pender's* division to move promptly to *Heth's* support. *Longstreet* was to follow this movement with *McLaws'* and *Hood's* divisions.

Buford's cavalry division, on the left of the Union army, was approaching Gettysburg June 30th, on the Emmitsburg Road, and encountered *Pettigrew's* brigade entering the town from the west. *Pettigrew* fell back towards Cashtown to a position on Marsh Run, where he notified *Heth*, to whose division he belonged, that Gettysburg was occupied by the Union forces. Buford's cavalry passed through the town of Gettysburg about half-past eleven o'clock in the forenoon. Halting west of Seminary ridge he went into camp, with Gamble's brigade south of the railroad to cover the approaches from Chambersburg and Hagerstown. Devin's brigade went to the north of the railroad, posting his videttes on all the roads north and northwest. Buford sent information to Reynolds of the presence of the enemy; and Reynolds, who was instructed to occupy Gettysburg, advanced the First Corps from Emmitsburg to Marsh Creek, about five and one-half miles from Gettysburg. Meade moved his right wing forward to Manchester. On the night of the thirtieth, Buford held a conference with Reynolds at Marsh Creek, and returned, during the night, to his headquarters in Gettysburg with one of Reynolds' staff, who was to report to his chief early in the morning of the next day.

At this time, *Lee* appears to have been fearful that his communications might be interrupted, and he was troubled by the naked defenses of Richmond. *Lee*, therefore, determined to draw back and make a diversion east of the South Mountain range to engage Meade's attention. Although *Lee's* plan of invasion had been thwarted, he determined to defeat Meade's army. On the other hand, Meade, having selected the general line of Pipe Creek for his defense, had thrown his left wing, preceded by Buford's cavalry, forward to Gettysburg as a mask. Both generals aimed to secure Gettysburg for the reason that it controlled the roads towards the Potomac. Its occupation by the Union army proved to be of great importance when we consider the subsequent events.

FIRST DAY.

The first day's battle was fought on the west and north of Gettysburg. It began with Buford's cavalry holding back the enemy's infantry beyond and along Willoughby Run until the arrival of the First Corps, followed by the Eleventh Corps. A severe engagement, especially along the front of the First Corps, ensued, in which Reynolds lost his life; and the Union forces, under Howard, were driven from the field after *Ewell* came from the north. Hall's Second Maine Battery opened the infantry fight as soon as it arrived on the ground and was placed in position north of the Chambersburg Pike. The principal fighting by the Confederates along the front of the First Corps was by two divisions of *Hill's* corps, who did not succeed after several attacks until reinforced by *Ewell*. It was then that the Sixteenth Maine Regiment was ordered to take position on the extreme right of the First Corps, at the Mummasburg Road, and to hold the enemy in check so that the remnant of the division might fall back; and thus, under imperative orders to stay there at all hazards, it was delivered to the enemy by relentless capture.

Stevens' Fifth Maine Battery, which occupied a position near the Lutheran Seminary, was sharply engaged during *Hill's* final assault, and aided by its rapid and severe fire in checking the enemy. The two corps of the Union army fell back through the town of Gettysburg, with heavy loss, but were not vigorously pursued by the enemy. The check given to the enemy's advance by the hard and desperate fighting of the First Corps led to results worth all the sacrifice; but to this day full credit has hardly been given to the great services rendered by that corps, familiar as we all are with the fearful losses inflicted upon it. The remnants of the two corps fell back upon Cemetery Hill, which lies to the south of the village of Gettysburg, and there awaited the arrival of the remainder of our army.

The chief features of the ground occupied by the Union army during the remainder of the battle, July 2d and 3d, may be described briefly as follows: South of Gettysburg there is a chain of hills and bluffs shaped like a fish-hook. At the east, which we will call the barb of the hook, is Culp's Hill; and turning to the west is Cemetery Hill, which we will call the shank, running north and south until it terminates near a slope in a rocky, wooded peak called Round Top, having Little Round Top as a spur. The credit of selecting this position has been equally claimed by both Hancock and Howard. At Hancock's suggestion Meade brought the army forward from Pipe Creek to secure it.

Lee, having arrived at Seminary Ridge with his troops near the close of the first day's battle, made an examination of the field and left *Ewell* to decide for himself how far he should follow up the attack upon the Union army at the east of the town at the close of the first day's battle. At this time *Ewell*, observing the strong position occupied by the Union forces upon Culp's Hill by the arrival of the Twelfth Corps under

Slocum, decided not to make an attack. Cemetery Hill at the same time was well occupied by infantry and artillery.

On the second day *Lee* determined to assume the offensive and resolved to give battle, although it seems that when he opened his campaign he had declared that it should be an offensive-defensive one. Probably his success on the first day may have induced the belief that a change from his original plan was well warranted. He was also influenced by the belief that the attacking party has the moral advantage, and in the light of his experience at Fredericksburg and Chancellorsville he thought he could succeed. *Longstreet* urged him to move around the Union left, and manœuvre Meade out of his position by threatening his communications with Washington; but he declined to accept the advice.

SECOND DAY.

On the morning of the second, *Lee's* general line was in concave order of battle, fronting the Union army, parallel to Cemetery Hill, and about a mile distant, with his left thrown to the east and through the town to a point opposite Culp's Hill. *Longstreet* was on his right, occupying Seminary Ridge, and about a mile distant from Cemetery Hill, with *Hill* in the centre and *Ewell* on the left.

The Union position was in the following order, beginning on the right: Slocum on Culp's Hill; Howard on Cemetery Hill; Newton, who succeeded Doubleday, commanding the First Corps; Hancock; and Sickles; the latter occupying the low ground between Hancock on his right and Little Round Top on his left. The Twelfth Corps had come upon the ground after the fighting of the first day. The Second Corps arrived on the morning of the second day. Graham's and Ward's brigades of the First Division of the Third Corps came upon the ground about seven o'clock on the night of the first day, followed by two brigades of the Second Division late in the night. One brigade from each division, left at Emmitsburg with artillery to guard the mountain pass, came up to Gettysburg in the forenoon of the second. The Fifth and and Sixth corps, by a hard night's march, arrived upon the ground the second day. The morning of the second day was occupied by Meade in strengthening his position and watching for *Lee's* attack. He believed that *Lee* would attack him on the right of our line, and prepared to move against *Lee* from that point. He finally decided to remain on the defensive.

Lee having perfected his plans, directed *Longstreet*, with his two divisions, then upon the field, consisting of more than 15,000 men, to attack a salient thrown out by Sickles from the general line on our left at the Emmitsburg Road. Neither army then occupied Round Top and *Longstreet* endeavored to capture it by extending his right in that direction. Sickles' thin line, of less than 10,000 men, resisted *Longstreet* for three hours along the front of the Third Corps position; the main fighting of the First Division being from 4:15 to 6:30 P. M., and of the Second Division from 6 to 8 P. M. Towards the last of it, on both fronts, other troops came to the assistance of the Third Corps. A portion of the Fifth Corps, thrown into the support of Sickles, after a desperate struggle, secured Round Top; and though *Longstreet* forced Sickles back from his salient reinforced by troops from the Second, Fifth, Sixth, and Twelfth corps, he secured only a small benefit commensurate with his loss after a long and bloody engagement lasting from 4 o'clock P. M. until it was dark and late in the night.

The centre of the Union line was occupied by the Second Corps, under Hancock, who assumed command of the left soon after Sickles was wounded. The Nineteenth Maine Regiment, under Colonel Heath, assisted in repulsing the attack of *Hill* at the close of the day, and made a charge driving the enemy beyond the Emmitsburg Road, recapturing the guns of one of our batteries which had been abandoned. The casualties of the regiment in killed and wounded exceed those of any other Maine regiment on this field.

In the Third Corps position between Round Top and the Peach Orchard on the Emmitsburg Road, the Fourth Maine Regiment, Col. Elijah Walker, was in the Devil's Den; the Seventeenth, Lieut.-Col. Charles B. Merrill, was in the Wheatfield; and the Third Maine, Col. Moses B. Lakeman, was in the angle of the salient at the Peach Orchard.

The Fourth Maine, with great sacrifice, successfully repelled a determined attempt of *Law* to gain the rear of Birney, and by counter charges was largely instrumental in holding back the overwhelming forces brought against Devil's Den until our lines were established farther back. The Seventeenth Maine, substantially alone, held the Wheatfield against successive onslaughts of thrice its numbers of the veterans of *Longstreet* until it was relieved by Hancock's troops, after more than two hours of fighting, in which it sustained a loss of one-third of its strength in killed and wounded. The Third Maine with two other regiments in the Peach Orchard defeated the fierce attacks of *Kershaw's* South Carolinians upon the south front of that position, and held the ground until the enemy gained the rear of the Orchard, nearly surrounding the small remnant of the command.

When *Longstreet*, late in the day, was forcing the Union troops back upon our main line with the help of *Hill*, who aided to dislodge the Second Division of the Third Corps from the Emmitsburg Road, the reserve artillery under Major McGilvery assisted in repelling the enemy's final attack. The Sixth Battery, under Lieut. E. B. Dow, took part in the stand then made and enabled our infantry to re-form.

On the extreme left of the Union line was the Twentieth Maine Regiment, under Col. Joshua L. Chamberlain. His regiment was on the left of the Fifth Corps troops that took possession of Little Round Top and prevented the enemy, after desperate fighting, from turning our left. After expending all his ammunition, Colonel Chamberlain, by a timely charge, drove his opponents down the west side of the hill and captured many prisoners. After dark the regiment seized and held Big Round Top.

The Seventh Maine Regiment, Lieut.-Col. Selden Connor, took position on high ground east of Rock Creek, the extreme right of the Union infantry line, where it protected our flank, but was not severely engaged after having driven the enemy's skirmishers out along its front.

Capt. Jacob McClure, Co. D, 2d U. S. Sharpshooters, was out on the skirmish line in front of the First Division of the

Third Corps, between Round Top and the Emmitsburg Road, and was under constant fire from morning until the general advance of *Longstreet* in the afternoon. When the company fell back, some of the men remained in line of battle and filled vacant places in the thin line of the division. Others came under the command of Colonel Chamberlain on Little Round Top and assisted his company under Captain Morrill, who had command of a skirmish line on the left, where both delivered a flank fire upon the enemy at a critical moment.

On the right of the Union army *Ewell* gained after dark a foothold on Culp's Hill, where a portion of the Twelfth Corps had vacated its ground when ordered near night to other parts of the Union army.

During the movement against Culp's Hill, *Early's* division was directed to carry Cemetery Hill by a charge, preceded by an artillery fire from Benner's Hill from four Confederate batteries. These batteries, however, were silenced by our batteries on Cemetery Hill and Stevens' Fifth Maine Battery in position between Cemetery and Culp's Hill. Then *Early's* infantry moved out, but were handsomely repulsed, suffering severe loss, especially from the enfilading fire on their left flank by the Fifth Maine Battery.

THIRD DAY.

At the close of the second day, *Lee* believed that he had effected a lodgment in both flanks of the Union army. Meade called a council of his corps commanders and decided to remain and hold his position, and at daylight attacked *Ewell* in force and compelled him to give up the ground that he had occupied the night before that had been left vacant by a portion of the Twelfth Corps. Then *Lee* determined to attack the centre of the Union line held by the Second Corps. He accordingly ordered *Longstreet*, who was opposed to the movement, to make this assault which is generally called "Pickett's Charge." *Lee* massed nearly one hundred and fifty guns of his artillery along Seminary Ridge and the Emmitsburg Road and opened fire against the Union line. Barely eighty guns from our side could be put in position to reply, and a tremendous artillery duel followed that lasted for two hours. Then *Pickett, Pettigrew,* and *Trimble,* under order of General *Longstreet,* with a column of about fifteen thousand men, made a charge into the centre of the Union line; but the charge failed, although some of *Pickett's* men broke through a portion of Hancock's first line, where they were met, in front and flank, by other forces of the Second Corps, including the Nineteenth Maine Regiment, and some of the First Corps, which rolled them back with great losses in killed, wounded, and prisoners. This ended the fighting along the infantry line of the Union army. The farthest point reached by the Confederates in this charge is marked by the "High-Water Mark" monument.

After the repulse of *Pickett* Kilpatrick made a charge from the extreme Union left without accomplishing much success. This was succeeded by an infantry reconnaissance composed of portions of the Fifth and Sixth corps — in the latter a part of the Fifth Maine Regiment participated — in the direction of the Peach Orchard, which resulted in the retirement of the enemy from nearly the entire front of the left of the Union lines to and beyond the Emmitsburg Road, the capture of a batch of prisoners, and the re-capture of a piece of artillery from the enemy. This successful and promising movement, however, was not followed up. There was a sharp and hard cavalry battle between Gregg, in conjunction with Custer, and *Stuart,* when the latter endeavored with his cavalry to pass around the Union right flank on the third day. Charges and counter charges were made there, and the Confederates, being defeated, withdrew from the field.

Lee spent all of the fourth day and until daylight on the fifth preparing for retreat, but in the meantime intrenching for any attack that might be made. But Meade did not attack; nor would he adventure anything. He permitted *Lee* to fall back to the Potomac without following up the advantage that he had gained. *Lee* crossed the Potomac at Williamsport and was followed some days after by Meade.

Of the forces actually engaged, the Union loss in the battle of Gettysburg was twenty-three thousand out of seventy-eight thousand ; the Confederate was twenty-three thousand out of seventy thousand, — about one-third of the entire number engaged.

In the following chapters will be found the accounts of the Maine troops at Gettysburg arranged in chronological order as follows :—

Second Maine Battery, Capt. James A. Hall.

Sixteenth Maine Regiment, Col. Charles W. Tilden.

Fifth Maine Battery, Capt. Greenlief T. Stevens.

Third Maine Regiment, Col. Moses B. Lakeman.

Fourth Maine Regiment, Col. Elijah Walker.

Seventeenth Maine Regiment, Lieut.-Col. Charles B. Merrill.

Twentieth Maine Regiment, Col. Joshua L. Chamberlain.

Nineteenth Maine Regiment, Col. Francis E. Heath.

Sixth Maine Battery, Lieut. Edwin B. Dow.

Co. D, 2d U. S. Sharpshooters, Capt. Jacob McClure.

Fifth Maine Regiment, Col. Clark S. Edwards.

Sixth Maine Regiment, Col. Hiram Burnham.

Seventh Maine Regiment, Lieut.-Col. Selden Connor.

First Maine Cavalry, Col. Charles H. Smith.

Tenth Maine Battalion, Capt. John D. Beardsley.

MONUMENT

OF

HALL'S SECOND MAINE BATTERY.

The monument, of white Hallowell granite, stands upon the spot selected for the Battery by General Reynolds on the morning of July 1st. It stands a few feet from the Chambersburg Pike on the north side. Upon one face of the shaft there is countersunk in relief the head of a volunteer artillerist. On the summit are five balls of black Addison granite; four of which rest on projecting corners of the cap, and the fifth, of larger size, crowns the central apex.

ADMEASUREMENTS.

Base: six feet, by six feet, by two feet; plinth: four feet, by four feet, by two feet two inches; die: three feet, by three feet, by six feet; cap: two feet eleven inches, by two feet eleven inches, by one foot nine inches; ball: one foot four inches diameter; four balls, each one foot diameter. Total height, thirteen feet and three inches.

INSCRIPTIONS.

HALL'S

2ND MAINE BATTERY.

1ST BRIG.

2ND DIV.

1ST CORPS.

JULY 1, 1863.

On the other side facing the Chambersburg Pike is inscribed:

CASUALTIES

2 MEN KILLED

18 WOUNDED.

Beside the monument stands a cannon mounted upon an iron carriage, which has been purchased and placed there by the survivors of the Battery.

HALL'S SECOND MAINE BATTERY,

ARTILLERY BRIGADE, FIRST ARMY CORPS,

AT THE BATTLE OF GETTYSBURG.

HALL'S Second Maine Battery went into action first of all the Maine troops. It was attached to the artillery brigade of the First Corps (a) ; and was the battery selected, in accordance with the practice of the army of the Potomac at that time, to accompany the leading division of the Corps upon its march. This arrangement brought it upon the field in the very van of the First Corps. Calef's battery of horse artillery, which had been assisting Buford, retired as the Second Maine came up to take its place ; and the latter battery at once opened upon the enemy the first cannonade after the arrival of the Union infantry and the action of General Reynolds had committed the army definitely to a battle for the possession of Gettysburg.

The men who brought the six three-inch guns of the Battery into position to join in the deepening roar of the great battle were volunteers principally from Knox County, but there were also men from Lincoln, Cumberland, York, Kennebec, Franklin, Androscoggin, and Oxford. Thirty-eight infantry-men, detailed from the Sixteenth Maine Regiment, also did duty with the Battery on this day. Captain James A. Hall, of Damariscotta, a young soldier whose conduct in other campaigns had earned his promotion from the first lieutenantcy, commanded the Battery.

General Reynolds in person selected the position for the Battery, on the right of and near the Chambersburg Pike, on the left of and several yards (b) from the deep cut of an unfin-

(a) The inscription upon the monument assigns the Second Battery to the First Brigade, Second Division, First Corps. General Hall states, however, that after January, 1863, all batteries ceased to be attached to brigades and divisions of infantry, and constituted an artillery brigade, their commanders reporting directly to corps headquarters. This rule did not apply to the reserve artillery, which was under an independent commander.

(b) In 1887 General Hall visited the field and found the position occupied by the right guns of the Battery. By a measurement made by him, the distance from it to the cut was found to be only twenty-one yards.

ished railroad which extended from Gettysburg in a direction nearly parallel with the Chambersburg Pike. The position which General Reynolds selected is the spot upon which the State of Maine has erected its monument of the Battery. It commanded the approaches along the Chambersburg Pike, and overlooked, as it does to-day, a broad and beautiful expanse of country, which rises and falls in gentle slopes of fields, pastures and forests as far as the blue South Mountain range to the west and north.

As General Reynolds and Captain Hall rode up to this position on the morning of July 1, 1863, the nearest of those slopes was already occupied by the deploying columns of Heth's division of Hill's corps, the van of Lee's army. At the same time, from a ridge to the westward, nearly twenty Confederate cannon were cannonading the ground upon which the infantry of the First Corps was forming. "Pay your attention to those guns," said General Reynolds to Captain Hall, "and draw their fire from our infantry while it is forming." And to General Wadsworth, commander of the First Division of the Corps, who rode up at that moment, he said: "Put a strong support on the right of this battery; I will look out for the left." With these words (a) General Reynolds rode away to the left, where he was soon after killed in the thick of the fight. To this position, hastily chosen amid the crash of the rapidly increasing battle, the Second Maine Battery moved up at once. It was then between 10 and 11 o'clock in the forenoon.

The Second Maine, galloping up to the position designated by General Reynolds, formed, "by piece, to the left into battery" and opened fire, enfilading the Chambersburg Pike and playing with effect upon the Confederate batteries that were annoying General Reynolds' infantry. It was a critical moment when the Battery came upon the field, and its commander had no time to examine closely the ground about him,— apparently the field extending away to his right, and covered with un-mown grass, was smooth and unbroken. Of the deep railroad cut along the right of his position he saw no sign

(a) Gen. J. A. Hall remembers these orders, which were given in his presence.

whatever; and as he naturally took position on the left of his Battery and nearer the Chambersburg Pike, he received no intimation of the existence of the cut until the Battery had been firing some time (a). He was suddenly undeceived when Lieutenant Carr reported that a body of the enemy were within twenty yards of the right gun of the Battery.

The movement which had taken place was most menacing to the Second Maine. About the time the Battery came into position, or a little before, Gen. Joseph R. Davis' Confederate brigade, of Heth's division, was also deploying on the same side of the Chambersburg Pike, fronting the Battery, but masked by an intervening ridge. Davis' brigade brought into line that morning three regiments, the 42d Mississippi on the right, 55th North Carolina on the left, and 2d Mississippi in the centre (b). These regiments advanced against Gen. Lysander Cutler's (c) brigade, of the First Division, the greater part of which General Wadsworth had stationed to the right of the Second Maine's position in compliance with General Reynolds' directions.

Cutler's troops, however, did not withstand the advance of Davis, which struck their right flank with force and compelled a large portion of the brigade to retire. This left the Battery exposed to the enemy, who could advance upon its right flank or annoy it from the shelter of the railroad cut. Captain Hall did not at first believe it possible that the enemy could be in the position described by Lieutenant Carr; but riding to the right he was convinced at once that the line of soldiers levelling their muskets at his men were the enemy. Lieutenant Ulmer, who was commanding the guns of the right section, with great coolness and judgment had anticipated the orders of Captain Hall, and, turning two pieces towards the advancing line, opened upon them with double-shotted canister. This discharge sent the Confederates tumbling back into the cut; but the Confederate skirmishers, shielding themselves

(a) Statement of Captain Hall in 1889.
(b) Official report of Confederate General J. R. Davis, Aug. 26, 1863. Confederate corps, divisions, and brigades were respectively larger than the corresponding organizations in the Union army.
(c) General Cutler was long a resident of Maine; moved west in 1857; his brigade was composed of N. Y., Penn. and Ind. regts.

behind such natural protections as the ground afforded, were able to pick off the gunners who had just repelled the battle line so gallantly. For obvious reasons a battery, though effective against troops in a body, is at the mercy of scattered skirmishers unless it is protected by an infantry support. Having no such support, the Second Battery found it necessary to retire at once, before the enemy's skirmishers should succeed in disabling it by killing men and horses. Lieutenant Ulmer was directed to take his two guns of the right section, retire with them two hundred and fifty or three hundred yards, and take position to enfilade the railroad cut, which was affording shelter to the Confederates. The other four guns were kept at work in the old position by Captain Hall, who intended to remain there until Lieutenant Ulmer could open fire from the new position. But Lieutenant Ulmer was not allowed to carry out his part of this plan. As he retired the Confederates followed in the cut ; and before he could fire a shot they charged upon him. They shot down horses and men, and he succeeded in getting his guns beyond their reach with the greatest difficulty. One gun was dragged off by hand, all the horses attached to it having been shot.

Meanwhile the other guns of the Battery were in the greatest jeopardy. The Confederate infantry were forming in the cut for another charge. Not a moment could be lost. A high fence and an enfilading fire from Confederate batteries rendered a movement into the Chambersburg Pike impracticable. The only way open for a retreat was through the field between the pike and railroad cut. The order was given at once ; and the intrepid artillery-men began the movement obediently, under a heavy fire. The Confederates shot all the horses attached to one gun, and the artillery-men were obliged to leave it temporarily (a) ; but the remainder were brought to a place of safety on the Chambersburg Pike. Captain Hall was about to return to take off his unhorsed and abandoned gun, when General Wadsworth gave him a peremptory order to lose no time in getting his battery into position on the heights near

(a) The Confederate troops were Davis' brigade. Davis was shortly after driven out of his advanced position with a large loss of prisoners, caught like mice in the railroad cut by a gallant charge of Union regiments.

the town to cover the retiring of the First Corps. So that gun remained upon the field until, later, Captain Hall with his own men and horses took it off.

The conduct of the Battery during the half hour in which it had been engaged had been conspicuously gallant. It had maintained itself against the concentrated fire of the Confederate guns massed against its position, returning their fire with such effect that several of the enemy's pieces were disabled; and had, without the assistance of infantry, repulsed one Confederate charge (a). But the little command had suffered severely. Two men had been killed outright and eighteen had been wounded. Twenty-eight horses had been killed, and Captain Hall's horse had been severely wounded under its rider. Three of the six guns had been temporarily disabled, one gun carriage and two axles being broken. Of this part of the battle General Hall has written (in 1889) as follows :—

"For one, who, under the blessings of a kind Providence, has been carried through a trying ordeal on the field of battle, to write the story which is in a limited degree the chronicle of his own acts is not agreeable to me. A generous country has given the Second Maine Battery full credit for what it performed on the field of Gettysburg July 1, 1863, while eminent soldiers, high in military renown, have been more than generous in commendation of the conduct of the company on that day. It was one of those moments when fortune seems to come to men beyond expectation, and by dealing kindly with tried humanity permits mortals to accomplish results which they could not hope for. If I should be asked if I could again take the Second Maine Battery as it was July 1, 1863, into that action, do what we then did, and get away with so little loss, I should answer, 'I do not think I could.' If repeated a thousand times I would have no hope of once being so highly favored as we were then. It was one of those rare occasions in warfare when unexpected favors were at hand, and when some invisible protection was very kind. Hence the command was rescued, while another company, in the same position and equally as well commanded, might have been destroyed, with no one at fault. I am sure that no mistakes were made by my officers and men,—not one. Every man did his full duty and far more. My Lieutenants, William N. Ulmer, of Rockland, Me., afterwards Captain of the Battery, Albert F. Thomas and Frank Carr, both of Thomaston

(a) General Hall has always regretted that the enemy's infantry could not have been kept off the flank of the Second Maine that morning. Although his Battery was overmatched three to one by the enemy's guns so far as number was concerned, he is of the opinion that the Maine gunners would have come off with the honors of the duel. Before the Confederates appeared on the right flank the Second Maine had silenced three or four of the Confederate guns and was in good condition for a long cannonade. But the Union right had been overlapped, and without infantry support the Battery could not remain.

and both now dead, with all the non-commissioned officers and men, were possessed with but one mind on that field; namely, to save the guns or die in the attempt. I have always given Ulmer great credit for his prompt, soldierly, and heroic work in meeting the first appearance of the enemy on our right.

"One ridiculous thing in some of the histories of the battle has caused me annoyance, namely: as our last gun was retiring into the pike from the second ridge to the rear, all the horses on it were killed, and that gun remained on the field in jeopardy for some time, until with a pair of horses, a sergeant, and two men I was able to take it off safely. It has been claimed by several other commands that they fired that gun with telling effect upon the enemy. As the gun while standing upon the field without horses was not moved, and was not even unlimbered, of course it was not fired and could not have been fired during that time."

It was between 11 and 12 o'clock in the forenoon when the Battery was brought to a safe position near the town on the Chambersburg Pike (a). The First Corps, until this time the only Union troops upon the field, were hard pressed; and it was to prepare for their retirement to the strong position of Cemetery Hill that General Wadsworth ordered the Second Maine to move through the town and take that position in advance. The Battery retired according to orders and took a commanding position in the old cemetery. But meanwhile General Howard with the Eleventh Corps had appeared; and the Battery was scarcely in position before an aide came from General Wadsworth saying that the front line was to be held and directing the Battery to return.

The Battery at once moved down the hill, through the streets of the town, and, taking the line of the unfinished railroad, proceeded to Seminary Ridge. The enemy's artillery were at that time enfilading this cut, but the movement was made without casualties. At Seminary Ridge the Battery received the order to move by a wood road along the ridge towards the Union right and "go into battery" on the open ground beyond. But before the movement was completed it was found that the enemy were in possession in that direction; and the Battery was forced to return to the Chambersburg

(a) In his official report of the battle Gen. Abner Doubleday, who commanded the First Corps, says: "The dispositions made by Captain Hall to meet the emergency were both able and resolute." This refers, of course, to the repulse of the charge from the railroad cut.

Pike. There it was met by Colonel Wainwright, chief of artillery of the First Corps, who, seeing that the Battery had but three guns left for work, ordered it to return to the position upon Cemetery Hill (a). Before obeying the order Captain Hall was allowed to recover the gun left in the forenoon, which had been kept from the Confederates by an opportune advance of the Union infantry soon after it had been abandoned.

On July 2d, the second day of the battle, the three effective guns of the Battery were stationed on the extreme left of the line of artillery in the cemetery. Here at 4.15 p. m. the Battery opened fire in reply to the enemy's guns, and continued in action until the latter ceased firing for the day. In this action one of the gun carriages was disabled by the force of a recoil, and the Battery was retired that night for repairs (b). During the battles of the two days it had fired six hundred and thirty-five rounds of ammunition.

The monument erected by the State of Maine stands, as has already been stated, upon the spot selected for the Battery by General Reynolds on the morning of the first day. Cut from the granite of Maine it is, both in size and design, an appropriate memorial.

In the Evergreen Cemetery, at Gettysburg, a granite tablet has been erected to mark the position of the Battery on the second day of the battle, bearing this inscription:

HALL'S

BATTERY.

2ND MAINE.

JULY 2, 1863.

(a) In retiring through the town the second time the Battery was unmolested, as the Union lines had not begun to give way extensively enough to allow the enemy to advance to the town. General Doubleday, in his history of the battle, says of the retreat of the First Corps: "I remember seeing Hall's Battery and the 6th Wisconsin Regiment halt from time to time to face the enemy and fire down the streets." Captain Hall says that some other battery must have been mistaken for his, as the Second Maine passed through the streets before the general retreat.

(b) In the afternoon of the second day Captain Hall had command of several batteries of reserve artillery. On the third day he was on duty with General Hunt, Chief of Artillery of the army of the Potomac.

OFFICIAL REPORT OF CAPT. JAMES A. HALL.

NEAR BERLIN, MD., July 16, 1863.

COLONEL: — I have the honor to submit the following as my report of the part taken by my Battery at the battle of Gettysburg, on July 1st, 2d, and 3d:—

We were in camp on the morning of July 1st at Marsh Creek, four miles from Gettysburg. At 9 A. M. marched, following the advance brigade of the First Division, First Army Corps, to the battlefield, about a half a mile south and west of town, where we were ordered into position by General Reynolds on the right of the Cashtown Road, some 400 yards beyond Seminary Hill. The enemy had previously opened a battery of six guns directly in our front at 1,300 yards distance, which they concentrated upon me as I went into position, but with very little effect.

We opened upon this battery with shot and shell at 10.45 A. M., our first six shots causing the enemy to change the position of two of his guns and place them under cover behind a barn. In twenty-five minutes from the time we opened fire a column of the enemy's infantry charged up a ravine on our right flank within sixty yards of my right piece, when they commenced shooting down my horses and wounding my men. I ordered the right and centre sections to open upon this column with canister, and kept the left firing upon the enemy's artillery. This canister fire was very effective and broke the charge of the enemy, when, just at this moment, to my surprise I saw my support falling back without any order having been given me to retire. Feeling that if the position was too advanced for infantry it was equally so for artillery, I ordered the Battery to retire by sections, although having no order to do so. The support falling back rapidly, the right section of the Battery, which I ordered to take position some seventy-five yards to the rear, to cover the retiring of the other four pieces, was charged upon by the enemy's skirmishers and four of the horses from one of the guns shot. The men of the section dragged this gun off by hand.

As the last piece of the Battery was coming away, all its horses were shot, and I was about to return for it myself, when General Wadsworth gave me a peremptory order to lose no time, but get my Battery in position near the town, on the heights, to cover the retiring of the troops.

I sent a sergeant with five men after the piece, all of whom were wounded or taken prisoners. I had got near to the position I had been ordered to take, when I received another order from General Wadsworth to bring my guns immediately back; the officer bringing the order saying he would show me the road to take, which was the railroad grading leading out from town, which was swept at the time by two of the enemy's guns from the hills beyond, through the excavations at Seminary Hill.

Having gotten on to this road, from its construction I could not turn from it on either side, and was obliged to advance 1,200 yards under this raking fire. Arriving at Seminary Hill, I found no one to show me the position I was to occupy, and placed my Battery in park under cover of the hill, and went forward to see where to take position, when I again met an aide of General Wadsworth, who ordered me to go to the right along the woods, pass over the crest and over a ravine, and there take position.

Obeying this order, I moved towards the right until met by an orderly, who informed me I was going directly into the enemy's lines, which were advancing from this direction. I halted my command and rode forward, but before reaching the described position was fired upon by the enemy's skirmishers. I then countermarched my Battery and moved to near the seminary, and was going forward to ascertain, if possible, where to go, when I met Colonel Wainwright, who informed me my abandoned gun was still on the field, and that he had refused to put the Battery into the position desired by General Wadsworth. I then took a limber and went back upon the field with one sergeant, and recovered the abandoned gun with parts of all the harness, and immediately moved back through the town, putting my only three guns which were not disabled in position, by order of General Howard, on the left of the cemetery.

On the second we opened fire in reply to the enemy's guns at 4.15 P. M., and continued in action until the enemy's artillery ceased for the day, during which time another gun was disabled by its axle breaking by the recoil, when I was relieved by a battery from the reserve artillery, and, by order of General Newton, went to the rear to repair damages, and the Battery took no further part in the engagement.

Casualties, first day, eighteen men wounded and four taken prisoners; twenty-eight horses killed and six wounded; one gun-carriage rendered useless, two axles broken. Second day, one axle broken. Fired during engagement, 635 rounds of ammunition.

Very respectfully, your obedient servant,

JAMES A. HALL,
Captain, Commanding Second Maine Battery.

COL. C. S. WAINWRIGHT,
Commanding Artillery Brigade, First Army Corps.

—Rebellion Records, Series I, Vol. xxvii, p. 359.

PARTICIPANTS.

At the battle of Gettysburg the Second Maine Battery carried the names of one hundred and fifty officers and men on its rolls, thirty-five of whom were detailed from the Sixteenth Maine Infantry, two from the 13th Mass. Infantry, and two from the 97th New York Infantry, thus leaving but one hundred and eleven of its own men. The present for duty (including three on daily duty and seven present sick) is made up from ninety-two names of the battery men proper, thirty-one from the Sixteenth Maine, two from the 13th Mass., and two from the 97th New York, a total of one hundred and twenty-seven. The six on detached service are all battery men, while the seventeen absent sick are made up of thirteen battery men and four from the Sixteenth Maine. A large portion of this detail from the Sixteenth Maine was later transferred permanently to the Fifth Maine Battery.

PRESENT FOR DUTY.

(INCLUDING THREE ON DAILY DUTY AND SEVEN PRESENT SICK.)

COMMISSIONED OFFICERS.

Captain, James A. Hall, Damariscotta.
First Lieutenant, William N. Ulmer, Rockland.
Second Lieutenant, Albert F. Thomas, Thomaston.
Second Lieutenant, Benjamin F. Carr, Thomaston.

SERGEANTS.

John Montgomery, Boothbay,	Austin Reed, Boothbay,
Asia F. Arnold, Damariscotta,	William A. Davis, Damariscotta,
Charles E. Stubbs, New Gloucester,	Anthony N. Greely, Rockland,
Thomas E. Barry, Cape Elizabeth,	Oscar Spear, Warren.

CORPORALS.

Nathan Batchelder, St. George,	George F. Thomas, Rockland,
John W. Turner, Camden,	Charles Allen, Rockland,
Asbury Staples, Cape Elizabeth,	James Ward, Philadelphia, Pa.,
Cyrus T. Parker, Windham,	Warren Ott, Camden,
Franklin Tolman, Rockland,	John Marsh, Portland.
Cyrus N. Mills, Rockland,	

MUSICIANS.

Alexander Burgess, Warren,	Ezekiel F. Demuth, Thomaston.

ARTIFICERS.

Percy Montgomery, Rockland,	Thomas G. Huntington, Richmond.

PRIVATES.

Achorn, Washington, Rockland,	Ames, Charles E., Damariscotta,
Barnard, Alvin, Waldoboro,	Barnes, George E., Camden,
Barrington, John, Rockland,	Blackington, Leland, Camden,
Brackley, Orrin, Freeman,	Bunker, George, Rockland,
Burns, George W., Vinalhaven,	Colby, James, Fox Island,
Corhaulen, Cornelius, Camden,	Crie, Reuben F., Matinicus Isle Pl.,
Davis, Alpheus S., Warren,	Davis, Harrison H., Liberty,
Derby, Samuel, Rockland,	Fales, Abner A., Thomaston,
Farrington, Jacob U., Rockland,	Fletcher, Charles D., Camden,
Gardiner, Benjamin B., Rockland,	Greely, Almond, Rockland,
Green, Alva F., Rockland,	Hall, Henry E., Matinicus Isle Pl.,
Harding, Samuel J., Camden,	Harrington, Thomas J., St. George,
Hewitt, Anson, Rockland,	Hysom, George W., Jr., Bristol,
Ingraham, Clarence, So. Thomaston,	Ingraham, Elbridge G. S., Camden,
Jameson, Charles A., Rockland,	Jones, Charles, Athens,
Jones, Samuel E., Camden,	Kellar, John M., Rockland,
Kellar, Moses J., Camden,	Kirkpatrick, Benjamin, Rockland,
Knowles, Joseph P., Rockland,	Linnekin, Alonzo D., Warren,
McCollum, James D., Warren,	McDonald, Ambrose, Portland,
Marsh, Robert N., Rockland,	Melvin, Hartwell, Camden,
Meservey, Morrill J., Camden,	Nash, John B., Warren,
Nichols, Henry, Thomaston,	Nutter, John F., Wellington,
Orbeton, William N., Camden,	Ott, William H., Camden,
Parks, George T., Damariscotta,	Pinkham, Orrin G., Strong,

Plaisted, Orin, Searsmont,
Rhines, Isaiah, Damariscotta,
Snowdeal, Joseph, South Thomaston,
Spaulding, Robert, Rockland,
Thompson, James L., Rockland,
Ulmer, Frank H., Rockland,
Vining, James, Avon,
Witham, Franklin P., Rockland,
Wood, Jerome B., Rockland.

Ray, Myron, Camden,
Ripley, Frederick, Appleton,
Spaulding, Charles H., Rockland,
Starrett, Augustus, Warren,
Thorndike, Richard N., Camden,
Ulmer, Frederick H., Rockland,
Walsh, Spencer G., Rockland,
Witham, Odbrey, Rockland,

DETACHED SIXTEENTH MAINE MEN PRESENT WITH THE BATTERY.

Allen, Lorenzo D., Canton,
Brann, Charles P., Gardiner,
Christophers, Christopher, Washburn,
Davis, Charles F., Gardiner,
Gardiner, George W., Gardiner,
Gray, Enoch P., Lovell,
Hilton, Smith, Lewiston,
Kingdon, John, Maysville,
Leavitt, James, Patten,
McCollum, John, Ellsworth,
McGrath, Charles E., Brownfield,
Murphy, Jeremiah, Augusta,
Roberts, Matthew, Lewiston,
Sawyer, John L., Passadumkeag,
Spear, Nahum, Gardiner,
Waterhouse, John W., Farmingdale.

Baker, Amos, Hartland,
Brown, William, Newcastle,
Cross, Charles E., Waterville,
Dodge, Frank, Newcastle,
Gowell, John B., Calais,
Hathorn, Charles, Veazie,
Jennings, Rollin F., Leeds,
Lane, Newman B., Augusta,
Little, Arno, Vienna,
McGinley, John, Biddeford,
McKeen, John H., Patten,
Priest, James S., Vassalboro,
Savage, William K., Gardiner,
Smith, Charles, Philadelphia, Pa.,
Turner, Henry, Rome,

ON DETACHED SERVICE.

PRIVATES: Gleason, George R., Thomaston; Oliver, Joseph, Thomaston; in Hospital Dept. Art. Brigade.

REVISED REPORT OF CASUALTIES.

SERGEANT: Thomas E. Barry, wounded July 1st.
CORPORAL: James Ward, Pennsylvania, wounded July 1st.

PRIVATES.

Knowles, Joseph P., wounded July 1st.
Orbeton, William N., wounded July 1st.
Thorndike, Richard N., wounded July 1st.
Ulmer, Frederick H., killed July 1st; reported missing or prisoner.

DETACHED MEN OF SIXTEENTH MAINE REGIMENT,
SERVING WITH THE BATTERY.

PRIVATES.

Brann, Charles P., Co. B, wounded July 1st.
Hathorn, Charles, Co. H, wounded July 1st.
McGinley, John, Co. H, wounded July 1st.
Smith, Charles, Pennsylvania, Co. D, wounded July 1st.

Note concerning the foregoing report of casualties.

Captain Hall in his official report states that eighteen men were wounded. An explanation between his report and the above will be found in the fact that those who were wounded slightly returned to duty, and their names do not thus appear in the official reports subsequently returned to the adjutant general.

HISTORICAL SKETCH OF SECOND MAINE BATTERY.

COMPILED BY CHARLES HAMLIN

FROM OFFICIAL AND OTHER SOURCES.

This battery was raised at large, and was mustered into the United States service November 30, 1861, organized as follows :

CAPTAIN: Davis Tillson, Rockland.

FIRST LIEUTENANTS.

James A. Hall, Damariscotta,   Samuel Paine, Portland.

SECOND LIEUTENANTS.

Samuel Fessenden, Portland,   William A. Perry, Rockland.

SERGEANTS.

William P. Simonton, Camden,   Albert F. Thomas, Thomaston,
William N. Ulmer, Rockland,   Benjamin F. Carr, Thomaston,
Benjamin Kirkpatrick, Rockland,   Homer Richmond, Warren,
John Montgomery, Boothbay,   Charles D. Jones, Waldoboro.

CORPORALS.

William Brown, Deer Isle,   Lewis L. Smith, Rockland,
Monroe Durgin, Thomaston,   Thomas E. Barry, Cape Elizabeth,
Charles E. Stubbs, New Gloucester,   Thatcher Burbank, Strong,
Charles H. Gloyd, Thomaston,   Charles L. Fletcher, Rockport,
Calvin P. Lincoln, Searsmont,   Asia F. Arnold, Damariscotta,
Timothy F. Goudy, Bristol,   Samuel Wier, Rockland.

MUSICIANS.

Alexander Burgess, Warren,   Ezekiel F. Demuth, Thomaston.

ARTIFICERS.

William Russell, Camden,   James E. Thorndike, Rockland,
Percy Montgomery, Rockland,   Anson Hewett, Rockland.
James H. Seely, Strong,

WAGONER: Isaac Young, Damariscotta.

BATTLES.

1862. Cross Keys, June 8; Cedar Mountain, August 9; Rappahannock Station, August 21, 22, 23; Thoroughfare Gap, August 29; Second Bull Run, August 30; Chantilly, September 1; Fredericksburg, December 13.

1863. Chancellorsville, May 1–6; Gettysburg, July 1, 2, 3.

1864. Wilderness, May 6; Spotsylvania, May 10–17; North Anna, May 24, 25; Bethesda Church, June 1, 2, 3; Cold Harbor, June 12; Petersburg, June 17–30; July 30 (550 rounds this day).

SKIRMISHES.

1862. Strasburg, June 1; Woodstock, June 2; Mount Jackson, June 4; New Market, June 5; Harrisburg, June 6; Port Republic, June 9.

The battery was organized in the winter of 1861–62 ; the first squad being mustered at Augusta for three years, November 30, 1861, and on December 14th and 28th others were mustered in ; and from that time to March 28, 1862, the ranks were being filled and the battery drilled by its captain. Later they went to Portland, where the battery remained stationed at Fort Preble until April 2d, when it left for Washington, and went into camp on Capitol Hill to prepare for active service in the field. April 22d Captain Tillson was promoted to Major of Maine Light Artillery, and assigned as chief of artillery to Ord's (afterwards Ricketts') division. He was succeeded by Captain Hall, who was promoted to the captaincy of the battery.

April 25th the battery, equipped with six 3-inch ordnance guns, took up its line of march, and four days after arrived at Manassas. From thence it went to Front Royal, Cross Keys, and Port Republic in the Shenandoah Valley. Its first engagement was at Cross Keys. On June 1st the right and left sections of the battery were sent forward to report to General Bayard, then on the road to Strasburg. On the 16th the detached portion returned to Front Royal, after which the army fell back and the battery encamped at Manassas, where it remained until the 5th of July. On that day it took up its line of march and, passing through Buckland and New Baltimore, it arrived at Warrenton on the afternoon of the next day.

On July 20th Lieutenant Fessenden was appointed aide-de-camp on the staff of General Tower. Three days after, the battery moved and went to Waterloo, where it remained encamped until August 5th, when it went to Culpeper Court House. Four days after, the battery engaged the enemy five miles beyond Culpeper, at Cedar Mountain, for about half an hour and silenced their batteries. During this battle at Cedar Mountain the battery came up gallantly to the fire, and opened upon the flank of the rebel camp near morning. The principal engagement with the enemy here was in a midnight attack August 9th. The splendid service of the battery was evidenced the next morning by the enemy's losses seen in front of its position. This was the beginning of the engagements with the enemy in the Pope campaign. On the fifteenth the battery moved from its encampment, at Cedar Mountain, and after marching eight or nine miles, went into camp on the plantation formerly owned by the rebel general Ewell. Two days later it marched to Mitchell's Station, on the Rapidan River. The bridges across this river having been destroyed, the Battery proceeded to the Rappahannock River, where August 21st it engaged the enemy all day, holding its position until the twenty-third, when it was sent to guard a bridge which was burned by our army before its retreat. August 22d the battery was reinforced by thirteen recruits. These recuits were enlisted by Lieut. W. N. Ulmer, who was sent to Maine for that purpose. They were mustered at Augusta, August 16th, and sent to the front as fast as steam could take them. One of their survivors, R. Fred Crie, speaks thus of this incident: "We were welcomed as 'raw recruits' and provided with coffee and hard tack. Then each was assigned to his future place in the ranks, and given the best possible place for a night's rest. You know by experience what the bed was and how far it was from the floor to the ceiling of our new apartment, as the only thing to be seen above us was the stars, and beneath us, mother earth. We had heard that a soldier's duty was to obey orders and that we did. Before we had taken rations the next morning, the 'Johnnies' sent their compliments over to us and we were not slow to reply; and for a few hours the artillery duel went on, our loss being two horses killed."

The battery having proceeded to Thoroughfare Gap, it engaged the enemy on the twenty-ninth, having one piece disabled. On the thirtieth it engaged the enemy on the old battle-field of Bull Run, where it took an active part. In this fight Lieut. Samuel Fessenden lost his life, two men were wounded and one missing — probably killed in action. Lieutenant Fessenden, acting as aide-de-camp to General Tower, was mortally wounded the afternoon of August 30th, having his horse killed under him at the same instant, while in the advance of his command in immediate proximity to the enemy, and leading a regiment of his brigade under a murderous fire of musketry into close action, during one of the most critical and sanguinary periods of the disastrous engagements of that day. He died September 1st at Centreville.

From an unpublished paper by Brevet Maj. A. B. Twitchell, who was at the time mentioned connected with the Fifth Maine Battery (Leppien's), we extract the following to show the desperate situation and hot work :

"The Fifth Battery on the afternoon of August 30th followed Tower's brigade towards Bald Hill and went into position some considerable distance in rear and a little to the right of the hill, and the battery opened fire leisurely to get range of the enemy's position. Very shortly we became aware of the seriousness of the engagement on our left and at Bald Hill; Tower's troops seemed to be yielding; a battery that had been in position at the hill limbered up and went to the rear, and immediately thereafter Maj. Davis Tillson, Chief of Artillery, galloped up to our battery and gave the order: 'Limber up and follow me!' and we complied in hot haste. As we moved rapidly to the front he ordered us into position at Bald Hill, a little to the front and left of Tower's troops. We succeeded in placing our guns in position and attempted to open fire, but it was an abortive attempt, as the Confederate infantry were already close upon us, firing as they advanced, shooting down our cannoneers and horses in a moment and taking possession of our guns (all but one)."

The next engagement was at Chantilly, September 1st, after which the battery was ordered to turn over its guns and horses to Capt. James Thompson, battery C, Penn. artillery, and proceed to Washington for a new outfit.

Arriving in Washington on September 11th, the battery remained in the defenses of that city until October 13th, when it crossed over into Maryland and marched to Sharpsburg. During its stay in Washington, the battery received a new supply of guns, horses, and equipments, also a few recruits. It arrived at the front during the battle of Antietam, but did not reach that battlefield in time to take part in the battle. Remaining at Sharpsburg about a week, it then moved again into Virginia, going into camp at Brook Station, November 23d, after having been on the move nearly four weeks. Here a detail of about thirty men from the Sixteenth Maine Regiment joined the battery, which by sickness and otherwise had lost a number of its men. These men proved to be of the best quality; two of whom were killed and many wounded. After a year's service with this battery the remnant of this detail was transferred permanently to the Fifth Maine Battery.

On the 9th of December it took up the line of march in the movement upon Fredericksburg under General Burnside. It took its first position on the north side of the Rappahannock River under direction of Captain De Russy, U. S. A. On the night of the eleventh it fired a few shots at the enemy, and the next day crossed the river.

On the following day, December 13th, on which the crisis of the battle of Fredericksburg took place, the battery was ordered into position at nine o'clock in the forenoon in a cornfield on the south side of the pike road, and on the left of General Gibbon's division to support its left flank, where it opened fire upon a rebel battery, sixteen hundred yards diagonally on the right flank, which was playing on it, and which soon turned its fire in another direction. As the heavy mist which hung over the battlefield cleared away, Captain Hall found he was exposed to a cross-fire from a battery of the enemy, seven hundred yards directly on his left flank, which opened with a well-directed and rapid fire of solid shot, that was very galling. The battery maintained its position nearly thirty minutes, when, by order of General Gibbon, Captain Hall sent his caissons back across the road under cover; not however until a limber chest of one of them was blown up. The guns were kept in position, firing only occasionally into the woods, until two o'clock in the afternoon, when the battery commenced shelling the woods in their front, where our infantry were about to advance. On the advance of General Gibbon's line the battery was posted within two hundred yards of the woods, into which they directed a rapid fire of shell, which was continued until Gibbon's division fell back, retiring some distance in the rear. Captain Hall now discovered a body of the enemy advancing from the woods in front of his left, upon which at a distance of two hundred yards he opened with case shot and canister, cutting down men and colors, until his last round was expended, when he was obliged to retire. On the morning of the fourteenth the Battery took a position on the extreme left of the line assigned by General Reynolds' chief of artillery. Late in the after-noon of the fifteenth it recrossed the river and took position on the heights, covering the bridge over which General Frank-lin's troops were crossing. The casualties during the battle were two men killed, fourteen wounded; twenty-five horses killed and six wounded. In this hard-fought and severe battle the survivors of this battery claim to have blown up one of the enemy's caissons and to have completely silenced the bat-tery to which it belonged. The battery occupied, as will easily be seen, a most trying position. A charge was made by the enemy against the battery across the field from the woods at the foot of the heights in front of the battery. They came on with a determination to take the battery, but in this they were mistaken, though they succeeded in shooting the horses of the left gun of the left section; but a counter charge by the infantry supporting the battery drove the enemy back and the gun was replaced in its former position. The battery expended 1,100 rounds of ammunition in this battle, which is known as the Fredericksburg campaign under Burnside.

Under cover of the darkness during Monday night, the fif-teenth, it silently recrossed the river and not long after went into temporary winter quarters at Fletcher's Chapel, where it drew a supply of horses to replace those killed in battle, and also received a detail of men from the 136th Pa. Regiment. The next movement was what is called "Burnside's mud march." The survivor before quoted says of this move: "No doubt we did our part of the growling, as we tried to keep from freezing during the storms by getting so near our camp fires as to scorch our clothes and curl our cap visors. Well, we got back into the camp and voted this move a failure."

The battery sustained an untarnished reputation for promptness, discipline, and courage during all these campaigns.

In the reorganization of the army of the Potomac under General Hooker, who had succeeded General Burnside, the battery was assigned to the Artillery Brigade of the First Corps. Col. C. S. Wainwright was chief of artillery of this corps commanded by General Reynolds.

On the 3d of May it took part in the battle of Chancellorsville, holding the extreme right of the lines of the army, and making a reconnoissance the next day with General Robinson towards Ely's Ford, where they had a short but brisk fight. After the battle it went into camp near White Oak Church.

On the 12th of June commenced the Pennsylvania campaign. Broke camp and marched northward, crossing the Potomac on the twenty-third and keeping in the advance until on the morning of July 1st it engaged the enemy about two miles beyond Gettysburg, on the westerly side of the town, in conjunction with the First Division of the First Army Corps. The march for that day had been so arranged that it was nearly two hours after it became engaged before other batteries arrived, during which time its guns were under a heavy fire of artillery, which they were gradually silencing when they were charged by the enemy's infantry in column. This charge they repulsed, but their infantry support failing them they were left with their right flank exposed to the sharpshooters who had taken cover in a ravine, and were obliged to retire, when the rebel infantry rallied, and a hand-to-hand encounter took place over two of the guns, the combatants mingling together in their struggle for the prize. The guns were all brought safely off. Later in the day, being so reduced in men and horses, and the gun carriages having been smashed, but three pieces could be manœuvred, which were the first placed in position in the graveyard on Cemetery Hill, sweeping the road leading up through the town where the enemy were advancing. On the second day they fought the enemy's artillery from this position with great success. Near night of the second day the battery, having been relieved by another one, was ordered into the reserve, where it remained through the third day.

Returning to Virginia through Maryland, following General Lee's retreat from Gettysburg, the Battery, August 2d, went into camp at Kelly's Ford, where it remained until September 16th, then marching near to Culpeper and thence to the Rapidan River. Later in the fall the battery was ordered into Camp Barry, artillery depot, Washington, where it arrived on the 8th of November.

Soon after the Gettysburg campaign Captain Hall, having been promoted to Major of Maine Light Artillery, was placed in command of Camp Barry under Gen. A. P. Howe, an artillerist of the regular army and who had commanded previously a division in the Sixth Army Corps. Lieut. W. N. Ulmer, having been promoted to Captain in the meantime, resigned November 18th and Lieut. Albert F. Thomas became the Captain of the battery. During the remainder of the year and until April 25, 1864, the battery remained at Camp Barry, recruiting and refitting for the field. Under the immediate command of Captain Thomas, seconded and aided by Major Hall, the battery was brought to a very creditable condition of drill and discipline. The battery having been assigned to the Ninth Army Corps, under General Burnside, left Camp Barry April 25, 1864, to join in the 1864 campaign of the Army of the Potomac under General Grant. On this last named day it marched to Alexandria, thence to Fairfax Court House, Bristoe Station, Warrenton Junction, and Bealeton Station, at which place it remained in camp until May 4th, when they marched to Germanna Ford, on the Rapidan River, crossing the river the next day and taking position on the south bank. May 6th it marched to the left about one mile and again went into position; on the seventh, in compliance with orders, joined the division of the Ninth Corps on the Brock Road; on the ninth, reached St. Mary's bridge on the Ny River; on the tenth and eleventh, engaged the enemy about four miles from Spotsylvania Court House; on the twelfth, participated in a severe engagement with the enemy, in which two guns were disabled, two men wounded, and one horse killed; on the thirteenth, remained in position; on the fourteenth, engaged the enemy for about three hours; on the seventeenth, erected earthworks;

on the eighteenth, again fought the enemy during the greater part of the day; on the twenty-eighth, moved in the direction of the Pamunkey, which it crossed and encamped; on the twenty-ninth, marched three miles toward the front and halted in line of battle; and on the thirtieth marched and took position on the right.

On June 1st the battery engaged the enemy about five miles south of the Pamunkey; on the second, marched two miles to the right and went into position; on the third, engaged the enemy at short intervals; on the fifth, took position in a new line of battle then forming near Cold Harbor, remaining until the twelfth when the battery marched in the direction of the White House, on the Chickahominy, crossing the James River at Wilcox Landing on the fifteenth, and on the sixteenth marched towards Petersburg, encamping within three miles of the city; on the seventeenth marched to the front and took position in the line of battle then forming in front of Petersburg; on the twentieth changed position to relieve the 27th N. Y. Battery.

The battery being relieved by the 11th Mass. on the fifth of July, moved on the sixth two miles to the rear and went into camp, remaining until the twenty-fourth, when its guns were ordered into position; and on the twenty-sixth had a short engagement with the enemy. It remained in position in front of Petersburg at this time from July 24th to the 31st. At daylight on July 30th it opened fire on the enemy's works, keeping up a brisk fire nearly all day and firing 550 rounds,—this being the occasion of the explosion of the mine. On September 17th the battery was ordered to report to Colonel Gates at City Point, Va., where it went into position in the fort on the left of the road leading to Petersburg, and where it remained until the 13th of October, when it moved about two miles to the front, occupying the outer defenses of City Point. This battery did not participate in any subsequent engagements.

During Grant's campaign Lieutenant Carr, one sergeant, and two privates were wounded at Spotsylvania; June 25th one man was killed and one wounded. Private Thomas F. Simpson was mortally wounded by a sharpshooter on June 30th. Six men were wounded and some horses were lost between June 25th and July 5th. Lieutenant Montgomery was discharged for disability June 18th, leaving the Battery with only two officers present for duty; but on June 30th Sergeant Reed was promoted and mustered Second Lieutenant. Lieutenant Perry was on the staff of General Tillson.

On the 3d of May, 1865, orders were received to march for Alexandria via Fredericksburg and Fairfax. On the thirty-first of the same month the battery was further ordered to proceed to Augusta, Maine, where it arrived on the 6th of June, and was mustered out of service June 16, 1865.

Lieut. Charles E. Stubbs was promoted Captain, succeeding Capt. Albert F. Thomas, who had resigned; and Lieut. Anthony N. Greely commanded the battery after Lee's surrender until mustered out, Captain Stubbs in the meantime being absent on leave.

Major Hall remained on duty at the artillery depot, Camp Barry, Washington, during the remainder of the war. His commission as Major bears date June 23, 1863. On September 9, 1864, he was promoted Lieutenant-Colonel, and on March 7, 1865, he was breveted Brigadier-General.

The last promotions in the battery were those of Anthony N. Greely, May 8, 1865, and Asia F. Arnold, May 24, 1865, to be First Lieutenants.

ROSTER OF SECOND MAINE BATTERY.

CAPTAINS.

Date of Commission.	Name.	Remarks.
Nov. 29, 1861,	Davis Tillson,	promoted Major and Lieut.-Col. First Regt. Maine Mtd. Artillery and Brig.-Gen'l of Vols.
June 3, 1862,	James A. Hall,	promoted Major and Lieut.-Col. and brevet Brig.-Gen'l to date March 7, 1865.
Aug. 15, 1863,	William N. Ulmer,	resigned Nov. 18, 1863.
Dec. 1, 1863,	Albert F. Thomas,	discharged Jan. 22, 1865.
Jan. 31, 1865,	Charles E. Stubbs,	mustered out June 16, 1865.

FIRST LIEUTENANTS.

Nov. 29, 1861,	James A. Hall,	promoted Captain.
Nov. 30, 1861,	Samuel Paine,	resigned March 7, 1863.
June 3, 1862,	Samuel Fessenden,	died Sept. 1, 1862, of wounds received in battle Aug. 30th.

Oct. 17, 1862,	William A. Perry,	discharged May 13, 1865.
Mar. 26, 1863,	William N. Ulmer,	promoted Captain.
Aug. 15, 1863,	Albert F. Thomas,	promoted Captain.
Dec. 1, 1863,	Benjamin F. Carr,	discharged Feb. 7, 1865.
Jan. 11, 1865,	Charles E. Stubbs,	promoted Captain.
Jan. 31, 1865,	Austin Reed,	discharged May 1, 1865.
May 8, 1865,	Anthony N. Greely,	mustered out June 16, 1865.
May 24, 1865,	Asia F. Arnold,	mustered out June 16, 1865.

SECOND LIEUTENANTS.

Nov. 30, 1861,	Samuel Fessenden,	promoted First Lieutenant.
Nov. 29, 1861,	William A. Perry,	promoted First Lieutenant.
June 3, 1862,	William N. Ulmer,	promoted First Lieutenant.
Oct. 17, 1862,	Albert F. Thomas,	promoted First Lieutenant.
March 26, 1863,	Benjamin F. Carr,	promoted First Lieutenant.
Aug. 15, 1863,	John Montgomery,	resigned July 18, 1864.
Dec. 1, 1863,	Charles E. Stubbs,	promoted First Lieutenant.
Jan. 25, 1864,	Austin Reed,	promoted First Lieutenant.
Jan. 11, 1865,	Anthony N. Greely,	promoted First Lieutenant.
Jan. 31, 1865,	Asia F. Arnold,	promoted First Lieutenant.

MONUMENT.

The monument of the Sixteenth Maine Regiment, a simple granite obelisk twenty-four feet high, stands on Seminary Ridge north of the Chambersburg Pike, on the ground where the regiment fought for nearly three hours in the afternoon before it was ordered up to the Mummasburg Road, and where it met with its principal loss in killed and wounded. Upon one face of the obelisk is the coat of arms of the State of Maine, upon another draped flags, and upon a third side the badge of the First Corps with this inscription:

16TH ME. INF'Y.
1ST BRIG. 2D. DIV.
1ST CORPS.
JULY 1ST, 1863 FOUGHT HERE
FROM 1 O'CLOCK UNTIL 4 P. M.
WHEN THE DIVISION WAS FORCED
TO RETIRE, BY COMMAND OF
GEN. ROBINSON TO COL. TILDEN
THE REGIMENT WAS MOVED TO
THE RIGHT, NEAR THE MUMMAS-
BURG ROAD, AS INDICATED BY
A MARKER THERE, WITH ORDERS
"TO HOLD THE POSITION AT
ANY COST."
JULY 2D & 3D IN POSITION WITH
THE DIVISION ON CEMETERY HILL

CASUALTIES.
KILLED   2 OFFICERS,   9 MEN
WOUNDED 8   "   54 "
CAPTURED 11   "   148 "
STRENGTH OF REGIMENT
25 OFFICERS, 250 MEN.

SIXTEENTH MAINE REGIMENT.

FIRST BRIGADE, SECOND DIVISION, FIRST ARMY CORPS,

AT THE BATTLE OF GETTYSBURG.

FROM 10 to 11.30 o'clock on the forenoon of this first day of July, while Hall's Second Maine Battery was having its perilous experience at its position north of the Chambersburg Pike, the battle was sustained by Wadsworth's division alone. Meredith's brigade, extending between the Hagerstown Road and the Chambersburg Pike, had succeeded in worsting the Confederate brigade of General Archer, which had utterly failed to establish itself on the eastern bank of Willoughby Run, capturing Archer with part of his command. North of the Chambersburg Pike the fortunes of the forenoon had been less favorable. Hall's battery had been left unsupported and in great peril by the breaking of the line which should have held back Davis' Confederate brigade. But prompt action had checked Davis and re-established the Union line, so that at 11.30 Wadsworth's men were still holding the line which they had received from Buford in the morning.

At this hour the two other divisions of the First Corps, under Generals Rowley and Robinson, arrived from Emmitsburg. General Rowley's men were distributed to strengthen the line already formed. General Robinson's division took position in reserve around the seminary, fortifying itself with hastily-dug trenches. With this division, in General Paul's brigade, was the Sixteenth Maine Regiment, under Col. Charles W. Tilden. Men and officers, the regiment numbered about two hundred and seventy-five, remaining with the colors, of one thousand strong who left Maine on the 19th of August, 1862. In the preceding campaigns of the army of the Potomac the regiment had seen arduous service; but it had never made a march so difficult as the march up to Gettysburg. From White Oak Church, in Virginia, whence it had moved

on the 12th of June, the regiment had marched by way of
Bealeton Station, Bristoe Station, and Centreville Heights to
Middletown, Md., where it was assigned to picket duty on
the afternoon of June 27th. The army was hurrying northward in pursuit of Lee. On the afternoon of the twenty-eighth
the Sixteenth was ordered on the hardest forced march they
had ever made. As the column pressed northward through
the long hours of a damp and foggy night, many of the men
became so exhausted that they would fall to the ground the
instant the word was given for a brief halt. At about 2 A. M.
of the twenty-ninth it reached Frederick City, where it rejoined
the brigade. Resuming the forced march at 5 o'clock A. M., it
pushed on all day, passing through Emmitsburg at 6 P. M., and
camped near the town. Every man knew that some great
action was pending. As they had moved northward rumors
came through every mountain gap that in the valley beyond
Lee was marching towards Harrisburg and the north. In
twenty-five hours the regiment had marched forty miles,
encumbered with all the arms and accoutrements of the soldier, and over muddy roads crowded with the columns of the
division. More fortunate than several other Maine regiments
which moved in the forced marches of the great concentration
at Gettysburg, the Sixteenth was allowed a breathing space
before plunging into battle. Encamping at Emmitsburg during the night of June 29th, it marched on the next morning
only two miles to Marsh Run on the road to Gettysburg.
There it encamped during the day and night of June 30th.

On the morning of July 1st the regiment marched towards
Gettysburg. Arriving at the seminary, which is upon a slight
ridge, the Sixteenth occupied the oak-covered campus and
there threw up breast works about west-southwest. Reynolds
had been killed and Doubleday was in charge of the field at
that front; three-fourths of a mile westward, down by the
banks of Willoughby Run, the men of Wadsworth's and
Rowley's divisions were engaged with the Confederates of
Heth's division. At the same time heavy Confederate reinforcements were moving down by the northern roads, changing
all the conditions of the battle and forcing the commander of

the First Corps to summon all his reserves to the front. About 1 o'clock P. M. the Sixteenth received the order to go into battle.

At this time the conditions of the battle had changed greatly from what they were when studied last in connection with the exploits of the Second Maine Battery. The First Corps had been reinforced by the Eleventh Corps under General Howard, who had assumed command of the field by right of seniority. But the Confederates had at the same time received still heavier reinforcements, which were appearing not only from the west-ward along the Chambersburg Pike, but also from the north. Along the Mummasburg and Harrisburg roads the heads of columns of Ewell's corps, which had been recalled in haste from Harrisburg, were approaching, threatening the First Corps line in right flank and rear. The Eleventh Corps were hurried into position between the Mummasburg Road and the Harrisburg Road to meet Ewell's men, while the First Corps continued to face Hill on the west, its line extending from the Hagerstown Road across the Chambersburg Pike to the Mum-masburg Road. The extreme right of this line was formed by Baxter's brigade of Robinson's division, which had been taken from the reserve at the seminary. Baxter had formed on the right of Cutler's men, who were fighting like heroes in nearly the same place where they had met their reverse of the morn-ing. Baxter was at once actively engaged with the right of Rodes' division of Ewell's corps. Soon it became necessary to relieve him, and Paul's brigade, which was still in reserve at the seminary, was sent. The Sixteenth, with the brigade, responded to the order at once.

The regiment moved towards the northwest, over the ridge upon which the seminary stands, and, going about a quarter of a mile, advanced on the west side of the ridge in full view of the enemy. It was about one o'clock. The regiment at once deployed, its left facing nearly west while its right was swerved to meet a fire from a Confederate battery posted on Oak Hill to the northwest. The two hundred and seventy-five officers and men of the Sixteenth extended a battle line about four hundred and fifty feet, and were at once made the target of a deadly fire from the enemy. The Colonel's horse was shot from under him, Captain Whitehouse of Company K was killed instantly, Captain Waldron of Company I was wounded, and the rank and file suffered severely. For three hours, as nearly as hours could be measured in such a conflict (a), this battle was maintained with the superior forces which the Confederate General Rodes launched against this portion of the First Corps line. Finally a bayonet charge, gallantly participated in by the Sixteenth, cleared the Confederates from the immediate front of this part of the line.

This success was merely incidental and temporary, however. The battle of the afternoon had been going sadly against the 16,500 men of the First and Eleventh corps, who were contending against at least 25,000 Confederates; and about half-past three o'clock the Eleventh Corps line was broken and swept back to the town in disorder. This fatal disaster left the rear of the First Corps line exposed; and that portion of it north of the Chambersburg Pike was in immediate jeopardy. Paul's brigade, being upon the extreme right of this line, was most exposed to the overwhelming assaults launched by Ewell upon the staggering remnant of the First Corps.

Already the First Corps had prolonged its gallant resistance beyond the limit of prudence; and it could be saved from destruction only by heroic sacrifices. It fell to the lot of the Sixteenth Maine to make one of these sacrifices. In the last moments of the defense an aide of General Robinson rode up to the regiment bearing an order for it to move to the right along the ridge and take position by the Mummasburg Road. Immediately General Robinson himself rode up and repeated the order. The Sixteenth Maine was to advance alone when brigades and divisions, even two army corps, were retiring! Colonel Tilden stated to General Robinson the strength of the enemy and expressed the opinion, which was the opinion of every beholder, that it would be impossible to hold the position. "Take the position and hold it at any cost," was the answer of

---

(a) This is the length of time recorded on the monument. It corresponds with General Tilden's recollection. Maj. S. C. Belcher judged the time to be two hours and a half. The reports of general officers show that neither of these estimates is far out of the way.

General Robinson (a). "You know what that means," was the comment of the Maine Colonel as he turned to his brother officers and gave the command to move forward.

It was at the crisis of this battle of July 1st when the Sixteenth Maine advanced. The lines of the First Corps, until now held with desperate tenacity, were crumbling before the crushing weight of superior numbers. Brigades were shrinking into regiments and regiments were withering into companies. It was an hour when bands of brave men did heroic things which have been obscured in history by the turmoils and confusion of the general agony of the army (b).

MARKER OF SIXTEENTH MAINE REGIMENT.

A massive granite marker, designating the final position of the Sixteenth Maine Regiment, stands near the Mummasburg Road and bears the following inscription:

POSITION HELD JULY 1, 1863,
AT 4 O'CLOCK P. M., BY THE
16TH MAINE INFANTRY,
1ST BRIG. 2ND DIV. 1ST CORPS,
WHILE THE REST OF THE DIVISION WAS
RETIRING, THE REGIMENT HAVING MOVED
FROM THE POSITION AT THE LEFT WHERE
ITS MONUMENT STANDS, UNDER ORDERS
TO HOLD THIS POSITION AT ANY COST.
IT LOST ON THIS FIELD,
KILLED 11, WOUNDED 62, CAPTURED 159
OUT OF 275 ENGAGED.

(a)   The exact expression of General Robinson in giving this remarkable order was "at any cost," as is well remembered by General Tilden, who received it.

(b)   General Paul, commander of the brigade, was shot through both eyes, so no adequate report of the part of his brigade was ever made. Neither the division commander nor the corps commander mentioned this action of the Sixteenth.

It was about four o'clock in the afternoon when the Sixteenth Maine was ordered to advance (a). It obeyed at once, and took position in line of battle facing the Mummasburg Road. On the left and rear of its position the long lines of Hill's brigades, so often repulsed during the day, were advancing for their final and successful effort, reinforced by the fresh one of Ramseur. And as the soldiers of the Sixteenth anxiously scanned the low ground which stretches for a mile north and east of the Mummasburg Road, they saw a heavy column of Ewell's infantry move across their front to deploy against them. But when they turned from the spectacle of the hosts advancing against them and looked anxiously to the rear, whence support and encouragement should be expected, they saw only the retiring columns of their companions in arms. It is remembered to the lasting glory of the officers and enlisted men of the Sixteenth that in this bitter moment not one of them wavered. The two Confederate lines were approaching steadily, that from the west cutting off their line of retreat, that from the north and east about to strike them in front. The volleys of the little regiment detained Ewell's line not long. In a short time, perhaps twenty minutes — no one measured time then—the enemy were upon them in irresistible force. As Ewell's line came within close range, the regiment retired gradually along the ridge until it reached the railroad cut and grade.

In this last stand the Sixteenth's forlorn hope ended with a deed worthy of remembrance among the gallant deeds crowded so thickly into this day of battle. The two long lines of gray were closing upon the handful of men from Maine. The annihilation of the regiment as an organization seemed inevitable and immediate. Yet in that moment of the most trying experience that can come to any soldiers, the men of the Sixteenth performed an act which may convey to this generation some of the spirit animating the volunteers who repelled Lee's invasion of 1863. The two flags of the regiment, the stars and stripes

(a) General Robinson says in his report that his division withdrew about five o'clock. General Meade, in his report, says that General Howard, who commanded the field in the afternoon, gave the order for the First Corps to retire about four o'clock.

and the flag of Maine, the old pine tree on the golden shield in the field of blue, were taken from their staves, torn into pieces and secreted about the persons of the officers and men. These fragments were carried through Southern prisons and finally home to Maine, where they are still treasured as precious relics more than a quarter of a century after Gettysburg.

The two Confederate battle lines, closing together, struck the regiment simultaneously. Ewell's men appeared upon the north side of the cut and Hill's upon the south side so nearly at the same time that both lines, with levelled muskets, claimed the prisoners.

Colonel Tilden fell to Ewell's share (a). In all, twelve officers and ninety-two enlisted men, nearly the entire regiment as it had survived the day, were captured. A few men, thirty-five in all, and four officers succeeded in evading the Confederates and made their way to the rest of the army on Cemetery Hill (b). The thin lines of the weary soldiers of the First Corps had already filed off the field which they had contested so long and so gallantly, and where they had left nearly four thousand of their comrades dead or wounded. Of the two hundred and seventy-five men and officers who composed the Sixteenth Maine in the morning, less than forty represented the regiment in the ranks of the First Corps on Cemetery Hill, where it was arrayed in line of battle in the evening. This remnant of the regiment was in action July 2d under command of Capt. Daniel Marston. In the movements on this day, one officer and seven enlisted men were wounded. July 4th Major A. D. Leavitt succeeded in rejoining the regiment and it was afterwards led back to Virginia by Lieut.-Col. A. B. Farnham, who was absent sick during the battle (c).

(a) A tall skirmisher from Alabama, seeing Colonel Tilden standing with his sword drawn, drew up his musket and, at a distance of not over one hundred feet, shouted: "Throw down that sword or I will blow your brains out." Sticking his sword into the ground, Colonel Tilden passed to the rear, a prisoner. He was taken South to Libby Prison and there became one of the daring band who escaped through the famous tunnel.

(b) Thirty-six men of this Regiment, previously detailed into the Second Maine Battery, served with that battery this day.

(c) The Sixteenth Maine is among the "three hundred fighting regiments" enumerated by Fox in his statistics of Regimental Losses in the Civil War. Those were the regiments that during their term of service suffered a loss of killed in battle or died from wounds of 130 or more.

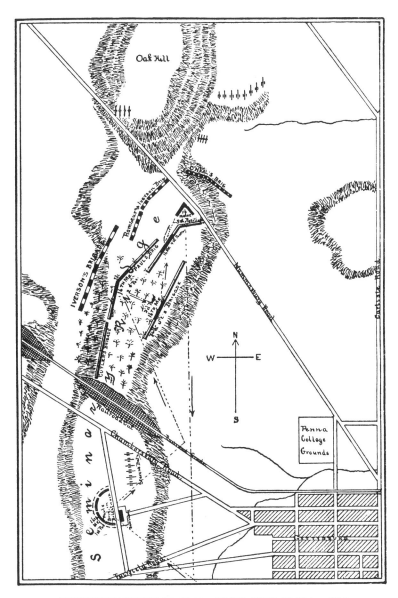

SUCCESSIVE POSITIONS OF 16TH MAINE INFY. JULY 1ST, 1863.

16TH MAINE.   UNION TROOPS.   CONFEDERATES.

MILE SCALE.

Drawn by C. K. Tilden.

INCIDENTS OF THE BATTLE

AND REMARKS THEREON

BY ADJUTANT ABNER R. SMALL,

LATE MAJOR OF THE SIXTEENTH MAINE REGIMENT.

By command of General Robinson, the First Brigade hastily threw up a redoubt of earth and fence rails, in a circular form, just in front of the seminary. About one o'clock rang out the command: "Fall in! Forward Sixteenth!" "Good-by, Adjutant, this is my last fight," cried Captain Whitehouse. He turned, repeated the command to his company, and I never saw him afterward. We double-quicked to the right, and took position behind a rail fence, in a piece of woods and nearly parallel with the Chambersburg Pike, and were at once engaged with the enemy, who were also in rear of a fence and some two hundred yards distant. Corporal Yeaton, of the color guard, was the first man killed. While cautioning his men to keep cool and aim low, Captain Waldron, of Company I, was struck, a ball entering just back of the jugular vein and penetrating to the lung. Colonel Tilden, the only mounted regimental officer in the brigade, had his horse shot from under him. Now came the order to charge bayonets. Color-sergeant Mower was the first to jump the fence, and the regiment followed with a ringing cheer, and in the face of a galling fire went double-quick, scattering the rebel line pell-mell to the rear into the woods. Our boys would have followed them, but were recalled, and moved with the division still further to the right, fighting until overpowered by numbers pressing upon our right flank.

Now two frowning war clouds were rolling upon the First Corps with thunders and lightnings. Shot and shell opened great gaps; musket balls cut like comb-teeth; and victorious rebel cheers gave irresistible impetus to their charging columns.

When our whole force was falling back it was necessary to save as much of the Second Division as possible. General Robinson rode up to Colonel Tilden. "Advance and hold that hill at any cost," was the order of the Division commander. "Boys, you know what that means," shouted Colonel Tilden.

It meant the saving of the rest of the division. It meant death to many, and a captivity worse than death to the survivors of that little band of already exhausted troops, forced by an imperative order to the foot of a sacrificial altar.

There was no thought of wavering, but with compressed lips and tense nerves these manly boys silently obeyed their loved commander. They looked to him for inspiration; they prayed to God for support, as they received the command: "About face! Forward Sixteenth!"

The regiment advanced, took position behind the stone wall, and broke the right wing to the right, parallel to the Mummasburg Road, the color company holding the apex,—the identical spot where the 88th Penn. have since placed a tablet. They held the position bravely against fearful odds.

Every moment was precious to the retiring division, more than precious to the troops going into position on Cemetery Hill. The deep, hoarse growl of the battle storm grew into a lion-like roar. The rebels fired upon us from all sides,—from behind the wall, from the fences, from the Mummasburg Road. They swarmed down upon us, they engulfed us, and swept away the last semblance of organization which marked us as a separate command. To fight longer was useless, was wicked. For this little battalion of heroes, hemmed in by thousands of rebels, there was no succor, no hope. Summoned to surrender, Colonel Tilden plunged his sword into the ground and broke it short off at the hilt, and directed the destruction of the colors. A rebel officer sprang to seize the flag, when the men, once more and for the last time, closed around the priceless emblems, and in a moment of fury rent the staves in twain and threw the pieces at the officer's feet. Eager hands from every direction seized the banners and tore them piece by piece beyond reclaim or recognition,—but now to be held doubly dear. To-day, all over Maine, can be found in albums and frames and breast-pocket-books gold stars and shreds of silk, cherished mementos of that heroic and awful hour.

And so the Sixteenth Maine was the last regiment that left the extreme front on the 1st of July, — if four officers and thirty-six men can be called a regiment.

What if the enemy took our swords, seized our guns, and confiscated our persons with whatever they bore? They left our honor untarnished and in our hearts a consciousness of duty faithfully done, too dearly testified by the bleeding and broken forms stretched upon the crimson field.

The contest was almost absurd in its great one-sided pressure. We were crushed as between the upper and nether millstones of fate, but not humiliated. General Robinson's order made of the Sixteenth Maine a forlorn hope, as it were. The irresistible force of circumstances dashed the hope to atoms, but not until after the Second Division of the First Army Corps was saved.

On the 2d of July, Ewell occupied the town, posting his line within half a mile of the cemetery. General Newton, assigned to command of the First Corps, placed it in reserve in rear of the cemetery, and within thirty minutes' march of any part of the Union line. Early in the morning the brigade was reorganized, Col. Richard Coulter commanding, with Adjt. A. R. Small detailed as acting Assistant Adjutant-General. The regiment under Captain Marston changed position from time to time as ordered, and with the brigade was ordered to the left centre of our general line late in the afternoon (a). While it was moving by the right flank past General Meade's headquarters, a rebel shell exploded in the regiment, severely wounding Lieut. Fred H. Beecher and seven enlisted men. Moving eight hundred yards, the command was given, "By the right flank! March!" and in line of battle the brigade dashed on through the smoke, over the bowlders, but only to find that the enemy had already been driven back.

In terrible suspense, on the 3d of July, moments crept by until one o'clock, when the stillness of the air was suddenly broken by a signal gun. Instantly one hundred and fifty guns were discharged as if by electricity, answered on the Union side by about one hundred more, and tons of metal parted the air, which closed with a roar, making acres of earth groan and tremble. The hills and the huge bowlders take up the sound

(a) Colonel Coulter, commanding the brigade on July 2d, speaks of this movement as occurring "about seven o'clock in the evening." *Vide* his Official Report Rebellion Records, Serial No. 43, p. 294.

and hurl it back, to add its broken tones to the long roll of sound that strikes upon ears thirty miles away. For two hours the air was filled with a horrible concordance of sounds. The air, thick with sulphurous vapor and smoke, through which came the sharp cry of agony, the hoarse command, and the screaming shell, almost suffocated those supporting the batteries. Guns are dismounted and rest their metallic weight upon quivering flesh. Caissons explode, and wheels and boxes strew the ground in every direction. Horses by the score are blown down by the terrible hurricane and lie moaning in agony almost human in its expression. One battery at our immediate front lost forty horses in twenty minutes. In the vicinity of Meade's headquarters shells exploded at the rate of sixty per minute. Solid shot would strike the ground in front, cover a battalion with sand and dirt, ricochet, and demon-like go plunging through the ranks of massed men in the rear. For a mile or more a lurid flame of fire streams out over the heads of our men in long jets, as if to follow the tons of metal thrown through the murky air, which parts to receive it and shudders as if tortured by screaming furies.

Our artillery ammunition was reduced to a few rounds, and there came a signal from Little Round Top that the enemy was rapidly massing for a charge behind the dense smoke which afforded them a screen. Notwithstanding our infantry would become more exposed if our batteries were silent, the order was issued and the firing ceased. The rebels jumped at conclusions and sent up a wild yell. We had heard it too often to lose heart or courage; but nerves were at their extreme tension as we watched the splendid lines of Confederate infantry which stretched in our front, as if for parade; and a second and yet in the rear a third debouch from the woods into view. Such a sight is given only once in a life-time, and once seen never to be forgotten. Pickett's division leads the front on the right with Pettigrew's on the left. In their rear moved Anderson's and Trimble's commands; the right was covered by Perry and Wilcox, and the left by McGowan and Thomas. Down the slope into the valley they come; and now it is our turn, and from the black muzzles of more than eighty cannon pour round shot, spherical case and canister, in an incessant torrent which cuts great swaths of living grain. Men go down by scores, but others fill the gaps, and the undaunted tide sweeps on in perfect order fairly across the Emmitsburg Road, when from behind the stone-wall the Union line pours in a shower of hissing bullets, carrying death and destruction to those brave but mistaken men. They go down like jackstraws; they lie in windrows. With a desperation born of madness, they force their way through a shower of leaden hail. Hot with passion born of war, stained and blinded with blood, the living fail to see the terrible harvest of death in their rear, and, utterly reckless of personal results, they press on and on, and with a yell of victory plant their tattered flags of rebellion upon the Union stone-wall. They turn to beckon on the next line. The next line! Where is it? Exultation is drowned in despair and defeat, for from both flanks the Union boys are giving a deadly fire, while shot and shell enfilade their rear. Thousands fall to the ground and hold up their hands in token of surrender, and others flee through the storm of bullets, shell and canister that reaches the Emmitsburg Road. A brave man can but pity the victims of such a terrible disappointment. Looking down upon all this, I could see, shorn of all wordy description, simply a square mile of tophet.

The remnant of the Sixteenth is sadly depressed. The loved colonel on his way to Richmond, to the prison-pens of the South; our valued surgeon, Alexander, wounded and a prisoner; all the line officers but four either killed, wounded, or missing, and a fearful list of casualties among the men. We thought of the brave fellows started on a pilgrimage worse than death. There is said to be a time in every man's life when he learns to cry. I believe many of us graduated in this accomplishment that night. While we were in the slough of despond, and trying to assist as skirmishers in the front line, Major Leavitt joined the regiment and assumed command at ten o'clock P. M. The heavy rain pressing down our spirits could not dampen our joy at his coming.

From "Benny" Worth, who escaped from the enemy's hands, we learned that Corporal Bradford with others rendered timely aid to many of the wounded inside the rebel lines. He found Captain Lowell, of Company D, where he fell mortally wounded, a short distance from the Mummasburg Road and near the stone-wall. Although conscious, he was speechless. He was carried to a vacant room in the seminary on the first floor. Before Bradford could find a surgeon, he with others was marched to the rear some two miles.

PARTICIPANTS.

FIELD, STAFF AND NON-COMMISSIONED STAFF.

Colonel, commanding, Charles W. Tilden, Castine.
Major, Arch D. Leavitt, Turner (commanding on and after evening of July 4th).
Acting Major, Capt. Samuel Clifford Belcher, Farmington.
Captain, Daniel Marston, Phillips, commanding July 2d-4th.
Adjutant, Abner R. Small, Waterville (Acting Assistant Adjutant-General of brigade from morning of July 2d).
Quartermaster, Isaac N. Tucker, Gardiner.
Surgeon, Charles Alexander, Farmington.
Assistant Surgeon, Joseph B. Baxter, Gorham (at brigade hospital).
Assistant Surgeon, William W. Eaton, Brunswick.
Chaplain, George Bullen, Skowhegan.
Acting Sergeant-major, Cherbury F. Lothrop, Chesterville.
Color Sergeant, Wilbur F. Mower, Greene (National flag).
Color Corporal, Sampson A. Thomas, Turner (State flag).
Quartermaster Sergeant, George W. Brown, Augusta.
Commissary Sergeant, Charles H. Parlin, Skowhegan.
Ordnance Sergeant, James P. Hamblen, Limington.
Hospital Steward, Joseph B. Dow, Farmington.

COMPANY A.

Captain, Isaac A. Pennell, New Portland.
First Lieutenant, Nathan Fowler, Skowhegan.
Second Lieutenant, Nathaniel W. Coston, Athens.

SERGEANTS.

Daniel A. Spearin, Blanchard,   James S. Parsons, Lexington,
Winslow A. Morrill, Patten.

CORPORALS.

John W. Watson, New Portland,   Aretas H. West, New Portland,
Henry E. Dexter, Vienna,   Bray Wilkins, Fairfield,
Phineas McCollar, Madison,   Clement C. Williams, New Portland.

PRIVATES.

Achorn, Jacob, Rockland,   Brackett, Hiram, Detroit,

Butts, Isaac H., New Portland,   Carvill, Benjamin, New Portland,
Chamberlain, Stephen A., Mayfield,   Clark, Henry R., Solon,
Cook, Moses W., West Waterville,   Fuller, Horatio G., New Portland,
Furbish, Jairus H., Lexington,   Goodwin, Lyman O., Detroit,
Gould, George H., Lexington,   Hackett, Alden T., Patten,
Holbrook, Abel C., Embden,   Hurd, Joel B., Harmony,
Kealiher, John D., Moose River Pl.   Knowles, Freeman T., Skowhegan,
Morrill, Hiram A., New Portland,   Murch, Albert J., Starks,
Piper, Thomas B., Blanchard,   Reed, William H., Stetson,
Thompson, John F., New Portland,   Whitcomb, Tilston T., Concord.

ON DETACHED SERVICE: Levi Berry, Embden, hospital nurse; George A. Downing, Skowhegan, ambulance corps; Edward P. Snow, Skowhegan, hospital nurse; John Young, New Portland, division wagoner.

COMPANY B.

Captain, Eleazer W. Atwood, Gardiner.
First Lieutenant, Fred H. Beecher, Gardiner.
Second Lieutenant, Melvin C. Wadsworth, Pittston.

SERGEANTS.

Leander L. Taylor, Gardiner,   Charles E. Deering, Gardiner,
Reuben M. Farrington, China,   Gustavus Moore, Gardiner.

CORPORALS.

Augustus W. McCausland, Gardiner, Charles O. Wadsworth, Gardiner.

PRIVATES.

Atkins, Alonzo C., Manchester,   Austin, Henry D., Augusta,
Britt, James, Augusta,   Brookings, Edmund J., Farmingdale,
Bruce, William W., Augusta,   Campbell, Hiram W., Manchester,
Chenery, George W., Gardiner,   Doyle, Thomas, Augusta,
Ewer, Henry A., Vassalboro,   Hooker, George H., Gardiner,
Huntington, William H., Gardiner,   Maury, Joseph, Waterville,
Palmer, Ambrose H., Winslow,   Phillips, Charles M., Augusta,
Phillips, Joseph P., Augusta,   Palmer, John, Winslow,
Pooler, Joseph, Waterville,   Plummer, Evarts P., Augusta,
Pullen, Elias, Winthrop,   Richardson, Joseph W., Turner,
Robie, John G., Litchfield,   Robinson, William H., Gardiner,
Smith, Charles D., Gardiner,   Smith, Thomas E., Gardiner,
Strong, George F., Gardiner,   Tallow, Martin, Waterville,
Thayer, Adin B., Waterville,   Webber, Samuel L., Richmond,
Welch, Joseph W., Gardiner,   Welch, Warren E., Gardiner.

MUSICIAN: Wesley Webber, Gardiner.

ON DETACHED SERVICE: Sergeant George H. Stone, Farmingdale, ambulance corps; Albert H. Norcross, Augusta, quartermaster dept.; George F. Wentworth, Gardiner, quartermaster dept.

COMPANY C.

Captain, Daniel Marston, Phillips.
First Lieutenant, Marshall S. Smith, East Livermore.
Second Lieutenant, George D. Bisbee, Peru.

SERGEANTS.

Charles M. Adams, Wilton,   William Farnham, Wilton,
Henry D. Fisk, Presque Isle,   Charles C. Small, Wilton.

CORPORALS.

Edwin C. Jones, Fayette,   William N. Yeaton, Farmington,
John M. Keene, Phillips,   Dorillus Hobbs, East Livermore,
George H. Farnham, Wilton,   Francis A. Crane, Fayette,
Robinson Fairbanks, Sharon,   Charles F. Soule, Mapleton.

PRIVATES.

Adams, George G. B., Wilton,   Bartlett, Nathan, Jr., Livermore,
Bascomb, Thomas A., Wilton,   Blackwell, William T., Jay,
Blanchard, Charles M., Phillips,   Brown, Orville, East Livermore,
Brown, Rice, Vienna,   Butterfield, Henry J., Bethel,
Butterfield, Martin, Mapleton,   Chaney, Farwell, Wilton,
Chandler, Alphonso L., Mapleton,   Davis, Colamore P., Freeman,
Grindle, Madison J., Maysville,   Hinds, David H., East Livermore,
Lufkin, Loren, Phillips,   Moulton, Joel D., Phillips,
Newton, Abraham, Canton,   Phinney, Archibald, Washburn,
Reed, Elias, Wilton,   Ridley, James, East Livermore,
Sharp, Henry A., Lyndon,   Stratton, Albion W., Washburn,
Tuttle, John, Freeman,   Witham, Sidney T., Chesterville.

MUSICIANS.

Hartson W. McKenney, Phillips,   James A. Barrows, Peru,
John B. Hall, Washburn.

ON DETACHED SERVICE: Calvin Beals, East Livermore, cattle guard; Alburn C. King, Dixfield, cattle guard; Thomas S. Hopkins, Mt. Vernon, Adjutant's clerk; Israel S. Lovell, Fremont Plantation, ambulance corps; Winthrop A. Rowe, Phillips, Orderly, regimental headquarters; John H. Stickney, Phillips, cattle guard.

COMPANY D.

Captain, Oliver H. Lowell, Gorham.
First Lieutenant, Samuel H. Plummer, Waterford.
Second Lieutenant, William H. Broughton, Portland.

SERGEANTS.

John M. Webster, Waterford,   William F. Lombard, Peru,
Joseph H. Hamilton, North Yarmouth.

CORPORALS.

Sanford M. Reed, Mexico,   Benjamin F. Fuller, Brunswick,
Laforest Kimball, Waterford,   Charles H. Putnam, Bethel.

PRIVATES.

Adams, Hosea, Stoneham,
Bailey, Edwin, Lovell,
Bancroft, Columbus, Litchfield,
Bowie, Edwin R., Portland,
Downey, John, Windsor, Nova Scotia,
Foster, John F., Gray,
Lane, Nelson A., Poland,
Plummer, Charles, Waterford,
Rider, Charles D., North Yarmouth,
Small, William H., Dixfield,
Stevens, Charles H., Waterford,
Townsend, Horatio G., Newfield,
Warren, Jonathan, Lovell,
Wood, Isaac W., Waterford.

Andrews, Henry F., Lovell,
Bean, Peter T., Bethel,
Butters, Timothy, Waterford,
Conture, Charles, Quebec,
Dunnells, Joseph, Newfield,
Gray, Samuel, Jr., Stoneham,
Park, Silas H., Dixfield,
Richards, Prentiss M., Roxbury,
Roberts, Albert W., Falmouth,
Smith, Charles, Philadelphia, Pa.,
Stone, Moody R., Waterford,
Twitchell, Fordyce P., Bethel,
Whitman, Gilbert M., Woodstock,

MUSICIANS.

George P. Hall, Bethel,
Charles A. Locke, Bethel.

Cyrus L. J. Cook, Madrid,

ON DETACHED SERVICE: Stephen Coffin, Lovell, hospital nurse; Abel H. Harriman, Lovell, regimental headquarters' guard; Edward E. Hayes, Mexico, division teamster; Erastus Hayes, Mexico, division teamster; Oliver H. McKeen, Waterford, wagoner.

COMPANY E.

Captain, William A. Stevens, Waterville.
First Lieutenant, Lincoln K. Plummer, Jefferson,
Second Lieutenant, Aubrey Leavitt, Turner.

SERGEANTS.

Edwin C. Stevens, Waterville,
Warren Seaward, Vassalboro,
Martin B. Soule, Waterville.

Jones Whitman, Turner,
Joseph G. Lamb, Leeds,

CORPORALS.

William Ballantine, Waterville,
Octavius H. Tubbs, Hebron,
Sampson A. Thomas, Turner, color bearer (State flag).

Consider F. Blaisdell, Jay,
Harrison Merchant, Weld.

PRIVATES.

Abbott, Charles, Newport,
Bradford, Luther, Turner,
Foster, William G., Pittsfield,
Harmond, George C., Turner,
Knight, Joseph F., Newport,
Lyon, Charles C., Newport,
Monk, Isaac J., Turner,
Pulcifer, Alexander W., Weld,
Tibbetts, Andrew J., Newport,
Webber, Gustavus V., Vassalboro,
Winship, Charles P., Turner,

Bates, William T., Waterville,
Fales, Curtis V., Turner,
George, Francis, Leeds,
Hoyt, Stephen A., Vassalboro,
Lyford, James M., Waterville,
Mills, Albion B., Vassalboro,
Priest, Hiram T., Vassalboro,
Thomas, David S., Carthage,
Trask, Ezra W., Belgrade,
Webber, Virgil H., Vassalboro,
Worth, Benjamin F., Vassalboro.

MUSICIAN: Benjamin W. Johnson, Jay.

ON DETACHED SERVICE: Sergeant Robert C. Brann, Vassalboro, pioneer corps; Asel A. Littlefield, Belgrade, ambulance corps; Daniel A.

Soule, Waterville, Brigade commissary dept.; Granville Richmond, Leeds, brigade commissary dept.; Mark Towle, Newport, guard at regimental headquarters; Roscoe B. Townsend, Jay, teamster Division train; Francis Worth, Vassalboro, ambulance corps; Otis Wood, Jr., Turner, wagoner.

COMPANY F.

Captain, Thomas F. Wentworth, Gorham.
First Lieutenant, George A. Deering, Saco.
Second Lieutenant, Daniel L. Warren, Standish.

SERGEANTS.

Charles W. Ross, Biddeford,	John McPhee, Gorham.

CORPORALS.

Edward L. Varney, Brunswick,	William Cannell, Gorham,
William Manchester, Jr., Standish.	

PRIVATES.

Andrews, Abram S., Gorham,	Barker, Levi D., Sweden,
Blair, Samuel, Gorham,	Brocklebank, Nathan C., Bridgton,
Burnham, George R., Hollis,	Fenderson, Benjamin, Saco,
Follett, William A., Scarboro,	Greene, Joseph, Saco,
Harding, John F., Dover, N. H.,	Harmon, Alpheus S., Standish,
Hodgdon, Abram B., Hollis,	Johnson, Albion, Gorham,
Leavitt, Frank J., Buxton,	March, John D., Bridgton,
Palmer, George, Saco,	Pierce, Charles R., Wareham, Mass.,
Powers, Albert, Windham,	Reynolds, Charles, Saco,
Rhodes, Frank, Dayton,	Seavey, Charles L., Saco,
Smith, George W., Saco,	Smith, Melville B., Hollis,
Tarbox, Frank L., Hollis,	Thorpe, David H., Saco,
Tibbetts, Sheldron H., Saco.	

MUSICIAN: Henry C. Crockett, Westbrook.

ON DETACHED SERVICE: Sergeant James P. Hamblen, Limington, ordnance sergeant; Larkin E. Barker, Bridgton, hospital guard; John M. Burnham, Parsonsfield, cattle guard; Royal L. Cleaves, Bridgton, nurse in hospital; Aaron Cross, Bridgton, guard brigade headquarters; Thomas J. Dorset, Standish, division teamster; William F. Green, Gorham, division teamster; Granville B. Jordan, Sweden, guard regimental headquarters; Lorenzo D. Libby, Windham, division teamster; William R. Loud, Denmark, ambulance corps; Eugene Savage, Anson, hospital guard; Gideon M. Tucker, Standish, wagoner.

COMPANY G.

Capt. Samuel Clifford Belcher, Farmington, acting Major;
Second Lieutenant, Isaac H. Thompson, Anson, commanding Company.

SERGEANTS.

Thomas H. B. Lenfest, Palmyra,	John H. Frain, Madison,
Byron D. Babcock, Palmyra,	Joseph R. Ricker, Chesterville,
Joseph P. Austin, Skowhegan.	

CORPORAL: Gorham Lord, Detroit.

PRIVATES.

Blunt, David F., Skowhegan,
Crocker, Sylvester, Strong,
Cross, Josiah W., Detroit,
Fairbrother, Frank, Palmyra,
Gibbs, Thomas A., Skowhegan,
Hodgkins, Jacob T., New Sharon,
Mace, John W., Farmington,
Moore, Levi M., New Sharon,
Prince, Edward M., New Sharon,
Quint, George R., Anson,
Snow, Daniel B., Skowhegan,
Williamson, Boardman, New Sharon,
Works, Lewis, New Sharon.

Chamberlain, William H., Skowhegan,
Crocker, Abner, Strong,
Emery, Luke, Anson,
Farnham, Samuel T., Palmyra,
Gleason, Sumner A., Farmington,
Lake, John W., New Vineyard,
Merrow, John E., Skowhegan,
Neal, Andrew, New Sharon,
Pullen, Harrison, Anson,
Quint, William F., Anson,
Wade, Gardner B., Farmington,
Wilson, Edward, Skowhegan,

ON DETACHED SERVICE: First Lieut. Joseph H. Malbon, Skowhegan, commanding ambulance corps; Elisha G. Baker, New Sharon, wagoner.

COMPANY H.

Captain, John D. Conley, Bangor.

Second Lieutenant, James U. Childs, Farmington.

SERGEANTS.

John McDonald, Calais,
Frank Wiggin, Limestone Plantation,

Lewis C. Richards, Limerick,
George H. Fisher, Winterport.

CORPORALS.

Joel S. Stevens, Frankfort,
Charles L. Favour, Limerick,
William Fennelly, Mt. Desert.

Nelson Hewey, Veazie,
Thomas D. Witherly, Bangor,

PRIVATES.

Atkins, Charles R., Pittsfield,
Chick, Winfield S., Thorndike,
Day, Calvin, Cornish,
Dyer, George F., Biddeford,
George, Timothy A., Holden,
Gregory, Amasa, Montville,
Hayes, Charles J., Limerick,
Middleton, Thomas, Ellsworth,
O'Connor, Patrick, Tremont,
Patten, Jacob M., Pittsfield,
Pierce, James S., Limerick,
Pugsley, Francis, Scarboro,
Rich, Tyler F., Tremont,
Smith, William H., Portland,
Wilson, George W., Parsonsfield,

Bean, Dudley B., Passadumkeag,
Clement, Samuel H., Winterport,
Dearborn, George F., Monson,
Foss, James C., Winterport,
Goodwin, Charles, Cornish,
Hagan, John, Calais,
Lonely, Danforth, Mapleton,
Neal, Adam J., Waite Plantation,
Patten, George W., Pittsfield,
Phillips, David, Pittsfield,
Potts, Thomas, Biddeford,
Redding, George F., Calais,
Rupert, Moses J., Passadumkeag,
Whitten, Martin L., Etna,
Yeaton, James P., Waite Plantation.

MUSICIAN: Samuel R. Garey, Limerick.

ON DETACHED SERVICE: William L. Moore, Princeton, cattle guard ; Joseph Simpson, Corinth, cattle guard.

COMPANY I.

Captain, William H. Waldron, Lewiston.
First Lieutenant, Lewis C. Bisbee, Canton.

SERGEANTS.

Zelotes Rowe, Lisbon,
Jabez P. Parker, Greene.

Wilbur F. Mower, Greene, color
bearer.

CORPORALS

Hosea D. Manley, Auburn,
George B. Haskell, Webster,
John S. Brown, Augusta.

George D. Marston, Auburn,
William Davis, Durham,

PRIVATES.

Allen, William, Presque Isle,
Anderson, George W., Byron,
Blake, Isaac A., Lisbon,
Churchill, Charles C., Buckfield,
Estes, Jeremiah, Durham,
Flugil, George B., Monmouth,
Garcelon, Benjamin F., Webster,
Gould, Thomas J., Lisbon,
Howard, Elias, Manchester,
Hutchins, George A., Canton,
Littlefield, Thomas C., Hallowell,
Patten, Lora S., Greene,
Piper, George T., Turner,
Small, Daniel, Lisbon,
Shurtleff, William D., Turner,

Anderson, Charles R., Lewiston,
Batchelder, William H., Wilton,
Briggs, Arannah, Greene,
Davis, Robert, Gardiner,
Farris, Freeman H., Turner,
Frost, George W., Greene,
Gilbert, Roscoe, Greene,
Holmes, Stewart, Turner,
Howland, Enoch, Topsham,
Jordan, Ephraim L., Webster,
Mower, Eugene S., Greene,
Peabody, Samuel, Canton,
Powers, Roderick, Presque Isle,
Stover, Oliver, Webster,
Vose, Sabastian S., Lewiston.

ON DETACHED SERVICE : Second Lieut. Charles A. Garcelon, Lewiston, commanding brigade ambulance corp ; Charles W. Allen, Livermore, brigade commissary dept. ; Henry Hackett, Durham, ambulance corps ; William W. Marston, Buckfield, division teamster ; Dennis Sullivan, Portland, cattle guard ; Charles H. Young, Peru, guard at corps headquarters.

COMPANY K.

Captain, Stephen C. Whitehouse, Newcastle.
First Lieutenant, Joseph O. Lord, Biddeford.
Second Lieutenant, Edward F. Davies, Castine.

SERGEANTS.

Wilmot H. Chapman, Nobleboro,
Joseph B. Varnum, Castine,
Francis C. Mayo, Bluehill.

Atwood Fitch, Bristol,
Walter Dunbar, Nobleboro,

CORPORALS.

Reuel W. Higgins, Deer Isle,
Albert C. Stevens, Bluehill,
Frank Devereux, Castine,

John J. Blodgett, Castine,
Charles A. Devereux, Penobscot,
Charles T. Choate, Bluehill.

PRIVATES.

Allen, Charles P., Brooklin,
Bickford, Isaac B., Pittsfield,
Bowden, Lorenzo D., Castine,
Cunningham, Edward, Jefferson,
Hatch, Mark E., Castine,
Gregory, Lambert, Bluehill,
Morgrage, Andrew J., Castine,
Peacock, Joseph, Bluehill,
Savage, Hiram, Washington,
Wescott, Henry D., Castine,

Bickford, Elisha F., Castine,
Bowden, Frank M., Castine,
Butler, Henry B., Castine,
Dow, Reuben A., Brooklin,
Joyce, Moses S., Deer Isle,
Marks, James B., Sedgwick,
Page, Ira, Sedgwick,
Sanborn, Alonzo B., Brooklin,
Spaulding, Daniel, Pittsfield,
Wilson, Thomas J., Sedgwick.

ON DETACHED SERVICE: Seth K. Chase, Bluehill, guard brigade headquarters; Daniel Coligan, Washington, division teamster; Daniel M. Curtis, Deer Isle, ambulance corps; Francis M. Willens, Bluehill, cattle guard; Walter J. Willens, Bluehill, guard at corps headquarters.

Note to foregoing list of participants.

It will be observed that the list above given presents a total of one hundred more men and six more officers than the numbers given respectively in the inscription on the monuments.

It is to be said in regard to the officers that those of the field and staff were inadvertently omitted in making up the account for the inscription, attention being drawn to the companies and the officers of the line more than to the field and staff. Adding the latter, not including Lieut.-Col. Augustus B. Farnham absent sick, the accounts agree precisely.

With regard to the discrepancy in the two reports of men present, it is to be said that the numbers given in the inscription are those reporting present for duty at the last roll-call before the battle. It is certain that men came up to the regiment while it was in its first position, before its engagement. There can be little doubt that others came up in like manner at some time during the three days of the battle. It is quite possible that there may be some named on this list who were not able to get up, and consequently were not engaged in the fighting. But it is believed to be more nearly just to run the risk of including in this list some who were not in the battle than to leave off some because there is no other proof of their being present than the presumption from their well-known soldierly and manly character.

REVISED REPORT OF CASUALTIES.

FIELD AND STAFF.

Colonel Charles W. Tilden, prisoner.
Captain and Acting Major Samuel Clifford Belcher, prisoner.
Surgeon Charles Alexander, wounded and prisoner; paroled.
Assistant Surgeon William W. Eaton, prisoner; paroled.
Acting Sergeant-Major Cherbury F. Lothrop, prisoner; paroled.

COMPANY A.

Captain Isaac A. Pennell, wounded.

SERGEANTS.

Daniel A. Spearin, wounded.
Winslow A. Morrill, mortally wounded.

CORPORALS.

Bray Wilkins, prisoner.   Clement C. Williams, prisoner.

PRIVATES.

Carville, Benjamin, prisoner.   Clark, Henry R., wounded.
Cook, Moses W., wounded.   Downing, George A., prisoner.
Fuller, Horatio G., prisoner.   Furbish, Jairus H., prisoner.
Goodwin, Lyman O., prisoner.   Gould, George H., prisoner.
Holbrook, Abel C., wounded.   Hurd, Joel B., wounded.
Murch, Albert J., prisoner.   Piper, Thomas B.,
Thompson, John F., wounded.   missing; never heard from, probably killed.

COMPANY B.

Captain Eleazer W. Atwood, prisoner.
First Lieutenant Fred H. Beecher, wounded July 2d.
Second Lieutenant Melvin C. Wadsworth, prisoner.

SERGEANTS.

Charles E. Deering, prisoner.   Gustavus Moore, prisoner.

Corporal A. W. McCausland, wounded.

PRIVATES.

Austin, Henry D., missing.   Bruce, William W., missing.
Ewer, Henry A., wounded.   Huntington, William H., killed.
Palmer, John, prisoner; paroled.   Phillips, Charles M., wounded.
Robinson, William H.,   Thayer, Adin B., missing.
wounded and prisoner.

COMPANY C.

Second Lieutenant George D. Bisbee, prisoner.
Sergeant Charles N. Adams, prisoner.

CORPORALS.

Francis A. Crane,   George H. Farnham, wounded.
missing; never heard from since, prob- John M. Keene, prisoner; paroled.
bly killed.

Dorillus Hobbs, pris'r; died in prison. William N. Yeaton, killed.

PRIVATES.

Bartlett, Nathan, Jr.,
prisoner; died in prison.
Brown, Orville, wounded.
Butterfield, Martin, prisoner; paroled.
Chandler, Alphonso L.,
prisoner; escaped.
Hinds, David H., wounded.
Reed, Elias, wounded.

Blackwell, William T.,
prisoner; paroled.
Butterfield, Henry J., killed.
Chaney, Farwell, prisoner; paroled.
Davis, Colamore P., pris'r; escaped.
Newton, Abraham, prisoner.
Stratton, Albion W., wounded.

COMPANY D.

Captain Oliver H. Lowell, killed.
First Lieutenant Samuel H. Plummer, wounded.
Sergeant John M. Webster, prisoner.

CORPORALS.

Benjamin F. Fuller, wounded.
Charles H. Putnam,
prisoner; died in prison.

Laforest Kimball, wounded.
Sanford M. Reed, missing.

PRIVATES.

Adams, Hosea,
wounded; prisoner; died in prison.
Bean, Peter T., prisoner.
Foster, John F.,
missing; not heard from, probably killed.
Park, Silas A., killed.
Rider, Charles D., wounded.
Smith, Charles, wounded.
Twitchell, Fordyte P., prisoner.

Bancroft, Columbus, killed.
Downey, John,
missing; not heard from, probably killed.
Gray, Jr., Samuel, killed.
Richards, Prentiss M., prisoner.
Roberts, Albert W., prisoner.
Stevens, Charles H.,
missing; not heard from, probably killed.

COMPANY E.

Captain William A. Stevens, wounded, prisoner ; paroled.
Second Lieutenant Aubrey Leavitt, wounded.

SERGEANTS.

Martin B. Soule, wounded.
Edwin C. Stevens, prisoner.

Luther Bradford, prisoner.
Joseph G. Lamb, prisoner.

CORPORALS.

Consider F. Blaisdell, prisoner.
Octavius H. Tubbs, prisoner.

Harrison Merchant, pris'er; paroled.

PRIVATES.

Abbott, Charles, prisoner.
Fales, Curtis T., prisoner.
Hammond, George C., pris'r; paroled.
Lyford, James M., prisoner.
Mills, Albion B., wounded.
Priest, Hiram T., killed.
Tibbetts, Andrew J., prisoner.
Webber, Virgil H., killed.

Bates, William T., killed.
Foster, William G., wounded.
Hoyt, Stephen A., prisoner.
Lyon, Charles C., wounded.
Monk, Isaac J., prisoner; paroled.
Thomas, David S., prisoner; paroled.
Webber, Gustavus V., wounded.
Winship, Charles P., wounded.

COMPANY F.

Captain Thomas F. Wentworth, prisoner.
First Lieutenant George A. Deering, prisoner.

SERGEANTS.

Charles W. Ross, prisoner.   John McPhee, prisoner.

CORPORALS.

William Cannell, killed.   Edward L. Varney, prisoner.

PRIVATES.

Andrews, Abram S., prisoner.   Barker, Levi D., prisoner.
Burnham, George R., wounded.   Fenderson, Benjamin, wounded.
Greene, Joseph, prisoner.   Harding, John F., prisoner.
Palmer, George, wounded.   Powers, Albert, prisoner.
Smith, George W., prisoner.   Tibbetts, Sheldon H., wounded.

COMPANY G.

Sergeant Byron D. Babcock, wounded and prisoner.
Corporal Gorham Lord, prisoner.

PRIVATES.

Emery, Luke, prisoner.   Fairbrother, Frank, killed.
Farnham, Samuel T., prisoner.   Gibbs, Thomas A., prisoner.
Hodgkins, Jacob T., wounded, pris'r. Pullen, Harrison, killed.
Quint, George R., wounded.   Quint, William F., prisoner.
Snow, Daniel B., prisoner.   Wade, Gardiner B., prisoner.
Williamson, Boardman, wounded.   Works, Lewis, prisoner; paroled.

COMPANY H.

Second Lieutenant James U. Childs, prisoner.
Corporal Charles L. Favour, wounded.

PRIVATES.

Chick, Winfield S., wounded.   Clement, Samuel H., prisoner.
Day, Calvin, killed.   Hayes, Charles J., missing.
Neal, Adam J., wounded.   Redding, George F.,
                                        prisoner; died in prison.

COMPANY I.

Captain William H. Waldron, wounded.
First Lieutenant Lewis C. Bisbee, wounded and prisoner.
Sergeant Zelotes Rowe, prisoner; died in prison.

CORPORALS.

John S. Brown, pris'r; died in prison. William Davis, wounded.
Hosea D. Manley, missing.   George D. Marston,
                                        killed or died of wounds.

PRIVATES.

Anderson, George W., missing.   Batchelder, William H., wounded.
Blake, Isaac A., killed.   Davis, Robert, wounded.
Estes, Jeremiah, prisoner.   Farris, Freeman H., wounded.
Garcelon, Benjamin F., prisoner.   Holmes, Stewart, missing.
Patten, Lora S., missing.   Piper, George S., missing.
Stover, Oliver, pris'r; died in prison.

COMPANY K.

Captain Stephen C. Whitehouse, killed.

SERGEANTS.

Francis C. Mayo, prisoner.   Joseph B. Varnum, prisoner.

CORPORALS.

Charles T. Choate, prisoner.   Frank Devereaux, killed.
Charles A. Devereaux, wounded.   Albert C. Stevens, wounded.

PRIVATES.

Bickford, Elisha F., killed.   Bickford, Isaac B., prisoner.
Bowden, Frank M., killed.   Butler, Henry B., prisoner.
Cunningham, Edward, prisoner.   Low, Reuben A., wounded.
Marks, James B., prisoner.   Morgrage, Andrew J., prisoner.
Sanborn, Alonzo B., wounded.   Savage, Hiram, killed.
Wescott, Henry B., prisoner.   Wilson, Thomas J., prisoner.

Note on the foregoing report of casualties.

The foregoing list shows the following totals :

Killed : officers, 2 ; men, 19 ; total, 21. Wounded : officers, 8 ; men, 45 ; total, 53. Prisoners and missing : officers, 9 ; men, 88 ; total, 97. Missing, never heard from : 5 men. Total loss, 176. Seven of the wounded were captured.

This differs widely from the inscription upon the monument and official report of casualties made shortly after the battle. The latter gives the losses as follows :

Killed, 9 ; wounded, 59 ; captured, 164. Total loss, 232.

This discrepancy is partly explained by the following considerations :

1. The official report was based naturally on the results of the roll-call of the regiment after the disaster of the day on the evening of July 1st. It is undoubted that many then properly reported as prisoners or missing contrived to escape or find their way back on the next and following days ; and probable that many who were both wounded and captured were originally placed in both lists.

2. As to the discrepancies in the lists of killed and wounded, it is to be said that many at first reported wounded proved to be mortally wounded, and when these died soon after, they are now properly placed on the lists of the killed, and deducted, of course, from the wounded.

3. There is a considerable number hitherto borne on the rolls of the Adjutant-General of Maine, and also of the Adjutant-General of the U. S. Army, as missing in action, who were seen in the line of battle bearing themselves bravely, but not accounted for at its close. Some in the above list who were so seen and who have never been heard from since, now thirty-three years, have been placed above in a separate list, and several others are almost as clearly entitled to be so discriminated. In truth, these might properly and with a high degree of probable truth be borne on the lists of the killed.

We cannot refrain from expressing the feeling that such a rule should be applied by authority of Congress to all cases of faithful and honorable record where men seen in their place in a disastrous battle of our war for the Union, and never heard from again, should no longer have their honorable title clouded by so ambiguous a final report as "missing."

ADDRESS OF GENERAL CHAMBERLAIN.

General Chamberlain's response to the toast "Gettysburg" at a banquet in honor of the Sixteenth Maine Infantry and the Fifth Battery at the city of Gardiner.

Comrades of the Sixteenth and of the Fifth Battery:

It is an honor to be held worthy of your remembrance on an occasion like this. The reason of it is to be found in your own generous hearts. Something there may be in the suggestion that the flag of the Sixteenth in the field was finally furled within my own lines. In the closing days of our service, when all those varied experiences grouped under the wide and deep word, "casualties," together with the gradual expiration of terms of enlistment, brought men of the same state nearer and nearer together, it happened that the men of the Sixteenth left in the field (as had been those of the Second and the Sharpshooters) were consolidated with those of my old regiment, the Twentieth, and so were mustered out of the service in the division of which I was the commanding officer. I have evidence of my ability at that time to recognize merit in that I, forthwith upon the opportunity, invited one of your gallant field officers to a place on my staff (a).

(a) Major Abner R. Small.

Another thing which perhaps gives me footing here is that queer "back action" attraction by which "extremes meet." This is often from deep, underlying likeness, and not apparent antagonism. Here it is like service in opposite extremes of position. You were at one post of peril and responsibility; I was at another, the most remote from you in place, but so similar in circumstance, that I can understand and appreciate all your experience. With you, on the first day, the army put her right foot forward; with us, on the second, she put her left foot forward. She changed steps, but she stood.

You have given me a great theme. It is large enough to occupy our minds as many days as it held us, body and soul, breasting that tidal wave of July, 1863. I have not now, for this, so many minutes at my disposal. I pass it with a glance.

Gettysburg was a great battle; — its action, its tension, its hazards, its consequences. In it were involved questions of gravest import, the decision of which makes history; interests social, political, moral, personal; of gravest import for ourselves, for others, for our Country, for man everywhere; — for the present time, and for the future, for which also we hold a trust. The pressing question before us was whether we had a Country; whether we were a people, or only a populace; whether we were a mere chance partnership holding only by human will, or a Nation, constituted in the purpose and calling of Divine Providence, bound together for the noblest ends of living by ties of mutual interest and honor,—bonds both of love and of law. All the great ruling sentiments which have their vital source in this idea,—patriotism, loyalty, self-devotion for the sake of others,— nay, what we consider the supreme of earthly blessings,— largest scope for individual life, endowments, powers, genius, character,—these were the prize for which we wrestled in that terrible arena. More than this. Involved here, too, were widest human interests. We fought for the worth of manhood; for law and liberty, which mean freedom for every man to make the most of himself, with good-will of all others, without oppression or depression.

We had a deep, inward vision of this at the time, though unspoken and perhaps unclear; but no man even now can realize in thought, or recognize in fact, all the reach of good coming forth out of that struggle and that victory for the Country and for mankind. But I must leave that line of thought with you.

Looked at in its outward aspect, this battle will be a great example in military history,—a study in military science;—the strong features of the ground affording great variety of offensive and defensive measures, of grand and minor tactics, in a sudden and unplanned great battle; not without exemplification, too, of the tactics of the moral forces and the desperate strategy of sacrifice. In its inward aspect, example, also, of the value of character in the stress and strain of battle, where mature experience and intelligent comprehension have enforced the lesson that manly fortitude, heroic valor, and pride of honor must be organized into the habit of discipline and unquestioning obedience, without which all generalship is vain. But this thought, also, leading so far and so deep, I must leave for you to finish.

Many have claimed the honor of selecting the final standing-ground of our great defense. To this sudden change of position, some participants were "accessory before the fact," and some "after the fact." But if there was any selection here, it was a very "natural selection." Whether, in every instance, it led to the "survival of the fittest," there may be some question. The manner of its occupancy is not suggestive of deliberate premeditation, but our people certainly may be said to have chosen this ground and promptly taken it, in decided preference to matters and things they had found at the further front.

But who, let me ask, made it possible to select this ground but the men who on that first of July, all day long, held Lee's advance at bay, until our scattered corps could come up by forced marches and take advantage of the field? Who but John Buford with his cavalry, and Reynolds with his First Corps,—you of his infantry and artillery,—with masterly skill, stubborn courage, and unexampled devotion, wrought that marvelous opening by which it was Meade, and not Lee, who secured that heart of hills made awful in memory and immortal in history? That magnificent fighting of the First Corps, I do not know where it was ever surpassed!

But my theme grows intense as it narrows and nears. I know how you of the Fifth Battery, after holding your salient angle at the front until it was an island in the raging sea of foes, galloped straight through their enveloping masses, through embarrassing masses of fugitives as well, and with your brazen throats calling a halt to the astonished enemy thinking to sweep away our right flank, where for a sublime moment you alone gave check to the battle tide.

I know what you men of the Sixteenth did, when your General of Division, seeing that it must be a stricken field, and that he must save what he could of his command by the last resort of falling back with his main body while a few should hold the fighting front, and that this could be done only by men who would make a stand equal in every test of character to the desperate charge of a "forlorn hope," calling to Colonel Tilden, said: "Take that hill and hold it at any cost!" I know how you stood, and where, and when, and at what cost! Your General knew what men you were. You knew perfectly well what your service was to be. It is a terrible duty, but a glorious honor. You saw what was coming, front and left and right. You saw the last of the Union army leave the field. You saw the blades of the great shears coming down and down, and closing in and in—and you knew they must meet, and cut and crush all that was between. But you stood; you fought it out to the last and "at any cost" indeed. Environed, enveloped, crushed, overwhelmed,—as truly heroic, as much to be held in highest honor and dearest memory, as if you had died at your posts, every man of you!

Some such example as yours, the great Apostle must have had in mind when he exhorts his followers to "put on the whole armor of God, that ye may be able to withstand in the evil day, and having done all, *to stand.*"

So many of you were captured,—not because you were placed in a false position, with flank unguarded and rear cut off; not because you were not well handled; not because you were "caught napping" or "cooking coffee"; but because you would not yield your post, though disaster and death swirled and swept around and over you.

Your colors, it was said, were lost. That word came to me when, on the morning of the second, I reached the crest far to the rear of that where you had stood; and I felt a shock, but not of shame. For I knew something terrible must have befallen, and that there could have been no dishonor where you were. But when I came to know the truth of it all, I saw that instead of your colors being lost, they were eternally saved! Not laid down, but lifted up; not captured nor surrendered, but translated,—the shadow lost in substance! The flag,—it is the symbol of the Country's honor, power, law, and life. It is the ensign of loyalty, the bond of brotherhood for those who stand under it; a token and an inspiration. Hence it is held sacred by the soldier; as in great moments it is also by the citizen. All which that flag symbolized you had illustrated and impersonated; had absorbed into your thoughts and hearts—if I should not rather say, itself had absorbed your thoughts and hearts,—your service and suffering into its own deeper meaning and dearer honor. Now it had done all a symbol could do; you had stood for all it stood for. Now the supreme moment had come. Nothing could be averted; nothing could be resisted; nothing could be escaped. That was an awful moment; passing that of death, it seems to me. Then the soul is born anew. No thought of yielding up the token of the Country's honor enters the heart of any one of you, though it has fulfilled its ends; though you are to go to prison and to death. Your Colonel, calm and dauntless,—commander still,—bids you break the staff that had borne it aloft, and tear that symbol single as your souls into as many pieces as you had bosoms, and shelter them with your lives, lest that flag be touched by hostile hand, or triumphed over by living man! And they went with you to prison. And these bars and stars next your hearts helped you to endure those other bars, besetting you because you were true; helped you to look up to those other stars, where we dream all is serene and safe and free. [Here the long repressed feelings of the hearers broke into wildest demonstration, in the midst of which a member of the regiment arose and took from his breast pocket a star of the old flag, at which the assembly lost all control of itself; and the General continued.] Yes, and through this tumult of cheers and tears, I see that you hold them still to your hearts, precious beyond words, radiant with the glory of service and suffering nobly borne; potent to transmit to other souls the power that has made them glorious!

Lost? There is a way of losing that is finding. When soul overmasters sense; when the noble and divine self overcomes the lower self; when duty and honor and love,—immortal things,—bid the mortal perish! It is only when a man supremely gives that he supremely finds.

That was your sacrifice; that is your reward.

HISTORICAL SKETCH.

BY LIEUTENANT FRANCIS WIGGIN.

The Sixteenth Regiment of Infantry for three years' service was authorized by a call from the War Department of May 21, 1862, for the enrolment of fifty thousand troops to be drilled and held in reserve, to be drawn upon as needed. At that time it was supposed by those in authority, and by people generally, that the six hundred thousand soldiers in the field would be amply sufficient for the putting down of the Rebellion. The seven days' battles in the vicinity of Richmond, and the falling back of McClellan's army to Harrison Landing, undeceived the country as to the magnitude of the task on hand, and a call for three hundred thousand additional troops was issued, the fifty thousand under the call of May 21st being included in the latter call.

Although recruiting for the regiment commenced in May, it was not till August 13th that the complement was full. The regiment on that date consisted of 960 enlisted men and 39 commissioned officers. The organization was as follows :

FIELD, STAFF, AND NON-COMMISSIONED STAFF.

Colonel, Asa W. Wildes, Skowhegan.
Lieutenant-Colonel, Charles W. Tilden, Castine.
Major, Augustus B. Farnham, Bangor.
Adjutant, Abner R. Small, Waterville.
Quartermaster, Isaac N. Tucker, Gardiner.
Surgeon, Charles Alexander, Farmington.
Assistant Surgeon, Joseph B. Baxter, Gorham.
Chaplain, George Bullen, Skowhegan.

Sergeant-Major, Francis A. Wildes, Skowhegan.
Quartermaster-Sergeant, George W. Brown, Augusta.
Commissary-Sergeant, Charles H. Parlin, Skowhegan.
Hospital Steward, William W. Eaton, Brunswick.
Drum-Major, William H. Palmer, Calais.

COMPANY OFFICERS.

Co. A. Captain, Charles A. Williams, Skowhegan.
First Lieutenant, S. Forrest Robinson, Skowhegan.
Second Lieutenant, Isaac A. Pennell, New Portland.

Co. B. Captain, Charles K. Hutchins, Augusta.
First Lieutenant, Eleazer W. Atwood, Gardiner.
Second Lieutenant, George W. Edwards, Gorham.

Co. C. Captain, Daniel Marston, Phillips.
First Lieutenant, Hovey C. Austin, Presque Isle.
Second Lieutenant, Marshall S. Smith, East Livermore.

Co. D. Captain, Moses W. Rand, Waterford.
First Lieutenant, Humphrey E. Eustis, Dixfield.
Second Lieutenant, Henry P. Herrick, North Yarmouth.

Co. E. Captain, Arch D. Leavitt, Turner.
First Lieutenant, William E. Brooks, Skowhegan.
Second Lieutenant, William A. Stevens, Waterville.

Co. F.   Captain, Thomas E. Wentworth, Gorham.
First Lieutenant, Oliver H. Lowell, Gorham.
Second Lieutenant, George A. Deering, Saco.

Co. G.   Captain, S. Clifford Belcher, Farmington.
First Lieutenant, Joseph H. Malbon, Skowhegan.
Second Lieutenant, Isaac H. Thompson, Anson.

Co. H.   Captain, John Ayer, Bangor.
First Lieutenant, Ira S. Libby, Limerick.
Second Lieutenant, Israel H. Washburn, Orono.

Co. I.   Captain, William H. Waldron, Lewiston.
First Lieutenant, William Bray, Turner.
Second Lieutenant, Charles A. Garcelon, Lewiston.

Co. K.   Captain, Stephen C. Whitehouse, Newcastle.
First Lieutenant, Augustus T. Somerby, Ellsworth.
Second Lieutenant, Augustus C. Peters, Bluehill.

Company A was raised in Somerset and Kennebec counties; Company B in Kennebec county; Company C in Franklin and Oxford counties; Company D in Oxford and Cumberland counties; Company E in Androscoggin, Kennebec, and Penobscot counties; Company F in York and Cumberland counties; Company G in Somerset and Franklin counties; Company H in Waldo and Penobscot counties; Company I in Kennebec and Androscoggin counties; Company K in Hancock and Lincoln counties; and men from all parts of the state were scattered throughout the companies.

The regiment was mustered into United States service at Augusta, August 14, 1862. August 19th it started for Washington, where it arrived on the 21st, and on the 22d it marched across Long Bridge to Arlington Heights. Here the several companies were distributed among the forts on the Heights, for the purpose of being drilled in heavy artillery practice, under the instruction of the officers and sergeants of the 14th Mass.

Three weeks were spent here, and the men were fast acquiring the bearing and skill of soldiers, when the defeat of General Pope's army at the Second Bull Run battle, and the invasion of Maryland by General Lee, called every available regiment to the field. On September 6th at eleven P.M. came the order to rendezvous at Fort Tillinghast, leaving tents, knapsacks and overcoats behind, whence we took up the march towards the South Mountain in Maryland, under command of Colonel

Wildes, who shortly afterward gave over the command to Lieutenant-Colonel Tilden, who remained at the head of the regiment and was promoted Colonel, January 8, 1863, Colonel Wildes having resigned. On September 9th the regiment was assigned to Hartsuff's brigade, Ricketts' division, Hooker's corps. The Sixteenth did not participate in the battle of Antietam, but marched over the battlefield the next day after the conflict, before the dead had been buried, and went into camp near Sharpsburg. The men had no shelter-tents; knapsacks and overcoats had been left at Arlington Heights and were now stored in Washington. The men were exposed to all the inclemencies of the weather by night and by day, with only such protection as could be made from boughs and fence rails. The services of many a noble and patriotic soldier were lost to the country by reason of the two months' severe and unnecessary exposure to which they were subjected. The army was at last put in motion for Virginia. To guard against cold, rain, sleet and snow we were accustomed to wrap our blankets around our shoulders; and our brother soldiers in other regiments, disregarding our pitiable condition, jeered at us and called us the "Blanket Brigade." The men of this regiment were of that heroic temper which bears insult in silence. They resolved that when the proper time came they would show the army and the country of what stuff they were made. But in this pitiful plight they marched from Sharpsburg to Rappahannock Station, and from that place to Brooke's Station near Fredericksburg, where on Thanksgiving Day, November 27, 1862, they received their knapsacks and overcoats from Washington. Never had men more cause for thankfulness than the patient, shivering men of the Sixteenth.

Col. Adrian R. Root, of the 94th N. Y., had then the command of the brigade to which the Sixteenth had lately been assigned, the other regiments being the 94th and 104th N. Y. and the 107th Penn.

The battle of Fredericksburg, December 12–13, 1862, was a disastrous and overwhelming defeat for the Union army; but there never was a battle where greater bravery was shown than by the men of the North at Fredericksburg. The Sixteenth Maine was in General Franklin's grand division, on the left of the Union position. At about two o'clock P. M. the brigade was ordered into action. The regiment numbered at this time 417 guns. The enemy were posted behind the Fredericksburg and Richmond railroad, which they were using for a breastwork. Under cover of a ridge our brigade removed knapsacks and fixed bayonets. It then advanced steadily over the ridge and at the order, "Double quick! Charge!" the men went forward with a cheer, under a terrific and destructive fire, but with no wavering. The Sixteenth remembers the taunts and jeers of the last three months and feels that its opportunity has come. Ahead of all the others it rushes over the railroad embankment and springs down upon an astonished and terrified line of battle. The rebels throw down their arms and give themselves up. Over two hundred prisoners are taken and sent to the rear. Then the Sixteenth advanced to the edge of the woods and fired sixty rounds of ammunition at a second line of battle, and would have charged a second time if it had not been restrained. Its loss in this battle in killed, wounded and missing was two hundred and thirty-one (a)—more than one-half the number engaged. The missing were mostly wounded and prisoners. The losses in the regiment amounted to one-half the losses in the whole brigade. Colonel Root, the brigade commander, in his official report spoke in the highest terms of the conduct of the officers and men of the Sixteenth in this battle. He further says: "Previous to the action thirty-eight men of the regiment had volunteered to do duty with Hall's battery, and I am assured by Captain Hall that their conduct was creditable in the highest degree." The injustice of the past was overcome; the voice of insult and reproach was forever silenced; the term "Blanket Brigade" was never heard again.

The monotony of camp life in winter quarters near Belle Plain was broken once by a forward movement of the army in what is known among soldiers as the "Mud March" of January 19–23, 1863, in which the severe experiences of cold, wet, mud and hunger were intensified by the sensation of a complete failure in our attempt.

(a) See nominal list in 1862, A. G. R. Maine, page 877.

On April 29th the regiment took its place in the movements around Chancellorsville. During this battle Adjutant A. R. Small of the Sixteenth made a most daring and successful reconnaissance on the right of our army, and brought back important information concerning the withdrawal of the rebel forces and their movement toward Fredericksburg. The losses of the Sixteenth in this battle had not been great, but the results of exposure and fatigue had been fearful, and the whole army was disgusted at the result of a campaign that was so well begun.

At the opening of the Gettysburg campaign the 94th and 104th N. Y., the 107th Penn., the 13th Mass., and the Sixteenth Maine constituted the first brigade of the second division, First corps. On the morning of June 12th tents were struck and the regiment began its long march northward, with 281 men and 32 officers. June 15th it reached Centreville; on the 19th Guilford, where it remained in camp till the 23d. The march from Fredericksburg had been most arduous; the temperature 90 degrees above zero every day, and the terrors of sunstroke added to the fatigue and thirst. On the 29th of June our corps reached Emmitsburg.

On the morning of July 1st we were suddenly marched in the direction of Gettysburg, the sound of cannonading quickening every step until the brigade was put into position near the seminary. Not long afterward it was ordered to "the front," where it commenced its action by a bayonet charge executed in such fashion as to drive the enemy entirely from their position. The brilliant but terrible chapter of the part of the Sixteenth in the battle of Gettysburg need not be recounted here, as it is set forth, faithfully and fully, in a preceding account. It is sufficient to say that its heroism and devotion make a conspicuous instance of service and suffering, which history has not failed to note.

The little remnant — thirty-eight men and four officers — which managed to escape the terrible catastrophe of the afternoon of July 1st made its stand with its division on Cemetery Hill and rendered such service as it could in the second and third days' battle.

The regiment was for a time almost unrecognizable as such. The Colonel and most of the officers were prisoners in the hands of the enemy; its Adjutant was detached as acting assistant adjutant-general of the brigade, and Major Leavitt exerted himself to bring together the broken fragments of the regiment as fast as circumstances would allow. On July 18th the First corps recrossed the Potomac and went into camp near Waterford, Va. By a special order from corps headquarters a detail from the regiment was ordered to proceed to Maine, for the purpose of securing recruits and drafted men to fill up its depleted ranks. Men were now returning from prison and from hospitals, and with the 168 drafted men now assigned, the regiment began to assume a respectable appearance as to size. Lieutenant-Colonel Farnham had returned from severe illness at hospital and assumed command, and the regiment was ready for action early in September. It participated in all the peculiar movements, known among soldiers as the " Culpeper and Centreville Express," over the old battlefields about Bull Run. On the 20th of November the regiment numbered 650 men, and with its two new stands of colors sent by friends in Maine it had an appearance worthy of its early days and a heart proud of its later fame.

In the Mine Run campaign the regiment had something of its earlier experience. Exposure, fatigue and hunger, sowing more seeds of disease and death, began their terrible and long effect. But the prudence of General Meade doubtless saved us another great slaughter, even more disastrous than Fredericksburg. On December 3d the regiment went into winter quarters at Kelly's Ford.

In March, 1864, changes took place in the organization of the army. The First corps, to which the Sixteenth had been attached, was absorbed into the Fifth corps, our division constituting its Second division, under General Robinson. March 28th Colonel Tilden returned to the regiment, having boldly and skilfully escaped from Libby Prison through the famous Rose Tunnel. On the day following, the men of the Sixteenth presented to him the magnificent black horse which he rode during the remainder of the war and brought home with him when the regiment went out of service.

On May 4, 1864, commenced the campaign of the Wilderness. The regiment was actively engaged in the three battles ;
its losses, however, were comparatively small. But in a desperate charge on the 8th of May it lost several of its officers
and nearly a hundred men. In the battle of Laurel Hill at
Spotsylvania, on the tenth, the regiment took a prominent part
and lost four officers and fifty men in a charge upon the
enemy's works. On the twelfth charged the enemy's works,
but without success. No soldiers in the world could have carried those tiers of earthworks, yet our division was hurled
against them again and again. Major Leavitt was mortally
wounded and every company suffered great loss. From May
5th to the 21st the regiment had lost nineteen men and two
officers killed or mortally wounded ; one hundred and sixteen
men and two officers wounded, and thirty-eight men and two
officers missing,—doubtless taken prisoners.

On May 23d the regiment took part in the brilliant engagement on the North Anna River, where the enemy were repulsed
with great loss. In the severe battle of Bethesda Church —
which was our part in the famous Cold Harbor battle — the
regiment lost four men killed and fourteen wounded.

On the 8th of June our brigade was transferred to the Third
division of the Fifth corps, and took part in the movements
and engagements about the Chickahominy River. On the 16th
the brigade crossed the James River and moved up toward the
outer defenses of Petersburg. It had part in the severe
actions of June 17th and 18th ; in the latter the Fifth corps
by desperate assault and with great loss gained a commanding
advanced position across the Norfolk railroad, which was afterwards known among our soldiers as "Fort Hell." Thereafter
the regiment shared the fortunes of the Fifth corps in the
entrenchments in front of Petersburg and the various operations upon the enemy's right flank. It participated in the
aggressive movement of the First corps, August 18th, to extend
our lines to the left beyond the Weldon railroad. The enemy
was on the alert, taking advantage of every disjunction of our
troops in the formations for battle. Severe fighting occurred
that day and the next, in a rather disconnected way but gener-

ally with an enemy upon one flank or the other. The Corps however planted itself firmly and for good astride the railroad. In repelling a front and flank attack too long on the 19th the Sixteenth, endeavoring to retire, found itself surrounded, and lost heavily. During the enterprise it lost two men killed, twenty-eight wounded, and a hundred and fifteen prisoners. Among these prisoners were Colonel Tilden, Adjutant Small, Captains Conley and Lord, Lieutenants Broughton, Fitch, Chipman and Davies. Colonel Tilden, however, wouldn't stay captured and Lieutenant Davies as well, although they were taken to Petersburg and started for Richmond. They managed at the risk of their lives to elude their guards and coolly return to the front with Confederates on all sides. Watching their opportunity they walked over into their own brigade picket line on the twenty-second.

The regiment had now been assigned to the Second brigade, under General Baxter. The regiment was stationed in Fort Wadsworth and there remained until December 5th. December 7th it took up the march with the Fifth corps to destroy the Weldon railroad to the North Carolina line. In this expedition it lost four men.

On January 1, 1865, there were present for duty in the Sixteenth sixteen officers and five hundred and twelve men. On the 5th of February it moved to the left and took part in the battle of Hatcher's Run, losing one officer and seventy-three men killed and wounded, including two color bearers. On the 29th of March the last campaign of the war opened, in which the Fifth corps operated with General Sheridan's cavalry; General Chamberlain's brigade opening the campaign with a decisive blow upon the enemy on the "Quaker Road." On the White Oak Road, on the 31st, the Sixteenth lost one man killed and four wounded, and one officer and twenty-three men missing. In the brilliant action of Five Forks,—a cyclone attack on the enemy's position, one of the picturesque battles of the war,—the regiment was closely engaged, Lieut.-Col. Farnham being severely wounded through the lungs and one man killed and twelve wounded. In the rapid and brilliant movements which taxed our men to the utmost, but resulted in

Lee's surrender at Appomattox Court House, the regiment took an active and earnest part and had the honor of being at Appomattox at the time of Lee's surrender. After about a month of occupation in taking possession of Confederate property and maintaining and administering peace and order along the line of the South Side railroad, the Fifth corps took up its march through Petersburg and Richmond and across almost all the great and terrible battlefields of the war toward Washington, and encamped at Arlington Heights on the 12th of May. This return march over fields of such tremendous experiences was an incident never to be forgotten. The regiment took its part in that last grand review of the army in Washington, where it laid down its own arms before the constituted authorities of the nation in the most magnificent spectacle ever beheld on this continent. On the 5th of June the regiment, as such, was mustered out of the service of the United States; its later recruits, whose term of service had not expired, were assigned to the Twentieth Maine regiment. When leaving for the homeward journey, on June 6th, the regiment passing through Washington, marched by the hospital where Colonel Farnham lay, as was then supposed at the point of death, that he might take a last look at the command he loved so well. Reaching Augusta on the 10th of June the regiment was quartered in the cavalry barracks, where it was disbanded on the 16th and its heroic men, having honored themselves and their country, modestly returned to their place and work as peaceful and worthy citizens.

The Sixteenth Maine Regiment was emphatically a fighting regiment. On three several occasions it was almost extinguished by deaths, wounds or capture. At Fredericksburg it lost more than half its number; at Gettysburg it had at the close of the first day only thirty-eight men and four officers left; at Laurel Hill it lost nearly one-third of its men; at the Weldon Railroad it lost more than half the men engaged. First or last, every member of its color-guard was killed or wounded. The regiment left Augusta in 1862 with 960 enlisted men. It received in all 916 recruits. It lost in killed and mortally wounded 10 officers and 168 men. It had wounded in action

22 officers and 266 men. There died of disease one officer and 240 men. It had discharged for disability 17 officers and 260 men. Resigned and discharged for promotion, 25 officers; discharged by order and for promotion, 126 enlisted men; missing in action fate unknown, deserted, and transferred to other organizations in the service, 673 enlisted men. There belonged to it during the three years of its existence 1,876 enlisted men and 86 officers, and its total diminutions as above stated for the same period from all causes were 1,467 men and 53 officers; the remainder — 33 officers and 409 men — were mustered out with the regiment or elsewhere (a). It was fortunate in its field officers, whose ability and character commanded respect and affection, and the mutual regard between officers and men of this regiment is something perhaps remarkable. It is not too much to say that this regiment will have place in history as one of the most intelligent, patriotic, reliable and faithful regiments that went out from the State of Maine, and one whose part and office of fortitude and self-sacrifice on the first day of the battle of Gettysburg was to check the victorious advance of the rebel army and enable the shattered remnants of the First Corps to form a new line on Cemetery Ridge, thus having no small part in determining the final fortunes of that memorable field.

REGIMENTAL ROSTER.

COLONELS.

Date of Commission.

Aug. 9, 1862.   Asa W. Wildes, resigned Jan. 7, 1863.

Feb. 5, 1863.   Charles W. Tilden, brevet Brigadier-General March 13, 1865; mustered out June 5, 1865.

LIEUTENANT-COLONELS.

June 23, 1862.   Charles W. Tilden, promoted Colonel.

Feb. 5, 1863.   Augustus B. Farnham, brevet Colonel April 1, 1865; mustered out June 5, 1865.

MAJORS.

Aug. 9, 1862.   Augustus B. Farnham, promoted Lieutenant-Colonel.

Feb. 5, 1863.   Arch D. Leavitt, died May 31, 1864, of wounds received at Spotsylvania May 12th.

(a) The figures are derived from *History of the Sixteenth Maine* by Major A. R. Small, page 323.

June 1, 1864.	S. Clifford Belcher, not mustered, absent wounded.
Oct. 31, 1864.	Abner R. Small, mustered out June 5, 1865.

ADJUTANTS.

Aug. 16, 1862.	Abner R. Small, promoted Major.
Dec. 9, 1864.	Cherbury F. Lothrop, mustered out June 5, 1865.

QUARTERMASTERS.

Aug. 16, 1862.	Isaac N. Tucker, discharged July 28, 1864.
Aug. 13, 1864.	George W. Brown, mustered out June 5, 1865.

SURGEONS.

June 3, 1862.	Charles Alexander, discharged Nov. 8, 1864.
Nov. 25, 1864.	William W. Eaton, mustered out June 5, 1865.

ASSISTANT SURGEONS.

July 22, 1862.	Joseph B. Baxter, mustered out May 23, 1865.
Oct. 24, 1862.	Warren Hunter, resigned Jan. 24, 1863.
Feb. 5, 1863.	William W. Eaton, promoted Surgeon.
Feb. 10, 1865.	David P. Bolster, mustered out June 5, 1865.

CHAPLAINS.

Aug. 2, 1862.	George Bullen, resigned Oct. 3, 1863.
Dec. 8, 1863.	Uriah Balkam, discharged Oct. 8, 1864.
Feb. 8, 1865.	John Mitchell, mustered out June 5, 1865.

CAPTAINS.

July 29, 1862.	Charles A. Williams, Co. A, died Nov. 10, 1862.
Nov. 19, 1862.	S. Forest Robinson, Co. A, resigned Jan. 24, 1863.
Mar. 2, 1863.	Isaac A. Pennell, Co. A, discharged for disability Oct. 14, 1864.
Sept. 15, 1864.	Charles T. Hildreth, Co. A, mustered out June 5, 1865.
Aug. 9, 1862.	Charles K. Hutchins, Co. B, killed in battle Dec. 13, 1862.
Dec. 31, 1862.	Eleazer W. Atwood, Co. B, discharged Nov. 25, 1864.
Dec. 9, 1864.	Joseph H. Malbon, Co. B, mustered out June 5, 1865.
Aug. 9, 1862.	Daniel Marston, Co. C, discharged Dec. 22, 1864.
Jan. 28, 1865.	Edward F. Davies, Co. C, mustered out June 5, 1865.
Aug. 16, 1862.	Moses W. Rand, Co. D, died Dec. 8, 1862.
Dec. 31, 1862.	Oliver H. Lowell, Co. D, killed in battle July 1, 1863.
Dec. 1, 1863.	Samuel H. Plummer, Co. D, discharged Oct. 20, 1864, for disability.
Nov. 9, 1864.	William H. Broughton, Co. D, mustered out June 5, 1865.
Aug. 9, 1862.	Arch D. Leavitt, Co. E, promoted Major.
Feb. 5, 1863.	William E. Brooks, Co. E, resigned Feb. 26, 1863.
Mar. 22, 1863.	William A. Stevens, Co. E, killed in battle June 17, 1864.
Aug. 8, 1864.	Lincoln K. Plummer, Co. E, brevet Major and Lieut.-Colonel Mar. 13, 1865; mustered out June 5, 1865.
Aug. 9, 1862,	Thomas E. Wentworth, Co. F, discharged July 1, 1864.
Aug. 8, 1864.	George A. Deering, Co. F, mustered out June 5, 1865.
Aug. 16, 1862.	S. Clifford Belcher, Co. G, discharged Sept. 13, 1864, on account of wounds received in battle May 8, 1864.
Dec. 26, 1864.	Isaac H. Thompson, Co. G, mustered out June 5, 1865.

Aug. 16, 1862.	John Ayer, Co. H, died Feb. 22, 1863, of wounds received in battle Dec. 13, 1862.
May 22, 1863.	John D. Conley, Co. H, mustered out June 5, 1865.
Aug. 16, 1862.	William H. Waldron, Co. I, wounded and prisoner July 1, 1863; discharged Sept. 27, 1863, for disability.
Dec. 1, 1863.	Lewis C. Bisbee, Co. I, mustered out June 5, 1865.
Aug. 16, 1862.	Stephen C. Whitehouse, Co. K, killed in battle July 1, 1863.
Dec. 1, 1863.	Joseph O. Lord, Co. K, mustered out June 5, 1865.

FIRST LIEUTENANTS.

July 21, 1862.	S. Forest Robinson, Co. A, promoted Captain Co. A.
Nov. 19, 1862.	Isaac A. Pennell, Co. A, promoted Captain Co. A.
June 13, 1863.	Nathan Fowler, Co. A, discharged Oct. 26, 1864, on account of wounds received May 8th.
Sept. 5, 1864.	S. P. Newman Smythe, Co. A, mustered out June 5, 1865.
Aug. 9, 1862.	Eleazer W. Atwood, Co. B, promoted Captain Co. B.
May 23, 1862.	Abner R. Small, Co. B, promoted Adjutant.
Mar. 26, 1863.	Frederick H. Beecher, Co. B, wounded at Fredericksburg and at Gettysburg; discharged Sept. 30, 1864; transferred to V. R. C.
Dec. 9, 1864.	Jones Whitman, Co. B, mustered out June 5, 1865.
Aug. 16, 1862.	Hovey Austin, Co. C, discharged March 30, 1863.
Apr. 10, 1863.	Marshall S. Smith, Co. C, prisoner May 5, 1864; discharged May 15, 1865.
Aug. 16, 1862.	Humphrey E. Eustis, Co. D, resigned Dec. 8, 1862.
Dec. 31, 1862.	Samuel H. Plummer, Co. D, promoted Captain Co. D.
Dec. 1, 1863.	William H. Broughton, Co. D, promoted Captain Co. D.
Nov. 9, 1864.	Atwood Fitch, Co. D, mustered out June 5, 1865.
Aug. 9, 1862.	William E. Brooks, Co. E, promoted Captain Co. E.
Feb. 5, 1863.	William A. Stevens, Co. E, promoted Captain Co. E.
Mar. 16, 1863.	Lincoln K. Plummer, Co. E, promoted Captain Co. E.
Aug. 8, 1864.	Aubrey Leavitt, Co. E, brevet Captain and Major to date March 13, 1865; mustered out June 5, 1865.
Aug. 16, 1862.	Oliver H. Lowell, Co. F, promoted Captain Co. D.
Dec. 31, 1862.	George A. Deering, Co. F, promoted Captain Co. F.
Aug. 8, 1864.	Cherbury F. Lothrop, Co. F, promoted Adjutant.
Aug. 16, 1862.	Joseph H. Malbon, Co. G, promoted Captain Co. B.
Dec. 9, 1864.	Lewis G. Richards, Co. G, discharged Feb. 4, 1865.
Mar. 15, 1865.	Frank Wiggin, Co. G, mustered out June 5, 1865.
Aug. 16, 1862.	Ira S. Libby, Co. H, resigned Oct. 31, 1862.
Dec. 13, 1862.	Israel H. Washburn, Co. H, resigned June 12, 1863.
Aug. 16, 1862.	William Bray, Co. I, resigned Aug., 1862, not mustered.
Aug. 23, 1862.	Lewis C. Bisbee, Co. I, promoted Captain Co. I.
Dec. 18, 1863.	Isaac H. Thompson, Co. I, promoted Captain Co. G.
Aug. 16, 1862.	Augustus T. Somerby, Co. K, resigned March 12, 1863, for disability.
May 23, 1863.	Joseph O. Lord, Co. K, promoted Captain Co. K.
Dec. 1, 1863.	Edward F. Davies, Co. K, promoted Captain Co. C.
Jan. 28, 1865.	Jabez P. Parker, Co. K, mustered out June 5, 1865.

SECOND LIEUTENANTS.

July 29, 1862.	Isaac A. Pennell, Co. A, promoted 1st Lieutenant Co. A.
Dec. 3, 1862.	Francis A. Wildes, Co. A, resigned Feb. 26, 1863.
May 22, 1863.	Nathan Fowler, Co. A, promoted 1st Lieutenant Co. A.
June 13, 1863.	Nathaniel W. Coston, Co. A, died May 27, '64, of wounds.
Sept. 22, 1864.	William T. Dodge, Co. A, brevet 1st Lieutenant to date March 13, 1865; mustered out June 5, 1865.
Aug. 9, 1862.	George W. Edwards, Co. B, died in rebel prison, May 27, 1863, of wounds received; commissioned 1st Lieutenant Co. B, not mustered.
Jan. 24, 1863.	Frederick H. Beecher, Co. B, promoted 1st Lieut. Co. B.
Mar. 26, 1863.	Melvin C. Wadsworth, Co. B, mustered out June 5, 1865.
Aug. 19, 1862.	Marshall S. Smith, Co. C, promoted 1st Lieutenant Co. C.
Apr. 10, 1863.	George D. Bisbee, Co. C, mustered out June 5, 1865.
Aug. 16, 1862.	Henry P. Herrick, Co. D, killed in battle Dec. 13, 1862.
Dec. 31, 1862.	William H. Broughton, Co. D, promoted 1st Lieut. Co. D.
Dec. 1, 1863.	Atwood Fitch, Co. D, promoted 1st Lieutenant Co. D.
Nov. 9, 1864.	Charles H. Parlin, Co. D, mustered out June 5, 1865.
Aug. 9, 1862.	William A. Stevens, Co. E, promoted 1st Lieut. Co. E.
Mar. 2, 1863.	Lincoln K. Plummer, Co. E, promoted 1st Lieut. Co. E.
May 22, 1863.	Aubrey Leavitt, Co. E, promoted 1st Lieutenant Co. E.
Nov. 25, 1864.	Jones Whitman, Co. E, promoted 1st Lieutenant Co. B.
Dec. 9, 1864.	Gustavus Moore, Co. E, mustered out June 5, 1865.
Aug. 16, 1862.	George A. Deering, Co. F, promoted 1st Lieut. Co. F.
Mar. 17, 1863.	Daniel L. Warren, Co. F, discharged Oct. 27, 1863, for disability.
Dec. 1, 1863.	Cherbury F. Lothrop, Co. F, promoted 1st Lieut. Co. F.
Dec. 9, 1864.	Daniel A. Spearin, Co. F, mustered out June 5, 1865.
Aug. 16, 1862.	Isaac H. Thompson, Co. G, promoted 1st Lieut. Co. I.
Dec. 18, 1863.	Isaac R. Whitney, Co. G, discharged Dec. 17, 1864.
Aug. 2, 1862.	Israel H. Washburn, Co. H, promoted 1st Lieut. Co. H.
Dec. 13, 1862.	John D. Conley, Co. H, promoted Captain Co. H.
May 22, 1863.	James U. Childs, Co. H (promoted 1st Lieutenant, not mustered), mustered out June 5, 1865.
Aug. 16, 1862.	Charles A. Garcelon, Co. I, discharged Feb. 5, 1864, for promotion.
Nov. 25, 1864.	Jabez P. Parker, Co. I, promoted 1st Lieutenant Co. K.
Jan. 28, 1865.	Wilbur F. Mower, Co. I, discharged May 15, 1865, for disability from wounds.
Aug. 16, 1862.	Augustus C. Peters, Co. K, discharged March 30, 1863, for disability from wounds.
July 16, 1862.	Charles A. Williams, Co. K, promoted Captain Co. A.
May 22, 1863.	Edward F. Davies, Co. K, promoted 1st Lieut. Co. K.
Dec. 1, 1863.	Wilmot H. Chapman, Co. K, promoted 1st Lieutenant Co. I, not mustered; mustered out June 5, 1865.

MONUMENT

OF

STEVENS' FIFTH MAINE BATTERY.

The monument of Stevens' Fifth Maine Battery stands on a knoll, a spur of Culp's Hill east of the village of Gettysburg. Since the battle that knoll has been named Stevens' Knoll or Hill. (See Plate 95, Atlas to accompany Rebellion Records; Penn. at Gettysburg, Vol. i, p. 48.) The earthworks thrown up on the night of July first for the protection of the men and pieces have been preserved. In those earthworks cannon have been placed to mark their position.

The monument is of the most substantial character. The first and second bases are of Hallowell granite. The die is of red granite, the color indicating artillery. The apex is a large cannon ball of black granite two and one-half feet in diameter; both die and ball are highly polished.

ADMEASUREMENTS: Base: five feet four inches, by five feet four inches, by one foot eight inches; plinth: four feet, by four feet, by two feet four inches, of Hallowell granite; die: three feet, by three feet, by six feet, of Red Beach granite; ball: two feet eight inches diameter, of black Addison granite. Total height, twelve feet eight inches.

The monument on two faces (first view) bears the following inscriptions:

STEVENS' BATTERY

5TH MAINE 1ST CORPS

FOUGHT HERE JULY 1, 2, 3, 1863.

ALSO ENGAGED

JULY 1ST NORTH OF THE SEMINARY.

AMMUNITION EXPENDED

979 ROUNDS.

BULL RUN 2nd,

FREDERICKSBURG,

CHANCELLORSVILLE,

GETTYSBURG,

WILDERNESS,

SPOTTSYLVANIA,

COLD HARBOR,

PETERSBURG,

OPEQUAN,

FISHER'S HILL,

CEDAR CREEK.

See page 81 for inscriptions on the other two faces, second view.

INSCRIPTIONS ON MONUMENT.

(Second view, shown at page 95.)

LOSSES.
BULL RUN 2ND,
1 OFFICER AND 3 MEN KILLED
8 MEN WOUNDED
6 MEN MISSING.

CHANCELLORSVILLE,
6 MEN KILLED
3 OFFICERS AND 19 MEN WOUNDED.

GETTYSBURG,
3 MEN KILLED
2 OFFICERS AND 11 MEN WOUNDED
6 MEN MISSING.

OPEQUAN,
6 MEN WOUNDED.

CEDAR CREEK,
2 MEN KILLED
16 MEN WOUNDED.

"IN THE ASSAULT UPON
EAST CEMETERY HILL
IN THE EVENING OF
JULY 2ND THE ENEMY
(HAYS' AND HOKE'S BRIGADES)
EXPOSED THEIR LEFT FLANK TO
STEVENS' BATTERY
WHICH POURED A TERRIBLE FIRE
OF DOUBLE CANISTER INTO
THEIR RANKS."

DOUBLEDAY.

STEVENS' FIFTH MAINE BATTERY,

AT THE BATTLE OF GETTYSBURG.

THE Fifth Maine Battery, belonging to the artillery brigade, First Army Corps, was also in the first day's battle. This battery at Chancellorsville two months before had passed through one of the most trying ordeals experienced by a battery in the war of the rebellion, when it lost six men killed, three officers and nineteen men wounded and forty-three horses killed. One officer, Captain George F. Leppien, whose wound proved mortal, died at Washington, D. C., May 24, 1863.

The battery after that engagement was at once refitted and placed on a war footing by a detail of fifty-three men from the 83d and 94th New York regiments. These men, more than one-third of its number, had never served in mounted artillery before. They however were drilled, disciplined and made efficient as light artillery-men before the battery arrived at Gettysburg. This detachment, with the eighty men belonging to the battery proper, with three commissioned officers, present for duty, made the battery at Gettysburg on the morning of July 1st, one hundred and thirty-six strong.

The battery, six light 12-pounders, under Captain Greenlief T. Stevens, with Lieutenants Edward N. Whittier and Charles O. Hunt, made its way up through Virginia and Maryland with the First corps, of which it then formed a part, and at daylight on that eventful day was with the artillery brigade between Marsh Creek and Gettysburg. The corps that morning resumed its march in the following order: Wadsworth's First division with Hall's Second Maine battery; Rowley's Third division; then the artillery brigade to which the Fifth battery belonged; lastly Robinson's Second division with the Sixteenth Maine regiment. General Reynolds, in command of the left wing of the army, accompanied Wadsworth's division.

Immediately west of the village of Gettysburg there are two parallel ridges of land extending in a northerly and southerly direction, the first about one-third of a mile from the outskirts of the village, on which the Theological Seminary is located; and the other about one-third of a mile west of the Seminary, and sloping down gradually towards the west to Willoughby Run. On the most westerly ridge and facing west General Wadsworth's division was first formed, with Hall's Second Maine battery on his right.

The Fifth Maine battery reached the vicinity of Gettysburg between ten and eleven o'clock A. M. It turned off the Emmitsburg road to the west in the vicinity of the "Peach Orchard," and marched across the fields in the direction of a furious conflict then raging between the enemy and Wadsworth's division. On reaching a piece of lowland the carriages were cleared and the battery made ready for action. At this point orders were received by Captain Stevens from Colonel C. S. Wainwright, chief of artillery, First army corps, to take position in the southerly part of a grove some two hundred yards south of the Seminary and relieve Lt. Stewart's battery B, Fourth U. S. artillery.

At this hour the first Confederate advance down by Willoughby Run had been checked by Wadsworth's division, and there was a temporary lull in the battle. The battery unengaged remained in this position nearly two hours. Rowley's division, which had preceded the battery on the march, had been divided by General Doubleday, and Stone's brigade assigned to the open space between the woods where General Reynolds was killed and the Chambersburg pike, and Biddle's brigade to the left of our line near the Hagerstown road.

By this time the battle was again raging to the front and right, and with the greater number of contestants had increased in the volume of its tumult and fury. General Doubleday, who succeeded General Reynolds in the command of the corps, was establishing with prudent forethought a fortified position on the ridge around the Seminary when orders were received by Captain Stevens from General Doubleday to change position from the south to the north of the Seminary, where he took his second position on the right of Cooper's battery B, First Penn. ; Cooper was next to the Seminary building and Stevens was next to Cooper.

It was about two P. M. when this movement was made. At this hour the Sixteenth Maine had already moved from the entrenchments at the Seminary and was facing or about to face the onset of Rodes' right. The Eleventh corps was already engaged with Rodes' left and Early's division of Ewell's corps. The battle was now raging from Rock Creek and the Harrisburg road on the right around by Willoughby Run to the Hagerstown road on the left. The hours from two until four o'clock were to be crowded with thrilling events in which the batteries at the Seminary were to play a prominent part. In all twelve guns were massed at this point so closely that they were hardly five yards apart ; four guns of Cooper's battery B, First Penn., six guns of Stevens' Fifth Maine battery and two guns of Reynolds' battery L, 1st N. Y., under command of Lt. Wilber. The other four guns of Reynolds' battery, under Lt. Breck, at this hour were on the same ridge south of the Seminary.

Stewart's battery B, 4th U. S. artillery, was also on the same line but further to the north or right, one-half — three guns — being between the Chambersburg pike and the railroad cut, and the other half north of the railroad cut in the edge of the woods.

Robinson's division was on the right of Stewart's battery and formed the right of the line of the First corps.

The Fifth Maine opened fire as soon as it was in position, throwing spherical case and shell at first over our infantry in the lower ground in front.

The whole line of battle from right to left was then one continuous blaze of fire. The space between the two ridges was completely filled with the thin blue smoke of the infantry, making it difficult to distinguish friend from foe, while the artillery from their higher position belched forth a tremendous fire of shot and shell, throwing their deadly missiles in rapid succession into the ranks of the enemy advancing on our direct front, covering themselves for the moment in dense clouds of white smoke. Our infantry, by the overwhelming numbers of the enemy, five to one, were forced back upon a line with the artillery, some of them crouching under the very muzzles of the guns of the Fifth battery to avoid its fire. When our front was clear and within canister range, using double charges, the guns of the Fifth battery were turned to the right on the columns of the enemy, and when their first line was within about one hundred yards of the Seminary it was brought to a halt by Stewart's, Stevens', Reynolds' and Cooper's batteries, — Stevens' expending about fifty-seven rounds of canister (a).

But the enemy's second line, supported by a column deployed from the Cashtown or Chambersburg pike, pushed on, and in the face of the most destructive fire that could be put forth from all the troops in position succeeded in dislodging our infantry, driving in the cavalry and completely outflanking and enfilading our line both on the right and on the left. At this hour, nearly four o'clock, the Eleventh corps which had been facing north and forming nearly a right angle with the First corps line, and in full view of our position at the Seminary, was fast falling back toward the town, closely pressed by the enemy.

Colonel Wainwright in his official report, referring to this hour, said: "An order was now received by Captain Stevens from General Wadsworth to withdraw his battery. Not knowing that he had received such an order, and still under the false impression as to the importance attached to holding Seminary Hill, I directed all the batteries to remain in position. A few minutes, however, showed me our infantry rapidly retreating to the town. All the batteries were at once limbered to the rear and moved at a walk down the Cashtown pike until the infantry had left it" (b). * * *

By this time the enemy's skirmishers had lapped our retreating columns and opened a severe fire within fifty yards of the road in which the artillery was obliged to pass. The pike being clear, the batteries now broke into a trot, but it was too late to save everything. Battery L, 1st N. Y., lost one gun

(a) The battery expended in the battle of Gettysburg 103 rounds of canister. See Rebellion Records, Vol. 27, page 362. Lt. Whittier in his report of the engagement on the evening of July 2d says: "When within six hundred yards I opened with canister and fired, before they were repulsed, upwards of 46 rounds." This leaves 57 rounds expended at the Seminary on July 1, as canister was used at no other times.

(b) Rebellion Records, Vol. 27, part 1, page 357.

and five horses; three caissons of battery B, 4th U. S. artillery, broke down before they reached the town and had to be abandoned. Another caisson of the same battery was struck by a shell and destroyed. While at a trot-march a gun wheel of one of the guns of the Fifth battery came off, the axle dropping in the road; the team was halted, the gun raised by the cannoneers and wheel replaced, Captain Stevens springing from his horse and seizing the gunner's pinchers, inserted the handle for a linch-pin, and the gun was saved from capture.

At this point, near where a brook crosses the Chambersburg pike, not far from the westerly outskirts of the village, private William Widner, a driver, detached from the 94th N. Y. and serving with the battery, was killed, falling from his horse beside the road. Charles M. Bryant was killed near the Seminary as the battery was limbering to the rear, and Lieut. Charles O. Hunt was severely wounded in the thigh while at the same point.

Privates Aaron Simpson, William Leonard, Sylvester L. Brown, John A. Paine, Warren B. Bailey and Edwin T. Witham were also wounded; and privates J. P. St. Clair, Charles Smith, Jno. Dwyer, Jno. Bessey and A. C. Marvin were taken prisoners, the last three being detached men from the 94th N. Y. regiment.

Such were the losses in this battery up to this hour, four o'clock in the afternoon.

A MARKER

stands in the road west of the Seminary buildings to indicate the position of the Battery at that point in the first day's battle. (See map of the First Day.) The marker, of Maine granite, is a large rectangular block, cut away on the upper half of one side in a slope, presenting a polished raised table inscribed with the following legend:

STEVENS'

BATTERY,

5TH

MAINE.

JULY 1, 1863.

The First corps had lost heavily. General Reynolds had been killed. He was on horseback in the easterly edge of an open wood, surrounded by his staff. The enemy were in the wood. Without doubt he felt anxious in relation to the result and frequently turned his head to see if Robinson's and Rowley's divisions, which had not then arrived, would be up in time to assist Wadsworth who was hotly engaged, and while he was looking back in that way a rebel sharp-shooter shot him through the back of the head, the bullet coming out near the eye. He fell dead in an instant without uttering a word. He had served in the 3d U. S. artillery with Generals Sherman, Thomas and Doubleday, and had fought in the same battles with the latter in the Mexican war.

Our troops never fought with greater spirit, believing that Gettysburg was to be held at all hazards. "We have come to stay" was the battle cry that passed along the line. As it proved, a great portion of them did come to stay, laying down their lives to save this country for the present and future generations. When out of ammunition many a soldier replenished his box from that of his killed or wounded comrade.

When the left of the Eleventh corps nearest the First corps fell back, a force of nearly 20,000 Confederates was thrown upon the First corps, which in the beginning of the contest only numbered 8,200 and which was reduced at the close of the engagement to 2,450 (a).

General Wadsworth in his official report said: "The severity of the contest during the day will be indicated by the painful fact that at least half of the officers and men who went into the engagement were killed or wounded" (b).

General Robinson, commanding the Second division, went into the battle with less than 2,500 officers and men and sustained a loss of 1,667, of which 124 were commissioned officers (c).

The Confederate general A. M. Scales, who advanced directly against our position at the Seminary, in his official report said:

(a) Rebellion Records, Vol. 27, part 1, page 251.
(b) Rebellion Records, Vol. 27, part 1, page 266.
(c) Ibid, page 291.

"We passed over them (the first Confederate line of battle) up the ascent across the ridge and commenced the descent just opposite the Theological Seminary. Here the brigade encountered a most terrific fire of grape and shell on our flank, and grape and musketry in our front. Every discharge made sad havoc in our line, but still we pressed on at a double quick and we reached the bottom, a distance of seventy-five yards from the ridge we had crossed and about the same distance from the college in our front. Here I received a painful wound from a piece of shell and was disabled. Our line had been broken up and only a squad here and there marked the place where regiments had stood. Every field officer in the brigade save one had been disabled; and the following list of casualties will attest sufficiently the terrible ordeal through which the brigade passed. Killed 48, wounded 381, missing 116. Total 545 " (a).

On the retreat the guns of the Fifth were intermingled with those of Captain Cooper's battery B, 1st Penn., and, passing through the town whose streets were crowded with the columns of the First corps and encumbered by stragglers from the Eleventh corps upon whose heels the Confederates were closely following, moved along Baltimore street and up the hill on the Baltimore pike to the Cemetery gate. This was the rallying point of broken and disordered regiments and batteries. Of the sixteen thousand five hundred men of the First and Eleventh corps who went into the battle, not more than five thousand five hundred were rallied on this hill in fighting condition; while stretching through the village of Gettysburg and to the right and left of the same were the heavier columns of the Confederate army. Nearly four thousand of their comrades were lying upon the field in full view beyond the town. Five thousand more had been captured and two thousand dispersed (b). The annals of war present no instance of more desperate, stubborn, gallant and persistent fighting than that offered July 1, 1863, by the First corps.

With several hours of sunlight the situation of the remaining Union forces was perilous indeed. "But sometimes, at a critical moment," says the Comte de Paris, "a single individual may bring a moral force on the battlefield worth a hundred battalions." Such a person was General Hancock at this moment. He was sent by General Meade to take charge of the field. He arrived on Cemetery Hill about four o'clock, and was by the gate of the Cemetery as the Fifth Maine

(a) Rebellion Records, Vol. 27, part 2, page 670.
(b) Estimate made by the Comte de Paris, Hist. Civil War, Vol. III, page 570.

battery came up. He called for the captain of "that brass battery." Captain Stevens heard what he said and put himself in
Hancock's presence; he ordered Stevens to "take (his) battery
on to that hill," pointing to Culp's Hill, and "stop the enemy
from coming up that ravine." "By whose order?" was the
inquiry. "General Hancock's," was the reply.

When the order was given, "Fifth battery, forward!" each
gun and caisson separated from Cooper's battery and the
infantry with which it had been retiring, and dropped into its
proper place and marched easterly down the Baltimore pike
until it reached a lane leading to a cottage in the direction of
Culp's Hill. Passing through that lane and up the elevation, it
reached the summit of a knoll at the westerly extremity of
Culp's Hill. This position commanded completely the easterly
slope of Cemetery Hill and the ravine at the north. As the
battery reached this position the enemy was sweeping through
the village and up across the lowlands in our front. The battery was unsupported. No Union infantry was on the right,
and none on the left nearer than Cemetery Hill where the
other troops were turned off to the right and left by General
Hancock and put into line of battle. The battery at once
went into position and opened so vigorous a fire that the
advance of the Confederates in that direction was stopped and
the desire of General Hancock was fully achieved. The enemy
took shelter by lying down behind any object that furnished
protection.

General Hunt, chief of artillery of the Army of the Potomac, attracted no doubt by the rapidity and vigor of the battery's fire at this hour, paid it a visit. On learning that the
battery had no supports, and that a body of the enemy had
gone so far to the right that their position and movements were
covered by the woods on the northerly slope of Culp's Hill and
that there was nothing to prevent their skirmishers from
approaching within one hundred yards of the battery without
being observed, he said to Captain Stevens: "I don't like the
look of this; send some of your men and tear gaps in the
fences between here and the Baltimore pike, and on the opposite side of the pike, so that you can reach the high land beyond

in case you're driven out." The order was promptly obeyed. The non-military reader should observe that while a battery can keep back or destroy masses of the enemy, it cannot successfully contend with a line of skirmishers. To resist them would be like shooting mosquitoes with musket balls. But the battery was not forgotten by Hancock. In this connection General Doubleday in his report of the engagement says: "Major-General Hancock now rode up and informed me he had been placed in command of both corps. He at once directed me to send a force to support a battery which had been established on a lower range of hills some one hundred yards to the east of our position, protecting our flank in that direction. I complied with the order and sent the remainder of Wadsworth's division there. Immediately afterward orders came from General Howard, who ranked Hancock, to send the troops in another direction. This occasioned at the time some little delay and confusion" (a).

General Wadsworth, however, with the remainder of his division did not go in another direction, but went directly to the battery, passing between the line of limbers and caissons of the battery and taking position on the right and a little in advance of the same where it remained during the remainder of the battle, planting his headquarter-colors near its right gun. At intervals the battery maintained its fire until dark to keep down the enemy that were in our front and prevent the movement of their troops as far as possible within its range.

In this connection Colonel A. C. Godwin, commanding Hoke's Confederate brigade after Colonel Avery was mortally wounded, said:

"The brigade continued to advance toward the town, but while yet in the outskirts was wheeled to the left and re-formed on the railroad. The enemy had now succeeded in planting a battery upon a high sloping spur on the mountain side immediately in our front. Under cover of the railroad cut we were moved by the flank about 400 yards to the left and then moved forward. The shells from the enemy proving very effective, we were soon after halted in a depression on the hillside and the men ordered to lie down. Skirmishers were thrown forward and this position held through the night and until 8 P. M. on the next day, July 2, when the brigade moved forward to the attack" (b).

(a) Rebellion Records, Vol. 27, part 1, page 252.
(b) Rebellion Records, Vol. 27, part 2, page 484; also see map of the first day.

Between five and six o'clock P. M. the Union troops that were not in the first day's battle began to arrive. Slocum's Twelfth corps, between eight and nine thousand strong, was the first to appear. While yet in the distance the lone star upon their banners told us who they were, causing the Fifth battery boys to send up cheer after cheer. The First division of that corps was put in position on our right down by Rock Creek, while two brigades of the Second division wended their way up across the country in our rear and took position on the left of our line between Cemetery Hill and Little Round Top (a).

But this is not a chronicle of the Twelfth corps. On that ground it was evident that the contest would be renewed the next day, and preparations were accordingly made for the same. During the night earthworks were constructed "under the direction of Captain Stevens, which on the two days following proved of the greatest service in covering and protecting the men and pieces" (b). It will be observed elsewhere that the losses were largely sustained on the first day. When all was quiet except occasional picket firing, the teams having been cared for, the men, regaled with their usual allowance of hardtack and coffee, tired and exhausted, repulsed but not routed, beaten but not dismayed, wrapped their blankets about them and camped down beside their guns and horses for a little rest, with mother earth for a pillow, and the starry heavens above them for a shelter. Thus passed one of our days and nights on this battlefield destined to become the Waterloo of the western world.

The forenoon of the second day passed similarly to the closing hours of the first day, — troops arriving, picket firing, sharpshooting and artillery duelling at long range. From an early hour in the morning the enemy's sharp-shooters, posted behind walls and fences in the lowlands in front of the battery, were very annoying and were only partially dislodged by our skirmishers sent out to oppose them.

During the afternoon while observing movements of the enemy Captain Stevens was severely wounded, being shot through both legs below the knee, and was removed from the

(a) See Rebellion Records, Vol. 27, part 1, page 758.
(b) See Official Report on file, Adjutant-General's office, Maine.

field.   Sergeants Lorrin E. Bundy and James W. White, performing the duty of commissioned officers, evinced quite as
plainly as on other occasions courage and discretion of a high
degree.   Lieutenant A. B. Twitchell being absent, wounded,
the command of the battery then devolved upon Lieutenant
Whittier, who has recently furnished the following account of
the battery in the battle of Gettysburg while under his command.
He writes in part as follows :

"To take up my topic, the part borne by the Fifth Maine
battery in the battle after Captain Stevens was wounded.
About one o'clock the enemy ran guns into position just opposite the end of East Cemetery Hill, to enfilade our lines which
from that point ran in a southerly direction towards the Round
Tops.   We could just reach the enemy, and joining fire with
the rifled guns on East Cemetery ridge their batteries were soon
silenced.   Great annoyance was experienced later from sharpshooters in our front concealed in bushes, behind fences and
even in the trees along the course of Rock Creek.   A company
of riflemen was deployed and made its way out some distance,
and after some difficulty dislodged the enemy and drove their
men back towards their main skirmish line.   And so the afternoon wore on, our anxiety increasing as we saw the fight raging
with what seemed doubtful success on our part, way off on our
left, in front of the Round Tops and out on the Emmitsburg
road, while troops were hurrying from the right of our line
across to the succor of the Third and Fifth corps, until it seemed
as if the whole Twelfth corps was in motion, and it was, excepting Greene's brigade, as we afterwards learned ; and the roar
and crash of artillery, the rattle of musketry, the vast clouds
of smoke rolling down from Little Round Top and filling the
valley, all joined to make us feel that the day was going against
us.   In the urgent desire of reinforcing the Third corps
(Sickles'), only Greene's brigade was left to hold the works
protecting the extreme right of the line against any attempt of
the enemy to gain a foothold on the Baltimore pike (a).

"About 4 P. M. those who were on the left of our position,
where the view of Benner's Hill was unobstructed by the trees

(a) The movement of Twelfth corps to reinforce other portions of the line
occurred between 6 and 7 o'clock P. M.

LOSSES.

BULL RUN 2ND,
1 OFFICER AND 3 MEN KILLED,
1 MEN WOUNDED,
6 MEN MISSING.

CHANCELLORSVILLE,
6 MEN KILLED,
3 OFFICERS AND 19 MEN WOUNDED.

GETTYSBURG.
3 MEN KILLED,
2 OFFICERS AND 11 MEN WOUNDED,
6 MEN MISSING.

OPEQUAN,
6 MEN WOUNDED,

CEDAR CREEK,
2 MEN KILLED,
16 MEN WOUNDED.

"IN THE ASSAULT UPON
EAST CEMETERY HILL
IN THE EVENING OF
JULY 2ND THE ENEMY
(HAYS AND HOKE'S BRIGADES)
EXPOSED THEIR LEFT FLANK TO
STEVENS' BATTERY
WHICH POURED A TERRIBLE FIRE
OF DOUBLE CANISTER INTO
THEIR RANKS." —
DOUBLEDAY.

on the northerly slope of Culp's, had presented to their gaze the almost unexampled spectacle of a Confederate battery in full view, thrown into 'action front' as deliberately as on parade. This was the initial movement of Andrews' battalion of artillery, commanded by Major Latimer, taking position, with fourteen guns closely crowded together on the crest of this small hill. Two guns, 20-pounder Parrotts, went in-battery on an elevation to the right and rear of the position chosen. From the high ground further to the enemy's right, rifled pieces opened simultaneously with Andrews' battalion a converging fire on our batteries on East Cemetery Hill, and enfilading our infantry lines and the artillery, which, further south in the cemetery, were facing Seminary ridge and the Emmitsburg road. I doubt if more than six or eight projectiles came to the ground on the knoll where we had been ordered by General Hancock.

"At once, as if directed by the command of one man, our battery united with battery L, 1st N. Y., Lieut. Breck, with Cooper and Wiedrich on the hill, and with Taft's 20-pounders in the cemetery, and poured such destructive fire into the batteries on Benner's Hill that in less than half an hour four of their limbers or caissons exploded and their batteries were silenced. Nowhere on the field of Gettysburg was such havoc wrought by artillery on artillery, and the wreck of Andrews' battalion, in horses and shattered gun- and ammunition-carriages left on the field for months, was a noteworthy feature and was visited by throngs of eager sight-seers. Major Latimer died of wounds received here. One captain and one first lieutenant were severely wounded; two non-commissioned officers and eight men were killed; two non-commissioned officers and thirty-five men were wounded; thirty horses were killed.

"It was during this artillery duel that John F. Chase received the terrible wounds which so nearly cost him his life. Our guns grew so hot, in spite of using wet sponges, that it was quite an hour afterwards before one could bear his hand on the knob of the cascabel. Soon after General Howard, commanding on East Cemetery Hill, sent an aide with the General's compliments and congratulations for the efficient work done by

the battery on that occasion, and about this time Lieutenant
Matthewson came over from Colonel Wainwright, and finding
that our ammunition was running low, very kindly offered to
see that our chests were refilled. In considerable haste, all
that was left in the caissons was transferred to the limber-chests
of the guns, and we soon saw our teams disappearing down the
pike in the direction of the ammunition trains in the fields
towards General Slocum's headquarters, a mile and a half or so
in our rear, and we were left there with a scanty supply of
shot and shell, a larger equipment of case shot and all the
canister left over from the first day's fight.

"Our guns cooled all the more rapidly from the use of wet
sponges which at the same time left the guns clean; the sun
dropped behind the western mountains, and all grew quiet save
for the scattered fire of skirmishers, an occasional gun flashing
from Little Round Top and the distant sound of the exploding
shells; the dusk of evening was creeping down the valley of
Rock Creek and shutting out the town from view, and there
was abundant promise of a peaceful night in our immediate
front, when suddenly one of our sergeants on the lookout
shouted, 'Look! look at those men,' and he pointed to our left
front in the edge of the town and between our position and
the farm buildings of William Culp, where, in line of battle
extending nearly to Rock Creek at the base of Benner's Hill,
the enemy could be seen climbing the walls and fences and
forming for the assault. The assaulting column was Hays'
brigade ('Louisiana Tigers') and Hoke's brigade of North Carolinians, with Gordon's brigade in the reserve. Time 7 :45 P. M.

"It must be borne in mind that Johnson's division was
already in possession of our works on the right of our line,
directly in our rear and within a few hundred yards of the
Baltimore pike, and that Rodes' division, struggling to free
itself from the hindrances of the streets and houses of Gettysburg, was taking position on the west of the town, in the fields
fronting our infantry and artillery on Cemetery Hill.

"All comrades of the old Fifth know how quickly and how
well our guns opened the artillery fire that evening, for the
order, 'Case, 2 1-2 degrees, 3 seconds time,' had hardly been

heard before up went the lids of the limber-chests, the fuses were cut in another moment, and the guns were loaded as if on drill. Slap went the heads of the rammers against the faces of the pieces, a most welcome sound, for at the same moment came the order 'Fire by battery,' and at once there was the flash and roar of our six guns, the rush of the projectiles, and along the front of the enemy's charging line every case shot— ' long range canister'—burst as if on measured ground, at the right time and in the right place above and in front of their advance. This was the first intimation given by artillery of the rebel attack on East Cemetery Hill. General Underwood, at that time commanding the 33d Mass. regiment, wrote me afterwards :

" 'I had just placed my regiment in line behind the stone wall at the head of the valley separating Culp's from Cemetery Hill, and had no knowledge, the evening was so far advanced, of any artillery near me, when right over my head, it seemed to me, there was a flash of light, a roar and a crash as if a volcano had been let loose.'

" It was the Fifth Maine battery turned loose on the enemy. In another moment the battery was 'firing at will,' while Breck, Ricketts and Wiedrich, on East Cemetery Hill, made the ground tremble with their volleys plowing through the lines of the enemy now in full movement and charging on their position. Two important causes contributed to delay the rebel advance : first, the front fire of fifteen guns on East Cemetery Hill and the flank fire of the Fifth Maine on the northern slope of Culp's Hill ; second, the delay arising from firing and loading, for their lines opened fire in reply even to the feeble resistance offered by our skirmishers.

" When the enemy started on this movement their lines nearly faced our position, but as they advanced they obeyed the order given at the outset, and, pivoting on their right which rested on and moved along the outskirts of the town, they so changed direction by an almost right half-wheel of their whole force, that at 8 : 30 we had an oblique fire on them ; and when they were under the steep acclivity of Cemetery Hill, where the guns on the crest couldn't touch them, the Fifth Maine had an enfilading fire on their whole left and centre. In this position no other artillery could reach them, and they were delivered over to the hot, unsparing havoc of our canister, and it wrought their ruin.

"One battery alone was placed so as to fire canister down the valley and to deliver a direct fire on the enemy's front from East Cemetery Hill. It was Breck with battery L, 1st N. Y., on the low ground on the side of the slope nearest our position; but in his published report he says: 'I did not use canister for fear of the infantry in my front,' etc. (a).

"A few minutes before this it was found that the right guns of the battery were almost useless because of the position of the enemy's line rapidly changing and soon to be quite in rear of our left flank; the left half of the battery was already firing at nearly right angles to the direction taken at the opening, the gunners having followed the enemy's advancing line by firing more and more left oblique. As soon as it was reported that the left half-battery only could be worked, the right half-battery was 'limbered up' and the ʼguns placed in position on the slope to the left and rear of our earthworks and facing the town, and the whole battery was once more effective and this time with canister.

"It was now so dark that the enemy's line could be made out only by the fire from their rifles. The extreme left, bent back, nearly faced us, but their left and centre were still facing the slopes of Cemetery Hill, and a desperate effort was made by their officers under this 'terrible enfilade fire of double canister' to rally a sufficient number of their men to enable them to secure foothold among the batteries. General Hays writes:—

"'Here we came upon a considerable body of the enemy and a brisk musketry fire ensued. At the same time his artillery, of which we were now within canister range, opened upon us, but owing to the darkness of the evening now verging into night, and the deep obscurity afforded by the smoke of the firing, our exact locality could not be discovered by the enemy's gunners, and we thus escaped what in the full light of day could have been nothing else than horrible slaughter.'—*Official Records, Vol. 27, part 2, page 480.*

"Colonel Godwin, commanding Hoke's brigade after Colonel Avery was wounded, writes:—

"'After the summit of a hill had been gained it was discovered that the batteries we had been ordered to take were considerably to the right of our

(a) Rebellion Records, Vol. 27, part 1, pp. 362-364.

right flank and in front of Hays' brigade. We continued to advance, however, under a terrific fire, climbed a rail fence and still farther beyond descended into a low bottom and dislodged a heavy line of infantry from a stone-wall running parallel with our front. The enemy's batteries now enfiladed us, and a destructive fire was poured into our ranks from a line of infantry, formed in rear of a stone-wall running at a right angle with our line of battle and immediately below the battery. Colonel Avery now ordered a change of front and succeeded in wheeling the brigade to the right, a movement which none but the steadiest veterans could have executed under such circumstances; three stone-walls had to be surmounted in swinging around; the ground was rocky and uneven. The men now charged up the hill with heroic determination; in this charge the command had become much separated, and in the darkness it was now found impossible to concentrate more than forty or fifty men at any point for a further advance. Major Tate with a portion of the 6th N. C. regiment, aided by a small number of the 9th La., succeeded in capturing a battery on the right.'

"Major Tate, in a letter to the governor of North Carolina, writes : —

"'Longstreet charged on the south face (of the heights) and was repulsed; A. P. Hill charged on the west face and had been repulsed; and our two brigades were, late in the evening, ordered to charge the north front, and after a struggle such as this war has furnished no parallel to, seventy-five North Carolinians of the sixth regiment and twelve Louisianians of Hays' brigade scaled the walls and planted the colors of the 6th N. C. and the 9th La. on the guns. It was now fully dark.'—*Rebellion Records, Vol. 27, part 2, pp. 484–486.*

"That is, only eighty-seven men out of Hoke's and Hays' brigades succeeded in reaching the crest of East Cemetery Hill.

"Colonel Wainwright states : 'Their centre and left never mounted the hill at all, but their right worked its way up under cover of the houses and pushed its way completely through Wiedrich's battery into Ricketts'' (a).

"Our only loss of any importance this evening took place about this time ; a volley from that portion of their line nearest us killed four out of six horses on the left piece, the one most exposed to their fire, the piece which nearly touched the right of the 33d Mass. regiment, and was firing obliquely across their front. We had nearly or quite expended the contents of our chests, and some 46–49 rounds of canister had been hurled across the valley and up the slopes of the ridge, occupied by the enemy's left and centre, when the cry went up from one end of the battery to the other for more canister and for more

(a) Rebellion Records, Vol. 27, part 1, page 358.

friction primers ; but our work had already been accomplished. Little by little, rapidly at first and then more slowly, their lines retreated, and we could see that they were falling back by their receding line of fire, and soon all was quiet in our immediate front. I gave the order to limber to the rear, and then, and before the battery moved, I crept down the slope on the right of the battery and found it to be true as reported, that the enemy was in full retreat from our front; then, and only then, was the battery withdrawn to the Baltimore pike and halted while I went up to the cemetery gate, there found Colonel Wainwright, and reported to him what I had done and why. Infantry was at once placed in our works, and in obedience to Colonel Wainwright's orders, after finding Lieutenant Matthewson, then on his return to us with full chests, returned to our position, turned out the infantry sleeping there, and at 10 : 30 everything was in the same condition as before the fight of the evening, only better, because our supply of ammunition was more nearly complete than it had been at any previous hour of that day.

"While it is true that on this occasion the battery sustained no material loss, it should not be lost sight of that our position was not the enemy's objective point; it is also true, that the enemy could not have comprehended the importance of the position we occupied with reference to the protection it afforded our troops on Cemetery Hill; for we could enfilade any line advancing to the assault of that crest, and could cover with our canister the sharp acclivity of the hill and its immediate foreground, searching their advance with the most demoralizing and destructive of all that is possible from artillery, an enfilading fire of double canister; and more than all this, it is not what a battery loses, it is the loss it inflicts which is the true measure of its effectiveness.

"Some rain during the night refreshed while it wet us thoroughly, though many of the men slept through it all, so great was their fatigue. 'The last sound slumbers of the night held us in their soft but sure embrace' until early dawn, when we were violently aroused by an outburst from artillery posted on the hill where the Twelfth corps headquarters were, and on a small knoll a little nearer our position. Twenty guns in all (a) opened at 4 A. M., at the short range of 600–800 yards, on the enemy holding possession of that portion of our line vacated the evening before by the Twelfth corps. This cannonade was continued with but short intervals until 10 A. M. Meanwhile the enemy had pushed his lines, strongly reinforced, up to the base and along the slopes of Culp's Hill for its whole length, and their bullets swept the crest of the knoll where we were, and at one time they seemed so near breaking through in our front that canister was brought up from the limbers and caissons, and piled up inside our works behind which our men sought protection. The nearness of the woods in our right front, through which they would have come had they broken through, made this course with reference to ammunition imperative. An attempt was made in the morning to place one or two of our guns in the woods and behind the earthworks on the higher part of Culp's Hill, where a flank fire could have been obtained, but the attempt was given up because of the impossibility of moving the guns through the woods without first cutting down many trees,—an undertaking considered by General Wadsworth's aide too hazardous.

" The battery was not actively engaged during the 3d. Orders had been received early in the morning to fire at any and all considerable bodies of troops within range, and this was done with the good effect of forcing all troops moving to reinforce Johnson to make a long detour behind Benner's Hill and the high ground on the further side of Rock Creek. During the forenoon Col. Wainwright came over to the battery and looked us over, and took note of our condition and the opportunities our position gave us to command the open country from Culp's Hill to the edge of the town, and the fields from Benner's Hill along the high ground towards what was afterwards known as Hospital Hill ; and he said to me that he hoped we realized that we held ' one of the most important, if not the most important position on the whole line.'

" I need not refer to any other incident during the remaining portion of the 3d than the sad circumstance of the wounding

(a) Rebellion Records, Vol. 27, part 1, page 871.

and death of corporal Sullivan Luce.   *   *   *   I can never forget that hour, for we were firing into the town, word having been sent us that the enemy was forming there for another assault on Cemetery Hill, and aide after aide galloped across to our position with orders for us to be watchful and active. When the prisoners of Pickett's division were brought over the slope of Cemetery Hill towards our position, and before we could tell that the enemy had been repulsed, it seemed as if our lines were broken, and that our way out was blocked. The battery was then thrown into position to fire to the rear, and in a moment more would have been in action, but then came the cheers and the fight was ended.

"General Hunt, chief of artillery at Gettysburg, wrote me under date of June 13, 1887, concerning the part borne by the battery at Gettysburg in the evening of the second day :   'Its splendid service in the repulse of Ewell's attack on Cemetery Hill was one of the marked features of the battle.'

"In another letter written in 1887, General Hunt wrote : 'The excellent service of the Fifth Maine battery, posted at the head of the ravine, was one of the prominent causes of the success.'

"Concerning the battery and at an earlier date in its history than Gettysburg, General Hunt said :   'No better battery than Leppien's could be found in the United States service, either volunteer or regular.'   (See A. G. R. Maine, 1863, pp. 123–125.)

"Maj.-Gen. Doubleday, commanding First corps at Gettysburg, replying to a request that he would write some words of commendation of the work done by the battery while in his command and on the evening of July 2, 1863, wrote of 'the brilliant service the battery performed at Gettysburg in repelling or rather crushing the attack of the Texan troops in their attempt to make a permanent lodgment among the Eleventh corps troops on Cemetery Hill, — the battery's enfilading fire was so destructive and so well directed that only a remnant of Avery's and Hays' brigades returned to their original positions in line.   It gives me pleasure to testify to the very important part borne [by the battery] and to its great influence in deciding the victory in our favor.'

"The battery came into my charge, as it did into the care of Captain Stevens my immediate predecessor, a terrible engine of war, tried and proven, and in the highest degree perfected, fresh from the hands of a master in the science and art of war, one who was highly accomplished in all that pertained to a light artillery organization; for it was said of Leppien as early as November, 1861, by an authority no less distinguished than General Barry, chief of artillery of the defenses of Washington : ' He knows all about artillery from the face of the piece to the tips of the leader's ears.' Well and nobly did he fulfill the promise of his earlier years; how well, the record bears abundant and indisputable evidence."

PARTICIPANTS.

Officers and men of the Fifth Maine Battery present for duty in the battle of Gettysburg, July 1, 2, and 3, 1863.

COMMISSIONED OFFICERS.

Captain, Greenlief T. Stevens, Augusta.
First Lieutenant, Edward N. Whittier, Gorham.
Second Lieutenant, Charles O. Hunt, Gorham.

SERGEANTS.

Lorrin E. Bundy, Columbia, N. H.,   James L. Loomis, Colebrook, N. H.,
James C. Bartlett, Bethel,   James W. White, Vassalboro.

CORPORALS.

Lemuel A. Cummings, Augusta,   Edward P. Stearns, Bethel,
James H. Lebroke, Lewiston,   David I. Black, Hanover, N. H.,
Andrew J. Welch, Wells,   Charles A. Hinckley, Belgrade,
Roliston Woodbury, Sweden,   Michael Hickey, Lewiston,
Hiram M. Paul, Stewartstown, N. H.

MUSICIAN: Calvin W. Richardson, Lewiston.

ARTIFICERS.

John Murphy, Portland,   Alden S. Dudley, Augusta,
William H. Huskins, Belgrade.   Charles O. Kennard, Portland,
Isaiah W. Spiller, Gilead.

PRIVATES.

Bailey, Warren B., Lisbon,   Berry, William, Portland,
Blackman, Joseph B., Augusta,   Bradley, Michael, Portland,
Brown, Charles E., Carratunk Pl.,   Brown Rufus, Brighton,*
Brown, Sylvester L.,Colebrook, N. H. Brown, William C. A., Poland,
Bryant, Charles M., Winslow,   Cannon, Joseph B., Farmingdale,
Casey, James, Portland,   Chase, John F., Augusta,
Clapp, Andrew J., Portland,   Cook, Charles W., Athens,

* Given as Bridgton on company rolls.

Connor, Maurice O., P. Edward's Is.,
Cummings, Henry A., Augusta,
Dutton, Ruel W., Augusta,
Hamilton, Henry A., Vassalboro,
Harmon, Algernon S., Portland,
Heath, Albert, Pittsburg,
Hussey, John F., Augusta,
Leonard, William, Lewiston,
Luce, Sullivan, Auburn,
Mennealy, Thos. B.,Columbia, N. H.,
Morse, Bennett, Grafton,
Paine, John A., Hallowell,
Powers, Corydon, Hanover,
St. Clair, Isaac P., Lisbon,
Smith, Charles, Hallowell,
Sukeforth, James L., Washington,
Towne, William I., Vassalboro,
Varney, Alden M., Houlton,
Warren, Edward, Lewiston,
Whittier, George W., Gorham,
Witham, Edwin F., Lovell,
Woods, John, Portland,
Worster, John, Belgrade.

Crane, Charles L., Fayette,
Dunton, David H.,Pleasant Ridge Pl.,
Greene, Patrick, Lewiston,
Hanson, John H., Lewiston,
Harris, Horace, Stewartstown, N. H.,
Hinkley, Alonzo, Lisbon,
Kelly, Patrick, Portland,
Lombard, James A., Belgrade,
Maxwell, Richard E., Minot,
Mitchell, Stephen, Paris,
Nevers, William H., Sweden,
Pike, Charles E., Bridgton,
Ryan, William, Augusta,
Simpson, Aaron, Sheffield, Vt.,
Spiller, Francis J., Gilead,
Thompson, Eben, Portland,
Tuttle, Wilbert D., Athens,
Varney, John H., Manchester,
White, Henry, Stratford, N. H.,
Witham, Charles C., Portland,
Withee, Charles A., Madison,
Woods, Joseph, Portland,

ON DAILY DUTY AND DETACHED SERVICE.

SERGEANTS: George W. Woodbury, Sweden, in quartermaster and commissary department; John A. Brown, Portland.

WAGONER: Joseph L. Marston, Portland, forage master.

PRIVATES: Henry H. Hunt, Gorham, acting hospital steward; Frank E. Pearson, Orono, and John P. Ryan, Augusta, in invalid detachment.

Not included in the above there were fifty-three men serving with the battery detached from the 83d and 94th N. Y. regiments.

REVISED REPORT OF CASUALTIES.

Captain: Greenlief T. Stevens, wounded July 2, both legs.
Second Lieutenant: Charles O. Hunt, wounded July 1, leg.

PRIVATES.

Bailey, Warren B., wounded July 1, leg.
Brown, Sylvester L., wounded; died Sept. 13.
Bryant, Charles M., killed July 1.
Chase, John F., wounded July 3, arm and eye.
Leonard, William, wounded July 1, chest.
Lombard, James A., wounded July 3, leg.
Luce, Sullivan, killed July 3.
Paine, John A., wounded July 1, arm.
St. Clair, Isaac P., prisoner July 1.
Simpson, Aaron, wounded July 1, wrist.
Smith, Charles, prisoner July 1.
Witham, Edwin F., wounded July 1, ankle.

The following casualties occurred among the men from the 94th N. Y. :

Privates: John Berry, prisoner July 1; John Dwyer, prisoner July 1; —— Huntermark, prisoner July 1; Hosea Kenyon, wounded July 3; A. C. Marvin, prisoner July 1; Homer Nichols, wounded July 3; James F. Seacoy, wounded July 3; William Widner, killed July 1.

HISTORICAL SKETCH OF FIFTH MAINE BATTERY.

BY BREVET MAJOR GREENLIEF T. STEVENS.

This battery was raised at large and entered the service under favorable auspices. It was mustered into the United States service December 4, 1861, officered as follows :

George F. Leppien, Portland, Captain ; William F. Twitchell, Portland, Greenlief T. Stevens, Augusta, First Lieutenants ; Adelbert B. Twitchell, Bethel, Ezra Clark, Portland, Second Lieutenants.

The battery was rendezvoused at Augusta until the tenth day of March, 1862, on which day it left for Portland, and remained quartered at Fort Preble until April 1st, when it proceeded to Washington. There it remained until the 19th of May, when it embarked for Acquia Creek, Va. Then field operations commenced which continued to the close of the war.

Gettysburg was only one of the many engagements in which the battery bore an honorable part. During its entire term of service it was continually at the front excepting a brief period in the fall of 1862, refitting after being roughly treated by the enemy. It served in succession under McDowell, Pope, McClellan, Burnside, Hooker, Meade, Grant and Sheridan. On August 9, 1862, at Cedar Mountain, Va., the battery was first under fire (a). It took position at night during a heavy cannonade but was not engaged, and sustained no losses.

On the twentieth day of August, 1862, the battery was at Rappahannock Station in position on the northerly bank of the river covering and protecting the bridge at that place, and on the two days following engaged the enemy's artillery and assisted

(a)   Sometimes called Cedar Run and Slaughter's Mountain.

in dispersing a body of their infantry attempting to form near the bridge.

On the 23d the battery covered the retreat to Warrenton during which one of the guns was disabled by recoil and was sent to the rear. On August 28th the battery fell back with the division to Thoroughfare Gap; but the enemy was there in advance, holding possession, and were masters of the situation. In the afternoon the battery was engaged, taking position on a steep knoll and firing across the gorge.

Three days previous to this "Stonewall" Jackson (Thomas J.) by a circuitous route had stolen quietly away under the direction of his chief and marched his entire corps around the right flank of our army by way of Amissville, Orleans and Salem, keeping thus far west of the Bull Run Mountains. He passed the main body of his corps through Thoroughfare Gap in these mountains two days before the Fifth battery was there, and on the night of the 26th was at Bristoe Station on the Orange and Alexandria Railroad in rear of our army and between it and Washington, thus breaking General Pope's communication by railroad with his base of supplies and compelling him to abandon his position on the Rappahannock and make a hasty retreat without a decisive battle being fought (a).

On August 30th the battery was on the battlefield of Bull Run. On the afternoon of that disastrous day, when the battle had become general and was raging with great violence along the whole line, our left was sorely pressed, and quickly General Tower was sent with the Second and Third brigades of Ricketts' division and the Second and Fifth Maine batteries, for its relief. This position our troops endeavored most gallantly to maintain. But infantry and artillery alike were overwhelmed and the enemy were at once in the midst of the battery. Our troops suffered severely. Four guns of the Fifth battery were captured. One gun and the line of caissons were saved. General Tower fell, seriously wounded. Lieutenant William F. Twitchell, who was in command of the battery, was killed and left on the field; his body, however, was afterwards recovered and sent to his friends in Maine. He was mounted when shot.

(a) Rebellion Records, Vol. 12, part 2, page 181.

The fatal bullet struck him in the right side through the vest pocket. A buck-shot hole was also found through one of his gloves (a). Sergt. Orrison Woods and George W. Stone of Augusta and James Thompson of Houlton were also killed. Sergt. George E. Freeman of Portland and privates John Finley of Lewiston and Ezra T. Fletcher of Stewartstown, N. H., were mortally wounded. George T. Bishop and Horace Harris of Stewartstown, John McCormic of Vassalboro, Jonathan B. Wescott of Athens and Eli Whitney of Denmark were wounded.

General Ricketts, in speaking of the artillery of his division in that engagement in his official report, said : "Captains Mathews' and Thompson's Penn. batteries and Captains Leppien's and Hall's Maine batteries deserve to be mentioned not only for their uniform attention to their duties, but for their efficiency throughout the 30th of August."

After this engagement the battery was ordered to Washington to refit and rejoin the division at the earliest possible date.

The battery next confronted the enemy at Fredericksburg. It crossed the Rappahannock December 12, 1862, on the lower pontoon bridge. It was in the left Grand Division which was commanded by General Franklin. After crossing, the battery parked some ten or twelve hundred yards southwest of a large stone mansion, where it remained until the morning of the 13th. Then it moved with the division in a southeasterly direction along the enemy's front and took position in rear of an embankment at a sunken road, which furnished a partial protection for men, horses and pieces.

About three o'clock and thirty minutes in the afternoon the battery under orders moved to the left of the division, crossed the road and took position in front of Birney's division. At four o'clock P. M. or perhaps a little later the enemy opened a brisk cannonade from the woods in our direct front at a distance of 900 yards, which the Fifth and the other batteries on that part of the line answered by a rapid and effective fire. The enemy's guns were silenced in less than twenty minutes. About five o'clock the enemy again opened from a position

(a) Captain Leppien, disabled by painful disease, was riding in an ambulance on that occasion. Lieutenant Stevens was absent under special orders. The command of the battery thus devolved upon Second Lieutenant A. B. Twitchell.

further to our left and were again readily silenced. The battery maintained that position during the night of the 13th. On Sunday, the 14th, it threw several shots at the enemy without reply, after which it was withdrawn and resumed its former position in rear of the embankment at the sunken road.

During the engagement Captain Leppien was also acting chief of artillery of Gibbon's division, and in his absence, which was a large portion of the time, the battery was under the immediate command of Lieutenant Stevens.

Captain Randolph, chief of artillery of Birney's division, Third corps, which was serving with the First corps, after complimenting the batteries under his own command in his official report said: "The batteries of Captains Cooper and Leppien on my left did good service. The practice of the Fifth Maine (Captain Leppien's) attracted my special notice and admiration" (a).

In this engagement the battery lost no men either killed or wounded, and from any data at hand we are unable to give the number of horses killed or ammunition expended.

After the battle at Fredericksburg the battery went into quarters near Fletcher's Chapel, Va., where it remained until the twentieth day of January of the following year, when it broke camp and marched to near Banks' Ford on the Rappahannock. The storms of winter had been heavy. The ground had been frozen and thawed, and the roads, after a few thousand troops with their artillery and wagons had passed over them, became beds of deep mire. They were next to impassable, and the whole army was virtually stuck in the mud. This was known as "Burnside's Mud March." On the return of the army to its winter quarters the battery re-occupied its old camp. After General Hooker succeeded General Burnside, the battery was assigned to the artillery brigade of the First corps. On the twenty-eighth day of April the battery again broke camp and moved to the bank of the Rappahannock near General Franklin's crossing; and on the second day of May marched up the river and crossed the same at United States Ford and encamped for the night between the river and Chan-

(a) Rebellion Records, Vol. 21, page 365.

cellorsville. On Sunday, the third of May, about eight o'clock in the forenoon, orders were received by Captain Leppien from Colonel Wainwright, chief of artillery of the First corps, to move the battery to the front and report to General Reynolds, commanding the corps.

While on the way to the front, orders were received from General Hooker that the batteries in reserve should move along to Chancellorsville, which was near the centre of our line, and report to the chief of artillery there. On arriving and reporting, the battery was ordered to take position in an open field just to the right of the Chancellor House, the left piece being near one of the outbuildings. The enemy's line extended along the southerly edge of the field and into the woods at an estimated distance of 450 or 500 yards.

As soon as the battery emerged from the woods and made its appearance upon the open field their infantry was removed from our front, which disclosed their artillery posted in the rear and partially covered by a slight elevation. The enemy had our exact range. He immediately opened upon us the most galling and destructive fire that the battery ever experienced; its location furnished not the slightest protection, and our men and horses began to fall before the battery was in position. The following communication to the Adjutant-General of Maine tells the sad story in brief:

"HEADQUARTERS FIFTH BATTERY MAINE VOLS.,
CAMP NEAR WHITE OAK CHURCH, VA., MAY 8, 1863.
GENERAL: — Enclosed I have the honor to hand you Monthly Returns for the month of April of the battery under my command, also a list of killed and wounded of the battery in the recent action of May 3, 1863. I shall as soon as possible transmit to you a detailed report of the part performed by the battery in that action.

I remain, General, very respectfully your obedient servant,
G. T. STEVENS, *Lieutenant, Commanding Battery.*
BRIG.-GEN. JOHN L. HODSDON, *Adjt.-Gen'l State of Maine,*
AUGUSTA, MAINE."

List of killed and wounded in action of May 3, 1863:

KILLED.

Sergt. William F. Locke,	Corp. Benjamin F. Grover.

PRIVATES.

William W. Ripley,	Timothy Sullivan,*
James Nason,	James P. Holt.

WOUNDED.

Capt. George F. Leppien, severely, left leg amputated.
Lieut. G. T. Stevens, slightly, flesh wound left side.
Lieut. A. B. Twitchell, severely, flesh wound in leg, two fingers amputated.
Sergt. James C. Bartlett, slight, leg.
Sergt. Andrew McRae, severely, right breast.
Corp. Lemuel A. Cummings, slight, neck.

PRIVATES.

Alonzo Hinkley, slight, face.
Charles L. Crane, slight, foot.
Edwin F. Witham, slight, foot.
Joseph Woods, slight, face.
Charles M. Kimball, severely, arm.
William H. Nason, severely, hand.
James Russell,* severely, back.
Joseph Holsinger,* slight, arm.

John Bolinger,* slight, head.
Roliston Woodbury, slight, back.
Heylep Powers,* slight, arm.
Napoleon B. Perkins, severely, leg.
Edward A. Stewart, severely, leg.
Edwin L. Knowlton, severely, leg.
Cornelius O'Neil, severely, leg.
George Dennison, severely, side.

Total: Six men killed, three officers and nineteen men wounded.

* Detached from the 136th regiment Penn. Vols. and serving in the battery.

Captain Leppien was the first officer wounded. He was on his horse. The battery was in full play. Every gun was being worked to its utmost capacity. An exploded shell struck his leg not far from the ankle joint nearly severing the foot. Amputation followed, after great loss of blood, then extreme prostration and finally death on Sunday, May 24th, in the city of Washington. He held a Lieut.-Col's commission in the Maine Mounted Artillery, but on account of some delay was not mustered into the United States service as such until May 18th. He rests in a patriot's grave in Laurel Hill Cemetery on the banks of the Schuylkill near Philadelphia, the city in which he was born.

Lieutenant Stevens was the next officer wounded. He was hit or grazed by a shot or shell which felled him to the ground, tearing the clothing from his side and giving him a severe shock with a slight flesh wound.

The command of the battery then devolved upon Lieut. A. B. Twitchell, who continued to work the battery until it was nearly silenced for want of cannoneers, most of them being killed or wounded, and he himself severely wounded.

The battery was thus deprived of its three ranking officers, when Lieutenant Edmund Kirby of Battery I, 1st U. S. artillery, was ordered by General Couch to its assistance.

He had scarcely arrived when his horse lost a fore leg by a cannon shot. Kirby called for a pistol which was handed him and he shot his horse on the spot. That scene had hardly been enacted when Lieut. Kirby received a fatal wound, his thigh being smashed by a ball from a spherical case shot. He lost his leg and lost his life.

Beside the three officers of the battery who had been disabled, not including Lieut. Kirby, six men had been killed and nineteen men wounded and forty-three horses killed. Corporal James H. Lebroke then informed General Hancock of the condition of affairs, who ordered a detail from the infantry which removed the pieces by hand to a place of safety. One gun and the caissons had previously been taken from the field. The gun was disabled. It was struck on the face by a solid shot and its muzzle closed. Notwithstanding the disadvantages under which the battery labored, the men behaved in the most gallant manner, continuing to work their pieces until their ammunition at hand was exhausted.

The Chancellor house, which was being used as a hospital, was shelled and fired by the enemy. The wounded were removed from within and around it, and by ten o'clock in the forenoon our whole line fell back in the direction of the United States Ford and established a new line half a mile to the rear of its former position. No Union troops thereafter occupied the position vacated by the battery.

Lieut.-Col. C. H. Morgan, chief of artillery, Second corps, in his official report said: "I do not think it [the ground] could have been held by any number of guns I could have placed in the contracted ground near the Chancellor house" (a). With great exertion the battery was brought to White Oak Church, refitted, and a large detail obtained from the infantry was drilled and made efficient by the time the army moved north on the Gettysburg campaign.

Batteries of mounted artillery in the service were called or named after their captains or permanent commanders who were chargeable with and accountable for all of the property belonging to the same. As their commanders changed, the name of

(a) Rebellion Records, Vol. 25, part 1, page 310.

the battery changed also. Thus the Fifth Maine Battery was known as Leppien's battery up to and including the battle of Chancellorsville. Subsequently the same battery, in the official reports and in history, having changed its captain and permanent commander was known and called Stevens' battery. The same applied to all batteries, regulars and volunteers alike.

It is well known that the Maine Mounted Artillery was raised and mustered into the United States service as independent batteries. Under this arrangement there was no promotion beyond a captaincy. The captain was the highest officer. To obviate this seeming hardship the several batteries in the field formed a quasi-regimental organization among themselves and asked the appointment and muster of field officers. This was granted by the war department rather as an act of favoritism towards the Maine artillery than a strict military right.

In chronological order the battle of Gettysburg, an account of which has already been given, came next. In November of that year the battery took part in the Mine Run campaign. Its service consisted only in marching and counter-marching until it finally went into winter quarters at Culpeper, Va., and was at that place when General Grant arrived and established his headquarters there.

In the spring of 1864 the Army of the Potomac was reorganized. The old First corps that had won renown under General Reynolds was merged into the Fifth corps. The Third corps (formerly Sickles') became a part of the Second corps and the Fifth battery was temporarily assigned to the artillery reserve.

On May 4th the army commenced its colossal campaign of that year. The battery crossed the Rapidan at Ely's Ford and encamped for the night near the battlefield of Chancellorsville. On the 5th the enemy were encountered in force in the Wilderness and from subsequent events both Grant and Lee were evidently fired with determination to win. There was but little skirmishing to foreshadow the coming storm, the strangest battle ever fought, one that no man could see. Its progress could only be determined by the crashing volleys of musketry and the Union cheer and rebel yell as the lines swayed back and forth. It is impossible to conceive of a field worse adapted to the movements of a great army. The country was thickly wooded, with an occasional opening and intersected by a few narrow roads. "It is the region of gloom and the shadow of death." Manœuvring for advantage was out of the question. The troops could only receive direction by point of the compass. Commanders could not see their own lines of battle, but there came out of the depth of the forest the roll and crash of musketry, volley upon volley, that told the sad story of death.

Artillery was almost entirely ruled out of use, and cavalry was but a little more useful. The contest continued two days, but it decided nothing. It was in every feature a drawn battle, and its result was only shown in the thousands of dead and wounded in blue and gray that lay scattered through that dismal forest. The battery stood in harness both night and day and was once or twice in position but, like most of the 274 field guns that crossed the Rapidan with the army, was not engaged in the battle of the Wilderness. (a) On May 17th the battery was withdrawn from the artillery reserve and assigned to the Sixth corps under General Wright and ordered to report to Colonel C. H. Tompkins, chief of artillery. This was Sedgwick's old fighting corps, but Sedgwick was not then living. He was killed on the 9th, eight days before the battery joined the corps. On the 21st the battery was in line near Spotsylvania Court House and engaged the enemy, expending 118 rounds of ammunition without loss.

On the 24th the battery crossed the North Anna at Jericho Ford, and the next day struck the Virginia Central Railroad and shelled the enemy near Little River while reinforcing their pickets. The railroad was effectually cut, the track torn up, the ties piled and burned and the rails heated and bent, rendering them useless. On May 26th the battery recrossed the North Anna, marched to the Pamunkey, crossed the river and entrenched, and on the 27th was in the advance guard; the next day was in the rear guard, and fired eight or ten rounds at the

(a) The 274 guns do not include eight Coehorn mortars and 42 guns of the Ninth corps (Burnside's) which joined the army in May. The Confederates had 213 field guns which were but little used.

enemy's cavalry that harassed the rear of our column. This was during the march to Cold Harbor where the battery arrived on the first day of June; but Sheridan was there in advance, and with his ever present cavalry had driven the enemy from their barricades, capturing half a regiment of cavalry and a few of Hoke's infantry.

The battery was not at once ordered into position; but on the second day of June, by direction of the corps chief of artillery, Lieut. Bucklyn, aide-de-camp, and the captain of the battery made a reconnaissance, on their hands and knees, in front of the First division through the ferns and low bushes to ascertain whether the position would be tenable for artillery, and they decided that, if proper earthworks were thrown up, artillery could be used to good advantage, and so reported at headquarters. No man in that position could stand upright without being shot in a moment. Consequently the services of Captain Walker of the Fifth Maine regiment with his company of pioneers were secured, and as soon as dark, earthworks, rude but of a substantial character, were constructed on the right bank of the Gaines' Mill road, and at two o'clock at night the pieces of one section (two guns) were quietly placed in the works by hand, it being imprudent to bring the horses within 100 yards, as the least noise would draw the enemy's fire who were not more than 275 yards away. Four ammunition chests were dismounted and placed in trenches dug for their security, and such other ammunition as was deemed requisite was taken from the caissons, wrapped in ponchos and placed in the gun pits for immediate use. The horses and limbers were sent to a ravine in the woods some 400 yards to the rear. The captain and seven men with each gun took position in the gun pits, and at four o'clock on the morning of the 3d our lines were advanced, when these two guns immediately opened, showering the enemy's rifle pits with canister and driving and keeping the enemy in front down in their trenches. During the early part of the day no attention was paid to the enemy's artillery as their fire was principally directed at these two guns and doing but little harm, their projectiles either striking and stopping in the earth in front or passing harmlessly over head and exploding, many of them, far to the rear. A battery that was posted directly in front, less than 300 yards distant, when it became troublesome was twice shelled into silence during the day. The enemy's shells having the plug fuse would not work at such short range, while our battery was furnished with the Bormann fuse, which could be cut to explode at any distance required within range of the guns.

On that day and at that point no other artillery was on the front line, but these two guns made themselves heard both far and near. An eye-witness reported as follows : " In the battle of Cold Harbor, Stevens' battery, belonging to the Sixth corps, was so near the rebel line that the soldiers nicknamed it ' Battery Insult.' It stirred up the rebels in a most aggravating manner, and was an excessively dangerous spot to be seen in. After the discharge of the pieces hundreds of bullets would zip through the embrasures and around the earthworks ; occasionally round shot would batter down portions of the work, but the artillerists stuck to it and did good execution."

On June 4th the battery was not engaged, and on the morning of the 5th between two and three o'clock these two guns were withdrawn, having expended 16 canister, 16 shell, 64 solid shot and 128 spherical case without the loss of a man either killed or wounded.

On the 7th the battery was ordered to report to Major–General Birney, commanding a division of the Second corps, as he was short of artillery, and was immediately ordered into position at Barker's Mill on the right of Mott's brigade, which at that time formed the left of our line. On the evening of the 8th received orders from General Birney that for every shot that the enemy threw at his headquarters, which were on an elevation across the mill pond in rear of the battery, to throw one on Turkey Hill, which was at right angles with the enemy's battery. This practice was continued for an hour or more, when the enemy discovering the *modus operandi* ceased their fire. Ammunition expended, 19 shot and 16 shell. The enemy, using the Whitworth gun, were at least one mile distant across the Chickahominy.

On the 9th engaged the enemy at a distance of 1,000 yards,

expending 32 shot, 159 spherical case and 19 shell. No casualties were met with as the battery was well protected by earthworks thrown up during the first night under Birney. From that time nothing worthy of note occurred in the battery during the forward movement of the army until June 16th, when the battery was ordered into position with the corps, covering the crossing of the James by the army. On the 18th the battery went into position before Petersburg and at once remodeled an old rifle pit of the enemy, in their outer line of works, making it appropriate for artillery, and opened on the enemy, expending eight shot and 24 spherical case, with the loss of one man wounded (a).

By direction of Colonel Tompkins one section of the battery was withdrawn that night and ordered to report to General Wheaton, who directed it to take position some 800 or 900 yards to the front, on the right of the road leading up the Appomattox to a point nearer Petersburg. Nearly the same operations were repeated here as at Cold Harbor. The guns were unlimbered and run into position by hand, ammunition chests dismounted and sunk into trenches, and the horses and limbers were sent to the rear.

"In the early part of the night Lieutenant Charles O. Hunt, whose section was to take this advanced position, went out in advance to acquaint himself with the location. Owing to a wrong direction given him by General Wheaton, and to the fact that there was a gap in our picket line at this point, he fell into the hands of the enemy. He remained a prisoner until February 22, 1865, when he was paroled, and was finally exchanged and rejoined the battery in the field on April 13, 1865" (b).

On the 29th day of June the battery with the Sixth corps marched to Reams Station, south of Petersburg, ordered there to reinforce General James H. Wilson, who was returning to the army of the Potomac from his cavalry raid against the South Side and Danville railroads; but we were too late to render him assistance.

On the 6th day of July the battery returned to Petersburg

(a) Private John Worster, Belgrade. Only man wounded in the battery during this campaign under Grant.

(b) Statement of Lieutenant Hunt.

and reported to General Getty, commanding the Second division, Sixth corps, and went into position near the left of our line, which was thrown back facing in a direction nearly opposite to that of Petersburg, and commenced work on an unfinished redoubt. On the night of the 9th marched to City Point. On the evening of the 10th embarked the cannoneers and guns on the steamer *Jefferson* and the drivers and horses on another transport, under orders to sail for the city of Washington and rejoin the corps, — the city being threatened by the rebel army under Early.

The battery arrived in Washington and reported at artillery headquarters of the corps at Crystal Spring, at two o'clock on the morning of the 13th, and immediately went into position. The enemy had pushed up around Fort Stevens, and had been driven back by Getty's division of the Sixth corps, temporarily under command of General Wheaton. After the arrival of the Fifth battery the remainder of the night, or rather the morning of the 13th, was occupied in strengthening our position, burying the dead and caring for the wounded. At daylight on the 13th it was discovered that the enemy were moving from our front in the direction of Rockville, Md.

Then commenced a new campaign which culminated in Sheridan's crowning victories in the valley of the Shenandoah. For the next two months the battery participated in the general movements and operations of the corps; marching to Snicker's Gap in the Blue Ridge Mountains by way of Poolesville, White's Ford and Leesburg, and returning to Georgetown, D. C., by way of Leesburg and the Chain Bridge across the Potomac.

From Georgetown, D. C., the battery with the corps proceeded to Harper's Ferry by way of the Monocacy and Frederick City, thus taking an active part in the defensive campaign for the protection of Baltimore and Washington. On August 5th General Grant directed a concentration of the forces of Generals Wright, Emory and Crook in the vicinity of Harper's Ferry without delay, with orders that if the enemy moved north of the Potomac to follow him and attack him wherever he went. On the 6th Sheridan crossed the Potomac and entered his new field of operations, the Shenandoah Valley.

On the 21st the battery entrenched on the Berryville pike near Charlestown, W. Va., and that night fell back to Halltown, within four miles of Harper's Ferry, and again entrenched, the corps being largely outnumbered by the enemy. But Sheridan soon assembled a powerful army, afterwards known as the Army of the Shenandoah. It embraced the Sixth corps, 13,344, infantry and artillery, under General Wright; the Nineteenth corps, 13,025, under General Emory; the Eighth corps (a), 7,507, under General Crook; and the cavalry, with its accompanying artillery, 6,818, under General Torbert, making the sum total of 40,694 troops south of the Potomac by September 10th, 1864. The above number does not include 4,815 troops included in the district of Harper's Ferry, which were also south of the Potomac. This was the most effective Union force ever assembled in the Shenandoah Valley. From the twenty-first day of August to the eighteenth day of September nothing unusual occurred, the battery making the usual marches and counter-marches with the corps incidental to a campaign.

On the evening of the 18th orders were received to be ready to march at two o'clock the next morning, the 19th. The battery was in harness at the appointed time and soon after moved with the artillery brigade, Sixth corps, from a point near Clifton to Opequan Creek, a distance of some five or six miles, beyond which, and within about three miles of Winchester, the enemy were encountered in force. The Union line of battle, facing to the west, was formed from left to right in the following order: Wilson's division of cavalry; Sixth corps, General Wright; Nineteenth corps, General Emory; Merritt's and Averell's divisions of cavalry. General Crook's command was held in reserve at the Opequon until a later hour in the day. The batteries of the Sixth corps were ordered into position on the corps front by Colonel C. H. Tompkins, chief of artillery. The formation was effected under an annoying fire of the enemy. Notwithstanding the early hour in which the army moved, it was not in line of battle ready to advance until past eleven o'clock in the forenoon. In the attack the Sixth and Nineteenth corps

(a) Crook's command—two divisions—was more strictly designated: "Army of West Virginia," by Sheridan, and in the official reports. See Rebellion Records, Vol. 43, part 1, pp. 40, 403.

advanced in fine order and in great spirit, driving for the time everything before them.   After an advance of several hundred yards of both infantry and artillery a most determined charge of the enemy was made on the left of the Nineteenth corps, crowding it back and turning the flank of the Third division of the Sixth corps (Ricketts') and threatened a disaster.   "The moment was a fearful one.   Such a sight rarely occurs more than once in any battle as was presented in the open space between two pieces of woodland into which the cheering enemy poured.   The whole rebel line, reckless of bullets, even of the shells of our batteries, constantly advanced."

General Getty, commanding the Second division of the Sixth corps, in his official report said: "The success of the enemy, however, was but momentary.   He was promptly met, held in check, and finally repulsed by several batteries, prominent among which was Stevens' (Maine) battery of light twelve-pounders, of the corps, and troops of the First division" (a).

"When the Nineteenth army corps was repulsed," said Col. C. H. Tompkins, "and the enemy had passed the right flank of the 1st N. Y. [battery] I ordered it withdrawn to the ridge about 100 yards in rear and on the left of the Fifth Maine.

"To the front and right of this position the enemy was checked, the Fifth Maine enfiladed his line with canister, and finally was driven to the cover of the woods."   *   *   *

"I cannot speak," he says, "in too high terms of the conduct of the officers and men of the command.   Particular mention should be made of Capt. G. T. Stevens, commanding the Fifth Maine battery, and First Lieut. W. H. Johnson, commanding 1st N. Y. Independent battery, for the gallant manner in which they handled their batteries when charged by the enemy, at which time Lieutenant Johnson was seriously wounded" (b).   *   *   *

Colonel Tompkins further said in the same report: "To the following named officers of my staff I am expressly indebted for valuable assistance, and would respectfully recommend them to the major-general commanding for promotion

(a)   Rebellion Records, Vol. 43, part 1, page 192.
(b)   Rebellion Records, Vol. 43, part 1, pages 271, 272.

for gallant and meritorious conduct in both engagements: First Lieut. E. N. Whittier, acting Assistant Adjutant-General, Fifth Maine battery; First Lieut. J. K. Bucklyn, acting aide-de-camp, 1st R. I. Light Artillery."

General Wright, commanding the corps, gave the following concise account of the enemy's repulse: "The First division [Russell's] moved admirably on the enemy, and the batteries with canister opened upon them with murderous effect, the two driving them back in much disorder. This was the turning point in the conflict" (a).

The Fifth Maine and the 1st N. Y. Independent were the only batteries having a fire on that part of the line. Lieutenant Johnson was mortally wounded and soon died. General Russell in the hour of triumph was instantly killed, a piece of shell penetrating his chest in the region of his heart. "His death," said Sheridan, "brought sadness to every heart in the army." Among other losses, that charge and temporary advantage cost the enemy the loss of Major-General Robert E. Rodes, one of their most experienced and skillful division commanders.

It was now long past noon, and the broken portion of Ricketts' line was quickly reformed in rear of Russell's division, now under Upton. Dwight's division of the Nineteenth corps took the place of Grover's. The latter, however, was promptly rallied and brought up; and the Eighth corps, which had been held in reserve down by the Opequan, was ordered to move rapidly to the front, and was placed in line on the right of the Nineteenth corps. Sheridan was now prepared for his culminating effort. Our whole line was then advanced, and the enemy driven at every point and pushed steadily back, contesting every foot until five o'clock in the afternoon, when, to use the language of Sheridan, "We sent them whirling through Winchester," and the victory was complete.

General Wheaton, commanding the First brigade, Second division, Sixth corps, described the closing scene of the engagement as follows: "With little difficulty we advanced to the brick house on the north side of the pike and at the foot of the slope east of Winchester. A severe artillery fire was here

(a) Rebellion Records, Vol. 43, part 1, page 150.

encountered and here some of the enemy's infantry seemed inclined to delay for a short time our advance. Sending to General Getty for a battery to confront the one that was giving us so destructive a fire, I soon had Captain Stevens' Fifth Maine battery trotting up to our support. From the moment it opened, our forward movement was without opposition, and the enemy could be seen in the distance running, routed, to the rear in the direction of the Winchester and Strasburg pike. Our men were wild with delight at this evidence of their glorious success, and could hardly be restrained and kept in the ranks " (a).

In the engagement the battery did its full share of the work. It expended 283 solid shot, 220 spherical case, 66 shell, and 39 canister, total 608 rounds; or in other words it burned 1,520 pounds of powder and hurled 7,296 pounds of iron into the enemy's ranks with the loss of only six men wounded (b). The ground on which the battle was fought was, for the most part, rolling, and every advantage was taken of the same to save our men and punish the enemy. The Union losses were 697 killed, 3,983 wounded, 338 missing; total 5,018.

The enemy reported their total loss to be 3,611 not including their cavalry, which is not given. Among the trophies captured were five pieces of artillery, nine battle flags, a number of caissons and 4,000 stand of small arms (c).

On September 20th at an early hour in the morning Sheridan's victorious army moved up the Shenandoah Valley in pursuit of the enemy. The cavalry preceded the infantry and artillery on the march. The valley to the north of the Strasburg is at least twenty miles in width. There it narrows up to four miles, being intersected by other mountains; and at Fisher's Hill, two miles further south, it is still more narrow. To the latter point, eighteen miles from Winchester, Early had hastily fallen back. In that position, with mountains on his right and left, he felt himself secure.

(a) Rebellion Records, Vol. 43, part 1, page 198.

(b) Rebellion Records, Vol. 43, part 1, page 273; Maine Adjutant-General's Report, 1864, page 238. Two of the wounded were Michael Bradley, of Portland, and Henry Turner, of Rome.

(c) Rebellion Records, Vol. 43, part 1, page 25.

The twenty-first was spent in driving the enemy's skir-mishers through Strasburg back upon their defenses at Fisher's Hill, and in securing a commanding lodgment on the ridge to the north of Tumbling Run in front of the enemy's main posi-tion. Their right was found to be impregnable and Sheridan concluded to repeat the tactics of the Opequan and turn the enemy's left, which was admirably accomplished. The Fifth battery was in line, but there being no position near where the Napoleon gun, with which the Fifth was armed, could be effectively used, none of those guns belonging to the Sixth corps were engaged. Following up the success of the infantry the Fifth battery took from the field three iron 12-pounder guns of the enemy, two limbers, four horses, four sets of har-ness and thirty rounds of artillery ammunition (a).

From Fisher's Hill Sheridan's army moved rapidly up the valley in pursuit of Early's shattered forces. The battery went as far up as Harrisonburg. The enemy was so closely followed and hardly pressed that a portion of them left the valley and took to the mountains. Early could not be induced to offer further resistance.

October 6th our army commenced to retrace its steps, and then the devastation of the valley commenced in earnest. It was no pleasurable duty. The battery had but little hand in it. That task was assigned to the cavalry. It however was a mil-itary necessity, and designed to prevent the subsistence of the Confederate army in that vicinity.

The Union losses at Fisher's Hill were as follows in killed, wounded and missing: Sixth army corps, 238; Nineteenth army corps, 114; army of West Virginia, 162; Cavalry, 14. Total, 528 (b).

We now come to Cedar Creek, Sheridan's last battle in the Shenandoah Valley, and the last battle in which the Fifth Maine battery was engaged. That battle was a complete surprise to the Union army, but the result was as favorable as though the whole scheme had been deliberately planned and faithfully executed.

(a) Rebellion Records, Vol. 43, part 1, page 273.
(b) Rebellion Records Vol. 43, Part 1, page 124.

On the eighteenth day of October, the day before the engagement, the army was at rest and encamped near Cedar Creek,
some four or five miles north of the battle-field of Fisher's Hill.
The troops were posted facing up the valley in a southerly
direction. General Crook was on the left; the Nineteenth
corps, General Emory, in the centre; and the Sixth corps,
General Ricketts, on the right. The front lines of the Eighth
and Nineteenth corps were entrenched; that of the Sixth corps
was not, as it occupied a naturally strong position.

The cavalry was upon the flanks of the army, and the Fifth
battery with the other artillery of the corps was in park near
the infantry. General Sheridan being absent, General Wright
was in command. The enemy having been largely reinforced,
again turned their faces towards our army and were at Fisher's
Hill, but in what force was not known. Both armies were then
on the westerly side of the north branch of the Shenandoah
River. The day had been warm and the night cool, and a heavy
fog hung over the valley on the morning of the 19th. As soon
as dark on the night of the 18th three divisions of the enemy
left their encampment at Fisher's Hill, crossed the river and
worked their way down opposite the left flank of our army,
recrossed the river which was fordable at that season of the
year, and made their attack at early dawn on Thoburn's division
of Crook's command. Those of the division that were not killed
or captured were routed and fled to the rear. The gallant Thoburn was killed. Then the bugles' shrill notes, the rattle of
harnesses, the command of officers, the crash of musketry coming still nearer in that chill morning, created a pandemonium not
easily described. The enemy next struck Hayes' division of
Crooks' command, which shared a similar fate, although Hayes
got his troops in line and made a stubborn resistance. The whole
Sixth corps turned out at once. Tents were struck, baggage
loaded, and teams directed to the rear. The left of the Nineteenth
corps was turned and the enemy were sweeping down in rear of
their entrenchments, rendering them useless, and carrying all
before them. The Fifth battery was then ordered by Colonel
Tompkins to take position on a knoll to the left and engage the
enemy that were approaching from that direction. The battery
had no supports. A stone-wall, however, in tumble-down con-

dition was about 50 yards in front of the battery, in rear of which a body of our infantry had taken position and was then holding it. The battery at once opened on the enemy that were coming down over the hill just across a ravine. The fog had now partially cleared away. Soon our infantry in rear of the wall withdrew from the position and passing along the hillside to the right of the battery went to the rear.

The battery held that position until charged by the enemy. In that charge two guns which had recently been received from battery A, 1st Mass., manned by men from that battery and temporarily assigned to the Fifth Maine battery, fell for the time being into the hands of the enemy, the horses being shot and tangled up in harness in the attempt to limber to the rear. The other guns with difficulty succeeded in reaching our line then forming to the right and some distance back in the edge of the woods, some of the horses falling in harness while on the way.

In retiring from that position the Fifth Maine came across one gun of McKnight's battery M, 5th U. S., that was left upon the field. The gun was secured by order of Captain Stevens, attached to the carriage hook of a caisson, moved back to our line in the edge of the woods and turned over to McKnight's battery by direction of Colonel Tompkins. Other guns of McKnight's battery had been recaptured and drawn off by the infantry.

The army fell back to a ridge of land about a mile north of Middletown and some four miles from where the enemy made their attack in the morning, the Sixth corps taking position and contesting the ground on the way back, holding the enemy in check and giving the troops of the Eighth and Nineteenth corps time to reorganize and re-form.

At that point Sheridan came up and took command, General Wright resuming command of the Sixth corps. The formation then effected was similar to that of the morning except the Sixth and Nineteenth corps had changed places in line. All of the Eighth corps that could be assembled were still on the left. The Fifth battery was in position on or near the right of Getty's division. All were enthusiastic at Sheridan's arrival. He rode along in rear of the line from left to right encouraging the troops by saying : " We will whip them yet," " You haven't begun to fight," " We will camp on the old ground to-night." Troops that had started on the retreat were turned back and put into position, and stragglers returned to the line of battle like bees to a hive, not waiting to find their own command but going into line wherever they struck it.

The enemy made one or two persistent attacks upon this position but were repulsed and compelled to take shelter, the Fifth battery doing at least its share of the work. Everything having been prepared and the men refreshed by a bite of hard-tack and a little water,—the only refreshment since the night before,—and somewhat rested from the fight and fatigue of the morning, an advance of the whole line was then ordered by General Sheridan.

Colonel Tompkins riding up to the battery said to Captain Stevens : " Now we are going to attack and, if we drive them, I want you to follow and push them as hard as you can." He appeared satisfied to have the battery fight on ground of its own selection and in its own way.

The advance of the whole army was made between three and four o'clock in the afternoon. The Fifth battery with the other artillery opened at once and the enemy was driven at every point for more than half a mile, until near Middletown. There a part of Getty's division, coming under a terrific fire of infantry and artillery, experienced a temporary check and was compelled to fall back, but soon rallied and returned to the line. The attack was then renewed with great spirit, and with the assistance of the Fifth Maine battery, which General Getty had requested, and one gun of battery C, 1st R. I. light art., under Lieutenant Lamb, which had survived the storm of the morning, the enemy was driven in confusion through the town and over the plains to Cedar Creek. The cavalry was then hurled upon the routed and disorganized enemy, securing many of the trophies and substantial fruits of the great victory.

At Middletown five of their dead were found in one spot, the victims of a single 12-pounder spherical case shot fired by the Fifth battery (a). General Getty in his official report of

(a) Maine A.-G. Report for 1864-5, Vol. 1, page 239.

the battle said : " During the advance in the afternoon Stevens' Maine battery of light 12-pounders and a section of Lamb's battery 10-pounder Parrots * * * were served with rapidity and effect " (a).

The battery in that engagement sustained a loss of twenty-eight men, including the attached men, as follows :

KILLED.

PRIVATES: John H. McKeen, Patten; Jeremiah Murphy, Augusta.

WOUNDED.

SERGEANTS: James L. Loomis, Colebrook, N. H.; Lemuel A. Cummings, Augusta.

CORPORAL: Hiram M. Paul, Stewartstown, N. H.

PRIVATES: Charles E. Brown, Carratunk; Seth W. Terrill, Stewartstown, N. H.; Henry White, Stratford, N. H.; Amos Baker, Hartland; Arno Little, Mt. Vernon; Charles F. Merry, Boothbay; James S. Priest, Vassalboro; Lucius Smith, Readfield; Samuel Stevens, Augusta; John W. Waterhouse, Gardiner.

The remainder of the wounded were attached men whose names do not appear on our Maine records.

Among other things too numerous to mention, Sheridan and his victorious army in the space of three months and six days captured from the enemy 94 pieces of artillery, 40 battle flags, 19,230 stand of small arms and about 13,000 prisoners (b).

ROSTER.

COMMISSIONED OFFICERS.

CAPTAIN GEORGE F. LEPPIEN.—November 18, 1861, mustered into U. S. service; February 27, 1863, on leave of absence for 15 days; March, present for duty; May 3, wounded at Chancellorsville; May 18, mustered Lieutenant-Colonel; May 24, died from wounds in Washington.

FIRST LIEUTENANT WILLIAM F. TWITCHELL.—December 4, 1861, mustered into U. S. service; June, 1862, absent sick; June 21, returned from absent sick; July, present for duty; August 30, killed at Second Bull Run.

FIRST LIEUTENANT GREENLIEF T. STEVENS.—January 31, 1862, mustered into U. S. service; July 27, on detached service, Special Order No. 35; September 9, returned from detached service; October 20, absent sick; November, present for duty; May 3, 1863, wounded at Chancellorsville; June 18, promoted Captain; July 2, wounded at Gettysburg; August 27, present for duty; December 31, absent with leave; February, 1864, present

(a) Rebellion Records, Vol. 43, part 1, page 195.
(b) Rebellion Records, Vol. 43, part 1, pages 37, 57.

for duty; January 17, 1865, absent with leave for 20 days; February, present for duty, and appointed Brevet-Major U. S. V., to rank from October 19, 1864; July 6, 1865, mustered out of the U. S. service at the close of the war.

SECOND LIEUTENANT ADELBERT B. TWITCHELL.—December 4, 1861, mustered into U. S. service; September 1, 1862, promoted 1st Lieutenant; March 30, 1863, on leave of absence; April, present for duty; May 3, wounded at Chancellorsville; August, present sick; September 9, absent sick; December 11, discharged, commissioned Captain Seventh Maine Battery.

SECOND LIEUTENANT EZRA CLARK.—January 31, 1862, mustered into U. S. service; February 13, 1863, sick in hospital, Georgetown; March 24, on recruiting service; February, 1864, present for duty; December 16, on detached service, Augusta, Maine; January 31, 1865, mustered out U. S. service, term expired.

FIRST SERGEANT EDWARD N. WHITTIER.—September 1, 1862, promoted 2nd Lieutenant; March 18, 1863, on leave of absence 15 days; April, present for duty; May 18, promoted 1st Lieutenant; February 13, 1864, on recruiting service; April 16, on detached service 2nd Brig. Art. Reserve; May 17, on special duty Brig. Hd. Qrs. Sixth corps; December 16, returned from detached service; February, 1865, appointed Brevet-Captain U. S. V., to take rank from October 19, 1864; April 13, 1865, on detached service art. brig. h'dqrs. A. of S.; July 6, mustered out of U. S. service at close of the war.

QUARTERMASTER SERGEANT CHARLES O. HUNT.—May 18, 1863, promoted 2d Lieutenant; July 1, wounded at Gettysburg; July 28, absent with leave; September, present for duty; January 24, 1864, absent under orders; February, present for duty; March 24, promoted 1st Lieutenant; June 18, taken prisoner; April 13, 1865, present for duty; July 6, mustered out with the Battery.

SERGEANT JAMES C. BARTLETT.—June 17, 1864, promoted 2nd Lieutenant; January 31, 1865, on detached service at Alexandria, Va.; February 15, absent with leave for 20 days; March 8, absent sick; May 5, 1865, discharged for disability.

QUARTERMASTER SERGEANT GEORGE W. WOODBURY.—March 30, 1865, promoted 2nd Lieutenant; July 6, mustered out with the Battery.

SERGEANT DAVID I. BLACK.—June 1, 1865, promoted 2nd Lieutenant; July 6, mustered out with the Battery.

NOTE. On the 10th of January, 1865, the battery proceeded to Frederick, Md., where it remained encamped until the 4th of April, when it returned to Winchester. April 6th it was assigned to the artillery brigade, the Nineteenth corps having been discontinued. After that the duties were battery and brigade drill. On June 21st the battery was ordered to Maine, where it was mustered out and discharged from the United States service at Augusta on the 6th of July, having served three years and seven months.

MONUMENT
OF
THIRD MAINE REGIMENT.

The monument stands in the historic "Peach Orchard" near the Emmitsburg road, upon a commanding elevation which overlooks the undulating fields and woods where Longstreet's lines advanced on the afternoon of July 2d. It is cut from Maine granite, surmounted by a red diamond block highly polished.

ADMEASUREMENTS: Base, five feet by five feet by one foot six inches; plinth, three feet six inches by three feet six inches by one foot six inches; shaft, two feet six inches by two feet six inches by eight feet one inch; cube, of Red Beach granite, two feet by two feet two inches by two feet. Total height, thirteen feet one inch. The following are the inscriptions upon the die.

3RD
MAINE INF'TY.
2ND BRIGADE
1ST DIVISION
3RD CORPS
STRENGTH OF REGIMENT
MORNING OF JULY 2ND.
14 OFFICERS AND 196 MEN.

DETACHED FROM THE
BRIGADE, FOUGHT HERE
IN THE AFTERNOON OF
JULY 2ND, 1863,
HAVING BEEN ENGAGED
IN THE FORENOON AT
POINT IN ADVANCE AS
INDICATED BY A MARKER.

JULY 3RD
IN POSITION ON LEFT
CENTRE OF LINE, UNTIL
AFTERNOON, WHEN WITH
OTHER REGIMENTS OF THE
BRIGADE, IT MOVED TO
SUPPORT OF THE CENTRE
AT TIME OF THE ENEMY'S
ASSAULT.

---

1 OFFICER AND 17 MEN
KILLED, 2 OFFICERS AND
57 MEN WOUNDED, 45 MEN
MISSING.

THIRD MAINE REGIMENT,

SECOND BRIGADE, FIRST DIVISION, THIRD ARMY CORPS,

AT THE BATTLE OF GETTYSBURG.

IN the battle of July 1st the three Maine organizations in the First corps, the Sixteenth regiment, Colonel Tilden, and Hall's and Stevens' batteries, were the only Maine troops engaged. But when General Sickles with part of his command arrived on the field on the evening of July 1st, after the first day's battle, he brought two more Maine regiments, the Third and Fourth, of Gen. J. H. Hobart Ward's brigade, of Gen. David B. Birney's division. There was in this division another Maine regiment, the Seventeenth, which was attached to Col. P. Regis de Trobriand's brigade, that had been left at Emmitsburg to guard the pass of the mountains, so the Seventeenth did not arrive until the forenoon of July 2d.

The Third Maine, as it marched onto the field of Gettysburg on the evening of July 1st, was in every respect, except that of numbers, as fine a veteran regiment as there was in the army of the Potomac. Two years before it had left the Kennebec Valley, a thousand strong, under its Colonel, Oliver O. Howard, who, as Major-General commanding the Eleventh corps and the field, bore a prominent part in the first day's battle. During the two years of its service two hundred fresh recruits had been sent from Maine, yet at the roll-call on the morning of July 2d, only a little upwards of two hundred men and officers answered, — a striking testimonial of the arduous services of the regiment in the campaigns of Virginia. At the battle of Chancellorsville, a few weeks before, its loss had been heavy. The regiment was under command of Colonel Moses B. Lakeman.

Early on the morning of July 2d, Colonel Lakeman formed his regiment in line of battle parallel to and facing the Emmitsburg road and on the right of the brigade. This was on the line which General Sickles was establishing with the Third corps before he had determined to advance his line to the angle of the Peach Orchard. But as the forenoon advanced General Ward ordered Colonel Lakeman to move forward as support to one hundred of the 1st U. S. Sharpshooters, under Colonel Berdan, who were to cross the Emmitsburg road and penetrate the woods beyond with the intention of ascertaining what force of the enemy might be there. It was well known that the Confederate forces had been arriving during the night, a fact very evident already to the Fourth Maine which had been on picket duty all night beyond the Emmitsburg road.

The Third Maine, preceded by the Sharpshooters, advanced to and moved southward along the Emmitsburg road for some distance, then left it and advanced toward a dense wood on the west side. In approaching this wood, believed by both officers and men to be concealing the foe, the command was forced to move three-quarters of a mile through an open field. But they were unmolested as they made this movement, so trying to the soldier ; and entering the wood, formed to support the Sharp- shooters, who were advancing as skirmishers. It was between 11 and 12 o'clock when the regiment advanced into the thick coverts of oak and chestnut.

They had proceeded about fifteen rods when they espied men in butternut gray dodging among the trees. These men were from Alabama,—the 8th, 10th and 11th,—and belonged to Wil- cox's brigade of five Alabama regiments, of Anderson's division of A. P. Hill's corps (a). With the skirmishers of these Confederates the Sharpshooters were already engaged when the Third Maine came up in support. The regiment advanced on the double-quick, and drove in the opposing skirmishers. Then, through the trees and the smoke, suddenly loomed three distinct lines of the enemy, one behind another in close column, and stretching a distance of one hundred and fifty yards in front (b). The advance of this overwhelming force the Third

(a) Statement of Lieut. Hannibal A. Johnson (1889) a First Sergeant that day, and wounded and captured by these Alabamians in the wood. See also Wilcox's Report, Rebellion Records, Vol. 27, part 2, page 617.

(b) Statement of Lieutenant Johnson (1889). Colonel Lakeman states that the Third had little protection, as the Sharpshooters, who had been advancing as skir- mishers, had secured nearly all the trees.

3RD
MAINE
INFANTRY
ENGAGED HERE
FORENOON OF
JULY 2ND
1863.

Maine met with an audacity and firmness in keeping with its reputation as one of the hardest fighting regiments of the army of the Potomac. "We felt," one of the survivors of that day has said, "that the life of the Nation was at stake, and every man in the ranks was conscious of personal responsibility." The combatants were in plain sight of each other, probably not over three hundred yards apart, and for twenty-five minutes, — the Confederates say twenty minutes, — this unequal contest was maintained. At the end of the twenty-five minutes the bugle sounded the retreat. In this short time the regiment sustained a loss of forty-eight men, killed, wounded and missing, over thirty of whom were captured. The presence of the enemy was disclosed, and his movement to attack the Union left uncovered. Leaving its dead and some of the disabled wounded, who could not be taken on account of the rapidity and force of the Confederate advance, the regiment retired, followed vigorously by the yelling foe, upon whom the audacious skirmishers did not cease to keep up a constant fire as they retired (a).

The marker of the Third Maine Regiment to indicate the position of the regiment during this action near the noon of the second day stands in the grove west of the Emmitsburg road on the west slope of Pitzer's Run, a tributary of Willoughby Run, and bears the following inscription on its face:

3RD
MAINE
INFANTRY
ENGAGED HERE
FORENOON OF
JULY 2ND
1863.

The Confederates ceased their fire on the edge of the woods, and the Third, going back over the open field unmolested, took position in the Peach Orchard, where it was to be stationed in conformity with the new plan of battle which General Sickles was about to adopt. For General Birney had no sooner communicated to his corps commander the information secured by the

(a) Fox, the author of "Regimental Losses in the Civil War," considers worthy of especial note "the tenacity with which the Third Maine held that skirmish line at Gettysburg."

Third Maine and the Sharpshooters than he was ordered to advance his division of three brigades, and swing to the left so that its right should be at the Peach Orchard while its left should be at Devil's Den (a). Ward's brigade, to which the Third and Fourth Maine belonged, but from which the Third Maine was to be detached during this battle, was on the left near Devil's Den; in the centre was de Trobriand's, among whose soldiers was the Seventeenth Maine; on the right was Graham's brigade; and connecting to the left of the latter it was to be the fortune of the Third Maine to fight on this afternoon.

After returning from the reconnaisance, Colonel Lakeman was moving his regiment to join its brigade when he received an order from General Birney to take position in the Peach Orchard. There to the left of Graham the regiment went into line of battle without any greater delay than was necessary for the soldiers to take a hasty luncheon from their haversacks. The regiment was posted behind the fence that bounded the Peach Orchard on the southwest side, its right resting along the east side of the Emmitsburg road.

The regiment waited in line until about 4 o'clock in the afternoon before there were any signs of an attack in force by the enemy, who, with an unaccountable sluggishness, was letting the long July day slip away. There was more or less firing, however, and the Third Maine being midway between batteries of the two armies suffered somewhat from exploding shells. Several times during the afternoon the enemy's skirmishers also advanced on the position of the Third. At one time the regiment was quite hard pressed by a force of them coming up on the front and right flank. These however were repulsed, and there was no other advance for a time. But as Colonel Lakeman scanned the country across the Emmitsburg road and to the westward, he soon saw the glistening bayonets of long and continuous columns of infantry passing toward Round Top and the Union left, where the battle was about to burst with fury at Devil's Den and in the Wheatfield, around the positions of the Fourth and the Seventeenth Maine regiments. Those marching columns were of Hood's division of Longstreet's

(a) Report of Gen. David B. Birney (1863).

corps; and behind the walls and fences by the left flank of these columns were Kershaw's and Barksdale's brigades of LaFayette McLaws' division of the same corps, ready to advance upon the Peach Orchard and the defenses near it so soon as Hood should develop his attack farther to the Union left (a). Colonel Lakeman at once sent notice of his discovery to Captain Randolph, chief of artillery of the Third corps, who sent up a battery. This battery took a position near the regiment and threw shell into the distant Confederate columns. These shots were among the very first in the opening of the battle of the second day (b). The columns of the enemy continued their movements; but the fire of the battery was very annoying to them and caused a detour in their line of march to avoid discovery of their plan.

Soon detachments of the enemy were seen advancing towards the Orchard in force against the position occupied by the Third Maine. Towards the front of the regiment came the left wing of Kershaw's South Carolina brigade (c), while from across the Emmitsburg road the Mississippi regiments of the fiery Barksdale were soon to sweep in upon the rear and right flank of the Third. While meeting the attack of Kershaw in his front Lakeman learned that Barksdale had broken through Graham's line, which, posted on the Emmitsburg road to the right of the Peach Orchard, formed the extreme right of Birney's division. This disaster left the rear of the Third Maine exposed, so Colonel Lakeman at once changed the line of his regiment to face the Emmitsburg road. This angle of the Peach Orchard, the very apex of Sickles' line, was at this instant menaced on its two sides by overwhelming forces. As the Third Maine turned from Kershaw to meet Barksdale it received a withering fire. The color company (K) was just forming on the prolongation of the line, when, struck by an enfilading volley, it literally melted away. Every man of the color-guard was either killed or wounded. In a short time, measured by minutes, a third at least of the one hundred and fifty men left from the morning's

(a) Report of Gen. J. B. Kershaw, 1863.

(b) Statement of Colonel Lakeman, 1889. The battery would appear to be Ames' battery G, 1st N. Y., subsequently relieved by battery I, 5th U. S.

(c) Eighth South Carolina and James' South Carolina battalion.

fight were killed or wounded; and the regiment, "wrapped in a vortex of fire," as the Comte de Paris has said, was hurled out of the Orchard by overwhelming numbers (a). To Graham's brigade, which was nearest on Birney's line, the remnant of the Third Maine gravitated; but as evening came on the entire line which Sickles had established gave ground. In the general movement the Third Maine retired behind the second Union line that Hancock had established and which checked the Confederate onsets. That night the regiment rejoined Ward's brigade, which had retired from the ridge of Devil's Den. The official report of General Ward (1863) calls particular attention to the gallantry of Colonel Lakeman and his regiment on this day.

Of the fourteen officers and one hundred and ninety-six men who entered the battle in the morning only ninety-seven reported at night. One-half of the others were lying on the field, dead or wounded. The survivors slept upon their arms that night. After noon the next day they were sent to support the Second division of the Second corps; but the attack had been repulsed before their arrival. On July 4th the Third was on skirmish duty, but sustained no losses.

A MARKER

to designate the position of the Third Maine when in support of the Second corps, afternoon of July 3d, at the close of the enemy's assault, stands upon the east side of Hancock Avenue in a northeasterly direction from "High Water Mark" monument. It is cut from Maine granite, adorned with a red granite diamond, and has the following inscriptions:

3RD MAINE REGIMENT
COLONEL M. B. LAKEMAN
IN SUPPORT
JULY 3RD 1863.
ENGAGED   JULY   2ND
IN PEACH ORCHARD.

OFFICIAL REPORT OF COL. MOSES B. LAKEMAN.

NEAR WARRENTON, VA., July 27, 1863.

CAPTAIN: — I have the honor to submit the following report of the part taken by my regiment at the battle of Gettysburg, Pa., on the 2d instant:—

By order, I formed my regiment in line of battle parallel to and facing

(a) The regiment of Barksdale's brigade advancing nearest the Third Maine at the time was probably the 21st Mississippi.

3rd MAINE REGIMENT
COLONEL M.B. LAKEMAN
IN SUPPORT
JULY 3rd   1863

ENGAGED   JULY 2nd
IN PEACH ORCHARD

the Emmitsburg road, on the right of the brigade, at early morn. Soon after, by order of General Ward, I moved my regiment as a support for a body of sharp-shooters, under command of Colonel Berdan, to whom I was ordered to report, by Captain Briscoe of General Birney's staff. Advancing to and for some distance on the Emmitsburg road, I approached a dense wood on the west side of the road, and on entering it formed my regiment (as ordered) to support the advancing line of skirmishers, and followed at supporting distance. They soon, however, became hotly engaged, * * * and I advanced double-quick to the line they occupied, and instantly formed my regiment under a heavy fire from the enemy, which we returned with a good will. Here I labored under a decided disadvantage, which will account for my heavy loss. The skirmishers were well secured behind trees, while my battalion filled the intervals. The enemy showed himself in overwhelming force, but so well did we hold our position that his advance was much checked and very disastrous, and not until ordered * * * to fall back did a single man leave the ranks, with the exception of those slightly wounded, when I retired, giving an occasional volley to check his advance, which now became quicker.

I was obliged to leave my dead and seriously wounded on the field, and on arriving at the road formed my regiment, which had gotten somewhat confused from loss of men and obstructions in our retreat.

This engagement was short but very severe, and serves to give me a renewal of confidence in the men I command. I sustained a loss of forty-eight in killed, wounded and missing.

While on the move to join my brigade, I received an order from General Birney to take position in a peach orchard on the right of my previous one, and accordingly moved my regiment there and occupied it. Here I was enabled several times during the day to repulse the enemy's skirmishers (who seemed very anxious to drive us from it) and also to seriously harass the left flank of their advancing columns to the position which the other regiments of the brigade were holding, changing my front as circumstances required. In this position my regiment lay about midway between our own and the enemy's batteries, and a few of my command were more or less seriously injured from the frequent explosion of shells immediately over us.

I was heavily pressed in front and on my right flank about 4 P. M., but succeeded in repulsing, with considerable loss, the force, which was much greater than mine, and sent them flying back to their covers. An hour later they came forward again with a force much greater than before, but I engaged them and held them for some fifteen minutes, when I received a severe flank fire on my left. I then saw a large force marching round to cut me off, and ordered my regiment to retire, and while doing so we received a most distressing fire, which threw my command into much confusion, and mixing them up with a portion of the First brigade, which was also falling back.

I regret to report the loss of my national colors, or no men fought harder under it that day than did my regiment, but Captain Keene of the color company and his 1st—and only—lieutenant, Henry Penniman, fell, the former pierced by four bullets, the latter severely wounded in the leg. The color-bearer fell, wounded; two of the guard were killed and four others seriously wounded; and, as darkness was fast approaching, I did not miss it till the following morning. If I had, they would have had me and my little squad or I would have had my flag.

As soon as I could rally the remainder of my shattered regiment, I joined the brigade, and the men lay on their arms during the night.

I am proud to say the conduct of my officers and men throughout the entire day is deserving the highest praise. Their coolness and courage in resisting a force which they could plainly see was four times their number I cannot pass over lightly, but feel somewhat recompensed for my loss by the knowledge that the few I have left are of the same material as the gallant spirits that have fallen.

I entered the engagement of the morning with 14 officers and 196 rifles, and lost during the day 113 killed, wounded and missing, including Major Lee wounded, Captain Keene killed, etc., a list of which has already been sent to headquarters.

I have the honor to be, captain, very respectfully, your obedient servant,

MOSES B. LAKEMAN,
Colonel, Commanding Third Maine Regiment.

CAPT. JOHN M. COONEY,
Asst. Adjt.-Gen., Second Brig., First Div., Third Corps.
—Rebellion Records, Series I, Vol. xxvii, p. 507.

HEADQUARTERS THIRD MAINE REGIMENT, July 27, 1863.

COLONEL: — I herewith respectfully report the movements of my regiment under your command at the battle of Gettysburg, on the 3d, 4th and 5th instants.

On or about noon of the 3d instant, I was, by order of General Ward, sent as support to the Second division of the Second corps, which was being heavily pressed by the enemy, but who had succeeded in repulsing them before my arrival. I reported to General Webb, and placed my regiment, as ordered by him, in support of a battery in our front, but our services were not required throughout the afternoon or night.

Early on the morning of the 4th instant, I, with the Fourth Maine, 99th Penn. and 20th Indiana regiments, advanced to the front, sending forward the skirmishers of the Second corps, and taking position on the Emmitsburg road, previously the skirmish line, relieved the skirmishers in my front, thereby being supported by, instead of supporting, the Second corps. Quite brisk skirmishing took place during the day, but without loss, I am happy to state, to my regiment.

I remained on this line until about 12 M. on the 5th, when I retired to the position occupied the previous morning, leaving my skirmishers still to the front, when, finding the enemy had gone, my skirmishers were relieved, and I, with the other regiments, joined the brigade.

Respectfully submitted.

MOSES B. LAKEMAN,
Colonel, Commanding Third Maine Regiment.

P. S. Permit me to add that the conduct of my officers and men throughout the whole of the trying engagement was admirable in the extreme, and they are highly deserving of special mention.

ITINERARY.

The following itinerary of the Third regiment during the Gettysburg campaign is taken from the diary of Col. Moses B. Lakeman, commanding the regiment:

Thursday, June 11, 1863. Fair. Relieved from picket; arrived in camp at 1 o'clock P. M.; started on march at 2 P. M. — Rappahannock Station. Marched about ten miles, bivouacked for night at 11 o'clock P. M.

June 12th. Fair. Started on march at 9 o'clock A. M.; marched about twelve miles; arrived at bivouac one mile from Bealeton at 5.30 P. M.

June 13th. Fair. Moved bivouac one and a half miles to Bealeton. Division officer of day.

June 14th. Fair. Struck bivouac at 4.30 P. M.; arrived near Catlett's Station, eight miles, at 10 o'clock.

June 15th. Fair. Started at 5 o'clock A. M. on march; arrived near Centreville at 6 o'clock P. M.; distance marched ten miles; very warm and dusty.

June 16th. Fair. Started at 5.30 o'clock A. M., and marched about three miles to rifle pits.

June 17th. Fair. Started at 3.30 o'clock P. M., and marched about three miles in rear of Centreville.

June 18th. Rain. Remained in bivouac. Smart rain in afternoon and evening. Lt.-Col. Burt left on fifteen days' sick leave.

June 19th. Rain. Started at 3 o'clock P. M.; marched to Gum Spring; distance marched ten miles; a very severe march on account of rain, mud and darkness; arrived at 10.30 P. M.

June 20th. Rainy. Remained in bivouac. Lts. Day, Anderson, Gilman and Blake missing, supposed to be captured by guerillas.

June 21st. Rainy. Remained in bivouac until 3.30 o'clock P. M., when we changed position to front. Heavy firing in direction of Aldie.

June 22d. Fair. Remained in bivouac until 5 P. M. Part of regiment went on picket, rest moved to rear on reserve. Sat on court martial on case of Major D——— of —— N. Y. Vols. at Col. Berdan's headquarters.

June 23d. Fair. Remained in bivouac.

June 24th. Fair. Remained in bivouac.

June 25th. Rainy. Regiment relieved from picket; struck bivouac at 6 o'clock A. M., and marched to Monocacy, where we arrived at 10 P. M.; distance marched about twenty-four miles.

June 26th. Rainy. Started at 6 o'clock A. M.; marched to near Point of Rocks; distance six miles. Division officer of day.

June 27th. Rainy. Started at 10 o'clock A. M.; passed through Jefferson and bivouacked near Middletown; distance about twelve miles.

June 28th. Fair. Started at 8 o'clock A. M.; passed through Middletown and Frederick to Walkerville, distance about sixteen miles, and bivouacked for the night.

June 29th. Rainy. Started at 6 o'clock A. M.; passed through Walkerville, Woodsborough, Middleburg and Taneytown, distance marched about eighteen miles, and bivouacked for night.

June 30th. Rain. Started at 2.30 o'clock P. M. and marched to near Emmitsburg; distance eight miles.

July 1st. Rain. Started at 2.30 o'clock; bivouacked near Gettysburg, Pa.; distance nine miles. Enemy in our front. Severe march; distance marched fourteen miles.

July 2d. Fair. Took position early; went to the front in woods with one hundred sharp-shooters; met enemy in force; lost in the charge forty-eight men killed, wounded and missing; remained in advance until evening when we retired with First brigade, losing great many men, reported seventy-four. Maj. Lee, Capt. Keene, Lt. Penniman, Sergt.-maj. Small, killed or wounded.

July 3d. Fair. Took position on left in movement. Went to support of Second corps; no casualties. Rained at night. Enemy completely repulsed in our front entire day. Commanding brigade.

July 4th. Rain. No casualties. Moved to first line and relieved skirmishers of 15th Mass. Occupied the line until midnight, when we retired in rear of second line. Very heavy rain all night; skirmishers to front all night; enemy left at night.

July 5th. Fair. Relieved from support of Second corps; rejoined brigade and occupied line of 2d instant. Found and buried our dead.

July 6th. Stormy. Remained in same position; visited hospital. Lieut.-Col. Burt joined regiment. 16 K., 59 W., 10 P., 22 M. [These figures evidently refer to the losses at Gettysburg in killed, wounded, prisoners and missing.]

July 7th. Rain. Started from bivouac at 4 o'clock A. M.; passed through Emmitsburg and Mechanicstown and bivouacked there for the night; distance marched fourteen miles.

July 8th. Rain. Started 6.45 A M.; passed through Katoctin Furnace and Pass, on pike; three hours' rest at noon on account of extreme bad road; passed through Frederick; bivouacked on road to Middletown; distance marched sixteen miles.

July 9th. Fair. Started at 5 o'clock; passed through Middletown and bivouacked at South Mountain Pass; distance marched five miles.

July 10th. Fair. Started at 5 o'clock; moved towards the front, very short marches to change position; distance marched ten miles. Passed through Cadysville; bivouacked near Antietam Creek.

July 11th. Fair. Started at 4 o'clock; passed through Rocks Mills; crossed Antietam Creek; bivouacked for night; distance six miles. Presented with set spurs by Co. E.

July 12th. Rain. Moved to front in reserve; formed line in afternoon and bivouacked for night; advanced about one mile.

July 13th. Fair. No charge; remained on same line.

July 14th. Rain. Struck bivouac at 12 o'clock; passed Jones' Cross Roads and bivouacked for night in field near and in rear of reb's works— (two miles). Division officer of the day.

July 15th. Fair. Started at 4 o'clock en route for Harper's Ferry; passed through Fairplay and Sharpsburg and bivouacked three miles beyond; —eight miles.

July 16th.   Rain.   Started at 6.30 o'clock A. M. and bivouacked near Maryland Heights; marched about six miles.

July 17th.   Rain.   Started at 6 o'clock P. M. and crossed Potomac at Sandy Hook to Harper's Ferry; crossed Shenandoah River and bivouacked for night; marched eight miles.

PARTICIPANTS.

FIELD, STAFF AND NON-COMMISSIONED STAFF.

Colonel, Moses B. Lakeman, Augusta.
Major, Samuel P. Lee, Hallowell.
Surgeon, Thaddeus Hildreth, Gardiner.
Assistant Surgeon, William H. Jewett, Turner.
Second Assistant Surgeon, James D. Watson, Brooks.
Chaplain, S. Freeman Chase, Camden.
Quartermaster, Charles T. Watson, Bath.
Sergeant-major, Henry S. Small, Bowdoinham.
Quartermaster-sergeant, Thomas McFadden, Bath.
Commissary-sergeant, Lorenzo W. Grafton, Augusta.
Hospital Steward, John Littlefield, Jr., Skowhegan.
Drum-major, Charles Ellis, Waterville.
Fife-major, Charles Elliott, Bath.

COMPANY A.

Captain, George W. Hervey, Bath.
First Lieutenant, Abner W. Turner, Bath.
Second Lieutenant, George C. Hudson, Bath.

SERGEANTS.

First Sergeant, Charles T. Hooper, Bath,
Charles N. Osgood, Bath,   William B. Parris, Bath.

CORPORALS.

Jonathan Newcomb, Jr., Bath,   John L. Little, Bath,
Charles T. Butler, Phippsburg,   Wesley Oliver, Bath.

PRIVATES.

Adams, John W., Bath,   Barton, George H. B., Bath,
Campbell, Thomas G., Bath,   Crooker, William F., Bath,
Durgin, William H., Bath,   Emery, Augustus F., Phippsburg,
House, Henry H., Bath,   Hughes, William, Woolwich,
King, Eleazer, Bath,   Lord, John A., Bath,
Norton, Charles M., Bath,   Preble, Edgar W., Woolwich,
Ramsey, Edwin R., Bath,   Sprague, Gilman S., Bath,
Trull, Phineas A., Bath,   Wall, Amos H., Bath,
Webber, Oliver, Bath.

ON SPECIAL DUTY OR DETACHED SERVICE: Sergeant Lincoln Litchfield, Bath, div. com. dept. Privates: Lewis K Blair, Bath; John E. Foley, Bath, ambulance driver; Adam Lemont, Brunswick, prov. gd. div. h'dqrs.; Franklin Shepherd, Bath, corps h'dqrs.

COMPANY B.

SERGEANTS.

Hannibal A. Johnson, Hallowell,   Asa C. Rowe, Augusta,
Frederick Gannett, Augusta.

CORPORALS.

Edward L. Smith, Belgrade,   Frank White, Augusta,
John W. Jones, Augusta.

PRIVATES.

Barker, Enoch M., Troy,   Call, Nathan H., Augusta,
Crummett, George L., Augusta,   Delano, Charles S., Augusta,
Foss, William T., Belgrade,   Gannett, Charles, Augusta,
Kittredge, Orrin, Richmond,   Pease, Thomas O., Augusta,
Sawyer, Charles E., Bath,   Winslow, Joseph F., China.

MUSICIAN: Frank Carlin, Augusta.

ON SPECIAL DUTY OR DETACHED SERVICE: Capt. Edward C. Pierce, Augusta, signal corps. Wagoner Frank E. Sager, Hallowell. Privates: William Bagley, Canton; George M. Bean, Augusta; Orrin G. Farnham, Bath; Harry W. Gardiner, Hallowell, signal corps; Reuel Merrill, Augusta; Stephen M. Scates, Augusta; Benjamin Sedgerly, Bowdoinham.

COMPANY C.

Captain, John S. Moore, Gardiner.

SERGEANTS.

Parlin Crawford, Gardiner,   George F. Spear, Gardiner,
George M. Houghton, Gardiner.

CORPORALS.

Charles H. Martin, Canaan,   Danforth M. Maxcy, Gardiner,
Charles M. Landers, Danville.

PRIVATES.

Brookings, Daniel, Pittston,   Colburn, Hiram W., Pittston,
Crosby, Reuben H., Winthrop,   Dale, Horace W., Gardiner,
Dean, Westbrook, Gardiner,   Dennis, John S., Gardiner,
Fall, Harnden A., Gardiner,   Foy, Charles H., Gardiner,
Heath, Andrew, Whitefield,   Hutchinson, Albion T., Gardiner,
Leighton, William, Augusta,   Moody, Daniel M., Pittston,
Morrill, George T., Wiscasset,   Neal, Lyman C., Augusta,
Packard, Almon J., Gardiner,   Pettingill, William H., Winthrop,
Spear, Charles H., Gardiner,   Sturtevant, William H., Gardiner,
Wakefield, Stephen D., Gardiner,   Walker, Nathan N., Gardiner,
Washburn, George M., Gardiner.

ON SPECIAL DUTY OR DETACHED SERVICE: Privates: Moses S. Wadsworth, Gardiner, hosp. nurse; George S. Wedgewood, Litchfield, clerk brig. h'dqrs.; Charles H. Welch, Gardiner; William Wight, Gardiner, brig. h'dqrs.

COMPANY D.

Captain, Alfred S. Merrill, Bath.
First Lieutenant, Woodbury Hall, Woolwich.

SERGEANTS.

Eben S. Allen, Bath,   Henry H. Shaw, Woolwich,
Alvin Kennerson, Bath.

CORPORAL. George Farnham, Woolwich.

PRIVATES.

Carlton, Jotham S., Bath,	Campbell, Archibald, Bath,
Dearborn, Charles H., Wentworth,	Fletcher, James, Bath,
Getchell, Charles, Woolwich,	Hartnett, Patrick T., Bath,
McIntire, Josiah K., Bath,	Pushard, Joseph, Bath,
Ring, David, Bath,	Roach, Joseph A., Bath,
Scammell, Timothy, Bath,	Snell, Charles F., Bath,
Wakefield, Jeremiah, Bath,	Williams, Melville C., Bath.

MUSICIAN: Warren W. Goud, Topsham.

ON SPECIAL DUTY OR DETACHED SERVICE: Wagoner Lyman P. Wildes, Bath, teamster div. h'dqrs. Privates: Chandler Ayers, Bath, div. h'dqrs.; Isaac Durgin, Bath, teamster brig. h'dqrs.; James Jameson, Bath, div. pro. guard; Edward C. Stinson, Woolwich, brig. h'dqrs.

COMPANY E.

Captain, George O. Getchell, Hallowell.
First Lieutenant, George S. Fuller, Hallowell.
Second Lieutenant, George A. Nye, Hallowell.

SERGEANTS.

First Sergeant, Charles M. Bursley, Hallowell,
George F. Chamberlain, Hallowell.

CORPORALS.

George W. Hubbard, Hallowell,	Charles J. Dalton, Chelsea.

PRIVATES.

Bailey, George W., West Gardiner,	Bancroft, Charles, Hallowell,
Bragg, William F., Hallowell,	Bryant, John W., Hallowell,
Burns, Hugh, Hallowell,	Buswell, Albert S., Hallowell,
Carter, Henry C., Farmingdale,	Crosby, Rodney, Albion,
Douglass, Isaac M., Bath,	Emerson, Hazen H., Hallowell,
George, Sherburn S., Hallowell,	Gilman, Charles C., Hallowell,
Leighton, Silas F., Manchester,	Murch, Alden F., Foxcroft,
Packard, Horatio M., Bridgewater,	Roach, Henry J., Bath,
Rogers, Charles B., Hallowell,	Russell, George G., Harpswell,
Simmons, Stephen M., Hallowell,	Sprague, Allen H., St. Albans,
Sweetland, Frank, Farmingdale,	Sweetland, Seth, Farmingdale,
Towns, Elijah C., Wilton,	Towns, Elisha, Wilton,
Towns, Reuben A., Wilton,	Turner, Iddo B., Palermo,
Williams, Frank, Gardiner.	

ON SPECIAL DUTY OR DETACHED SERVICE: Sergeant Thomas S. Allen, Bowdoin, brig. ambulance corps. Privates: William C. Bartlett, Bethel; James S. Choate, Hallowell, teamster; William E. Mathews, Hallowell, brig. ambulance corps; William B. Potter, Dubuque, Ia.; clerk brig. h'dqrs.; Noah F. Weeks, Hallowell, teamster.

COMPANY F.

Captain, William C. Morgan, Cornville.

SERGEANTS.

Anson R. Morrison, Skowhegan,	Joseph P. Durgin, The Forks pl.
Ora H. Nason, Clinton.	

CORPORALS.

Amos H. Cole, Starks,	Henry H. Chase, Skowhegan.

PRIVATES.

Currier, Thomas S., Anson,
Luce, Alsbury, Norridgewock,
Maxwell, Charles N., Canaan,
Rackliff, William J., Fairfield,
Savage, Brooks D., Skowhegan,
Smith, Wilson C., Farmington,
Swan, Franklin, Anson,
Towle, Charles L., Winthrop,
Williamson, Luther A., Starks.

Dorathy, George E., Walpole, Mass.
Maxim, William H., Norridgewock,
Parlin, John A., Skowhegan,
Rich, George F., Skowhegan,
Shattuck, Luke F., Madison,
Stevens, John H., Clinton,
Swan, Henry B., Anson,
Weston, William H., Skowhegan,

ON SPECIAL DUTY OR DETACHED SERVICE: Corporal George Keef, Fairfield. Wagoner Luther Dean, Madison. Privates: John L. Fish, Starks; John F. Frost, Skowhegan; Benjamin Greenlief, Starks; Heman Hunnewell, Jr., Solon; John W. Jones, Winthrop, orderly div. h'dqrs.

COMPANY G.

First Lieutenant, George A. McIntire, Waterville.
Second Lieutenant, Charles W. Lowe, Waterville.

SERGEANTS.

First Sergeant, William E. Brown, Sidney,
William H. Copp, Waterville,
George C. Drummond, Winslow.

George W. Davis, Waterville.

CORPORALS.

Algernon P. Herrick, Brooklin,

Orrin Austin, New Sharon.

PRIVATES.

Arnold, Charles H., Sidney,
Field, Henry, Sidney,
Frost, Samuel E., Belgrade,
Hallett, Leander T., Mercer,
Marshall, John T., Southport,
Perry, James, Waterville,
Pullen, Frank D., Waterville,
Spofford, Amherst, Southport,
Webber, Hiram C., Winslow.

Derocher, Henry, Waterville,
Fossett, John E., Vassalboro,
Grover, Charles C., Skowhegan,
McClausland, Simon, Winslow,
Perley, Nathaniel, Waterville,
Pollard, Otis, Winslow,
Sawtelle, Augustus M., Sidney,
Sylvester, Charles E., Bath,

MUSICIAN: Llewellyn E. Hodges, Winslow.

ON SPECIAL DUTY OR DETACHED SERVICE: Corporals Jonathan Bigelow, Jr., Lowell; Charles W. Derocher, Waterville. Wagoner John G. Wiley, Boston, Mass. Privates: Charles Bacon, Waterville, hosp. nurse; Charles H. Buswell, New Sharon; Luther N. Eames, Waterville; George Lashus, Waterville; Hiram G. Robinson, Sidney; Moses W. Young, Calais.

COMPANY H.

SERGEANTS.

William W. Livermore, Vassalboro,
Albro Hubbard, Waterville.

CORPORALS.

John H. Bacon, Waterville,
Eben Farrington, Livermore,

John F. Stanley, Smithfield,
Philander F. Rowe, Smithfield.

PRIVATES.

Bow, Horace, Waterville,
Cochran, Robert, Waterville,
Dixon, George, Fairfield,

Bragg, Lewis, Vassalboro,
Corson, Albert, Waterville,
Dyer, Lorenzo, Brighton,

Eaton, James R., Vassalboro,
Farrington, Frank, Chesterville,
Freeman, George R., Vassalboro,
Hunter, Melvin, Clinton,
Jones, Charles H., Jay,
Preble, William T., Winslow,
Rowe, Isaac, Smithfield,
Woodman, Alvin B., Waterville.

Emery, Joseph R., Fairfield,
Fish, Hiram, Waterville,
Hursom, Milford, Waterville,
James, Isaiah H., Waterville,
Major, Cyrus M., Vassalboro,
Robinson, Charles H., Sidney,
Tallus, John, Waterville,

MUSICIANS.

Henry Crowell, Waterville,   Baxter Crowell, Waterville.

ON SPECIAL DUTY OR DETACHED SERVICE: Privates Samuel W. Austin, New Sharon; Solomon B. Lewis, Waterville; Nathan P. Taber, Vassalboro.

COMPANY I.

SERGEANTS.

First Sergeant, John B. Dodge, Somerville,
Andrew Nicholas, Augusta,   Nelson W. Jones, Palermo,
Henry Lyon, Vassalboro.

CORPORALS.

Daniel Chadwick, Augusta,   Henry A. Griffith, Augusta,
Wilbert Boynton, Palermo,   Warren W. Cooper, Somerville.

PRIVATES.

Bailey, Andrew J., Chelsea,
Bolton, William, Augusta,
Brown, William A., Augusta,
Day, David, Augusta,
Goodwin, Adam B., Newfield,
Lewis, Alexander, Somerville,
Livermore, Leonard H., Augusta,
Mann, John A., Augusta,
Orrick, James, Augusta,

Bachelor, Charles M., Augusta,
Brann, Levi W., Somerville,
Burden, Calvin H., Augusta,
Fellows, George L., Augusta,
Hill, Reuben, Sanford,
Lewis, Andrew J., Somerville,
Maher, William, Gardiner,
Neal, Harrison W., Palermo,
Palmer, William V., Newfield.

ON SPECIAL DUTY OR DETACHED SERVICE: Corporal George P. Wentworth, Augusta. Musicians William Stover, Augusta; Marcellus Gale, Augusta. Wagoner William H. Spofford, Augusta, teamster div. h'dqrs. Privates: Byron C.Bickford, Augusta; Byron Branch, Augusta, div. h'dqrs.; Benjamin C. Campbell, Somerville; Augustus Chadwick, Augusta, ambulance corps; Samuel Gowell, Augusta; Frank S. Martin, Augusta, teamster brig. h'dqrs.; Rufus S. McCurdy, Augusta, pro. guard. div. h'dqrs.; Hezekiah Ridley, Richmond, ambulance corps; John H. Spaulding, Augusta, teamster div. h'dqrs.; Edward A. Stewart, Augusta, div. h'dqrs.; William S. Thoms, Augusta, corps mail agent.

COMPANY K.

Captain, John C. Keene, Leeds.
First Lieutenant, Henry Penniman, Winthrop.

SERGEANTS.

First Sergeant, Fred H. Strout, Durham,
Bradford W. Smart, Vassalboro,   Edward K. Thomas, Winthrop,
Dexter W. Howard, Leeds.

CORPORALS.

Hugh S. Newell, Readfield,	Charles A. Smart, Vassalboro,
Alexander T. H. Wood, Winthrop,	Andrew P. Bachelder, Winthrop.

PRIVATES.

Burgess, William H., Winthrop,	Butler, George A., Winthrop,
Caswell, Lloyd B., Leeds,	Chandler, Samuel G., Winthrop,
Cochran, Hiram, Waterville,	Frost, Albert H., Winthrop,
Heald, William, E. Livermore,	Holmes, James M., Winthrop,
Johnson, Henry C., Farmington,	Keay, Ruggles S., Greene,
Norris, Daniel S., Mt. Vernon,	Perkins, George, Winthrop,
Raymond, William R., Wayne,	Ricker, James C., Winthrop,
Stearns, Joseph H., Winthrop,	Thompson, Gustavus A., Winthrop,
Turner, Henry S., Leeds	Wilson, William G., Winthrop,
Wood, Elias, Winthrop.	

ON SPECIAL DUTY OR DETACHED SERVICE: Privates: John W. Russell, Winthrop, blacksmith; Franklin Dwyer, Winthrop; William Elder, Winthrop, pro. guard, div. h'dqrs.; Charles H. Smiley, Winthrop, brig. ambulance corps; Patrick H. Snell, Winthrop, brig. ambulance corps.

The condensed morning report of the Third Maine regiment June 30, 1863, shows:

Present for duty, 22 officers, 244 enlisted men; total, 266.

Present sick, 2 men; present daily duty, 3 men.

Note on foregoing list of participants.

It will be observed that the monument inscription and Col. Lakeman's official report show less in number than this nominal list. The non-combatant officers here given were omitted in the former, and one staff officer, present June 30th, was not on duty July 2d. The discrepancy of two line officers remains; it is possible that two were commissioned and acting as officers, but not mustered as such at the time; all those named in the list are well vouched for as present.

As to the difference of fifty in enlisted men: some fell out sick after June 30th; a number in every regiment were mustered as present for duty June 30th who did not carry arms in battle, — stretcher-carriers, temporary details, etc. Having been denied all information from the departments at Washington, the difficulty of separating the names at this late day is insurmountable.

REVISED REPORT OF CASUALTIES.

FIELD AND STAFF.

Major, Samuel P. Lee, wounded, right arm dislocated.
Sergeant-major, Henry S. Small, killed.

COMPANY A.

SERGEANTS.

Charles N. Osgood, w'd, leg, severe. William B. Parris, wounded, leg.

CORPORALS.

Jonathan Newcomb, Jr., prisoner.   John L. Little, killed.

PRIVATES.

Crooker, William F., prisoner.   Emery, Augustus F., w'd, side, severe.
Hughes, William, prisoner.   Ramsey, Edwin R., wounded, hand.
Trull, Phineas A., prisoner.   Webber, Oliver, prisoner.

COMPANY B.

SERGEANTS.

Hannibal A. Johnson, w'd and pris'r.   Asa C. Rowe, killed.
Fred Gannett, w'd, right foot.

Corporal John W. Jones, killed.

PRIVATES.

Barker, Enoch M., prisoner.   Call, Nathan H., wounded.
Gannett, Charles, prisoner.   Winslow, Joseph F., prisoner.

COMPANY C.

SERGEANTS.

Parlin Crawford, w'd, arm, severe.   George F. Spear, killed (rep'd miss'g).

CORPORALS.

Charles H. Martin, prisoner.   Danforth W. Maxcy,
Charles M. Landers, w'd, head, severe.   wounded, died Aug. 13, 1863.

PRIVATES.

Dale, Horace W., killed.   Dennis, John S., w'd, thigh, severe.
Foy, Charles H., wounded, foot.   Heath, Andrew, wounded, hand.
Moody, Daniel M., w'd, thigh, ampt'd. Neal, Lyman C., wounded, leg.
Sturtevant, William H., w'd, leg.

COMPANY D.

SERGEANTS.

1st Sergt. Eben S. Allen,   Henry H. Shaw, wounded, severe.
wounded, died Aug. 6, 1863.
Corporal George Farnham, wounded, foot.

PRIVATES.

Hartnett, Patrick T., prisoner.   Roach, Joseph A., w'd, died July 11,'63
Wakefield, Jeremiah, wounded, leg.

COMPANY E.

Sergeant George F. Chamberlain, wounded, died Aug. 21, 1863.

PRIVATES.

Bailey, George W., w'd, severe.   Bancroft, Charles, killed (rept'd w'd).
George, Sherburn S., w'd, severe.   Leighton, Silas F., w'd, shoulder.
Murch, Alden F., wounded, leg.   Packard, Horatio M., wounded.
Rogers, Charles B., killed.   Simmons, Stephen M., prisoner.
Sprague, Allen H., w'd, died Aug. 3,'63 Sweetland, Seth, prisoner.

COMPANY F.

SERGEANTS.

Joseph P. Durgin, wounded.   Ora H. Nason, prisoner.

CORPORALS.

Amos H. Cole, killed.   Henry H. Chase, wounded.

PRIVATES.

Currier, Thomas S., killed.   Dorathy, George E., wounded.
Luce, Alsbury, killed.   Maxim, Wm. H., killed (rep'd mis'g).
Rackliff, William J., wounded.   Shattuck, Luke F., prisoner.
Stevens, John H., wounded.   Swan, Franklin, prisoner.
Swan, Henry B., reported killed ;   Towle, Charles L., wounded.
   rejoined regiment from missing.

COMPANY G.

SERGEANTS.

1st Sergt. William E. Brown, w'd, leg. George W. Davis, wounded.

CORPORALS.

Algernon P. Herrick,   Orrin Austin, reported prisoner.
   prisoner; died Oct. 28, 1863.

PRIVATES.

Arnold, Charles H., prisoner.   Derocher, Henry, prisoner.
Fossett, John E., wounded.   Frost, Samuel E., wounded.
Grover, Charles C., prisoner.   Perry, James, wounded.
Webber, Hiram C., wounded; died Aug. 18, 1863.

COMPANY H.

Sergeant William W. Livermore, wounded.

CORPORALS.

John H. Bacon, wounded,   Eben Farrington, killed.
Philander F. Rowe, prisoner; died in prison, Nov. 27, 1863.

PRIVATES.

Corson, Albert, killed.   Dixon George, wounded.
Major, Cyrus M., prisoner; died in prison, Dec. 9, 1863.

COMPANY I.

SERGEANTS.

Nelson W. Jones, killed.   Henry Lyon, killed.
Corporal Warren W. Cooper, wounded.

PRIVATES.

Bailey, Andrew J., wounded.   Bachelor, Charles M., wounded.
Burdin, Calvin H., killed.   Fellows, George L., killed.
Lewis, Alexander, prisoner.   Lewis, Andrew J., wounded.
Neal, Harrison W., wounded.   Palmer, William V., prisoner.

COMPANY K.

Captain John C. Keene, killed.
First Lieutenant Henry Penniman, wounded.

CORPORALS.

Charles A. Smart, wounded.   Alexander T. H. Wood, wounded.

PRIVATES.

Burgess, William H., killed.
Chandler, Samnel G., wounded.
Frost, Albert H., killed.
Heald, William, wounded.
Perkins, George, wounded.
Ricker, James C., prisoner.
Wilson, William G., missing.

Butler, George A., prisoner.
Cochran, Hiram,
prisoner; died in prison, Dec. 29, 1863.
Keay, Ruggles S., prisoner.
Raymond, William R., wounded.
Turner, Henry S., wounded.
Wood, Elias, prisoner.

Note on the foregoing report of casualties.

The monument inscription gives an aggregate of 122 killed, wounded and missing ; Col. Lakeman's official report 113 ; the foregoing nominal list 109. This list agrees with the inscription in the aggregate of killed and wounded—77, although those who died of their wounds are separated from the wounded here and counted with the killed, but not so on the monument. In this list, the "missing" are those who were captured, whether wounded or not, and those never heard from (there being 2 of the latter). A careful research brings the list of missing down to 32, instead of 45 as on the monument. It is probable that the number 45 was adopted for the monument inscription from Fox's statistics ; it does not tally with the information obtainable in the Adjutant-General's office at Augusta. The total discrepancy of 4 between this list and Col. Lakeman's report probably arises from 4 falling out and not accounted for with their command, but soon after rejoining for duty.

HISTORICAL SKETCH.

COMPILED FROM OFFICIAL AND OTHER SOURCES
BY THE EDITORS.

The Third Maine regiment of infantry was organized for active service May 28, 1861, and mustered into the U. S. service at Augusta, June 4th. It was raised in the central portion of the state, and went into camp at Augusta on the State grounds fronting the Capitol. Company A was the only company which existed under former militia laws, and was known as the Bath City Greys. While in camp at Augusta it was under constant drill of Sergeant Burt, U. S. A., assisted by Mr. Frank Pierce, a native of Augusta and a graduate of the Vermont Military School. The regiment was armed with the Springfield smooth-bore musket.

The original organization of the regiment was as follows :

FIELD AND STAFF.

Colonel, Oliver Otis Howard, Leeds, a graduate of West Point.
Lieutenant-Colonel, Isaac N. Tucker, Gardiner.
Major, Henry G. Staples, Augusta.
Chaplain, Andrew J. Church, Augusta.
Surgeon, Gideon S. Palmer, Gardiner.
Assistant Surgeon, George E. Brickett, China.
Adjutant, First Lieut. Edwin Burt, Augusta.
Quartermaster, William D. Haley, Bath.

Sergeant-Major, James H. Plaisted, Waterville.
Quartermaster-Sergeant, Joseph S. Smith, Bath.
Commissary-Sergeant, Lorenzo D. Grafton, Augusta.
Hospital Steward, Frank H. Getchell, Waterville.
Drum-major, Charles H. Howard, Leeds.
Fife-major, Moses M. Wadsworth, Gardiner.

COMPANY OFFICERS.

Co. A.   Captain, William O. Rogers, Bath.
First Lieutenant, Reuben Sawyer, Bath.
Second Lieutenant, John S. Wiggin, Bath.

Co. B.   Captain, Edwin A. Bachelder, Augusta.
First Lieutenant, Albert B. Hall, Augusta.
Second Lieutenant, Edwin Burt, Augusta.

Co. C.   Captain, William E. Jarvis, Gardiner.
First Lieutenant, James M. Colson, Gardiner.
Second Lieutenant, George S. Andrews, Gardiner.

Co. D.   Captain, Charles A. L. Sampson, Bath.
First Lieutenant, William H. Watson, Bath.
Second Lieutenant, Warren R. Mattson, Bath.

Co. E.   Captain, James M. Nash, Hallowell.
First Lieutenant, John W. Sanborn, Hallowell.
Second Lieutenant, Gorham S. Johnson, Hallowell.

Co. F.   Captain, Elbridge G. Savage, Solon.
First Lieutenant, Royal B. Stearns, Skowhegan.
Second Lieutenant, Henry A. Boyce, Skowhegan.

Co. G.   Captain, Frank S. Hesseltine, Waterville.
First Lieutenant, Nathaniel Hanscom, Benton.
Second Lieutenant, William A. Hatch, Waterville.

Co. H.   Captain, William S. Heath, Waterville.
First Lieutenant, Francis E. Heath, Waterville.
Second Lieutenant, John R. Day, Waterville.

Co. I.   Captain, Moses B. Lakeman, Augusta.
        First Lieutenant, A. R. Quimby, Augusta.
        Second Lieutenant, H. M. Rines, Augusta.
Co. K.   Captain, Newell Strout, Durham.
        First Lieutenant, Binsley S. Kelley, Winthrop.
        Second Lieutenant, William Elder, Winthrop.

The Third regiment, with Col. O. O. Howard, left Augusta June 5, 1861, and arrived at Washington on the evening of the 7th. On their passage through New York city a beautiful regimental flag was presented to them by Hon. Stewart L. Woodford, U. S. District Attorney, in behalf of the sons of Maine. The next day after their arrival in Washington they were ordered to a camp of instruction on Meridian Hill, where they remained until July 6th, when they crossed the Potomac and encamped in front of Fort Ellsworth, being at that time the advance regiment. On the 10th they moved their camp to Clermont, where they were brigaded, Colonel Howard, acting Brigadier-General, commanding. July 14th they commenced the march for Bull Run, under the command of Major Staples, arriving at Centreville on the 17th, and at Bull Run on the 21st. In the disastrous battle at the latter place, the Third sustained itself nobly. Its loss was eight killed, twenty-nine wounded and twelve taken prisoners.

On the 23d, returning to its previous camp at Clermont, it remained there until August 10th, when it moved to the right of Fort Ellsworth, and was put into Sedgwick's brigade, formed of Third and Fourth Maine, 38th and 40th N. Y. regts.

On the 27th and 28th of August, a portion of the regiment under the command of Major Staples had a brilliant skirmish with the enemy at Bailey's Cross Roads, but met with no loss. The Third remained near Fort Ellsworth, doing picket duty, working on fortifications and drilling, until September 27th, when the brigade was ordered forward to the Fowle's estate, on the old Fairfax road, and was posted in Heintzelman's division. During this time Colonel Howard was promoted to Brigadier-General, and Major Staples succeeded him as colonel.

On the 17th of March, 1862, broke camp, marched to Alexandria and then proceeded to Hampton, where they remained until April 3d, when they moved with the army of the Potomac to

Yorktown, at the siege of which they bore an honorable part, and when the enemy evacuated they were among the first in pursuit.

At the battle of Williamsburg, May 5th, the regiment was detached by General Heintzelman to guard the left flank, which position they held until sunset, when they marched to the relief of the regiments then engaged. Gen. Phil. Kearny, who commanded the division, says that the Third and Fourth Maine " by their steady and imposing attitude contributed to the success of those more immediately engaged." The Third lost but two men, wounded.

May 15th they arrived at Cumberland Landing on the Pamunkey river, where they remained a few days, when they marched to within a few miles of Bottom's Bridge, on the Chickahominy. On the 23d they crossed this bridge and marched within half a mile of Fair Oaks. The battle of Seven Pines took place on the 31st and June 1st. On the former date, during the attack on the enemy's left, the Third was ordered to the front by General Birney. It moved up the railroad by the flank, and occupied several positions on the right and left of the road during the afternoon, resting at night in line of battle upon the first opening on the right of the railroad, above the bridge. The next morning it was ordered into the field on the left of the railroad, where it formed a line of battle under the edge of the woods. The presence of the enemy in force in their front was revealed by his terrific fire, opened upon the skirmishers under the command of Major Burt, who checked them until the main body came up. A charge was then ordered, and the movement was gallantly executed. The enemy was pursued a half mile when the Third encountered his reserve, who returned our fire with terrible effect, but which was soon silenced. During this battle the regiment did its duty nobly and bravely. General Kearny told Colonel Ward, commanding the brigade at the time of the action, that " The brigade have done nobly, sir, and the Third and Fourth Maine can't be beat ! " The loss in killed and wounded was nearly one-third of the regiment.

The Third remained in the advance line of the army until June 25th, when they were engaged in the battle of White Oak

Swamp, in which the regiment by having a good position was enabled to do excellent service with very slight loss. On the 29th they were withdrawn from the advance line of fortifications before Richmond at an early hour in the morning, and under command of Major Burt crossed White Oak Swamp at Jordan's ford in the evening, covered by the left flank company as skirmishers, under command of Lieutenant Cox, who, after an advance of nearly two miles in the direction of Charles City Cross Roads, came upon the rebels in considerable force, when a brisk skirmish took place ; but in consequence of the disparity of force, Lieutenant Cox was forced to retire after a loss of one man killed and one taken prisoner. By order of General Birney the regiment then recrossed the swamp, followed its bank about six miles, and again crossing, gained the highlands and bivouacked for the night.

On the morning of the 30th they went forward on the Charles City Road and took an active part in the battle of Charles City Cross Roads. Before daybreak on the morning of July 1st they marched to Malvern Hill, where during the battle at that place they assisted in supporting Randolph's 6th R. I. battery. For eight hours they were exposed to a severe fire from the enemy's batteries, during which time the conduct of the men was admirable in the extreme. Their loss was very light. At an early hour the next morning they removed to Dr. Mung's plantation near Berkley's Station, where they bivouacked that night, and on the following morning, after having their camp shelled by the enemy, advanced three miles in the direction of Harrison's Landing, where they encamped. From this time until August 15th, the Third remained in front, when they joined in the retrograde movement towards Yorktown, where they arrived on the 19th, and on the 21st embarked on transports for Alexandria, at which place they arrived the following day. From thence they proceeded on the 23d by rail to within four miles of the Rappahannock river, thence to Greenwich, Bristoe's Station, Manassas and Centreville, and finally on the 29th of August they marched for Bull Run, arriving on the battlefield at about 9 A. M., and participating in the engagement of that day. The next day they supported Randolph's battery until 3 o'clock P. M., when they retired to the rear. The regiment shortly returned to the attack with the lamented General Kearny at their head, but meeting a rebel brigade they were forced to retire under a murderous fire. A portion of the Third also encountered another heavy fire, while supporting a section of a battery, when with the rest of the forces they fell back to Centreville.

The next day the regiment took up the line of march for Fairfax, when took place the battle of Chantilly, during which it sustained unflinchingly a murderous fire from a superior force, losing four killed, thirty-eight wounded and eight missing.

On the 2d of September they marched to Alexandria and encamped in the vicinity of Fort Lyon. On the 8th they moved to Fort Worth, and from thence to Fort Barnard, where they remained until the 15th, when they proceeded to Poolesville, Md., and thence to White's Ford, on the upper Potomac. The several fords from the Monocacy to Conrad's Ferry were guarded by the regiment. At the last named place Colonel Staples had temporary command of the brigade.

On the 11th of October the regiment, together with the Fourth Maine, proceeded to the mouth of the Monocacy, to intercept the return of Stuart's cavalry into Virginia. A brisk engagement ensued, which resulted in the enemy's making his escape. Returning to Poolesville, they marched to White's Ford, thence to Leesburg, Warrenton, on the Rappahannock (Nov. 7th), where they remained at Waterloo bridge until the 16th, when they were ordered to Falmouth, arriving there November 22d. In the meantime Col. Staples resigned, and Lieut.-Col. Lakeman was promoted to the colonelcy.

Remained at Falmouth until Dec. 11th, when they joined in the forward move on Fredericksburg. Late in the afternoon of the following day they marched six miles down the river in order to cross the Rappahannock and reinforce General Franklin, who had been giving battle to the enemy since morning. On arriving within about a mile of the pontoon bridge, it was found that the troops previously sent by this route had not yet crossed, and the Third was ordered to bivouac. The next day at daybreak they were under arms, and at 10 o'clock they crossed the Rappahannock, when General Birney, commanding division, immediately formed his brigades and pushed forward to the left of the ground occupied by General Whipple, and prepared for action. Colonel Lakeman marched to the rear some one hundred and seventy-five yards, and took position amid a shower of shot and shell, when he was ordered to the support of Hall's Second Maine battery, remaining in position nearly six hours, under a most trying fire. The position was a post of honor and danger. The battery having been ordered to change position, an attempt was made by the enemy to capture it, but the unerring aim of a well-sustained fire from the Third sent him back to the cover of his intrenchments. At an early hour the next morning they were withdrawn from the front and placed in the second line, where they remained through the day, when at midnight they took up their previous position in the advance. The regiment was from necessity compelled to lie on wet ground, in front of the enemy, for nearly fifty hours, which accounts for the slight loss they sustained, — three killed, twenty-five wounded and four missing. On being withdrawn from the lines, they marched to the camp they previously occupied, on the north bank of the Rappahannock.

The regiment broke camp on the 20th of January, 1863, and with the army participated in General Burnside's movement, afterwards known as the "mud march"; the movement being abandoned, it returned to its former camp on the 23d, where it remained until March 4th, when with the division it moved to Potomac Creek, four miles, and remained there until April 28th, during which time the regiment was almost constantly employed, under Captain Morgan, building military roads.

During the winter of 1863, after General Hooker had succeeded General Burnside in the command of the army, the system of badges to be worn upon the cap was invented. The Third corps badge thus adopted was the diamond, evidently carrying out the idea of General Kearny, in whose division the Third Maine regiment belonged. Accordingly, those of the First division, including the Third, Fourth and Seventeenth Maine regiments, and company D, 2d U. S. Sharpshooters, retained the red diamond patch of Kearny, the white diamond designating the Second and the blue diamond the Third division.

April 28th, with the army, the Third regiment crossed the Rappahannock river, proceeded to and participated in the battle of the Cedars and Chancellorsville, May 2d and 3d, in which engagements it lost Lieutenants Cox and Witham, killed, Lieutenant Emery wounded, Lieutenants Fuller and Nye, prisoners; also fifty-six men wounded and prisoners, four of whom afterwards died of wounds.

The movements of the regiment at the battle of Chancellorsville were as follows: The regiment bivouacked near United States Ford on the night of April 30th. At daybreak, on the morning of May 1st, the brigade crossed the Rappahannock and marched to the Plank road, where it took position in line of battle and there remained until the morning of the 2d. On the 2d the regiment moved farther up the Plank road, awaiting an attack until two o'clock in the afternoon, when the whole division advanced out beyond our lines several miles, striking the enemy's train-guard and capturing many prisoners. This action was called the Cedars. Shortly after sunset returned towards the previous position, but halted at Hazel Grove, remaining there, in line of battle, until nearly midnight, when the brigade was ordered to charge upon a force which had gained possession of the Plank road, and the road leading to it, by defeating the Eleventh corps. The regiment advanced and engaged in a severe fight which lasted nearly an hour; the first and second lines of earthworks were carried and held until daylight, notwithstanding the stubborn resistance of the enemy who outnumbered our forces very largely. This movement and its success resulted in keeping open the communication with the Twelfth corps, from which we had been substantially cut off by Jackson's movement around our right flank, and by which he had driven back the Eleventh corps in disorder. At daylight, May 3d, the enemy occupied the woods on two sides and opened a sharp fire on the brigade, which was briskly returned, until our troops were re-arranged nearer the Chancellor house. Around this as a centre the battle on May 3d was fought, in which Major-General Berry was killed. The brigade supported such batteries as was ordered and otherwise participated in the action that took place. The regiment after several changes of position, at times under severe fire, finally took up a position with its brigade in the new line of works, occupying the first line of defense. In this position it was subjected to a heavy artillery fire from the enemy, and several men were more or less wounded. The brigade was highly complimented by General Ward, its commander, for the gallantry of its officers and men. They occupied the front line of earthworks until daybreak of the 6th, being the last to leave the front, recrossing the Rappahannock in the forenoon and returning to their former camp. Here it remained until June 11th, when it took its line of march with the army that terminated in the battle of Gettysburg, July 1, 2 and 3, 1863.

In this engagement at Gettysburg, July 2 and 3, 1863, the Third Maine regiment took a most conspicuous part, being the first to attack the enemy on the morning of the 2d, a long distance in advance of the line, where it sustained a loss of forty-eight killed, wounded and missing. The regiment during the remainder of the day held an advanced position in the ever memorable Peach Orchard until evening, when it was attacked by an overwhelming force and compelled to fall back, sustaining the loss of Captain Keen, killed, Major Lee and Lieut. Penniman, severely wounded, and fifty-eight men killed, wounded and prisoners. In this attack the regiment was not connected with its brigade. On the morning of the 3d the regiment, under command of Captain Morgan, with three others, were detached under the command of Colonel Lakeman to support the Second division, Second corps, where it remained until the morning of the 4th, when the four regiments formed an advance line of battle on the Emmitsburg road and, relieving the advanced skirmishers, remained there until the morning of the 5th, when it rejoined the brigade, the enemy having left its front. The regiment then rested in position until the morning of the 7th, when, with the rest of the army, it started in pursuit of the enemy.

July 23d the regiment, with the Fourth Maine, under command of Colonel Lakeman, engaged and routed the enemy at

Wapping Heights; the regiment, deployed as skirmishers, charged and cleared the heights. At night the enemy retreated. Next morning the regiment moved towards Warrenton, where it arrived the 26th, and on the 31st moved to Warrenton Sulphur Springs, where it remained in camp until September 16th, when it marched to Culpeper, arriving on the 18th, and remained there until October 11th, when, with the army, it commenced a retrograde movement, and with the division engaged the enemy at Auburn Mills, on the 12th, routing them.

The Third arrived at Fairfax Station on the 14th and remained there until the 19th, when it advanced with the army to Catlett's Station, arriving there the 22d and remaining there until November 7th, during which time it was engaged repairing the railroads.

On November 7th the regiment was engaged in the skirmish at Kelly's Ford, with slight loss, and the following day advanced towards Brandy Station, arriving there the 9th. On the 26th, with the army, it crossed the Rapidan river at Jacob's Ford, and took part in the engagements of Orange Grove on the 27th and Mine Run on the 30th, with loss of one killed, eight wounded and twenty-three missing. The regiment remained in position until December 1st, when it recrossed the Rapidan and returned to camp near Brandy Station.

On the 1st of January, 1864, the regiment was encamped near Brandy Station, Va., where it remained until May 4th, when it moved, under General Grant, across the Rapidan towards Richmond, and encamped the same night on the battlefield of Chancellorsville. The Third corps had been consolidated with the Second, and the regiment still remained in the First (Ward's) brigade, Third (Birney's) division, the corps being commanded by Hancock. It participated the next day in the battle of the Wilderness, being in position near where the Brock road crosses the Plank road. Here it fought on the afternoon of the 5th and the forenoon of the 6th, with heavy loss. The regiment made and repelled several charges during this memorable battle, and its men won fresh laurels by their courage and steadiness under the furious attacks of the enemy. Among the killed was Lieut.-Col. Burt, and of the wounded was Captain

Getchell, who afterwards died of his wounds. After remaining one day in their rifle-pits, they on the 8th joined in the movement towards Spotsylvania Court House, doing but little fighting however. On the 10th the regiment was held in reserve until sunset, when they joined their brigade in a charge in which they were repulsed. In the assault at Spotsylvania by the Second corps, on the 12th, it took part. The assaulting column succeeded in carrying the works of the enemy at the celebrated "salient," capturing Johnson's division and many cannon, and the repeated counter-assaults of the enemy failed to dislodge the Union troops; the ground was thickly covered by the dead and wounded of both sides. The loss of the regiment in these engagements was severe, Captain Nye being mortally wounded, acting-Adjutant Bursley killed, and Captain Merrill missing. On the evening of the 19th the division to which the Third belonged relieved those of our forces who had been engaged, including the heavy artillery regiments, in repelling the furious assaults of the enemy at the Frederickburg road. On the morning of the 23d the regiment moved towards the North Anna, where it arrived during the afternoon, and where it participated in the assault upon the enemy's works commanding the bridge, losing severely; among others were Major Morgan killed and Colonel Lakeman wounded. On the 28th the regiment reached and crossed the Pamunkey, pushing along until the morning of the 30th, when it was engaged in throwing up intrenchments, losing during the change of position by the army sixteen men on picket, most of whom were taken prisoners. On the 3d of June the regiment with its division supported General Barlow's division in the engagement at Cold Harbor. On the 4th the regiment, after being highly complimented by General Birney, in general orders, left for Maine, its term of service of three years having expired, arriving in Augusta on the 11th, where the veterans were greeted with a public reception and partook of a handsome collation prepared by the city authorities. The regiment, numbering about 112 men, was mustered out of the U. S. service on June 28, 1864. The re-enlisted men and recruits were transferred to the Seventeenth Maine regiment before their departure from the front.

The Third Maine was one of the best regiments in the service from Maine and was held in high esteem by those in whose commands it served.

In Fox's work, Regimental Losses of the Civil War, the Third Maine is classed among the three hundred fighting regiments of the Union armies, so distinguished on account of their losses in battle.

ROSTER.

The following information relating to the Third Maine regiment will be found in the Volunteer Army Register (part 1), published by the War Department August 31, 1865:—

OFFICERS AT MUSTER–OUT, JUNE 28, 1864.

COLONEL: Moses B. Lakeman, Nov. 14, 1862.

CAPTAINS: John S. Moore, Feb. 12, 1862; Alfred S. Merrill, Oct. 26, 1862; George A. McIntire, Dec. 31, 1863; Henry P. Worcester, Jan. 8, 1864; Edward C. Pierce, Feb. 5, 1863 (*a. w. m.*).

FIRST LIEUTENANTS: John R. Day, Sept. 12, 1861 (paroled prisoner, discharged June 5, 1865); Charles T. Watson, R. Q. M., July 1, 1862; Daniel W. Emery, Aug. 19, 1862; Woodbury Hall, Oct. 26, 1862; George S. Fuller, Nov. 14, 1862; Holman M. Anderson, Feb. 27, 1863 (paroled prisoner, discharged Jan. 30, 1865); William H. Higgins, Jan. 20, 1864; Abner W. Turner, Feb. 5, 1863 (*a. w. m.*).

SECOND LIEUTENANTS: George S. Blake, Oct. 15, 1862; Charles W. Lowe, Dec. 6, 1862; Samuel L. Gilman, Feb. 27, 1863; George C. Hudson, Feb. 27, 1863; John B. Dodge, Jan. 3, 1864; Bradford W. Smart, Apr. 2, 1864; Hannibal A. Johnson, Apr. 7, 1864.

SURGEON: Thaddeus Hildreth, Oct. 23, 1861; ASSISTANT SURGEON: James D. Watson, Dec. 22, 1862.

CHAPLAIN: Stephen F. Chase, Mar. 23, 1863.

(The dates given above refer to rank or commission; those hereafter given refer to the date of event.)

DIED.

Lieut.-Col. Edwin Burt, killed at Wilderness, May 6, 1864; Major William C. Morgan, killed at North Anna river, May 23, 1864; Captain *Nathaniel Hanscomb, June 16, 1862, at Fair Oaks, Va., of fever; Captain John C. Keene, killed at Gettysburg, July 2, 1863; Captain George W. Harvey, May 9, 1864, of wounds received in action; Captain George O. Getchell, May 30, 1864, of wounds received in action; Captain George A. Nye, June 4, 1864, of wounds received in action; First Lieut. *Charles B. Haskell, July 2, 1862, of wounds received in action at Fair Oaks, Va.; First. Lieut. *Warren W. Cox, killed at Chancellorsville, Va., May 3, 1863; First Lieut. William H. Briggs, killed at Totopotomy, Va., May 30, 1864; Second Lieut. Denola Witham, killed at Chancellorsville, Va., May 2, 1863.

*Not mustered to this grade.

PROMOTED OUT OF REGIMENT.

Colonel Oliver O. Howard, to Brigadier-General U. S. Vols., Sept. 7, 1861; Captain William S. Heath, to Lieut.-Colonel Fifth Maine Vols., Sept. 23, 1861; Captain William A. Hatch, to Major 3d U. S. V., Mar. 8, 1863; First Lieut. James H. Tallman, R. Q. M., Mar. 24, 1862, to Captain and A. Q. M.; Surgeon Gideon S. Palmer, Oct. 23, 1861, to Brigade Surgeon; Captain Francis E. Heath, resigned July 26, 1862, to accept promotion as Colonel, Nineteenth Maine; Captain Frank S. Hazeltine, discharged Nov. 14, 1861, to become Major, Thirteenth Maine.

TRANSFERRED.

Major Samuel P. Lee to Invalid Corps, July or Nov., 1863; Chaplain Henry C. Leonard to Eighteenth Maine regiment, Oct. 28, 1862.

RESIGNED AND DISCHARGED.

Colonel Henry C. Staples, Nov. 14, 1862; Lieut.-Col. Isaac W. Tucker, Nov. 4, 1861; Lieut.-Col. C. A. L. Sampson, July 7, 1862.

CAPTAINS: John M. Nash, July 30, 1861; Newell Strout, Aug. 8, 1861; E. G. Savage, Sept. 11, 1861; W. E. Jarvis, Oct. 3, 1861; G. S. Johnson, Aug. 4, 1862; W. L. Richmond, Oct. 16, 1862; W. H. Watson, Oct. 25, 1862; Reuben Sawyer, Jan. 15, 1863; J. S. Wiggin, Mar. 23, 1863; J. H. Plaisted, Mar. 26, 1863.

FIRST LIEUTENANTS: G. B. Erskine, July 24, 1861; A. R. Quimby, July 27, 1861; B. S. Kelly, Aug. 7, 1861; W. D. Haley, R. Q. M., Sept. 7, 1861; R. B. Stearns, Nov. 4, 1861; J. M. Colson, Nov. 8, 1861; Albert B. Hall, Adjt., Nov. 28, 1861; G. S. Andrews, Feb. 11, 1862; E. P. Donnell, Apr. 6, 1862; Henry Penniman, Nov. 4, 1863.

SECOND LIEUTENANTS: H. M. Rines, July 27, 1861; W. R. Mattson, Aug. 12, 1861; H. A. Boyce, Aug. 2, 1861; W. Elder, Aug. 20, 1861; E. C. Low, Mar. 11, 1862; S. Hamblen, Dec. 5, 1862, to be Lieut.-Col. 10th U. S. Col. Hy. Arty.; C. A. Hill, Dec. 28, 1862, to be Capt. 1st U. S. Col. Infty.; T. J. Noyes, Mar. 24, 1863; A. C. Wilson, May 6, 1863.

ASSISTANT SURGEONS: G. E. Brickett, Aug. 27, 1861; F. H. Getchell, Oct. 28, 1862; W. H. Jewett, May 6, 1863.

CHAPLAIN: A. J. Church, July 11, 1861.

OTHERWISE LEFT THE SERVICE.

Captain E. A. Bachelder, Dec. 22, 1862; Lieut. J. Savage, Aug. 19, 1862; Lieut. F. Elliot, Aug. 19, 1862; Adjt. C. C. Drew, Mar. 29, 1864.

MONUMENT
OF
FOURTH MAINE REGIMENT.

The monument is placed in the gorge of Devil's Den, where the regiment suffered its heaviest loss. With one of the huge bowlders of that wild place for its foundation, it is a conspicuous memorial of Maine valor. It is a five-sided shaft of Maine granite and bears on each face the red diamond of the First division of the Third corps.

ADMEASUREMENTS: Base, six feet from angle to angle by two feet four inches; plinth, three feet six inches between the angles by two feet; shaft, two feet nine inches between angles by twelve feet in height. Total height, sixteen feet four inches.

On the several sides are the following inscriptions:

4TH MAINE
INFANTRY.
COLONEL ELIJAH WALKER.

THIRD CORPS, FIRST DIVISION,
SECOND BRIGADE.

22 KILLED AND DIED.
38 WOUNDED.
56 MISSING.
ERECTED BY THE
STATE OF MAINE.

IN REMEMBRANCE
OF OUR CASUALTIES
JULY 2D. 1863.

FOURTH MAINE REGIMENT,

SECOND BRIGADE, FIRST DIVISION, THIRD ARMY CORPS,

AT THE BATTLE OF GETTYSBURG.

THE Fourth Maine regiment was involved in the desperate battle upon the advanced line projected by General Sickles, and belonged to Ward's brigade. Like the Third Maine, it was one of the truest veteran regiments in the army of the Potomac. It left Maine June 17, 1861, bearing upon its banner the inscription "From the Home of Knox," indicating the portion of the state in which it had been recruited. Major-General Hiram G. Berry, who had but recently met a glorious death at Chancellorsville, was its first colonel. It was led to Gettysburg by Colonel Elijah Walker, who had won an honorable reputation for bravery in the campaigns of Virginia.

The Fourth Maine arrived on the field with Sickles' corps about 7 o'clock in the evening of July 1st, the first day of the battle, having moved up with the corps from Taneytown by the way of Emmitsburg. The regiment brought onto the field about three hundred men and officers. About nine o'clock in the evening of their arrival Colonel Walker received orders from Major-General Sickles to establish a picket line to extend along a portion of the front of the left wing, as the Union line was formed at that hour. In obedience to this order the regiment moved out, crossed the Emmitsburg road, and after advancing thirty or forty rods, established a picket line. In the woods to the front were the Confederate pickets also, and in those same woods the latest accessions to the Confederate strength were gathering after their march from the passes of South Mountain. The night passed quietly, but at daybreak a desultory skirmish fire began between the opposing picket lines, which was continued until 9 or 10 o'clock in the forenoon of July 2d. From that time until afternoon, when the Fourth was relieved by the 1st Mass. (a), there was quiet on this part of the picket line.

When the Fourth went onto the picket line the evening before, the Union line was extending from Cemetery Hill towards Little Round Top in a line nearly straight. But as the regiment rejoined the brigade, events were so shaping themselves, as has been noticed already in connection with the advance of the Third Maine, that General Sickles felt impelled to advance his corps to the higher ground in his front, where it made the angular line from Devil's Den up to the Peach Orchard, thence northerly along the Emmitsburg road. This new line was formed between two and three o'clock in the afternoon. The station of this brigade was at the left extremity of this line, and the Fourth Maine was at the left extremity of the brigade. The official report of the regiment, made directly after the battle and before history had made famous every hill and valley on the field, speaks of taking position on a "rocky hill." This was the hill to the right of Devil's Den, that wonderful ravine where nature has disposed precipices and huge bowlders in a wild combination meriting the name which is given it. The Fourth Maine was stationed to support two sections of Smith's 4th N. Y. battery of 10-pounder Parrott's. To the left was a gorge where flows towards the south a small stream called Plum Run. Across and to the east of the Run rise the precipitous sides of the two Round Tops. On the right of the battery and extending through the timber to the Wheatfield were the 124th and 86th N. Y., the 20th Ind. and 99th Pa. in the order named, the direction of the line trending towards the Peach Orchard. The 2d U. S. Sharpshooters, also of Ward's brigade, were thrown forward as skirmishers about one-third of a mile in advance beyond Devil's Den in a southerly direction.

Hood's division of Longstreet's corps had been creeping upon concealed roads southward out beyond the left of our lines that occupied a section of the Emmitsburg road, and had at length advanced to that road beyond the Union pickets, in a wood behind a ridge, at a point about 1,300 yards south from

(a) There is some disparity in the several sources of evidence as to the exact time when the Fourth was relieved at the picket line.

the Peach Orchard and about the same distance westerly from
Devil's Den.

A group of signal men on Little Round Top had detected
the enemy's movement and signaled the fact to Meade's headquarters. Approaching 4 o'clock Smith's battery opened fire
into the woods at the Emmitsburg road, quickly receiving a
reply from some batteries pushed out on a hillock near the road.
West of that road, along a general ridge diverging from the
road as it extended northward, the enemy's battalions of artillery were admirably posted, and some of them joined in the
opening attack. They threw shell at the Devil's Den position
as well as at the group of signal men, and paid their respects
to the Peach Orchard batteries, not overlooking Winslow's battery in the Wheatfield,—light twelves, — not very effective in
reply at that range. There was no longer doubt where the
heavy hand of battle would fall. The audacious advance of
Sickles brought upon his thin, extended lines the first and most
furious attack of the enemy.

It was about 4 o'clock when the soldiers of Ward's right,
looking in the direction of the Emmitsburg road, saw clouds of
Confederate skirmishers emerge from the woods, followed by
heavy lines of infantry. They were Robertson's and Law's
brigades of Hood's division, and, as they came on " in line and
en masse, yelling and shouting," as General Ward described it
in his official report, in 1863, with the memories of the day
fresh in his mind, they were opening the second day of the
battle of Gettysburg. On Robertson's right, moving directly
towards Round Top, Law's Alabama brigade advanced, but
more silently. The position at Devil's Den had been pointed
out to the subordinates of Longstreet as first to be attacked and
carried. Doubtless it appeared to Longstreet to be the left of
the Union line, and indeed it was at that hour.

But General Hood had discovered the importance of Little
Round Top, and sent Law's Alabama brigade, with which the
changes of the advance associated two regiments of Robertson's
Texans, to pass around Devil's Den, scale the heights and
attempt the seizure of Little Round Top. By order of his superior officer, but contrary to the judgment of Colonel Walker,

the Fourth Maine was moved from its position in the rear of the battery to the left, and extended across the gorge of Plum Run in such a way as to defend Ward's left flank and rear, and in a measure the approaches to Little Round Top. When the exigency of the contest demanded it Ward gave a further support to the battery position with the 99th Pa., taken from his right. The battle now began with Ward's line, directly against which the two remaining regiments of Robertson — 1st Texas and 3d Arkansas — advanced under Robertson's immediate command. The attack was fierce, and the first struggle for possession of the battery was chiefly between the 1st Texas and the 124th New York, the latter seconded by the 86th New York. About this time Ward's line was reinforced upon its right flank by the coming-in of the Seventeenth Maine to the south edge of the Wheatfield, which struck the 3d Arkansas and diverted it from the attack upon the battery, at the same time menacing the left flank of Robertson, who fell back a short distance without securing the coveted prize.

Robertson's next attack with his two regiments was directed more upon the right of Ward's line in an attempt to outflank him, which was spiritedly made but steadfastly resisted during a prolonged contest, ending by Robertson falling back again. In these first two attacks the Fourth Maine had taken no part except by about 70 men, with 3 officers, whom Colonel Walker had deployed south of Devil's Den as skirmishers; these men, reinforced to some extent by the retiring U. S. Sharpshooters and the skirmishers of other regiments of Ward, had caused the on-coming Confederates much annoyance and delay, besides quite a loss, as the latter were taken in flank on their first advance; these skirmishers were in fact one of the causes of the separation of Robertson's brigade into two parts, (a) and the detour made by Law's troops in getting to Little Round Top. These skirmishers held their ground while Robertson attempted the battery position, and until at a later time when Benning came in, which will be seen further on.

Meanwhile, Hood being wounded, the command of his division fell to General Law, who with his brigade was moving upon Little Round Top. Finding as he advanced beyond the Plum

(a) Official report of Major Bane, 4th Tex., Rebellion Records, serial no. 44, p. 401.

Run valley that insufficient strength was exerted against the Smith battery position to capture it, Law detached two regiments from his extreme right, the 44th and 48th Alabama, and directed them to move across to the left and attack the battery in reverse. Following out these instructions, the two regiments moved by their left flank to a point about two hundred yards from Devil's Den on its easterly approach, halting there in the thin growth which fringed Plum Run and in view of the Fourth Maine. Here the two Alabama regiments were swung into line facing the gorge. The 44th Alabama, being immediately opposed to the position taken by the Fourth Maine, became at once the particular antagonist of the latter. (See diagrams on pages 251 and 194.)

The 48th Alabama, advancing northerly along the sloping side of Little Round Top, parallel with Plum Run, passed the position of the Fourth Maine after exchanging a few compliments, and presently had a duel with the 40th New York. When the Fourth Maine first stretched across the Plum Run gorge there were no Union troops on Little Round Top. Colonel Walker, mindful of his left flank, sent out some skirmishers into the woods on the slope, but before they met the advancing enemy, Vincent had arrived upon the crest and the skirmishers of his 83d Penn., 16th Mich., and 44th N. Y. regiments advanced down the hill; this advance of skirmishers, immediately engaging those of Law, induced Walker to believe a line of battle would follow to connect with him on his left, and so he drew in his flankers. The 4th Alabama of Law and the 4th and 5th Texas of Robertson passed up Little Round Top in their circling advance; and the 47th and 15th Alabama up the slope of Big Round Top. The firing began on the slopes of Little Round Top fifty rods or so to the left and rear of the Fourth Maine, which, posted in the valley, had not yet fired a shot. It was now nearly 5 o'clock, perhaps nearer 4.45, when in the edge of the wood of small pines appeared the 44th Alabama, its right upon the flank of Colonel Walker and uncomfortably near; the latter immediately opened a destructive fire upon the enemy while he was forming his lines, and at the same time arranged the Fourth Maine as well as possible to confront the advancing line, making use of the bowlders, which sprinkled the ground, as much as circumstances permitted. The Alabamians came on in a truly heroic manner, but were met with equal firmness by the Maine men, although the latter were much less in numbers. The advance was checked and they soon gave it up, retiring into the woods, where they were completely concealed behind trees and rocks. From behind these natural protections they kept up a biting musketry fire upon Walker's men, who in the open valley were placed at great disadvantage and suffered large loss (a).

It was now past 5 o'clock. The two contending forces were in a close grapple, extending from the left of the Union line, — which now was Vincent's spur on Little Round Top occupied by the Twentieth Maine, — around its south crest to Plum Run and thence southerly to Devil's Den ; and on the other side of the battery ridge Robertson's line had been prolonged westward by Anderson's Georgia brigade about half the distance to the Emmitsburg road. The whole line was alive with burning powder. Smith's battery, at Devil's Den, was abandoned by orders of its captain. The other section of the battery, located up the valley northerly some distance, was now manned for action. All the desperate efforts so far made, from both sides of this flat-iron-shaped position, where the field pieces rested, to capture it had proved futile. Robertson was desperately anxious to take those guns, and finding that Benning's brigade of four Georgia regiments was nearly in his rear, as a support to the right of their lines, he asked Benning to help him. Benning had intended to support Law's brigade, and supposed the troops contesting with Ward to be Law's, not distinguishing them in the wooded lands. This error on his part, possibly, saved the crest of Little Round Top from capture. Perhaps it seemed important to the Confederates to wrest this ridge from our troops in order to protect their own at

(a) Colonel Walker has recently requested the Commissioners of the Gettysburg National Park to move the flanking stones marking the direction of his line at this period. The position of these stones as found Sept. 21, 1897, would make the Fourth Maine face the Smith-battery position; whereas, as he stated to the Commissioners, at date named, upon the ground, his line faced a quarter-circle to the left of this; that he met the 44th Ala. in his front, at first a little upon his left flank, and that his line if prolonged to the left would strike upon Little Round Top. Stakes were then driven into the ground to mark the corrected places for the stones.

our left rear on Little Round Top from being surrounded and captured by an attack from their rear, as was easily feasible by an enterprising general with a smart brigade, so long as they were only protected by two regiments, the 44th and 48th Alabama. The Confederates also desired to secure possession of a stone-fence which starts at the summit of this ridge near the battery, and runs westerly, affording a complete curtain and breastwork to hold that ground and dominate the woods in front to the Wheat-field. (See diagram on page 194.) Robertson had twice essayed to seize and hold this fence without success. After the second attempt, General Ward advanced his centre and right to take possession of it; (a) this occurred just as Benning was also advancing.

Without delay Benning had formed his brigade in a line east and west, perpendicular to the trend of the ridge, and moved forward, his left centre regiment aiming directly at the battery position, the right centre regiment having Devil's Den in its course, and the regiment on the right of that moving up Plum Run. Benning's left regiment as it advanced mingled with the 1st Texas of Robertson and they became amalgamated. As his lines, advancing through the growth that fringed the stream, emerged into view, they were subjected to a plunging shell fire from Hazlett's battery of 10-pounder rifles placed on the summit of Little Round Top. This battery played an effective part in the struggle, both against Longstreet's guns at the Emmitsburg road and with its sweeping fire down the slopes, searching out the recesses where troops were ambushed, and demoralizing their charges. The 44th Alabama had felt its power, and, until night closed, this battery and its infantry supports on the crest completely dominated the southerly end of the gorge and the ridge near Devil's Den. Benning's reinforcement to Robertson for attack, moving directly upon the point, thus taking both sides of the line of Ward in flank, must in the end be irresistible to the small and decimated regiments arraying themselves to meet it. As Benning advanced, the two wings of his brigade converged somewhat towards Smith's battery. Taken unawares, the skirmishers of the Fourth Maine and other regiments, being virtually surrounded while hotly

(a) Official Report of General Ward. — Rebellion Records, serial no. 43, page 493.

contesting the advance on the Den from one direction, were scooped up by Benning as prisoners. The 44th Alabama, seeing the column of Benning coming up the Run and through the rough fastness of Devil's Den, at once came forth to join in the fray. The Fourth Maine gallantly held them at bay, but in conjunction with this overwhelming force at his front, Colonel Walker became at length aware that others had advanced as far as his right flank, close up to the abandoned guns of Smith. What followed is well described by Colonel Walker himself in his address at the dedication of the monument, given on another page.

The experienced eye of Colonel Walker at once convinced him that the key to the whole position rested at the battery, although the possession of the guns themselves amounted to nothing; it formed the sharp angle to Ward's line, and once in the possession of the enemy he could rake the line of Ward, as first established, its entire length, and destroy the organizations that were attending to the advance of Anderson towards their front. Without hesitation Walker drew his small remaining force from the nest of bowlders in the gorge, hastily got it into line and charged home with the bayonet upon Benning's men, who had entered the battery, and drove them out in a fierce encounter. Assisted by the 99th Penn. (a) in keeping off the Confederates from the gorge side of the hill, and by the 124th N. Y. on his right, he succeeded in repelling repeated assaults in a hand-to-hand contest for some considerable time, which enabled Ward to arrange the 6th N. J., (b) and 40th N. Y. regiments, that had been brought in to his left rear in Plum Run valley, so that a withdrawal of the brigade could be safely effected, its thrust-out angle being no longer of importance as a tactical point. Colonel Walker claims with good reason, that after he recaptured the battery its guns might

(a) Major Moore, commanding the 99th Penn., in his official report of the battle says: "* * * the engagement became very general with the enemy, who was throwing a large force against our brigade in hopes of breaking through our lines. I was now ordered by General Ward to march my regiment double-quick from the right to the left of the brigade. This movement rapidly executed placed my command on the brow of a hill overlooking a deep ravine, interspersed with large bowlders of rock. Here the conflict was fierce. I held my position for over thirty minutes * * *." See Rebellion Records, serial no. 43, page 513.

(b) The regiment commanded by Lieut.-Col. Gilkyson with others of the Third, or Jersey, brigade of the Second division had been sent by General Humphreys, under orders of General Sickles, to the support of the First division, and was made subject to the orders of General Birney. — Rebellion Records, serial no. 43, page 534.

have been used safely and effectively in defending that position. The Fourth Maine and the brigade retired by order of General Ward. After safely reaching the rear the command was turned over to Capt. Edwin Libby, the wound of the Colonel proving very severe. The retirement of the brigade from this advanced position, probably after 6 o'clock P. M., was not followed up by the enemy beyond the stone fence, and about the same time Cross' brigade of Caldwell's division of the Second corps advanced into the woods where the right of Ward had rested. This ended the fighting of the Fourth Maine on July second.

July third the regiment was with the brigade in reserve. At the crisis of the assault upon our lines in the afternoon the regiment, together with the Third Maine, 99th Penn., and 20th Ind., all under Col. Lakeman, were hurriedly moved to the right to the support of the Second division, Second corps, and were ordered into a position in rear of a battery at that point. The enemy, however, had just been repulsed, and the regiment was not actively engaged. It remained here during the night, and early July fourth was advanced to the front on the skirmish line, having two men wounded.

The regiment's entire loss was, killed and mortally wounded, 4 officers, 19 men; wounded (not mortally), 1 officer, 43 men; missing and prisoners, 4 officers, 69 men.

A MARKER

to denote the position of the Fourth Maine when in support of the Second corps, afternoon of July 3d, at close of the enemy's assault, stands upon the east side of Hancock avenue in an easterly direction from " High Water Mark " monument. It is cut from Maine granite, adorned with a red granite diamond, and has the following inscription:

4TH MAINE REGIMENT
JULY 3 IN SUPPORT HERE
CAPTAIN EDWIN LIBBY
IN COMMAND.
JULY 2 ENGAGED AT DEVIL'S DEN
COLONEL ELIJAH WALKER
IN COMMAND, WOUNDED.

PARTICIPANTS.

FIELD, STAFF, AND NON-COMMISSIONED STAFF.

Colonel, Elijah Walker, Rockland.
Major, Ebenezer Whitcomb, Searsport.
Adjutant, Charles F. Sawyer, Rockland.
Quartermaster, Isaac C. Abbott, Rockland.
Surgeon, Seth C. Hunkins, Windham.
Assistant Surgeon, Albion Cobb, Otisfield.
Sergeant-Major, William H. Gardner, Belfast.
Hospital Steward, Samuel S. Hersey, Belfast.
Quartermaster-Sergeant, Henry C. Tibbetts, Rockland.
Commissary-Sergeant, Lemuel C. Grant, Frankfort.
Drum-major, Fred J. Low, Winterport.
Fife-major, John F. Singhi, Rockland, leader division band.

COMPANY A.

Second Lieutenant, Andrew J. Gray, Montville.

SERGEANTS.

Marcian W. McManus, Unity,   Thomas H. Gurney, Waldo,
Henry W. Ladd, Searsmont,   Tolford Durham, Waldo.

CORPORALS.

Joseph P. Libby, Unity,   Timothy W. Abbot, Freedom,
Michael Dorsey, Bangor,   Jerry Denning, Bangor,
James Gall, Searsmont,   Horace Speed, Pittsfield.

PRIVATES.

Allenwood, Ephraim F., Belmont,   Bryant, Demetrius J., Montville,
Buker, Alpha, Ellsworth,   Cooley, Melvin, St. Albans,
Colly, James M., Belfast,   Crosby, William, Rockland,
Curtis, Stephen O., Monroe,   Daggett, Stephen, Liberty,
Doten, Charles, Freedom,   Flye, Daniel D., Unity,
Hall, Henry C., Belmont,   Hatch, Sylvanus, Lincoln,
Hatch, Hiram H., Lincoln,   Law, Melvin, Union,
Lincoln, Llewellyn, Searsmont,   Lord, Augustus S., Belfast,
Nichols, Melvin, Bangor,   Ordway, Lewis, Belmont,
Philbrick, Benjamin F., Rockland,   Piper, Albert, Waldo,
Russ, George A., Belfast,   Sidelinger, Manuel, Union,
Sweeney, Dennis, Belfast,   Sylvester, George W., Belfast,
Sylvester, Sanford B., Lincolnville. Walker, Andrew P., Belmont,

ON SPECIAL DUTY OR DETACHED SERVICE: John B. Smith, Burnham, brig. h'dqrs.; E. W. Stinson, Oldtown, div. h'dqrs.; Eben M. Sanborn, Belfast, amb. corps. Musician, William H. Clifford, St. Albans, amb. corps.

COMPANY B.

Captain, J. B. Litchfield, Rockland.
First Lieutenant, Arthur Libby, Rockland.

SERGEANTS.

First Sergeant, Havillah Pease, Rockland,
Henry O. Ripley, Rockland, color bearer, Edgar L. Mowry, Rockland.

CORPORALS.

Otis G. Spear, Rockland,   Thaddeus S. Pillsbury, Rockland,
Henry T. Mitchell, Rockland,   Wyman W. Ulmer, Rockland,
George E. Wall, Rockland,   Charles W. Hopkins, Bangor.

PRIVATES.

Bigdoll, Ellis, Dedham,   Dow, Dana Y., Thomaston,
Gardner, Andrew J., Lincoln,   Goodwin, Albert, Monson,
Grant, Robert, Bangor,   Kallock, John J., Rockland,
Maguire, Edward C., Glenburn,   Norris, Daniel C., Pt. Tobacco,
Philbrook, Levi A., Thomaston,   Spear, Josiah C., Rockland,
Stetson, George F., Rockland,   Simmons, Hanson B., Rockland,
Taylor George F., Rockland,   Titus, John W., Rockland,
Totman, Samuel S., Rockland,   Turner, Charles A., North Haven,
Ulmer, Alonzo N., Rockland,   Willis, Aruna, Rockland,
Wooster, Alden F., Rockland,   Waterman, Edward K., North Haven.

ON SPECIAL DUTY OR DETACHED SERVICE: James W. Clark, Rockland, and Morton A. Blackington, Rockland, brig. h'dqrs. team; Charles E. Gove, Union, and H. J. Dow, Rockland, div. h'dqrs. guard; G. H. Tighe, Rockland, ambulance corps.

COMPANY C.

First Lieutenant, Charles H. Conant, Rockland.
Second Lieutenant, Joseph R. Conant, Rockland.

SERGEANTS.

First Sergeant, Kendall K. Rankin, Rockland,
Charles H. Miller, Rockland,   Rufus O. Fales, Thomaston.

CORPORALS.

Warren W. Austin, Thomaston,   John Colburn, Rockland,
George G. Gardiner, Camden.

PRIVATES.

Brown, James M., Thomaston,   Butler, Ephraim K., Thomaston,
Brown, Orlando F., Rockland,   Cain, James A., Palermo,
Collins, William J., Camden,   Caswell, William, Warren,
Cunningham, Alfred W., Jefferson,   Cunningham, Austin, Warren,
Cain, James A., Palermo,   Knight, Francis E., Jefferson,
Kellar, Thomas, Rockland,   Martin, Patrick, Jefferson,
Perry, Charles C., Rockland,   Pottle, Andrew, Rockland,
Snowdeal, Thomas E., S. Thomaston, Walker, John F., Rockland,
Walter, Benjamin F., Warren,   Wade, Edwin, Rockland.

ON SPECIAL DUTY OR DETACHED SERVICE: Sergeants: John H. Young, Rockland, Ord. Sergt. ammunition train; E. S. Rogers, Rockland, div. prov. guard. Privates: Leonard C. Rankin, Rockland, B. F. Palmer, Thomaston, and A. Shepherd, Jefferson, div. prov. guard; Alden Crockett, Rockland, charge of div. supply train; Horatio G. Collins, Rockland, J. G. Whitney, Rockland, James F. Tuttle, Rockland, G. A. Staples, Rockland, and O. F. Brown, Rockland, in div. supply train; James Bolcomb, Thomaston, brig. wagon-master; Nathaniel C. Matthews, Rockland, and Rufus Robbins, Rockland, brig. train; Jacob Winslow, Rockland, amb. team; Walter Sutherland, Rockland, brig. cook.

COMPANY D.

Captain, Edwin Libby, Rockland.
Lieutenant, George R. Abbott, Thomaston.

SERGEANTS.

First Sergeant, James McLaughlin, Rockland,
William Fountain, Rockland, Samuel L. Meservey, Rockland,

CORPORALS.

John Witham, Washington, Levi G. Perry, Rockland,
William Perkins, Thomaston, Edward Hall, Rockland.

PRIVATES.

Clark, Abial B., Jefferson, Clark, John M., Belmont,
Clark, Joseph E., Northport, Cunningham, Jacob C., Rockland,
Davis, Charles A., Rockland, Eaton, Isaiah V., Deer Isle,
Fields, Anthony, Washington, Gray, John S., Deer Isle,
Hodges, Charles, Gardiner, Joy, Edward H., Washington,
Marshall, Henry P., Ruperts, Martin, Christopher, Hope,
Morrissey, John, Rockland, Peasly, George, Somerville,
Pushor, Eben E., Pittsfield, Richards, Horatio, Rockland,
Shepherd, Almon, Jefferson, Stickney, Alonzo H., Belfast,
Townsend, Appleton, Somerville, Taylor, Simon, Rockland,
Trim, Joseph O., Camden, Watson, Jerome, Union.

ON SPECIAL DUTY OR DETACHED SERVICE: Sergeant, Allen P. Farrington, Rockland, brig. blacksmith. Privates: Mark Perry, Rockland, charge of amb. train; Joseph Thompson, Rockland, Charles P. Burns, Rockland, and Elias Davis, Warren, brig. teamsters; John Miller, Rockland, div. prov. guard; Joseph Dunbar, Deer Isle, amb. corps; John R. Chase, Swanville, butcher.

COMPANY E.

First Lieutenant, Jason Carlisle, Boothbay.
Second Lieutenant, Charles S. McCobb, Boothbay.

SERGEANTS.

First Sergeant, Artemas Robinson, Damariscotta,
Thomas B. Campbell, Thomaston, Zuinglas C. Gowan, Nobleboro.

CORPORALS.

Nathaniel B. Waters, Newcastle, Francis K. Chapman, Nobleboro,
Ira A. Waltz, Damariscotta, Willard T. Barstow, Damariscotta,
William B. Perkins, Newcastle, John P. Blake, Boothbay.

PRIVATES.

Bryer, Albert W., Boothbay, Chapman, Charles K., Newcastle,
Chapman, Everett B., Nobleboro, Corey, John K., Boothbay,
Fountain, Isaac W., Bristol, Giles, Harvey H., Boothbay,
Gove, Oscar C., Newcastle, Hall, Almond, Newcastle,
Hall, Harlow M., Waldoboro, Hatch, Moses W., Newcastle,
Hodgkins, James H., Nobleboro, Kinney, Jesse S., Newcastle,
Lailer, Frank H., Bristol, Mears, Joseph E., Bristol,
Perkins, Thomas R., Newcastle, Skinner, John R., Damariscotta,
Smith, William M., Boothbay, Thompson, John L., Damariscotta,
Turner, Charles C., Bremen. Waters, Isaac T., Newcastle.

ON SPECIAL DUTY OR DETACHED SERVICE: W. M. Hathorn, Thomaston, D. E. Gammage, Damariscotta, and E. G. Snow, Nobleboro, div. prov. guard; John W. Lamour, Baltimore, Md., and Lucius B. Varney, Bristol, amb. corps.

COMPANY F.

Captain, George G. Davis, Brooks.
First Lieutenant, Solomon S. Stearns, Portland.
Second Lieutenant, George M. Bragg, Lincolnville, commanding Co. K.

SERGEANTS.

First Sergeant, Albert H. Rose, Brooks,

Henry Leach, Knox,
Hiram G. York, Dixmont,

Francis O. J. S. Hill, Newburg,
Joseph G. Hilt, Lincolnville.

CORPORALS.

Charles B. Parsons, Newburg,
Rufus G. Bickford, Bangor,
Freeman M. Roberts, Jackson,

Winthrop H. Chick, Dixmont,
William C. Rowe, Monroe,
George R. Hall, Brooks.

PRIVATES.

Barlow, Elisha J., Knox,
Crocker, Albert D., Dixmont,
Forbes, Francis M., Brooks,
Hall, Harrison, Troy,
Hollis, James M., Thorndike,
Nickerson, Daniel C., Swanville,
Patterson, Nathan, Belmont,
Piper, Enoch F., Newburg,
Rowe, Frank, Jr., Brooks,
Stone, John F., Dixmont,
Whitcomb, Thomas O., Knox,

Condon, Albert J., Dixmont,
Evans, Amos, Brooks,
Gardiner, John H., Brooks,
Hines, James H., Unity,
Jackson, Edward W., Washington,
Overlock, Warren, Liberty,
Pierce, Daniel, Jr., Monroe,
Rowell, Charles H., Montville,
Shepherd, John J., Appleton,
Tasker, Ephraim D., Dixmont,
Wood, Charles A., Belfast.

ON SPECIAL DUTY OR DETACHED SERVICE: E. H. Bean, Hampden, orderly div. h'dqrs.; Robert Waterman, Jr., Montville, and Freeman Jones, Washington, hosp. attendants.

COMPANY G.

First Lieutenant, William A. Barker, Rockland.
Second Lieutenant, George L. Crockett, Wiscasset.
Sergeant, James T. McKenney, Wiscasset.

CORPORALS.

John R. Rittal, Dresden,
Crosby R. Brookings, Wiscasset,

Bradford Lowell, Wiscasset,
Nathaniel Stewart, Dresden.

PRIVATES.

Blinn, Bradford H., Wiscasset,
Erskine, Joseph, Wiscasset,
Howard, Daniel O., Alna,
Howard, Leander, Washington,
Light, Elwell, Washington,
Munsey, William, Wiscasset,
Nute, Alexander, Wiscasset,
Piper, James R., Belmont,
Seavey, William, Wiscasset,
Tibbetts, George, Wiscasset,

Call, Timothy, Dresden,
Fredson, Peter, Jr., Wiscasset,
Howard, Elijah, Washington,
Jones, Leonard, Washington,
McCorrison, Thomas J., Knox,
Nelson, Joseph, Washington,
Overlock, Eben, Washington,
Rittal, James F., Dresden,
Stewart, Thomas, Dresden,
Young, Zealor W., Searsmont.

ON SPECIAL DUTY OR DETACHED SERVICE: Onesimus Clark, Alna, regt. hosp.; John Downey, Wiscasset, and John B. Carlton, Woolwich, with trains.

COMPANY H.

Second Lieutenant, Nathaniel A. Robbins, Union.

SERGEANTS.

First Sergeant, Francis P. Ingalls, Bluehill,
Joseph B. Babson, Brooklin,   George P. Wood, Penobscot.

CORPORALS.

Daniel W. Barker, Levant,   John H. Thomas, Warren,
Horace C. Clough, Rockland,   Jared R. Reed, Mt. Desert,
William H. Tripp, Sedgwick.

PRIVATES.

Allen, Charles W., Sedgwick,   Ames, George L., Camden,
Brackett, Charles W., Belfast,   Blackington, Alfred, Thomaston,
Carter, Edwin J., Sedgwick,   Cox, George, Bangor,
Crowley, Patrick, Rockland,   Downes, Samuel N., Winterport,
Farnham, Joseph E., Knox,   Furbish, Abram J., Rockland,
Gilmore, William D., Hope,   Grindle, Elijah H., Penobscot,
Higgins, Simon, Tremont,   Jackson, Joel, Montville,
Jones, Silas S., Lincolnville,   Keefe, John, Thomaston,
McMahan, Daniel, Prospect,   Moore, Charles F. Knox,
Mink, Edwin, Waldoboro,   Noonan, James, Searsport,
Page, Amos, Kenduskeag,   Rose, Charles, Bangor,
Saunders, Thomas C., Rockland,   Sherman, Frank A., Knox,
Simmons, William H., Union,   Stahl, Isaac, Rockland,
Wallace, Alexander M., Waldoboro,   Whitney, Adolphus M., Bangor,
Young, Harrison, Searsmont,   Young, Morrison, Searsmont.

ON SPECIAL DUTY OR DETACHED SERVICE: James W. Page, Sedgwick, col.'s regtl. orderly; Stillman Mink, Waldoboro, brig. teamster.

COMPANY I.

Captain, Robert H. Gray, Stockton.
Second Lieutenant, Orpheus Roberts, Stockton.

SERGEANTS.

First Sergeant, Christopher C. Gray, Stockton,
Ivory W. Baird, Camden,   Daniel Carley, Prospect,
Abiather S. Merrithew, Green Isle.

CORPORALS.

Clarendon W. Gray, Stockton,   Elias B. Moore, Frankfort,
Moses H. Witham, Plymouth.

PRIVATES.

Burgin, Augustus, Belfast,   Burgin, Chesbrook, Belfast,
Calderwood, Henry D., Camden,   Chase, Nathan, Searsport,
Donahue, John, Bangor,   Doyle, Thomas, Searsport,
Fillmore, Richard T., Swanville,   Forbes, Frank, Vassalboro,
Fowler, John C., Searsport,   Jellerson, Lemuel B., Frankfort,
Kent, Edward E., Brewer,   Millano, Juan, Plymouth,
Parker, Charles P., St. Albans,   Pendleton, Lewis E., Frankfort,
Phinney, Charles A., Winterport,   Rich, Wesley, Jackson,
Sidelinger, Oliver P., Troy,   Sidelinger, Rufus P., Troy,
Small, Samuel D., Swanville,   Snow, Benjamin F., Orrington,
Staples, Alvah, Prospect,   Towers, William S., Searsport,
Whittam, Clifton, Searsport.

ON SPECIAL DUTY OR DETACHED SERVICE: Benjamin Nickerson, Eden, with Randolph's battery; Robert G. Ames, Searsport, brig. wagon-master; William H. Irving, Vassalboro, brig. h'dqrs.; Oscar F. Colson, Stockton, brig. hosp. cook; Prentice Colson, Frankfort, and Otis Colson, Winterport, brig. hosp.

COMPANY K.

[Lieutenant George M. Bragg, of Company F, in command.]

SERGEANTS.

First Sergeant, Amos B. Wooster, Belfast,

David H. Kimball, Belfast,   John A. Toothaker, Belfast.

CORPORALS.

Sears Nickerson, Belfast,   Silas M. Perkins, Belfast,
Elisha Hanning, Belfast,   James E. Doak, Belfast,
Dennis Moody, Monroe,   Henry A. Davis, Belfast.

PRIVATES.

Baker, Edward, Belfast,   Carter, Preston J., Belfast,
Collins, Charles C., Belfast,   Deane, James E., Belfast,
Gordon, Ephraim A., Frankfort,   Hawkins, Aurelius, Waldo,
Herrin, Andrew, Augusta,   Hilton, Alvin, Appleton,
Johnson, George F., Windham,   Merrick, Isaiah B., Newport,
Rariden, Michael, Belfast,   Ray, Jacob D., Knox,
Robinson, John A., Belfast,   Rogers, Frederick H., Bangor,
Sawyer, John K., Belfast,   Shuman, John F., Belfast,
Ware, Horace L., Northport,   Whitehead, Robert, Belfast,
Woodbury, William H., Frankfort.

MUSICIANS, Frederick J. Low, Frankfort, Eleazer J. Young, Lincolnville.

ON SPECIAL DUTY OR DETACHED SERVICE: John A. Rines, Belfast, brig. teamster; A. A. Dailey, Searsmont, and B. F. Young, Lincolnville, amb. corps; E. B. Richards, Lincolnville, and Samuel Jackson, Rockland, brig. guard; George L. Feyler, Thomaston, regt. hostler.

REVISED REPORT OF CASUALTIES.

FIELD, STAFF AND NON-COMMISSIONED STAFF.

Colonel Elijah Walker, wounded, *tendo Achilles.*
Major Ebenezer Whitcomb, wounded, died Oct. 5th.
Sergeant-Major William H. Gardner, prisoner.

COMPANY A.

SERGEANTS.

Marcian W. McManus, prisoner.   Thomas H. Gurney, prisoner.
Henry W. Ladd, leg wounded.   Tolford Durham, prisoner.

CORPORALS.

Jerry Denning, wounded, hip.   James Gall, wounded, foot, the 4th.

PRIVATES.

Allenwood, Ephraim F., w'd, side.   Cooley, Melvin, prisoner.
Crosby, William, prisoner.   Curtis, Stephen O., prisoner.
Flye, Daniel D., prisoner.   Hall, Henry C., prisoner.
Hatch, Hiram H., prisoner, died.   Hatch, Sylvanus, prisoner, died.
Law, Melville, prisoner.   Sweeney, Dennis, w'd, hand, the 4th.
Sylvester, George W., pris'r, died.   Sylvester, Sanford B., prisoner.
Walker, Andrew P., wounded, slight.

COMPANY B.

Captain J. B. Litchfield, prisoner.

CORPORALS.

Wyman W. Ulmer, wounded, shoulder and breast.
Henry T. Mitchell, wounded, prisoner; died in Richmond Dec. 17, 1863.

PRIVATES.

Stetson, George F., w'd, shoulder and breast.
Ulmer, Alonzo N., wounded, face.
Simmons, Hanson B., wounded, face.
Turner, Charles A., wounded, hand.

COMPANY C.

Sergeant Rufus O. Fales, prisoner, died in Richmond, Nov. 12, 1863.

CORPORALS.

John Colburn, wounded, eye.
George G. Gardiner, killed.

PRIVATES.

Brown, James M., prisoner.
Caswell, William, prisoner, died.
Cunningham, Austin, prisoner.
Martin, Patrick, wounded, shoulder.
Snowdeal, Thomas E., prisoner.
Butler, E. K., prisoner.
Collins, William, Jr., prisoner, died.
Kellar, Thomas, prisoner, died.
Pottle, Andrew, prisoner.

Musician Alfred W. Cunningham, prisoner.

COMPANY D.

Corporal John Witham, killed.

PRIVATES.

Clark, John M., wounded, leg.
Dunbar, Joseph, amb. corps,w'd, arm.
Fields, Anthony, prisoner.
Hodges, Charles, prisoner.
Peasly, George, prisoner, died in Ga.
Shepherd, Almon, wounded, breast.
Townsend, Appleton,wounded, pris'r.
Trim, Joseph O., wounded leg.
Davis, Charles A., wounded.
Eaton, Isaiah V., w'd, died in July.
Gray, John S., wounded, died July 28.
Martin, Christopher, wounded, hand.
Richards, Horatio, pris'r, died in Ga.
Stickney, Alonzo H., killed.
Taylor, Simon, prisoner.
Watson, Jerome, wounded, face.

COMPANY E.

Second Lieutenant Charles S. McCobb, killed.
Sergeant Zuinglas C. Gowan, prisoner.

CORPORALS.

Ira A. Waltz, prisoner.
William B. Perkins, wounded, leg.
Willard T. Barstow,w'd, died Aug. 28.
John P. Blake, wounded, hand.

PRIVATES.

Hatch, Moses W., wounded, arm.
Turner, Charles C., prisoner.

COMPANY F.

Captain George G. Davis, prisoner, escaped old Libby prison.
First Lieutenant Solomon S. Stearns, prisoner.
Second Lieutenant George M. Bragg, commanding Co. K, w'd, died July 5.
Sergeant Henry Leach, prisoner.
Corporal William C. Rowe, wounded, side.

PRIVATES.

Bickford, Rufus G., prisoner.
Gardiner, John H., prisoner.
Hall, Harrison, wounded.
Forbes, Francis M., prisoner.
Hall, George R., killed.
Hollis, James M., prisoner; died
Nov. 27, 1863, at Richmond, Va.

Nickerson, Daniel C., prisoner.
Patterson, Nathan, prisoner.
Shepherd, John J., prisoner.
Tasker, Ephraim D., prisoner.

Overlock, Warren, wounded.
Rowe, Frank, Jr., prisoner.
Stone, John F., wounded, arm.
Whitcomb, Thomas O., prisoner.

COMPANY G.
CORPORALS.

John R. Rittal, killed.
Crosby R. Brookings, w'd, died Aug. 10.

Bradford Lowell, prisoner.

PRIVATES.

Blinn, Bradford H., prisoner.

Erskine, Joseph, prisoner,
    died, Richmond, November 22.
Fredson, Peter, Jr., wounded, head. Howard, Daniel O., wounded, leg.
Howard, Leander, prisoner.
Munsey, William, prisoner.
Piper, James R., prisoner.
Seavey, William, wounded, head.

McCorrison, Thomas J., wounded.
Overlock, Eben, prisoner.
Rittal, James F., prisoner.
    died, Richmond, November 12.

COMPANY H.
Lieutenant Nathaniel A. Robbins, prisoner.
First Sergeant Francis P. Ingalls, killed.
Corporal Daniel W. Barker, wounded, leg.

PRIVATES.
Brackett, Charles W., wounded, arm. Carter, Edwin J., wounded, shoulder.
Emerton, Andrew L., captured at Gilmore, William D., prisoner,
    Emmitsburg.
Higgins, Simon, wounded, back.
Rose, Charles, wounded and prisoner. Simmons, William H., prisoner.
Steele, George W., capt'd at Emmits- Young, Harrison, pris'r, died at Rich-
    burg; escaped.
    mond.

COMPANY I.
Second Lieutenant Orpheus Roberts, killed.

SERGEANTS.
Ivory W. Baird, prisoner.

Daniel Carley, wounded, hand.

PRIVATES.
Burgin, Augustus, wounded.
Chase, Nathan, wounded, died July 21.
Doyle, Thomas, wounded, died July 5.
Phinney, Charles A., prisoner.
Small, Samuel D., prisoner.
Whittam, Clifton, prisoner.

Calderwood, Henry D., prisoner.
Donahue, John, prisoner.
Parker, Charles P., prisoner.
Rich, Wesley, prisoner.
Towers, William S., wounded.

COMPANY K.
First Sergeant Amos B. Wooster, wounded in face, slight.
Sergeant John A. Toothaker, wounded, died July 20.

PRIVATES.
Collins, Charles C., prisoner.
Hawkins, Aurelius, wounded, arm.
Hilton, Alvin, wounded, died July 9.
Merrick, Isaiah B., w'd, neck, pris'r.
Ray, Jacob D., wounded, hand.
Sawyer, John K., killed.
Ware, Horace L., missing.
Woodbury, William H., missing.

Gordon, Ephraim A., w'd, ankle.
Herrin, Andrew, prisoner.
Johnson, George F., w'd, died July 9.
Rariden, Michael, w'd, died July 24.
Rogers, Frederick H., killed.
Shuman, John F., w'd, died July 15.
Whitehead, Robert, wounded, foot.

Note on the foregoing report of casualties.

This nominal list shows a total loss in the battle of 140, men and officers. Of these 23 were killed or died of their wounds; 44 simply wounded; 73 prisoners, of whom 4 were also wounded. Of the prisoners, many died in southern prisons. The monument inscription of "22 killed and died" did not include Isaiah V. Eaton, who died of his wounds, and lies in the National Cemetery. The disparity in the wounded is explained in the address of Colonel Walker. The inscription of 56 missing was an error, the number being, according to the nominal list, too small by 17; an application has been made to the Gettysburg Park Commissioners to have the inscription of "56 missing" rectified, if it can be done without marring the monument.

REGIMENTAL DEDICATION OF MONUMENT,

OCTOBER 10, 1888.

ADDRESS OF COLONEL ELIJAH WALKER.

Comrades, Ladies and Gentlemen: —

I am not here to deliver an oration of such rhetorical finish as that which characterizes the efforts of my learned comrades at the exercises around the Seventeenth Maine regiment's monument to-day on the Wheatfield, but as the representative of the Fourth Maine, to accept this granite shaft and turn it over to the protecting care of the Battlefield Memorial Association, pending a formal and more befitting dedication. You will pardon me if, as one speaking from personal knowledge and experience, I take this opportunity to briefly review the Fourth Maine regiment's history, and tell of a few of the movements in which the command participated in the course of its long term of service in the field.

In the latter part of April, 1861, four companies were enlisted and organized in Rockland, two in Belfast, one in Brooks, one in Searsport, one in Wiscasset and one in Damariscotta. May 8th the officers of these companies met in Rockland,

in obedience to orders, and elected Hiram G. Berry as their colonel. The regiment went into camp in Rockland May 17th, was mustered into the United States service June 15th, left the state on the 17th, arrived in Washington the 21st, crossed the Potomac to Alexandria July 8th, and encamped at Bush Hill.

On the 12th a reconnaissance was made by companies B and C, and three Confederate soldiers were captured with loaded muskets in their hands. On the 16th we marched in pursuit of the rebels. On the 21st we came upon and engaged them at Bull Run, where our army was defeated, with a loss to our regiment of 23 men killed, 3 officers and 24 men wounded, and 3 officers and 38 men missing. Few are the regiments that suffered more by fatalities than this, on that hard-fought field. We returned to Alexandria and the camp we left, on the 16th. From that time until March 17th, 1862, the regiment was employed in drill, picket duty, felling trees and building fortifications. We also made several reconnaissances, and were the first to report the retreat of the enemy from Manassas. On the 18th we were on board a steamboat en route for Fortress Monroe, whence we went to Hampton, Va.

March 25th Colonel Berry, who had been promoted and assigned to the command of a brigade, took leave of the regiment, and I assumed command. April 4th we left Hampton, and arrived near Yorktown the next day. Here we remained until May 4th, when we followed the retreating enemy to Williamsburg, where we found them, strongly fortified, on the 5th, Here we escaped without loss of men, although we were the first to occupy Fort Magruder on the morning of the 6th. The enemy were defeated and were followed to Fair Oaks, where the left of our army was attacked on the 31st. Here, for two days, our (Kearny's) division had severe fighting. June 15th, 22d, and 25th the regiment had skirmishing on the picket line. On the 27th, a retreat having been ordered by the army commander, our regiment was assigned to prepare two roads across White Oak Swamp, and we were the last infantry troops to cross the swamp on the morning of the 30th. We held the advanced position in the battle of Glendale during that day, and when the retreat began at night were the last to leave the field.

At Malvern Hill, July 1st, with our food supply exhausted, we held the front line of our division, and were the last infantry to leave that famous battlefield. At Harrison's Landing we were obliged to endure miasma and bog water until Aug. 15th, when we marched to Yorktown, took a steamer for Alexandria, going thence by rail to Warrenton Junction, where we arrived on the 21st. We were sent five miles in advance, to Rappahannock Station, where on the 27th we were left, without rations, to serve as a "blind" and be captured by the enemy, if need be; but we succeeded in extricating ourselves, by hard marching, with the loss of a few who became exhausted and fell into the hands of the rebels. These unfortunates were stripped of their outer garments, paroled and permitted to rejoin us. On the morning of the 29th we arrived on the Bull Run battlefield, where we had severe fighting nearly all day, losing 10 men killed, 2 officers, the sergeant-major, and 33 men wounded, and 8 missing. I escaped without injury, but thereafter my horse carried Confederate lead in his flesh. On the 30th our division was on the reserve, but late in the day we had a lively time, and the Fourth Maine and 40th N. Y., were the last to leave the field.

September 1st, at Chantilly, we were sent by General Kearny to open an attack on the enemy, and had desperate fighting, losing 12 men killed and 2 officers and 52 men wounded. My horse was shot and killed. We then fell back to Alexandria, moving thence up the Potomac to Point of Rocks, Md. October 12th we had a skirmish with Stuart's cavalry near the mouth of the Monocacy. The Third and Fourth Maine were under my command, and we were successful in turning the cavalry into a road leading to an ambush at the ford; our troops, however, that were to spring the trap, hastily left on the approach of the horsemen, who crossed the Potomac in safety. On the 28th we left the upper Potomac and marched to Falmouth, arriving on the 20th of November. The first duty assigned us here was to load 300 wagons with logs. We then moved twelve miles down the river and built a corduroy bridge across a swamp. This work accomplished, we joined our division, by a forced march, and crossed below Fredericksburg, where, on December 13th, I led 211 men and officers in a charge upon the enemy's fortified position, having 3 officers and 19 men killed, and 7 officers and 59 men wounded ; 36 men were reported missing, of whom 8 have never been heard from. Our army retreated on the morning of the 16th, when I withdrew and followed the last pickets across the river.

At Chancellorsville, May 2d and 3d, we had our share of the fighting, taking the lead in the moonlight charge and being the last to cross the pontoon bridge on the retreat. Here we lost 1 officer and 2 men killed, 3 officers and 15 men wounded, and 7 men missing. Things remained quiet until June 11th, when we marched from camp to Bealeton Station, thence successively, to Catlett's Station, Manassas Junction and Blackburn's Ford, and on the 17th arrived at Centreville. On the 19th our Third corps bivouacked at Gum Springs, where we remained until the 25th, when we again moved and bivouacked at the mouth of the Monocacy. On the 26th we marched to Point of Rocks, Md. ; on the 27th to Middletown ; on the 29th to Taneytown, and on the 30th to near Emmitsburg, occupying the village the next morning, July 1st, at 11 o'clock. At 1 P. M. our corps commander, General Sickles, led the larger part of his command to Gettysburg, arriving at 7 o'clock that evening. We heard there had been a severe engagement in which our troops encountered a force much superior in point of numbers, and were driven back past Seminary Ridge, through the village of Gettysburg, and having made a stand on Cemetery Hill, were there re-forming their lines. This was unwelcome news to us who had been so often defeated, but every soldier knew we were on the free soil of a free people, and all were determined to defend it or die in the attempt.

The sun disappeared, and presently the stars became dimly visible through a vaporous and smoky atmosphere. The soldiers were seeking rest for their wearied limbs, and the officers were engaged in readjusting the lines and forming new ones, and in seeing that their men were supplied with ammunition. With my regiment of about 300 men and 18 officers I made a bed of that soil destined to become the Union veterans' Mecca, and to be immortalized in song and story ; and we were trying to get a little sleep in preparation for the morrow when I heard a familiar voice inquiring for Colonel Walker, and I answered, " I am here, captain. Is it our turn to establish a picket line ? " " Yes, it is the order of General Sickles that your regiment establish a picket line, the right to connect with the First corps pickets and the left with those of the Second corps."

I reluctantly obeyed, moved to the front about half a mile and established a line by a rail fence, some 30 or 40 rods west of the Emmitsburg road, making connection with the First corps pickets, as directed, but I failed to find any troops on my left, except a few cavalry scouts. The enemy's pickets, at this time, occupied the woods directly in our front, 30 and 50 rods from our line, in which woods the enemy were assembling throughout the night. All was quiet until daybreak, when they opened fire upon us and several times advanced into the opening, but were as often glad to regain the shelter of the woods. Early that morning I reported a large force in the woods in front of me, but the report was disregarded by my superiors, and I was twice ordered to advance and drive the enemy's pickets out of the woods. These orders I did not attempt to execute. At 9 o'clock Colonel Berdan reported to me with 250 of his Sharpshooters with orders to join me in dislodging the rebels. I soon convinced Colonel Berdan that it would be foolhardy to make the attempt, and he agreed with me that an attack on the rebels' flank was the only practicable move that could be made, if our superiors could not be otherwise convinced of the strength of the concealed Confederates. He left, saying he would report the result of his observations, and at about 9.30 the Third Maine and the Sharpshooters did attack the rebels' flank, as I had suggested, by which movement the correctness of my conclusions was soon demonstrated. From that time until 2.30 P. M. it was quiet in our front, but there was some sharp fighting on our left, and we were then relieved by the 1st Mass. We at once joined our brigade, which we found packing up to move, advanced with it to the front and were assigned a position on the high ground to the left of the corps and, at that time, the left of the army, connecting with the 124th N. Y. At my front and centre was the 4th N. Y. battery, Captain Smith.

It was now 3 o'clock and my men were hungry, having drank water for supper, breakfast and dinner. Fires were kindled, a heifer was found near by and slaughtered, coffee was steeped and beef impaled on sticks was warmed over the blaze. We drank our coffee and ate the very rare and thoroughly smoked meat, sprinkling it with salt, of which condiment every soldier carried a little in his pocket.

At 3.45 the enemy came out of the woods half a mile from us and opened fire with their artillery, Smith's battery responding. Their infantry appeared in large numbers. They first met the 2d U. S. Sharpshooters, commanded by Lieut.-Col. Stoughton, who checked the advance, but fell back as the strong rebel force came on. I was ordered to the left, leaving Smith's guns without support and creating a space of about two hundred yards without infantry. To this move I objected, but was assured by the adjutant-general of the brigade, who brought the order, that other troops would take my place to protect the battery. I unwillingly moved to the low ground, — the valley now memorable in history, — sending a few skirmishers, commanded by Capt. Arthur Libby, into the woods between the two mountains, and also a strong line of skirmishers to my front. I soon withdrew the men from the woods, as troops were coming down Little Round Top in the rear of Libby's line. The line in front had a severe time with the advance of the enemy, but was not dislodged.

The troops of the Fifth corps had occupied Little Round Top and were advancing down its southern slope, being 40 or 50 rods to my rear and left, when they met the enemy. Musketry fire commenced with severity. At this time I had not been engaged, except with my skirmish line in the valley, but in a moment the 44th Ala. regiment appeared at the edge of a wood of small pines on our left flank. The colonel of that regiment says that while he was getting his men into position, and before they fired a shot, one-fourth of them had been killed or disabled; but when he did open fire upon us we soon found, to our sorrow, that we had no mean foe to contend with. They soon gave up and retired into the woods, where they were completely concealed.

Smith, on the high ground, abandoned his guns, and the rebels came over on my right flank and in rear of my skirmish line, many of the latter surrendering. I moved back about 100 yards, fixed bayonets, and charged forward by the right oblique, driving the enemy from Smith's guns and connecting with the 124th N. Y. We had a sharp encounter on our left, at the brow of the hill, a little to the right of Devil's Den. It was at close quarters. I was on foot and wounded, my horse having been killed. My sword was wrenched from my hand, but my men saved me and I recovered the sword. At this critical moment the 99th Penn. came to our assistance, forming on our left along the brow of the hill, and the enemy fell back, taking cover behind the rocks and bowlders and in Devil's Den. The 6th N. J. regiment soon arrived, taking position to the left of the 99th Penn. and the 40th N. Y., extending the line further to the left, swinging their right and advancing into the low ground. The low, wet ground, which we had been obliged to abandon, was occupied by large numbers of the advancing enemy, but that valley, which we had christened, had received its name for all time, — the "Valley of Death."

We held our position until about sunset, when our brigade fell back and the troops from the Second and Fifth corps had a line in our rear. When I gave the order to fall back I was unable to walk, but was saved from prison, and possibly from death, by Sergeant Mowry of company B and Corporal Roberts of company F, who wrested me from the foe and assisted me to the rear. Our flag was pierced by thirty-two bullets and two pieces of shell, and its staff was shot off, but Sergt. Henry O· Ripley, its bearer, did not allow the color to touch the ground, nor did he receive a scratch, though all the others of the color-guard were killed or wounded.

I turned the regiment over to Capt. Edwin Libby, a tried, brave and faithful officer, and took my first ride in an ambulance. July 3d the regiment was with the brigade, in reserve, and with the Third Maine, 99th Penn. and 20th Ind., under Colonel Lakeman, moved to support the Second corps when the enemy was assaulting it. On the 4th it was on picket.

The Fourth Maine was with the troops that followed the

defeated enemy into Virginia, our division meeting and engaging the rebels at Wapping Heights on the 23d.   I was absent, but I rejoined the regiment in time to be with it in the manœuvres from Culpeper to Centreville, in October.

At Kelly's Ford, November 7th, I commanded the second attacking brigade, composed of 99th Penn., 86th and 124th N. Y., Third, Fourth, and Seventeenth Maine.   I had the Fourth Maine in support of Randolph's Rhode Island battery, but it escaped without casualties.   At Orange Grove, November 27th, seeing the supports leaving Randolph's battery, I took my regiment to his assistance, dragged his guns out of the mud, placed them on high ground, and the enemy were repulsed with great slaughter.   At Mine Run, November 29th and 30th, the Fourth Maine and 20th Ind. had special orders to charge the rebel batteries, at a signal gun announcing General Warren's attack on the left; had the signal gun been fired we would have been given over to destruction, but Warren refrained from assaulting.

During the winter of 1864 I was recommended by my superior officers and a long list of Maine officials, including the governor, for promotion; having, in an unguarded moment, expressed my favoritism for George B. McClellan, our representative, who had been intrusted with my cause, failed to present the recommendations.

May 5th we were the first of the Second (Hancock's) corps to meet and attack the enemy, losing 1 officer killed and 3 mortally wounded; 4 other officers were wounded, 1 of whom being disabled; 17 men were killed, 104 wounded and 2 missing. Myself and horse were wounded, but I remained on duty.

May 6th I was in command of the brigade.   We had severe fighting all day, the Fourth Maine losing 1 officer killed, and myself and another slightly wounded but not disabled; also 4 men killed, 26 men wounded and 6 missing.   On the 7th, 4 men were wounded and 1 missing, probably killed, as he was never heard from.

Small engagements often afforded as critical situations as great battles.   One such occasion befell me on May 10th, when I was ordered to cross the Po River and, using the Fourth and

part of the Seventeenth Maine and the picket men, to force
the enemy's outposts and learn what force he had.   The stream
was some 10 or 12 feet broad, bordered with swamps, and
varied in depth up to six feet.   With Captain Briscoe, of General Birney's staff, I crossed and reconnoitered; decided to
advance the Seventeenth and pickets on the road nearest the
river, while I led the Fourth by another road farther out, running nearly parallel.   The enemy's mounted videttes retired as
we approached them.   During our advance of about two miles
we wounded and took two of them with their horses.   While
scouting in advance of my men, I suddenly came within 150
yards of a gray-appareled line of battle which a scrub growth
had concealed from view.   We then retraced our steps to the
road on which Briscoe had advanced and was now skirmishing
with the "graybacks," as I wanted to recall him and cross the
stream, for I knew they would be after us in large numbers.
But an order came from division headquarters to go in and
assist Briscoe's force to drive back the enemy's pickets.   I pro-
tested but could not disobey the order.   Sending my color-
guard and prisoners across the river, and leaving Lieut. Henry
O. Ripley with a squad of men to guard the road, I attempted
to carry out my instructions.   Captain Briscoe was then a mile
away.   Advancing about half a mile I received an order to
rejoin the division on the other side of the river.   Sending out
Capt. Arthur Libby with a few men to learn whether our road
was open, he found that the "woods were full of them," and
commanding the road.   This was one of the situations that tests
a man's nerves.   I formed my men under the brow of a hill,
where they bravely held the enemy in check while I got word
to Briscoe to retreat across the river.   We then dashed through
the swamp and into the water, which with the mud was up to
our armpits; this was our only chance, as the enemy had gained
the river on our right and left.   My horse followed the men,
and both he and his rider were safely landed on the other side
with the assistance of two gallant boys.

Here my beloved and reliable Lieutenant Ripley was brought
in a blanket, fatally wounded.   On the enemy's approach to
the point where he had been stationed, he had rallied his men

to check their advance, and the next instant a bullet had passed through his neck. His men retreated and crossed on the road. In this spirited affair two enlisted men of the regiment were also wounded, — one mortally, — and four were missing. Ripley was the sixth officer of the regiment killed or mortally wounded since this short campaign began, the others being Captains Amos B. Wooster and Edwin Libby, killed ; Major Robert H. Gray and Lieutenants C. C. Gray and J. R. Conant, mortally wounded ; four others besides myself had been wounded, but only one disabled from duty.

On the 12th, at Spotsylvania, we were exempt from casualties. On the 15th one man was wounded. On the 23d, at North Anna, in a successful charge upon the enemy's works, which, on the north side of the river, defended a bridge, we had 5 men killed and 19 wounded. I was again hit by a rebel bullet, adjutant Sawyer was also wounded,—both continued on duty. On the 24th one man was killed, private Juan Millano, the last on our long "roll of honor." June 2d, at Cold Harbor, two men were wounded. June 14th we crossed the James River, and on the 15th I turned over to the Nineteenth Maine the 217 re-enlisted men and later recruits, and with the balance of my command, including 4 staff and 9 line officers and 113 men, proceeded to Maine, where we were mustered out of the service July 19, 1864.

When General Berry was called to a more exalted position, he recommended me for the colonelcy of the regiment he so dearly loved. I accepted the honor reluctantly, conscious of my inability to adequately fill his place ; but I am satisfied that while under my command the name and fame of the regiment were bravely upheld, and that fresh laurels were added to those it had already won.

[I desire to say here, that the 99th Pennsylvania monument stands on ground from which that regiment did not fire a shot July 2, 1863. Their right was where their left marker is now placed, and extended along the brow of the hill. The Fourth Maine are entitled to the ground from the 124th N. Y. to the base of Little Round Top, except that occupied for a time by Smith's 4th N. Y. battery.]

The number of wounded recorded on our regimental shaft includes only such as were seriously disabled.

In conclusion, I desire to say that, as a Commissioner appointed by the governor, I accept this monument (which is of my own design) from the granite and lime district of Maine in which the regiment whose heroism it commemorates was raised, and to you, Major Krauth, representative of the Battlefield Memorial Association, I entrust it, with the fervent hope that when the stone shall have yielded to the disintegrating hand of time, our flag will still be floating over an undivided country and a free people.

HISTORICAL SKETCH.

The Fourth Maine regiment of infantry was composed of volunteers mainly from Knox, Lincoln and Waldo counties. It was raised and organized under an act of the legislature of Maine approved April 25, 1861, authorizing the raising of ten regiments in anticipation of requirements that were soon to be made by the general government to aid in suppressing the rebellion.

The original organization when mustered into U. S. service was as follows :

FIELD, STAFF AND NON-COMMISSIONED STAFF.

Colonel, Hiram G. Berry, Rockland.
Lieutenant-Colonel, Thomas H. Marshall, Belfast.
Major, Frank S. Nickerson, Belfast.
Adjutant, Jabez B. Greenhalgh, Rockland.
Quartermaster, Isaac C. Abbott, Rockland.
Surgeon, William A. Banks.
Assistant Surgeon, Elisha Hopkins.
Chaplain, Benjamin A. Chase, Unity.

Sergeant-Major, S. H. Chapman.
Quartermaster-Sergeant, John H. Crowell, Winterport.
Commissary-Sergeant, Julius S. Clark.
Hospital Steward, Charles S. McCobb, Boothbay.
Principal Musician, Isaac Prince, Belfast.
Fife-major, Henry E. Burkmar, Belfast.

COMPANY OFFICERS.

Co. A.   Captain, Henry W. Cunningham, Belfast.
          First Lieutenant, Richard S. Ayer, Montville.
          Second Lieutenant, Isaac C. Abbott, Rockland.

Co. B. Captain, Elijah Walker, Rockland.
      First Lieutenant, Orrin P. Mitchell, Rockland.
      Second Lieutenant, Julius B. Litchfield, Rockland.
Co. C. Captain, Oliver J. Conant, Rockland.
      First Lieutenant, Charles A. Rollins, Thomaston.
      Second Lieutenant, Charles B. Greenhalgh, Rockland.
Co. D. Captain, Lorenzo D. Carver, Rockland.
      First Lieutenant, Thomas B. Glover, Rockland.
      Second Lieutenant, Charles L. Strickland, Rockland.
Co. E. Captain, Stephen C. Whitehouse, Newcastle.
      First Lieutenant, James O. Dow, Newcastle.
      Second Lieutenant, Frederick E. Hussey, Newcastle.
Co. F. Captain, Andrew D. Bean, Brooks.
      First Lieutenant, James S. Huxford, Brooks.
      Second Lieutenant, Charles H. Burd, Belfast.
Co. G. Captain, Edwin M. Smith, Wiscasset.
      First Lieutenant, William H. Clark, Wiscasset.
      Second Lieutenant, Gustavus Rundlett, Wiscasset.
Co. H. Captain, G. J. Burns, Rockland.
      First Lieutenant, John C. Cobb, Rockland.
      Second Lieutenant, B. P. Brackley, Rockland.
Co. I. Captain, Ebenezer Whitcomb, Searsport.
      First Lieutenant, William E. Burgin, Searsport.
      Second Lieutenant, James N. Fowler, Searsport.
Co. K. Captain, Silas M. Fuller, Belfast.
      First Lieutenant, Alden D. Chase, Belfast.
      Second Lieutenant, Horatio H. Carter, Belfast.

The organization, after the first battle of Bull Run, began to change by resignation. The vacancies in the company officers were filled by promoting non-commissioned officers and privates, so that by January 1, 1862, the regiment got firmly upon a war basis. Captain Elijah Walker had become Major, and before the spring campaign of 1862 opened, was promoted to the colonelcy. The original company H was disbanded September 21, 1861. The officers left the service; but the enlisted men were not discharged, they remained in service, and faithfully performed their duties to the end. To take the place of this a new company H was recruited at Bangor and Belfast, and in November, 1861, organized with William L. Pitcher for Captain, and Albert L. Spencer and George F. Bourne, as Lieutenants, all from Bangor.

The active service in the field performed by the Fourth Maine is so fully outlined in the dedication address of Colonel Walker, which appears on the preceding pages, that a recounting of the same is omitted here.

ROSTER.

The following information relating to officers of the Fourth Maine regiment is obtained from the Volunteer Army Register (part 1), published by the War Department, August 31, 1865, and other reliable sources.

OFFICERS AT MUSTER-OUT, JULY 19, 1864.

COLONEL: Elijah Walker, March 17, 1862.

LIEUTENANT-COLONEL: George G. Davis, May 10, 1864.

CAPTAINS: Julius B. Litchfield, August 1, 1862, prisoner of war, discharged March 3, 1865; Ezra B. Carr, April 2, 1863; William A. Barker, September 1, 1863; Arthur Libby, December 9, 1863; Jason Carlisle, December 23, 1863; Charles H. Conant, December 31, 1863; George R. Abbott, January 13, 1864,—while Lieutenant of company D served as Quartermaster from July 22, 1863, to January 13, 1864; after muster-out with Fourth Maine he served as Captain in 1st Maine S. S. and as Major Twentieth Maine regiment; brevet Colonel.

FIRST LIEUTENANTS: Charles F. Sawyer, Adjutant, February 26, 1862, afterwards Captain Twentieth Maine, brevet Major; Solomon S. Stearns, May 12, 1862; Edward D. Redman, October 9, 1863; Elisha S. Rogers, October 16, 1863; George L. Crockett, December 8, 1863; Artemas Robinson, January 1, 1864; Kendall K. Rankin, January 13, 1864, — served as Quartermaster until muster-out.

SECOND LIEUTENANTS: Nathaniel A. Robbins, March 12, 1863, promoted to Quartermaster, not mustered, prisoner of war, discharged March 15, 1865; Marcian W. McManus, July 23, 1863.

SURGEON: Seth C. Hunkins, June 14, 1861. ASSISTANT SURGEON: Albion Cobb (*a. w. m.*).

CHAPLAIN: Benjamin A. Chase, June 15, 1861.

(Dates given above refer to rank or commissions, those given hereafter refer to date of the event.)

DIED.

MAJORS: William L. Pitcher, killed in action at Fredericksburg, Va., December 13, 1862; Ebenezer Whitcomb, October 5, 1863, of wounds received at Gettysburg; Robert H. Gray, May 9, 1864, of wounds received in battle of the Wilderness.

CAPTAINS: Daniel H. Adams, April 29, 1863, of disease; Andrew J. Gray, August 22, 1863, of disease; Edwin Libby, killed at battle of the Wilderness, May 5, 1864; Amos B. Wooster, killed at battle of the Wilderness, May 6, 1864.

FIRST LIEUTENANTS: George F. Bourne, killed at battle of Fredericksburg, Va., December 13, 1862; Joseph R. Conant, May 8, 1864, of wounds received May 5; Christopher C. Gray, May 29, 1864, of wounds received May 5, Wilderness; Henry O. Ripley, June 13, 1864, of wounds received in action of Po river.

SECOND LIEUTENANTS: Walter S. Goodale, killed in battle of Fredericksburg, Va., December 13, 1862; Sheridan F. Miller, killed in battle of Chancellorsville, May 2, 1863; Orpheus Roberts, killed in battle of Gettysburg, July 2, 1863; Charles S. McCobb, killed in battle of Gettysburg, July 2, 1863; George M. Bragg, July 5, 1863, of wounds received at Gettysburg.

PROMOTED OUT OF REGIMENT.

Col. Hiram G. Berry, March 17, 1862, to Brig.-General of Vols.; Lieut.-Col. Thomas H. Marshall, Sept. 9, 1861, to Colonel 7th Maine Vols.; Lieut.-Col. Frank S. Nickerson, November 29, 1861, to Colonel 14th Maine Vols.; Capt. Edwin M. Smith, April 1, 1862, to Captain and A. A. G.; First Lieut. and R. Q. M. Isaac C. Abbott, July 8, 1863, to Captain and A. Q. M.

RESIGNED AND DISCHARGED.

RESIGNED: Lieut.-Col. Silas M. Fuller, March 1, 1862.

CAPTAINS: Oliver J. Conant, September 9, 1861; Stephen C. Whitehouse, October 31, 1861; Henry W. Cunningham, December 16, 1861, became Lieutenant-Colonel 19th Maine regt.; Joseph L. Havener, April 3, 1862; Charles B. Greenhalgh, April 27, 1862; Andrew D. Bean, May 12, 1862; Orrin P. Mitchell, July 31, 1862; Gustavus Rundlett, August 12, 1862; Levi R. Bisbee, September 30, 1862; Thomas B. Glover, October 28, 1862; James D. Erskine, November 29, 1862; Charles A. Rollins, January 7, 1863; Albert L. Spencer, January 23, 1863; William H. Clark, January 27, 1863; Richard S. Ayer, March 22, 1863, — afterwards Captain in Inv. corps; George F. Crabtree, June 21, 1863; John G. Auld, December 14, 1863.

FIRST LIEUTENANTS: James O. Dow, July 8, 1861; Alden D. Chase, July 15, 1861; William E. Burgin, August 15, 1861; John C. Cobb, September 27, 1861; James S. Huxford, October 28, 1861; Benjamin Kelley, Jr., February 22, 1862; Charles L. Strickland, May 4, 1862; James N. Fowler, July 18, 1862; Alonzo E. Libby, November 13, 1862; Otis C. McGray, April 3, 1863; Jabez B. Greenhalgh, May 27, 1863; William Shields, September 27, 1863, — became Lieut. U. S. Army; Frank D. Ames, October 8, 1863.

SECOND LIEUTENANTS: Fred E. Hussey, July 8, 1861; Horatio H. Carter, August 12, 1861; Beniah P. Brackley, September 19, 1861.

SURGEON: Abial Libby, July 17, 1862. ASSISTANT SURGEON: William R. Benson, September 30, 1862.

DISCHARGED: Lieut.-Col. Lorenzo D. Carver, December 16, 1863, for disability; 2d Lieut. Charles H. Burd, January 1, 1862; Surgeon George W. Martin, May 12, 1863; Surgeon W. A. Banks, July 18, 1861; Asst. Surgeon Elisha Hopkins, July 18, 1861.

OTHERWISE LEFT THE SERVICE.

SURGEONS: Freeland S. Holmes, never joined regiment, commissioned into 6th Maine; Capt. G. J. Burns dismissed October 10, 1861; 2d Lieut. Eben Harding dismissed April 27, 1863.

MONUMENT

OF

SEVENTEENTH MAINE REGIMENT.

This monument, of Hallowell granite, stands at the south edge of the Wheat-field, between the Peach Orchard and Devil's Den, by the stone fence, where its colors were July 2, 1863, at the position where the regiment successfully resisted all assaults of the enemy upon it. Two square bases of single blocks support a four-sided shaft or die, which, inlaid with diamond-shaped blocks of red granite, rises to the capital with a projecting cornice. This forms a platform on which is a sculptured group, chiseled from a block of white granite, representing a section of stone-wall, with wheat, and the statue of a typical soldier of 1863, true in every detail, posed alert, resting upon one knee in the wheat, holding his rifle, at the "ready," across the wall.

ADMEASUREMENTS: 1st base, 8 feet by 8 feet by 2 feet 3 inches; 2d base, 6 feet by 6 feet by 2 feet 8 inches; shaft, tapering from 4 feet 3 inches to 3 feet 8 inches, each side, by 9 feet; cap, 4 feet 9 inches by 4 feet 9 inches by 2 feet; statue, 4 feet 9 inches by 4 feet 9 inches by 4 feet 6 inches. Total height, 20 feet 5 inches.

Upon two sides are the following inscriptions:—

130 KILLED AND WOUNDED, 350 ENGAGED.

JULY 2, 1863.

17TH MAINE

INFANTRY.

LT. COL. CHAS. B. MERRILL,

COMMANDING.

3RD BRIGADE,

1ST DIVISION,

3RD CORPS.

WHEAT-FIELD,

JULY 2, 1863;

PICKETT'S REPULSE,

JULY 3, 1863.

—See page 191 for legend upon the monument.

LEGEND.

Upon a bronze panel set into the north side of the second base is this legend:—

THE SEVENTEENTH MAINE FOUGHT HERE IN THE WHEATFIELD 2 1-2 HOURS, AND AT THIS POSITION FROM 4:10 TO 5:45 P. M., JULY 2, 1863. ON JULY 3, AT TIME OF THE ENEMY'S ASSAULT, IT REINFORCED THE CENTRE AND SUPPORTED ARTILLERY. LOSS, 132. KILLED OR MORTALLY WOUNDED, 3 OFFICERS, 37 MEN. WOUNDED, 5 OFFICERS, 87 MEN.

THIS REGIMENT OF VOLUNTEERS FROM WESTERN MAINE WAS MUSTERED INTO THE UNITED STATES SERVICE AT PORTLAND, AUGUST 18, 1862, FOR THREE YEARS. IT TOOK PART IN THE BATTLES OF FREDERICKSBURG, CHANCELLORSVILLE, GETTYSBURG, WAPPING HEIGHTS, AUBURN, KELLY'S FORD, LOCUST GROVE, MINE RUN, WILDERNESS, PO RIVER, SPOTTSYLVANIA, FREDERICKSBURG ROAD, NORTH ANNA, TOTOPOTOMY, COLD HARBOR, PETERSBURG, JERUSALEM ROAD, DEEP BOTTOM, PEEBLE'S FARM, FORT HELL, BOYDTON ROAD, SIEGE OF PETERSBURG, HATCHER'S RUN, FALL OF PETERSBURG, DETONSVILLE, SAILOR'S CREEK, FARMVILLE, APPOMATTOX.

AGGREGATE ACTUAL STRENGTH IN SERVICE, 91 OFFICERS, 1,475 MEN. KILLED AND DIED OF WOUNDS, 12 OFFICERS, 195 MEN. DIED OF DISEASE, 4 OFFICERS, 128 MEN. DIED IN CONFEDERATE PRISONS, 31 MEN. WOUNDED, NOT MORTALLY, 33 OFFICERS, 519 MEN. MISSING IN ACTION, FATE UNKNOWN, 35 MEN. TOTAL LOSS, 957. MUSTERED OUT JUNE 4, 1865.

SEVENTEENTH MAINE REGIMENT,

THIRD BRIGADE, FIRST DIVISION, THIRD ARMY CORPS,

AT THE BATTLE OF GETTYSBURG.

WE have followed the fortunes of the Third and Fourth Maine regiments, the one upon the right and the other upon the left of Birney's line. At a point near the centre of this line another Maine regiment, the Seventeenth infantry, of de Trobriand's brigade, defended a no less important position. This was one of the two brigades which Sickles left near Emmitsburg to guard the mountain passes while he pressed on to Gettysburg, eleven miles away, with the rest of the corps, in response to Howard's call for assistance. But before daybreak of July 2d Colonel de Trobriand received orders to come up to Gettysburg. The brigade marched rapidly, but cautiously, up the Emmitsburg road, arriving near Gettysburg late in the forenoon. The regiment was under command of Lieut.-Colonel Merrill, ably seconded by Major West. As it passed northerly along the road beyond the Peach Orchard it received a fire from the Confederate skirmishers, screened by the woods in which they were posted, west of the road. The regiment filed off the road to the east and, passing through grass fields and across lots, halted near a growth, where the hungry boys made a hasty luncheon of hard tack and coffee.

In the line, which Sickles was forming, de Trobriand first occupied the ridgy, wooded ground between the Peach Orchard and the Wheatfield. The Wheatfield was of triangular shape, about 400 yards each side; the highest portion was bounded by a cross road running along by the Peach Orchard and easterly across the north slope of Little Round Top. The Wheatfield sloped down southerly from this road, and along its westerly side by a wood, to quite low ground, making a corner near a branch of Plum Run, with a thick alder growth on the

Apex of 17ᵗʰ Maine Reg't Monument.

west; the third or southerly side was bounded by an open growth of sizable trees, a stone-wall intervening, and this wood separated the Wheatfield from Devil's Den.

The Seventeenth was at first placed south of the Peach Orchard, supporting the skirmish line of the 3d Mich. De Trobriand had two regiments at the front, to the left of the latter,—the 5th Mich., whose skirmishers connected to the 3d, near the Rose barn, also the 110th Penn., a small regiment. The largest regiment in the brigade, the 40th N. Y., was in the wood, in reserve, behind these.

The ball opened by a shot from a battery at the Peach Orchard, soon taken up by Smith's battery at Devil's Den, the latter drawing fire from the enemy's batteries near the Emmitsburg road farther south. Ward's brigade extended from Devil's Den, through the wood, nearly to the Wheatfield. The advance of the enemy's line of battle was such that Ward received the first contact, on an attempt by the enemy to capture Smith's battery. There was a gap between Ward and de Trobriand at the south corner of the Wheatfield. To occupy this gap the Seventeenth Maine was hastened upon the double-quick by the left, taking up its position at the stone-wall, the right of the regiment extending beyond the wall to the alders. Some time after, the 40th N. Y. was also taken from de Trobriand and sent to Ward's left rear, in the Plum Run valley.

Shortly after 4 P. M. the Seventeenth planted its colors at the stone-wall on the southern edge of the historic Wheatfield (a). There were no immediately connecting troops upon its left or right. The regiment took position just in time to receive the first and furious attack made by the enemy on that part of the line. This was made by Robertson's brigade of Hood's division, and the first struggle of the Seventeenth was with the 3d Ark. regiment. The latter, advancing towards the battery, struck the line of the Seventeenth obliquely; the Seventeenth overlapping its left flank, threw it into confusion by a spirited enfilading fire. Their line recoiled. After a short delay they made a change of front, and brought in some of the

(a) The authority for this account of the Seventeenth's battle is Captain George W. Verrill, a participant in the battle as Second Lieutenant of company C. He is also the author of all that part relating to the battle in the Wheatfield.

1st Texas from their right.   Advancing again they made an
effort to dislodge the Seventeenth from its position, but without
avail.   Their lines were again broken, causing a partial withdrawal of their attacking forces here, and likewise at that part
of the line where they had previously pressed hard upon Ward's
brigade (b).

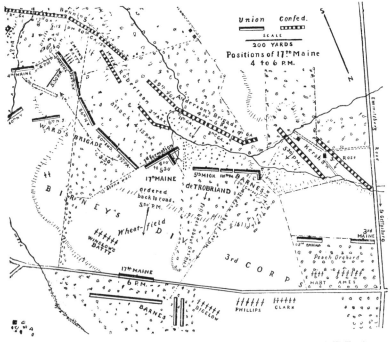

DIAGRAM 1.   Drawn by G. W. Verrill.
SEVENTEENTH MAINE IN THE WHEATFIELD.

The enemy re-formed his lines and brought in Anderson's
Georgia brigade with these scattered portions of Robertson's,
making another determined assault.   As this developed an
attack extending from Little Round Top westward, and beyond
the right of the Seventeenth, it brought into action the 5th Mich.
and 110th Penn. regiments, which were posted on the wooded
ground west of the Wheatfield, as well as some regiments
of the Fifth corps, posted on the right of these.   As the

(b) General Ward said in his official report, "The valuable services rendered by
Col. T. W. Egan, Lieut-Col. Merrill and their noble regiments (40th N. Y. and Seventeenth Maine), at an opportune moment, cannot be over-estimated.   Also see Rebellion Records, Vol. 27, part 2, page 408, reports of 3d Ark. and 1st Texas.

right wing of the Seventeenth, prolonging the course of the stone-wall beyond its west end, extended obliquely towards the enemy, in advance of the general position, and was thus in the air, the Georgians outflanked it when they advanced. Perceiving this, the Seventeenth promptly took measures to avert disaster. One-third of the regiment from its right was swung back to a slight rail fence which, starting from the stone-wall at nearly a right angle, formed the boundary of the real wheat field. Thus two fronts were presented by the regiment, forming a salient angle at the stone-wall. The movement was accomplished, although with considerable loss, so quietly that the rest of the regiment, engaged as they were with the enemy, were not aware of it, a steady fire being kept up. The tables were turned. As the veterans of Georgia moved directly forward upon the 5th Mich. and 110th Penn., who received them face to face, this new line of the right wing of the Seventeenth took them in flank. They changed front to match the flank line of the Seventeenth and again advanced, and thus exposed their left to the reliable men of the 5th Mich. Meanwhile the enemy, that was not affected by this flanking fire, pressed forward, even up to the stone-wall, and a desperate struggle at close quarters ensued for this coveted position. At the salient angle was company B, with H, K and C at the right; at the left of B was G the color company, and on its left, along the stone-wall, were D, I, F, A and E. All received a raking fire, particularly G, B and H, but all remained steadfast, and routed the enemy, some of whom were taken prisoners, their color-bearer, who had advanced nearly to our line, narrowly escaping capture. On that portion of the line the enemy had made no impression, and Anderson's brigade retired out of range. The fight had continued over an hour; many had fallen, but success inspired confidence.

To complete his line so as to attack the Peach Orchard in reverse, Longstreet now brought in Kershaw's South Carolina brigade of McLaws' division, which advanced, holding its left upon the Emmitsburg road and pushing forward its right to gain ground to the east, so as to assault the Orchard from the south, as it advanced, and at the same time secure a foothold

at the Wheatfield, thus taking de Trobriand in the right flank
and rear. Semmes' brigade, on the right of Kershaw, was expected to assist Kershaw and connect with Anderson's brigade.

The troops of Barnes' division of the Fifth corps that had
taken an excellent position on the right of de Trobriand, and
had assisted in repulsing the last previous assault, were in a
situation to receive a part of Kershaw's force in line. Kershaw's advance, at about 5 : 30 P. M. could be plainly seen as his
regiments gained the Rose building; as they advanced, Anderson's brigade also made another attack. The assault was most
desperate, with a strength at least double that of ours; if successful it would sweep directly across the Wheatfield, converging as it advanced. Again the Seventeenth at the stone-wall
held the enemy at bay; at its angle it repelled the attempts of
Anderson after a long and persistent struggle; but Kershaw
forced back the Fifth corps forces at the " loop " and struck the
flank of de Trobriand's brigade in the woods. Pushing ahead
for a junction with Anderson, a portion of the assailants made
for the west corner of the Wheatfield through the thick alder
growth, happily there, which both impeded their rush and broke
the solidity of their ranks; they emerged through the alders
within fifty paces of the flanking right wing of the Seventeenth,
which awaited them at the rail fence. Here were a hundred
muskets, in the hands of steady veterans, to receive them:
" Aim low, boys! make every shot tell! " With the most
frantic efforts to re-form his lines for a charge, the enemy was
unsuccessful; the men dropped as they emerged from the
alders; in a few minutes they gave it up and retreated out of
sight. The Seventeenth breathed easier. But the attack of
Kershaw, forcing Barnes away, in turn compelled the 5th Mich.
and 110th Penn. to move rearward. Kershaw thus gained
lodgment in the woods west of the Wheatfield, considerably in
rear of the position of the Seventeenth. Winslow's battery,
posted at the north side of the field, withdrew from its position. The Seventeenth was thus left alone, far in advance of
its brother regiments and well outflanked upon its right by
Kershaw. It was ordered back across the field in line of battle
to the cross road before spoken of. Another attack followed
before a new general line could be arranged.

The enemy seeing the retrograde movement across the Wheatfield, at once moved up to the abandoned stone-wall and over it, and also to the edge of the woods west of the Wheatfield. General Birney rode up, saw the desperate situation, and also saw the Seventeenth Maine near him, which had just squatted down in the cross road and had sent for ammunition. It had expended already over forty of the sixty rounds with which it was provided (a). Birney called upon the Seventeenth for a charge. He placed himself at the head of the regiment,

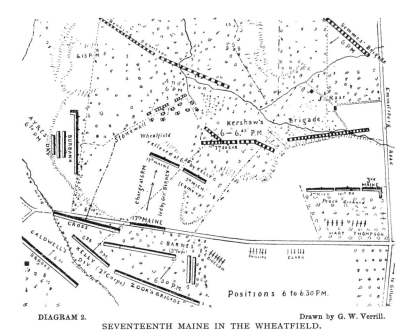

DIAGRAM 2.   Drawn by G. W. Verrill.
SEVENTEENTH MAINE IN THE WHEATFIELD.

and with a cheer and a rush it moved down into the Wheatfield. The enemy disappeared over the stone-wall and into the

(a) Sergeant Pratt of company C (afterwards a captain), and some others, carried 80 rounds into the fight. Captain Pratt has positive knowledge that he fired 60 rounds from the stone-wall position, although there were lulls in the battle, a change of position by the company, and a slight wounding, to interrupt him in his work. This proves the time that the regiment remained at the wall to have been nearly two hours. The Sergeant did not quit the field until he received his third wound, after the charge under Birney.

woods. Placing the Seventeenth about midway of the Wheatfield he ordered it to remain there and keep back the enemy. (a)

The Seventeenth took upon itself without flinching this task
of a forlorn hope. It was past 6 o'clock. General Sickles had
just been wounded. Birney was notified and took command
of the corps. Leaving the Seventeenth, he went to another
part of the field, but he was not unmindful of the situation he
left; (b) the gallant 5th Mich. was brought up and extended
the line of the Seventeenth to the right; the two small brigades
of Barnes, who had retired from the front woods, were now
resting in the woods one hundred yards in rear of the Wheatfield, but not engaged (c); General Birney had sent to Hancock
for Second corps troops. Meanwhile the raking musketry fire
of the enemy at short range, both from the stone-wall in front
and the wood nearer and to the right, was making sad inroads
upon the attenuated ranks of the Seventeenth and its brother
regiment, as there was no protection of any sort; occasionally
the enemy would form a line and emerge from the woods as
for a charge, but the firmness and confidence displayed by the
Seventeenth and the 5th Mich., ready to meet him with the
bayonet, apparently disheartened him.

The cartridges were giving out; every box of a dead or
wounded comrade was appropriated to eke out the supply.
Twenty minutes,—a half-hour,—passed, and still no signs of
help; the last cartridge was gone and the men were grimly
told by the commanding officer that the Seventeenth would
stay there and hold the ground with the bayonet until the last
man had fallen! (d) This small band of Third corps men successfully held the line at this critical time without assistance

(a) Of this Gettysburg charge General Birney said in his official report, concerning the Seventeenth: "This regiment behaved most gallantly, and evinced a high
state of discipline. Their enthusiasm was cheering, and the assistance rendered by
their charge most important."

As accounts of various military writers have injected several regiments into this
charge led by General Birney, it is desired to emphasize the fact, that no other regiment took part in it, and no troops were brought up to aid the Seventeenth except
as here narrated.—G. W. V.

(b) See de Trobriand's report,—Rebellion Records, serial no. 43, page 520.

(c) See Birney's report,—Rebellion Records, serial no. 43, page 483; also Sweitzer's report,—Ibid., page 611.

(d) See Lieut.-Col. Merrill's official report,—Rebellion Records, serial no. 43, p. 522.

from other infantry. The batteries in and to the east of the Peach Orchard nobly performed their work and helped to keep Kershaw's men under cover by their rapid and well-aimed fire.

At last, at just about 6 : 40 o'clock, deliverance came. Caldwell's division of the Second corps readily assumed the battle on that portion of the line. Cross' brigade went in where Ward's right had rested; after this, Kelly's brigade advanced, in line of battle, through and beyond the small remnant of the Seventeenth Maine and 5th Mich., into the edge of the wood, with a rush upon Kershaw's troops, with whom the Maine and Michigan veterans had been contending.

The Seventeenth, thus relieved, collected and took along its wounded who were disabled on the field, and then, in good order, finally left the Wheatfield, handing it over, still intact, into the keeping of other Union troops.

[It may not be amiss to state briefly the events of that evening, on this part of the field, after the Seventeenth was relieved. Cross' brigade advanced upon the enemy posted behind the west end of the Wheatfield stone-fence, and the wall running westerly from Devil's Den. A hot contest ensued for thirty or forty minutes, the enemy holding his ground, when the regulars of Ayres' division, Fifth corps, came in up to the east side of the Wheatfield and relieved Cross' brigade. Kelly's brigade, with that of Zook upon its right, fought fiercely with Kershaw in the woods where we left him, finally driving the latter out. About this time Brooke, with his brigade of Caldwell's division, charged across the Wheatfield, almost unresisted by the used-up and disconnected troops of Anderson, Kershaw and Semmes. By these three brigades of Caldwell the line was advanced to the farthest point held by the Third corps and extended farther south. This was about 7 P. M., when, Barksdale having pushed back our regiments and batteries just north of the Peach Orchard, Longstreet brought up Wofford's fresh brigade, which advanced through the Orchard and easterly on the cross road. There was nothing to resist him ; Tilton's brigade of Barnes' division had been resting in Trostle's grove, in an excellent position to defend from Wofford, but had retired. Kershaw joined to Wofford, and taking our lines about the Wheatfield in the right flank and rear, easily whirled out the three brigades of the Second corps, Sweitzer's brigade of the Fifth corps which was then in the Wheatfield, also the regulars of Ayres, causing heavy loss, and advanced the Confederate line to the Plum Run valley, west of Little Round Top. Here it was met by a charge of about three brigades of the Sixth and Fifth corps. These with the timely aid rendered at this point by McGilvery's batteries, in driving back Barksdale's troops, not far distant, north of the cross road, turned the tide of battle. This was about 7 : 30 P. M. The Confederates retired to the southerly and westerly sides of the Wheatfield, about where they were when the Seventeenth was relieved, nearly an hour before.]

On July 3d, when Longstreet's assault was made upon the centre of Hancock's line, the Seventeenth was brought into the general line to receive it, at a point where Wilcox's column would have struck, had it got so far, but our batteries pounded this column to pieces before it reached our infantry line ; lying there, supporting the batteries, the regiment was exposed to a severe artillery fire, losing in it two killed and ten wounded, — small loss compared to that of the day before.

A MARKER

located upon the ground held by the regiment July 3d, during the charge, stands upon the west side of Hancock Avenue, near the monument of the 9th Mich. battery and to its right. This marker, cut from Maine granite, assumes the size and appearance of a small monument. The upper portion of the die shows rather more than the half of a square block, with one of its angles making the apex. Upon the face, matching the angles of the top, a red granite diamond, or lozenge, is inlaid, beneath which is the following inscription:

POSITION OF THE 17TH MAINE INFTY. JULY 3, 1863.

LOSING HERE KILLED 2, WOUNDED, 10.

THIS REGT. FOUGHT JULY 2, IN THE WHEATFIELD,

AS SHOWN BY MOMUMENT THERE, LOSING 120.

POSITION OF 17TH MAINE INF'TY. JULY 3.1863
LOSING HERE KILLED 2, WOUNDED 10
THIS REGT. FOUGHT JULY 2, IN THE WHEATFIELD
AS SHOWN BY MONUMENT THERE LOSING 120

PARTICIPANTS.

FIELD, STAFF AND NON-COMMISSIONED STAFF.

Lieutenant-Colonel, Charles B. Merrill, Portland, commanding regiment.
Major, George W. West, Somerville, Mass.
Adjutant, First Lieutenant Charles W. Roberts, Portland.
Quartermaster, First Lieutenant Josiah Remick, Portland.
Surgeon, Nahum A. Hersom, Sanford.
Assistant Surgeon, William Wescott, Standish.
Chaplain, Jeremiah Hayden, Raymond.
Sergeant-Major, Henry L. Bartels, Portland, acting 2d Lieut., see company F.
[Acting Sergeant-Major, Frederick W. Bosworth, Portland, Private co. A.]
Quartermaster-Sergeant, John Yeaton, Jr., Portland.
Commissary-Sergeant, John F. Putnam, Lewiston.
Hospital Steward, Nathaniel B. Coleman, Portland.

COMPANY A.

Captain, Charles P. Mattocks, Portland.
1st Sergt., act'g 2d Lieut. Grenville F. Sparrow, Portland (com., not must'd).

SERGEANTS.

Alvin F. Blake, Portland, act'g 1st Serg. Fayette M. Paine, New Vineyard,
Benjamin Doe, So. Berwick,   Edward H. Crie, Portland.

CORPORALS.

Jesse A. Stone, Portland,   Robert M. Low, Pownal,
Joseph F. Lake, Portland, color-bearer, George T. Jones, Richmond.

PRIVATES.

Andrews, Albert H., Jr., Portland,   Armstrong, Jacob L., Portland,
Barker, Alonzo J., New Vineyard,   Bodkin, Peter P., Portland,
Brown, Daniel W., Baldwin,   Brown, Jacob C., Portland,
Burns, Michael, Portland,   Chick, William H., So. Berwick,
Delihanty, Thomas, Portland,   Dresser, Albion K. P., Pownal,
Goodenow, Charles, Gray,   Herrick, Ira J., New Vineyard,
Hodsdon, Joseph A., Falmouth,   Ingraham, Octavius C., Portland,
James, John W., Portland,   Joy, Granville W., So. Berwick,
Marston, Edward H., Falmouth,   Marston, Horace G., Falmouth,
Marston, Joseph S., Falmouth,   McDonald, Peter, Compton, Can.,
Miller, Alonzo, Portland,   Milliken, Charles, Portland,
Pettengill, Albion C., Portland,   Pratt, Jeremiah L., New Vineyard,
Pray, Ivory, So. Berwick,   Sawyer, Alonzo W., Westbrook,
Sawyer Henry H., New Gloucester,   Spaulding, David M., New Vineyard,
Skillings, Franklin, Portland,   Totman, John F., Portland,
Tuttle, John F., Freeman,   Waterhouse, Robert, Portland,
Wilkinson, Frederick N., So. Berwick.

ON SPECIAL DUTY OR DETACHED SERVICE: 2d Lieut. Edwin B. Houghton, Portland, act'g A. D. C. brig. staff, commiss'd 1st Lieut., not mustered. Corporal Anson F. Ward, Portland, div. provo. guard. Privates: Frederick W. Bosworth, Portland, act'g Sergt.-Major, see Field and Staff; Robert Hamilton, Portland, corps provo. guard; Samuel D. Roberts, Portland, 4th N. Y. batt'y; Henry C. Allen, New Gloucester, corps amm'n train; Edward Fabyan,

Portland, teamster; Cornelius Boyle, Portland, regt'l pioneer; John B. Miles, New Vineyard, cattle guard; Obed W. Paine, New Vineyard, blacksmith; Jonas Reynolds, So. Berwick, cook; Mark H. Sawyer, Portland, and George H. M. Taylor, Portland, div. supply train; James S. Spaulding, Anson, Oliver Waite, Anson, and Oliver Walker, So. Berwick, brig. amb. train. Musicians: Henry B. Berry, Portland, and Augustus Vaughn, New Vineyard, hosp. dept. Wagoner Charles R. Hale, Portland, div. supply train.

COMPANY B.

First Lieutenant, Benjamin C. Pennell, Portland, commanding company.
Second Lieutenant, William H. Green, Portland.

SERGEANTS.

Horace A. Smith, Portland, acting First Sergeant,

Edwin J. Hawkes, Portland,	Daniel Gookin, Portland,
Cyrus M. Hall, Portland.	

CORPORALS.

David C. Saunders, Sweden, color gd.,	George W. Jones, Portland,
Edward A. Roberts, Portland,	Charles H. Merrill, Portland,
George W. H. Roach, Portland,	Aaron Hubbard, So. Berwick.

PRIVATES.

Brackett, Byron, Sweden,	Carruthers, Charles E., Portland,
Charles, Frank C., Fryeburg,	Davis, Samuel C., Portland,
Doughty, John, Jr., Portland,	Duran, George E. H., Portland,
Elliot, William S., Portland,	Emery, Moses D., Stowe,
Fabyan, Charles H., Portland,	Flannagan, James, Portland,
Foster, R. G. W., Albany,	Grover, Alpheus, Portland,
Holt, James G., Fryeburg,	Lehane, John, Portland,
Libby, Seth B., Portland,	McKeen, James, Stowe,
McKenzie, Matthew, Portland,	Morton, Sidney G., Fryeburg,
Morton, William B., Fryeburg,	Norton, George L., Portland,
Noyes, Alvin A., Portland,	Quint, Monroe, Stowe,
Smith, Daniel, Jr., Fryeburg,	Walker, Alden B., Fryeburg,
Wiley, Gardner B., Stowe,	Wiley Joseph, Fryeburg,
Winn, Andrew, Portland.	

ON SPECIAL DUTY OR DETACHED SERVICE: Corporal John Witham, Portland, provo. guard. Privates: Augustus A. Kimball, Portland, 6th R. I. batt'y; Edwin G. Thorne, Portland, Smith's 4th N. Y. batt'y; Samuel Buxton, Portland, amm'n train; Samuel C. Holden, Fryeburg, surgeon's detail; Orlando Hooper, Portland, George F. Moulton, Portland, and Joseph Wescott, Windham, brig. amb. corps; Edward Kelly, Portland, cook. Musicians: James F. Bartlett, Portland, and William H. Colby, Portland, assisting wounded. Wagoner Samuel E. Silsby, Portland, tools wagon.

COMPANY C.

First Lieutenant, Edward Moore, Portland, commanding company.
Second Lieutenant, George W. Verrill, Norway.

SERGEANTS.

First Sergeant, Jordan M. Hall, Casco,	Asa L. Downs, Minot,
William F. Morrill, Durham,	Gustavus C. Pratt, Oxford.

CORPORALS.

Josiah G. M. Spiller, Casco,	Cyrus T. Pratt, Poland,

Jas. F. Strout, Raymond, color guard, James L. Fuller, Minot, George B. Dunn, Poland.

PRIVATES.

Allen, Joseph A., Raymond,
Black, Lawson S., Bethel,
Campbell, Alexander, Minot,
Dean, Abraham, Jr., Oxford,
Durgin, George A., Minot,
Graffam, Henry, Casco,
Hawley, John, Farmington,
Mills, Fessenden M., Norway,
Perkins, George F., Minot, in part,
Ricker, Wentworth P., Poland,
Strout, Charles W., Minot,
Welch, Stephen S., Casco,
Berry, James, Naples,
Brown, Horace J., Poland, in part,
Churchill, Allen M., Poland,
Duran, Josiah, Poland,
Faunce, William, Oxford,
Haskell, Samuel F., Poland,
Maybury, Enoch, Naples,
Pattee, Andrew J., Poland,
Pratt, Addison B., Minot,
Strout, Albert, Raymond,
Verrill, Richard, Raymond,
Witham, Henry, Casco.

On Special Duty or Detached Service: Privates: Preble Soper, Hebron, in provo. guard; George G. Bridgham, Poland, hostler brig. h'dqrs; Orrin Downs, Oxford, teamster supply train; Chester J. Dunn, New Gloucester, assist. to wounded; John B. Evans, Raymond, cook; D. S. N. Thurlow, Raymond, regt'l pioneer. Musician Stephen W. Gammon, Poland, in charge of stretcher bearers. Wagoner James E. Fulton, Raymond, supply train.

COMPANY D.

Captain, John C. Perry, Portland.
First Lieutenant, Newton Whitten, Portland.
Second Lieutenant, Stephen Graffam, Portland.

SERGEANTS.

First Sergeant, Franklin I. Whittemore, Portland,
Daniel J. Chandler, Lewiston,   Newton W. Parker, Lewiston.

CORPORALS.

Bernard Hogan, Lewiston, color guard, George A. Parker, Lewiston,
Melvin Davis, Lewiston,   George F. Hanna, Portland.

PRIVATES.

Austin, Joseph, Lewiston,
Bickford, Nathaniel G., Lewiston,
Cobb, Daniel, Windham,
Dwelley, Samuel L., Lewiston,
Faunce, Gilman, Lewiston,
Gammon, Samuel H., Portland,
Groves, Laphorest, Lewiston,
Holt, John, Lewiston,
Lane, William N., Lewiston,
Parker, George I., Lewiston,
Rogers, Ezra P., Lewiston,
Skillin, Hiram B., Portland,
Toole, Thomas, Lewiston,
Baker, Edwin G., Lewiston,
Chadderton, Joseph, Lewiston,
Currier, George O., Lewiston,
Fall, Melvin, Lebanon,
Fowler, Levi, Lewiston,
Goodwin, Henry G., So. Berwick,
Hays, Charles H., Portland,
Hulme, James, Lewiston,
Mills, Joseph N., Portland,
Penley, Henry H., Lewiston,
Rounds, Isaac, Lewiston,
Sweeney, Michael, Lewiston,
Winter, Amos G., Lewiston.

On Special Duty or Detached Service: Privates: Charles H. Pinkham, Lebanon, Livingston's N. Y. battery; Charles W. Peasley, Lewiston, div. provo. guard; William Bodge, Lewiston, orderly div. h'dqrs; Warren S. Butler, Lewiston, regt'l hosp. nurse; Thomas M. Dennett, Portland, hostler; Edmund D. Field, Portland, in amb. corps, stretcher bearer; John Hogan, Lewiston, regt'l pioneer, stretcher bearer; Thomas C. Haley, Lewiston, and John E. Newman, Portland, div. supply train; Elijah P. Harmon, Lewiston, hostler div. h'dqrs; Frank A. McDonald, Lewiston, and Bradford Stevens, Lewiston, div. amb. train; Charles McCarty, Portland, guard at hospital; Isaiah G. Mason, Lewiston, brig. blacksmith. Wagoner Frank C. Houghton, Lewiston.

COMPANY E.

Captain, Ellis M. Sawyer, Cape Elizabeth.
Second Lieutenant, Frederick A. Sawyer, Portland.

SERGEANTS.

First Sergeant, Herman Q. Mason, Portland.

Charles F. Vanhorn, Portland,   Oliver E. Jordan, Cape Elizabeth.

CORPORALS.

George F. Small, Cape Elizabeth,   William M. Loring, Yarmouth,
Herbert Soule, Yarmouth,   Albert O. Baker, Yarmouth, color gd.

PRIVATES.

Adderton, Josiah M., No. Yarmouth,   Allen, Albion S., Freeport, (part July 2).
Anthoine, Edwin D., Cape Elizabeth,   Baker, Charles W., Yarmouth,
Barstow, Jeremiah R., Cumberland,   Blackstone, Jordan, Pownal,
Blake, Elijah, No. Yarmouth,   Brown, John N., Cape Elizabeth,
Bruce, Rufus S., Yarmouth,   Colley, Charles L., No. Yarmouth,
Doughty, George W., Cape Elizabeth,   Goff, Lucius S., Gray,
Hall, James H., Yarmouth,   Harmon, Arthur A., Cape Elizabeth,
Hayes, David P., No. Yarmouth,   Hayes, Francis E., No. Yarmouth,
Holyoke, Charles G., Yarmouth,   Huff, Samuel, Jr., Portland,
Johnson, Albert A., Freeport,   Jordan, Simon, Cape Elizabeth,
King, William H., Woolwich, Eng.,   Lombard, John T., Cape Elizabeth,
Loring, Joseph H., Yarmouth,   Marston, E. Greeley, Yarmouth,
Milliken, Samuel, Cape Elizabeth,   Mitchell, Tristram P., Yarmouth,
Pargade, Cheri, No. Yarmouth,   Plowman, Oliver, Scarborough,
Rideout, Joseph M., Cumberland,   Ross, George E., Gray,
Seabury, Ammi D., Yarmouth,   Soule, George O. D., Yarmouth,
Sparks, James E., Yarmouth,   Thompson, Charles H., Gray,
True, Hollis, Pownal,   Whitney, William J., No. Yarmouth.

ON SPECIAL DUTY OR DETACHED SERVICE: Privates: Standish P. Reed, Yarmouth, R. I. battery; Aaron Hodgdon, Pownal, cook; Francis H. Hale, Paris, and Moses McKenny, Cape Elizabeth, div. provo. guard; William H. Gore, Gray, and Lewis A. Simpson, Gray, amb. corps; David V. Lovell, Pownal, and William F. Roberts, Cape Elizabeth, teamsters. Wagoner Lewis W. Lombard, Portland, with trains.

COMPANY F.

First Lieutenant, Joseph A. Perry, Portland, commanding.
[Act'g Second Lieut., Serg.-Major Henry L. Bartels, com'd, not mustered.]
First Sergeant, Hannibal S. Warren, Norway.
Sergeant, Charles P. Jackson, Woodstock.

CORPORALS.

Zephaniah E. Sawtelle, Paris,   Asa G. Charles, Norway,
George R. Fickett, Portland,   William D. Merrill, Norway, color gd.,
Albert C. Gammon, Norway,   Austin Hanson, Hiram,
Otis H. Dyer, Paris.

PRIVATES.

Allen, George H., Shapleigh,
Burgess, Joseph P., Brownfield,
Day, Henry, Jr., Brownfield,
Farnham, Luther B., Woodstock,
Gannon, William, Greenwood,
Kenniston, George G., Brownfield,
Libby, Richard L., Windham,
Morse, Moses H., Paris,
Newcomb, Charles A., Sebago,
Parker, Isaac, Hiram,
Stone, Henry F., Lebanon,
Thorne, Edgecomb N., Brownfield,
Washburn, Almon T., Paris,
Whitman, George W., Woodstock,

Ames, Willard O., Greenwood,
Curtis, Oliver G., Paris,
Estes, Joshua P., Bethel,
Farr, Solomon, Greenwood,
Holt, Calvin, Norway,
Knapp, James H. S., Paris,
Morse, Edward F., Norway,
Morton, Melville, Westbrook,
Newhall, Eugene P., Paris,
Pratt, Levi A., Paris,
Thorne, Barnett, Woodstock,
Twitchell, Charles H., Paris,
Washburn, Linas G., Paris, July 2,
Woodman, John M., Hiram.

ON SPECIAL DUTY OR DETACHED SERVICE: Sergeant Frank L. Berry, Paris, amb. corps; Privates: Hosea R. Allen, Hiram, and William Spencer, Baldwin, hospital nurses; William H. Day, Brownfield, in 4th N. Y. battery; Ephraim H. Brown, Norway, corps provo. guard; Lemuel B. Carter, Paris, and William H. Gray, Brownfield, amb. corps; William H. Downs, Paris, teamster supply train; Isaac E. Osgood, Hiram, guard to convalescents; William H. Thorne, Bridgton, amb. train; Cyrus S. Tucker, Norway, brig. saddler; Wentworth H. Shaw, Bridgton, provo. guard; Seth Wadsworth, Hiram, surgeon's detail. Musician John C. McArdle, Paris, assistant for wounded. Wagoner Nathaniel LeBarron, Greenwood, quartermaster's dept.

COMPANY G.

Second Lieutenant, Hiram R. Dyar, Farmington, commanding company.

SERGEANTS.

First Sergeant, John N. Morrill, Strong,
Walter F. Noyes, Jay,
Stephen H. Roberts, Berwick,

James Snowman, Weld,
Lloyd W. Lamos, Berwick.

CORPORALS.

Johiel B. Blethen, Madrid,
Jeremy P. Wyman, Strong,

Albert L. Bradbury, Avon,
Benjamin F. Huff, Buxton, color guard.

PRIVATES.

Arnold, Edgar W., Farmington,
Butterfield, Augustus F., Farmington,
Dunnell, Alvah L., Buxton,
Frederic, George A., Temple,
Ham, Charles H., Berwick,
Houston, Elbridge L., Weld,
Kannady, George H., Phillips,
Kimball, John H., Jay,
Manson, John S., Buxton,
Pinkham, Francis, Berwick,
Rollins, Albert G., New Sharon,
Stearns, Albert M., Weld,
Vaughan, Sylvester, New Vineyard,
Wentworth, Henry R., Berwick,
Wilder, Silas, Temple.

Bean, Nelson O., Industry (July 3d),
Colomy, Elbridge, Berwick,
Eastman, George A., Berwick,
Hackett, Sumner S., Strong,
Hanscomb, Eben B., Buxton,
Hurd, Francis E., Berwick,
Kannady, Warren, Avon,
Lawrence, James B., Weld,
Norton, Oliver D., Industry,
Roberts, James A., Berwick,
Sawyer, Isaac D., Buxton,
Thompson, John, Madrid,
Wallingford, George, Berwick,
Whitehouse, Charles T., Berwick,

ON SPECIAL DUTY OR DETACHED SERVICE: Corporal John W. Copeland, Worcester, Mass., provo. guard. Privates: Francis O. Bean, Industry, teamster div. train; Luther Childs, Salem, R. I. batt'y; George L. Hosmer, Farmington, regt'l detail; Asa Jennings, Farmington, hosp. nurse; Joseph L. McLaughlin, Weld, 4th N. Y. batt'y; John Plaisted, Temple, stretcher bearer; James E. S. Pray, Berwick, field hosp. ass't; Charles M. Rand, Weld, cook; Ebenezer Roberts, Berwick, div. provo. guard; John Vaughan, Berwick, hosp. attend't. Wagoner Leonard T. Vosmos, New Sharon, with trains.

COMPANY H.

Captain, Almon L. Fogg, Westbrook.

Act'g 2d Lieut., 1st Sergt. George A.Whidden,Westbrook; com'd not must'd.

SERGEANTS.

Stephen P. Hart, Westbrook, acting First Sergeant,

William H. Sturgis, Standish, Charles J. Bond, Windham,

James H. Loring, Westbrook, color bearer.

CORPORALS.

Sumner Winslow, Westbrook, James M. Webb, Westbrook,
George Barrows, Harrison, Robert B. Whitcomb, Standish,
Charles R. Meserve, Hallowell.

PRIVATES.

Adams, Frank, Westbrook, Barber, William, Westbrook,
Bond, Benjamin F., Gorham, Brackett, Horace N., Harrison,
Chute, Charles A., Westbrook, Cobb, Solomon, Westbrook,
Cobb, Uriah, Windham, Crosby, Leonard E., Westbrook,
Davis, Albert S., Standish, Davis, John S., Hollis,
Dow, Benjamin A., Standish, Dyer, Roscoe G., Sebago,
Hatch, Royal S., Westbrook, Hicks, Ephraim, Gorham,
Jones, Edward H., Westbrook, Libby, Darius S., Falmouth,
Martin, Ira L., Sebago, Plaisted, Trafton S., Westbrook,
Rand, Royal, Windham, Sanborn, Charles W., Otisfield,
Scribner, Bourdon, Harrison, Small, Oliver F., Limington,
Spurr, Llewellyn, Otisfield, Thomas, Charles W., Westbrook,
Thomas, Manuel, Windham, Winslow, Nathaniel P., Westbrook.

ON SPECIAL DUTY OR DETACHED SERVICE: Corporal Albion P. Stiles, Gorham, corps postmaster. Privates: Andrew Saunders, Sebago, 3d R. I. batt'y (wounded July 2d); John G. Scott, Westbrook, Smith's 4th N. Y. batt'y; Franklin E. Morse, Otisfield, battalion of convalescents; Cyrus Chaplin, Naples, and Luther E. Hall, Harrison, stretcher bearers; William S. Hanscomb, Windham, div. hosp. nurse; Andrew J. Larrabee, Westbrook, and Mesach P. Larry, Windham, surgeon's detail; Charles A. Warren, Standish, amb. corps; Leonard Pride, Westbrook, cook; James G. Sturgis, Standish, hosp. ass't; Daniel W. Haskell, Harrison, and Van R. Morton, Westbrook, div. provo. guard; Horace B. Cummings, Portland, and Thomas D. Emery, Standish, quarterm'r dept.; Jabez Marriner, Westbrook, commiss'y dept.; Alonzo Moses, Standish, hostler; Thomas Sands, Standish, brig. h'dqrs; Alphonzo A. Spear, Standish, teamster; Henry C. Hatch, Sebago.

COMPANY I.

Captain, William Hobson, Saco.

First Lieutenant, James O. Thompson, Portland.

SERGEANTS.

1st Sergeant, Frank C. Adams, Saco,   Charles C. Cole, Hiram,
Oliver D. Blake, Biddeford,   Charles J. Goodwin, Saco.

CORPORALS.

Samuel E. Jenness, Biddeford,   Charles H. Parcher, Biddeford,
Aurelius A. Robertson, Bethel,   Owen Stacy, Saco,
Frederick A. Mitchell, Saco, color guard.

PRIVATES.

Benson, Robert, Saco,   Bradbury, Thomas C., Biddeford,
Brand, Thomas, Saco,   Brown, James B., Gorham,
Goodwin, Charles E., Saco,   Haley, John, Saco,
Harmon, Andrew J., Saco,   Hill, Joseph, Saco,
Holmes, Hiram G., Biddeford,   Irish, Melville, Gorham,
Jordan, Charles A., Saco,   Jose, James W., Saco,
Kimball, George, Saco,   Libby, Henry H., Scarborough,
Richardson, George A., Limington,   Roberts, John H., Gorham,
Rounds, Walter, Scarborough,   Sawyer, Charles F., Baldwin,
Simpson, John H., Scarborough,   Small, Edwin, Limington,
Sweetsir, James F., Biddeford,   Tasker, George F., Saco,
Waterhouse, Winfield S., Scarboro',   Wentworth, David A., Brownfield,
White, Charles M., Standish.

ON SPECIAL DUTY OR DETACHED SERVICE: Musician William H. Atkinson, Limington, clerk brig. h'dqrs. Privates: Allen H. Abbott, Saco, brig. h'dqrs; James C. Blaisdell, Lebanon, amb. corps; Thomas Clark, Saco, hostler; Alvin Hodge, Biddeford, 4th N. Y. batt'y; John A. Kilham, Saco, amm'n train guard; Michael McGrath, Biddeford, teamster; William H. H. Pillsbury, Shapleigh, regt'l surgeon's clerk; Thomas F. Perkins, Biddeford, at corps h'dqrs; Benjamin P. Ross, Biddeford, brig. quarterm'r dept.; Eliphaz Ripley, Buckfield, blacksmith div. h'dqrs.

COMPANY K.

Captain, Milton M. Young, Lewiston.
First Lieutenant, Putnam S. Boothby, Biddeford.
First Sergeant, Isaac O. Parker, Kittery.
Sergeant, Harry Crosby, Kittery.

CORPORALS.

Andrew J. Miller, Auburn,   William H. Neal, Kittery,
Robert H. Mathes, Durham, N. H.,   Edwin A. Duncan, Kittery, color guard,
James A. Bennett, Auburn,   George J. Strout, Auburn.

PRIVATES.

Achorn, Casper, Kittery,   Austin, Robert W., Gardiner,
Beals, Charles A., Auburn,   Bunker, Daniel B., Kittery,
Burnham, John C., Kittery,   Butland, F. Augustus, Kittery,
Churchill, Robert J., Kittery,   Cotton, John H., Auburn,
Goodwin, Valentia H., Kittery,   Grace, Andrew J., Jr., Kittery,
Hall, Silas P., Oxford,   Hatch, Samuel O., Auburn,
Hussey, Daniel H., Kittery,   Keith, Augustus H., Auburn,
Lord, Oren, Waterford,   Lunt, Horace, Kittery,
Lyon, George W., Auburn,   Phillips, Hiram B., Kittery,
Remick, John H., Kittery,   Wardwell, Cyrus T., Oxford,
Young, Augustine, Auburn.

ON SPECIAL DUTY OR DETACHED SERVICE: Privates: John M. Crocker, Auburn, div. provo. guard; George H. Holt, Albany, at corps h'dqrs; John Holden, Kittery, corps provo. guard; Elisha Hall, Auburn, amm'n train guard; John F. Hewey, Auburn, and Nathan B. Lord, Abbott, teamsters; Addison A. Miller, Auburn, cook. Musician Wesley D. Rowell, Kittery, ass't to wounded.

REVISED REPORT OF CASUALTIES.

FIELD AND STAFF.

Adjutant Charles W. Roberts, right leg, amputated.

COMPANY A.

Acting First Sergeant Alvin F. Blake, wounded, died Aug. 2.
Sergeant Fayette M. Paine, wounded, both legs.
Corporal George T. Jones, wounded, leg.

PRIVATES.

Brown, Jacob C., killed.   Hodsdon, Joseph A., killed.
Marston, Horace G., wounded, foot.   Milliken, Charles, wounded, arm.
Skillings, Franklin, wounded, thigh. Spaulding, David M., wounded, leg.
Tucker, George W., missing, fell out before battle.

COMPANY B.

Second Lieut. William H. Green, July 3, shell concussion; resumed duties.

SERGEANTS.

Horace A. Smith, wounded, leg.   Cyrus M. Hall, July 3, killed.
Corporal George W. Jones, wounded, leg; died July 23.

PRIVATES.

Brackett, Byron, wounded, head.   Carruthers,Charles E.,w'd; died July 9.
Davis, Samuel C., w'd; died July 4.   Duran, George E. H., July 3, w'd.
Elliot, William S., wounded, shoulder. Emery, Moses D.,w'd, hip; died July 9.
Flannagan, James, wounded.   Lehane, John, wounded, leg.
McKeen, James, July 3, w'd, head.   McKenzie, Matthew, wounded, arm.
Morton, Sidney G., wounded, foot.   Norton, George L., July 3, w'd sh'lder.
Noyes, Alvin A., wounded, groin.   Quint, Monroe, killed July 3.
Walker, Alden B., wounded, groin.   Wiley, Joseph, wounded, leg.

COMPANY C.

Second Lieutenant George W. Verrill, wounded, thigh.

SERGEANTS.

William F. Morrill, wounded, leg.   Gustavus C. Pratt, three wounds, arm.

CORPORALS.

James F. Strout, color guard,w'd, thigh. George B. Dunn, wounded, shoulder.

PRIVATES.

Black, Lawson S., wounded.   Dean, Abraham, Jr., wounded, thigh.
Faunce, William, wounded, side.   Mills, Fessenden M., w'd; died July 3.
Pattee, Andrew J., w'd; died July 9. Pratt, Addison B., wounded, thigh.
Strout, Charles W., July 3, w'd, neck. Witham, Henry, killed.

COMPANY D.

First Lieutenant Newton Whitten, July 3, wounded, foot.
Second Lieutenant Stephen Graffam, wounded, arm.

CORPORALS.

Bernard Hogan, color guard, w'd; died July 18. Hanna, George F., w'd, leg.

PRIVATES.

Bickford, Nathaniel G., wounded, leg. Cobb, Daniel, wounded, head.
Dwelly, Samuel L., w'd; died July 8. Fowler, Levi, killed.
Hulme, James, wounded, leg. Hays, Charles H., wounded.

COMPANY E.

Sergeant Oliver E. Jordan, wounded, leg.

CORPORALS.

George F. Small, wounded, thigh. Albert O. Baker, color guard, w'd, hand.

PRIVATES.

Baker, Charles W., wounded. Brown, John N., July 3, wounded, leg.
Goff, Lucius F., wounded, hand. Harmon, Arthur A., killed.
Hayes, Francis E., wounded, breast. Johnson, Albert A., wounded, arm.
Sparks, James E., wounded. Whitney, William J., wounded, side.

COMPANY F.

Sergeant Charles P. Jackson, killed; first man hit; reported w'd and missing.

CORPORALS.

Zephaniah E. Sawtelle, wounded, hand. William D. Merrill, color g'd, w'd, hand.
Austin Hanson, killed.

PRIVATES.

Ames, Willard O., w'd; died July 24. Day, Henry, Jr., wounded, leg.
Day, William H., w'd; died Aug. 31. Farr, Solomon, wounded, head.
Holt, Calvin, w'd; died Jan. 6, 1864. Kenniston, George G., w'd, bowels.
Libby, Richard L., wounded, arm. Morse, Moses H., wounded, hand.
Twitchell, Charles H., w'd, arm and leg. Washburn, Almon T., wounded, side.

COMPANY G.

Second Lieutenant Hiram R. Dyar, killed.
Sergeant James Snowman, July 3, wounded, hip.
Corporal Benjamin F. Huff, color guard, wounded.

PRIVATES.

Arnold, Edgar W., wounded, arm. Childs, Luther, det'd R. I. batt'y, w'd.
Colomy Elbridge, wounded. Eastman, George A., wounded.
Hackett, Sumner S., wounded, arm. Hanscomb, Eben B., wounded, hand.
Houston, Elbridge L., wounded. Hurd, Francis E., killed.
Lawrence, James B., w'd and prisoner. Rollins, Albert G., killed.
Sawyer, Isaac D., killed. Thompson, John, wounded.

COMPANY H.

Captain Almon L. Fogg, wounded, abdomen; died July 4.

SERGEANTS.

Stephen P. Hart, acting First Sergeant, wounded, leg.
Charles J. Bond, wounded, leg. James H. Loring, color bearer, killed.

CORPORALS.

George Barrows, killed. Robert B. Whitcomb, wounded, leg.
Sumner Winslow, killed.

PRIVATES.

Cobb, Solomon, wounded, arm. Dyer, Roscoe G., killed.
Hicks, Ephraim, killed. Jones, Edward H., wounded, breast.
Martin, Ira L., wounded; died Aug. 9. Rand, Royal, w'd July 2; died July 3.
Sanborn, Charles W., wounded, foot. Saunders, Andrew, det'd R. I. batt'y,
Spurr, Llewellyn, wounded, leg. wounded.

COMPANY I.

First Sergeant, Franklin C. Adams, wounded, hand.

CORPORALS.

Aurelius A. Robertson,w'd; died July 5. Owen Stacy, wounded.

Frederick A. Mitchell, on color guard, wounded, leg amputated; died July 10

PRIVATES.

Brand, Thomas, wounded, leg.	Jordan, Charles A., wounded, leg.
Kimball, George, wounded, leg.	Small, Edwin, wounded, shoulder.
Wentworth, David A., wounded, leg.	White, Charles M., wounded, arm.

COMPANY K.

Captain Milton M. Young, wounded July 2; died Aug. 13.

SERGEANTS.

First Sergeant Isaac O. Parker, wounded; died July 7.

F. Augustus Butland,w'd; died Sept. 6. Harry Crosby, wounded, left leg.

CORPORALS.

William H. Neal, killed.	James A. Bennett, wounded, hand.

PRIVATES.

Austin, Robert W., wounded.	Beals, Charles A., July 3, wounded.
Bunker, Daniel B., killed; reported wounded and missing.	Grace, Andrew J., Jr., July 3, w'd, hip.
	Hall, Silas P., wounded, hand.
Hatch, Samuel O., w'd; died July 5.	Hussey, Daniel H., wounded, leg.
Lord, Oren, wounded, chest.	

REGIMENTAL DEDICATION OF MONUMENT,

OCTOBER 10, 1888.

Brevet Lieut.-Col. Edward Moore, President of the Seventeenth Maine Regiment Association, called the large assembly to order at the monument in the Wheatfield and introduced Rev. Charles G. Holyoke, late Sergeant-Major of the regiment, who offered the following

PRAYER.

Almighty God, our Heavenly Father, we have reason to thank thee that thou hast spared our lives until this day. We thank thee that in thy good providence we are permitted to gather here to pay this tribute of respect to the memory of our departed comrades. O God, we thank thee for our land, the land bequeathed to us by our forefathers, the land of liberty and freedom. We thank thee that when war broke forth upon our land, with all its ruin, terror and woe, and there were those who would gladly have torn asunder our country, that there came forth from their homes and firesides friends and dear ones, those who were loyal and true, to defend our beloved land. And we are here to-day to dedicate this monument to the memory of those who on this sacred spot shed their blood and laid down their lives in defending our flag and nation. We would remember what they endured and suffered for the cause of freedom. Grant that, as in time to come, to all who shall visit this ground and this region made sacred by the blood of patriots shed, they shall remember at what cost and sacrifice our Union, our Country, was preserved. God bless our land, and may peace evermore prevail throughout all our borders, for thy name's sake. Amen.

ADDRESS BY BREVET LIEUTENANT-COLONEL MOORE.

Comrades: —

A quarter of a century has passed by since you were upon this field, a field which you helped to make historic by your deeds of valor on July 2 and 3, 1863. You visit this field to-day for the purpose of dedicating this beautiful monument, erected by our state to commemorate the gallant deeds of her sons, and to perpetuate the memory of those of the Seventeenth Maine regiment who fell upon this decisive battlefield of the war.

You will pardon me if, on this occasion, I refer briefly to the war record of the regiment, aside from the part it took in the battle of Gettysburg. During its term of service the regiment took part in twenty-seven battles, besides doing duty in petty engagements and on the picket line during one-fifth of the whole term of enlistment. In the statistical tables by W. F. Fox of losses in battles, we find a list of "300 fighting regiments," comprising those whose aggregate deaths by battle amounted to 130 or more; we also find his list of 45 infantry regiments that lost over 200, killed or died from wounds in battles; we also find a list of 22 regiments out of all the regiments of the Union armies whose mortality by battle exceeded fifteen per cent of their enrolment. In regard to the last list he says: "The regiments in this list can fairly claim the honor of having encountered the hardest fighting in the war. They may not have done the most effective fighting, but they evidently stood where the danger was thickest, and were the ones which faced the hottest musketry. They were all well-known, reliable commands, and served with unblemished records. The maximum of loss is reached in this table." We find the Seventeenth Maine in all these lists.

Your connection with the battle of Gettysburg dates back to June 11, 1863, when you left "Camp Sickles," Va. After tedious marches, covering over 200 miles, you arrived at the college near Emmitsburg, the afternoon of July 1st. On the morning of July 2d, at 1 : 30 o'clock, the regiment received orders to assemble for a march. At 4 : 30 A. M. it started for Gettysburg, and at 10 o'clock arrived on the field of battle, having marched thirteen miles in five and a half hours. Lee was just extending his lines to his right, his skirmishers threatening the Emmitsburg road. A little after noon the regiment was placed at the left of the Peach Orchard to support the brigade skirmish line, where it remained until the battle began. A few minutes after the first shot was fired, at about 4 o'clock P. M., we entered this Wheatfield with 350 rifles, 20 officers and 3 acting as officers, commissioned but not mustered, and became actively engaged with the troops of Hood's division of Longstreet's corps. We moved at double-quick across this Wheatfield under fire, until we gained possession of this stonewall in our front. Our right extended some distance beyond the rivulet, our colors resting on the spot where this monument stands, our left along the wall as far as a large bowlder.

The contest for this wall became very severe along our whole front, the lines of battle being not over one hundred yards apart, and a number of times during the contest the enemy were upon one side while the Seventeenth was upon the other. Winslow's battery, which was located in rear of our left flank, on the ridge up there, did splendid service, and assisted the regiment to drive the enemy back. Shortly after the regiment became engaged, a small command, said to be the rallied portions of two regiments, was brought up in rear of the right flank of the Seventeenth, with the evident intention of placing them in line, connecting on our right ; but while they were yet some seventy-five yards in our rear, the mounted officer leading them fell from his horse, wounded, and these troops disappeared from our sight without delay. Our right flank being unprotected, the enemy attempted to gain our rear, but his movements were discovered, and our right wing was refused to nearly a right angle with this wall. Those of the enemy who attempted to gain our rear were exposed to a murderous fire from our right wing, and they retired. After every repulse the enemy would re-form, bringing up fresh troops and extending his lines for fresh assaults, and so the fight continued along this wall until about 6 o'clock, when we received orders to fall back across this field to the cross road on the ridge, and replenish our ammunition. Our boys left this position, which they had so long and successfully defended, with reluctance, but the enemy had gained ground on both our right and left, and Winslow's battery had been withdrawn. The enemy followed up and attempted to gain our flanks. His movements were noticed, just as we reached the road, by our gallant division commander, Gen. David Bell Birney, who rode up, took the Seventeenth, and led it in a charge. With cheers the regiment, in line of battle, came down this Wheatfield and forced the enemy back over this wall. Although our ammunition was low, the fighting was continuous and of a most deadly character. The loss in officers and men was very severe in this part of the fight. After a contest prolonged until about dusk, our men being in the open field without shelter, but yielding no ground, the regiment was finally relieved by other troops, and was ordered to withdraw from the Wheatfield.

The colors of the regiment, our two flags, had their stand in two places in this field, as the manœuvres of the battle carried the regiment. First, here at the wall, where this monument stands ; later on, after our upheld standards advanced, at the centre of the regimental line, in that glorious charge under Birney, they found their stationary place to be nearly in the centre of this field, about 100 yards east of the woods which yet bounds it on the west. The colors of the regiment, — the national and the state, — our glory and our pride ! emblems of progress and of achievements ! And the Color-Guard ! let us recall our Color-Guard : National Color-Bearer, Corporal Lake of A ; State Color-Bearer, Sergeant Loring of H ; the others were Corporals Saunders of B, Strout of C, Hogan of D, Baker of E, Merrill of F, Huff of G, Mitchell of I and Duncan of K, — ten in all, counting the bearers. The first to be hit was Strout, almost as soon as we reached this wall, — wounded, and left for dead on the field ; here he lay, part of the time unconscious, as the lines and missiles of warfare passed back and forth over him ; at length, on July 4th, to be restored to us, not mortally wounded. Then Baker's turn came, and he lost a portion of his hand; then Mitchell, mortally wounded. And so the guard grew less, the casualties being about equally divided between the two positions. At the second position, Sergeant Loring was instantly killed. The color, crimsoned with the blood of his fallen companion, was seized by Lake, who for a minute held both standards in his grasp, and then handed Loring's over to Corporal Merrill; the latter was wounded, and he in turn passed the color over to Corporal Duncan, who got it safely into bivouac that night. Corporals Huff and Hogan were wounded, the latter mortally; only three of the ten were unscathed. Lake and Duncan were promoted to Sergeants on the field. This is what it meant to belong to the Color-Guard at Gettysburg.

On the morning of July 3d the regiment was moved to the right, and assembled with the division in reserve. It so remained until noon, when we were startled by two signal guns from the Confederate side, which were the prelude to the most terrific cannonading our army ever experienced. For nearly two hours 160 guns sent shot and shell into our ranks, preparatory to Longstreet's assault upon the centre of the Union line. During this artillery duel we received orders to move to the right and reinforce the lines of General Doubleday. Proceeding at double-quick, we were soon at the front in position to aid in repelling the assault generally known as Pickett's charge. The regiment was formed in line supporting the 9th Mich. battery. Throughout the assault the regiment was exposed to a severe artillery fire, and suffered a loss in both officers and men.

At 9 P. M. you were sent to the front to perform picket duty, where you remained for the night. On the morning of the 4th the regiment, relieved from picket, was set to work throwing up earthworks. On the morning of July 5th, the Confederate army was on the retreat, and the battle of Gettysburg was at an end.

The list of casualties in the regiment during the engagements of July 2d and 3d numbered 132 killed and wounded. I deem it appropriate to read this roll of honor. [The killed and mortally wounded appear in the whole nominal list of casualties following the list of " participants," on another page.]

With justice to the memory of those heroes of the Seventeenth Maine who here laid down their lives, defending this
position as if it typified their country ; and speaking for its survivors, sixty of whom, participants in this battle, being now
present and ready to bear witness to the truth, I cannot close
without stating that no circumstance, condition or act occurred
on this Wheatfield July 2, 1863, that would warrant the placing of that monument where it now stands, a few paces to the
west of this of the Seventeenth Maine, as marking a place in
line of battle ; for upon that very spot the ranks of the Seventeenth stood July 2d, and fought from the opening of the contest until nearly 6 o'clock that afternoon.   We protest against
the placing of that monument of the 115th Penn. on that spot,
or within 200 feet of it.   We also protest against the inscription upon that monument which, without justification, recites
that July 2d "this regiment" [115th Penn.] "engaged the
enemy here at 4.30 P. M."

POEM.

THE SEVENTEENTH MAINE IN THE WHEATFIELD.

BY CAPTAIN GEORGE W. VERRILL.

The foe! the foe advances! Mark you now his course,
Straight for the Union left, where half-formed lines are seen.
He aims to hurl his columns with resistless force
Upon and through the Orchard, blushing with its fruit,
The Hillock, slumbering in the shadow of its trees,
Across the Wheatfield, happy with its ripening grain,
Over the crags and pits and sloughs of Devil's Den,
Around and up the steeps of Round Top's rugged sides;
To smite, to pierce and crush, to tear and sweep away,
The slender thread of Blue stretched out to bar his way!

This only done, yea less, for at the Wheatfield's verge
The thread its centre finds;—unchecked even here the surge,
And on and through will pour the torrent of the foe,
To wreck the Union lines, engulf and overthrow.

The foe comes on! and now the Wheatfield bare of troops!
Haste, Birney and de Trobriand! fill up the gap—
This open gateway—quick! or you will be too late!
Even now the skirmish challenge rings through rifle tube,
And spatters of the coming storm fall here and there!
Nearer the Southron comes,—a mighty wave of Gray!
No line of Blue, no Northern breasts his course to stay!

Up now, ye sons of Maine!—in double-quick go in
And fill the gap!—though thin your line, stretch out and fill!—
Ah, none too soon! for even while the bending grain
Still kisses Northern feet that press it as they speed,
The angry Southern missiles clip its nodding plumes!

Stand firm, O Pine Tree Sons;—upon you now is laid
The safety of the whole!—Guard well the Wheatfield gate,
You boys with Diamond Red and " 17 " shining there,
Laughing in face of foe!—Can you be brave as gay?
To stand, though comrades none, on right or left, are nigh?
To stand, till succor comes? If so it chance, to die?

Breaks now the storm! the iron bolts of war fly free!
Mercy affrighted flies to Heaven!—but leaves a wall,—
Blest wall of precious stones, with sparkling jets of fire!—
Fierce flashes gleam; the leaden hail pours in;
Thunder of guns, shrieking of shell, and hissing ball!
Death and Destruction rampant in the sulphurous air;
The Rebel yell, the Union cheer; and face to face
The bayonet!—This is the hour that calls for manhood's best!

And is the Seventeenth Maine still there?—It wavers not;
Its colors still, though rent in shreds, defiant float.
Its veterans firm! the earth beneath them quakes with dread!
Hearts strong, nerves tempered in the flame of battle, theirs;
Their true aim reaps its harvest; death and crippling wounds
They deal to foe. But what they give, they take.
Alas! by ones and tens our noble lads go down.
The weeping grain wraps its soft mantle round the slain,
And tenderly supports the wounded on its breast.

No succor yet!—and thin and thinner are the ranks,
And fast the lessening store of cartridge goes—
No aid! though eager thousands wait the word to come!—
But more the honor due, as aid is less, in strife.

Still there, our boys! Though foiled, recoiling from the shock,
The foe, persistent, gathers up his scattered strength,
Compact, full four to one, determined now to gain
The field still firmly held by sturdy boys from Maine!
Still held as if each stalk of grain with life-blood red,
Were precious as the living hearts this life-blood shed.

Again the yell! More withering now the battle blast!
Lead to the tender flesh, iron to the brittle bone!
Foes at the front charge in, and from the left and right
Focus their fury here;—rages and roars the fight!

By ones and tens and scores our best and bravest fall,
Yet still undaunted there the rest!—Secession's wave
Breaks on the Northern rocks! Disaster here is curbed

In mid career!—hurled back the foe!—the Wheatfield saved!—
Your duty done, O Seventeenth! here come two lines of Blue
To guard and keep the ground, thus long hours held by you,
The red-stained Wheatfield at immortal Gettysburg!

Upon the spot where these men fought, to manhood true,
Raise high the granite shaft, nor art nor treasure spare,
To evidence, in lasting stone, the honor due
To them, who battled thus, for love of country there;—
And register the debt of gratitude, anew.

ORATION.

BY BREVET BRIGADIER-GENERAL WILLIAM HOBSON.

Comrades and Fellow Citizens :

If a stranger from foreign lands should finish his inspection of our famous battlefields of the late war by a visit to Gettysburg, he might ask why this only of those many fields is covered with monuments of various designs, but all tasteful and elegant, and why this field in special manner is the Mecca of pilgrimage to all lovers of our Constitution and Union. The answer is not far to seek. The battle of Gettysburg enjoys a distinction which cannot be accorded to any other of the great conflicts of which the history of the war is full. It has been well said that it marks the high water of the tide of rebellion. The waves of fire which surged around these heights on the first three days of July, 1863, ever after receded until they sank into an eternal calm at Appomattox. Again, it was the only battle of magnitude which was fought on distinctively free soil, never again to be vexed by the tread of hostile armies. It was fought, too, at a point not far distant, at that time, from the centre of population of the United States, and at a time not far away from the middle of the four years' conflict. All previous battles led up to Gettysburg; all subsequent battles led away from it.

Still further, the fighting of the battle at this point was not the work of human design. Neither General Meade nor General Lee had the least intention or idea of making this the scene of conflict. As the meeting in the summer sky of two little clouds differently charged with electricity calls in all the neighboring forces of nature on either side until earth and heaven resound with the roar of nature's artillery, so the accidental meeting on the first day of July, 1863, of Buford's cavalry with the forces of the enemy naturally and irresistibly drew to the conflict on both sides all the powers of the opposing armies.

As to no General belongs the credit of causing the battle to be fought here, so to no one in particular more than another belongs the credit of conducting it to a successful issue. General Reynolds' orders on the first of July were not to bring on a general engagement. He did not know when he moved to Buford's assistance that he was bringing on a general engagement, and, unfortunately for him and his country, he never knew it. Whether, if he had known it, he would have done differently, we never learned from him. This much we do know, that he was not a man to march away from the sound of the enemy's guns, or to remain quiet when his comrades needed his assistance.

To General Howard, when he arrived upon the field, a serious problem was presented, the preservation of the shattered remnants of Reynolds' corps, and the selection of a position where that corps, united with his own, could make a stand against the forces of the rebels already flushed with victory. His keen, practised military eye rested upon Cemetery Hill, and to him belongs the credit of first placing our forces in position there. The arrival of the Twelfth corps, which was stationed on his right on Culp's Hill and Rock Creek, the arrival of the Third corps which was put in position on his left, only later to be moved further to the left to let its first position be occupied by the Second corps, put our army in array for the movements of the second day.

Of those movements it is hardly necessary to say to any one who is at all conversant with strategy, and has studied the topography of the country, that the action of Major-General Sickles, our gallant and beloved corps commander, in advancing a portion of his forces to the Emmitsburg road, and there meeting the first brunt of the rebel attack, was the salvation of our army in that second day's fight. It shattered their lines in the first onset; it retarded their advance, and when they finally swung around and met our obstinate resistance here, in the Wheatfield, and that of the 124th N. Y., the Fourth Maine, the 40th N. Y. and other regiments on our left, by the "Devil's Den" and in the "Valley of Death," time had been gained for the Fifth corps to come up, hold and successfully defend the "Round Tops" and other points on our left. If Sickles had formed his line on the prolongation of the line of the Second corps, in the depression of the land which you see, and had there awaited the rebel attack, with their outnumbering forces they would have gained possession of the "Round Tops," and our left flank would have been irretrievably turned. So, too, is due to the gallant and accomplished General Warren the credit of seeing the strategic importance of the "Round Tops," and of ordering them to be occupied by the Fifth corps, which, after as brave and desperate fighting as was ever seen on any field, completed the repulse of the rebels on our left. On our right, the morning of the 3d, by attacking and driving back Ewell's corps, General Slocum made amends for his still unexplained failure to come to the help of Reynolds and Howard on the afternoon of the 1st, while General Hancock's magnificent repulse of Pickett's charge in the afternoon is too well known to need praise or comment here. Each of these general officers, with the possible exception hinted at, did the right thing at the right time. Together, but not simultaneously, they forged a chain of defense in which the breaking of any link would have been disastrous to the Union cause.

As to no general officer belongs the special credit for what was accomplished here, so no particular corps, division, brigade or regiment can claim precedence of its fellows in contributing to the successful result. There was, probably, no battle in the war where the fighting was more evenly distributed among the troops engaged. With the exception of the Sixth corps, which, through no fault of its own, did not arrive on the field until late in the afternoon of the second day, and was only partially engaged on our left, every corps in all its parts was actively engaged at some period of the battle, as the official reports of losses show. It is worthy of note, too, in the light of the subsequent history of the war, that this battle was fought entirely by troops who had voluntarily enlisted for the defense of their country. No conscript nor bounty jumper aimed here his unwilling musket at his country's foes. The cohorts of the lame, the halt, the deaf, the blind, and the aged, with their gray hair dyed to the semblance of youth, who, from the following fall to the close of the war, filled our ambulances and hospitals, and obstructed the prosecution of the war, had not then made their appearance. The rapacious and unscrupulous recruiting officer had not then sent forward his levies from the slums of the cities and the jails of the counties. None of these can claim any share in this glorious victory. It was won by men who had a personal interest in the issue, who knew what that interest was, and were willing to risk their lives for the success of the cause for which they fought. For this reason, and because they recognized the supreme importance of the crisis, I think there was no battle in the war where it was so little necessary for officers to look out for, or watch over, their men. Every man was an officer to himself. So it can be said, in all truth, and must be said that to the humblest rear rank private, who fought here, is due as much honor and reverence for what he did, as even to the commander-in-chief.

In addition to the special characteristics of the battle heretofore mentioned, it may also be said that, if we consider the extent of territory covered by the conflict, the number of troops engaged, the proportion of losses to the number engaged in the action, the length of time the contest continued, the skill and bravery and even the desperation shown on both sides, and last and greatest of all, the magnitude of the issues involved, it must be reckoned as one of the greatest and most important battles ever fought upon the face of the globe. I said the magnitude of the issues involved. The other elements to be considered can be weighed with almost mathematical accuracy, but no human scales can determine the weight and value of the victory at Gettysburg. Fortunately for us, fortunately for the world, we shall never know what the result would have been if victory had perched on the other banners. We only know that the hands on the dial which mark the progress of civilization would have been turned back for an indefinite period.

The history of that one word, civilization, in its primary and derived meanings, would give a more complete idea of the world's progress than all the histories that have ever been written. In its primary, active sense it denotes simply the making a man a citizen. In its later, derived and passive sense it includes all those advances and improvements in the arts, sciences, literature and morals which entitle a nation to call itself civilized. That word civilized has no synonyms, nor does it need any. You all know what it means.

Now, I undertake to say, that there is a logical and historical connection between the active and the passive sense of this word; that in all ages and in all nations the development and advance of what we call civilization, in its ordinary sense, has been in direct ratio to the exercises of the rights, duties and powers of a citizen on the part of all the inhabitants of the different nations. And as, in a democracy only, does a citizen obtain the full exercise of his rights, duties and powers, so only in a democracy can be found the highest development of civilization.

All the forms of government which have ever existed may be brought under one of three classes, a theocracy, an aristocracy, or a democracy. Of these three forms theocracy is suited to man's lowest, and democracy to his highest, development. The failure of the republics of Greece and Rome was owing to the fact that they did not recognize the vital principles of democracy, the equality of all people before the law. They undertook to reconcile liberty and slavery under the same form of government, a mistake which must always prove fatal to a democracy. It was the same mistake which came so near proving fatal to our form of government, and which culminated in the war of the rebellion. The founders of our government saw this danger, and, if they had forecast the future, would undoubtedly have made the abolition of slavery one of the conditions of the formation of the Federal Union. They knew perfectly well, from the logic of ethics and from the lessons of history, that liberty and slavery could not co-exist for any length of time under the same form of government. But the necessity of superseding the old confederation, which was a mere rope of sand, by a Union which should create a Nation, and the fact that slavery was dying out from natural causes, and at that time bade fair to be eliminated before many years, led to a compromise in the formation of the Constitution which flatly contradicted the first clause of the Declaration of Independence, the foundation principle of the Revolutionary struggle, by recognizing the institution of slavery, and throwing certain safeguards around it, without even mentioning the word slave.

It is needless to recount how the hopes and expectations of the founders of the Constitution were disappointed. The history of the country from 1789 to 1861 is familiar to you all, as also that slavery, from being regarded as an institution merely to be tolerated for a limited time, came to claim, and did actually obtain, a dominant influence in national politics, as a matter of right. The history of the compromise in the formation of the Constitution was the same as the history of all compromises between right and wrong. It merely postponed the evil day. Wrong intrenched itself, and only made it more difficult for right to prevail, when it was finally forced to the conflict, as it always must be.

The inevitable tendency of the existence of slavery, in the midst of institutions otherwise free, had not been unobserved. More than fifty years ago, De Tocqueville, the eminent French statesman, visited this country and spent two years in the careful study of the working of our institutions. He seems to have been the only foreigner who ever thoroughly understood them, and in his famous book, "Democracy in America," published after his return, he pointed out slavery as the chief source of our danger, and foretold the troubles to which it would give rise. He could only foretell, however, nor could any one prevent. Moral laws work as certainly and as remorselessly in the domain of politics as do the laws which govern the operations of nature.

"Mute thought has a sonorous echo," says an eminent French writer. He might have added that the reverberations of the echo are proportioned to the moral power of the thought. The thunders of the artillery at Gettysburg, louder than had ever before been heard on an open field of battle, were the echoes of the preamble to the Declaration of Independence. They proclaimed that none but free men should live in a free country, and that they all should have equal rights and power under the laws. Only in this way can a free government exist, as the framers and signers of the Declaration well understood. The war of the rebellion was, then, a contest on the part of the government for self-preservation, a duty as incumbent on a democracy as upon an individual.

The nation had shown its power to resist foreign foes; would it be able to overcome those of its own household? Should the balance between the centripetal and centrifugal forces, under which it had been intended that the members of our political system should move in harmony around a common centre, be disturbed, and these members be allowed to drift off into space at their own will, perhaps hereafter to be constantly coming into collision with one another? These questions were decisively answered at Gettysburg. The end did not come then, but it was made certain. No rational person doubted the outcome after Gettysburg. The red-handed perjurer and usurper who then sat on the throne of France, waiting and wishing and plotting, but not daring to interpose for the destruction of a government which his own nation had helped to establish, concealed more carefully, if he did not cease, his machinations. The tories of England, the enemies of everybody but themselves, confined their assistance to the Confederates to such acts as could not be made the pretext for war. Thenceforward to a much greater extent than before, the sympathies and the moral support of the civilized world were on the side of the Union. The battle of Gettysburg had shown the possibility and the probability, ay, the certainty, of the fulfillment of Bishop Berkeley's famous prophecy:

> "Westward the course of empire takes its way,
>   The four first acts already past;
> A fifth shall close the drama with the day,
>   Time's noblest offspring is the last."

The fulfillment of this prophecy will result from the lessons taught by the war, lessons which ought to be self-evident, that a democratic form of government can be permanent only when all men living within it have equal rights under the laws, and have sufficient intelligence and moral sense to exercise those rights and discharge the duties arising from them. The government being under obligation to prolong its own existence, as the expressed wish of the people, has the right and the power to enforce the performance of these conditions. An education sufficient to enable a man to transact the ordinary business of life, which shall include those principles of morals which underlie all religions, should be made compulsory upon those who hereafter may aspire to the privilege of suffrage. Intelligence and morality are the foundation of republican institutions. Beyond that every man may safely exercise his own belief, be he heathen or Christian, Hebrew or Mohammedan, or, to speak in a paradox, even have no religious belief at all. Recent developments seem to make plain also that it is the duty of the government in the exercise of the instinct of self-preservation to prevent the immigration of those misguided people who are hostile to all forms of government. Their belief may be due to the unfortunate conditions under which they were born and bred in foreign lands, but it is clearly not the duty of this country to harbor those who confess allegiance to none.

In considering the supreme importance of the victory at Gettysburg, I could not help making these suggestions. They seem naturally to arise from the subject. They might be expanded into volumes, but I can trust the common sense of this audience to take them and work them out to their proper conclusion.

One more peculiarity of the victory at Gettysburg, considered as the turning point of the war. Although only twenty-five years have elapsed, yet already, both victors and vanquished unite in expressions of satisfaction at the result. Nowhere else in the past history of the world can this be paralleled. It was hundreds of years after the conquest of England by William the Conqueror before Anglo Saxon and Norman grew together into a homogeneous nation, and the Frenchman of to-day has still an antipathy to "perfidious Albin," because it humbled the eagles of Napoleon at Waterloo. This heretofore has always been the case between conquerors and conquered. Family quarrels have ever been proverbial for their bitterness, and this was bitter enough while it lasted. The era of fraternal feelings between north and south, which has already arrived, is an auspicious omen for the future.

And here let me say, we could take no credit for what we did on this field if we had not been confronted by men as brave as ourselves. I saw the famous charge of Pickett's division on the third day. A more magnificent sight I never saw than when, after forming, they advanced across the fields towards the Emmitsburg road. I have read the history of many famous charges, but never of one that marched so far and so steadily into the very jaws of hell. No straggling, no falling out, except by those disabled by our merciless fire, they advanced till further advance was an impossibility. As the Seventeenth Maine lay on picket that night on the ground over which they advanced, and I saw, the next morning, eight or ten files front lying on their faces, side by side, as evenly as if placed by hand, where our canister had swept through them, ending their forward movement and their lives at the same time, I realized more than ever the horrors of war and the bravery of the men we had been fighting.

So, with all honor to the men we fought here, and with no desire for self-laudation, we have come to dedicate this monument, set up in the interest of history to mark the spot where the Seventeenth Maine regiment, the first in the famous "Wheatfield," the "Whirlpool," as it has been aptly called, did its duty to the best of its ability. We should be doing injustice to them and to ourselves did not those monuments do honor also to the brave men who here gave up their lives. The pathetic and eloquent words of our martyred President, chiseled upon the stone in yonder cemetery, immortal as the deeds they commemorate, will never be equalled; but it is a question whether those who die for their country, even as he also died, are not rather to be congratulated. "*Dulce et decorum est pro patria mori,*" "It is pleasant and honorable to die for one's country," said the Latin poet, 2,000 years ago, and modern sentiment echoes his words:

> "Come to the bridal chamber, death!
> Come to the mother when she feels,
> For the first time, her first-born's breath;
> Come when the blessed seals
> That close the pestilence are broke,
> And crowded cities wail its stroke;
> Come in consumption's ghastly form,
> The earthquake shock, the ocean storm;

Come where the heart beats high and warm,
With banquet song, and dance, and wine;
And thou art terrible—the tear,
The groan, the knell, the pall, the bier,
And all we know, or dream, or fear,
Of agony are thine.

" But to the hero, when his sword
Has won the battle for the free,
Thy voice sounds like a prophet's word,
And in its hollow tones are heard
The thanks of millions yet to be.''

After the oration was concluded remarks were made by Colonel Bachelder, in which he highly complimented the Seventeenth regiment.

Brevet Brig.-Gen. George W. West, formerly Major and Colonel of the Seventeenth, also made a few remarks, describing the movements of the regiment in the Wheatfield, and his great gratification that this worthy memorial had been erected to commemorate the services of those who fell here, and likewise of those who survived.

Lieutenant-Colonel Merrill, the representative of the Seventeenth as one of the Maine Commissioners, sent a letter of regret that illness prevented his attendance.

The monument was then turned over to the Gettysburg Memorial Association by Colonel Moore, to be cared for until such time as the State of Maine should present this and the monuments of the other organizations in a more formal manner.

HISTORICAL SKETCH.

BY CAPTAIN GEORGE W. VERRILL.

(NECROLOGIST OF SEVENTEETH MAINE REGIMENT ASSOCIATION.)

The Seventeenth Maine Regiment of Volunteers was raised by voluntary enlistments under President Lincoln's call of July 2, 1862, for three hundred thousand for three years' service. Those in the most western part of the state naturally gravitated to an appointed rendezvous at Portland, Me. The ranks were full and overflowing within about thirty days after the proclamation went forth. The following counties contributed to make up the thousand strong which formed the organization :

Androscoggin, 152 ; Cumberland, 398 ; Franklin, 84 ; Kennebec, 6 ; Knox, 17 ; Oxford, 168 ; Sagadahoc, 2 ; Somerset, 3 ; York, 178 ; Aroostook, Lincoln, Penobscot and Piscataquis, 1 each ; 7 were residents of other states and 3 out of the country.

Few had seen service ; some had belonged to military companies. All were anxious to learn and the "awkward squad" was apparent about "Camp King," our rendezvous, across Fore River from Portland. Some of the officers had been selected in advance—Thomas A. Roberts, for our Colonel, had been Captain of an independent military company of Portland; his son, Charles W., a Lieutenant serving in the Tenth Maine, for our Adjutant. We were also fortunate in securing Captain George Warren West from the Tenth Maine, for our Major, a strict disciplinarian and a thorough military man. Charles B. Merrill, a lawyer of Portland, for our Lieutenant-Colonel; his patriotic fervor impelled him into the service. As was customary, the line officers were mostly selected in recognition of recruiting services. By the time the regiment was mustered into the United States service it could perform some simple evolutions ; with its long line formed in dress parade it greatly edified the ladies who graciously attended the function. The muster-in occurred August 18, 1862. The following was the original organization :—

FIELD, STAFF, AND NON-COMMISSIONED STAFF.

Colonel, Thomas A. Roberts, Portland.
Lieutenant-Colonel, Charles B. Merrill, Portland.
Major, George W. West, Somerville, Mass.
Adjutant, First Lieutenant Charles W. Roberts, Portland.
Quartermaster, J. T. Waterhouse, Portland.
Surgeon, H. L. K. Wiggin, Auburn.
Assistant Surgeon, William Wescott, Standish.
Chaplain, Harvey Hersey, Calais, Vt.

Sergeant-Major, Henry L. Bartels, Portland.
Quartermaster-Sergeant, Charles W. Richardson, Portland.
Commissary-Sergeant, Josiah Remick, Portland.
Hospital Steward, Nathaniel B. Coleman, Portland.
Drum-Major, John C. McArdle, Paris.

COMPANY OFFICERS.

Co. A.   Captain, William H. Savage, Portland.
First Lieutenant, Charles P. Mattocks, Portland.
Second Lieutenant, James M. Brown, Portland.

Co. B.   Captain, George W. Martin, Portland.
First Lieutenant, Willard M. Jenkins, Fryeburg.
Second Lieutenant, Benjamin C. Pennell, Portland.
Co. C.   Captain, Augustus Goldermann, Minot.
First Lieutenant, Otho W. Burnham, Poland.
Second Lieutenant, Joseph A. Perry, Portland.
Co. D.   Captain, Isaac S. Faunce, Lewiston.
First Lieutenant, Milton M. Young, Lewiston.
Second Lieutenant, John C. Perry, Portland.
Co. E.   Captain, Ellis M. Sawyer, Cape Elizabeth.
First Lieutenant, George W. S. Fickett, Cape Elizabeth.
Second Lieutenant, William Roberts, Yarmouth.
Co. F.   Captain, Albion Hersey, Paris.
First Lieutenant, Uriah W. Briggs, Norway.
Second Lieutenant, James M. Safford, Portland.
Co. G.   Captain, Edward I. Merrill, Farmington.
First Lieutenant, Benjamin G. Ames, Phillips.
Second Lieutenant, Prescott Newman, Phillips.
Co. H.   Captain, Almon L. Fogg, Westbrook.
First Lieutenant, Dudley H. Johnson, Presque Isle.
Second Lieutenant, Edward Moore, Portland.
Co. I.   Captain, William Hobson, Saco.
First Lieutenant, Putnam S. Boothby, Biddeford.
Second Lieutenant, James O. Thompson, Portland.
Co. K.   Captain, Andrew J. Stinson, Kittery.
First Lieutenant, John P. Swasey, Canton.
Second Lieutenant, Madison K. Mabry, Hiram.

The new regiment made a brave show when on August 21st it broke camp, marched through the streets of Portland lined with enthusiastic people, and started south " for three years or the war." We journeyed to Washington by rail and boat without interruption or accident, except the shock occasioned by finding ourselves packed into box cars at Baltimore instead of ordinary passenger cars as previously. We survived the shock, however, as we did many others afterwards, common to a soldier's life. August 23d relieved the 9th R. I. in a line of forts on east branch of the Potomac, running up from the main river. The situation was admirable,—an ideal camping ground. Sickness, however, incident to change of climate, prevailed. We drilled with the heavy ordnance, as well as in infantry tactics. While we were here the battles of Second Bull Run and Antietam both occurred. The boom of cannon and steady roll of small arms in both engagements were plainly heard, although in a direct line they were distant from us thirty-five and fifty miles respectively.

JOINING THE ARMY. — October 7th we bade adieu to fort life to join the Army of the Potomac in the field. On the capitol steps we rested three hours before crossing Long bridge. Our course was up the Potomac. At Upton's Hill joined Berry's brigade, Birney's (First) division, Third corps. The brigade was then composed of 1st, 37th, 55th N. Y., 2d, 5th Mich. and Seventeenth Maine, regiments. The square, red patch marking Kearny's men was proudly worn by the veterans. Raw troops were not allowed them until proof of worthiness in battle was shown.

October 11th crossed into Maryland over Chain bridge, and arrived two days later near Edward's Ferry, where we remained picketing the river and canal until October 28th. Our regiment had not been supplied with tents or "shelter pieces" until October 26th, although the weather all along was cold and rainy. The hardships endured thus far doubtless lessened the effective strength of the regiment by more than 100 men, equivalent to a large battle loss, many being permanently used up. Thus we became soldiers. A remaining badge of our rawness, however, was the knapsack, bloated with relics of a past refinement, weighing from twenty pounds upwards. The knapsack became obsolete in our division in the 1864 campaign.

October 28th forded the Potomac at White's Ford, where the river was waist-deep and about one-third mile wide. The army, under McClellan, moved along the foot-hills, keeping pace with Lee, who moved up the Shenandoah valley beyond the Blue Ridge. We marched via Middleburg, White Plains and Salem to Waterloo on the north fork of the Rappahannock, and we remained in this vicinity several days, during which time Burnside succeeded McClellan in command of the army. Here a new plan of operations was made, with Falmouth, on the Rappahannock, as a point for concentration. Accordingly, on November 16th the march began ; on the 22d we went into camp around Falmouth. The time in camp was fully occupied in drills, inspections and ineffectual attempts to keep comfortable and in health, during a very cold spell in a bleak situation, until December 11th.

BATTLE OF FREDERICKSBURG. — Early on December 11th the regiment, under Col. Thomas A. Roberts, numbering 628 men and officers, broke camp and marched towards Fredericksburg, remaining on the north side of the river that night. Next morning we moved down the river to the left of our lines. Crossed the Rappahannock on Saturday, December 13th, at noon, on a pontoon bridge, and marched to our allotted place under shelling from the enemy's guns.   Soon the enemy made an advance of infantry to turn Birney's left or seize his batteries posted in our front.   To repel this attack General Berry threw out the Seventeenth to the left of the batteries in line of battle, speedily checking the onset with a few rounds.   We lay on the field subjected to frequent shelling until our army retired on the night of December 15th.   Our loss was three killed and mortally wounded, and seventeen wounded.

Next day returned to our camp, when General Birney declared in orders that the new regiments had shown themselves "fully worthy of the 'Red Patch,' and I, in the name of the division, acknowledge them as members in full standing." General Berry also complimented the Seventeenth in his official report.   Nevertheless, there was a feeling of disappointment in the air ; visions of valiant deeds and fierce personal encounters faded unrealized.   A soldier appreciates his individuality never so much as in his first battle.   The regiment changed camp ground twice during the succeeding inactivity of the army.

January 20, 1863, Burnside's second campaign began.   His general order was read to each regiment announcing that we "were about to meet the enemy again."   Fortified with this assurance we started out, and at night brought up at Scott's Mill, near the Rappahannock, where we went into bivouac without any fires or loud sounds, for it was intended to surprise the enemy, and next morning our brigade was to lead and force the crossing.   With this pleasing anticipation, and a drizzling rain, and no coffee, we slept the sleep of the just.   The rain continued, and it is matter of history that we did not meet the enemy ; but we could read the derisive placard of the Johnnies across the river :   " Stuck in the mud."

General Hooker succeeded Burnside January 26th in command of the army. Improvement in rations and morale followed the change. We lost General Berry by his promotion to Major-General and command of the Second division of our corps.

Before the spring campaign opened many deaths occurred, and many were discharged for "disability," including several officers who resigned. Promotions followed, to fill vacancies, and the Seventeenth was "boiled down," well-seasoned and proficient in drill.

THE CEDARS AND CHANCELLORSVILLE. — April 28th the Third corps, under General Sickles, moved down the river as a feint ; thence on the 30th we marched rapidly up river, in a tortuous course, to United States Ford, arriving after midnight, and crossed the river early on May 1st. The men carried on the person eight days' rations and sixty rounds of ammunition. May 1st the regiment numbered nearly 500, rank and file, under command of Lieut.-Colonel Merrill (Colonel Roberts being absent on sick leave). The brigade was under Colonel Hayman, a regular army officer. The day passed in manœuvring, and that night we lay upon the Plank Road, connecting to left of Eleventh corps. May 2d Sickles pushed forward several miles on a reconnaissance in force ; a lively and successful skirmish with the enemy ensued until sundown, taking prisoners. At dusk word came of the crushing attack of Jackson upon the Eleventh corps, reporting the latter to be destroyed, and that we were cut off by Jackson from the rest of our army. We silently and gloomily retraced our steps to Hazel Grove, an open plateau about a half mile from the Chancellor House. From this plateau our division made a night attack, known as the "midnight charge," upon Jackson's troops lying between us and the Plank road. The operations of Sickles' corps May 2d were known as the battle of The Cedars. Stonewall Jackson was mortally wounded in the evening, and this great loss to the Confederate cause is directly traceable to General Sickles' operations. Sunday, May 3d, about 5 o'clock, General Stuart, who succeeded Jackson, resumed the battle, the weight of it falling upon Sickles' corps and a division of the Twelfth, the Eleventh corps infantry having been re-formed near the river. The battle raged furiously and incessantly until about noon. The

Seventeenth, with its brigade, was placed south of the Chancellor House, in an advanced position, lying flat on the ground, supporting a battery, when the onslaught was made. The enemy's artillery played upon and over us from many cannon at Hazel Grove, and our own artillery fired over us in reply. Musketry fire from two directions also came into us from beyond our infantry lines. The enemy at one time broke through in front, and came for the battery. Our brigade at once, under the lead of General Birney, made a counter-charge, putting them to rout and taking a batch of prisoners. We then took up a new position, as the battery was withdrawn. The Seventeenth was the last infantry to go from the field south of the Chancellor House. Later in the day it was placed in a line of works at the White House. Except by heavy shelling we were not greatly molested there. At 4 P. M. our brigade was advanced outside the breastworks, prepared to charge if the enemy broke our skirmish line in the woods ; but the battle in that vicinity was over.

May 5th Colonel Roberts returned. May 6th we recrossed the river, our division being the last withdrawn from the front lines, and thence returned to our camp, as likewise did all others to their own. The loss in the Seventeenth in this battle was : killed and mortally wounded, 1 officer (1st Lieut. Dudley H. Johnson) and 10 enlisted men ; wounded, 5 officers (Capt. Augustus Goldermann, acting as field officer, Capt. Edward I. Merrill, 1st Lieuts. James M. Brown, Putnam S. Boothby ; 2d Lieut. Thomas W. Lord) and 54 men ; also 41 taken prisoners. Total, 111.

June 11th broke camp and began the march northward which culminated in the battle of Gettysburg, our route taking us to Manassas Junction, Centreville and Gum Springs, Va., from thence, on June 25th, to the Potomac, which we crossed at Edwards Ferry, on a pontoon bridge, continuing along the canal towpath to the Monocacy, where we bivouacked for the night. This day's march of thirty miles was the highest record of the regiment. Next day proceeded to Point of Rocks ; thence to Jefferson Village, Middletown, Frederick City, Taneytown, Emmitsburg and Gettysburg. The regiment took an active part in the battle of Gettysburg ; engaged in the Wheatfield

July 2d for two hours and a half; July 3d supported Daniel's 9th Mich. battery, under severe shelling. A narration of this battle is given on another page, with an account of our losses.

In the pursuit of Lee's army after Gettysburg the Third corps started from the field July 7th. The regiment was reduced, through casualties and sickness, to about 150 men. The march was through Emmitsburg, Frederick City, Middletown and South Mountain Pass, reaching Antietam battlefield on the 10th. The enemy made a stand, covering Williamsport, which nearly paralyzed Meade, and caused a halt. It was a question whether to attack or not. The rank and file were eager to pitch in, but uncertainty or timidity at headquarters lasted several days, during which time Lee decamped across the Potomac into the Shenandoah Valley.

Our army crossed the river on the 17th and marched on east side of Blue Ridge, reaching Manassas Gap July 22d.

WAPPING HEIGHTS. — July 23d we ran into the rear guard of Lee. The Seventeenth was in the second line, supporting the skirmishers. Our only casualty was the mortal wounding of Sergt.-Major Fred W. Bosworth by a shell.

Resuming the march the army passed through Salem and Warrenton, and on July 31st went into camp at Sulphur Springs, on the north fork of the Rappahannock. The Confederate army encamped beyond Culpeper; ours around Warrenton. Both settled down to rest and recuperate. To fill our ranks three officers, Capt. Charles P. Mattocks, Lieuts. J. A. Perry and W. H. Green, with a recruiting squad, had been sent to Portland for recruits July 24th.

September 15th our army advanced down to Culpeper; September 23d we received 160 recruits from Maine. They proved to be of good material. October 11th General Lee took the bit in his teeth. Very adroitly deceiving Meade, he got a good start upon the right flank of the latter, and a complicated race began for Centreville or some intermediate point.

AUBURN. — In a blind fashion both Union and Confederate columns occasionally attempted to march on the same road at the same time. This occurred on October 13th, when Stuart's cavalry got upon our road at Auburn on Cedar Run. Our brigade ran into a brigade of this cavalry and a brisk skirmish ensued for a couple of hours, engaging both arms of the service. The enemy was routed, leaving his dead and some prisoners and horses behind. The Seventeenth had one man wounded and three missing. This astounding retrograde movement ended when our troops reached Fairfax Court House on the 15th of October. Lee did not attack our forces, but spent a couple of days destroying the railroad track. On the 19th he disappeared, and Meade moved forward. Our division went into camp near Catlett's. Maj. George W. West, having been commissioned as Colonel, was mustered to that grade October 22d, and assumed command of the regiment, which had now acquired a strength of about 375, rank and file.

KELLY'S FORD.—November 7th our army advanced across the Rappahannock, the Seventeenth crossing at Kelly's Ford where, behind works, some resistance was made and a few hundred prisoners secured who appeared glad to be taken in out of the cold. Next day pushed forward in line of battle to Brandy Station, from which our southern neighbors fled at our approach. We prepared comfortable quarters and enjoyed them until Meade, doubtless remembering the ides of October, attempted a counter-stroke upon Lee's right, beyond the Rapidan.

LOCUST GROVE AND MINE RUN.—We crossed the Rapidan at Jacob's Ford in the evening of November 26th, and stopped for the night about a mile farther on. Next day, November 27th, the Third division took the lead and struck the enemy. Our (First) division moved forward, formed, and was held in support. Those in front gave way. Advancing in line beyond these men, new to battle, we met the enemy, and a fierce musketry conflict ensued, until every round of our ammunition was expended. Just at this moment a brigade of the Sixth corps (in which was the Sixth Maine regiment) came up, moved beyond our right flank, turned that of the enemy, gave him some volleys routing him, and the field was ours. This action occurred at a villa called Locust Grove. This stand-up fight caused us a grievous loss, inflicted unnecessarily through the incompetency or recklessness of some officer, superior to the regimental, who directed the Seventeenth to take the place of

the regiment it relieved ; thus bringing the line of the regiment
nearly perpendicular to, and in front of, that of the enemy,
who, at short range, made great havoc with our right companies, while the left of the regiment was untouched.   Our loss
was : killed or mortally wounded, eleven, of whom were Capt.
Ellis M. Sawyer (acting as Major) and 1st Lieut. James M.
Brown ; and thirty-nine wounded, of whom was 1st Lieut. F.
A. Sawyer.   Our picket, under Lieut. W. H. Green, scooped
in about a dozen prisoners the next morning.

On the 28th we moved some miles and came to our general
line, confronting the enemy posted and waiting for us on the
heights, in his works, beyond the Mine Run, a stream of some
width but generally fordable.   Remained here the 29th and
30th ready to assault the works, which were of a most formidable character, at sound of a signal gun.   We formed on both
days to make this hopeless sacrifice, momentarily expecting the
signal to advance.   It did not sound, and the enterprise was
abandoned.   We marched all night, from dusk to sunrise, and
recrossed the river without molestation ; many stragglers
doubtless fell into the enemy's hands.   We lost one, taken
prisoner.   Returned to encampment at Brandy Station and
went into winter quarters.

A new stand of colors, in silk, National and State, with
eagles, presented by the merchants of Portland to the Seventeenth, was received February 22d.   These were safely borne
through the campaigns of 1864.   March 24th the unwelcome
order of consolidation was received.   The Third corps was
merged into the Second, under command of General Hancock ;
the First and Second divisions becoming the Third and Fourth
divisions of the Second corps.   General Birney retained command of our division.   The veterans of the Third corps
retained their diamond patches.   Brigades were also consolidated.   Ours, to be commanded by Gen. Alexander Hays,
thus became the Second brigade of Third division, Second
corps, and was composed of the Fourth and Seventeenth Maine,
3d and 5th Mich., 63d, 57th and 105th Penn., 93d N. Y. and
1st U. S. Sharpshooters.

Lieutenant-General Grant joined the army in April.   We

vacated the winter huts on the 26th of that month, encamping in shelter tents in open fields. We lay here until the general movement began on May 3d.

GRANT'S CAMPAIGN. — The Seventeenth Maine began this campaign with 21 officers, 5 acting officers (commissioned but not mustered) and 439 enlisted men in the ranks. The officers were : Colonel, George W. West ; Captains, John C. Perry (acting as Field officer), Joseph A. Perry, Benjamin C. Pennell, William H. Green, Isaac S. Faunce, Sumner S. Richards, George W. Verrill ; First Lieutenants, Frederick A. Sawyer, John N. Morrill, James S. Roberts, Grenville F. Sparrow, George A. Whidden, Henry L. Bartels, Wellington Hobbs ; Second Lieutenants, Stephen Graffam, Franklin C. Adams, Gustavus C. Pratt, Robert H. Mathes, William H. Sturgis, Benjamin Doe. Acting officers : Sergeant-Major, Edward H. Crie ; Sergeants, Charles C. Cole, Jordan M. Hall, Joseph S. Hobbs, and Newton W. Parker. In addition to these the following combatant officers of the regiment were on detailed duty in the division : Maj. Charles P. Mattocks, commanding 1st U. S. Sharpshooters ; Capt. Edwin B. Houghton, acting A. I. G. on First brigade staff ; Second Lieut. Walter F. Noyes, commanding brigade pioneers (these went into action).

Taking up the line of march at midnight, May 3d, we crossed the Rapidan on morning of the 4th at Ely's Ford ; proceeded thence to the battle ground of Chancellorsville, remaining there during the day and night.

BATTLE OF THE WILDERNESS.—May 5, 1864, marched and reached Todd's Tavern about noon. The enemy—Hill's corps —having struck the Sixth corps, marching on the Brock road, we were turned upon that road and marched northward to the point where it crosses the Orange Plank road. The Seventeenth was on the right of the Second corps. About 4 P. M. we advanced in line of battle, parallel with the Brock road through thick undergrowth, until we felt the enemy. In an unsuccessful effort to find connections upon our right, as ordered, the regiment became separated from the troops on our left, but advanced upon Hill and forced him back at his left flank, after a fierce stand-up fight, lasting until dark, taking about thirty prisoners.

May 6th, at 5 o'clock A. M., in the same formation, we advanced again, in a general attack in line of battle, capturing a line of breastworks, routing the enemy and driving him before us a mile and a half. The Seventeenth and Fourth Maine, side by side, pushing forward, had become the point of a wedge, well driven through the enemy's lines. Arriving at an opening, crossed by the Plank road, we halted under a sharp infantry fire, and that of a couple of unfriendly field pieces, for our connections to come up. The broken lines of the enemy on our right rear, finding we had outflanked them, retreated in a mob, hundreds of them falling into our hands as prisoners, whom we directed to the rear, as we had directed those taken in the advance. Doubtless all of them were claimed by troops at our rear as their captures. Colonel West, who had already lost his horse,—shot under him,—was severely wounded and helped to the rear. Longstreet, having made dispositions, put in his corps. We successfully resisted his attack in front, but he forced an opening somewhere on the left and towards our rear, which caused our line to fall back, under orders of Colonel Walker of Fourth Maine, then commanding the brigade. Thus a glorious victory was allowed to slip which we had held firmly in our grasp ; a single brigade at the front, with us, could have secured the harvest. At noontime our whole line, thus out-generaled, retired, fighting, in good order to the Brock road, along which breastworks were built. Later in the day we received an assault upon this line by Longstreet's corps, which was repulsed.

May 7th advanced with the division, massed by brigades in columns of regiments, to find the enemy,—and we found him, lively enough with his buck shot and artillery, behind works.

The regiment lost in the three days 201. Of this number 62 were killed outright or died of their wounds. The loss of officers was : killed, 2d Lieut. Benjamin Doe and acting 2d Lieut. Newton W. Parker ; wounded, Col. George W. West, Capt. Joseph A. Perry, 1st Lieuts. George A. Whidden (re-joined for duty May 16th), Wellington Hobbs (rejoined for duty June 28th), Henry L. Bartels, Frederick A. Sawyer, 2d Lieut. Franklin C. Adams and acting 2d Lieut. Joseph S.

Hobbs (rejoined for duty May 11th). Major Mattocks was captured on the skirmish out-posts, May 5th, at the first collision ; had this not occurred the regiment might have regained this field officer, after the loss of Colonel West. Owing to our lack of officers, Major Moore of the 99th Penn. was temporarily assigned to command the Seventeenth, the word coming from General Birney that he had so high a regard for the Seventeenth that he gave us the best available field officer in the division. Major Moore gallantly led us until May 16th.

May 8th moved towards Spotsylvania as far as Todd's Tavern, where we built works ; not engaged, although under fire. May 9th marched southward towards the Po river. The greater portion of the regiment was sent on picket across the river under Capt. W. H. Green, senior of the regimental detail.

PO RIVER.—May 10th the picket line with some supports advanced as skirmishers and drove the enemy's cavalry a long distance, back upon their infantry supports. A large force of the latter rapidly advanced upon our scattered line and upon its flanks, intending to capture the whole. Our detachments and the Fourth Maine, the whole under command of Col. Elijah Walker of that regiment, were skillfully, although with difficulty and some loss, withdrawn, rejoining the brigade on north side of the stream. The remainder of the 10th and the 11th was employed in supporting charging columns, batteries and skirmishers. Loss in the two days was one mortally wounded, seven wounded (including Capt. S. S. Richards), and two missing (never heard from and probably killed).

SPOTSYLVANIA. — Roused from sleep at 10 o'clock in the evening of May 11th, we silently moved out of our works on the right of the line, and marched away in the darkness and rain. The regiment reached its destination just before daybreak May 12th, and was immediately placed in the column already formed to charge the enemy's works at the "Salient." A short rest while waiting for the heavy fog to clear. About daybreak the charging column, composed of Barlow's (First) division and our own division, moved forward side by side, without noise until the picket line was reached and captured, when some shots were fired. Then with loud cheering we rushed forward for the works, through the obstructions and up over the steep glacis, without a halt. The Seventeenth entered in the first line at the very angle of the Salient, on the inner side of which were deep traverses, a long line of hitched-up artillery, and a mass of Confederates paralyzed with consternation, probably both at our appearance and the previous disappearance of most of their comrades into our protection. Gen. Edward Johnson's division was extinguished; about 5,000 men of it captured and he himself and his subordinate, General Steuart, prisoners of war in our hands. General Johnson was taken by Sergeant S. Frank Haskell and Private J. F. Totman of the Seventeenth Maine, and escorted by them to General Hancock. The six batteries and horses fell into our hands. Without stopping to re-form we pushed forward for an inner line of works, but were met by a wide-awake enemy defending it, and by the advance of converging formations. We retired, fighting, back to the captured works, and from the outside used them as a breastwork. One of the bloodiest encounters of the war, in a hand-to-hand struggle, ensued across the works, continuing all day and until nearly midnight, when the determined foe gave it up, leaving eighteen cannon and the whole Salient in our possession.

A part of the Sixth corps at the proper moment came in on our right at the west angle of the Salient, and gallantly took and carried on the fierce battle. To these heroic veterans an equal share of glory and credit is due for holding fast the captured position and artillery.

We took into the battle 225 muskets, with 13 officers and 4 acting officers. Our loss : 12 men killed or mortally wounded ; 41 wounded, of whom were 1st Lieut. John N. Morrill and 2d Lieut. Stephen Graffam ; 5 taken prisoners ; 1 missing, probably killed ; Captain Houghton, detailed on First brigade staff, also wounded. Sergt. Edward G. Parker, carrying our national color, was killed, and Sergt. Edwin Emery, bearing the state color, was badly disabled by two wounds, the Color-guard nearly annihilated. Acting Sergt.-Major G. A. Parker was wounded.

Maine was well represented here : the Third, Seventeenth, Fifth, Sixth and Seventh regiments all fought at the Salient. The Sixteenth, Nineteenth, Thirty-first and Thirty-second also co-operated by assaults upon the works near by.

From the 13th to 19th not engaged, except on picket.   On the 16th Lieut.-Colonel Merrill returned to duty, taking command.   Capt. Edward Moore also returned from a leave of absence.

FREDERICKSBURG ROAD. — On the 19th, at 2 A. M., the division marched about five miles to the Anderson House, on the Fredericksburg road.   The army supplies came this way. Ewell circled our right to strike this road in our rear.   Near the trains he ran against the First Maine heavy artillery regiment, used as infantry, and another of same kind, who fought with steadiness, holding the enemy.   Our division went at double-quick to the rescue, supporting the line and advancing the battle.   The Seventeenth relieved the First Maine, that had lost heavily, and advanced upon the enemy, who fell back. Next morning advanced again, and the enemy fled.   The regiment secured 47 prisoners (the division 500), with a loss of only one wounded and one missing.

NORTH ANNA. — May 21st, at 1 A. M., with 184 muskets, we took the Guiney Station road, passed through Bowling Green, crossed the Mattapony, beyond which we bivouacked, — a twenty miles march ; 22d built breastworks ; 23d marched at 5 A. M. southward, approaching the North Anna.   The enemy held a redoubt near the bridge on the north side, with flanking lines to the river.   Our division charged in line of battle ; our brigade, under Col. B. R. Pierce, advancing, met a fusilade, and was raked by artillery from across the river, but carried everything handsomely to the river.   Next day intrenched under fire on the south side.   Remained here until the 27th.   Loss : killed and mortally wounded, four (of whom were 1st Lieut. James S. Roberts and 2d Lieut. Walter F. Noyes), and seventeen wounded.

TOTOPOTOMY. — At midnight, May 26th, recrossed river and marched to the Pamunkey, crossing it on the 28th, near Newcastle.   Several positions and advances were made in the ensuing four days.   On June 1st the enemy's line at the Totopotomy Creek, which flows into the river, was assailed with success by our division, the First brigade leading, supported by ours — our regimental loss being slight.   The Seventeenth was

this day transferred to the First brigade, commanded by Colonel
Egan, and served with it until March 15, 1865. The Third
Maine belonged to this brigade. Marched at midnight without halting, passing Salem church and around our army towards
the left until, at 6 A. M., we halted for breakfast, after which,
to the left until we joined Barlow's (First) division at the front.

COLD HARBOR. — June 3d a general assault was made upon
the enemy's strong works, ending in failure and a fearful loss ;
we were held as a support to the First division and suffered
slightly. Remained in this vicinity until June 12th. On June
4th the re-enlisted men and recruits of the Third Maine were
transferred to the Seventeenth. Many names were on the transfer rolls, but we received only 129 men carrying muskets ; these
were sterling men, many of them being non-commissioned
officers, for whom we found places.

The vigor of our men, which had kept up remarkably until
this time, suddenly collapsed. We had nearly fifty prostrated
in one day. A portion of them recovered before the 12th.
Losses since May 24th : one killed, four wounded, five captured.
The sergeants remaining to us, who had served as officers since
the campaign opened, were here mustered according to their
commissions.

June 12th left the works at Cold Harbor, and on the 13th
marched to the James river, crossing next day at Windmill
Point, and remained on the south side waiting for rations that
day and night. June 15th marched to the line in front of
Petersburg and bivouacked behind captured earthworks. Our
strength was 16 officers and 224 enlisted men.

PETERSBURG ASSAULTS. — June 16th, while the roll was
being called, a well-aimed shell burst in our ranks, injuring
several, among them Capt. John C. Perry, commanding the
regiment, — Lieut.-Col. Merrill being off duty, — and the command devolved upon Capt. Benj. C. Pennell. Soon the Seventeenth Maine and 20th Ind. were moved out and formed in line
of battle without supports ; the orders were to advance and take
the enemy's intrenchments and battery about fifty rods distant.
We moved forward in line of battle, over stubby but level
ground, under a storm of bullets, shell and solid shot, poured

into us as we advanced, coming from the veterans of Lee's army. Our line shriveled and the alignment was broken. We failed to reach the main line, but took and held an out-work about midway the lines. A short time elapsed when we re-formed the two regiments at this point, expecting to have a support, but none came, and we moved forward a second time, gaining some ground, but with no better success; holding the advanced position, however, under a murderous fire until we were withdrawn towards night. Colonel Egan was wounded. The whole First division charged at sunset upon the same line, and were likewise repulsed. Our loss was : killed and mortally wounded, 16 (amongst them one of the color-bearers, Corporal Leonard Pride) ; wounded, 2 officers, Capt. John C. Perry and 2d Lieut. Jordan M. Hall, and 37 enlisted men. Next day the Seventeenth occupied a portion of the advanced line used for skirmishing, keeping up a galling fire which drove the opposing skirmishers from their pits. Captain Pennell was instantly killed while attempting to bring down with a Sharp's rifle the " stars and bars " planted on their works opposite our colors. The command of the regiment then devolved upon Capt. Edward Moore, who was succeeded the same evening by Major Gil-braith, of the 20th Ind., detailed temporarily by General Birney to this special duty with our regiment, which he well performed until July 10th, when relieved by return of Lieut.-Colonel Merrill to duty.

June 18th a general assault on the enemy's works was made, with very small success but with frightful casualties. We charged at the Hare House along a ridge (overlooking the plain where the First Maine Heavy charged). The small ad-vancement of our lines was secured by earthworks thrown up in the night in close contact with the enemy. Here we remained in the works until relieved on the 20th by the Ninth corps.

Loss since June 16th, killed and mortally wounded, one officer and 13 enlisted men ; wounded, 18 enlisted men.

JERUSALEM ROAD. — June 21st the Second corps extended the lines to the left beyond Jerusalem Road. Next day a por-tion of our division in this movement was outflanked and cap-tured in the new breastworks. Our brigade was ordered to charge and retake these works at daybreak of the 22d. As we were drawn up in an open field to undertake this task each man nerved himself and prepared for the worst, in many instances leaving valuables and messages with the surgeon. The word was given ; the line moved forward in splendid style. Before half the distance was gained the enemy gave a feeble volley and left the work, which we occupied without trouble, with loss of one killed, two wounded and three missing. The regiment lay behind works after this, not engaged although at the front.

July 12th the corps moved from the front and encamped, doing daily fatigue duty, levelling old works, etc. An official nominal list of our casualties for May and June was compiled, showing the number to have been 376, of whom only 32 were missing, which included those taken prisoners. Five officers were killed and fifteen wounded, being a much higher percentage than that of the enlisted men.

July 26th marched to the James, crossing at Jones' Point.

FIRST DEEP BOTTOM. — Moved forward about two miles and performed picket duty until relieved on 28th, when at dusk we recrossed the river and marched in rear of the investing lines until morning ; next evening after dark we marched to the Hare House and quietly relieved Hicks' troops of the Ninth corps in the intrenchments. This was in preparation for the famous Mine Explosion which occurred next morning, July 30th, near by us. Returned at nightfall to our camp in reserve, where we stayed until August 12th.

SECOND DEEP BOTTOM. — August 12th marched to City Point and embarked on steamers. At 10 P. M. steamed up the James to Deep Bottom, where we landed in the morning.

Advancing on the 14th, the enemy fell back into his strong works. We were established on the picket line at a large cornfield, doing that duty until the 19th. The main attack was made on the right, by the Tenth corps and a portion of the Second corps, all under General Birney. Failure followed temporary success. Skirmishing was continuous on the picket line, punctuated with artillery fire. Colonel Chaplin of the First Maine H. A., in command of the picket, was killed quite near the Seventeenth. Our loss was only four, wounded.

Returning to the Petersburg lines we were put into the trenches, relieving the Thirty-second Maine and another regiment. The opposing works were about 500 yards away; with us was Ames' N. Y. battery, relieved by White's Fourth Maine battery. One-third of our men were held constantly under arms in the works, with pickets in front. This was north of Fort "Hell" in an ordinarily healthy location; many deserters came in. The opposing pickets were at first peaceable, with commercial dealings; September 10th our picket line was advanced, which brought on a scrimmage. The brigade Officer of the Day was Capt. Edward Moore, whose duties brought him into this affair. We had a few wounded, amongst them Lieut. Joseph S. Hobbs at the main works. Then there began constant picket firing, day and night, except for a half hour at sunset, each day, by consent, when pickets were changed on both sides. We suffered a useless loss from this picket firing.

PEEBLES' FARM AND FORT HELL. — October 1st moved from the trenches, making a movement " to the left," to extend our lines and establish them with earthworks, which being accomplished we returned on the 5th and were placed in Fort Sedgwick (known as Fort " Hell "). Mortar shelling was frequent, and on the evening of the 11th a concentrated fire from many came into our fort, descending all around and causing some loss. October 15th were withdrawn and encamped back from the works. Colonel West, who had been absent, wounded, since May 6th, returned to duty. Lieut.-Colonel Merrill resigned, and took his leave of us. The regiment furnished picket details for the front. October 24th Lieut. Wellington Hobbs was killed and Lieut. George A. Whidden permanently disabled by the same bullet; Lieut. George B. Dunn also slightly wounded, same night.

BOYDTON ROAD. — October 26th the Second and Third divisions, under Hancock, marched to the left, crossing Hatcher's Run on the 27th, and pushed to the Boydton Road. The enemy nearly surrounded us. The Seventeenth was finally posted to guard our line of retreat, and constructed a barricade which General Hancock commended, adding," fix them so that you can fight on either side." The regiment was selected to escort the ambulances, filled with wounded, back to the works, in advance of the troops, after nightfall. An all-night march. October 30th we were placed in Fort Rice, remaining until November 29th, when we moved again to the left near the Peebles' House, at the southerly turn of our lines. December 7th the Fifth corps and our division, with some cavalry, all under General Warren, made an infantry raid, marching beyond the Nottaway River to Jarrett's Station on the Weldon railroad, and then destroying the railroad in a most thorough manner. Twenty miles of it was put *"hors de combat,"* from the Nottaway to Belfield. Our troops burned many buildings on the return, as revenge upon inhabitants who had murdered men that fell out. No encounter with the enemy. After this we encamped, out of the works, near Fort Dushane, as in winter quarters.

1865.

Colonel West, who had been appointed to Brevet Brigadier-General for his conduct at battle of the Wilderness, arrived at the front January 8th and was placed temporarily in command of the brigade, General de Trobriand being absent, and later was assigned to command another brigade. He did not return to duty with the regiment. Captain William Hobson, in command by seniority, was promoted to Lieutenant-Colonel of the regiment January 18th.

HATCHER'S RUN.—February 5th our division, under General Mott, followed by the Second division, marched to Hatcher's Run, and our brigade forced the passage of the stream under fire. The crossing was secured by forming the brigade in a crescent, one flank resting upon the south bank. The object being an extension of our works to the left, the line was established and intrenchments built, when we encamped near the Smith house, resuming camp duties, picketing, etc., and the usual routine. February 22d the 2d U. S. Sharpshooters was disbanded and its company D was transferred to the Seventeenth; by this we gained about a dozen fine soldiers. March 15th the regiment was re-transferred to the Second brigade, now commanded by Brig.-Gen. Byron R. Pierce, formerly Colonel of the 3d Mich. regiment, an ideal leader.

March 25th a demonstration was made against the enemy's picket lines in our corps front, as a diversion to aid in the recovery of Fort Steadman, which the enemy had captured from the Ninth corps. Our move was successful, provoking an attack upon our corps that we repulsed, and captured prisoners. The loss of the regiment was small.

Counting up the regimental casualties from August 19, 1864, to March 26, 1865, we found them to be one officer and eleven enlisted men killed and mortally wounded, and three officers and twenty-five enlisted men wounded.

March 29th broke camp at 6 A. M., marched on the Vaughan road, crossed Hatcher's Run and advancing towards Boydton Road, made connection on our left with the Fifth corps. Next morning advanced in line about a mile and found the enemy's skirmishers, in view of his main line of works, from which his artillery opened. Our lines were strengthened with breastworks.

At this time the strength of the regiment was about 300, rank and file. The following officers were on duty with the regiment : Lieutenant-Colonel William Hobson, commanding ; Major, Charles P. Mattocks (rejoined for duty March 31st from prisoner of war since May 5, 1864) ; Adjutant, George A. Parker ; Captains, William H. Green, Isaac S. Faunce, Gustavus C. Pratt, Charles C. Cole, George B. Dunn ; First Lieutenants, Robert H. Mathes, William H. Sturgis commanding company B, Parlin Crawford commanding company F, Joseph S. Hobbs commanding company H, James M. Webb commanding company C, Schollay G. Usher, Dexter W. Howard commanding company E, William H. Copp ; Second Lieutenants, Fayette M. Paine, Albert L. Bradbury, Edwin A. Duncan, Asa G. Charles, Charles H. Parcher, Sumner W. Burnham, Edwin W. Sanborn, Thomas Snowman. Other line officers, on detailed duty in the field, were Capt. Joseph A. Perry, at division hospital ; Capt. George W. Verrill, A. A. D. C. on staff of General Pierce ; 1st Lieut. Edward H. Crie, acting regimental quartermaster ; 2d Lieut. Edwin Emery, brigade ambulance officer ; quartermaster Josiah Remick, as 1st brigade quartermaster.

FALL OF PETERSBURG. — The general assault upon the defensive works was ordered for 4.30 A. M. April 2d, to commence on right of our army, after a night of cannonading. Early in the morning General Pierce sent two regiments, with an aide, to "feel" the works in front, which we found nearly evacuated, and they were secured by these, being the first from the division ; the remainder of the brigade then advanced to the works. Without delay the brigade marched towards Petersburg upon the Boydton Plank Road, sending in advance an aide and orderly to scout the way ; the enemy had fallen back to the outskirts of Petersburg, where Lee had stretched a breastwork across to the Appomattox.   Approaching this line we found resistance, also an artillery fire from across the river.   The Ninth and Sixth corps had carried their front, except a couple of forts.   We formed, connecting with the troops of the latter on our right. It is related that while the Seventeenth was throwing up a breastwork here, about twilight, two strangers came along and stopped on the line of work, conversing together, peering and pointing in a peculiar manner.   Colonel Hobson ordered them to "get out of the way," which they did without any "back talk."   The strangers were afterwards discovered to be Lieut.-General Grant and Maj.-General Wright.

Lee evacuated that night.   In the morning the pursuit began, and we marched twenty miles.   Stragglers from Lee were plenty.   The pursuit continued energetically, and on the 5th we came up with his rear guard.

DEATONSVILLE AND SAILOR CREEK. — April 6th the First brigade had the lead.   Lee had changed his course.   About 2 P. M., when the enemy made a stand, the Seventeenth, with another of our regiments, was lent to the First brigade, to prolong its line, which at once formed and impetuously charged under a hot musket and artillery fire.   The Seventeenth, after breaking their line, wheeled to the left and charged upon those Confederates who still held to their works, capturing about seventy-five prisoners, including several officers, and the battle-flag of the 21st N. C.   Lieutenant-Colonel Hobson was wounded in the first advance.   The command of the regiment then devolved upon Major Mattocks, who detailed Captain Green to act as a field officer. The division then, in line of battle, advanced about two miles, where the enemy was again found. Then the Seventeenth was returned to its own brigade, which in turn took the advance to charge. Moving forward under musketry and artillery fire, we crossed a small stream, where we routed a skirmish line, and kept on up a ridge ; the rest of the brigade separated and moved to the left, while the Seventeenth alone made connection with the First division on our right, as planned. General Humphreys, the corps commander, was present, who at once ordered another charge, when we pressed on, completely routing the enemy, who had made a stand at some buildings, and driving him across and beyond Sailor Creek. His wagon train fell into our hands with a large batch of prisoners. It was a headquarters train, and proved rich plunder. Six barrels of whiskey was the load of one wagon, which was wisely poured into the brook. The loss was : killed and mortally wounded, seven, including 1st Lieut. Schollay G. Usher ; wounded, twenty-seven, including Lieut-Colonel Hobson, Captain Dunn, 1st Lieut. Webb, 2d Lieut. Duncan ; 1st Lieut. Hobbs was slightly wounded, but not disabled from duty.

The pursuit continued next day, the Second division in the lead ; crossed the Appomattox at High Bridge, then on fire, where the enemy made some resistance, but gave way, leaving eighteen guns behind. In the afternoon came up with him, strongly intrenched, in a strong position at Farmville. Skirmishing followed, and feints of attack, the object being to detain them. In the night our foe decamped, and on the 8th the hunt began again, passing through New Store. Late at night, or rather at daylight of the 9th, got within striking distance. Sunday, April 9th, we continued the march until about noon and halted, about two miles from Appomattox C. H.

THE SURRENDER. — About four o'clock in the afternoon General Meade, coming from the front, announced the surrender of General Lee and the Army of Northern Virginia, at Appomattox Court House.

April 11th marched for Burkesville Junction, remaining there until May 2d, when the long march began for Washington ; on the way passing through Richmond, Fredericksburg, and other places memorable in the long strife; finally reaching Bailey's Cross Roads, near Washington, where we encamped and remained until mustered out of service, June 4, 1865.

The regiment, under Colonel Mattocks, took part in the Grand Review in Washington on May 23d.

The men whose terms of service held beyond September 30, 1865, were transferred to the First Maine Heavy Artillery regiment; this transfer also included three officers. About 300 enlisted men and thirty officers were present June 4, 1865, to be mustered out, and these came back to Maine with the organization. A large number of our comrades were absent, wounded and sick in hospital, who were thus deprived of the great joy of returning home under the colors.

The Seventeenth, returning to Maine, arrived in Portland June 8th, where it, and the Twentieth regiment, were received with enthusiasm and were highly honored by a public reception. June 10, 1865, the organization was disbanded.

ROSTER.

The following information relating to officers of the Seventeenth Maine regiment is obtained from the Volunteer Army Register (part 1), 1865, and other reliable sources.

OFFICERS AT MUSTER-OUT, JUNE 4, 1865.

COLONEL: Charles P. Mattocks, May 15, 1865,—brevet Colonel from Major, April 9, 1865; brevet Brigadier-General from Colonel, May 13, 1865.

LIEUTENANT-COLONEL: William Hobson, Jan. 18, 1865, mustered out June 6, 1865,—brevet Brigadier-General, April 6, 1865.

ADJUTANT: 1st Lieut. George A. Parker, Jan. 18, 1865.

QUARTERMASTER: 1st Lieut. Josiah Remick, Nov. 8, 1862.

CAPTAINS: Joseph A. Perry, Nov. 1, 1863; Edward Moore, Nov. 16, 1863,—brevet Lieut.-Col., March 13, 1865; Edwin B. Houghton, Nov. 16, 1863, mustered out June 11, 1865,—commissioned Major, not mustered; William H. Green, Dec. 22, 1863,—brevet Major, April 9, 1865; George W. Verrill, March 14, 1864,—after Feb. 3, 1865, detached, on brigade staff, acting as Asst. Adjt.-Gen., Asst. Insp. Gen., and Aide-de-Camp, also served on Military Commission to examine officers; Grenville F. Sparrow, July 4, 1864; Gustavus C. Pratt, Jan. 18, 1865; Charles C. Cole, Jan. 31, 1865.

FIRST LIEUTENANTS: Edward H. Crie, June 5, 1864,—commissioned Captain, not mustered; Robert H. Mathes, July 4, 1864, — brevet Captain, April 9, 1865; William H. Sturgis, July 4, 1864,—brevet Captain April 9, 1865;

Parlin Crawford, Nov. 4, 1864,—formerly of Third Maine; Lloyd W. Lamos, Nov. 5, 1864; Joseph S. Hobbs, Nov. 17, 1864; James M. Webb, Jan. 18, 1865; William H. Copp, Feb. 12, 1865, formerly of Third Maine.

SECOND LIEUTENANTS: Albert L. Bradbury, Jan. 16, 1865; Asa G. Charles, Jan. 18, 1865; Edwin A. Duncan, Jan. 18, 1865,—brevet 1st Lieut., April 9, 1865, commiss'd 1st Lieut., not mustered; Charles H. Parcher, Jan. 18, 1865; Edwin Emery, Jan. 20, 1865; Sumner W. Burnham, Jan 26, 1865; Thomas Snowman, Jan. 31, 1865; Horace B. Cummings, Feb. 12, 1865; Charles G. Holyoke, Sergeant-Major,—commiss'd 2d Lieut., not mustered.

SURGEON: Nahum A. Hersom, April 11, 1863. ASSISTANT SURGEONS: Nathaniel B. Coleman, Nov. 21, 1863; James G. Sturgis, Nov. 3, 1864.

CHAPLAIN: Joseph F. Lovering, Dec. 7, 1863.

(Dates given above refer to rank or commission, those given hereafter refer to date of the event.)

DIED.

CAPTAINS: Almon L. Fogg, July 4, 1863, of wounds at battle of Gettysburg; Milton M. Young, Aug. 13, 1863, of wounds at battle of Gettysburg; Ellis M. Sawyer, Nov. 28, 1863, of wounds at battle of Locust Grove,—commissioned Major, not mustered; Benjamin C. Pennell, June 17, 1864, killed in battle of Petersburg.

FIRST LIEUTENANTS: G. W. S. Fickett, Sept. 24, 1862, of disease; Willard M. Jenkins, Nov. 18, 1862, of disease; Dudley H. Johnson, May 3, 1863, killed in battle of Chancellorsville; James M. Brown, Nov. 27, 1863, killed in battle of Locust Grove; James S. Roberts, May 23, 1864, killed in battle of North Anna; Wellington Hobbs, Oct. 24, 1864, killed in action at Petersburg,—commissioned Captain, not mustered; Schollay G. Usher, April 6, 1865, killed in battle of Deatonsville or Sailor Creek.

SECOND LIEUTENANTS: William C. Winter, Jan. 25, 1863, of disease; Hiram R. Dyar, July 2, 1863, killed in battle of Gettysburg; Benjamin Doe, May 6, 1864, killed in battle of Wilderness; Walter F. Noyes, May 24, 1864, killed in battle of North Anna; Newton W. Parker,—commis'd 2d Lieut., not mustered, killed in battle May 6, 1864; Edward G. Parker,—commis'd 2d Lieut., not mustered, killed in battle May 12, 1864.

QUARTERMASTER: 1st Lieut. Jacob T. Waterhouse, Oct. 23, 1862, of disease.

TRANSFERRED AND PROMOTED OUT OF REGIMENT.

CAPTAINS: Edward I. Merrill, Dec. 11, 1863, to Inv. corps as Captain,—brevet Major, March 13, 1865; Isaac S. Faunce, June 4, 1865, to First Maine H. A. FIRST LIEUTENANTS: Newton Whitten, Dec. 28, 1863, to Inv. corps; Dexter W. Howard, May 6, 1865, app't'd Captain in 128th U. S. Col. Troops, —formerly of Third Maine; Fayette M. Paine, June 4, 1865, to First Maine H. A. SECOND LIEUTENANTS: Edwin W. Sanborn, May 6, 1865, app't'd 1st Lieut. in 128th U. S. Col. Troops,—formerly of Third Maine; Daniel J. Chandler, June 4, 1865, to First Maine H. A.

DISCHARGED ON ACCOUNT OF WOUNDS.

COLONEL: George W. West, April 27, 1865,—brevet Brigadier-General, Dec. 2, 1864.

ADJUTANT: 1st Lieut. Charles W. Roberts, Dec. 16, 1863.

CAPTAINS: Augustus Goldermann, Aug. 19, 1863; John C. Perry, Sept. 14, 1864; Sumner S. Richards, Oct. 1, 1864; George B. Dunn, June 3, 1865. FIRST LIEUTENANTS: Frederick A. Sawyer, Sept. 24, 1864; Henry L. Bartels, Oct. 3, 1864; John N. Morrill, Oct. 20, 1864; George A. Whidden, Feb. 4, 1865,—commissioned as Captain, not mustered. SECOND LIEUTENANTS: Thomas W. Lord, Sept. 20, 1863,—afterwards in U. S. Army, retired as Captain; Franklin C. Adams, Oct. 1, 1864,—promoted to 1st Lieut., not mustered; Jordan M. Hall, Oct. 3, 1864.

RESIGNED AND DISCHARGED.

COLONEL: Thomas A. Roberts, June 2, 1863.

LIEUTENANT-COLONEL: Charles B. Merrill, Oct. 7, 1864.

ADJUTANT: 1st Lieut. Putnam S. Boothby, Oct. 31, 1864,—previously resigned as 1st Lieut., Dec. 2. 1862; re-commissioned.

CAPTAINS: Andrew J. Stinson, Oct. 5, 1862; William H. Savage, Dec. 4, 1862; Albion Hersey, Dec. 21, 1862; Isaac S. Faunce, Jan. 1, 1863, re-commissioned as Captain, Jan. 23, 1864; Uriah W. Briggs, March 21, 1863; George W. Martin, March 26, 1863. FIRST LIEUTENANTS: John P. Swasey, Nov. 19. 1862; Benjamin G. Ames, Nov. 20, 1862; Otho W. Burnham, Feb. 3, 1863; William Roberts, August 5, 1863; Charles E. Hubbard, August 28, 1863. SECOND LIEUTENANTS: Madison K. Mabry, Dec. 10, 1862; Prescott Newman, Dec. 29, 1862; James M. Safford, Dec. 31, 1862; Danville B. Stevens, May 20, 1863; Ralph H. Day, May 21, 1863.

SURGEON: Henry L. K. Wiggin, Jan. 31, 1863. ASSISTANT SURGEONS: Paschal P. Ingalls, March 2, 1863; Louis E. Norris, Oct. 1, 1863; William Wescott, Dec. 11, 1863.

CHAPLAINS: Harvey Hersey, Oct. 27, 1862; Jeremiah Hayden, Aug. 29, 1863.

OTHERWISE LEFT THE SERVICE.

Capt. James O. Thompson, Feb. 23, 1864; 2d Lieut. Stephen Graffam, Nov. 25, 1864.

MONUMENTS.

The positions of the Twentieth Maine on the field of Gettysburg on the second and third days are marked by two monuments. The survivors of the regiment placed, in 1886, on the spot and near where their colors were planted on the afternoon of July 2d, a simple monument, of Hallowell granite, four feet square at the base and five feet four inches in height, bearing upon one side of the shaft, around the Maltese Cross of the Fifth corps, this inscription:—

TWENTIETH MAINE

THIRD BRIG. FIRST DIV.

FIFTH CORPS.

Upon another side is the following inscription:—

HERE THE 20TH MAINE REGIMENT,

COL. J. L. CHAMBERLAIN COMMANDING, FORMING THE

EXTREME LEFT OF THE NATIONAL LINE OF BATTLE

ON THE 2ND DAY OF JULY 1863 REPULSED THE

ATTACK OF THE EXTREME RIGHT OF LONGSTREET'S

CORPS AND CHARGED IN TURN CAPTURING 302

PRISONERS. THE REGIMENT LOST 38 KILLED OR

MORTALLY WOUNDED, AND 92 WOUNDED, OUT OF

358 ENGAGED.

THIS MONUMENT, ERECTED BY SURVIVORS OF

THE REGIMENT A. D. 1886, MARKS VERY NEARLY

THE SPOT WHERE THE COLORS STOOD.

Upon the two other sides is the roll of those of the regiment who fell. The stone-wall thrown up hastily along the brow of the hill, to afford some slight shelter under the murderous fire, remains to emphasize the record of the monument.

MONUMENT

OF

TWENTIETH MAINE REGIMENT.

Upon Big Round Top is placed the monument erected by the state. It is of Hallowell granite. The base, of two tiers, shows as quarried, with cut angles; a single block forms the plinth which has chiseled borders and top; on this rests the massive die, nearly cubical in form, with a pointed apex.

ADMEASUREMENTS: Base, four stones, five feet by five feet by two feet; plinth, four feet nine inches by four feet nine inches by one foot seven inches; die, three feet six inches by three feet six inches by four feet six inches. Total height, eight feet one inch.

Upon one side of the die a panel is sunk, from a polished surface, leaving in relief the following legend:—

THE 20TH MAINE REG'T,

3D BRIG. 1ST DIV. 5TH CORPS,

COLONEL

JOSHUA L. CHAMBERLAIN,

CAPTURED AND HELD THIS

POSITION ON THE EVENING

OF JULY 2D 1863, PURSUING

THE ENEMY FROM ITS FRONT

ON THE LINE MARKED BY

ITS MONUMENT BELOW.

THE REG'T LOST IN THE BATTLE

130 KILLED AND WOUNDED

OUT OF 358 ENGAGED.

THIS MONUMENT MARKS THE

EXTREME LEFT OF THE UNION

LINE DURING THE BATTLE OF

THE 3D DAY.

There is by the monument here a wall of stone hastily thrown up for defenses by the regiment on the night of July 2d.

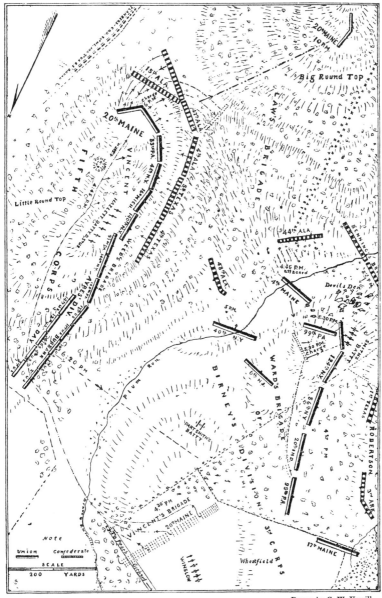

Drawn by G. W. Verrill.

Diagram showing Little Round Top and Devil's Den, with positions of Twentieth and Fourth Maine regiments.

Also a portion of the Wheatfield where Vincent's brigade entered, and Seventeenth regiment engaged.

TWENTIETH MAINE REGIMENT,

THIRD BRIGADE, FIRST DIVISION, FIFTH ARMY CORPS,

AT THE BATTLE OF GETTYSBURG.

WHILE the conflict was raging along Birney's line another was in progress on the slopes of Little Round Top. We have already seen the Alabama and Texas regiments, under Law, rushing up across the valley of Devil's Den, and passing beyond and around the Fourth Maine and the other defenders of that position. By this movement the approaches of Little Round Top were uncovered; and the Confederates, passing the ravine, began to swarm up the sides of that precipitous height, which was now recognized as a most important position in the battle of this day.

In the defense of this position a Maine regiment was to play a gallant part. The Twentieth Maine regiment, with the 16th Mich., 44th N. Y. and 83d Penn. formed Vincent's brigade of Barnes' division. It was the only Maine regiment now in the Fifth corps, the remnants of the Second Maine having been consolidated with the Twentieth. On the morning of June 29th the brigade had left its bivouac at Frederick City, Md., and by hard forced marches, on the last day of which this regiment acted as the advance guard for the Fifth corps, had arrived at Hanover, Penn., at about 4 p. m. July 1st. While preparing for much needed rest, the plans were suddenly changed by hurried messengers bringing word that our First and Eleventh corps had struck the enemy at Gettysburg, some sixteen miles away, and were being driven back. This was the signal for more hard marching. The worn and wearied men were enthusiastic to rush to the rescue of their fellow soldiers and the imperilled flag. They pulled out at 6 p. m. for a night's march to Gettysburg. It is fifty-five miles from Frederick City to Gettysburg by the route they took. The short time in which this distance was accomplished by soldiers weighed down with all the burdens of heavy marching order, and this at the end of a long, wearisome and worrysome march from the Rappahannock, under the fiery heats of a midsummer sun, will suggest the physical condition of men about to take strenuous part in a great battle. The cheers of welcome and blessing that met them on that Gettysburg night-march, from all the little homes along the road, struck a deep chord in every soldier's heart. Without a halt they arrived within striking distance of the anxious lines then holding front against the enemy, and were bidden to take a little rest. At daylight they pushed to the front, and were massed in rear of Cemetery Hill, under preliminary orders to prepare to attack the enemy on the right of our position.

Meantime the plans of the opposing commanders were taking shape. Suddenly, at about 4 o'clock P. M. July 2d, an artillery fire opened on our extreme left, where our Third corps had taken position; and the head of the Fifth corps, instead of attacking on the right, was hurried to the support of the Third corps on the extreme left. How our Twentieth regiment at the head of the brigade went in at first to Sickles' line of battle then under tremendous fire; how the gallant General Warren, seeing, with military eye, the importance of the Round Top heights, begged General Sykes to send Vincent's brigade to gain this position in advance of Longstreet's troops, then rushing for the same commanding heights; how Hazlett, aided by the infantry, lifted his guns by hand and handspike up the craggy sides; how Vincent fought and fell; how the Twentieth, at the critical moment, with a bayonet charge turned the confident Confederate onslaught into rout, on the left of our army,—all this makes one of the most famous passages of the battle of Gettysburg.

The brigade, moving instantly and at the double-quick, crossed Plum Run, and scaled the northern crest of Little Round Top, under the storm of shells from Longstreet's batteries across the valley, crashing among the rocks and trees along the path of the column toiling up the mountain side (a).

(a) Official Report of Colonel Chamberlain, July 6, 1863. Rebellion Records, Vol 27, part 1, page 622.

Passing to the southern slope of Little Round Top, making the extreme left of the Union line, where Vincent, entrusting the left of the line to the discretion and keeping of the Colonel of this regiment, saying to him, "You understand! hold this ground at all costs!" rested his defense. The Twentieth, in order to meet the fire then enveloping our left, was formed "on the right into line," the successive companies keeping somewhat under shelter until they reached their place in the line (a). On their right came up the other regiments of the brigade, the 83d Penn., the 44th N. Y. and the 16th Mich., making a somewhat convex line to cover the flank of our troops and artillery, then following, and in position to resist the formidable attack of the right of Hood's division, now intending to carry this southern crest and so command the whole Union left.

The Twentieth Maine, as it formed that rugged line of battle among the crags and bowlders of that crest now charged with a nation's defense, numbered twenty-eight officers and three hundred and fifty-eight men present for duty equipped (b). Although less than a year in the army the regiment had seen arduous service, entitling it to the name of veteran. Col. Joshua L. Chamberlain was its commander.

Such advantage as was possible was taken of the rough, rocky and wooded ground. Facing it on the south was Big Round Top, a commanding summit among the clustered hills, but impracticable for battle ground, which was separated from Little Round Top by a smooth, thinly wooded valley. In establishing his defense Colonel Chamberlain, regardful of his exposed left flank, sent out company B, under Captain Morrill, to operate as he found necessary on that flank. Moving to the left, this company deployed as a skirmish line to check a demonstration on the left of the regiment; but afterwards, in the crisis of the fight, it got in its volley on the enemy's right, which demoralized them.

(a) The order of companies from right to left was E, I, K, D, F, A, H, C, G, company B being detached as skirmishers.

(b) According to the official reports; but Colonel Chamberlain has since said that when the fight began some of those reported as absent sick came up and took their places, and that he also dismissed the "pioneers" and the "provost guard," as well as the prisoners under arrest in their charge, and all of these went into the fight and did gallant service.

These dispositions were scarcely made when a portion of Law's Alabamians, with two regiments of Robertson's Texans swarming up from beyond Devil's Den, threw themselves against Vincent's right-centre, where a fierce conflict began to rage. Very soon the left was assailed, and the Twentieth was at once plunged into furious conflict. The enemy threatening to outflank us and to envelop our left and rear, the Colonel had promptly, as occasion permitted, stretched his regiment to the left by taking intervals by the left, and at the same time bent back, or "refused" the left wing, so that it was nearly at right angles with the right. In this way the regiment was brought to occupy about twice the extent of its ordinary front, some of the companies being extended into single rank, where the ground gave sufficient shelter. The colors were planted where the original left had been, now in the angle of the line. Upon this salient fell a most deadly fire during the hour of desperate fighting which followed.

The most formidable assailants of the Twentieth did not, however, advance by way of the valley. They came over the summit of Big Round Top, having been drawn that way by an interesting incident of the battle. When the 2d U. S. Sharpshooters retired before the Confederate advance, a portion of them ambushed themselves on the side of Big Round Top, whence they poured an annoying fire upon Law's men as they passed up the gorge. To silence this fire the 15th and 47th Ala., under direction of Col. William C. Oates of the 15th, advanced up the slope of Big Round Top, against the Sharpshooters, who mysteriously disappeared. Reaching the summit of the hill, Colonel Oates, charmed by the commanding position, wished to hold it ; but, upon the receipt of an urgent order from Law to "get on the enemy's left as soon as possible," he moved the two regiments down the hillside and across the hollow towards the slope of Little Round Top (a).

They advanced in battle line with no skirmishers, the 15th Ala. on the right and opposing the left of the Twentieth Maine, cutting off as they advanced Captain Morrill's company. It was a most formidable advance. The 15th Ala. was one

(a) Statement of Colonel Oates (1890).

of the strongest and finest regiments in Hood's division, and largely outnumbered the Twentieth Maine. Suddenly, and to the Confederates unexpectedly, a most destructive volley burst from the line of the Twentieth (a). Surprised but not disconcerted, the Alabamians replied, and the fight grew fierce and tense. Coming in with vastly superior numbers on the flank of the Twentieth, the enemy made a left wheel in order to take it in what they supposed to be its flank and rear, or at least to rake it with an enfilading fire. But here was proved the great benefit of the tactical manœuvre of the "refused" left flank. The enemy was met by a firm front, instead of falling upon an unguarded rear. Their fire, falling on the left wing of the Twentieth in front, enfiladed the right stretched out beyond. Against both fronts of the regiment, however, the whole force of the enemy advanced in repeated charges. "The edge of the fight swayed backward and forward like a wave," are the words of the Colonel's report. Squads broke through each line in one place and another. Now the Maine men were driven back and the colors of the enemy for a moment are inside their line.

At one moment it looked as if the colors of the Twentieth Maine must be lost. Buried from sight in smoke, when the black cloud lifted for a moment the colors were seen almost alone. All the Color-Guard and the flanks of the companies on its right and left were cut away; but the Color-Sergeant, Andrew J. Tozier, was standing his ground, the staff planted on the earth, and supported within his left arm, while he had picked up a musket and was defending his colors with bullet, bayonet and butt, alone! Seeing this heroic example and the imminent peril of the colors in the whirl that wrapped the left and centre, the Colonel sent his brother, the acting Adjutant (b), to rally some men, wherever they could be found, for the support of the Sergeant and the rescue of the colors. In order to ensure the delivery of his order under the hot fire the Colonel dispatched immediately Sergeant Ruel Thomas (whom he had taken as a sort of staff-orderly) with the same instructions.

(a) Colonel Oates says (1890) that he did not know of the presence of the Twentieth Maine among the rocks and trees in front until this volley was delivered. The fire was most destructive; but he felt compelled to push on under the circumstances.

(b) Colonel Chamberlain's official report, July 6, 1863.

At the same time the Colonel asked the commanding officer of the 83d Penn., on his right, for a company to fill this perilous gap; but the 83d could not risk its own safety to spare a man.

The situation was desperate. The men had been using cartridges snatched from the boxes of their fallen comrades, and even from those of the enemy. A third of the regiment was down, dead or disabled on their line. As the last rounds of ammunition were expended, the men were preparing to club their muskets as the last resort of the defensive. They had so far maintained their swaying line in spite of the terrible pressure on point after point of it.

But in a moment the scene changed. The enemy suddenly drew back to the shrubbery and rocks in the bottom of the valley, as if to gather force for a supreme blow. At this crisis, with the quick and resolute instinct to strike before he was struck, Chamberlain staked all upon a desperate counter-charge. He repaired to the left centre to advise Capt. Ellis Spear (a), who, acting as field officer, was in charge there, of his new purpose. Great responsibility was to fall upon this officer, as his flank was to start the movement, and moreover to become the wheeling flank, as the movement must swing on the right as a pivot; otherwise the regiment would be cut in two by the enemy, massing on the centre, as they naturally would do. As the Colonel was returning to the centre to give the necessary order, Lieutenant Melcher of the color company came up to him, asking permission to move out and gather up some of the wounded who lay between the two lines. "Yes, sir. Take your place with your company. I am about to order a 'right wheel forward' of the whole regiment" was the reply. The brave young officer sprang forward, and at that moment Chamberlain's voice thrilled along the line, "Bayonet!" The Colonel placed himself at the centre, on the apex of the salient angle of his line, abreast with the colors. The enemy had in the mean time made a furious onset. But when the left wing whirled the enemy's right out of the shelter of rocks they had taken, our centre dashed upon their disordered mass, and the whole regiment swept forward with irresistible force.

(a) Commissioned Major, but not mustered as such.

In the first onset the Colonel came directly in contact with the commanding officer leading the enemy's centre, with uplifted sword in one hand and a heavy " Colt's " revolver in the other. He fired one barrel in the Colonel's face, and gave him his sword with the other hand (a).

The left wing had now fought its way up abreast with the right, what was left of the two centre companies closing on the colors; Capt. A. M. Clark, the senior captain, commanding on the right, holding that flank well to the 83d Penn., to prevent the enemy from trying to break through between, and the whole regiment, like a reaper, cutting down the disconcerted foe. Many in their first line threw down their loaded arms, threw up their hands and surrendered ; others were taken in hand-to-hand conflicts. Still sweeping in an extended right wheel, the Twentieth routed a second line, trying to rally for a stand (b). The Confederates did not rally. They had suffered severely at the hands of the Twentieth, and moreover had been subjected to a mysterious and alarming fire from their right and rear. They were not aware that some of the 2d U. S. Sharpshooters who had disappeared on Big Round Top had joined Captain Morrill's skirmishers behind a stone-wall, on the right of the 15th Ala., where these combined forces rendered most material aid in the final charge of the regiment. No less than 400 prisoners, including two field and several line officers, were captured, most of them from the 15th and 47th Ala., with a few from the 4th and 5th Texas (c).

The Confederates were driven completely and finally from the front of the Twentieth ; nor had Law's most desperate assaults succeeded in gaining a foothold in any other portion of the line held by Vincent's brigade. At the hour when the Twentieth Maine dashed upon the 15th and 47th Ala. regiments, Little Round Top was saved, not to be attacked again.

It was about 6 : 30 p. m. when the Confederates were driven

(a) See Rebellion Records, serial number 43, page 624.

(b) These were squads or groups of the 47th and 4th Ala. and some of the 4th and 5th Texas, which had been attacking the left centre of the brigade.

(c) According to Captain Prince's address at Gettysburg (1889) fifty dead of the 15th Ala. were buried in front of the Twentieth, and about 100 of their badly wounded were left to become prisoners.

from the south side of Little Round Top. But the withdrawal of the enemy did not leave the Twentieth Maine the much needed opportunity to take rest or even to perform the saddest duty of the soldier on the battlefield, the burial of his dead comrades. Of the wooded slopes of Big Round Top, towering 664 feet above the plain, the foot of it but a few rods from the position of the Twentieth, the enemy were still in possession. The commander of the brigade directed Colonel Chamberlain to advance and seize the crest of Big Round Top. Colonel Rice, Vincent's successor, says in his report: "I ordered Colonel Chamberlain, of the Twentieth Maine, to advance and take possession of the mountain. This order was promptly and gallantly executed by this brave and accomplished officer, who rapidly drove the enemy over the mountain, capturing many prisoners."

The regiment, including company B recalled, now numbering about 200 men, scrambled up the ascent. It was 9 o'clock before the advance began, and darkness shrouded the summit of the hill and had settled deep on its rocky, wooded and precipitous sides. With fixed bayonets and in extended order, the little band pressed up the black hillside. In front of them they could hear the movements of squads of the enemy falling back; and when near the summit they received a straggling and uncertain fire out of the darkness. Twenty-five prisoners were taken in this advance, among them a staff officer of General Law. Upon the crest of the hill Colonel Chamberlain placed the regiment in a strong position among the rocks, and sent back for reinforcements and ammunition,—for not the least gallant feature of this advance was the fact that the soldiers made it with empty cartridge boxes and without supports near at hand.

Through some misadventure the necessary supporting and connecting troops were wanting, and the Twentieth remained for some time detached from the other Union forces and within musket range of the enemy. To quote from Lieutenant Miller of the Twentieth Maine, in his address October 3, 1889, at the dedication of the monument erected by the state to the Twentieth, on Big Round Top:

"Apprehending that the rebels might seize this opportunity to envelop our right, Colonel Chamberlain hastily detailed a picket line on the front and left, and retired the main body to lower ground near the foot of the ascent. He then dispatched a request to Colonel Rice for the 83d Penn. and afterward for the 44th N. Y. to support the Twentieth on the right by echelon. In this formation, being partially supplied with ammunition, the line again advanced considerably beyond its former position, where the men lay on their arms till morning, expecting an attack at any moment.

" I have mentioned the detail of a picket line in the early part of the night. These pickets advanced down the side of the hill in our front until they could see the enemy by the light of their camp-fires and hear conversation, when they retired part way up to the crest. The Confederates had evidently seen their movements, for they soon sent a squad to ascertain whether they were friends or foes. Being halted by our pickets, they answered 'friends' and were told to come right along. This strategy was continued until twenty-five of the 4th Tex. regiment had been captured by company E on the right of the line. At this time some officer, farther to the left, gave an order to fire, and no more prisoners were taken that night. These prisoners were sent to the rear under the escort of John Bradford and Eugene Kelleran of company I, who tramped around in the darkness a long time trying to find the provost guard. Coming out into an open space they decided to bivouac till morning, when the prisoners were turned over to the proper officer.

"The only casualty in the Twentieth during this movement occurred in the morning, when Lieut. Arad Linscott took a musket and going out in advance of the picket line to get a shot at the enemy, who were firing in among our men, was mortally wounded in the thigh by a sharpshooter."

The following is an excerpt from Colonel Chamberlain's field notes made upon the battlefield, which further elucidates the exciting circumstances and events of the evening of July 2d :

"At about dusk Fisher came up with brigade of Penn. Reserves, in rear of our line of battle. Rice asked him to advance and seize Great Round Top. He declined. Rice then asked me to go. We formed—about 200 men—in extended order; one rank, bayonets fixed, no firing, little ammunition. Quite dark. Rough scrambling; few of enemy before us; took two officers prisoners, one Captain Christian, and five or six men. Arriving at crest, drew together; solid front; in half hour two regiments came up on right as supports. Tried to form them on our right rear; sharp, close volley from right; supports confused and withdrew. Dangerous situation. Divided regiment; half holding present ground; half withdrawn to ground abandoned by supports, half way down right rear. Sent for 83d Penn. Relieved my reserved line with these, and resumed former position with whole regiment. Formed two reliefs of skirmishers, sent down in front; relieved every two hours. Right of skirmish line took about twenty more prisoners. Texas troops. Linscott mortally wounded on skirmish line early in morning. Sharp skirmishing at daylight. Strong skirmish line of enemy all around right front. Two regiments of Reserves had come up towards morning on left, near summit. Some supplies of ammunition came up with 83d Penn. at once distributed; served well. Withdrawn with brigade at about 9 in morning and placed in support of troops on left centre of general line; to left of ' Pickett's charge.' Not engaged; under heavy artillery fire all forenoon. Remained all day and night."

The 83d Penn. and 44th N. Y. were posted on the right to guard this isolated position almost within the enemy's lines. With a strong picket line advanced nearly to the Confederates at the foot of the hill, and changing every two hours, the defenders of Big Round Top lay down upon their arms; and a broken sleep succeeded the deadly strife and wild tumult of the day. By our thus gaining possession of Big Round Top the enemy were induced to give up further attack upon the Union left.

At the opening of the fight there was no time for the men to take much heed to shelter themselves. But as the battle grew, the regimental line conformed itself to the nature of the ground, and availed itself of momentary lulls to throw up slight breastworks of loose rocks behind which the men, lying down, could find some protection. When the regiment was preparing to extend its front and refuse its left, extended as has been stated, the colors were placed where the extreme left had been; they were stationed where a decayed tree had been broken off but adhering to its stump about three feet from the ground, in the line of direction to the right. But between this stump and the great rock where the monument now stands there was no protection, nor means to make any.

It will be noticed in the list of casualties that all the corporals and one sergeant of company F, the color company, were killed or wounded; and that six corporals and two sergeants of company A, on its left, were killed or wounded. Only two of the color-guard escaped unhurt. The Colonel was struck twice, although not disabled,—a tearing cut in the right instep by a piece of shell or a splinter of rock, and a contusion on the left thigh by the steel scabbard being doubled against it, struck by a minnie ball; the Adjutant received several scratches, and several others, both officers and men, were slightly hurt, but remained on duty.

From the fact that the men fired at least sixty rounds to a man, it is evident that they fought for considerably more than an hour, closely engaged. If the enemy fired half that number, there were not less than 20,000 bullets directed upon the regiment. It is no wonder that the trees on that slope were completely "peppered" with bullets to the height of five or six feet. One tree, some three or four inches through, in front of the left of company F, was cut entirely off about two feet above the ground. The ragged edges of the cut showed that it was made by bullets, and not by a shell.

But even sheltered and spared as the men were, the casualties shown in the list of names entitle this regiment to be called one of the "fighting regiments," according to the popular judgment based on the number of men lost in action. This is proof of being exposed to hostile fire, but not necessarily of the degree of service rendered in action.

At 10 o'clock on the 3d the Twentieth took a position with the brigade to the right of Little Round Top to support the troops on our left centre. There it remained during the battle of the third day, not called upon to assist in repelling the charge of Pickett's division, which fell further to the right.

On the morning after Pickett's charge, the regiment with the brigade made a reconnaissance to the front, through the Peach Orchard and by the "burning barn" used as a hospital by both parties. Pushing on as far as Willoughby Run, no enemy being discovered, the brigade was brought back, and Colonel Chamberlain went up to Little Round Top and looked after his dead. The regiments gathered their dead from the sheltered places where they had been borne, and buried them on the southern side of the crest behind their line of battle. Rude headboards, made of ammunition boxes, marked each grave, and bore, rudely but tenderly carved, the name and home of every man (a). Detachments from the brigade buried many of the rebel dead at the foot of the slopes, on the edge of the valley near where they had fallen. The bodies of the Twentieth Maine have since been removed to the National cemetery, where several of them are marked "unknown." The headboards placed by comrades had evidently been unheeded or taken away.

(a) General Chamberlain's lecture, October, 1866, "Twentieth Maine at Gettysburg."

PARTICIPANTS.

FIELD, STAFF AND NON-COMMISSIONED STAFF.

Colonel, Joshua L. Chamberlain, Brunswick.
Acting Field Officer, Captain Atherton W. Clark, Waldoboro, company E.
Acting Field Officer, Captain Ellis Spear, Wiscasset, company G.
Acting Adjutant, First Lieutenant Thomas D. Chamberlain, Bangor, co. G.
Quartermaster, Alden Litchfield, Rockland.
Chaplain, Luther P. French, East Corinth; at hospital.
Acting Sergeant-Major, Samuel L. Miller, Waldoboro, company E.
Color Sergeant, Andrew J. Tozier, Plymouth, company I.
Colonel's orderly, Reuel Thomas, Thomaston, Sergeant company I.
Quartermaster-Sergeant, Howard L. Prince, Cumberland.
Commissary-Sergeant, Elmas M. Kalloch, Warren.
Hospital Steward, Granville M. Baker, Standish.

COMPANY A.

First Lieutenant, Addison W. Lewis, Waterville, commanding.

SERGEANTS.

First Sergeant, Charles R. Shorey, Waterville,

Henry W. Getchell, Winslow,	James H. Harrington, Burnham,
George W. Reynolds, Sidney,	Albert M, Clark, Waterville.

CORPORALS.

Charles H. Reed, Freedom,	David J. Lewis, Waterville,
Charles E. Avery, Sidney,	Joseph D. Simpson, Waterville,
Laforrest P. True, Clinton,	John Reed, Jr., Eustis,
Fred H. Mann, Sidney,	Henry M. Tozer, Waterville.

PRIVATES.

Bartlett, Charles H., Sidney,	Benson, Thomas S., Sidney,
Breen, John H., Augusta,	Church, Chandler K., Burnham,
Dawes, Calvin, Cumberland,	Foss, Washington, Cornville,
Fuller, Emulus S., Eustis,	Grindle, Joseph, Bangor,
Hall, Isaac C., Freedom,	Hill, William E., Burnham,
Hutchins, Alvah L., Freedom,	Longley, Samuel, Sidney.
Lore, Charles, Waterville,	Marden, Ezra B., Bangor,
Norton, Hiram, Solon,	Rankins, William, Waterville,
Stevens, Jeremiah C., Sidney,	Shaw, Resolvo, Waterville,
Surry, Joseph L., Castine,	Stinson, Merritt, Clinton,
Tarbell, Erastus, Clinton,	Sylvester, Ira R., Freedom,
True, Franklin, Clinton,	Taylor, Alfred, Eustis,
Whitten, Isaiah, Alfred,	Wardwell, David S., Clinton,
Willey, William E., Belgrade,	Young, Ervin S., Solon.

ON SPECIAL DUTY OR DETACHED SERVICE: William A. Estes, Bangor, battery C, 1st N. Y.; Henry H. Scribner, Bangor, George A. Webber, Ellsworth, and George W. Young, Bangor, battery L, 1st Ohio; John King, Waterville, and Edgar Scates, Waterville, regt'l hosp.; Eben Rowe, Belgrade, with regt'l baggage; Elijah G. Stevens, Belgrade.

COMPANY B.

Captain, Walter G. Morrill, Williamsburg.
Second Lieutenant, Frederic W. Lane, Milo.

SERGEANTS.

Acting First Sergeant, William Griffin, Stockton,

Samuel G. Crocker, Brownville,   Royal B. Decker, Lagrange.

CORPORALS.

George H. Moulton, Lagrange,   William H. Owen, Milo,
Walter S. Bray, Dover,   William T. Livermore, Milo,
Richard Hughes, Brownville,   Cyrus C. Durgin, Sebec,
Thomas F. Hodgdon, Milo.

PRIVATES.

Brown, William A., Sebec,   Burrill, Newell E., Dover,
Cotton, Richard G., Williamsburg,   Cross, Eli W., Dover,
Cummings, Leonard N., Albany,   Cummings, Wesley, Albany,
Edes, Augustus, Abbot,   Field, Benjamin R., Foxcroft,
Freeman, Samuel, Medford,   Frees, William L., Maxfield,
Higgins, David S., Sebec,   Hitchborn, George W., Medford,
Johnson, John, Solon,   Lamson, William P., Jr., Sebec,
Leach, George W., New Brunswick,   Leonard, Abial E., Milo,
Libby, Seth H., Lagrange,   Lyford, Danville B., Sebec,
Lyford, John, Sebec,   Morrill, Edwin, Sebec,
Oakes, Hudson S., Foxcroft,   Page, David F., Atkinson,
Parkman, Franklin B., Guilford,   Richardson, George H., Denmark,
Sanborn, Edmund R., Lagrange,   Sanborn, William S., Lagrange,
Sanders, Henry C., Brownville,   Skillings, Charles A., Guilford,
Spaulding, Randall H., Foxcroft,   Stone, George W., Richmond,
Warner, Sumner L., Dover.

MUSICIAN, William F. Gould, Eastport.

ON SPECIAL DUTY OR DETACHED SERVICE: Charles E. Bowker, Orrington, battery L, 1st Ohio; Arthur Jordan, Ellsworth, and Augustus N. Lufkin, Orrington, battery I, 5th U. S.; Daniel A. Jackson, Orneville, regt'l hosp.

COMPANY C.

Captain, Charles W. Billings, Clinton.
First Lieutenant, Rufus B. Plummer, Linneus, assigned to G.
Second Lieutenant, James H. Stanwood, Waldoboro.

SERGEANTS.

First Sergeant, Isaac W. Estes, Bethel,
George H. Wood, Hartford,   Andrew J. Roberts, Sumner,
Arad Thompson, Livermore,   Charles A. Knapp, Rumford.

CORPORALS.

Andrew C. Deering, Foxcroft,   Arthur B. Latham, Buckfield,
Nathaniel S. Estes, Bethel,   Vincent W. Pinhorn, Orrington.

PRIVATES.

Allen, Elliot C., Wilton,   Barker, Eugene A., Rumford,
Beadle, Charles M., Buckfield,   Bean, Arthur M., Bethel,
Bean, Edgar F., Bethel,   Bryant, Varano G., Bethel,
Buck, Charles T., Sumner,   Carpenter, Henry A., Charleston,
Chase, Benjamin F., Sumner,   Davis, Moses, Caribou,

Drake, Elisha O., Livermore,
Fogg, Elliott L., Sumner,
Heald, Llewellyn B., Sumner,
Hodgman, Osgood A., Rumford,
Mills, George V., Brooksville,
Moore, Henry H., Canaan,
Murdock, Sylvester E., Buckfield,
O'Connell, John, Waterford,
Powers, Charles P., Newry,
Royal, David H., Bangor,
Stevens, Oliver L., Livermore,
Thomas, Moses S., Woodland,
Turner, Winslow, Buckfield,
Whittier, Charles G., Caribou,
York, George H., Woodstock.

Faunce, Edward, Rumford,
Heald, Benjamin F., Sumner,
Hodgdon, Josiah S., Peru,
Melcher, Samuel G., Brunswick,
Monk, Decatur, Buckfield,
Morton, Daniel W., Windsor,
Neal, George D., Livermore,
Odlin, Waldo P., Bangor,
Roberts, Albert, Livermore,
Small, Alva B., Caribou,
Thomas, James, Rumford,
Tobin, John, Caribou,
Verrill, Moses F., Buckfield,
Wright, John, Veazie,

ON SPECIAL DUTY OR DETACHED SERVICE: Lafayette M. Crosby, Harmony, battery I, 5th U. S.; John Harmon, Buxton, Samuel F. Mallett, Lee, and John H. Wentworth, Veazie, battery C, 1st N. Y.; John E. Carlton, Hanover, and Erskine C. Smith, Hanover, in quarterm'r dept.

COMPANY D.

Captain, Joseph B. Fitch, Bristol.
First Lieutenant, Weston H. Keene, Bremen.
Second Lieutenant, Mattson C. Sanborn, South Berwick.

SERGEANTS.

First Sergeant, Joseph Walker, Jr., Atkinson,

Randall B. Morton, Windham,
George W. Card, Dexter,

Jonathan G. Johnson, Garland,
Joseph A. Young, Bingham.

CORPORALS.

John M. Safford, Corinna,
Sanford A. Carpenter, Portland,
Andrew D. Mabury, Windham,
Albert J. Swanton, Dexter.

Luther M. Rideout, Garland,
Oliver French, Solon,
Willard Pinkham, Charleston,

PRIVATES.

Ames, Addison M., Cornville,
Augustine, Peter, Dexter,
Baker, Sylvester P., Solon,
Coan, Elisha S., Garland,
Crocker, George A., Dexter,
Ellis, Augustus, Dexter,
Herrin, Benjamin F., Skowhegan,
Jones, Danville F., Cornville,
Libby, Leander M., Corinna,
McPhee, Michael J., Bangor,
Pennington, Christopher, Garland,
Prescott, Stephen A., Dexter,
Ramsdell, John N., Exeter,
Shay, Michael, Bangor,
Stevens, Daniel, Wellington,

Anderson, James, Bangor,
Bailey, George T., Dexter,
Barker, Isaac C., Exeter,
Coombs, Thomas A., Brunswick,
Curtis, Merrill G., Dexter,
Greeley, Cyrus S., Dexter,
Hunnewell, Franklin S., Portland,
Knox, Sumner, Garland,
Lynes, John, Jr., Bangor,
Moon, Moses, Ellsworth,
Prescott, Eli L., Dexter,
Ramsdell, Benjamin F., Gray,
Rich, George R., Charleston,
Skillings, Sumner L., Garland,
Swett, Henry A., Garland.

MUSICIAN : Alonzo P. Allen, Gray.

On Special Duty or Detached Service: John Grenier, St. Francis, and James Hickey, Bangor, battery C, 1st Mass.; Elsbra McCoy, Bangor, and Leander Shaw, Exeter, battery D, 5th U. S.; Edward P. Merrill, Portland, and Dennis S. Pullen, Dexter, hosp. dept.; Aaron M. Page, Charleston.

COMPANY E.

Captain, Atherton W. Clark, Waldoboro, acting Field Officer.
First Lieutenant, Henry F. Sidelinger, Union, commanding company.
Second Lieutenant, Thomas R. Hogue, Waldoboro.

SERGEANTS.

1st Sergt., John M. Sherwood, Bangor,   Charles H. Haynes, Ellsworth,
William H. H. Hasey, Bangor,   Gardiner Schwartz, Waldoboro.

CORPORALS.

George A. Hock, Waldoboro,   John M. Sherman, Waldoboro,
Raymond W. Hoffses, Waldoboro,   Albert E. Titus, Union,
Timothy F. Brown, Bristol.

PRIVATES.

Bates, Calvin, Waldoboro,   Benner, George G., Waldoboro,
Bickmore, Charles E., Waldoboro,   Brackett, Chandler, Union,
Brock, Lowell, Waldoboro,   Brown, Charles C., East Benton,
Bryant, Elbridge R., Bristol,   Caswell, George B., Bristol,
Chapman, Edward K., Waldoboro,   Conway, John, Bangor,
Cudworth, Levi, Bristol,   Cutler, Alvin, Bristol,
Davis, William L., Union,   Fernald, John Q. A., Waldoboro,
Humphrey, Albert E., Waldoboro,   Lenfest, John, Union,
Levensaler, Elijah S., Waldoboro,   Little, Thomas C., Bristol,
Maddox, Aaron W., Union,   Mank, Leander M., Waldoboro,
Mann, Patrick, Bristol,   McIntyre, John J., Bristol,
McIntyre, Joseph, Bristol,   McKim, William D., Bristol,
Mero, Charles H., Waldoboro,   Mink, Orchard F., Waldoboro,
Palmer, George, Bristol,   Townsend, Thomas, Houlton,
Trundy, Hiram W., Union,   Turner, Barden, Waldoboro,
Twomey, Thomas, Bangor,   Wentworth, William H., Bangor,
Whitney, Charles A., Etna,   Witherell, Edwin S., Augusta,

On Special Duty or Detached Service: Samuel L. Miller, Waldoboro, act'g Sergt.-Major; William H. Chamberlain, Sewall M. Cowan, Bangor, Edwin H. Dunn, Bangor, and Lewis F. Morse, Veazie, battery D, 5th U. S.; William P. Harvey, Bangor, battery C, 1st Mass.; Henry H. Butler, Union, comm'y dept.; Cyrus G. Stewart, Union, quarterm'r dept.; Reuben Walton, Waldoboro.

COMPANY F.

Captain, Samuel T. Keene, Rockland.
First Lieutenant, Holman S. Melcher, Topsham.

SERGEANTS.

First Sergeant, Hezekiah Long, Thomaston,
Ammi M. Smith, Parkman,   George Crocker, St. Albans,
James R. Martin, Parkman.

CORPORALS.

Albion Brown, Harmony,   John W. Morin, Embden,
Franklin B. Ward, Brighton,   Paschal M. Tripp, Ripley,
William S. Hodgdon, Embden,   John Foss, Athens.

PRIVATES.

Boothby, Adney D., Athens,
Brown, Elisha A., Solon,
Carr, Elijah, Bangor,
Clark, Seth W., Solon,
Collins, Elias S., Harmony,
Curtis, Frank B., Wellington,
Daniels, George G., Harmony,
Davis, William H., Cambridge,
Dinsmore, Eben F., Hartland,
Dunlap, Horace, Ripley,
Fox, Samuel A., Cornville,
Frost, Albert, St. Albans,
Gordon, Frank, St. Albans,
Grant, Benjamin W., Cornville,
Hall, Leonidas, Portland,
Johnson, Sullivan, St. Albans,
Palmer, Luther L., Cornville,
Poland, Samuel, Athens,
Stone, Jesse M., Ripley,
Wentworth, John, Athens,
White, Sylvanus R., St. Albans,
Witherell, Robert A., Bangor,
Young, Thomas J., Athens.

Bosworth, Michael, Solon,
Bussell, Oshea, Wellington,
Clark, Horace B., Cornville,
Clifford, John F., Bangor,
Coombs, Augustus F., Parkman,
Daggett, Isaac T., Bingham,
Davis, Gilman, Wellington,
DeWitt, Joseph E., Ripley,
Dunham, Dawson J., Cornville,
Foss, Elfin J., Embden,
French, Edward B., Athens,
Gordon, Edmund, Bangor,
Gordon, Isaiah L., St. Albans,
Hall, Charles F., Bangor,
Hilton, Daniel, Cornville,
Libby, Benjamin D., Athens,
Patten, David, Cornville,
Redmond, George K., Embden,
Weaver, Leander S., Parkman,
Wentworth, Sanford H., Athens,
Whitman, Ezekiel, Brighton,
Wyer, Oscar, Bangor,

MUSICIAN: Michael Quimby, Bangor.

ON SPECIAL DUTY OR DETACHED SERVICE: Crosby N. Crocker, teamster quartermaster's dept.; Henry Reaviel, Bangor, and William N. Witham, Bangor, battery C, 1st N. Y.

COMPANY G.

Captain, Ellis Spear, acting Field Officer (see Field and Staff).
First Lieutenant, Thomas D. Chamberlain, act'g Adjt. (see Field and Staff).
[First Lieutenant Rufus B. Plummer of co. C, commanding.]
Second Lieutenant, Warren L. Kendall, Belfast.

SERGEANTS.

First Sergeant, James C. Rundlett, East Pittston,
Abner S. Hiscock, Damariscotta,   Eugene R. Jackson, Jefferson,
William B. Greenwood, Wiscasset,   William S. Jordan, Bangor.

CORPORALS.

George W. Bowman, Jefferson,   Cyrus Osborn, Alna,
Elisha Meserve, Wiscasset,   Melville C. Day, Jefferson,
Samuel G. Bailey, Woolwich.

PRIVATES.

Averill, Edward, Jefferson,
Bailey, David A., Woolwich,
Baker, James H., Woolwich,
Barnes, Moody D., Nobleboro,
Buker, William G., Brunswick,
Butler, Alvin, Mt. Vernon,
Carter, Lewis D., Woolwich,
Cushman, Llewellyn, Woolwich,

Ayer, Charles N., Brewer,
Bailey, Harlan P., Woolwich,
Baker, Josiah H., Edgecomb,
Borneman, Luther C., Jefferson,
Burr, Frank, Brewer,
Carr, Almon P., Mt. Vernon,
Cunningham, Albert, Edgecomb,
Cushman, Wales H., Woolwich,

Dunbar, Harlow, Nobleboro,
Given, John T., Brewer,
Huff, Gilman P., Edgecomb,
Light, Alva, Edgecomb,
Kennedy, John M., Richmond,
Murphy, Jere, Bangor,
Pero, Henry, Wiscasset,
Preble, Henry C., Woolwich,
Smith, James H., Wellington,
Sweeney, Eugene, Newcastle,
Tibbetts, Jotham D., Woolwich,
Vinal, John, Jefferson,
Wright, Fred R., Wiscasset.

Erskine, James H., Bristol,
Herscomb, Andrew, Edgecomb,
Knight, James A., Edgecomb,
Lowell, Samuel T., Alna,
Moody, Albert A., Waldoboro,
Nash, James A., Nobleboro,
Preble, George, Edgecomb,
Rankin, William, Newcastle,
Smith, John T., Edgecomb,
Swett, Nathaniel L., Orrington,
Veazie, Samuel W., Bangor,
Wheeler, Henry L., Greenfield, Mass.,

MUSICIAN: George D. Hodgdon, Richmond.

ON SPECIAL DUTY OR DETACHED SERVICE: Marcellus Blake, Carmel, and Albert L. Spencer, Bangor, battery C, 1st Mass.; John T. Given, Brewer, battery C, 1st N. Y.; Joseph Linscott, Newcastle, regimental armorer; James G. Brann, Jefferson; Alexis F. Flagg, Alna; Jotham D. Williams, Alna.

COMPANY H.

Captain, Joseph F. Land, Edgecomb.
First Lieutenant, William W. Morrell, Brunswick.
Second Lieutenant, William K. Bickford, Thomaston.

SERGEANTS.

First Sergeant, Charles W. Steele, Oakfield Plantation,
Lewis Merriam, Jr., Houlton,   James A. Horton, Haynesville,
Isaac N. Lathrop, Bangor,   Charles W. Proctor, Oxbow Pl.,
George W. Buck, Linneus, promoted on the field, from Private.

CORPORALS.

Myron W. Harris, Littleton,   John M. Libby, Biddeford,
Andrew J. York, Pownal,   Nathan S. Clark, Masardis,
George F. Estabrook, Amity.

PRIVATES.

Adams, Aaron, Linneus,
Clifford, Benjamin F., Linneus,
Davis, Fred T., Freeport,
Fowles, Gowen W., Medway,
French, Benjamin F., Linneus,
Goff, Edmund, Patten,
Hilt, Byron, Presque Isle,
Ireland, John F., Presque Isle,
Lamson, Iredell, Presque Isle,
McGuire, Seth, Linneus,
Morrison, Edmund, Linneus,
Rogers, Frank M., Appleton,
Swett, Jas. H., No. 8, R. 5, Aroos Co.
Tibbetts, Caleb B., Haynesville,
Welch, Thomas, Houlton,
Whitten, Melvin W., Dexter,
Wyman, Thomas C., Phippsburg.

Chesley, Hiram H., Patten,
Crane, Daniel, Linneus,
Estabrook, Glazier, Amity,
Frederick, Edward, Bangor,
Gerrish, Theo.,No. 5, R. 3, Aroos.Co.,
Ham, Mansfield, Hodgdon,
Ireland, Goodwin S., Presque Isle,
Knowlan, Freeman H., Masardis,
Leighton, Adriel, Augusta,
Miller, George, Bangor,
Ring, William D., Freeport,
Spooner, William E., Hodgdon,
Tarbell, Joseph E., Merrill Plantation,
Walker, Gustavus F., Hodgdon,
West, Joseph, Carmel,
Winslow, Joseph, Oxbow Plantation,

ON SPECIAL DUTY OR DETACHED SERVICE: Charles W. Jackins, Bangor, and Frank C. Williams, Bangor, battery D, 5th U. S.; Frank A. Johnson, Bangor, battery C, 1st Mass.; Andrew C. Munsey, Bowdoin, and Moses G. Rice, Bangor, quarterm'r dept.; John Stockman, Oldtown, wagon master; William M. Gilman, No. 6, R. 4; Joseph Macomber, 2d, amb. corps.

COMPANY I.

Captain, Prentiss M. Fogler, Hope.
First Lieutenant, Arad H. Linscott, Jefferson.
Second Lieutenant, Elisha Besse, Jr., Oakfield Plantation.

SERGEANTS.

First Sergeant, Hiram Morse, Warren,
John D. Leach, Camden,   Andrew W. Stover, South Thomaston.

CORPORALS.

Emerson Creighton, Warren,   John D. Morse, Thomaston,
Thomas H. Buck, Biddeford,   Daniel W. Keene, Bremen.

PRIVATES.

Andrews, Aaron M., Camden,   Andrews, Obed, St. George,
Barron, George W., Warren,   Bickmore, Eli, Friendship,
Blackington, Rufus R., Hope,   Bradford, I. John L., Cushing,
Bradford, William B., Cushing,   Bresnahan, Timothy, Ellsworth,
Briggs, William J., Union,   Burding, George W., So. Thomaston,
Cleaves, Daniel, Biddeford,   Copeland, Charles A., Warren,
Davis, Milton H., Friendship,   Elwell, Freeman, St. George,
Elwell, Ira G., St. George,   Farrand, Austin, Thomaston,
Fish, Benjamin N., Union,   Geyer, Francis, Friendship,
Grant, George N., So. Thomaston,   Griffin, Benjamin N., Stockton,
Hall, Lewis, Warren,   Howes, Oliver, Washington,
Hussey, Wright W., Biddeford,   Hyler, Sylvanus, Cushing,
Ingalls, Joshua, Bridgton,   Jameson, John H., Cushing,
Jones, Charles A., Hope,   Kelleran, Eugene B., Cushing,
Lester, Alexander E., St. John, N. B., Libby, Findley B., Camden,
Light, Edward, Washington,   Lincoln, Oliver W., Washington,
Monroe, Horace, Thomaston,   Peabody, Jason T., Union,
Robinson, Hance, Cushing,   Roosen, Theodore, Thomaston,
Sterling, George, Thomaston,   Stevens, Colver, Biddeford,
Stevens, William H., Bucksport,   Thomas, Oscar, Lee,
Thorndike, Hosea B., Camden,   Torrey, Charles L., Bangor,
Weed, John E., South Thomaston,   Wescott, James B., Biddeford,
Witham, Charles J., Washington.

ON SPECIAL DUTY OR DETACHED SERVICE: Charles E. Foster, Dedham, William H. Jones, Augusta, and Alfred Trask, Augusta, battery I, 5th U. S. Sergeants: Reuel Thomas, Thomaston, special orderly for Colonel; Andrew J. Tozier, Plymouth, regt'l color-bearer. Privates: Thomas A. Davis, Warren, Eben F. Manchester, Windham, and Ambrose Whitcomb, Thomaston, teamsters in quarterm'r dept.; George L. Witham, Southport, hosp. dept.; Thomas Arnold, Warren; George H. Dow, Warren.

COMPANY K.

First Lieutenant, James H. Nichols, Brunswick, commanding company.
Second Lieutenant, Joseph Fuller, 2d, Brunswick.

1st Sergt., George S. Noyes, Pownal, Albert E. Fernald, Winterport,
Spencer M. Wyman, Freeport, Charles Allen, Brunswick.

CORPORALS.
Sylvester S. Richards, Knox, Vinal E. Wall, Rockland,
Edwin B. Foy, Brunswick, Thomas B. McLain, Brunswick,
Charles M. Chase, Freeport, George A. Ramsdell, Brunswick,
George H. Royal, Topsham.

PRIVATES.
Ames, John H., Rockland, Baker, Daniel S., Winterport,
Bowden, Levi O., Winterport, Buker, James J., Ellsworth,
Buxton, Willard W., North Yarmouth, Chase, Stephen G., Winterport,
Cobb, George W., Brunswick, Colson, Theophilus, Winterport,
Courson, David H., Harpswell, Cross, Frederick H., Rockland,
Fenderson, Lewis, Winterport, Fickett, Amasa W., Brewer,
Field, Ira M., Freeport, Freethy, John G., Brooklin,
Grant, Enoch T., Freeport, Gray, Samuel F., Ellsworth,
Keating, Edwin, Appleton, Lane, Clement W., Winterport,
Libby, Samuel B., Durham, Linnekin, John F., Appleton,
McLain, Jacob, Damariscotta, Merrill, James R., Auburn,
Merrill, William F., Freeport, Messer, Thomas G., Damariscotta,
Morse, Winfield S., North Yarmouth, Newell, Enoch F., Brunswick,
Newton, William F., Harpswell, Pennell, William B., Harpswell,
Reed, Herbert M., Pownal, Rhodes, Charles, Rockland,
Ring, Benjamin T., North Yarmouth, Smith, Andrew H., Denmark,
Southard, Joel, Harpswell, Thorn, John F., Brunswick,
Toothaker, George A., Brunswick, Town, Alfred M., Brunswick,
Tyler, Irving, Durham, Walker, Orrin, Stoneham,
Ward, William, Jr., Orono, Wentworth, William A., Hope,
Whitney, William H., Brunswick, Worthing, William A., Harpswell.

ON SPECIAL DUTY OR DETACHED SERVICE: George W. Carlton, Lewiston, and Samuel A. Littlefield, Winterport, medical dept.; Joseph Tyler, Durham, regimental bugler; Erastus C. Anderson, Rockland, cattle guard; Stephen Littlefield, Winterport, hosp. cook.

REVISED REPORT OF CASUALTIES.

COMPANY A.
SERGEANTS.
James H. Harrington, w'd, face. George W. Reynolds, w'd, hip and leg.
CORPORALS.
Charles H. Reed, wounded, wrist. David J. Lewis, wounded, head.
Charles E. Avery, wounded, arm. Joseph D. Simpson, killed.
Laforrest P. True, wounded, arms. John Reed, Jr., killed.
PRIVATES.
Grindle, Joseph, wounded, hand. Hill, William E., wounded, arm.
Lore, Charles, wounded, arm. Norton, Hiram, wounded, head.
Rankins, William, wounded, arm. Surry, Joseph L., wounded, leg.

Sylvester, Ira R., wounded, side.   Taylor, Alfred, wounded, hand,
True, Franklin, wounded, arm.   Willey, William E., wounded, head.

COMPANY B.

PRIVATES.

Leach, George W., wounded and prisoner; died Dec. 1, 1863, in prison.
Morrill, Edwin, wounded, leg.   Sanders, Henry C., wounded, hand.

COMPANY C.

Captain Charles W. Billings, mortally wounded; died July 15, 1863.
Second Lieutenant James H. Stanwood, wounded, leg.
First Sergeant Isaac W. Estes, mortally wounded; died July 14, 1863.
Sergeant Charles A. Knapp, wounded, arm.
Corporal Vincent W. Pinhorn, wounded, hip.

PRIVATES.

Beadle, Charles M., mortally w'd; died, Davis, Moses, mortally wounded; died
   Aug. 6, 1863.   July 3, 1863.
Fogg, Elliott, L., killed.   Heald, Benjamin F., wounded, hand.
Heald, Llewellyn B., wounded, leg.   Hodgdon, Josiah S., wounded, arm.
Monk, Decatur, w'd, arm broken.   O'Connell, John, wounded, head.
Powers, Charles P., wounded, side.   Small, Alva B., mortally w'd; died
Stevens, Oliver L., mortally w'd; died   Aug. 28, 1863.
   July 11, 1863.   Thomas, Moses S., wounded, leg.
Tobin, John, wounded, arm broken.   York, George H., wounded.

COMPANY D.

Captain Joseph B. Fitch, wounded, thigh
Sergeant George W. Card, wounded, face.

CORPORALS.

Oliver French, wounded.   Andrew D. Mabury, killed.
Willard Pinkham, killed.

PRIVATES.

Ames, Addison M., wounded, arm.   Crocker, George A., w'd, shoulder.
Curtis, Merrill G., wounded, shoulder. Prescott, Stephen A., killed.
Ramsdell, John N., wounded, face.   Swett, Henry A., wounded, shoulder.

COMPANY E.

PRIVATES.

Little, Thomas C., wounded, head.   Mink, Orchard F., wounded, leg.

COMPANY F.

Captain Samuel T. Keene, wounded, side, severely.
Sergeant James R. Martin, wounded, face, severely.

CORPORALS.

Albion Brown, wounded, hand, slight. John W. Morin, w'd, thigh, slight.
Franklin B. Ward, w'd, leg amput'd. Paschal M. Tripp, killed.
William S. Hodgdon, killed.   John Foss, killed.

PRIVATES.

Brown, Elisha A., wounded, head.   Clark, Seth W., killed.
Curtis, Frank B., killed.   Foss, Elfin J., killed.
Fox, Samuel A., wounded, head.   French, Edward B., wounded, side.
Grant, Benjamin W., killed.   Hall, Charles F., killed.
Libby, Benjamin D., wounded, hand. Patten, David, wounded, arm and side.

Wentworth, John, killed.
Whitman, Ezekiel, w'd, shoulder.
Young, Thomas J., wounded, arm.

White, Sylvanus R., wounded, hand.
Wyer, Oscar, killed.

COMPANY G.

Second Lieutenant Warren L. Kendall, killed.

SERGEANTS.

Abner S. Hiscock, w'd, arm amput'd.   William S. Jordan, killed.

CORPORALS.

Cyrus Osborn, wounded, arm.   Melville C. Day, killed.

PRIVATES.

Barnes, Moody D., w'd, arm.   Borneman, Luther C., wounded, face.
Cunningham, Albert, wounded, arm.   Cushman, Llewellyn, wounded, arm.
Erskine, James H., wounded, side.   Herscomb, Andrew, wounded, neck.
Knight, James A., killed.   Kennedy, John M., wounded, thigh.
Smith, John T., prisoner, w'd, slight. Sweeney, Eugene, prisoner.
Tibbetts, Jotham D., prisoner.

COMPANY H.

First Sergeant Charles W. Steele, killed.
Sergeant Isaac N. Lathrop, wounded; died July 3, 1863.
Sergeant George W. Buck, promoted from Private on field, killed.
Corporal John M. Libby, wounded, lost two fingers.

PRIVATES.

Adams, Aaron, killed.   Chesley, Hiram H., wounded, neck.
Clifford, Benjamin F., wounded, face. French, Benjamin F., wounded, leg.
Ham, Mansfield, wounded, side.   Hilt, Byron, wounded, shoulder.
Ireland, Goodwin S., killed.   Lamson, Iredell, killed.
Morrison, Edmund, wounded, side.   Walker, Gustavus F., wounded, knee.
West, Joseph, wounded, arm.

COMPANY I.

First Lieutenant Arad H. Linscott, wounded; died July 27, 1863.

SERGEANTS.

Reuel Thomas, wounded, shoulder.   Andrew W. Stover, wounded, leg.

PRIVATES.

Fish, Benjamin N., wounded, head.   Lester, Alexander E., killed.
Peabody, Jason T., w'd, lost finger. Witham, Charles J., lost finger.

COMPANY K.

First Sergeant George S. Noyes, killed.
Sergeant Albert E. Fernald, wounded, hip.

CORPORALS.

Sylvester S. Richards, wounded, face. George A. Ramsdell, wounded, breast.

PRIVATES.

Buxton, Willard W., wounded; died   Chase, Stephen G., killed.
  July 10, 1863.
Cobb, George W., wounded, neck.   Merrill, James R., killed.
Merrill, William F., killed.   Newell, Enoch F., wounded, hand.
Reed, Herbert M., wounded, thigh.   Rhodes, Charles, wounded, neck.
Ring, Benjamin T., wounded, head.   Thorn, John F., wounded, leg.
Walker, Orrin, w'd; died at Gettysb'g. Wentworth, William A., wounded, leg.

HISTORICAL SKETCH.

BY AN OFFICER OF THE REGIMENT.

This regiment was recruited from different parts of the state, its ten companies coming from at least as many counties. It was the last of those organized under the call for three hundred thousand men in 1862. Almost as soon as enlisted the men were hurried into camp at Portland, and on the 29th day of August, 1862, were mustered into the service of the United States for three years or during the war. The original organization was as follows :

FIELD, STAFF AND NON-COMMISSIONED STAFF.

Colonel, Adelbert Ames, Rockland.
Lieutenant-Colonel, Joshua L. Chamberlain, Brunswick.
Major, Charles D. Gilmore, Bangor.
Adjutant, John M. Brown, Portland.
Quartermaster, Moses W. Brown, Brownville.
Surgeon, Nahum P. Munroe, Belfast.
Assistant Surgeon, Nahum A. Hersom, Sanford.
Assistant Surgeon, Siroella A. Bennett, New Portland.
Chaplain, Luther P. French, Corinth.

Sergeant-Major, Weston H. Keene, Bremen.
Quartermaster-Sergeant, Howard L. Prince, Cumberland.
Commissary-Sergeant, Elisha Besse, Jr., Winthrop.
Hospital Steward, Lewis W. Pendleton, Gorham.
Drum-Major, Andrew J. Philbrick, Palmyra.

COMPANY OFFICERS.

Co. A. Captain, Isaac S. Bangs, Waterville.
First Lieutenant, Addison W. Lewis, Waterville.
Second Lieutenant, Charles W. Billings, Clinton.

Co. B. Captain, Phineas M. Jeffards, Foxcroft.
First Lieutenant, James Lyford, Sebec.
Second Lieutenant, Walter G. Morrill, Williamsburg.

Co. C. Captain, Isaac H. McDonald, Buckfield.
First Lieutenant, Frank G. Russell, Rumford.
Second Lieutenant, Augustus H. Strickland, Livermore.

Co. D, Captain, Isaac W. Haskell, Garland.
First Lieutenant, Edward B. Fifield, Dexter.
Second Lieutenant, Mattson C. Sanborn, South Berwick.

Co. E. Captain, Atherton W. Clark, Waldoboro.
First Lieutenant, Joseph B. Fitch, Bristol.
Second Lieutenant, George F. Sumner, Union.

Co. F. Captain, Timothy F. Andrews, Harmony.
First Lieutenant, Hosea Allen, Wellington.
Second Lieutenant, Edwin Folsom, Harmony.

Co. G.   Captain, Ellis Spear, Wiscasset.
          First Lieutenant, Joseph F. Land, Edgecomb.
          Second Lieutenant, Joseph J. A. Hoffses, Jefferson.
Co. H.   Captain, Henry C. Merriam, Houlton.
          First Lieutenant, Daniel Stimson, Biddeford.
          Second Lieutenant, William C. Bailey, Garland.
Co. I.   Captain, Lysander Hill, Thomaston.
          First Lieutenant, Samuel T. Keene, Rockland.
          Second Lieutenant, Prentiss M. Fogler, Hope.
Co. K.   Captain, Charles L. Strickland, Bangor.
          First Lieutenant, James H. Nichols, Brunswick.
          Second Lieutenant, William W. Morrell, Livermore.

Excepting the Colonel and Major, and two or three subordinate officers, both officers and men were substantially without military knowledge or experience. The exigencies of the public service allowed barely time for organization and enrolment and the furnishing of uniforms. The drilling was sufficient only to enable the companies to form line and march by the flank. Two companies only were armed; but one dress parade was attempted, and that was attended with much difficulty and many blunders. The regimental line first formed was indeed awkward, but it was made of good material and it was never broken. Thus scarcely organized, partially armed, substantially undrilled and uninstructed, under the urgent demands of the government, it was rushed by rail to Boston and from Boston by steamship to Washington. The voyage was utilized to the utmost by Colonel Ames for the instruction of the officers, and a good beginning was made in learning the duties of the soldier. These studies and exercises were continued whenever opportunity offered during the ensuing season, whether in camp or campaign. The arming of the regiment was completed at Washington, and it then moved directly across the Potomac and joined the Third brigade of the First division of the Fifth army corps, only a few days before the movement of the army in the Antietam campaign. It was a severe trial to new men, unacclimated, unaccustomed to arms and the equipments of a soldier, unused to the march and bivouac, to bear the full burden in a veteran brigade, of a very active and earnest campaign. Only a part of the regiment was actively engaged in the battle of Antietam, the corps being mainly in reserve, but it was engaged and under musketry fire as a regiment, for the first time, at Shepherdstown Ford, three days after the battle of Antietam. It suffered, however, but slight loss.

After Shepherdstown Ford it was held in that vicinity to guard the fords of the Potomac. The situation of the camp was one of the most malarious and unhealthy on the upper Potomac, and the immediate proximity of the terrible battlefield affected the streams and the air so that men could hardly drink the water or breathe the air. The time, however, was utilized to the utmost in the instruction and drilling of the regiment. This was, in some respects, the most trying period in the history of the regiment. The houses in the vicinity were used as hospitals and were filled with desperately sick men lying upon the floor, poorly attended and not supplied with proper food. Many died, many men were permanently disabled, and many others were sent to the hospitals who afterwards returned to the regiment. More than 300 men were left behind at this place, or in other hospitals, when the regiment moved.

Marching from the Potomac to the Rappahannock, the regiment went into camp at Stoneman's Switch. Quarters for the men were rudely constructed, better than any they previously occupied, but still imperfect and uncomfortable. The men had been supplied with shelter tents, but the line officers had no shelter excepting a " fly." With these and a few poles supplemented by excavation in some instances, they contrived to keep themselves sheltered from the rain. As far as possible drilling and instruction were continued.

At the battle of Fredericksburg the regiment, being in the Centre Grand division, crossed the Rappahannock in the afternoon of the first day of the battle under artillery fire, and advanced with the brigade through the town to replace the lines which had vainly attempted to reach the stone-wall at Marye's Heights. The advance was made under heavy fire of artillery and musketry, but secured a position close up to the enemy's lines, where, however, nothing could be effected against the enemy, but greatly exposed the regiment to a deadly fire at close range. The regiment was held in this position that night and during the next day ; but on the second night the brigade was drawn back into the town. On the night of the withdrawal of the army, the regiment was sent again to the extreme front as an advanced line, where it remained almost alone while the army recrossed the river, and at 2 o'clock in the morning it was withdrawn, the rear of the rear-guard which crossed the last pontoon bridge left in place. On the next day it returned to its old camp, and remained here until April with no interruption except that it shared in the fruitless and miserable movement made in January, designated by the men as the "mud march." The men, not yet acclimated, were still suffering from diseases incident to camp life, and a considerable number died during the winter.

In April by some mis-doing small-pox virus was administered instead of vaccine in the regiment, and it was detached from the brigade and removed to another camp where it remained until the battle of Chancellorsville. Though still in quarantine, the regiment, at the request of Colonel Chamberlain, then in command, was permitted to take part in the battle of Chancellorsville. The Colonel reinforced his request for such permission by the suggestion that if the regiment could do no more it might "give the enemy the small-pox." It was, however, assigned to the duty of guarding the telegraph line from the field of battle on the right to that on the left, at Fredericksburg. After the battle it was the last to recross the river, and in a drenching rain returned to its camp. In May, 1863, Ames was commissioned as Brigadier General, and Chamberlain was promoted to be Colonel.

During the movements which culminated in the battle of Gettysburg it shared in the engagement at Middleburg, June 21st, the Third brigade having been sent to the support of the cavalry. It charged and drove the enemy from their positions behind stone-walls, forcing them back beyond Goose Creek.

After some hard marching, which occupied the greater part of the night of the 1st of July, the regiment was upon the field of Gettysburg, and in the afternoon of the second day it moved with the brigade under artillery fire to the left and was advancing into the Wheatfield when it was turned sharply to the left and rear and moved back in rear of Little Round Top. The main part of the brigade occupied the crest of Little Round Top towards the left, and the Twentieth being on the extreme left was refused and faced towards Big Round Top. It occupied the southern and eastern slope of the hill directly fronting a valley or level space which lay between the two Tops. The slopes and the valley were covered with a forest of oak trees, for the greater part free from underbrush, and open. The ground of the slopes and in the valley was strewn with large bowlders. There was no protection for our men, and no time to throw up earthworks, even if that had been practicable in the rocky soil. Company B, under Captain Morrill, was promptly thrown forward as skirmishers. Almost immediately thereafter the enemy appeared coming down the slope of Big Round Top, and they seemed to be overlapping our left. By the direction of Colonel Chamberlain, Captain Spear, who was then acting as Major, bent back the left companies slightly, for the better protection of that flank. The advanced enemy at once opened fire, pressing more heavily on the centre and left. Many of them took position behind the bowlders which afforded them protection, and were firing at short range. The firing was very heavy and our men were rapidly falling, but a vigorous and well-directed fire was kept up in return. The line on the left gave back somewhat at times, closing up to fill the gaps. The fire from the enemy continued for some time, and then slightly slackened, and the contest was decided by a charge of the Twentieth, down the rocky slope. It was done so suddenly that many of the Confederates, sheltered behind the bowlders in advance of their line, were at once run over and captured, and the shock of the charge falling directly upon their line broke it instantly. Then occurred one of those accidents such as often determine the result of a battle. Morrill's company (B), which had been advanced as skirmishers, as before related, not having effected a junction on its right, was cut off, and had moved around and occupied a stone-wall in the rear of the position taken up by the enemy, and when the Confederates were driven back by the charge towards this wall Morrill's company fired a volley into the rear; this threw them into confusion, and there being nothing on their right, about 300 of them surrendered and others escaped in disorder in the woods. The Twentieth sustained heavy loss, about forty per cent of the entire number of about 350.

The regiment with which it had been engaged was the 15th Ala., commanded by Colonel Oates, which, as he reported, went into battle with 640 muskets. After the repulse of the enemy at Little Round Top, Chamberlain was directed to advance and occupy Big Round Top, and in accordance with these orders he moved with the Twentieth Maine alone, climbing the steep and rocky side of this high hill and took position on the crest. It was then about dark. Advancing his skirmishers he encountered a line of skirmishers of the enemy and captured some thirty-five of them. He occupied the crest without support for the greater part of the night, but towards morning the line was completed between his right and the left of the line on Little Round Top. After daylight of the 3d the Twentieth was relieved and returned to its brigade. During the battle on the third day the brigade lay exposed only to artillery fire on the left of the point assailed by Pickett. The regiment advanced on the 4th to the Emmitsburg road, and on the morning of the 5th moved with the brigade and corps in the pursuit of the enemy. On the 10th of July it was engaged with the enemy on the Sharpsburg Pike, losing ten men. After the enemy had fallen back behind the Potomac the regiment had some hard marching, across the South Mountain, and after a brief bivouac on the north bank of the Potomac, crossed and took part in the further movement through Manassas Gap. It was present but not actively engaged in the skirmish at Wapping Heights.

In August the regiment was encamped at Beverly Ford; Colonel Chamberlain, having been assigned to the command of the brigade, was succeeded in command of the regiment by Spear, who had in the meantime been commissioned as Major. No other field officers being present, Clark of company E was detailed as acting field officer. The regiment shared in the movement between Culpeper Court House and Centreville in the fall of 1863, but was not actively engaged with the enemy until the 7th day of November, when it took part in the battle of Rappahannock Station, losing, however, but few men. It was subsequently in the affair at Mine Run in the latter part of November; and with other regiments covered the corps front on the picket line in front of the enemy's works, holding that ground during the entire time in which the corps was at Mine Run. The regiment suffered extremely from the severe cold, but had very slight loss in wounded and none killed. Returning from Mine Run the regiment was assigned to the duty during the winter of '63–'64 of guarding the railroad bridge at Rappahannock Station, and occupied that position until the 1st day of May, 1864. At this camp the men built comfortable and convenient quarters of slabs, split and hewed; substantial company kitchens were established and regular camp rations were issued. The location was healthy, and not a man was lost from the regiment during the whole winter. The men were exercised by drilling as often as the weather permitted. The senior Captain, Clark, being absent on detached services, Captain Keene was detailed as acting Field officer.

On the 1st day of May, 1864, under the command of Major Spear, the regiment left this camp, in which the officers and men had passed a pleasant winter, and bivouacked near Ingalls' Station, and on the 3d moved and went into bivouac near Culpeper. At midnight moved again, and on the morning of the 4th crossed the Rapidan at Germanna Ford, and marched out on the Plank road to the Orange Court House road, and went into line of battle on the left of that road.

In the morning it was reported that the enemy were advancing, and some slight intrenchments were made, and the trees were cut down in front of the line. The enemy not attacking and an advance being ordered, the regiment moved with the brigade, in the second line, with its right on road. The advance was at first through a thick wood, but, emerging from that into an open field, the lines met a sharp fire from the enemy, posted in the edge of the wood on the opposite side of the field. The charge across this field was on the double-quick. The two lines were somewhat disordered by a ditch about midway of the field, but the enemy were driven through the wood into a second opening. Here it became apparent that the brigade had advanced more rapidly than the line on the right of the road, and firing was heard on the right and rear.   This checked the advance. The Twentieth moved to the front and one company was deployed on the right, across the road.   Its captain reported that that flank was unprotected, and that skirmishers of the enemy were crossing the road in our rear.

The 83d Penn., which had been in front of the Twentieth, was re-formed in the rear, and wheeled to face to the right, but in a few minutes the enemy concentrated upon the left of the brigade and broke it, leaving both flanks of the Twentieth unprotected.   The regiment fell back in good order to the original works, bringing off thirty-five prisoners, with the loss of Captain Morrill of B, severely, and three other officers, wounded, ten men killed and fifty-eight wounded, and sixteen missing. On the 6th the regiment was engaged with the enemy and lost two men killed and ten wounded.   On the 7th the regiment with three others advanced to push the enemy back as far as possible and ascertain their position and force.   The skirmishers of the enemy were driven in and through the woods to a line of breastworks from which the enemy opened with artillery and musketry. One officer, Lieutenant Sherwood, was killed here, and Lieutenant Lane mortally wounded ; and a considerable number of men killed or wounded.   The regiment followed the corps to Spotsylvania Court House, moving early on the morning of the 8th, and at 6 P. M. advanced, supporting General Crawford's line. It was very nearly dusk when the regiment was, with the other detachments of the brigade, charged by the enemy, who, after a sharp hand-to-hand fight, were repulsed.   The regiment lost one officer (Captain Morrell of A) killed and two wounded, five men killed, thirteen wounded and two missing.   About 100 of the enemy were captured, including four commissioned officers.

The regiment was under fire on the 10th and 11th, but not actively engaged, and lost one killed and two wounded.   During the 12th and 13th it was occupied in intrenching, and on the night of the 13th marched all night to the left and went into position near Spotsylvania Court House, where it remained until the 20th of May, constantly under fire.

On the 21st of May the brigade was in the advance in following the enemy in their retreat.   Encountering a heavy rear guard with cavalry and artillery, which checked the advance of the corps, Colonel Chamberlain, who had recently returned to the regiment for duty, taking with him the Twentieth and two other regiments, made a skillful movement to cut them off and capture their artillery. The demonstration made in crossing a deep stream gave the enemy warning, and they galloped their guns away and were routed from their advantageous position, with the loss of several as prisoners.

The regiment crossed the North Anna in the afternoon of the 23d and took an important part in the brilliant actions on that side of the river, but without severe loss.

The regiment marched to the vicinity of Mangohick Church on the 27th and crossed the Pamunkey on the day following. It was engaged in the minor actions during the last of May and bore an important part in the severe engagement at Bethesda Church on the 2d and 3d of June, and lost during that time about thirty men. Again under command of Major Spear, it lay on the left of the army at Chickahominy on picket until the 12th of June, when it crossed the Chickahominy and moved towards the James, and thence to Petersburg. On the 18th it was in the reserve and suffered but slight loss. Here Colonel Chamberlain, who had some time before been assigned to command another veteran brigade of the division, was severely wounded in a desperate charge, and was promoted to be Brigadier-General by General Grant, on the field. On the 21st the regiment moved across to the left and after dark went into position and threw up earthworks in front of the enemy nearer the Jerusalem Plank road, where it remained until the 12th day of August. It lost here one officer (Maj. Samuel T. Keene) and five men killed, and seven men wounded.

The regiment subsequently, in August, took part in the capture of the Weldon Railroad and was actively engaged during the three days' fight at that point. It lay upon the Weldon Railroad until the 30th of September, receiving here one hundred recruits. On the 30th of September it moved with the division and took part in the battle at Peebles' Farm. The regiment was upon the extreme right of the line in the formation for the charge, but later was brought to the centre and

formed upon the skirmish line and charged on that line directly
towards the artillery in an earthwork in the centre of the field,
from which a line of rifle-pits extended to the right and left.
The charge was led by Major Spear. Captain Prince, then serving on the brigade staff, had rejoined his comrades of the regiment, in this perilous work, and was the first man in the fort.
The entire line was captured and a considerable number of prisoners, with one piece of artillery, taken by Captain Fernald and
a small squad of his company. General Warren telegraphed
General Meade, reporting the charge as " one of the boldest I
ever saw." Here the command devolved upon Captain Clark,
Major Spear succeeding to the command of the brigade. On the
afternoon of the same day a division of the Ninth corps advanced
on the left to push the enemy further, and the regiment, with
the brigade, advanced to protect the right flank of that division.
That division giving way, the brigade became severely engaged
with the enemy, but held its position until dark. The regiment
lost in this battle one officer (Capt. Weston H. Keene), and
five men killed, and three officers and forty-nine men wounded,
nearly forty per cent of those engaged. The regiment occupied
intrenchments made at this point until the affair at Hatcher's
Run, or Boydton Road, on the 27th of October.

It was engaged in December in the raid upon the Weldon
Railroad and assisted in destroying that road down to near
Hicksford (a). It was engaged in the action of Hatcher's
Run, February 6th, with slight loss. Returning it remained in
camp until the 29th day of March, when it took part in the
final movement against Richmond. It was engaged at the
Quaker Road on the 29th supporting Chamberlain, whose brigade drove the enemy from that road. It was also engaged on
the 31st in the battle at Gravelly Run and on the 1st day of
April, 1865, at the battle of Five Forks, where it charged the
enemy's works (b). It was with its corps in the movement
within the enemy's right, at Petersburg, and in the pursuit to

(a) The aggregate casualties during 1864 are stated to have been 254. January 26,
1865, it had 275 muskets, and in addition an unassigned company. Losses in 1865 were
81. Combining the two years we find: Killed, 5 officers, 41 men; wounded, 16 officers, 246 men; missing, 27 men. Aggregate, 335.—[EDS.]

(b) Capturing a battle-flag and many prisoners.—[EDS.]

Appomattox Court House, but was not actively engaged until it reached the Court House.

The closing scene at Appomattox Court House was a fit end of the last campaign and indeed of the war. The regiment was fortunate in sharing in the closing act, as it had shared in the previous three years, the story of which has been so briefly and imperfectly told. How the Fifth corps and the cavalry, under Sheridan, broke in the extreme right of the enemy and compelled the thinning of their lines in the formidable works, which had so long confronted the army of the Potomac; how, on the morning of the 2d of April, corps after corps tore their way through musketry and artillery fire, through abatis and over ditches and breastworks, and then pushed on after the retreating Confederates, all the world knows. It fell to the lot of the Twentieth to be in that part which followed Sheridan and the cavalry, endeavoring to pass to the left of their army and block its way. In this earnest pursuit the last day's march was occupied from five in the morning until midnight; indeed, until it seemed that man could march no longer; only the sound of Sheridan's cannon in front kept them in motion. The writer saw men fall out as they marched, turning aside and falling as they turned from sheer exhaustion; and finally, on the last halt, they lay down by the roadside, and could not be moved. But the next morning the stragglers were up, and the corps moved out at 5 o'clock, to the sound of battle in front.

Gray April clouds hid the morning sun as the columns emerged from the woods into the open country about the unknown little Court House village, destined that day to become historic. The open field, bordered by woods, stretched far out to right and left. To the front, a half mile away, was a low hill, skirted by trees, which hid the village. At the left, along this skirt, near its edge, a line of white puffs showed where the cavalry were stubbornly resisting the pressure of Lee's infantry. As the Fifth corps swung into line of battle, with wings bent forward, and the color-bearers shook out the battle-flags, the sun was breaking through the clouds over the eastern woods.

Behind, and moving to the left of the Fifth corps, was the Twenty-fourth, with well-closed columns, in which were two brigades of colored troops, assigned by some whim of justice, to block the last line of retreat of the fleeing Confederates.

Before the concave line of infantry, visible from flank to flank, sprang out the skirmishers, dotting the greensward. Behind, the artillery was moving up. The lines of infantry in order of battle, a long array of bright muskets spaced with colors, on an open field, more than twenty thousand men in sight, formed an unusual and inspiring spectacle even to veterans. But in front of this, and between it and the enemy, appeared a moving panorama still more picturesque. A body of cavalry, apparently relieved by the infantry on the left, came galloping across the field towards the right. In front, apart from the rest, conspicuous, clear against the sky as if in silhouette, on a black horse, in swift gallop, rode Sheridan. A more striking military figure cannot be conceived. It was the same long, powerful stride of the black horse that carried victory to Cedar Creek. Sheridan, alert, eager, his bronzed face set as if carved from oak, seemed in shape and movement the very embodiment of fighting energy. Next behind him spurred on his color-bearer, with the broad and swallow-tailed flag marked with crossed swords, and standing out and quivering in the rapid motion, a flag borne in many battles, and never backward.

Behind this, in quick succession, followed staff and orderlies and a hurrying body of horsemen. Over all this and over the infantry lines shrieked the shells of the enemy, bursting in the air, with white puffs, that one after another drifted and disappeared; or, plowing the ground, rebounded in the air. Sheridan, with this staff and escort and their flutter of flags, passed the front, and the infantry moved on, silent and steady, for what they thought the final grapple with the enemy.

The writer was riding with the skirmish line, and as it entered the curtain of trees, heard a shout on the left, and spurring in that direction saw emerging from woods a mounted officer in Confederate uniform, waving a white flag. No tidings had reached us of the previous correspondence between Grant and Lee; but even the men on the skirmish line had at once understood the meaning of the white flag, and all its consequences, and were wildly shouting, "Lee surrenders! Lee surrenders!"

Indeed, an angel appearing from heaven, shining as the sun, could have meant no more than that mounted officer with his bit of white cloth. It signalled the decree of the Almighty. It meant the final and complete triumph of the army of the Potomac, after four years of severe struggle, mixed often with bitter defeat. It meant the vindication and re-establishment of the government, the end of slavery, honor instead of shame, and prosperity and peace instead of peril and disaster. For this a thousand battles had been fought, and hundreds of thousands of men had perished. No one of us doubted that it was the close of the war, and for us it meant home and friends restored.

The officer with the flag turned and rode to the right, followed by shouts. With quite different feelings the line moved on through the woods and into the open country in which stood the straggling village.

We lay there under orders to be "ready to make or receive an attack" the remainder of that day and the 10th, and on the 11th the regiment, with the remainder of the brigade, under General Chamberlain's orders, relieved General Gibbon's corps from the formalities in receiving the surrender of the Confederate arms and colors, so that the Twentieth had its share in the last part of the closing scene, and when this was done, saw the Confederate troops, a forlorn array, without arms or colors or military music, in straggling columns, march off towards their distant homes.

After this the regiment was stationed near the battlefield of Five Forks for some weeks, and returned to Washington and went into camp on the Columbia Pike, on the 8th day of May, 1865. Here the original members of the regiment were sent to Portland under Lieutenant-Colonel Morrill and mustered out, leaving only the recruits and men assigned subsequently to the original organization. In place of the men mustered out, those remaining of the Sixteenth Maine and the battalion of the First Maine Sharpshooters were consolidated with the Twentieth, and under this organization the regiment, under Colonel Spear, returned to Portland and was mustered out on the 16th day of July, 1865.

THE LAST ACT.

The distinguished honor fell to a Maine officer, Brigadier-General Joshua L. Chamberlain, to be selected to command the detachment of Union troops, as representing the whole, to be marshalled in the military function of receiving, in a proper parade, the surrender of their arms and colors from the hands of the Confederates who had carried them.

[This selection of Chamberlain by Generals Gibbon and Griffin could not have been accidental. The Rebellion Records pertaining to that campaign, serial numbers 95, 97, show complimentary mentions of his name, and on page 730 of the latter volume is a recommendation by General Griffin for Chamberlain's promotion, "as a reward for his conspicuous gallantry and meritorious services during this campaign, in the action on the Quaker Road, * * * in the battle of Five Forks, * * * and in the culminating battle at Appomattox Court House. In this last action, April 9th, his brigade had the advance and was driving the enemy rapidly before it when the announcement of the surrender of Lee was made."—*Communication, April* 13, 1865.]

General Chamberlain called for his old brigade for this special duty,—the Third brigade, First division, Fifth corps, composed of the Twentieth Maine, First Maine Sharpshooters, 32d Mass., 1st and 16th Mich., 83d, 91st, 118th, and 155th Penn. regiments. This body was augmented during the day by other parts of the same division.

Chamberlain formed his troops in brigade line of battle, standing at attention, and in silence, as the Confederates marched up, under the escort of Major Ellis Spear of the Twentieth, and other officers, on staff service, brigade after brigade, along our front from right to left; some of their officers, by a marching salute, responding to the courtesy shown to a gallant foe by Chamberlain when he ordered his line to a "shoulder arms" (known now as the "carry"), and in the perfect decorum preserved by our men. Matching their front to that of Chamberlain, they halted and formed their line, in succession as they arrived, facing ours, and about twelve paces away, and then sadly they stacked their arms, laid their colors down, and silently departed from sight. This ceremony occupied the whole day, and when it ended the work of the army of the Potomac was done, and peace was fully assured.

ROSTER.

The following information relating to officers of the Twentieth Maine regiment is obtained from the Volunteer Army Register, published by the War Department August 31, 1865, .and other reliable sources.

OFFICERS AT FINAL MUSTER-OUT, JULY 16, 1865.

COLONEL: Ellis Spear, May 29, 1865, — brevet Major from Captain, August, 1863; brevet Lieut.-Col. from Major, Sept. 30, 1864; brevet Colonel, from Lieut.-Col., March 29, 1865; brevet Brig.-Gen'l from Colonel, to rank March 13, 1865.

LIEUTENANT-COLONEL: Thomas D. Chamberlain, June 23, 1865,—brevet Major from Captain, March 13, 1865; and brevet Colonel from Lieut.-Col.

MAJOR: George R. Abbott, July 3, 1865,—brevet Major from Captain, April 9, 1865.

CAPTAINS: Holman S. Melcher, Oct. 22, 1864,—brevet Major, April 9, 1865; William O. Howes, Nov. 29, 1864; Charles F. Sawyer, Nov. 29, 1864; Albion Whitten, Dec. 4, 1864; William H. Harrington, Dec. 29, 1864; John Butler, June 30, 1865; Samuel W. Schofield, July 14, 1865; John H. Terry, July 14, 1865.

FIRST LIEUTENANTS: Adjutant William E. Donnell, Sept. 1, 1863,— brevet Captain July 6, 1864; George W. Sweetser, Nov. 29, 1864; Warren T. Noyes, Dec. 29, 1864; George W. Furbish, July 1, 1865; George A. Rider, Quartermaster, July 3, 1865.

SURGEON: William H. True, March 9, 1865. ASSISTANT SURGEON: Charles G. Stevens, July 3, 1865.

MUSTERED-OUT WITH ORIGINAL MEN, JUNE 4, 1865.

LIEUTENANT-COLONEL: Walter G. Morrill, March 13, 1865, — brevet Major from Captain, July 6, 1864.

MAJOR: Atherton W. Clark, March 13, 1865, — brevet Major from Captain, Oct. 28, 1864, and brevet Lieut.-Col. from Major.

CAPTAINS: Howard L. Prince, Dec. 1, 1864,—brevet Captain from First Lieut., Sept., 1864; William Griffin, Dec. 27, 1864; Rufus B. Plummer, Sept. 16, 1863; Joseph B. Fitch, March 26, 1863, — brevet Major, Sept. 30, 1864; Prentiss M. Fogler, March 26, 1863; Joseph F. Land, March 26, 1863; Henry F. Sidelinger, Feb. 13, 1864,—brevet Major, April 9, 1865.

FIRST LIEUTENANTS: Quartermaster Alden Litchfield, Dec, 1, 1862; William K. Bickford, June 10, 1864; Charles R. Shorey, Dec. 1, 1864; Royal B. Decker, Dec. 27, 1864; Mattson C. Sanborn, June 28, 1864; Albert E. Fernald, July 12, 1864, — brevet Captain, Sept. 30, 1864; Alden Miller, Jr., July 12, 1864; Hiram Morse, June 18, 1864; Edmund R. Sanborn, May 7, 1865.

SECOND LIEUTENANTS: Samuel L. Miller, Dec. 1, 1864; Samuel G. Crocker, Dec. 27, 1864; Joseph Walker, Dec. 1, 1864; Albert E. Titus, Dec. 1, 1864; Hezekiah Long, Dec. 1, 1864; Aaron M. Andrews, Dec. 6, 1864; Spencer M. Wyman, May 19, 1865.

ASSISTANT SURGEON: Granville M. Baker, June 23, 1863.

(The dates given above refer to rank or commission; those hereafter given refer to the date of event.)

DIED.

CAPTAINS: Timothy F. Andrews, Oct. 10, 1862; Charles W. Billings, July 15, 1863, of wounds received at Gettysburg; William W. Morrell, killed in action May 8, 1864; Samuel T. Keene, killed in action June 22, 1864,— commissioned Major, not mustered; Weston H. Keene, killed in action Sept. 30, 1864.

FIRST LIEUTENANTS: Arad H. Linscott, July 27, 1863, of wounds received at Gettysburg; John M. Sherwood, killed in action May 7, 1864; George H. Wood, May 25, 1865, of accidental wounds.

SECOND LIEUTENANTS: Warren L. Kendall, July 5, 1863, of wounds received at Gettysburg; Frederick W. Lane, May 14, 1864, of wounds.

TRANSFERRED AND PROMOTED OUT OF REGIMENT.

Colonel Adelbert Ames, W. P. R. A., May 20, 1863, to Brigadier-General Vols., brevet Major-Gen. U. S. Vols., January 15, 1865, brevet Major-Gen. U. S. A. from Captain 5th U. S. Art'y, March 13, 1865; Colonel Joshua L. Chamberlain, June 18, 1864, on the field, to Brigadier-General Vols., brevet Major-Gen. Vols., March 29, 1865; Captain Isaac S. Bangs, Feb. 26, 1863,— Lieut.-Col. 81st U. S. Col'd Troops, promoted to Colonel 10th U. S. Col'd Art'y, not mustered, brevet Brig.-General, March 13, 1865; First Lieut. John M. Brown, Adjutant, June 29, 1863, to Captain and A. A. G.,— Lieut.-Col. Thirty-second Maine regt., brevet Brig.-General Vols., March 13, 1865; Second Lieut. Geo. C. Getchell, July 30, 1863, to Captain 81st U. S. C. T.; Second Lieut. James C. Rundlett, May 22, 1865, to Captain 128th U. S. Col'd Troops; Assistant Surgeon Nahum A. Hersom, April 11, 1863, to Surgeon Seventeenth Maine Vols.

DISCHARGED.

CAPTAIN: Lysander Hill, Feb. 6, 1863. FIRST LIEUTENANTS: Arad Thompson, Feb. 15, 1865; David M. Overlock, March 10, 1865; James H. Stanwood, June 2, 1865; Joseph Fuller, 2d, Dec. 20, 1864. SECOND LIEUTENANT: Elisha Besse, Jr., Feb. 6, 1864.

SURGEONS: Nahum P. Monroe, May 6, 1863; John Benson, Aug. 27, 1863; Abner O. Shaw, Feb. 22, 1865.

CHAPLAIN: Alfred C. Godfrey, March 28, 1865.

RESIGNED.

COLONEL: Charles D. Gilmore, May 29, 1865.

CAPTAINS: Isaac W. Haskell, Nov. 20, 1862; Phineas M. Jeffards, Nov. 29, 1862; Isaac H. McDonald, Dec. 10, 1862; Henry C. Merriam, Jan. 7, 1863, —afterward Lieut.-Col. in U. S. Col'd Troops (brevet Colonel March 26, 1865), Colonel and Brig.-Gen'l U. S. A.; Charles L. Strickland, Feb. 5, 1863.

FIRST LIEUTENANTS: Addison W. Lewis, Nov. 6, 1863; Moses W. Brown, Quartermaster, Nov. 20, 1862; Edward B. Fifield, Nov. 20, 1862; Hosea Allen, Nov. 21, 1862; James Lyford, Nov. 29, 1862; Frank G. Russell, Jan. 10, 1863; Daniel Stimson, Jan. 11, 1863; James H. Nichols, March 1, 1864, brevet Captain.

SECOND LIEUTENANTS: Edwin Folsom, Oct. 14, 1862; George F. Sumner, Oct. 31, 1862; Joseph J. A. Hoffses, Nov. 20, 1862; Augustus H. Strickland, Dec. 10, 1862; William C. Bailey, Feb. 9, 1863; Edward Simonton, April 6, 1863; Thomas R. Hogue, April 14, 1863; Samuel H. Glidden, Nov. 3, 1863.

CHAPLAIN: Luther P. French, Jan. 12, 1864.

OTHERWISE LEFT THE SERVICE.

Assistant Surgeon Siroella A. Bennett, March 21, 1863.

MONUMENT.

The monument, of cut Hallowell granite, is a massive cube, surmounted by a pyramidal top. It stands west of Hancock avenue, to the left of the copse of trees known as the Bloody Angle, in the position held by the regiment while awaiting Pickett's charge.

ADMEASUREMENTS: Base, 7 feet by 7 feet by 1 foot 8 inches; die, 6 feet by 6 feet by 5 feet 4 inches; apex, 5 feet 4 inches by 5 feet 4 inches by 5 feet 7 inches. Total height, 12 feet 7 inches.

Upon the faces of the cube are the date 1863, the trefoil of the Second corps, and these inscriptions:

19TH MAINE INF'Y REG'T.
1ST BRIGADE, 2D DIVISION, 2D CORPS

IN THE EVENING OF JULY 2D THIS REGIMENT AT A POSITION ON THE LEFT OF BATT'Y G, 5TH U. S., HELPED TO REPEL THE ENEMY THAT HAD DRIVEN IN HUMPHREYS' DIVISION, TAKING ONE BATTLE FLAG AND RE-CAPTURING FOUR GUNS.

ON JULY 3, AFTER ENGAGING THE ENEMY'S ADVANCE FROM THIS POSITION, IT MOVED TO THE RIGHT TO THE SUPPORT OF THE 2D BRIGADE AND JOINED IN THE FINAL CHARGE AND REPULSE OF PICKETT'S COMMAND.

EFFECTIVE STRENGTH, JULY 2D, 405; KILLED & MORTALLY WOUNDED, 65; WOUNDED, NOT FATALLY, 137; MISSING, 4.

COLONEL FRANCIS E. HEATH.

NINETEENTH MAINE REGIMENT,

FIRST BRIGADE, SECOND DIVISION, SECOND ARMY CORPS,

AT THE BATTLE OF GETTYSBURG.

WHILE the desperate defense of Little Round Top was going on, the utmost efforts of the Third corps and its reinforcements from the Fifth and Second corps, were insufficient to maintain the advanced line taken up by General Sickles. We have already seen the Third Maine overpowered at the Peach Orchard, the Fourth as severely handled in Devil's Den, and the Seventeenth holding on until relieved in the Wheatfield, all with heavy losses. The fortunes of these Maine regiments were the fortunes of the whole of Sickles' line.

The success of Longstreet was the signal for the advance of the Confederate army along the whole Union line ; and the Twentieth Maine had hardly ceased fighting Hood's soldiers on Little Round Top, when the troops of Early were ready to dash on Cemetery Hill, after dark, in the charge already described in connection with the Fifth Maine battery. In this general attack, the place of greatest hope for the Confederates was on the left centre of the Union army, where Sickles' line was already crumbling. This advantage followed up successfully would cut Meade's army in two. How this disaster was averted cannot be told without giving lasting honor to two Maine organizations, the Nineteenth infantry and Sixth battery.

The Nineteenth infantry was attached to Hancock's Second corps, and was the only Maine organization in that corps. With the 15th Mass., 1st Minn. and 82d N. Y., it formed Harrow's brigade of Gibbon's division. The regiment was commanded by Col. Francis E. Heath, who had earned his promotion in the Virginia campaigns of the Third Maine. The regiment numbered four hundred and five, men and officers, recruited prin-

cipally in the counties of Knox, Waldo, Kennebec and Sagadahoc. They had come from Maine less than a year before ; and,
although they had seen hard service and all the experiences
of the soldier's life in the Rappahannock campaigns, this was
to be their first opportunity to show their worth in a great
pitched battle.

As the Second corps was the last body of troops to leave
the Rappahannock, the regiment had been moved north by very
hard marches. On June 29th it was at Monocacy, and that day
it marched about thirty miles to Uniontown, near the Pennsylvania line. During the forenoon of the 1st of July the regiment acted as guard of the corps trains, a duty which brought
it into the extreme rear of the corps column. At noon it
was relieved and ordered to take its place in column. At this
hour rumors of a battle at Gettysburg were heard. The corps
was near Taneytown, where at that hour General Hancock
met General Meade, and whence, after a consultation, the
former General rode on to Gettysburg. General Hancock
started about 1 P. M., and his corps followed at once. The
Nineteenth marched all the afternoon and until 1 o'clock the
next morning, when it went into bivouac about three miles from
Gettysburg on the Taneytown road.

Early in the morning of July 2d the Second corps was
placed in line of battle, its right resting on the left of Cemetery
Hill, while its left stretched towards Little Round Top. The
three divisions of the corps filled about half the interval between
Cemetery Hill and Little Round Top, Sickles' Third corps holding the remaining distance. Gibbon's division held the centre
of the Second corps line, two of his brigades being in the line,
and a third in reserve a hundred yards in the rear (a).

This brigade was Harrow's, to which the Nineteenth Maine
was attached. This arrangement was only temporary, however.
General Sickles, about 2 : 30 P. M., moved his corps out to the
new line ; and after an hour's desperate fighting in Birney's
front the left division of Hancock's line, under Caldwell, was
sent to assist. The left of the Second corps line was thus weak-
ened. Hancock made the most effective disposition of his troops

(a)   General Harrow's report, Rebellion Records, serial no. 43, page 419.

possible in preparation for the crisis which his soldierly instincts anticipated. In the course of these preparations he moved the Nineteenth Maine from its position in reserve to the left of, and in advance of, the line of Gibbon's division, and stationed it on the left of Weir's U. S. battery, to which it was to act as support. General Hancock gave the order for this movement in person. Indeed, both General Hancock and General Meade were present in this part of the line at this time, hurrying up all available troops and batteries to meet the deluge which was overpowering Sickles at the Peach Orchard salient.

About 6 : 30 P. M. the Second division line of the Third corps, along the Emmitsburg road, was attacked on that front. A part of Humphreys' men, who held that part of the line along the road, after the division began to change front to rear, made their line of retreat so as to bring some of the Excelsior brigade towards the advanced position of the Nineteenth. The Confederates, impelled by the ardor imparted by success and superior numbers, came pressing upon their flank and rear, threatening to make the retreat a disastrous rout. Fearing this, General Humphreys, commanding the Second division of the Third corps, after changing his front to the rear, rode back to the Nineteenth, which was lying down, and ordered it to arise and stop with the bayonet the soldiers of his command, who had by that time drifted back to within one hundred and fifty paces. Colonel Heath refused to obey the order, fearing that his men, once caught in the disorder caused by broken troops, would be swept to the rear. Then General Humphreys rode down the line of the Nineteenth giving the order himself. Colonel Heath followed countermanding it, and was obeyed by his men (a). As Humphreys' men passed to the rear some of them shouted to the Nineteenth, "Hang on, boys! we will form in your rear." Some of them did try to do this, for they were brave men. The

(a) Captain George L. Whitmore, of Bowdoinham, who heard the conversation between General Humphreys and Colonel Heath, says (in 1889) that when General Humphreys had tried to order the Nineteenth up in vain, he turned to Colonel Heath and ordered him to the rear. To this Captain Whitmore says Colonel Heath returned the reply, " I was placed here by an officer of higher rank for a purpose, and I do not intend to go to the rear. Let your troops form in the rear and we will take care of the enemy in front." General Hancock was the officer who had stationed the Nineteenth.

Excelsior brigade succeeded for a moment in establishing a line, but soon drifted away in the smoke and confusion (a). The Confederate battle line was now right upon the four hundred men from Maine, who arose unwaveringly to receive it. As the gray line emerged from the smoke, about fifty yards in front a tall color-bearer was first seen, running at double-quick and tossing his colors several yards in front of their line. In quick response to the order, given by the Colonel, "Drop that color bearer," a private of the Nineteenth drew up his musket and fired. The Confederate colors went down, and at this instant the Nineteenth poured in its first volley. This fire evidently stopped the Confederates, as they returned it at once. For a short time, no one can tell how long, the two lines exchanged volleys. During this fire Captain Starbird of the left company reported that a Confederate regiment was deploying on his flank. The Colonel went to that part of the line at once, and found the enemy in double column in the act of deploying. They were not over twenty-five yards from the left of the Nineteenth. The Colonel at once threw back the left files of Captain Starbird's company so as to pour an enfilading fire upon the Confederate regiment, at the same time telling Captain Starbird to "give it to them." The left company mustered that day forty men, and its volley, poured in at short range upon a body of men in column, had a terrible effect. The Confederate regiment melted away in the smoke and was seen no more.

The Colonel at once returned to the centre of the regiment. Presently the Lieutenant-Colonel reported to him that the enemy had advanced on the right and cut off the Nineteenth. Therefore the order was given at once to face to the rear and march in retreat. Weir's battery meanwhile had ceased firing. The Nineteenth retreated about twenty or twenty-five paces, when, getting out of the smoke, it was found that the report of a flank

(a) General Hancock in his official report, Rebellion Records, Vol. 27, part 1, page 377, says: "The force, etc., * * * approached the line of battle as originally established. Humphreys' command was forced back, contesting the ground stubbornly."

He also says: "I directed General Humphreys to form his command on the ground from which General Caldwell had moved to the support of the Third corps, which was promptly done. The number of his troops collected was, however, very small, scarcely equal to an ordinary battalion, but with many colors, this small command being composed of the fragments of many shattered regiments."—Rebellion Records, Vol. 27, part 1, page 371.

movement by the enemy had been incorrect. The regiment immediately faced about, and the Colonel gave the order to charge. The regiment responded instantly, and moved on the double-quick against the enemy remaining in their front (a).

This was the critical moment when the Confederate onset, that had swept Sickles from the Emmitsburg road, was stopped by the second line formed by Hancock for the emergency. As the Nineteenth advanced towards the Emmitsburg road, the Confederates in front were dispersed or captured. Several stands of colors, many prisoners and four Union cannon, abandoned in the retreat, were the trophies of this daring and gallant charge (b). The Nineteenth, after advancing to within one hundred yards of the Emmitsburg road, halted and remained in that position until recalled about dark.

As the men and officers marched back to the line on that evening they might justly have felt that whatever glories there are in war had been won by them. But they must have appreciated, as a generation born to the comforts of peace cannot, the cost of war. Their loss in killed and wounded had been remarkable even in that remarkable battle. Many years later, when the records of the Union armies should be studied, it was to be written in history that at Gettysburg Harrow's brigade, of Hancock's corps, suffered heavier losses than any other brigade of any Federal army in any battle of the civil war. And of the devoted regiments of that brigade the Nineteenth Maine was to stand second in the extent of its losses (c). In this day's fighting one hundred and thirty men and officers of the regiment had been killed or wounded. The field over which they marched was strewn with the ghastly evidences of battle.

(a) The Confederate troops engaging the Nineteenth Maine were probably the Perry-Lang brigade, of Anderson's division, of Hill's corps.

(b) General Hancock in his official report, speaking of this period of the battle, says: "In this last operation the Nineteenth Maine, Col. F. E. Heath, bore a conspicuous part." He also says: "Humphreys' division participated in this advance and in the recapture of its guns."—Rebellion Records, Vol. 27, part 1, page 371.

(c) Fox's Regimental Losses in the Civil War is the authority. Fox speaks of the Nineteenth as facing a *feu d'enfer* on the afternoon of the 2d. Of Harrow's brigade, the 1st Minn. only, had losses greater than those of the Nineteenth. The Nineteenth was one of the three hundred fighting regiments, and lost at Gettysburg in killed and mortally wounded, during the two days, 68 out of 440, or fifteen per cent, according to Fox's work. This is the highest per centage of any of the Maine regiments in this battle. Fox's statement, as above, makes the regiment stronger by 35 than the statement of its officers, and the number of the killed three more.

Exhausted by their labors, with no food except such as could be obtained from the haversacks of their fallen foes, they had yet to perform the sad duty of gathering their wounded comrades and burying the dead. And when they finally laid down on their arms, the cries of the enemy's wounded, whom no friends had cared for, drove sleep from the eyelids of many a soldier.

On the forenoon of July 3d there was no fighting along that portion of the line occupied by the Second corps. The Nineteenth Maine was in position about two hundred yards to the right of its position of the previous day. At daybreak four companies, under Capt. W. H. Fogler, were sent out to form a skirmish line, the right of which was to rest upon the Emmitsburg road at the Codori house. They remained there until Pickett's division deployed for its famous charge, when they retired to the left, some of them falling in with Stannard's Vermont brigade. Neither to these skirmishers, nor to the rest of the regiment, were any rations served until after the fighting of the day was ended.

*Although the forenoon of July 3d passed without incident on the Union centre and left, there was severe fighting on the extreme right where the Twelfth corps were driving Ewell's men from intrenchments on Culp's Hill, which were seized during the assault of the previous evening ; and in the woods in front of the Second corps the Confederates were preparing for that final charge, which, as they expected, was to pierce the Union line, divide the army of the Potomac, open the way to the great cities of the north, conquer peace and procure the recognition of the southern Confederacy as one of the nations of the earth. In the way of the realization of these magnificent dreams was the thin line of Hancock's corps, worn by long marches and one desperate battle, and half-famished by a fast prolonged for more than twenty-four hours. The Nineteenth Maine was lying directly in the pathway which Lee was pointing out to his soldiers.

PICKETT'S CHARGE.

About 1 o'clock, at a signal of two guns, well understood by the soldiers of both armies, the Confederate artillery of one hundred and fifty guns opened in the grand cannonade which was to prepare the way for the charge. No soldiers in the new world had ever yet faced such a fire as Hancock's men found rained upon them. More than a hundred cannon were concentrating upon them a fire of solid shot and shell. The Nineteenth Maine, lying in the midst of the Second corps line, had no more protection than could be afforded by a light stone-wall; but the thinness of the line was its salvation, as it prevented those extensive casualties which alone could have added anything to the terrors of the situation. For an hour and a half, a time during which the mind of every soldier was strained to the utmost limit of human suspense and anxiety, this cannonade continued. Then, from the distant woods upon which every eye was bent, appeared the magnificent spectacle of the enemy's skirmishers deploying from a column of 15,000 men, like the opening of a vast fan. But in spite of this splendid reminder of the discipline and ardor of their enemy, a feeling of relief and exaltation swept from heart to heart along Hancock's line. With the end of the artillery fire the feeling of helplessness disappeared. "We knew then that a decisive moment was coming; and we felt that we were equal to it," said an officer of the Nineteenth, as years afterwards he described the scenes of the hour.

Immediately following the skirmishers came the Confederate line,—Pickett's division of Virginians, the flower of the Confederate army, supported on the right by Wilcox and Lang as a shield and on the left by Pettigrew and Trimble as part of the charging column. Well flanked on either side by heavy supports, the advancing column moved forward over the mile and a quarter of intervening fields, with a steadiness described with admiration by every spectator and every historian. The Union batteries opened upon them at once. When they came nearer the infantry began to fire, the Nineteenth beginning when they were within three or four hundred yards. The Confederates, as they advanced, obliqued to their left, bringing the weight of their charge to the right of the Nineteenth, and impinging upon Webb's brigade, of Gibbon's division. Webb's Pennsylvanians gave way before it; but their comrades of the Second corps rushed up to restore the line. The Nineteenth Maine was among the first, followed by several regiments on its left. It was a wild charge, with little regard for ranks or files. Volleys were given and received at close quarters. In their anxiety to reach the foe, men thrust their rifles over the shoulders, under the arms and between the legs, of those in the front ranks of the melee. All this went on while batteries far and near, and of both friend and foe, were throwing shot and shell into the area crowded with the struggling combatants. A little copse of trees, which remains to this day, marked the place of severest conflict. As the Nineteenth arrived at this copse a piece of shell prostrated Colonel Heath, and the command devolved upon Lieut.-Col. Cunningham. He soon received an order from an officer to cease firing, form the colors on the left and wait for further orders. The Nineteenth was at the south edge of the copse of trees. The Confederates were at that moment holding the portion of the Union line where they had broken through, and were within a few yards of the copse. The Nineteenth, with the other troops at hand, were at once ordered forward by General Webb. They moved along the left of the copse down to the wall where the Union line had been, but which was now in possession of the Confederates; there the fighting was hand to hand until the enemy were, by sheer strength, pushed beyond the wall; then the line was saved. The great, decisive battle of the rebellion was ended.

The Nineteenth Maine lost in the two days of battle, 65 killed and mortally wounded, 137 wounded not fatally, and 4 missing who were killed undoubtedly as no one of them has since been heard from (a).

PARTICIPANTS.

FIELD, STAFF AND NON-COMMISSIONED STAFF.

Colonel, Francis E. Heath, Waterville.
Lieutenant-Colonel, Henry W. Cunningham, Belfast.
Major, James W. Welch, Augusta.
Adjutant, First Lieutenant Francis W. Haskell, Waterville.

(a) The casualties as returned after the battle and before the results of the injuries to the wounded were known, were, 1 officer and 28 enlisted men killed; 11 officers and 159 enlisted men wounded, and 4 enlisted men missing. See summary at end of list of casualties, page 310.

Quartermaster, First Lieutenant James W. Wakefield, Bath.
Surgeon, Adoniram J. Billings, Freedom.
Assistant Surgeon, Henry C. Levensaler, Thomaston.
Sergeant-Major, George A. Wadsworth, Bath.
Quartermaster-Sergeant, George H. Page, Warren.

COMPANY A.
(Including 3 present sick.)

Captain, J. Whitman Spaulding, Richmond.
First Lieutenant, David E. Parsons, Norridgewock.
Second Lieutenant, Alvirus Osborne, Smithfield.

SERGEANTS.

Thomas M. Heald, Norridgewock,   Charles H. Colburn, Richmond,
Asa Andrews, 2d, Moscow.

CORPORALS.

Leonard H. Washburn, Norridgewock, Payson T. Heald, Norridgewock,
Gardiner W. Bigelow, Smithfield,   Columbus S. Anderson, Richmond,
Elias T. Jordan, Richmond,   George R. Ridley, Richmond,
Hiram W. Gage, Norridgewock,   Abner Baker, Moscow.

PRIVATES.

Bigelow, Charles H., Smithfield,   Buker, John C., Richmond,
Buker, William F., Richmond,   Bumpus, Alson B., The Forks pl.,
Butler, Edward K., Norridgewock,   Charles, Arthur E., Rome,
Charles, Benjamin F., Rome,   Chase, Roger, Madison,
Church, John P., Gardiner,   Collins, Charles W., Starks,
Dawes, John D., Madison,   Dresser, Emerson, Madison,
Eastman, Franklin, Gardiner,   Foss, Kingman, Moscow,
Gage, S. Nelson, Madison,   Groves, Charles H., Norridgewock,
Groves, Robert W., Smithfield,   Heald, Perham, Norridgewock,
Ingalls, Joseph F., Mercer,   Jones, Amos R., Madison,
Joy, William P., Ellsworth,   Kennison, Andrew, Norridgewock,
Lancaster, John P., Richmond,   Leavitt, Henry, Richmond,
Leavitt, Samuel, Richmond,   Meader, John W., Mercer,
Merrill, John, Jr., Richmond,   Murphy, William B., Norridgewock,
Nottage, William H., Starks,   Rowe, Charles M., Smithfield,
Sawtelle, Levander, Starks,   Small, Richard, Richmond,
Tibbetts, Charles H., Mercer,   Tibbetts, Isaac W., Mercer,
Trott, William F., Richmond,   Vigue, Louis, Carratunk pl.,
Weaver, George M., Starks,   Wells, Bradford B., Mercer,
Williams, David, Perkins.

MUSICIAN: J. Loyalist Brown, Bowdoinham.
WAGONER: Samuel D. Jordan, Richmond.

ON SPECIAL DUTY OR DETACHED SERVICE: Privates: Elliot F. Collins, Starks, art'y brig.; Osborn W. Fish, Madison, Thomas J. Gaubert, Richmond, Isaac Powers, Norridgewock, and Hiram W. Varney, Norridgewock, amb. corps; Sherburne N. Rowe, Smithfield, and Alfred Taylor, Norridgewock, guard div. h'dqrs; John R. Webster, Norridgewock, clerk quartermaster dept., army h'dqrs.

COMPANY B.
(Including 2 present sick.)

First Lieutenant, Elisha W. Ellis, Monroe.

SERGEANTS.

Darius S. Richards, Lincolnville,   Edwin A. Howes, Liberty,
Benjamin S. Crooker, Lincolnville.

CORPORALS.

Martin Hannan, Montville,   William Briggs, Monroe,
Abial Turner, Palermo,   Samuel N. Robertson, Monroe,
David G. Bagley, Liberty,   John M. Wellington, Montville,
Washington Patterson, Monroe,   Alvin H. Ellis, Monroe.

PRIVATES.

Bullen, Hugh A., Montville,   Buzzell, Elijah K., Monroe,
Chapman, George F., Liberty,   Churchill, William H., Montville,
Cilley, Lorenzo D., Brooks,   Clifford, Wilbur M., Palermo,
Coffin, Frank, Thorndike,   Crockett, Wilbur, Lincolnville,
Cross, Israel H., Lincolnville,   Crummett, Orson E., Northport,
Curtis, Watson, Monroe,   Curtis, William H., Monroe,
Dean, Silas, Lincolnville,   Dunton, Hosea B., Liberty,
Flagg, Job P., Monroe,   Gray, James C., Monroe,
Gregory, Alonzo V., Montville,   Hannan, Horace I., Liberty,
Hardy, Willard R., Searsmont,   Hills, Isaac, Northport,
Hubbard, William, Palermo,   Hustus, Hiram A., Monroe,
Knowles, Andrew J., Thorndike,   Knowlton, Joshua T., Monroe,
Larrabee, Moses, Jr., Monroe,   Mayo, George M., Monroe,
Monroe, Joseph R., Thorndike,   Moody, Augustus R., Lincolnville,
Morong, George E., Lincolnville,   Noyes, Eli, Palermo,
Parsons, Henry, Thorndike,   Rand, Marshall H., Monroe,
Roberts, Oscar E., Brooks,   Tenney, Leonard, Northport,
Ward, Benjamin F., Thorndike,   Ware, Jabez G., Northport,
Ware, Jason, Northport,   Whitney, Mark L., Lincolnville,
Wilson, Erastus T., Searsmont,   Young, George W., Lincolnville.

MUSICIAN: Edward L. Mitchell, Liberty.

ON SPECIAL DUTY OR DETACHED SERVICE: Second Lieut. Ansel L. White, Belfast, acting A. D. C. on brig. staff. Sergt. Daniel Bachelor, Palermo, amb. corps. Wagoner John A. Porter, Lincolnville, div. h'dqrs. Privates: Ira Z. Bennett, Montville, battery B, 1st R. I.; William R. Bradstreet, Palermo, amb. corps; Morrison R. Heal, Searsmont, battery A, 4th U. S.; Mayberry Richards, Lincolnville, guard div. h'dqrs.

COMPANY C.

(Including 5 present sick.)

Captain, George L. Whitmore, Bowdoinham.
First Lieutenant, Albion Whitten, Troy.
Second Lieutenant, Francis H. Foss, Fairfield.

SERGEANTS.

First Sergeant, George Dunbar, Fairfield,
Henry W. Nye, Fairfield,   Eugene A. Boulter, Unity,
Alexander W. Lord, Fairfield,   William H. Emery, Fairfield.

CORPORALS.

Gershom F. Tarbell, Benton,   Lindley H. Whittaker, Troy,
George M. Cotton, Fairfield,   George A. Osborn, Fairfield,

Christopher Erskine, Whitefield,
Alphonzo Nichols, Fairfield,

Gustavus L. Thompson, Fairfield,
Russell B. Gray, Fairfield.

PRIVATES.

Adams, John B., Bowdoin,
Bickmore, Mayo, Troy,
Brann, Merrill, Whitefield,
Call, Frederick S., Richmond,
Clough, Harrison T., St. Albans,
Dodge, Charles H., Freedom,
Emery, Henry, Fairfield,
Gilman, Lorenzo D., Unity,
Greenleaf, Benjamin W., Starks,
Hodgdon, George E., Troy,
Jones, Charles W., Thorndike,
Lewis, Jonathan, Clinton,
Lewis, William E., Fairfield,
Maxim, Sullivan A., St. Albans,
McIntire, Ezra F., Fairfield,
Phinney, Thomas F., Unity,
Pratt, Elbridge P., Fairfield,
Reynolds, Josiah K., Unity,
Shaw, Johnson, Troy,
Snell, Cyrus F., Madison,
Spaulding, William, Benton,
Webb, Reuben R., Unity,
Woodman, Alfred, Troy.

Allen, Alfred F., Fairfield,
Blethen, James L., Unity,
Buzzell, Benjamin F., Benton,
Chisam, Theodore, Unity,
Crosby, Abijah, Benton,
Emerson, James D., Madison,
Fogg, Eben S., Fairfield,
Glidden, Franklin W., Whitefield,
Haskell, Joseph E., Fairfield,
Huntress, George H., Shapleigh,
Kimball, Lyman B., Clinton,
Lewis, Milford T., Fairfield,
Libby, Nathaniel P., Unity,
Mayo, Oscar F., Fairfield,
Oliver, James M., Fairfield,
Plummer, Myrick, Whitefield,
Reed, Thomas, Richmond,
Rhoades, Reuben, Troy,
Sinclair, David, Fairfield,
Spaulding, John, Benton,
Usher, Orin S., Albion,
Woodward, Joseph G., Troy,

ON SPECIAL DUTY OR DETACHED SERVICE: Privates: Franklin Burrill, Fairfield, and Edwin Garcelon, Troy, amb. corps; Albert Choate, Unity, and John G. Pierce, Clinton, art'y brig.; Charles C. Goodwin, 2d, Dresden, Henry C. Goodwin, Dresden, George W. Tibbetts, Unity, and Randall K. Whitten, Unity, battery B, 1st R. I.; John S. Hall, Fairfield, saddler brig. h'dqrs; William H. Morrill, Benton, teamster brig. h'dqrs; Daniel Sanborn, Fairfield, blacksmith brig. h'dqrs; Richard Whitten, Unity, guard div. h'dqrs.

COMPANY D.

(Including 5 present sick.)

Captain, William H. Fogler, Belfast.
First Lieutenant, Edward R. Cunningham, Belfast.
Second Lieutenant, Leroy S. Scott, Belfast.

SERGEANTS.

First Sergeant, Elbridge C. Pierce, Belfast,
George L. Starkey, Belfast,
John C. Knowlton, Montville,

Ralph Johnson, Belfast,
John A. Lord, Belfast.

CORPORALS.

John F. Frost, Belfast,
Edgar Paul, Belfast,
Francis C. Wood, Northport,
William H. Wording, Belfast.

Robert T. Newell, Belfast,
Jesse A. Wilson, Belfast,
Alfred P. Waterman, Belfast,

PRIVATES.

Beckwith, Silas, Belfast,
Brown, James C., Searsmont,

Blodgett, Joshua W., Morrill,
Buckling, William D., Waldo,

Byard, Henry D., Rockland,
Coffin, Augustus, Thorndike,
Cunningham, Alden, Waldo,
Dean, Horace, Belfast,
Haire, Roswell, Belfast,
Hartshorn, Henry H., Belfast,
Hatch, Gardiner L., Montville,
Hoffses, Hiram B., Waldoboro,
Hunt, Lewis, Pittston,
Knowlton, Elisha P., Swanville,
Lenfest, James, Swanville,
Merriam, John, Morrill,
Nickerson, Jonathan S., Belfast,
Perham, Myrick, Pittston,
Prescott, Franklin K., Northport,
Smally, Castanous M., Belfast,
Thomas, Hushai, Morrill,
Tufts, George F., Belfast,
Wentworth, Orlando F., Waldo,
White, John A., Belfast,
Young, John W., Belfast.

Clements, Charles H., Knox,
Cooper, Charles F., Belfast,
Cunningham, Cornelius, Belfast,
Gray, John, Belmont,
Hamilton, Charles R., Swanville,
Hatch, Barak A., Belmont,
Hinds, Prescott D., Belfast,
Hunt, Kingsbury, Pittston,
Kelley Louira A., Belfast, act'g Corp.,
Lear, Benjamin O., Northport,
Maker, Andrew R., Belfast,
Murch, Charles A., Belfast,
Palmer, George W., Pittston,
Poor, Levi M., Belmont,
Robbins, James, Belfast,
Thomas, Ezekiel R., Morrill,
Thomas, Hushai C., Morrill,
Wentworth, Franklin A., Belfast,
White, James W., Belfast,
Wyman, Frederick H., Belfast,

MUSICIAN: Henry McIntosh, Vinalhaven.

ON SPECIAL DUTY OR DETACHED SERVICE: Corporal Nelson N. Mayo, Belfast, provo. guard. Privates: James O. Bean, Belmont, Hazzard's batt'y; Annas S. Campbell, Belfast, and Lorenzo W. Hoffses, Waldoboro, provo. guard; John W. Carter, Belfast, carpenter corps h'dqrs; Elijah S. Chase, Pittston, William W. Hartshorn, Belfast, Enoch Hollis, Jr., Pittston, and Rufus Tripp, Swanville, guard div. h'dqrs; Jacob N. Cunningham, Waldo, art'y brig.; Emery Robbins, Belfast, forage-master corps h'dqrs; Bridges C. Sherman, Liberty, Franklin Wentworth, Waldo, and George Williams, Waldo, amb. corps.

COMPANY E.

First Lieutenant, Nehemiah Smart, Swanville, commanding.

SERGEANTS.

First Sergeant, James H. Pierce, Prospect,

William B. Sawyer, Searsport,
Alfred E. Nickerson, Swanville,
Andrew D. Black, Stockton, acting Sergeant-Major July 3.

George L. Merrill, Searsport,
Enoch C. Dow, Stockton,

CORPORALS.

John B. Campbell, Frankfort,
Frank A. Patterson, Stockton,
Collins McCarty, Jr., Belfast,

Milton W. Nichols, Searsport,
Charles B. Norris, Searsport,
Nahum Downs, Swanville.

PRIVATES.

Atwood, John R., Frankfort,
Bowden, Levi, Frankfort,
Campbell, Daniel A., Frankfort,
Cilley, Judah, Brooks,
Cookson, Joseph G., Frankfort,
Dearborn, Leonard, Manchester,

Blanchard, Thomas S., Stockton,
Campbell, Charles E., Frankfort,
Carter, William A., Stockton,
Colson, William J., Searsport,
Curtis, Americus J., Swanville,
Dickey, Manly L., Stockton,

Edwards, Joseph W., Searsport,
Holmes, John C., Frankfort,
Low, William H., Frankfort,
Moore, James S., Frankfort,
Nickerson, Fred A., Swanville,
Nickerson, John F., Swanville,
Patterson, Isaac W., Prospect,
Shaw, James H., Brunswick,
Staples, Robert F., Stockton,
Strout, Parish L., Swanville,
Waterhouse, Fred L., Searsport,

Harriman, Charles E., Searsport,
Keene, John F., Stockton,
Maddox, Jason, Appleton,
Moore, John B., Frankfort,
Nickerson, John E., Swanville,
Nickerson, Reuel, Swanville,
Pease, Samuel O., Frankfort,
Sheldon, Edward B., Camden,
Stinson, Alfred, Prospect,
Sweetser, James, Searsport,
Woodbury, Stephen E., Searsport.

MUSICIANS.

Freeman Waning, Frankfort,   Isaac L. Spaulding, Frankfort.

ON SPECIAL DUTY OR DETACHED SERVICE: Privates: Charles Clark, Frankfort, battery I. 1st R. I.; Nelson Curtis, Swanville, cook; William H. Grant, Prospect, and James E. Nason, Frankfort, amb. corps; Eugene Merrill, Searsport, ord'ly div. h'dqrs; Peleg S. Staples, Stockton, batt'y B, 1st R. I.

COMPANY F.

(Including 2 present sick.)

Captain, Isaac W. Starbird, Litchfield.
First Lieutenant, Charles E. Nash, Hallowell.
Second Lieutenant, Edwin H. Rich, Thorndike.

SERGEANTS.

1st Sgt., Thos. T. Rideout, B'd'nham,   Oliver R. Small, West Gardiner,
Andrew J. Goodwin, Litchfield,   Orville G. Tuck, Hallowell, color sergt.

CORPORALS.

William A. Wood, Bowdoinham,
Joshua F. Gross, Brunswick,
Moses S. Dennett, Lewiston,
Richard H. Spear, West Gardiner.

Phillip H. Foster, Topsham,
John Richards, Bowdoinham,
Samuel Smith, Litchfield,

PRIVATES.

Adams, Franklin, Bowdoinham,
Arris, George A., Topsham,
Blake, Samuel T., Monmouth,
Burke, Cyrus E., Litchfield,
Chase, James F., Topsham,
Crane, Jonathan, Topsham,
Davis, John H., Litchfield,
Dunnell, Edwin L., Monmouth,
Gardiner, Israel A., Richmond,
Gilbert, Addison, Leeds,
Glass, Rufus P., Bowdoinham,
Gowell, Nathaniel O., Litchfield,
Grover, Alford, West Gardiner,
Harmon, Stephen, Litchfield,
Hodgman, George W., Wales,
Leavitt, Frank M., Bowdoinham,
Potter, Roscoe H., West Gardiner,

Adams, Silas, Bowdoinham,
Berry, Andrew J., Topsham,
Brann, John E., West Gardiner,
Chase, George E., Topsham,
Cole, Daniel M., West Gardiner,
Crosby, William H., West Gardiner,
Dillingham, Charles E., W. Gardiner,
Durgin, George T., Bowdoinham,
Getchell, Phillip P., Augusta,
Given, Simeon S., Bowdoinham,
Gowell, John D., Litchfield,
Greenleaf, Joseph D., Litchfield,
Hanscom, Moses C., Bowdoinham,
Harrington, Charles D., Topsham,
Keen, Calvin B., Leeds,
Maxwell, Rufus S., Bowdoin,
Richardson, Lorenzo M., Litchfield,

Rose, Thomas S., Greene,
Small, William S., Wales,
Spear, Alvin, West Gardiner,
Tobey, Joseph A., Somerville,
White, George O., Hallowell.

Shorey, William H., Monmouth,
Smith, John D., Litchfield,
Stevens, James O., Litchfield,
Turner, Anson, Gardiner,

MUSICIANS.

Henry H. Williams, Bowdoin, Lauriston Chamberlain, Bowdoinham.

ON SPECIAL DUTY OR DETACHED SERVICE: Privates: James H. Bowie, Bowdoin, battery B, 1st R. I.; Robert H. Corey, Topsham, amb. corps; Edwin Fairbanks, West Gardiner, cattle g'd corps h'dqrs; William J. Nickerson, Topsham, and Thomas L. Palmer, Hallowell, guard div. h'dqrs; James W. Powers, Litchfield, battery I, 1st U. S.

COMPANY G.

Captain, Everett M. Whitehouse, China.
First Lieutenant, Loring Farr, Manchester.
Second Lieutenant, Henry Sewall, Augusta.

SERGEANTS.

George A. Barton, Augusta,
Albert N. Williams, Augusta,

William O. Tibbetts, Augusta,
Edward H. Hicks, Augusta.

CORPORALS.

Albert H. Packard, Augusta,
George L. Perkins, New Sharon,
Walter Jordan, Chesterville,
George W. Chapman, Windsor,

William P. Worthing, China,
George W. Andrews, Augusta,
Stephen P. McKenney, Augusta,
Charles R. Powers, Augusta.

PRIVATES.

Carpenter, Thomas E., China,
Chadwick, Judah A., Augusta,
Dain, Andrew J., Chesterville,
Fuller, George S., Chesterville,
Grady, William O., Augusta,
Hussey, George A., Augusta,
Jackson, Charles H., China,
Lane, Nathaniel, Augusta,
Littlefield, Ruel, Augusta,
Mahoney, Daniel, Augusta,
Mayers, James H., Dresden,
Murphy, William, Augusta,
Nelson, Erastus F., China,
Robbins, Franklin D., China,
Robbins, Philip M., Chesterville,
Smart, Orren P., Augusta,
Smith, Augustus C., Augusta,
Smith, George A., Vienna,
Trask, Lauriston G., Augusta,

Carroll, Charles J., Windsor,
Cowan, John F., Palermo,
Doe, George F., Windsor,
Gill, Elijah, Chesterville,
Haskell, Joseph H., China,
Jackman, William H., Mount Vernon,
Jones, Amos, China,
Leighton, Hampton W., Augusta,
Lord, Amasa, Augusta,
Marston, Alfred J., Augusta,
Moody, Isaac, Augusta,
Murray, Winthrop, China,
Rideout, Thomas B., Augusta,
Robbins, John L., China,
Rogers, Henry A., China,
Small, William B., Augusta,
Smith, Charles F., Augusta,
Tobey, William B., China,
Tyler, Elias, China.

MUSICIAN: Ansel B. Dorset, Chesterville.

ON SPECIAL DUTY OR DETACHED SERVICE: Privates: Albert Call, Augusta, Benjamin R. Marston, Augusta, and George W. Merrill, Windsor, guard div. h'dqrs; Warren C. Harlow, Augusta, Abner Haskell, Augusta, and Alfred Haskell, Augusta, teamsters brig. h'dqrs; Jeremy D. Hyson,

Windsor, cook brig. h'dqrs; George W. Keen, Windsor, hostler brig. h'dqrs; Edwin D. Lee, China, orderly brig. h'dqrs; Abram Merrill, Windsor, cattle drover corps h'dqrs; Lewis A. Moulton, Chesterville, battery B, 1st R. I.

COMPANY H.

Captain, Willard Lincoln, China.
First Lieutenant, Albert Hunter, Clinton.
Second Lieutenant, Stephen R. Gordon, Clinton.

SERGEANTS.

First Sergeant, John F. Stackpole, Albion,

Jesse A. Dorman, Canaan,	Charles P. Garland, Winslow,
George E. Webber, Gardiner,	James T. Waldron, Canaan.

CORPORALS.

Francis P. Furber, Clinton,	George F. Hopkins, Albion,
Hollis F. Arnold, Palermo,	George H. Willey, Clinton,
Alfred T. Dunbar, Winslow,	Samuel C. Brookings, Pittston,
James O. Seavey, Boothbay.	

PRIVATES.

Abbott, Daniel B., Winslow,	Carr, Rinaldo A., Palermo,
Coro, Joseph, China,	Dodge, Martin V. B., Palermo,
Estes, John H., Vassalboro,	Estes, Redford M., Vassalboro,
Gerald, William F., Clinton,	Goodridge, Drew, Canaan,
Hamlin, Charles L., Vassalboro,	Hodgdon, Isaac C., Clinton,
Hopkins, Lewis E., Albion,	James, Josephus, Pittston,
Leonard, William, Albion,	Libby, Charles H., Albion,
Martin, Reuben D., Canaan,	Merrow, Thomas W., Canaan,
Murphy, Hamlen H., Friendship,	Page, Isaac L., Chelsea,
Patterson, Henry L., Augusta,	Prescott, Charles, Hartland,
Reed, Jesse, Gardiner,	Richards, Elmerin W., Winslow,
Richardson, Luke T., Canaan,	Small, James L., Pittston,
Taylor, William, Winslow,	Washburn, Augustus, Canaan,
Wheeler, George E., Canaan,	Williams, Nicholas, West Gardiner,
Wilson, John S., Winslow,	Wood, William F., Winslow,
Wyman, James, Hermon,	Young, Benjamin, Pittston.

MUSICIAN: Henry B. Washburn, China.

ON SPECIAL DUTY OR DETACHED SERVICE: Corporal Samuel S. Holbrook, Athens, div. h'dqrs. Privates: Charles E. Burrill, Canaan, hostler; John S. Clark, Gardiner, nurse; Arnold L. Foye, Palermo, hosp. attendant; Henry S. Jewett, Westbrook, postmaster; Fairfield S. McKenney, Clinton, teamster; Sumner Merrill, Winslow, battery A, 4th U. S.; Charles E. Ramsdell, Pittston, and Ivory D. White, Canaan, prov. guard; Orrin F. Stinson, Albion, div. h'dqrs; James M. Tyler, Albion, battery B, 1st R. I.; Bradley B. Withee, Winslow, cook, brig. h'dqrs; Wagoner William G. Stratton, Albion, teamster div. h'dqrs; John Withee, Winslow, cattle guard.

COMPANY I.

Captain, George D. Smith, Rockland.
First Lieutenant, Edgar A. Burpee, Rockland.
Second Lieutenant, George R. Palmer, Camden.

SERGEANTS.

William E. Barrows, Rockland, acting First Sergeant.

Joseph L. Clark, Rockland,	Chandler F. Perry, South Thomaston.

CORPORALS.

Lafayette Carver, Vinalhaven,
Rufus Shibbles, 2d, Camden,
John Vinal, Vinalhaven,
Orrin T. Conway, Vinalhaven.

Daniel G. Lamb, Camden,
George E. Holmes, Rockland,
George W. Barter, Boothbay,

PRIVATES.

Anderson, Edwin, Camden,
Bowley, Harrison B., Camden,
Calph, John, Appleton,
Carver, Francis S., Vinalhaven,
Clark, Luther, Rockland,
Dodge, Adrian C., Rockland,
Farnham, Samuel, Whitefield,
Higgins, John H., Camden,
Joice, Harvey C., Camden,
Little, Thomas, Bremen,
Maddocks, Joseph G., So. Thomaston,
Mills, James P., Vinalhaven,
Oxton, Amos B., Camden,
Shepherd, George W., Camden,
Thorndike, Warren B., Camden,
Vinal, Calvin B., Vinalhaven,
Wilson, Joseph W., Camden,

Black, Gorham L., Rockland,
Butler, Caleb P., Appleton,
Carey, John F., Camden,
Clapp, Hiram, Appleton,
Cobb, George S., Camden,
Dyer, Alden W., South Thomaston,
Fisk, Franklin, Camden,
Hutchings, Zuinglous, Appleton,
Little, Otis, Bremen,
Little, William H., Jr., Bremen,
McIntosh James H., Vinalhaven,
Norton, Joseph H., Vinalhaven,
Rhoades, Francis W., Bremen,
Sherwood, George E., Camden,
Turner, George S., Bremen,
Vinal, Worster S., Vinalhaven,
Witherspoon, Alpheus L., Camden.

MUSICIAN: Alexander Dumphe, Vinalhaven.

ON SPECIAL DUTY OR DETACHED SERVICE: Sergeant George Studley, Camden, prov. guard. Privates: John H. Cables, Rockland, and Edwin S. Jacobs, Appleton, prov. guard; Reuben T. Carver, Vinalhaven, div. h'dqrs; William W. Kittridge, Vinalhaven, Hazzard's batt'y; William N. Rackliff, Rockland, amb. corps; Solomon Taylor, Rockland, brig. h'dqrs; David Tolman, Camden, teamster brig. h'dqrs; Wagoner Hiram Whitten, Rockland, teamster brig. h'dqrs.

COMPANY K.

Captain, Dumont Bunker, Fairfield.
First Lieutenant, Richard Crockett, Brunswick.
Second Lieutenant, Samuel E. Bucknam, Eastport.

SERGEANTS.

First Sergeant, James N. Hinkley, Georgetown,
George L. Grant, Phippsburg,
Thomas P. Beath, Boothbay,

William Boynton, Jr., Bath,
George E. Grows, Brunswick.

CORPORALS.

Edwin W. Swett, Arrowsic,
Weld Sargent, Boothbay,
Stephen P. Trafton, Georgetown,
George W. Cushman, Brunswick.

Samuel Pratt, Jr., Richmond,
Warren Proctor, Brunswick,
Joseph W. Winter, West Bath,

PRIVATES.

Blaisdell, Richard M., Phippsburg,
Boyd, Abijah P., Boothbay,
Child, Thomas, Bath,
Dunton, Ezekiel L., Westport,

Blake, Edwin, Bath,
Brown, George H., Bath,
Dolloff, Beniah P., Boothbay,
Eaton, George T., Bath,

Elliot, Henry H., Bath,
Francis, Nelson, Arrowsic,
Jellison, Alvah, Kennebunk,
Knights, James H., Bangor,
Lombard, David C., West Bath,
Marr, Calvin E., Georgetown,
McFarland, Nathaniel C., Boothbay,
Mitchell, Edward T., Bath,
Mitchell, Jesse, Bath,
Nichols, Oliver P., Phippsburg,
Rourke, Lawrence J., Bath,
Scott, Thomas E., Georgetown,
Swasey, John J., Bath,
Varell, Gilman N., Rye, N. H.,
Webber, Isaac, Jr., Boothbay,
Williams, Henry N., Richmond,

Fogler, George P., Boothbay,
Heal, James T., Phippsburg,
Kimball, George A., Bath,
Lewis, James H., Brunswick,
Lowe, Charles M., Bath,
McAvoy, Charles E., Bath,
McKenney, William, Westport,
Mitchell, Isaac W., Bath,
Mitchell, Simmons A., Bath,
Oliver, Loring C., Phippsburg,
Sawyer, Addison, Bath,
Shea, Samuel B., Georgetown,
Tobie, Philander H., Bath,
Wallace, James R., Phippsburg,
Webster, Lorenzo, Boothbay,
Willis, William T., Arrowsic.

MUSICIAN: Alpheus M. Holbrook, West Bath.

WAGONER: Charles T. Clifford, Bath.

ON SPECIAL DUTY OR DETACHED SERVICE: Privates: Charles Blackman, Bath, and Horace A. Little, Bath, guard div. h'dqrs; Robert B. Blaisdell, Phippsburg, teamster amm'n train; Edward B. Curtis, Bath, battery I, 1st R. I.; Ezra L. Fowles, Westport, battery B, 1st R. I.; Josiah B. Rogers, Phippsburg, artillery h'dqrs.

From consolidated, regimental, morning report, June 30, 1863:—
Present for duty, 33 officers, 510 men. Present sick, 1 officer, 31 men.
On daily duty and detached service, 1 officer, 88 men.

REVISED REPORT OF CASUALTIES.

FIELD, STAFF AND NON-COMMISSIONED STAFF.

Colonel Francis E. Heath, wounded, shoulder.
Major James W. Welch, wounded, scalp.
Sergeant-Major George A. Wadsworth, wounded, head.

COMPANY A.

Sergeant Charles H. Colburn, wounded, leg.

CORPORALS.

Payson T. Heald, wounded, arm; died Aug. 5, 1863.
Gardiner W. Bigelow, wounded, arm. Abner Baker, w'd, breast; died Aug. 6.

PRIVATES.

Buker, William F., wounded, hands. Charles, Benjamin F., wounded, leg.
Church, John P., wounded, arm. Collins, Charles W., killed.
Kennison, Andrew, w'd, leg amp'd. Leavitt, Samuel, wounded, shoulder.
Murphy, William B., wounded, leg. Vigue, Louis, wounded.

COMPANY B.

First Lieutenant Elisha W. Ellis, wounded, side; returned in October.

SERGEANTS.

Edwin A. Howes, killed. Benjamin S. Crooker, wounded, head.

CORPORALS.

William Briggs, wounded, ankle.   Abial Turner, wounded, side.
Alvin H. Ellis, wounded, thigh.

PRIVATES.

Bennett, Ira Z. (battery), killed.   Chapman, George F., w'd, arm, side.
Coffin, Frank, w'd, thigh, died July 14. Crummett, Orson E., wounded, head.
Curtis, Watson, wounded, hand.   Curtis, William H., wounded, side.
Flagg, Job P.,w'd,breast; died Dec.19. Hardy, Willard R., wounded, hands.
Hills, Isaac, wounded, thigh.   Hubbard, William, wounded, head.
Larrabee, Moses, Jr., wounded.   Noyes, Eli, missing; fate unknown.
Rand, Marshall H., wounded.   Whitney, Mark L., wounded, leg.

COMPANY C.

Second Lieutenant Francis H. Foss, wounded, neck.

SERGEANTS.

1st Sergt. George Dunbar, w'd, elbow. Henry W. Nye, w'd, head, shoulder.
Alexander W. Lord, killed.   William H. Emery, wounded, head.

CORPORALS.

Lindley H. Whittaker, wounded.   Christopher Erskine, killed.
Gustavus L. Thompson, killed.

PRIVATES.

Adams, John B.,w'd,hip and shoulder. Blethen, James L., w'd, head and arm.
Call, Frederick S., w'd; died Aug. 25. Crosby, Abijah, w'd; died July 8.
Emery, Henry, wounded, foot.   Gilman, Lorenzo D., wounded, knee.
Haskell, Joseph E., wounded, leg.   Hodgdon, Geo. E., w'd; died Aug. 24.
Jones, Charles W., wounded, head.   Lewis, Jonathan, wounded, elbow.
Maxim, Sullivan A., wounded, leg.   Pratt, Elbridge P., killed.
Shaw, Johnson, w'd, foot amputated. Spaulding, William, wounded, arm.
Webb, Reuben R., wounded, thigh.   Woodward, Joseph G., killed.

COMPANY D.

First Lieutenant Edward R. Cunningham, wounded, breast.
Second Lieutenant Leroy S. Scott, wounded July 2; died July 13.
Sergeant George L. Starkey, wounded July 2, leg amputated.

CORPORALS.

Robert T. Newell, w'd; died July 9. Jesse A. Wilson, w'd; died July 3.
Francis C. Wood, wounded, arm.   Alfred P. Waterman, wounded July 2;
                                    died July 4.

PRIVATES.

Brown, James C., wounded, leg.   Byard, Henry D., w'd, leg, July 2.
Clements, Charles H., w'd July 2.   Cunningham, Alden, killed.
Dean, Horace, wounded.   Haire, Roswell, w'd; died July 4.
Hamilton, Charles R., w'd, face, arm. Hartshorn, Henry H., w'd July 3.
Hoffses,Lorenzo W., pr. gd.,w'd, legs. Kelley, Louira A., act'g Corp'l, killed.
Lear, Benjamin O., w'd, arm, July 2. Lenfest, James, wounded, leg, July 3.
Merriam, John, act'g Corporal, w'd; Murch, Charles A., wounded, leg.
   died Aug. 25.   Robbins, James, killed, July 3.
Thomas, Hushai C., w'd; died July 21. Tufts, George F., w'd, arm and leg.

COMPANY E.

SERGEANTS.

1st Sergt. James H. Pierce, w'd, side. Enoch C. Dow, killed.

CORPORALS.

Frank A. Patterson, wounded, leg.   Nahum Downs, w'd, leg; died July 18.
Collins McCarty, Jr., w'd, arm amp'd.

PRIVATES.

Atwood, John R., wounded, leg.   Colson, William J., wounded, leg.
Cookson, Joseph G., wounded, hand. Dearborn, Leonard, wounded, hand.
Harriman, Chas. E., w'd; died July 10. Keene, John F., wounded, arm.
Low, William H., killed.   Moore, James S., wounded.
Nickerson, Fred A., wounded, hand. Nickerson, John E., wounded, leg.
Nickerson, Reuel, w'd; died July 18. Sheldon, Edward B., w'd, arm amp'd.
Waterhouse, Fred L., wounded, leg.

COMPANY F.

Captain Isaac W. Starbird, flesh wound.
First Lieutenant Charles E. Nash, wounded, leg.
Second Lieutenant Edwin H. Rich, wounded, leg.
First Sergeant Thomas P. Rideout, wounded; died July 18.

PRIVATES.

Dunnell, Edwin L., wounded.   Grover, Alford, wounded, thigh.
Keen, Calvin B., wounded.   Shorey, William H., w'd; died July 4.
Small, William S., wounded, arm.   Tobey, Joseph A., wounded, face.
White, George O., wounded, shoulder.

MUSICIAN: Lauriston Chamberlain, wounded, back.

COMPANY G.

Second Lieutenant Henry Sewall, wounded, face.

SERGEANTS.

Albert N. Williams, killed.   Edward H. Hicks, w'd, arm and groin.

CORPORALS.

George L. Perkins, killed.   George W. Andrews, w'd, missing;
Stephen P. McKenney, w'd, hands.   supposed dead.

PRIVATES.

Carroll, Charles J., w'd; died July 10. Hussey, George A., wounded, hip.
Jackman, William H., wounded, side. Jones, Amos, wounded, arm.
Leighton, Hampton W., w'd, arm.   Moody, Isaac, wounded.
Murray, Winthrop, wounded, head.   Small, William B., wounded, shoulder.
Smart, Orren P., wounded, breast.   Tyler, Elias, wounded; died July 15.

COMPANY H.

Captain Willard Lincoln, wounded, head.
First Lieutenant Albert Hunter, wounded, throat.

SERGEANTS.

First Sergeant John F. Stackpole, killed.
Jesse A. Dorman, w'd; died July 6.   Charles P. Garland, wounded, leg.
George E. Webber, w'd; died July 7. James T. Waldron, wounded, thigh.

CORPORALS.

Francis P. Furber, wounded, mouth. Hollis F. Arnold, killed.
George H. Willey, killed.   Samuel C. Brookings, killed.

PRIVATES.

Abbott, Daniel B., w'd, arm and side. Carr, Rinaldo A., wounded, thigh.
Coro, Joseph, wounded, arm and side. Dodge, Martin V. B., w'd, arm and side.
Estes, John H., wounded, leg; missing. Estes, Redford M., wounded, leg.

Gerald, William F., wounded, thigh.
Hamlin, Charles L., wounded, leg.
Leonard, William, wounded, leg.
Martin, Reuben D., wounded, hip.
Taylor, William, killed.
Wheeler, George E., wounded, legs.
Wyman, James, killed.

Goodridge, Drew, wounded, leg.
James, Josephus, w'd; leg amp'd.
Libby, Charles H., wounded, leg.
Richardson, Luke T., wounded, side.
Washburn, Augustus, w'd; arm amp'd.
Wood, William F., wounded, leg.
Young, Benjamin, wounded, neck.

COMPANY I.
Captain George D. Smith, killed.

SERGEANTS.
William E. Barrows, killed.   Chandler F. Perry, killed.

CORPORALS.
Daniel G. Lamb, wounded.
George E. Holmes, wounded, head.
George W. Barter, wounded.

Rufus Shibbles, 2d, wounded, hand.
John Vinal, wounded, hand.
Orrin T. Conway, w'd, leg; died Sept 1.

PRIVATES.
Black, Gorham L., wounded.
Clapp, Hiram, wounded.
Dodge, Adrian C., wounded, cheek.
Jacobs, Edwin S., prov. g'd,w'd, head.
Maddocks, Joseph G., wounded, arm.
Norton, Joseph H., wounded.
Rhoades, Francis W., killed.
Wilson, Joseph W., killed.

Carey, John F., killed.
Clark, Luther, wounded.
Dyer, Alden W., wounded, shoulder.
Little, Thomas, wounded, leg.
Mills, James P., wounded, leg.
Oxton, Amos B., wounded, hand.
Turner, George S., w'd; died July 19.

COMPANY K.
Second Lieutenant Samuel E. Bucknam, wounded, leg.

SERGEANTS.
George L. Grant, w'd; died Nov. 5.   William Boynton, Jr., killed.

CORPORALS.
Weld Sargent, wounded, arm.   Warren Proctor, wounded, groin.
Stephen P. Trafton, wounded, leg.

PRIVATES.
Blaisdell, Richard M., wounded, leg.
Dunton, Ezekiel L., wounded, leg.
Francis, Nelson, killed.
Jellison, Alvah, wounded, thigh.
Lewis, James H., killed.
Lowe, Charles M., killed.
McAvoy, Charles E., killed.
Mitchell, Isaac W., wounded, hand.
Mitchell, Simmons A., w'd, back.
Oliver, Loring C., w'd; died July 20.
Scott, Thomas E., w'd, leg amp'd.
Varell, Gilman N., wounded, legs.
Williams, Henry N., w'd; died July 18.

Blake, Edwin, wounded, hand.
Fogler, George P., killed.
Heal, James T., w'd; died July 8.
Kimball, George A, wounded, foot.
Lombard, David C., w'd; arm amp'd.
Marr, Calvin E., wounded, foot.
McKenney, William, w'd, breast.
Mitchell, Jesse, wounded, shoulder.
Nichols, Oliver P., killed.
Sawyer, Addison, wounded, hand.
Shea, Samuel B., w'd; died July 20.
Webster, Lorenzo, wounded.

Summary of Casualties.

KILLED AND MORTALLY WOUNDED: Officers, company D 1, company I 1; enlisted men, A 3, B 4, C 8, D 9, E 5, F 2, G 4, H 8, I 7, K 12.   Total, 2 officers, 62 enlisted men.

WOUNDED, NOT MORTALLY: Officers, field and staff 2, B 1, C 1, D 1, F 3, G 1, H 2, K 1; enlisted men, non-commissioned staff 1, A 9, B 14, C 15, D 13, E 13, F 7, G 11, H 21, I 16, K 18.   Total, 12 officers, 138 enlisted men (of these 1 of G and 1 of H missing, supposed dead).   Missing, B 1.   Aggregate loss, 215.

The foregoing casualties were compiled from lists that were furnished to newspapers at the time by Capt. Charles E. Nash and Lieut. Loring Farr, from the printed Adjutant-General's Reports, and from other records in the office of the Adjutant-General of Maine.

HISTORICAL SKETCH.

COMPILED BY OFFICERS OF THE REGIMENT.

This regiment was made up from men enlisted in Kennebec, Somerset, Knox, Waldo and Sagadahoc counties.   The various companies arrived at Bath, where the regiment was organized, early in August, 1862.   It was mustered into the United States service on the 25th of that month.   The original organization was as follows :

FIELD, STAFF, AND NON-COMMISSIONED STAFF.

Colonel, Frederick D. Sewall, Bath.
Lieutenant-Colonel, Francis E. Heath, Waterville.
Major, Henry W. Cunningham, Belfast.
Adjutant, Frank W. Haskell, Waterville.
Quartermaster, James W. Wakefield, Bath.
Surgeon, Adoniram J. Billings, Freedom.
Assistant Surgeon, Henry C. Levensaler, Thomaston.
Chaplain, Eliphalet Whittlesey, Brunswick.

Sergeant-Major, William P. Joy, Ellsworth.
Quartermaster-Sergeant, Benjamin D. Hanson, Pittston.
Commissary-Sergeant, Thomas D. Wakefield, Bath.
Hospital Steward, Delon W. Abbott, Orono.
First Principal Musician, Daniel R. Maddocks, Belfast.
Second Principal Musician, Carter N. Payson, Camden.

COMPANY OFFICERS.

Co. A.   Captain, James W. Hathaway, Mercer.
First Lieutenant, Joseph W. Spaulding, Richmond.
Second Lieutenant, David E. Parsons, Norridgewock.

Co. B.   Captain, Lindley M. Coleman, Lincolnville.
          First Lieutenant, William Clements, Monroe.
          Second Lieutenant, Levi Rackliff, Lincolnville.
Co. C.   Captain, George H. Rowell, Fairfield.
          First Lieutenant, Joseph H. Hunt, Unity.
          Second Lieutenant, Francis M. Ames, Fairfield.
Co. D.   Captain, William H. Fogler, Belfast.
          First Lieutenant, Horace C. Noyes, Belfast.
          Second Lieutenant, Edward R. Cunningham, Belfast.
Co. E.   Captain, Daniel L. Dickey, Stockton.
          First Lieutenant, James Johnson, Searsport.
          Second Lieutenant, John S. Tapley, Frankfort.
Co. F.   Captain, Isaac W. Starbird, Litchfield.
          First Lieutenant, George L. Whitmore, Bowdoinham.
          Second Lieutenant, Charles E. Nash, Hallowell.
Co. G.   Captain, James W. Welch, Augusta.
          First Lieutenant, Everett M. Whitehouse, China.
          Second Lieutenant, George C. Hopkins, Mount Vernon.
Co. H.   Captain, Joseph Eaton, Jr., Winslow.
          First Lieutenant, Willard Lincoln, China.
          Second Lieutenant, Albert Hunter, Clinton.
Co. I.   Captain, Edward A. Snow, Rockland.
          First Lieutenant, Gershom F. Burgess, Camden.
          Second Lieutenant, George D. Smith, Rockland.
Co. K.   Captain, Charles S. Larrabee, Bath.
          First Lieutenant, Joseph Nichols, Phippsburg.
          Second Lieutenant, Dumont Bunker, Fairfield.

Colonel Sewall had previously been A. A. G. on the staff of Brig.-Gen. O. O. Howard. Lieut.-Col. Heath was promoted from Captain in the Third Maine regiment, having served with that organization from its formation. Maj. H. W. Cunningham had also been a Captain in the Fourth Maine regiment. F. W. Haskell, Adjutant, had previously been a member of the Third Maine.

The regiment left Bath August 27, 1862 ; reached Washington on the afternoon of the 29th ; the next day, after marching into Virginia, was ordered to recross the Potomac and garrison some forts on the Eastern Branch. While performing this duty the several companies were instructed in artillery drill. On the 30th of September the regiment was ordered to Harper's Ferry, where it was assigned to the First brigade, Second division, Second army corps. During October the army remained in the vicinity of Harper's Ferry ; on the 30th it took up its march in the direction of Warrenton, the Second corps reaching that place November 9th. Here General McClellan was relieved from his command and Burnside took his place. On the 15th the regiment left Warrenton and with the corps marched towards Fredericksburg, arriving near Falmouth on the 17th. Owing to the lack of bridge material, inclination or incapacity, the army did not cross the Rappahannock at this time, but remained on the left bank until well into December, thus giving the enemy time to concentrate his force in the vicinity of Fredericksburg. From November 20th to December 5th the regiment was engaged in keeping the road from Belle Plaine to Falmouth passable ; this road being the one over which the army drew its supplies at this time. While returning from this duty to its proper place in the corps the regiment marched in a very cold rain which turned to snow in the afternoon. Every one lay down that night wet through, with little or no shelter ; this exposure killed more men of this regiment than any battle it ever engaged in.

On the 11th of December the army had orders to cross the river. After wasting a long time in attempting to lay a pontoon bridge at Falmouth, an attempt was made by Colonel Hall of the Third brigade to cross in boats. This attempt succeeded, and the division crossed that evening, the Third and Second brigades doing the murderous street-fighting, and driving the enemy out of the city. About noon on the 13th the First brigade was ordered to the front, the Nineteenth being on the right. The brigade was formed in column of battalions, in mass, some eight hundred yards in front of Marye's Heights. It was understood that the brigade was to make a charge upon the enemy as soon as another brigade formed in its rear to support it ; while waiting, the First brigade was exposed to a severe shelling, which was exceedingly destructive in the four rear battalions. The Nineteenth was protected by a very slight rise of the ground in its front, which prevented any ricochet-shots from striking it. The brigade to support the expected charge at last made its appearance, and while forming in rear of the First brigade the rebel battery, which had been shelling the latter, opened on the newcomers. The effect was decisive ; in five minutes not any of the supporting brigade was in sight, and the charge was not ordered. On the night of the 15th the regiment was ordered back to its old camp near Falmouth, at which time the whole army was withdrawn.

During the "mud" campaign the regiment was not moved. The winter was passed in the usual duties, and the regiment attained so high a degree of efficiency and discipline that it was ranked among eleven regiments in the army to which were granted extra leaves of absence and furloughs.

On February 21st Colonel Sewall resigned on account of ill health, and Lieut.-Col. Heath was promoted to be Colonel. On April 27th Hooker commenced the movements which culminated in the battle of Chancellorsville. The Second division of the Second corps did not participate in these movements at first. May 1st, at 9 P. M., the regiment received orders to guard the field telegraph line to U. S. Ford on the Rappahannock ; on the 3d it was ordered to join the brigade at Falmouth, which had been engaged in the support of Sedgwick.

From this time until early in June the army remained quiet. At this time the rebel army commenced its movement towards Pennsylvania, drawing Hooker after it. The Second corps was the last to leave the Rappahannock, which it did on June 15th. On its march it passed the first Bull Run battlefield, and at midnight of the 20th reached Thoroughfare Gap, where the regiment remained till the 25th ; on that day the corps started for the Potomac, crossing the same at Edward's Ferry. Shortly after leaving the Gap we ran into Stuart's cavalry, which opened fire upon the corps with a couple of guns ; one of our batteries went into action, and this, with the flankers, closed the disturbance. The regiment had one man killed in this skirmish.

We left Monocacy on the morning of the 29th and marched beyond Uniontown, covering about thirty miles. July 1st the regiment was detailed to guard the corps train, but at noon it was relieved from this duty and ordered to push on and join its brigade. At 1 o'clock A. M., July 2d, it bivouacked within three miles of Gettysburg ; at 3 o'clock the same morning it moved for the field of battle, going into position near the centre of the Union line, south of the "copse of trees" now marked by the High Water Mark Monument. Towards night it became heavily engaged, losing about 130 in killed and wounded. On the next day it participated in the repulse of Pickett, and its losses in the two days' fighting amounted to 206, including four reported as missing who were undoubtedly killed, as they were never heard of afterwards. On and after July 4th Colonel Heath commanded the brigade and Lieut.-Col. Cunningham the regiment.

July 5th, at 5 p. m., the regiment with the corps started in pursuit of Lee, who had retreated towards Falling Waters; nothing was accomplished towards attacking Lee, and he was allowed to cross the Potomac without more fighting, excepting some minor skirmishes with our cavalry. The corps moved up Loudon Valley without much haste. On the 23d the regiment marched through Manassas Gap, and immediately retraced its steps, as the rebels were not within reach. After reaching Morrisville on the 29th there was a quiet time, nothing going on but ordinary camp duties. September 12th the regiment moved to Rappahannock Station; on the 27th it relieved our cavalry on a part of the line of the Rapidan, and maintained an extensive picket line till October 8th, at which time it was removed to Culpeper. Three hundred and forty-two recruits were received during September and October.

October 10th the regiment together with the corps was ordered out in great haste, and marched in the direction of Thornton's Gap. For several days, as well as nights, the movement was continued, in a most perplexing way. Lee was attempting to get in Meade's rear by the right. On the 14th the regiment was marching with the rest of the brigade on the right of the corps; the route was on the Orange and Alexandria Railroad, and towards Washington. About 2 p. m. it arrived at Bristoe Station on Broad Run; at this point the enemy made their appearance, and an attack was made on the Second corps. This was repulsed in fine style, the rebels losing five guns and two colors, one of which, of a North Carolina regiment, was taken by the Nineteenth. In this engagement the regiment was under command of Lieut.-Colonel Cunningham, Colonel Heath being in command of the brigade. The loss in the regiment was one killed and twelve wounded. The small number of casualties was doubtless owing to the railroad embankment, behind which the regiment did most of its fighting. As soon as darkness would permit, the march was continued towards Centreville, that point being reached about midnight. After a day or two the regiment moved back to Bristoe, and thence to Warrenton, arriving there the 20th. November 7th it moved to Kelly's Ford, crossing the river on the 9th.

On the 26th of November it joined in the movement to Mine Run ; it was engaged in this attempt to fight Lee on equal terms until the withdrawal of the army to its former line. The loss in this demonstration was one wounded.

During the winter the regiment encamped near Culpeper. Lieut.-Col. Selden Connor, of the Seventh Maine, was promoted to be Colonel of the Nineteenth, joining the regiment in February, Colonel Heath having resigned by reason of ill health. On February 6th the Second corps made a reconnaissance to Morton's Ford, in which the Nineteenth participated, and returned to its camp on the night of the 7th. Two men were wounded during the movement.

The regiment remained in camp till the opening of the Wilderness campaign. At daybreak May 4th it crossed the Rapidan at Ely's Ford ; May 6th it was engaged with the enemy, losing heavily. In this fight Colonel Connor was wounded in the thigh, resulting in disability from further service. For his gallant conduct he was promoted to Brigadier-General.

On May 8th the regiment marched towards Spotsylvania ; on the 9th it did some skirmishing at Po River ; May 10th it formed part of column which made two assaults on the enemy's works ; on the 12th it was engaged in the assault made by the Second corps. Major Welch, who was in command of the regiment, was severely wounded in this engagement (a). On the 18th it was engaged in another attack ; May 21st the regiment, Lieut.-Col. Cunningham in command, moved towards the North Anna, arriving there in the afternoon of the 23d ; it crossed the river on the 24th and again engaged the enemy. May 27th the regiment marched to Pamunkey River ; the 30th moved to the Totopotomy ; the 31st it was under fire near Bethesda Church.

(a) Major Welch captured and took off the field, colors of the 33d Va.—See official report, A. G. R. Maine, 1864-5, Vol. 1, page 279.

June 1st the regiment was engaged again, and Captain Fogler, who commanded it, was wounded ; on the 2d it reached Cold Harbor, and on the 3d participated in the sanguinary and fruitless assault upon the enemy's strong works.

On the 11th it marched for the James River. From the opening of the campaign to this time the casualties in the regiment were 298. Lieut.-Col. Cunningham had resigned, and the regiment was now in command of Capt. Charles E. Nash. June 15th it arrived near Petersburg, having crossed James River the previous day ; on the 18th it was attached temporarily to the Third division, and placed on the right of the assaulting column ; on the 20th it was relieved from duty in front of Petersburg, and with the corps moved several miles to the left.

June 22d, under the command of Capt. J. W. Spaulding, it was again engaged ; owing to the troops on its left being outflanked, and retreating, it lost heavily in killed, wounded and prisoners. July 26th it marched for Deep Bottom, and was engaged at that point on the 27th ; on the 29th it recrossed the James, and on the night of the 30th reached its old camp.

The regiment had crossed the Rapidan, the 4th of May, with 490 enlisted men and officers, and had been joined by 57 men, in the field, from the Fourth Maine regiment ; it now numbered scarcely 150 enlisted men, present for duty, so great had been the losses in killed, wounded and prisoners, and from other casualties. It remained in this position until August 12th, when, without previous orders, it suddenly broke camp and, under the command of Captain Spaulding, marched to City Point with the Second corps. Towards night of the 13th it went on board transports, which dropped down the river a few miles and lay at anchor until in the night, when they returned and steamed up river to Strawberry Plains, where early in the morning of the 14th it disembarked and marched to Deep Bottom ; after considerable delay it formed line of battle along Bailey's Creek at right angles to the river, the Tenth corps on the left. The Nineteenth formed the extreme right of the Second corps, reaching to Fassett's mill, with Gregg's cavalry division on the right flank. General Barlow, who was to make the attack, as he was desirous of winning promotion, had been placed in command of the First and Second divisions of the Second corps. He had succeeded in getting only the extreme right brigade in position when the attack was ordered. The line was formed just back of the crest of a ridge; in front was a deep ravine, through which flowed the creek below the mill. The enemy was posted in rifle-pits on the opposite crest. Colonel Macy, a brave officer of the 20th Mass., who commanded the brigade, remaining on his horse on ground where no officer could go mounted, was soon injured by the stumbling of his horse and taken to the rear. The command to charge having been given, the brigade advanced double-quick; the left soon entered a heavy timber, the right moving over the crest, down the open bluff, across the creek, where it was obstructed by a thicket of underbrush so dense that a single man could not penetrate without difficulty. The only opening through this thicket was a narrow cart-road; the regiment halted immediately under the rifle-pits of the enemy, where it remained until after dark; not receiving any communication from general or staff officers, and finding itself deserted by the troops on its left, without orders it withdrew by the right flank across the mill-dam and joined its division in the rear. On the 18th it was under a severe artillery fire when two attacks were made by the enemy on our line. That night it moved to the extreme left of our line, and in the night of the 20th commenced its return march to the old camp in front of Petersburg, where it arrived early in the morning of the 21st. Gen. Francis A. Walker, in his History of the Second Army Corps, and, following him, Gen. A. A. Humphreys, have severely criticised the troops of the two divisions under command of General Barlow for their lack of spirit in this attack. These writers, who were in error even in regard to the brigade and division engaged, probably obtained their data from a distance, and evidently knew nothing of the conduct of the troops which they criticised. The regiment in this expedition lost fifteen in killed and wounded. After remaining in camp a few hours, the First division, Barlow's, under command of Gen. Nelson A. Miles, and the Second division, Gibbon's, of the Second corps, commenced a movement to the left, and on the morning

of the 24th reached Reams' Station on the Petersburg and
Weldon Railroad. Here it found some rifle-pits in the form
of an irregular horseshoe, or letter V, thrown up by the cavalry
during the June expedition. It was employed during the day
in burning railroad sleepers and destroying the rails. Next
morning the enemy commenced an attack and continued pressing our lines during the day. In the afternoon they made
three charges, which were repulsed; finally, after a terrific
cannonade, raking across both wings in front and reverse, they
advanced on our right and centre; the right wing gave way,
then the centre; our batteries were captured; a battery on the
right was turned upon the rear of the left wing; one, at the
junction of the centre and left wing, was turned on the flank of
the left wing. The Nineteenth was in the centre of the left
wing and held its position until they were the only troops on
the line; then withdrew and formed the nucleus of a new line,
across the heel of the horseshoe-shaped works, which had been
captured by the enemy. Several attempts had been made during the engagement, by the general officers, to rally the troops
and retake the part of the works lost; but the regimental officers and troops would not respond. The men who had repulsed
Pickett's charge at Gettysburg, who had repelled Lee's attacks
in the Wilderness, and stormed his works at Spotsylvania, who
had been hurled against his intrenchments at Cold Harbor, had
learned to distrust the judgment of their superior officers, and
by a tacit understanding with their regimental officers declined
any further useless slaughter. Two decimated divisions had
been sent to destroy a few miles of railroad; after having
accomplished their mission they remained idle more than twenty-four hours, only four miles from other troops; during all
this time it was known to all officers and men that Hill's whole
corps was on the march from Petersburg for their destruction.
This apparent challenge for a fight was one of the unaccountable blunders of the war which has never been explained; the
result indicated that the troops should have been withdrawn on
the night of the 24th, or reinforcements should have been sent
to hold the position. The commander of the army of the Potomac and the commander of the Second corps have each placed

the responsibility upon the other. No further attack was made by the enemy, and after dark the troops were withdrawn. The regiment lost twelve, killed and wounded, and many prisoners. From August 26th to September 24th the regiment was in the second and rear lines of works in front of Petersburg. September 7th Captain Spaulding left on sick leave, and until October 21st the command fell successively upon Captain Parsons and Colonel Welch, the latter returning from absence on account of wounds. September 24th it moved into the front line, and on the 30th took up its position at the right of Fort Sedgwick — nicknamed Fort " Hell," — where it remained until October 26th. Colonel Welch resigned October 21st, and Major Starbird became Colonel, and was present until winter quarters. October 26th it moved to the left, and on the 27th was in the engagement at Boydton Plank Road. The losses were not heavy in this engagement, but the regiment was in a most trying position ; upon the left came shell ; in front shell came through a pine wood ; and ricochet-shot from across the open field ; canister was scattered over it from the right, and musket bullets came from the rear, driving Surgeon Randall to the line of battle, — the only time the writer ever knew a Surgeon to ask for a musket. After dark it withdrew and returned to the line in front of Petersburg ; on the 31st it occupied Fort Haskell.

The fifth company, unassigned infantry, formed at Augusta, Maine, October 5, 1864, joined the regiment October 22d, with three officers and sixty-four enlisted men present for duty, and was consolidated with the companies of the Nineteenth. The three officers were Capt. Addison W. Lewis, First Lieut. Edward B. Sargent, Second Lieut. Charles Bennett.

In the night of November 5th the picket line to the right of Fort Haskell was captured by the enemy, the brigade losing thirty-five men, about one-half of them belonging to the Nineteenth. This was made possible by the right of the line having been established in front of a mill-pond, with no line of retreat except by the left flank ; the enemy had only to strike the line in the centre, cut off the retreat, move to our right, and their work was done. November 29th, in the night, the regiment being relieved from duty in Fort Haskell moved to the left, near to Patrick's Station, the terminus of the Grant railroad, and built winter quarters. For the first time for two months it was out of the reach of shot and shell. It had been on continuous duty in the front line for more than two months; much of the time one-half of the men were required for skirmish, picket and guard duty. All were under fire of artillery and musketry at all times, both day and night. The losses in killed and wounded during this period were thirty-four men and officers, which, added to the losses sustained at Strawberry Plains and Reams' Station, made a total loss of fifty-nine in officers and men. The regiment remained here in the quarters it constructed until the expedition to Hatcher's Run.

During the year 1864 the losses in the Nineteenth were : killed and mortally wounded, 101 ; wounded, not fatally, 299 ; prisoners, 133 ; making total of 533 out of 614.

Early Sunday morning, February 5, 1865, the corps moved to the left to feel the enemy's right flank and extend the lines. Near the Armstrong house General Smyth directed Lieut.-Col. Spaulding to move the regiment by the left flank out of the column. The regiment then advanced by itself, meeting the enemy's skirmish line at Hatcher's Run and, forcing them back, crossed the Run and pressed the enemy back from two lines of rifle-pits, and held the position until relieved by troops of the Fifth corps, when it rejoined the brigade. Three days followed of very severe weather, which occasioned great suffering and the death of the acting Adjutant, Lieutenant Gerrish, by disease. It was most of the time under fire. On the 11th the regiment went into new winter quarters near Hatcher's Run.

March 7, 1865, General Meade issued General Order No. 10, as follows :

" In accordance with the requirements of General Orders No. 19 of 1862 from the War Department, and in conformity with the reports of boards convened to examine into the service rendered by the troops concerned, and by authority of the Lieutenant-General commanding the armies of the United States, *it is ordered :* That there shall be inscribed upon the colors or guidons of the following regiments and batteries serving in the army, the names of the battles in which they have borne a meritorious part, as hereinafter specified, viz. :

"NINETEENTH MAINE VOLUNTEERS : *Fredericksburg, Chancellorsville, Gettysburg, Bristoe Station, Mine Run, Wilderness, Spotsylvania, River Po, North Anna, Totopotomy, Cold Harbor, Petersburg, Deep Bottom, Strawberry Plains, Reams' Station, Boydton Road.*"

It appears from that order that only one other infantry regiment (1st U. S. Sharpshooters) in the army, during the time that this regiment had been a part of the army of the Potomac, had been in a greater number of engagements. That regiment had the names of seventeen battles upon its colors. But four other infantry regiments (20th Mass., 61st N. Y., 57th Penn., 7th Mich.) had as many as the Nineteenth Maine during the same period. The order was issued upon reports made prior to the Hatcher's Run fight of February 5th.

The final campaign began Wednesday, March 29, 1865. The Second corps moved out to the left by the Vaughan Road. The Nineteenth and one other regiment, both under command of Colonel Starbird, advanced through the woods as skirmishers to Dabney's Mill, from which location the enemy had hurriedly departed. The next day the regiment again advanced as skirmishers to within a few rods of the enemy's fort near the Crow house, pushing the rebel skirmishers all the way.

The regiment again engaged the enemy March 31st, and still again Sunday, April 2d, when our troops entered the enemy's works, capturing many prisoners, and started off in pursuit of Lee's army on the Cox Road. April 3d Richmond and Petersburg were occupied by Federal troops. The regiment participated with the corps during the week in hot pursuit of Lee's army. April 7th the regiment, advancing as skirmishers, had a sharp and spirited fight with the enemy at High Bridge, in which Colonel Starbird was again severely wounded. The enemy had fired both the railroad bridge and wagon bridge across the Appomattox at this point, and the regiment fought the enemy and saved the traveled bridge upon which the two army corps (Second and Sixth) crossed that day in close pursuit of the enemy. Gen. A. A. Humphreys, who commanded the corps later in the day, addressing Lieut.-Col. Spaulding, commended the regiment in strong terms. He with General Barlow, the division commander, had personally witnessed the heroic fight that the regiment made, and had sent the gallant General Smyth with his brigade to its support. General Smyth, later in the day, gave his life to his country.

The regiment again that day, and for the last time as enemies, met the Confederates near Farmville just at nightfall.

On Sunday, April 9, 1865, it participated in the wild and joyous excitement over the news of Lee's surrender, which General Meade himself carried to the troops.

The return march was begun two days after the surrender. The corps remained for about a month near Burkeville; then marched, passing through Richmond and along familiar routes, till it approached Alexandria, and went into camp May 15, 1865, near Bailey's Cross Roads. Tuesday, May 23d, it participated in the Grand Review of the Army of the Potomac by the President in Washington.

On the 31st of May it was mustered out of United States service by Capt. H. Y. Russell, 10th N. Y. Vols., mustering officer of the division.

The regiment left its last camp early in the morning of June 1, 1865, for Maine, and was finally paid at Augusta, Maine, June 7th and disbanded. The only commissioned officers mustered at Bath in August, 1862, who were with the regiment at the final muster, were Lieut.-Col. Spaulding and Major Parsons, and only two more of the original officers (Colonel Starbird and Captain Lincoln) were still on the rolls of the regiment.

ROSTER.

The following information relating to officers of the Nineteenth Maine regiment is obtained from the Volunteer Army Register, published by the War Department August 31, 1865, and other reliable sources.

OFFICERS AT MUSTER-OUT, MAY 31, 1865.

COLONEL: Isaac W. Starbird, Nov. 16, 1864, mustered out June 7, 1865, —brevet Brig.-General, March 13, 1865.

LIEUTENANT-COLONEL: Joseph W. Spaulding, Nov. 16, 1864.

MAJOR: David E. Parsons, Nov. 16, 1864.

ADJUTANT: First Lieut. Henry Sewall, July 18, 1864.

CAPTAINS: Willard Lincoln, Nov. 1, 1862, mustered out June 10, 1865; Nehemiah Smart, Oct. 27, 1863; Ansel L. White, Oct. 31, 1864, — brevet Major, April 9, 1865; Elbridge C. Pierce, Nov. 3, 1864; Oliver R. Small, Nov. 16, 1864, — brevet Major, March 13, 1865; Calvin B. Hinkley, Dec. 2, 1864; John A. Lord, Jan. 11, 1865; Thomas P. Beath, Jan. 11, 1865; Addison W. Lewis, Oct. 4, 1864, discharged June 9, 1865.

FIRST LIEUTENANTS: Edwin H. Rich, Feb. 28, 1864; Albert Hunter, Quartermaster, March 9, 1864; Charles P. Garland, Sept. 14, 1864; William B. Sawyer, Oct. 29, 1864; George P. Wood, Oct. 29, 1864,—previously Sergeant, Fourth Maine; Alfred E. Nickerson, Dec. 2, 1864; James H. Pierce, Dec. 2, 1864; Beniah P. Dolloff, Jan. 11, 1865; Charles Bennett, Jan. 13, 1865; George Studley, Feb. 16, 1865; Edward B. Sargent, Oct. 4, 1864, discharged June 9, 1865.

SECOND LIEUTENANTS: George H. Page, Oct. 27, 1863; Joseph B. Babson, Oct. 29, 1864,—previously of Fourth Maine; William H. Tripp, Oct. 29, 1864, — previously of Co. H, Fourth Maine, brevet Captain, March 13, 1865; Clarendon W. Gray, Dec. 2, 1864; Franklin Adams, Jan. 13, 1865; George A. Barton, Jan. 31, 1865.

SURGEON: William H. Randall, Nov. 16, 1864.   ASSISTANT SURGEON: Benjamin Bussey, Jr., Nov. 21, 1864.

CHAPLAIN: George W. Hathaway, June 14, 1863.

(The dates given above refer to rank or commission; those hereafter given refer to the date of event.)

DIED.

CAPTAINS: Lindley M. Coleman, Oct. 18, 1862, of disease; George D. Smith, killed in battle of Gettysburg, July 2, 1863.

SECOND LIEUTENANTS: Leroy S. Scott, July 13, 1863, of wounds in battle of Gettysburg; Lafayette Carver, June 22, 1864, of wounds; James N. Hinkley (commissioned, not mustered), of wounds, Feb. 15, 1864; George E. Grows (commissioned, not mustered), of wounds, July 7, 1864; William L. Gerrish, Feb. 11, 1865, of disease.

PROMOTED AND TRANSFERRED OUT OF REGIMENT.

Colonel Selden Connor, July 1, 1864, to Brigadier-General of Volunteers.

Chaplain Eliphalet Whittlesey, March 11, 1863, to Captain and Assistant Adjutant-General, U. S. Vols.

Assistant Surgeon Henry C. Levensaler, promoted to Surgeon Eighth Maine regiment, Aug. 17, 1863.

DISCHARGED.

CAPTAINS: Asbury C. Richards, Sept. 18, 1863; Everett M. Whitehouse, Oct. 14, 1864, expiration of term of service,—previously Corp'l Third Maine; Dumont Bunker, Oct. 26, 1864; William H. Fogler, Nov. 2, 1864; Charles E. Nash, Nov. 28, 1864; Edgar A. Burpee, May 15, 1865.

FIRST LIEUTENANTS: Albion Whitten, Nov. 17, 1863; Francis W. Haskell, Adjutant, Feb. 6, 1864; Richard Crockett, April 26, 1864; George A. Wadsworth, April 27, 1864; Edward R. Cunningham, June 15, 1864; George R. Palmer, Aug. 9, 1864; Loring Farr, Sept. 15, 1864; William H. Emery, Oct. 13, 1864.

SECOND LIEUTENANTS: Francis H. Foss, Oct. 27, 1863; Henry W. Nye, Feb. 23, 1864; Alvirus Osborne, Mar. 4, 1864; Samuel E. Bucknam, April 1, 1864; Thomas B. Campbell, Nov. 22, 1864; Columbus S. Anderson, Mar. 17, 1865.

ASSISTANT SURGEON: Fred G. Parker, Mar. 5,1864.

RESIGNED.

Colonel Frederick D. Sewall, Feb. 19, 1863,—afterwards Colonel Third regiment V. R. C. and brevet Brig.-General, July 21, 1865.

Colonel Francis E. Heath, on account of ill health, Nov. 4, 1863,—brevet Brig.-General, Mar. 13, 1865.

Colonel James W. Welch, Oct. 21, 1864.

Lieut.-Colonel Henry W. Cunningham, June 11, 1864.

Captains: Charles H. Rowell, Oct. 12, 1862; Joseph Eaton, Jr., Oct. 31, 1862; James W. Hathaway, Nov. 5, 1862; Daniel L. Dickey, Jan. 1, 1863; Horace C. Noyes, Feb. 20, 1863; Edward A. Snow, Feb. 23, 1863; Charles S. Larrabee, Mar. 3, 1863: George L. Whitmore, Nov. 7, 1863.

First Lieutenants: James Johnson, Oct., 1862; Joseph H. Hunt, Oct. 21, 1862; William Clements, Oct. 17, 1862; Francis M. Ames, Nov. 18, 1862; Gershom F. Burgess, Feb. 10, 1863; John S. Tapley, Feb. 14, 1863; Jason Gordon, Feb. 17, 1863; James W. Wakefield, Quartermaster, Nov. 13, 1863; Elisha W. Ellis, Dec. 12, 1863; Josiah W. Tucker, Dec. 28, 1864.

Second Lieutenants: Levi Rackliff, Oct. 29, 1862; Almon Goodwin, Dec. 17, 1862; George C. Hopkins, Jan. 27, 1863; Benjamin B. Hanson, Jan. 23, 1863; Stephen R. Gordon, Nov. 5, 1863; Joseph L. Clark, Nov. 30, 1863.

Surgeons: Adoniram J. Billings, Jan. 11, 1864; John Q. A. Hawes, Nov. 2, 1864, — resigned as Assistant Surgeon, June 22, 1863, and commissioned as Surgeon, Feb. 29, 1864. Assistant Surgeons: Wallace Bolan, Mar. 22, 1864; Benjamin F. Sturgis, Oct. 22, 1864.

Chaplain Edwin B. Palmer, Feb. 10, 1863.

OTHERWISE LEFT THE SERVICE.

First Lieutenant Joseph Nichols, Feb. 16, 1863, cashiered.

MONUMENT.

The monument of the Sixth Maine Battery, of Hallowell granite, stands in a conspicuous position upon Hancock avenue, in the left centre of the Union line. The monument is surmounted by a pyramid of five black cannon balls made of Addison granite. Upon its plinth is a group of cannon, flags, swords, etc., carved in bas relief; and on the die above is a five-pointed star, also in relief.

ADMEASUREMENTS: Base, six feet by six feet by one foot six inches; plinth, four feet four inches by four feet four inches by two feet four inches; die, three feet six inches by three feet six inches by four feet eight inches; five balls, each one foot two inches in diameter. Total height, nine feet eight inches. On its front and two flanking sides are the following inscriptions:

Dow's

6TH MAINE

BATTERY.

CAMPAIGNS A. P.

1862———1865.

McGILVERY'S BRIGADE

RESERVE ARTILLERY.

DOW'S SIXTH MAINE BATTERY,

FIRST VOLUNTEER BRIGADE, RESERVE ARTILLERY,

AT THE BATTLE OF GETTYSBURG.

IN the line "patched up" to stay the tide which had rolled the
advanced Sickles' line back, another Maine organization
appeared and bore a conspicuous part in the repulse of the
final Confederate advance. It was Dow's Sixth Maine battery,
attached to the Fourth (a) volunteer brigade of reserve artillery.
This battery, consisting of four light twelve-pounder Napoleon
guns, brought onto the field one hundred and three men and
officers and ninety horses. It had been recruited from York,
Waldo and Aroostook counties, and had been in service since
January 1, 1862. First Lieut. Edwin B. Dow commanded at
Gettysburg. The battery arrived on the field from Taneytown
about 8 A. M., July 2d, with the other batteries of the artillery
brigade. During the forenoon and first part of the afternoon of
that day the battery was parked in a field near the Taneytown
road, whence its officers and men were anxious spectators of the
struggle between Sickles and Longstreet. At 6 o'clock General
Tyler, commanding the artillery reserve, ordered Lieutenant
Dow to report to Maj. Freeman McGilvery (b), commanding
the First volunteer brigade of the reserve artillery.

Major McGilvery, to whom Lieutenant Dow was ordered to
report, was at that hour commanding his own and some other
artillery at the front, where he had been heavily engaged with his
batteries, which lined the cross-road below the Peach Orchard,
sustaining Sickles' advanced position. In the crisis of the battle
attending the breaking up of the Third corps line along the

(a) The heading places the battery in the First brigade, with which it fought in
this battle, as the monument inscription indicates, although regularly attached to
Fourth brigade. When the army was "stripped" to follow Lee it was found necessary, on account of the lack of men, to leave two guns at Falmouth, Va.

(b) Major McGilvery, who rendered very distinguished services in this battle,
was a Maine soldier, and promoted from Captain of the Sixth Maine battery.

Emmitsburg road, McGilvery seized the opportunity to assemble some retreating batteries, and also to order up Dow, who had not been engaged, and posted them along the ridge assigned for the main line, which Hancock had been strengthening for the salvation of the army.

It was about seven o'clock when the Sixth Maine battery reported to McGilvery (a). The enemy had just overrun and captured four guns of Bigelow's Ninth Mass. battery near the Trostle house, as the Sixth Maine opened fire. Directing his fire towards the abandoned guns, Lieutenant Dow soon drove the enemy from them; and later in the evening was able to recover and restore three of them to their rightful owners.

As the enemy near the Trostle house were driven from Bigelow's guns, McGilvery discovered them advancing in force upon the left centre of our lines, intending to push through and complete the victory of the afternoon. This was the hour when McGilvery's genius as an officer of artillery shone brightest. He hurried into position battery I, 5th U. S., three guns of the 5th Mass., two guns of Thompson's Penn. battery, and a volunteer battery the name of which was not ascertained in the confusion. To these he added the Sixth Maine, which had made a flank movement from its first position. Lieutenant Dow posted his guns in full view of the enemy, whose line of artillery and infantry had advanced into the open field about seven or eight hundred yards in front; while in the bushes along the banks of Plum Run, which flowed just in front of the position of the batteries, the Confederate sharpshooters had sheltered themselves and were directing an annoying and dangerous fire upon the artillery-men. This was the hour when Barksdale's brigade of fiery Mississippians, whom we have already seen overwhelming the Third Maine at the Peach Orchard, were advancing with unabated ardor. As the Sixth Maine went into position it came under a heavy fire from two batteries in the enemy's line. Lieutenant Dow replied to them with solid shot and shell, until the enemy's line of skirmishers advanced from their shelter towards the batteries. Very soon, moreover, a battle line of the enemy

(a) Major McGilvery's official report, 1863. — Rebellion Records, serial No. 43, page 882.

appeared, moving up at a distance of about six hundred yards, and evidently bent upon dashing through the line of batteries to the Taneytown road. At this moment the situation of the battery was most perilous. Its anxious commander saw nowhere any infantry supports ; the batteries around it, unable to stand the terrible fire, were moving off to the rear or were deserted by their cannoneers. The guns of battery I, 5th U. S., became silent; Thompson's Penn. battery, getting out of ammunition, was sent to the rear ; Pettit's 1st N. Y. battery, which had come up about the time the Sixth Maine reported, moved off, as did also the volunteer battery which McGilvery had put in position beside battery I, 5th U. S. (a). Alone of the line Dow's Sixth Maine and Phillip's 5th Mass. stood to their guns. McGilvery, whose bravery and sagacity were invaluable at this hour, directed Lieutenant Dow to " hold the position at all hazards," until reinforcements could be brought up. The Sixth Maine and its commanding officer were equal to the demands of the hour and the orders of their chief. Upon the advancing enemy the Sixth Maine and 5th Mass. used spherical case and canister with such precision and rapidity that his line could not advance, and was forced to retire. Lieutenant Dow, perceiving the enemy advancing beyond his left flank, hastily moved his guns to fire in that direction, and contributed largely to the repulse of Wofford.

It was about 7 : 45 P. M. when the enemy was repulsed. The battery had expended two hundred and forty-four rounds of ammunition. Although under a severe artillery and skirmish fire, the battery had only eight men wounded and not one killed. Altogether it was in action about an hour and a half. At eight o'clock the Sixth Maine was relieved by battery K, 4th U. S., then commanded by Second Lieut. Robert James. Before retiring from the field, however, Lieutenant Dow and his men, assisted by others, recovered seven guns abandoned during the battle of the afternoon, but not carried off by the enemy (b).

(a)   Major McGilvery's report, 1863, cited *ante.*

(b)   Lieutenant Dow received his commission as Captain September 1, 1863. He was brevetted Major of Artillery "for gallant and meritorious service at the battle of Gettysburg."

On the morning of July 3d, having repaired damages and received a new supply of ammunition, the battery reported again to Major McGilvery. The latter was at that time bringing his batteries into line on the low ground on the Union left centre, in anticipation of a conflict with batteries which the Confederates were then massing in great force, on the high ground by the Emmitsburg road. Against those batteries McGilvery massed thirty-nine guns. First upon the left, resting upon an oak wood occupied by our infantry, was Ames' battery G, 1st N. Y., six guns, and next to Ames was Dow with the Sixth Maine, four guns. Then came other batteries, making the number of guns thirty-nine. In front of these guns a slight earthwork was thrown up, to cover the men in the cannonade which was anticipated. Supporting these guns at their rear was the First division of the Second corps, reinforced by General Humphreys with his brigades of Carr, Brewster and Burling; on their left were two brigades, under Torbert and Nevin, of the Sixth corps; and on their right, portions of the Third corps.

About 1 o'clock the enemy opened upon the Union centre, with about one hundred and fifty guns, that memorable cannonade which preceded Pickett's charge. But much of this fire that was directed against the line of McGilvery's guns was so inaccurate as to do little damage, and the cannoneers were ordered not to reply, but to shelter themselves behind the earthworks in front of their guns. It was not until an hour or more of this cannonade that the batteries under McGilvery began a slow, well-directed fire upon those single batteries of the enemy most plainly in view. Several of them were thus badly broken up and driven to the rear before the Confederate infantry was ready to advance.

About 3 o'clock the cannonade ceased and Pickett's division advanced, with Pettigrew's division on its left, and Trimble closing the charging column. On the right were Wilcox's and Lang's brigades, whose line of march was towards McGilvery's batteries. These two brigades, however, never reached the Union line; they did not even succeed in getting within musket range of the line of guns that poured upon them such a withering fire. These being repulsed, the guns were turned obliquely to the right upon Pickett's line, which could now be swept by a most destructive, raking fire. No hill or forest interrupted the level plain over which the Sixth Maine cannoneers and their comrades trained the guns of McGilvery's line. The effect of this raking fire was terrible for the Confederates, but most advantageous for the defenders of the Union line. The decimated brigades and regiments which finally rushed upon Hancock's line, where we have already observed the Nineteenth Maine under fire, had been doomed to defeat when they came within range of the Union batteries.

During this day's action five men of the Sixth Maine battery were wounded. Only one hundred and thirty-nine rounds of ammunition were expended, but it was used to the greatest advantage. In the two days of the battle the battery lost not a gun nor a carriage.

REPORT OF LIEUT. EDWIN B. DOW, SIXTH MAINE BATTERY.

CAMP NEAR BERLIN, MD., July 17, 1863.

CAPTAIN:—I have the honor to report the action taken by the Sixth Maine battery, under my command, at the battle of July 2d and 3d, near Gettysburg, Pa.

I received orders from General Tyler, through Lieutenant Blucher, to report to General Sickles' (Third) corps, on the left centre, about 6 P. M., 2d instant. I immediately marched my command to the front, meeting an ambulance with General Sickles in it badly wounded.

I had not gone far when Major McGilvery ordered me into position in rear of the first line, remarking that he had charge of the artillery of the Third corps. On going into position my battery was under a heavy fire from two batteries of the enemy, situated some one thousand yards in my front. I replied to them with solid shot and shell until the enemy's line of skirmishers and sharpshooters came out of the woods to the left front of my position and poured a continual stream of bullets at us. I soon discovered a battle line of the enemy coming through the woods, about six hundred yards distant, evidently with a design to drive through and take possession of the road to Taneytown, directly in my rear. I immediately opened upon them with spherical case and canister, and, assisted by a section of Captain Phillips' (5th Mass.) battery, drove them back into the woods. Their artillery, to which we paid no attention, had gotten our exact range, and gave us a warm greeting.

We continued to shell the woods after their infantry retired, and upon visiting the spot the same night, about 9 o'clock, found many rebels dead and wounded. It was evidently their intention, after capturing the 9th Mass. battery and company I, Fifth regular, to have charged right through our lines to the Taneytown road, isolating our left wing and dividing our army; but owing to the prompt and skillful action of Maj. Freeman McGilvery, in forming his second line as soon as he found the first line lost, their plan was foiled, for they no doubt thought the woods in our rear were filled with infantry in support of the batteries, when the fact is we had no support at all. At this crisis my orders from Major McGilvery were to hold my position at all hazards until he could reinforce the position and relieve me. It was about 7 o'clock when the enemy retired, and I was in action altogether about one hour and a half.

At 7:30 P. M. I was relieved by Major McGilvery, who placed Seeley's battery, under command of Lieutenant James, in my position, and I retired into the edge of the woods. Lieutenant Rogers, of this battery, in reconnoitering found the enemy had retired from the field in haste, and had not taken the captured guns with them nor even spiked them. He immediately reported the fact to me, and as many men as I could spare were sent under his charge to bring them off the field. With the aid of the Garibaldi Guard, of New York, he brought off, under a fire from the enemy's sharpshooters, four 3-inch rifled guns and two limbers belonging to company I, Fifth regular, which we immediately limbered on our caissons and ran to the rear.

I was then ordered by Major McGilvery to go to the front and see if any other public property was on the field, which order I obeyed, and discovered four light 12-pounder guns and a limber of the 9th Mass. battery. The remnant of the 150th N. Y. regiment, although tired and weary, took hold of the guns and ran them up to Lieutenant James' position, where I turned them over to Lieutenant James, not having force sufficient to bring them off the field. Lieutenant James brought the guns off, and, I understood, turned them over to the 9th Mass. battery (a).

By order of Major McGilvery I reported to Generals Tyler and Hunt what we had done. General Hunt ordered me to go to the rear near the reserve train with the guns. I did so, and next morning had the satisfaction of returning the guns of company I, Fifth regular, to their commanding officer.

I am happy to state that in this action, although under the most severe artillery and sharpshooters' fire, I had only eight men wounded, not one killed. Ammunition expended, 244 rounds.

After repairing damages and getting a new supply of ammunition, I reported to Major McGilvery on the morning of the 3d, and was ordered into position between the 2d Conn. battery and Ames' (1st N. Y) battery, supported by a brigade of the Second corps. I built earthworks in front of my guns.

Nothing of importance occurred until about 11 o'clock, when, at a signal of one gun, the whole rebel line opened a most terrific fire upon our position. Case shot and shell filled the air. The men were ordered to cease firing and take refuge behind their earthworks. This fire lasted without much abate-

(a) Only three of the guns of 9th Mass. battery were taken off by this detail.— See James' report, Rebellion Records, serial No. 43, page 590; also report of Colonel Ketcham, 150th N. Y., *ibid.*, page 409.

ment about one hour and a half, when we discovered the enemy advancing under cover of the artillery. A light 12-pounder battery of four guns ran some four or five hundred yards in front of the enemy's line, so as to enfilade the batteries on our right. We opened with solid shot and shell upon this battery, and succeeded in dismounting one gun, disabling the second, and compelled the battery to leave the field minus one caisson and several horses.

I deem it due to Major McGilvery to say that he was ever present, riding up and down the line in the thickest of the fire, encouraging the men by his words and dashing example — his horse receiving eight wounds, of which he has since died, the gallant Major himself receiving only a few scratches.

The enemy fired mostly case shot and shell at our position, nearly all of which passed over our line of artillery and supports and exploded in the woods behind, covering the road with their fragments. Our loss this day was only five men wounded and five horses killed.

Owing to an injunction from General Hunt not to reply to the enemy's fire, but save our ammunition, we expended only 139 rounds. In the two days' action we did not lose a gun or carriage, but reported for duty again as soon as our stock of ammunition was replenished. I was ably seconded by Lieutenant Rogers, to whom we owe much of our success.

Where all did well it is useless to specify any certain individual among the non-commissioned officers and privates.

I have the honor to be, Captain, most respectfully, your obedient servant,

EDWIN B. DOW,
First Lieutenant, Commanding Sixth Maine Battery.

CAPT. C. H. WHITTELSEY,
Assistant Adjutant-General, Artillery Reserve.
—Rebellion Records, Vol. xxvii., part I., Serial No. 43, page 897.

PARTICIPANTS.

Senior First Lieutenant, Edwin B. Dow, Portland, commanding the battery.
Junior First Lieutenant, William H. Rogers, Stockton.

SERGEANTS.

Marshall N. McKusick, Baring,   Jeremiah Gardiner, Portland,
Joshua J. Seamons, Cary Plantation,   Samuel Thurston, Portland,
Joseph W. Burke, Lee,   James A. Pray, Gardiner,
Timothy Hegarty, Miramichi, N. B.

CORPORALS.

Wilson W. Sawtelle, Dexter,   William S. Leavitt, New Limerick,
Andrew J. Brown, St. George,   Albert A. Fling, Gardiner,
Edward R. Lamb, New Portland,   John G. Deane, Portland,
Thomas J. Daggett, Cary Plantation,   Winslow Hutchings, Alexander,
Edward L. Merrithew, Searsport,   Joseph Winter, Carthage,
John Cronan, Houlton.

PRIVATES.

Adams, John Q., Hodgdon,   Annis, John, Houlton,
Appleby, George, Hodgdon,   Appleby, Murray, Hodgdon,
Bartlett, Henry D., Eustis,   Bonnar, Thomas, Frederickton, N. B.
Broderick, John, Houlton,   Brown, Edward E., Brewer,

Brown, William G., Dixfield,
Calkins, Ira, Hodgdon,
Clarence, Felix, Houlton,
Clement, Henry, Smithfield,
Driscoll, Timothy, Rockland,
Ellis, Luther, Waterville,
Esancy, William H. H., Appleton,
Finn, James, Biddeford,
Gilpatrick, Lyman, Weston,
Haskell, Harvey L., Dexter,
Hewins, Joseph T., Augusta,
Horr, Henry J., Portland,
Kelly, Daniel, Biddeford,
Law, Norris M., Union,
Libby, Elias D., Stockton,
Lothrop, Stillman H., Carroll,
McCue, Peter, Portland,
Merrill, Joshua P., Cary Plantation,
Moore, John W., Easton,
Nelson, Joseph G., Hartland,
O'Heron, Daniel, Houlton,
Pattee, Albert M., Mercer,
Perkins, Nathaniel, Chesterville,
Proctor, Uriah, Eustis,
Reed, Elias H., Dead River Pl.,
Rich, Charles H., Smithfield,
Riley, Thomas, Rockland,
Russell, Asa, Amity,
Seavey, Charles C., Meddybemps,
Taylor, Samuel, China,
Trefethen, Epps A., Portland,
Wallis, Robert, Crawford,
Welch, John W., Augusta,
Wilds, Joseph, Biddeford,
Woodbury, David L., Hartland,

Burns, George, Searsmont,
Chambers, John, Presque Isle,
Clarence, George, Houlton,
Daggett, Benjamin F., Houlton,
Dunton, Samuel F., Camden,
Emery, George, Biddeford,
Evans, Oscar W., Sidney,
Foster, Sanders P., Monticello,
Hanson, Albert N., Saco,
Herrick, Florin G., Hodgdon,
Hinkley, Joseph D., Argyle,
Jackson, Leroy, Camden,
Lane, Orestes H., Carroll,
Lermond, Ambrose L., Appleton,
Littlefield, Edward, Biddeford,
Maddocks, George, Warren,
McKenzie Michael, Houlton,
Metcalf, James, Talmadge,
Mosher, Albert, Smithfield,
Norton, Ervin C., Vinalhaven,
Orne, William A., Friendship,
Penley, Joseph A., Wayne,
Proctor, Erastus, Appleton,
Reed, Eben, Dead River Plantation,
Reed, Henry, Houlton,
Richardson, Henry, Belgrade,
Robinson, Joel F., Sidney,
Sawyer, Edward T., Danville,
Smith, William G., Saco,
Thorndike, Thomas W., Camden,
Walden, James, Camden,
Waters, Ruel W., Augusta,
White, Charles L., Chesterville,
Wiley, David M., Easton,
Woodman, Marston, Searsport.

BUGLER, Henry H. Crosby, Augusta.

ARTIFICERS AND BLACKSMITHS: Jonas C. Spooner, Houlton, William H. Charles, Smithfield, Aaron P. Kinney, Houlton. WAGONER, Watson Andrews, Saco.

DETACHED IN ARMY: Amos Metcalf, Talmadge pl., hospital cook.

Morning report for June 30, 1863: Present for duty, officers 2, men 101; total, 103. Absent, detached service, 2; absent sick, 13. Present and absent, 2 officers, 116 men.

REVISED REPORT OF CASUALTIES.

Sergeant Joseph W. Burke, wounded.
Corporal William S. Leavitt, wounded slightly.

PRIVATES.

Annis, John, wounded slightly.
Ellis, Luther, wounded slightly.
Lothrop, Stillman H., wounded.
Proctor, Erastus, wounded.
Wiley, David M., wounded slightly.
Woodman, Marston, wounded slightly.

Dunton, Samuel F., wounded slightly.
Jackson, Leroy, wounded slightly.
Maddocks, George, wounded slightly.
Reed, Elias H., wounded.
Woodbury, David L., w'd slightly.

All those marked as "wounded slightly" returned to the battery soon after the battle.

HISTORICAL SKETCH OF SIXTH MAINE BATTERY.

COMPILED BY BREVET BRIG.-GEN. CHARLES HAMLIN.

The Sixth battery, recruited principally in York, Waldo and Aroostook counties in the months of November and December, 1861, was mustered into the United States service at Augusta, January 1, 1862. The battery was officered as follows:

Freeman McGilvery, Stockton, Captain; George H. Smith, Hodgdon, Edwin B. Dow, Portland, First Lieutenants; Fred A. Morton, Augusta, William H. Rogers, Stockton, Second Lieutenants.

The battery lay in camp at Augusta until March, when it received orders to proceed to Portland and occupy the barracks called Camp Berry. Orders were received March 30th for all the light batteries in Maine to report at Washington, D. C., and April 1st the six batteries took the cars for that city; arrived in Washington April 3d, and went into camp at East Capitol Hill.

The Sixth battery remained in camp about a month, when it was ordered to march to Fort Buffalo and garrison that outpost. Fort Buffalo was a small redoubt, mounting four light guns, situate near the village of Falls Church, Va., about seven miles from the Potomac. A portion of the company was armed with muskets, while the remainder acted as artillery-men. Matters becoming quiet in the neighborhood of Washington the guns

in the fort were sent to Fort Ramsay, and the Sixth battery was ordered to relieve the Fourth Maine battery at that post. A few days afterwards orders came to dismantle Fort Ramsay, which mounted several heavy guns *en barbette* and had a large stock of ammunition. After several days the fort was vacated and the battery ordered to occupy the village of Falls Church, Captain McGilvery being appointed commander of the post. At this time the rebel general "Stonewall" Jackson made his advance down the valley, driving General Banks into Maryland, and great fears were entertained that an attack might be made on Washington. The Sixth battery held the extreme outpost and picketed as far south as Fairfax Court House. Communicating with the headquarters at Arlington Heights by a system of signals, Captain McGilvery received very complimentary notices for his energy and watchfulness on this occasion. Shortly after, the battery was ordered to Washington to receive its proper armament. After fitting up a camp at East Capitol Hill it received its battery, which consisted of four light 12-pound brass pieces (Napoleons), and two 3-inch rifle guns (10-pounders), with one hundred and twenty horse-harnesses, ammunition and accoutrements complete.

Before it was properly drilled the battery was ordered to report to General Banks at Harper's Ferry. It marched up the valley via Charlestown and Winchester to Cedar Creek, Va., where General Banks' army then lay, and remained at Cedar Creek until after the 4th of July, when the corps moved via Front Royal across the Blue Ridge to Little Washington, near Culpeper. It remained in camp at Little Washington nearly a month, during which time the battery was well drilled and perfected for the field.

About this time Jackson was reported to be advancing with a heavy force from Gordonsville towards Culpeper. The separate corps or armies under Generals McDowell, Banks and Sigel were consolidated under the command of General Pope, and designated the Army of Virginia. General McDowell's corps lay at Culpeper; General Banks was ordered near Culpeper, and General Sigel remained at Sperryville. News having arrived that Jackson had crossed the Rapidan, thirty thousand strong, General Banks' corps, six thousand six hundred strong, was ordered to move forward and engage him. The morning of August 9th Banks' corps passed McDowell's and met the enemy strongly posted at Slaughter's (or Cedar) Mountain. The attack was made immediately, and after six hours of most terrific fighting, General Banks was forced to retire, he having received no aid from Generals McDowell or Sigel. The Fourth and Sixth Maine batteries were in Banks' corps and fought their maiden fight on that day. The Sixth was posted on the extreme left flank of the corps and repulsed a most determined attack made by the enemy, who, after repeated charges, was driven in confusion.

The battery was attached to General Augur's division and was under a heavy fire of rebel artillery. The rebels hoped to disable and drive us from the field. After General Augur was wounded he sent word to Captain McGilvery, congratulating him and his battery on their gallant fight, and said the battery was the means of repelling the assaults on the left flank, and saved the division from being destroyed or taken prisoners. The last gun was brought off the field in the face of the enemy's infantry not fifty yards distant.

Next day General Banks' corps occupied Culpeper, and General McDowell's corps watched Jackson. August 20th the retreat to the Rappahannock River began, and from that time until the 29th they marched and counter-marched, fought night and day, the men living on half rations and the horses on what they could pick up.

The Sixth battery was engaged at Rappahannock Station, Sulphur Springs and Blackburn's Ford. At Catlett's Station orders were received detaching the Sixth battery from Banks' corps and ordering it to proceed by forced marches and report to Major-General Hooker, who had just arrived at Manassas with the advance of the army of the Potomac, and had fought and driven Jackson without any artillery. It reported, as ordered, on the morning of August 29th and fought at Second Bull Run all day, with its division, which was relieved about 4 P. M. by General Kearny's division.

At daylight on the 30th the army was re-formed; and as

Jackson had been reinforced during the night by General Long-street, our army awaited the rebel attack. At 2 o'clock P. M. it was made by a heavy column falling upon our left flank; at the same time an attack was made along our whole front. So sudden and overwhelming was this assault of the enemy that our whole line gave way before it, losing whole batteries, almost without firing a shot.

The Sixth Maine was the centre of three batteries. That on the right was captured entire and the one on the left got away. The enemy charged the Sixth on the right and front. It fought them until its support had left and all the horses of two guns had been killed. Captain McGilvery finding it use-less to maintain the unequal contest, and the enemy gaining his rear, gave orders to fall back, which was done, leaving the two disabled guns on the field.

Captain McGilvery made a stand at the brick (hospital) building and repulsed the enemy with great loss, amply paying for the loss of his two guns. The repulse at the hospital enabled us to get off many of the wounded.

The battery was ordered to fall back towards Centreville by General Heintzelman, as the army was in full retreat. It arrived at Centreville Heights the next morning and was ordered into position on the heights covering the Bull Run road. September 1st the army evacuated Centreville and fell back upon the defenses of Washington. At night the enemy made a grand attack upon the right of our army with the expectation of cutting off the column, but after a desperate resistance, wherein we lost two of our best generals, Kearny and Stevens, they withdrew. The Sixth battery was with Kearny's division but was not called into action. Next morning it continued its movement and arrived at Fort Lyon, near Alexandria, the same night. The battery remained at Fort Lyon ten days, refitting, and moved with its division, via Rockville, to Frederick, Md. General McClellan then assumed command of the combined armies of the Potomac and Virginia.

The enemy were reported crossing the Potomac at Shep-herdstown and moving on Frederick City. September 7th the army commenced its movement to encounter the enemy, and on the 14th he was found strongly posted at South Mountain and Crampton's Gap. The attack was ordered and both positions were carried by bayonet charges, the enemy falling back on the main body, which took position on the south side of Antietam Creek. On the 17th our army moved into position and commenced a furious attack on the rebel left and centre, commencing the battle of Antietam. The Fourth and Sixth Maine batteries were posted on an eminence covering the stone bridge over which Hooker's corps had passed in the morning and Franklin's corps later in the day; but neither of these batteries was engaged. On the morning of the 19th the rebel army had entirely disappeared from our front, and our forward movement commenced. Finding General Lee had recrossed into Virginia, General McClellan ordered our army into camp. Two corps encamped around Harper's Ferry, Va., and the remainder in Pleasant Valley, Md., where McClellan's headquarters were. The Sixth battery encamped at Sandy Hook, Md. Upon the reorganization of the army, Banks' old corps was incorporated into the Twelfth army corps, and General Slocum assigned to the command. General Geary commanded the Second division, to which the Sixth battery was attached. During its stay at Sandy Hook it received a number of recruits and a full section of guns, horses, harnesses and material to replace those lost at Manassas.

When the army made its flank movement to Falmouth the Twelfth corps was left at Harper's Ferry to guard the valley. General Burnside had succeeded McClellan in command, and had fought the battle of Fredericksburg.

The Sixth battery was ordered to cross the Potomac and take position on Bolivar Heights, covering the Winchester pike. The division made many reconnaissances up the valley as far as Berryville and Winchester, but developed no enemy. December 10th the Twelfth corps moved to guard the line of communications from Alexandria to Falmouth. The First division moved to Stafford Court House, the Second division halting at Fairfax Station. The First brigade of the Second division, with one section of the Sixth battery, was ordered to proceed to Dumfries and hold that important post. On the morning of

December 27th the enemy suddenly appeared before the town with three thousand cavalry and six pieces of artillery, under Stuart, and demanded the surrender of the post. Colonel Candy of the 66th Ohio, commanding the brigade, refused, and immediately made dispositions for defense. After a severe fight of three hours the enemy were compelled to withdraw. Colonel Candy spoke very highly of the firing of the section of the Sixth which prevented the cavalry from forming for a charge. Hearing the rapid artillery fire, Lieutenant Dow was permitted to take the balance of the battery to Lieutenant Rogers' assistance, and after a severe march through mud axle deep he arrived at Dumfries at dark and joined his comrade. The division shortly after moved to Acquia Creek, which was our base of supplies, leaving the First brigade and the Sixth battery at Dumfries, which immediately made preparations to resist any attack, and built winter quarters.

Lieutenant Smith, who had been absent on recruiting service since the battery was at Cedar Creek, returned to the battery here, but resigned and left for home. Lieutenant Morton resigned while the battery lay at Sandy Hook, and Sergt. Orville W. Merrill, of Portland, was commissioned in his place. Lieutenant Merrill resigned while in camp at Dumfries, and Sergeants William H. Gallison, of Portland, and Edward Wiggin, Jr., of Hodgdon, were commissioned Second Lieutenants. Captain McGilvery had been promoted to Major of Maine mounted artillery during his absence, and the command of the battery devolved upon Lieutenant Dow.

The battery remained at Dumfries until May 27th, when it was ordered to report to the reserve artillery camp at Falmouth, where it was again reduced to a four-gun battery, on account of the diminished number of men. Lieutenants Gallison and Wiggin were mustered out by order of the War Department on account of this reduction. June 13th the army commenced its movement towards the Potomac. On the 15th the battery, which was attached to the Fourth brigade of reserve artillery, arrived at Fairfax Court House and remained till the 24th, when it marched to the Potomac, crossed at Edwards Ferry, and encamped until the 28th, then marched via Frederick and Taney-

town to Gettysburg, arriving there early on July 2d.   In the
memorable contest at Gettysburg the Sixth Maine was kept in
reserve until 6 P. M., July 2d, when the crisis of the battle had
arrived.   Our artillery, posted on the road leading from Little
Round Top to the Peach Orchard and along the Emmitsburg
road northerly, had been charged by the rebel infantry and
forced to give way.   Many pieces were captured, while others
were limbered up and went to the rear in haste and confusion.
Our infantry fell back to the ridge running parallel with the
Taneytown road, connecting Little Round Top with Cemetery
Hill.   The Sixth battery was posted near a road that led from
the rebel position through our lines.   The rebel infantry halted
to re-form, and their batteries took up new positions.   At half
past six or later the final attack was made, and the enemy endeavored to pierce our lines by the road near which the battery was
posted.   For an hour the contest raged with great fury, but the
Sixth held the position.   Major McGilvery, who, after the
wounding of Captain Randolph, commanded all the artillery
along that part of the line, started after another battery, as the
men of the Sixth were hard pressed and their ammunition was
getting short, and just as the enemy was completely repulsed
at all points, he brought up Seeley's battery K, 4th U. S. artillery.   This battery had been engaged during the afternoon,
with the Second division of the Third corps at the Emmitsburg
road, near the Smith house, and Lieutenant Seeley having been
wounded and carried to the rear, left the battery in command of
Lieutenant James, who brought the battery off the field when
the division fell back to the main line.   Battery K suffered
severely, and went into position under Major McGilvery with
only four guns, one section having been sent to the rear for
want of men to handle it.   Lieutenant James during the night,
with the assistance of the Sixth Maine battery and an infantry
detail, succeeded in bringing from the field several guns which
had been abandoned by our troops during the day.

The Sixth battery was highly complimented by Major McGilvery and Generals Tyler and Hunt, respectively chiefs of the
reserve and army artillery, for its gallantry on this occasion.
On July 3d it was placed in McGilvery's line of batteries on

the left centre, supported by the First division, Second corps, and the Third corps. The battery participated in the terrific artillery duel of that morning, and assisted in the repulse of Longstreet's assault on our lines, a little south of Cemetery Hill, which decided the fate of the battle and compelled the rebel army to recross the Potomac.

Marching thence to Hagerstown they were ordered to report to Major-General Howard, commanding the Eleventh corps, in his advance on Williamsport; but without being engaged rejoined the artillery reserve at Berlin. On the 18th they crossed the Potomac into Virginia, and proceeded by easy marches to Warrenton, arriving on the 25th, remaining till August 1st, then marched to Warrenton Junction and camped. They broke camp at the Junction September 16th and marched to Culpeper, where they lay until October 12th, when they commenced their retreat to Centreville Heights, subsequently advancing to Brandy Station. During the retreat the battery was ordered to the First corps, and participated in the skirmishes in which that corps was engaged as rear guard; and in this retreat the battle of Bristoe Station was fought and won by the Second corps. From the 1st of November till the 26th the battery was posted by sections along the railroad, supported by infantry, to guard the communications with Washington. November 26th it moved towards the Rapidan, and crossed two days later, finding the enemy strongly posted at Mine Run. December 1st they recrossed the Rapidan at Ely's Ford, and marched towards Brandy Station, arriving on the 3d. On the 8th it was ordered to the reserve again, and went into winter quarters. Lieutenant Dow was commissioned Captain and mustered in September 1, 1863, having been Lieutenant commanding since December 10, 1862. Large and convenient log houses were built for officers and men and stables for the horses. During the winter the battery was recruited to the maximum standard.

Lieutenant Wiggin had been re-commissioned a First Lieutenant, and Sergeants Samuel Thurston and Marshall N. McKusick were commissioned Second Lieutenants. The recruits were being drilled constantly and the battery made efficient. In

April, 1864, upon the reorganization of the army, the battery was assigned to the Second corps, General Hancock. A very high compliment was given the battery by Colonel Burton, commanding the reserve, upon its high state of discipline and efficiency.

May 3d the battery, under Captain Dow, left camp near Stevensburg at 8 P. M. and marched towards the Rapidan; crossed next morning and bivouacked at night on the Chancellorsville battle ground. On the 5th it broke camp at daylight and took up the line of march towards Spotsylvania Court House. Arriving at Todd's Tavern it was announced that the enemy was advancing rapidly against us. Hancock's corps marched back by the Brock road to connect with another corps. The enemy, assaulting, had pitched the battle in the woods where but little artillery could be used. The Second corps line was formed on the Brock road, extending on either side of the Plank road. The battery was posted on the Brock road with the right section on the Plank road. The 1st N. H. battery was posted on the left of the Sixth Maine. A line of works had been thrown up hastily in our front, and a second line was formed, behind which the battery was posted, out of sight of the enemy. About 4 o'clock the armies met, and most terrific infantry fighting ensued, until darkness interposed.

The battle ground was truly a "wilderness." At 5 A. M., May 6th, the battle again opened fiercely, and our troops had driven the enemy two miles at 10 o'clock, but were in turn forced to retire to their own works. At 4 o'clock P. M. Longstreet made his grand attack upon our left and at the junction of the Brock and Plank roads. He advanced boldly against our hastily constructed line of breastworks, where he was checked. But the dry logs of which the works were built caught fire, and our troops at that point were forced to retire to our second line.

The rebel line now quickly advanced, little dreaming of what was in store for them. On they came with banners flying, confident of victory until within two hundred yards of their goal, when the Sixth Maine and the 1st N. H. batteries opened upon them with double-shotted canister, making great gaps in their lines and causing the greatest consternation. In vain they tried to re-form and advance. General, field and line officers fell beside their men and colors, while the artillery and infantry poured volley after volley into the broken rebel ranks. They could not stand such fire and, amid a storm of shot and shell, they sought their own lines, broken and discomfited. During the action, which lasted half an hour, our breastwork caught fire, but the men stood to their guns till they were blistered, and had to be sent to hospital after the action was over. The battery suffered a loss here of one officer and seven men wounded. "During this attack Dow's battery, Sixth Maine, rendered effective service, one section on the Plank road, the other near Mott's left, in the second line. It was served with great steadiness and gallantry " (a). Night coming on the men lay beside their guns, and next day remained in position repairing damages.

May 8th, at daylight, they resumed the line of march to Todd's Tavern, near which our flankers were furiously attacked. The battery was ordered into position north of the tavern, where it remained until the morning of the 9th, when it relieved the 10th Mass. battery south of the tavern, covering the roads. Two guns were detached for picket duty with Colonel Kitchings' brigade, about four hundred yards out on the road. May 10th it resumed its line of march for Spotsylvania, went into position near the Deserted House, and opened fire, covering the advance of the Fourth division. At night it was ordered to report to General Gibbon, Second division, on the right. It went into position till night of the 11th, when they marched and bivouacked near the Fifth corps hospital. On the morning of the 12th it marched and parked in rear of the Deserted House. At 4 A. M. the grand salient attack was made by the Second corps, in which twenty pieces of artillery, two general officers and a whole division of Confederates were captured. The Sixth battery hauled off six rebel guns. At 11 A. M. it advanced to the Landrum house and opened fire on the salient of the rebel line. Lieutenant Thurston was wounded by a rifle shot. During the night of the 13th the enemy retired, and the battery was ordered forward and posted at the captured works

(a) Virginia Campaign of '64 and '65, page 48, by Gen. A. A. Humphreys.

of the enemy. Leaving this position on the morning of the 15th it parked on the Fredericksburg road.

On the 17th it turned in one section of guns under a general order reducing all six-gun batteries to four guns. Several changes of positions were made and on the 20th marched with Tyler's Heavy Artillery (now infantry) division, via Bowling Green, around the right flank of the Confederate army, crossed the Mattapony River and formed in battery near Poplar Tavern. It was in position till May 23d, when it approached the North Anna River and went into battery, covering Birney's attack on the redoubt and works at Taylor's bridge, which were handsomely carried. On the night of the 24th it crossed North Anna River and relieved Clark's N. J. battery near Doswell's house. At 6 P. M. of the 25th it opened fire on the enemy's breastworks, driving them out, Smyth's brigade charging and capturing the works. At 9 P. M. it withdrew, recrossed the river and went into battery covering the pontoon bridge, and at 11 A. M. on the 27th moved towards the Pamunkey River and crossed, and was in position at different points on the line till night of June 1st, when it moved to Cold Harbor.

On June 3d the Second corps made a charge upon the enemy's works and the battery took an advanced position, one section going with an intrenching detachment, and received a counter-charge by the enemy after our own had failed. The enemy's artillery opened upon the position with a large number of guns, to which the Sixth responded. When their infantry advanced, the Sixth poured into it shell, case and solid shot, which, with the stout resistance made by Smyth's and Owen's brigades, hurled back the rebel line. After this, desultory firing occurred until the 11th, when the battery was withdrawn from the front and next day marched with the corps for Petersburg. On the 16th and 17th of June Dow engaged the enemy and drove him out of position at the Hare house, and on the 18th took up position farther in advance on the front line at the Hare house. Here he had a sharp duel with the enemy's intrenched battery, at short range, to assist in a desperate charge of our troops upon the enemy's intrenchments. In these operations the battery sustained a large loss in killed and wounded. The battery accompanied Mott's (formerly Birney's) division on its first movement north of the James in July, and again in the second movement, August 14th, when one section engaged a Confederate battery ; these engagements were termed Deep Bottom. On its return to Petersburg the battery was placed in Fort Davis on the Jerusalem Plank road, and took its place as one of the siege batteries. It remained in Fort Davis, frequently engaging the enemy, until October 22d, when it was removed to Fort McGilvery (named in honor of its former commander). Fort McGilvery overlooks the city of Petersburg and is situate about six hundred yards from the rebel forts, near the Appomattox River. The battery was engaged almost daily with the rebel batteries opposite, and established a reputation for the accuracy of its practice.

Lieutenant Wiggin resigned on the 1st of May, and Sergt. John G. Deane of Portland was promoted Second Lieutenant (a).

The battery's original term of service expired December 31, 1864, but it re-enlisted for three years. On the 29th of November Captain Dow was discharged for disability and Lieut. William H. Rogers was shortly after promoted to the Captaincy. Sergt. Joseph W. Burke of Lee was commissioned Second Lieutenant, November 28th, and afterwards promoted to First Lieutenant.

Captain McGilvery, after his promotion to field officer, was for some time in command of the First brigade of artillery reserve with the army of the Potomac. He was a daring and successful officer and distinguished himself at the battle of Gettysburg. At the time of his death, September 7, 1864, he had command of a hundred guns. Being wounded in one of his fingers at Deep Bottom, and it being necessary to amputate it, chloroform was administered to him for the purpose. He died during the operation.

The battery was filled and fully equipped, and under its new Captain (Rogers) bade fair to add new laurels to those already attained under his two predecessors. During the winter of 1864–5 it kept one section in comfortable quarters near Meade's

(a) During the closing portion of the battery's service Lieut. Deane served as acting aide-de-camp upon the staff of General Hazard, Chief of Artillery, Second corps.

Station on the line of the railroad. The right section, under Lieut. Samuel Thurston, was stationed in the right front of Fort McGilvery, the left section, under Lieutenant Burke, was allotted to " Battery No. 9," a dug-out redoubt on low ground in near proximity to the Confederate Spring Hill battery, and exposed to incessant picket firing. Both of these positions were under the enemy's guns, many of the latter well posted across the river. Daily artillery practice occurred with astonishingly few casualties. In the preliminary movements for the 1865 spring campaign the battery was withdrawn from its winter position, detached from the Second corps, and placed where need required. In the final assault and capture of the Petersburg works, April 2, 1865, it was in position in Fort Sampson on the Fifth corps line. Upon the evacuation of Petersburg the battery joined the artillery reserve at City Point. May 3d it commenced its homeward march, by way of Richmond, Bowling Green and Stafford, to Alexandria, Va., where it remained until transportation to Maine was furnished. Arriving at Augusta, Me., June 7th, it was mustered out of service June 17, 1865.

There were present at the muster-out 174 men and officers. It bore upon its rolls during its term of service 314 names, 45 of them, who were original members, had served more than three and a half years. While in service 33 were killed or died of wounds or disease. There were sent to the battery while in the field 163 recruits.

The following is a list of the principal battles and engagements of the Sixth battery as announced in general orders by the War Department : *Cedar Mountain, Second Bull Run, Chantilly, Antietam, Gettysburg, Mine Run, Wilderness, Spotsylvania, North Anna, Cold Harbor, Petersburg and Deep Bottom.*

ROSTER.

CAPTAINS.

Freeman McGilvery, Feb. 3, 1862; commissioned Major First Regt. Maine Mounted Art'y, Feb. 5, 1863; Lieut.-Colonel, June 23, 1863; Colonel, Sept. 1, 1863, — not mustered to last two grades. Died Sept. 2, 1864, from effects of wounds in action of Deep Bottom, Va.

Edwin B. Dow, Sept. 1, 1863, promoted from First Lieutenant; dis-

charged Nov. 29, 1864; brevet Major of Vol. Art'y, for gallant and meritorious conduct at battle of Gettysburg.

William H. Rogers, Dec. 7, 1864; mustered out with battery June 17,
1865; originally Second Lieut., pro. to First Lieut. Mar. 2, 1863, and to Capt.

FIRST LIEUTENANTS.

George H. Smith, Jan. 16, 1862; resigned Feb. 17, 1863.

Edward Wiggin, Jr., Mar. 1, 1864, discharged May 3, 1864; originally
Private, promoted to Sergt., promoted to Second Lieut., promoted to First
Lieutenant.

Samuel Thurston, July 12, 1864, mustered out with battery June 17, 1865;
originally Private, promoted to Sergt., promoted to Second Lieut., Mar. 1,
1864, promoted to First Lieutenant.

Joseph W. Burke, Jan. 11, 1865, mustered out with battery June 17, 1865;
originally Private, promoted to Sergt., promoted to Second Lieut., Nov. 28,
1864, promoted to First Lieutenant.

SECOND LIEUTENANTS.

Frederick A. Morton, Feb. 1, 1862; resigned Sept. 24, 1862.

Orville W. Merrill, commissioned Oct. 1, 1862; resigned Jan. 29, 1863;
originally Sergeant.

William H. Gallison, Mar. 2, 1863; resigned June, 1863; originally Sergt.,
promoted to First Sergt., promoted to Second Lieutenant.

Marshall N. McKusick, Mar. 1, 1864; discharged Nov. 17, 1864; originally Corp'l, promoted to Sergt., promoted to Second Lieutenant.

John G. Deane, June 28, 1864, mustered out with battery June 17, 1865;
originally Private, promoted to Sergt., promoted to Second Lieutenant.

Elias D. Libby, Jan. 11, 1865, mustered out with battery June 17, 1865;
promoted from Private.

MONUMENT

OF

COMPANY D, MAINE VOLUNTEERS,

SECOND UNITED STATES SHARPSHOOTERS.

The monument of company D, Second U. S. Sharpshooters, is placed on a cross-road leading easterly out of the Emmitsburg road, towards Big Round Top, and to the Slyder buildings.   Its position is about five hundred yards from the Emmitsburg road, and about seven hundred yards southwesterly from Devil's Den.   It is a polished die of white granite, resting upon a rough, white granite base.

ADMEASUREMENTS: Base, 3 feet 4 inches by 3 feet 4 inches by 1 foot 6 inches; die, 2 feet 6 inches by 2 feet 6 inches by 3 feet 3 inches.   Total height, 4 feet 9 inches.

The inscription is: —

COMPANY D,

MAINE VOLUNTEERS,

2ND U. S. SHARPSHOOTERS.

JULY 2, 1863.

KILLED 1.

WOUNDED 5.

MISSING 5.

COMPANY D, SECOND U. S. SHARPSHOOTERS,

SECOND BRIGADE, FIRST DIVISION, THIRD ARMY CORPS,

AT THE BATTLE OF GETTYSBURG.

COMPANY D, of the Second United States Sharpshooters, of Ward's brigade, was composed of Maine soldiers, volunteers from Rockland and various towns. Captain Jacob McClure, of Rockland, commanded the company at Gettysburg. The two regiments of Sharpshooters in Ward's brigade were the best known regiments in the army. Recruited from picked men from different states, they were enlisted like regulars for the reason that no single state could furnish the material for a regiment of such fine marksmen. No recruit was eligible who could not make ten consecutive shots whose aggregate distance from the centre of the target would "string" less than fifty inches, an average of less than five inches for each shot; the distance being six hundred feet at a rest, or three hundred feet off hand. Many of the men could at that distance put the shots inside the bull's eye. The class of men were on a high grade for physical qualifications and intelligence (a).

On the morning of July 2d, prior to the occupation of Little Round Top by our lines, the regiment was ordered (b) to take position near the northern base of that eminence, on the prolongation eastward of the cross-road which borders the Peach Orchard, to cover the valley of Devil's Den; and in the disposition of the several companies Captain McClure and his company were posted in the valley, or ravine as it seemed to them. This position was held until about 2 p. m., when the regiment was ordered to advance southwesterly towards the Emmitsburg road. It moved through the woods to the south of Devil's Den and the Wheatfield, advancing until it reached another cross-road which leads to the Emmitsburg road. The

(a) Fox's "Regimental Losses in the Civil War."
(b) See official report of Lieut.-Col. H. R. Stoughton, commanding the regiment, *post.*

right of the regiment stopped upon this road, company D being
the right company of the regiment; then the left of the regiment wheeled up to be more nearly parallel with the Emmitsburg road. Company D did not advance far beyond a house
known then as the Slyder house. Getting into a general line
conforming to the natural aspect of the country, the men rested
comfortably for nearly two hours. There were no skirmishers
or pickets or Union troops connecting on either flank of the
Sharpshooters. Ward threw forward skirmishers from the 20th
Ind. and 99th Penn. regiments when he had established his
line of battle; these did not go out so far as company D, but
were ordered to support the Sharpshooters. The result of this
disposition of troops was that, when Robertson advanced, he took
the skirmish lines in broken flanks, and they had to retire to the
general line of battle. Nor could they in any event have done
much to restrain the onward rush of heavy lines of battle.

Hood's division was at this time moving southerly, at the
west of the Emmitsburg road and gradually approaching it, to
get beyond and to strike the Union left; and the Sharpshooters
were sent out to watch that approach to our lines, and if the
enemy approached, to skirmish with him and retard his advance.
After a preliminary engagement of short duration with the
enemy's skirmishers, or his first line of battle in rather open
order, the heavy Confederate battle lines appeared. Hood's
men were advancing towards Little Round Top and the hill of
Devil's Den. This line covered the entire front and flank of the
Sharpshooters; but the latter nevertheless assailed it valiantly.
Their fire was so severe that one Confederate regiment broke
three times before it would advance. When Hood's line was
within one hundred yards, and when their skirmishers were
pressing in on the right flank of the Sharpshooters, the latter
retired, although they still kept up a vigorous fire upon the
Confederates. A portion of the company retiring, as the lines
of the enemy swiftly advanced, found themselves at the south
end of Devil's Den ridge, and made a stand behind the fences
and bowlders of that wild spot, falling in with the skirmishers
of the Fourth Maine, whence they all poured an annoying fire
into the flanks of Hood's line, as his men essayed to carry these
natural defenses. This interruption in the movement caused

the separation of the enemy's attack into two separate parts and places. The larger portion of the Second Sharpshooters fell back before Hood's troops, as they advanced across Plum Run valley, and took every advantage afforded by the nature of the ground to hinder and break the force of the attack, leading a portion of Law's brigade to follow them well up towards the summit of Big Round Top. It was a scattered regiment, but the men were trained for just such emergencies, and every man could fight his own battle.

When Benning made his assault, about 5 : 30 P. M., upon Devil's Den he took our skirmishers in flank and cut off their retreat to the main line, thus capturing many of the Fourth Maine skirmishers and some of company D with them.

On July 3d the regiment was on the line immediately in rear of Stannard's brigade of the First corps ; a squad volunteered to go out, and they silenced some advanced artillery of the enemy ; otherwise it was not engaged. July 4th it was sent out westerly of the Emmitsburg road, in front of the Union centre, as a picket or skirmish line, and came into close contact with the pickets of the enemy, who were posted in a wood. A sharp fire was kept up all day, with quite a loss to the regiment. Company D had men not over twenty paces from the Confederates. It lost First Sergeant Gray, instantly killed, and another man wounded ; the total loss of the company in the three days being eleven out of twenty-seven, including Captain McClure wounded. As the total loss of the regiment was forty-one, it will be seen that company D sustained a large percentage of it.

OFFICIAL REPORT OF MAJ. HOMER R. STOUGHTON.

H'DQRS SECOND REGIMENT U. S. SHARPSHOOTERS, July 27, 1863.

CAPTAIN: I have the honor to report the operations of the Second U. S. Sharpshooters at Gettysburg, Pa., as follows: —

On the morning of July 2d I was placed in line on the extreme left of the Third corps, remaining there for nearly one hour, when the Colonel commanding instructed me to place my command in a position to cover a ravine near Sugar Loaf Hill [Little Round Top], which I did by putting company H on the brow of the hill, with vedettes overlooking the ravine, and company D in the ravine near the woods, to watch the enemy's movements in that direction. Companies A, E, G and C formed a line perpendicular to the cross-road that intersects with the Emmitsburg pike. Companies B and F I held in reserve.

I remained in this position until about 2 P. M., when General Ward directed that I should deploy my regiment across the ravine and through the woods on the right, and advance. I moved forward to a brook [Plum Run] some two hundred yards beyond a second cross-road, running perpendicular to the Emmitsburg pike, and intersecting with it in front of Sugar Loaf Hill. I sent forward scouts to reconnoiter the ground. I then rode out perhaps the distance of half a mile, and discovered the enemy's skirmishers advancing on my right, which, being unsupported by any connection with skirmishers on my right, I was compelled to withdraw to protect my flank. In this position we had but little time to wait. The enemy's skirmishers advanced to the top of the hill in our front, and immediately after they placed a battery directly in our front, and being too far for our range, I sent forward a few men under cover of woods on the left, and silenced one piece nearest us.

The enemy then advanced a line of battle covering our entire front and flank. While they were advancing, the Second regiment did splendid execution, killing and wounding a great many. One regiment broke three times and rallied, before it would advance. I held my position until their line of battle was within one hundred yards of me and their skirmishers were pushing my right flank, when I ordered my men to fall back, firing as they retired. My left wing retreated up the hill and allowed the enemy to pass up the ravine, when they poured a destructive fire into his flank and rear.

Here Adjutant Norton, with about a dozen men, captured and sent to the rear twenty-two prisoners. Special mention should be made of this officer for his coolness and bravery during this day's engagement.

The right wing fell back gradually until they mingled with the regiments composing the Second brigade, and remained till night, when the brigade was relieved.

In this day's action were wounded Captains E. T. Rowell (acting Major), J. McClure and A. Buxton. Our loss was twenty-eight, killed, wounded and missing. Among the missing was Lieut. D. B. Pettijohn, company A.

On the 3d instant the Second regiment was not engaged, with the exception of about a dozen volunteers, who went out to the front of the breastworks of the First army corps to silence one of the enemy's guns, which was accomplished, losing one killed and one wounded.

On the 4th instant I was ordered to move forward to the Emmitsburg pike, a few hundred yards to the left of the cemetery, and to deploy four companies to skirmish through the field to the woods in front. The enemy was driven back to his earthworks, about one hundred and fifty or two hundred yards from his first position. We held this position through the day, under a sharp fire from his sharpshooters.

The regiment sustained a loss this day of three killed and eight wounded. Among the wounded was Lieutenant Law, company E.

At 7:30 P. M. I was relieved by a New Jersey regiment, of the Sixth corps, and rejoined the brigade.

I have the honor to remain, your obedient servant,

HOMER R. STOUGHTON,
Major, Commanding Second U. S. Sharpshooters.
CAPT. JOHN M. COONEY,
A. A. G., Second Brigade, First Division, Third Army Corps.
—Rebellion Records, Series 1, Vol. xxvii., page 518.

PARTICIPANTS.

Captain, Jacob McClure, Rockland.

SERGEANTS.

First Sergeant, Josiah Gray, Prentiss,

Stephen C. Barker, Island Falls,   John E. Wade, Rockland,
Edgar Crockett, Rockland,   James M. Matthews, Rockland.

CORPORALS.

George H. Coffin, Cherryfield,   George U. Leighton, Jonesport,
Argyl D. Morse, Rockland,   John H. Rounds, Portland,
Richard C. Boynton, Jefferson.

PRIVATES.

Allen, John B., Marshfield,   Bradbury, James C., Burlington,
Bragg, Barzillai E., Rockland,   Brown, Henry, Rockland,
Dunbar, Oscar, Cherryfield,   Emerson, Stillman M., Addison,
Jameson, John J., Rockland,   Ladd, Francis W., Vienna,
Lindsay, Edward, Rockland,   McLain, Simon, Lowell,
Morey, Albion, Machias,   Pendleton, James N., Rockland,
Salley, James F., Madison,   Sullivan, John, Addison,
Wentworth, Charles O., Rockland,   Young, William H., Sidney.

ON SPECIAL DUTY OR DETACHED SERVICE: Corporal Luther G. Davis, Cherryfield, pioneer corps at brig. h'dqrs. Privates, Albert Bickford, Carratunk Plantation, amb. corps; John M. Hussey, China, regt'l teamster; Wilson R. Woodward, Bangor, regt'l quarterm'r dept.; William A. McFarland, Cherryfield, Charles S. White, Greenbush, amb. corps; John M. Wilson, Rockland, teamster div. h'dqrs.

REVISED REPORT OF CASUALTIES.

Captain Jacob McClure, wounded, July 2.
First Sergeant Josiah Gray, killed, July 4.
Sergeant John E. Wade, wounded, July 2.

CORPORALS.

Argyl D. Morse, prisoner, July 2.
John H. Rounds, prisoner, July 2.
Richard C. Boynton, prisoner, July 2.

PRIVATES.

Allen, John B., wounded, July 2.
Bradbury, James C., wounded, July 2.
Ladd, Francis W., prisoner, July 2.
Pendleton, James N., wounded, July 4.
Wentworth, Charles O., reported missing; discharged Sept. 25.

The "prisoners" were reported at the time as missing, and so appear upon the monument.

HISTORICAL SKETCH.

COMPILED BY THE EDITORS.

This company was raised in accordance with the request in September, 1861, from the Secretary of War to the Governor of Maine, to have raised a company of Rifle Sharpshooters, selected from the best rifle shots in the state. James D. Fessenden, of Portland, the son of Senator William Pitt Fessenden, was appointed by the Governor to superintend the formation of the company, to consist of three commissioned officers and ninety-seven enlisted men, to be mustered into United States service for three years, or during the war. Fessenden secured the co-operation of Lieuts. Jacob McClure at Rockland, Silas C. Barker at Augusta, and R. R. Park of the Veazie Rifles at Bangor, to supervise the work.

The required number of marksmen having volunteered from different sections of the state, the equipment and organization of the company was completed at Augusta, Me., November 8, 1861. The original organization of the company was as follows :

Captain, James D. Fessenden, Portland.
First Lieutenant, Jacob McClure, Rockland.
Second Lieutenant, Silas C. Barker, Augusta.

SERGEANTS.

First Sergeant, Lorenzo Hall, Rockland,
Albion Morey, Machias,   Stephen C. Barker, Island Falls,
Asa Conary, Bluehill,   George E. Nash, Cherryfield.

CORPORALS.

James A. Stevens, Steuben,   Edwin P. Morse, Rockland,
William A. McFarland, Cherryfield,   Maxcey Hamlin, Winslow,
Bingham S. Edgeley, Greenbush,   Wilson R. Woodward, Bangor,
Josiah Gray, Prentiss.
MUSICIAN: Warren Ladd, Vienna.

The company left the state November 13, 1861, with the Eleventh regiment, and on arrival at Washington was attached to the Second regiment of Berdan's U. S. Sharpshooters as company D. It was known that an organization of such marksmen was being formed, under the influence of Hiram Berdan, a distinguished expert rifleman, drawn from various states, to which the Maine company should be attached, and to be armed with superior rifles. At first several sorts of arms were in use, in some cases those owned by the soldier; some were furnished with globe sights at great cost. In the course of time, however, the breech-loading Sharp's rifle was proved to be the best adapted and most effective, and was uniformly furnished by the government. The company was stationed at or near Washington, in Camp of Instruction, until March 19th, when the regiment broke camp and joined General Augur's brigade of King's division, then attached to General McDowell's corps. On Wednesday, May 31st, while being transported by railroad from Catlett's Station to Rectortown, a collision of the cars killed one and wounded twenty-two, materially reducing the strength of the company already diminished by sickness and discharge.

We copy from the active-service report of company D, Second U. S. Sharpshooters, since leaving Camp of Instruction at Washington, D. C., March 19, 1862, and ending December 31, 1863, made by Captain Jacob McClure:—

"Left Camp of Instruction March 19, 1862, for camp Williams, near Alexandria, Va., sixteen miles from former camp; arrived there March 20th, and there joined the brigade of General Augur, in King's division. Left camp Williams April 5th and arrived at Bristoe Station evening of April 6th, where we camped until April 15th, on which day we marched towards Falmouth, Va., via Warrenton Junction, arriving at latter place same night. Left there morning of April 17th for Falmouth, marching a distance of thirty miles within fifteen hours, and, with little opposition from rebel cavalry and infantry, we entered Falmouth. After entering the town, as the enemy had fired the bridges connecting it with Fredericksburg, our company was detailed to extinguish the flames within range of rebel sharpshooters on the opposite side of the river. We soon dispersed them by a few well-directed shots and partially saved the bridge. Encamped at Falmouth until May 25th, at which

time we left, camping for the night about eight miles south
of Fredericksburg, near Fairview. Counter-marching on the
morning of the 29th, we started to the relief of General Banks,
in the Valley. We arrived at Catlett's Station May 31st, and
there took cars for Front Royal, Va., via Manassas Junction.
When near White Plains, about 3 o'clock on the morning of
June 1st, the train in our rear by some mismanagement came
into collision with ours, nearly demolishing several cars, killing
one man and wounding twenty-two others, some severely, all
of our company. We left the scene of our disaster same
evening and arrived at Rectortown. Remaining there in the
cars until the evening of June 2d, we went back by rail to
Haymarket, Va., near Thoroughfare Gap. There we remained
in camp until June 6th, when we left for Warrenton, arriving
the same night, and remained there until June 8th; from there
we marched to Elk Run, Va. We remained there until June
14th, when we left for Falmouth, arriving there June 15th, and
there remained in camp until August 5th; this day we left on
reconnaissance, proceeding some thirty miles into the enemy's
country south of Fredericksburg. We returned August 8th,
having accomplished our object, destroying an important bridge
on the Bowling Green road and taking an immense quantity of
forage, horses, mules and cattle.

" We left Falmouth August 10th, arriving at Culpeper
evening of August 11th, making a distance of forty-six miles
in about thirty-one hours. Remained at Culpeper in camp until
August 16th, then marched toward the Rapidan, encamping near
Cedar Mountain until August 19th. A retreat was then ordered,
and we marched to Rappahannock Station, arriving there in the
morning of the 20th. Our regiment acted as rear guard, and
had hardly crossed the river when the rebel cavalry made their
appearance. We had lost but one man up to this time (private
A. W. Hutchins), who was unwell and was overtaken by the
advance guard of the rebels; he was afterwards exchanged,
but died at Fort Delaware. The enemy made several desperate
attempts to cross. We were in line of battle and under a terrific fire of shell and canister for three days, with occasional

firing during the nights. The company, commanded by Captain McClure, was detailed to go to the river and ascertain where the enemy were crossing to our side. While performing this important duty, and just as we discovered them, a company of rebel cavalry, sixty strong, charged on us; our little company of twenty-eight men, deployed as skirmishers, repulsed and scattered them in every direction, killing two, wounding several, and taking their Captain and two privates prisoners. None of our men were injured. While here we were supporting batteries at times, and in this duty our regiment lost six killed and several wounded.

" On the 23d of August our regiment was on picket and under a severe artillery fire, which lasted about two hours; several of the regiment were wounded, and one man in our company, private Washington Tucker, received a wound which resulted in his death shortly afterwards. On the 23d we started for Warrenton, where we remained until August 26th, when the regiment was detached to General Patrick's brigade, and marched to White Sulphur Springs. There we were deployed as skirmishers, and were ordered to drive the enemy's skirmishers to the other side. Brisk skirmishing ensued, which lasted some six hours and resulted in our driving the enemy across the river. This was the fairest test we have ever had between rebel sharpshooters and ours. The loss of the regiment was three killed. The rebels lost thirty.

" We marched August 27th in the direction of Manassas Junction. When near Groveton, next day, we discovered the enemy in force. During the night we were compelled to fall back to Manassas; remained there until the 29th, when we were ordered forward to the same ground we had before occupied, our company supporting two pieces of artillery stationed near the Seabury road. About dark the rebels attacked us in overwhelming force, and we were driven back. In this action Lieutenant Barker was taken prisoner. Private James F. Sally was wounded, and private John Jordan killed. We had but twelve enlisted men in this battle. The rest of the company were completely exhausted by the severe marching, counter-marching and fighting of the past ten days, with short rations.

" We lay by the roadside until about noon of August 30th, when another advance on the enemy was ordered. We were on the right and deployed as skirmishers ; the fighting became so fierce that we lost sight of the right wing of our regiment, and our company, with the remainder of the left wing, joined one of the Penn. Reserve regiments, where we fought in closed ranks during the remainder of the day. We fell back to Centreville on the night of August 30th, broken and disordered, where we remained until September 1st, when we moved to Fairfax and encamped for the night, and on the 2d fell back to Falls Church, where we encamped until September 7th ; we marched into Maryland September 9th, eight miles from Washington, D. C., on the Harper's Ferry road. From there we marched, by way of Brookville and Lisbon, to Frederick, Md., where we arrived September 12th. September 14th we marched to South Mountain, and came upon the enemy in force. We engaged them about 3 P. M., our regiment being deployed as skirmishers and leading the attack. Night found the enemy completely routed after a brisk fight. On the morning of the 15th we pursued them, encamping about two miles from Keedysville and the enemy's line. September 16th our regiment was deployed and sent forward to feel the enemy's line. Slight skirmishing ensued, in which one man in our company, private Wellington (Arthur W.) Tucker was wounded, and died the same night. After our object was accomplished we fell back a short distance, and lay on our arms all night. At Antietam, on the morning of the 17th, we advanced in close column line of battle, the regiment, with its brigade (First brigade, First division, Hooker's corps), forming the extreme right of Doubleday's division. We fought continually for four hours, during which time our regiment lost three officers and ten men killed, three officers and forty-eight men wounded, and two missing. The loss of the company was six.

" September 19th went into camp near Sharpsburg, Md. October 20th marched to Bakersville, where we remained until the 26th, when we marched to Berlin. On the 30th crossed the Potomac and encamped near Lovettsville, Va. November

1st marched to Purcellville, remaining there until the 3d, when we resumed the march and arrived at Warrenton on the 6th. November 11th marched for Brooke's Station, between Falmouth and Acquia Creek, where we remained in camp until December 10th, when we marched towards Fredericksburg, and crossed the river three miles below. On the night of December 12th camped under the enemy's guns, and on morning of December 13th we were ordered forward, deployed as skirmishers on the extreme left of Franklin's corps, our left resting on the river bank. During the day we advanced about a mile and a half, driving the enemy from their fortifications, capturing several men and one commissioned officer. Stood picket through night of 13th; the 14th we lay in line of battle all day; at night on picket; 15th on picket all day, skirmishing quite lively; recrossed the river night of December 15th. Our loss in battle was nothing. One man, a straggler (private Edwin Thompson, of our company), was left behind and was captured by the enemy. From this date until April 28, 1863, were in winter quarters, doing the usual camp duty." [The First and Second regiments of U. S. Sharpshooters now constituted the Third brigade, under Col. Hiram Berdan, of the Third division of Third corps.]

"Tuesday, April 28th, left camp near Stoneman's Station and marched with the corps towards Fredericksburg, and camped three miles below. Remained there in reserve for the First army corps until the 30th; marched and crossed the Rappahannock at U. S. Ford May 1st. May 2d advanced two miles south of the Gordonsville road, in the direction of Spotsylvania Court House, where we encountered the enemy, and after sharp fighting captured a number of prisoners, actually larger than our own force engaged. Owing to the disaster to the Eleventh corps, the regiment was compelled to fall back to within one-half mile of the Gordonsville road, where we were entirely cut off and surrounded by the enemy. After sharp fighting in the night, we opened communication with General Hooker, and fell back on the morning of the 3d to Chancellorsville. May 3d and 4th we were constantly engaged with the enemy's sharpshooters. On the morning of the 5th retreated with the army across the river and went into our old camp (a). June 1st were still in camp at Stoneman's Station. July 1st, after severe marching, were at Taneytown, Md.

"We were constantly engaged three days in the battle at and near Gettysburg, July 2d, 3d, and 4th, in which eleven were lost in killed, wounded, missing and prisoners from the company. August 1st were at Warrenton, Va.; September 1st were at White Sulphur Springs; October 1st, at Culpeper; December 1st, at Brandy Station, Va., where we remain, December 31st. The company has re-enlisted for the war."

After re-enlisting, the veterans received a furlough for a few weeks, and many homes in Maine were made happy by the presence of these heroes, whose lives were newly pledged to the Union. The ranks of the company had doubled in length with recruits when it again took the field, before the campaign opened. Captain McClure and Lieutenant Cummings having been discharged for disability, First Sergeant Stephen C. Barker was promoted to Captain, and Sergeant Crockett to First Lieutenant.

In the consolidation of the army under Grant, in the spring of 1864, the Second Sharpshooters remained in Ward's brigade, now belonging to Third division of the Second corps; the Third Maine was in this brigade, and both took part in the same engagements in the campaign of 1864 until the 4th of June; and after that, the Seventeenth Maine having been transferred to the First brigade on June 1st, the fighting and marching of company D of the Sharpshooters can be traced in the history of the Seventeenth until the end of the war; although the duties of the Sharpshooters differed somewhat from the other infantry, being to a greater degree as skirmishers. The record of company D attests that in the battles and engagements in 1864 at the Wilderness, Po River, Spotsylvania, Fredericks-

(a) After the battle of Chancellorsville, in which General Berry and General Whipple, commanding respectively the Second and Third divisions of the Third corps, were both killed, the Third division was broken up and its parts united to the First and Second divisions of the corps. The First and Second regiments of Sharpshooters were united to Ward's (First) brigade of the First division.

burg Pike, North Anna, Totopotomy, Cold Harbor, Petersburg, Jerusalem Road, Deep Bottom, Peeble's Farm, Boydton Road, Hatcher's Run and other minor actions during the siege of Petersburg, its men never faltered. These engagements, added to its list of previous years, which included Rappahannock Station, Sulphur Springs, Gainesville, Second Bull Run, South Mountain, Antietam, Fredericksburg, The Cedars, Chancellorsville, Gettysburg, Wapping Heights, Auburn, Kelly's Ford, Locust Grove and Mine Run, make the sequence through the three years complete.

During the months of May and June, 1864, the regiment lost two hundred and twenty-three, of whom one hundred and eighty were in killed and wounded; in the same time company D had seven killed, eleven wounded, including Captain Barker, and eight missing.

The great losses and hardships of the campaign reduced the ranks fearfully, and yet the men were of such good metal that when in winter quarters in January, 1865, after the consolidation of the First, which had only about sixty men whose terms of service had not expired, into the Second regiment, there were over two hundred present for duty. Captain Barker was discharged, and Lieutenant Crockett was promoted to Captain, and Sergeant James M. Matthews had been commissioned Second Lieutenant, and later First Lieutenant, and was acting as Adjutant of the regiment. On February 5th company D took part in the engagement of Hatcher's Run, which was its last, as an organization.

About this time the terms of many of the men who had not re-enlisted in most of the companies expired; and under the provisions of an order from the War department, A. G. O., Special orders No. 47, of January 30, 1865, both the First and Second U. S. Sharpshooters, as organizations, were broken up. The officers and men whose terms held beyond a certain date were ordered in bodies to be assigned to regiments of the various states from which the companies came. Under this, on the 18th of February, 1865, the officers and enlisted men of company D were ordered to be transferred to the Seventeenth Maine regiment. There was no vacancy in the latter regiment for either Captain Crockett or Lieutenant Matthews and, thus becoming supernumerary, they were discharged the service, the latter on February 23, 1865. The men who joined the Seventeenth were distributed and faithfully served to the end of the war. When the Seventeenth was mustered out June 4, 1865, the men of company D were again transferred, this time to the First Maine Heavy Artillery regiment, and with it were mustered out of service September 11, 1865.

During its term of service company D had on its rolls 156 men and officers. Of these 16 were killed in action or died of wounds; 16 died of disease; 5 were missing in action; 8 deserted; 3 were transferred to the Veteran Reserve corps and 2 to the navy; 46 were discharged for disability and 11 at expiration of term of service; 22 had re-enlisted, of whom 4 had been killed or died of their wounds, and the remainder of them and of the recruits, numbering in all 49, present and absent, were transferred to the Seventeenth Maine regiment as above stated.

When the Sharpshooters were about to be disbanded, General de Trobriand, commanding the division, issued an order, dated February 16, 1865, — General orders No. 12, — in which he says he " will not take leave of them without acknowledging their good and efficient service during about three years in the field. The U. S. Sharpshooters leave behind them a glorious record in the army of the Potomac, since the first operations against Yorktown, in 1862, up to the last movements of the army on Hatcher's Run. And few are the battles or engagements where they did not make their mark."

ROSTER.

CAPTAINS.

James D. Fessenden, Nov. 2, 1861; detached to staff of General Hunter March 27, 1862; promoted July 16, 1862, to Colonel and Add'l Aide-de-Camp of Vols., and assigned to staff of Major-General Hunter; Sept. 25, 1863, assigned to staff of Major-General Hooker in the Chattanooga and Atlanta campaigns; promoted to Brigadier-General of Vols. Aug. 8, 1864; rode with Sheridan from Winchester to Cedar Creek Oct. 19, 1864, and assigned to command of Third brigade, First division, Nineteenth corps, Nov. 1, 1864; commanded his brigade and the post at Winchester during the winter; brevet Major-General of Vols. Mar. 13, 1865; served in command of Military Districts; mustered out of service Jan. 15, 1866.

Jacob McClure, Oct. 17, 1862; discharged Apr. 12, 1864; commissioned Major, First Maine regiment of Sharpshooters, Sept. 16, 1863, and Lieut-Col. Feb. 2, 1864, but was not mustered on either of these promotions.

Stephen C. Barker, Apr. 27, 1864; promoted from First Sergeant; discharged for disability on account of wounds Nov. 30, 1864.

Edgar Crockett, Dec. 15, 1864; originally Private, promoted to Corporal and Sergeant, to First Lieutenant May 1, 1864, and to Captain; discharged 1865, rendered supernumerary by consolidation.

First Lieutenants.

Silas C. Barker, Oct. 17, 1862; promoted from Second Lieutenant; resigned May 28, 1863.

Daniel L. Cummings, Sept. 1, 1863; originally Corporal, promoted to Sergeant and First Sergeant, to Second Lieutenant Oct. 17, 1862, and to First Lieutenant; discharged for disability Mar., 1864.

James M. Matthews, commissioned Dec. 15, 1864; originally Private, promoted to Sergeant and First Sergeant, to Second Lieutenant, mustered Dec. 5, 1864, and to First Lieutenant; appointed acting Adjutant of regiment Dec. 23, 1864; rendered supernumerary by transfer of company D to Seventeenth Maine regiment Feb. 18, and discharged Feb. 23, 1865.

MONUMENT

OF

FIFTH MAINE REGIMENT.

The monument stands north of Little Round Top, on the north side of the road leading from the Taneytown road to the Emmitsburg road and intersecting the latter at the Peach Orchard. The monument has an elaborate design, showing upon its face the Coat of Arms of Maine, the Greek cross of the Sixth corps, and a group of war trophies.

ADMEASUREMENTS: Base, six feet by four feet by one foot ten inches; plinth, four feet six inches by two feet six inches by one foot five inches; tablet, four feet by two feet by eight feet. Total height, eleven feet three inches.

The following are the inscriptions:—

5TH

MAINE INFANTRY

2ND BRIG. 1ST DIV. 6TH CORPS

OCCUPIED THIS POSITION FROM

EVENING OF JULY 2ND UNTIL

CLOSE OF BATTLE.

MUSTERED INTO U. S. SERVICE, PORTLAND, ME.
JUNE 24, 1861. SERVED WITH THE ARMY OF THE
POTOMAC IN THE FIELD FROM 1ST BULL RUN TO
PETERSBURG. MUSTERED OUT, PORTLAND, JUNE 27, 1864.

5TH

MAINE INFANTRY

2ND BRIG. 1ST DIV. 6TH CORPS

OCCUPIED THIS POSITION FROM
EVENING OF JULY 2ND UNTIL
CLOSE OF BATTLE.

MUSTERED INTO THE U. S. SERVICE PORTLAND, ME.
JUNE 24, 1861 SERVED WITH THE ARMY OF THE
POTOMAC IN THE FIELD FROM 1ST BULL RUN TO
PETERSBURG. MUSTERED OUT, PORTLAND, JUNE 27, 1864.

FIFTH MAINE REGIMENT,

SECOND BRIGADE, FIRST DIVISION, SIXTH ARMY CORPS,

AT THE BATTLE OF GETTYSBURG.

MAINE'S record at Gettysburg is not complete without the records of several other regiments that underwent the labors of the campaign and were present on the field, although by the fortunes of the day they were spared hard fighting and heavy losses. In General Sedgwick's Sixth army corps, which was thirty-five miles away at Manchester, Md., when the battle began on the morning of July 1st, were three of Maine's famous veteran regiments, the Fifth, Sixth and Seventh. The Fifth Maine was attached to Bartlett's brigade of Wright's division. It had been one of the first regiments to respond to President Lincoln's call for volunteers in 1861, and had been in nearly all the famous battles of the army of the Potomac. Colonel Clark S. Edwards, one of the bravest officers in the service from the state, commanded the regiment, which numbered at Gettysburg about two hundred and seventy-five officers and men.

The regiment was in camp near Manchester during the day of July 1st, getting the rest much needed after the long march through Maryland. Just before dark on the evening of July 1st orders were received to move to Taneytown, and the corps was immediately put in motion. The Fifth Maine, moving in the van of the corps, started about 9 : 30 P. M. (a).

News of the battle of Gettysburg had already reached the corps, and the soldiers of the Fifth Maine sprang forward with alacrity when the order came to move in that direction. As the column crossed the broad pike which leads from Baltimore to Gettysburg, and which intersects the road from Manchester to Taneytown, orders were received to change the destination

(a) Statement of Colonel Edwards in his address at Gettysburg, October 3, 1889.

of the corps and move by rapid marches to Gettysburg. All night the column tramped up the Baltimore pike and all the forenoon of July 2d. The soldiers of the Fifth were allowed to make no halt for breakfast, but pressed on hour after hour under the increasing heat pouring from a July sun. At noon the regiment was within twelve miles of Gettysburg, but the orders were so urgent that no time was allowed for dinner. They continued to press on until, between four and five o'clock P. M., Rock Creek near Gettysburg was reached. Canteens were filled and preparations made for refreshment; but before coffee could be made the wayworn troops, who had eaten nothing except on the move since the night before, were hurried forward to support the Third corps. The Third division of the Sixth corps and Bartlett's brigade of the First division were formed in lines of battle in that portion of the left centre of the Union position which was menaced by the Confederates who had broken through Sickles' line. The Fifth Maine, being in Bartlett's brigade, participated in this movement, and the monument to the regiment stands in the position which it held in this line. The Confederate attack was so far exhausted that the Fifth did no fighting, although about 7 : 15 P. M., when the troops of Ayres of the Fifth corps were coming out, it moved thirty or forty rods to the front down into the Plum Run lowlands (a).

Later in the evening the regiment formed its line on the right of Little Round Top, throwing up a wall of stones which remains at the present time. The regiment held this position during July 3d, until after Pickett's charge. In the evening three companies made a reconnaissance out towards the Emmitsburg road. Colonel Edwards accompanied the detachment. He had noticed from the side of Little Round Top some horses near the Trostle buildings and some portions of a battery, and had determined to secure the same if possible. Taking two or three trusty men (b) with him, all armed with rifles, they crept out through the fringe of wood and approached near enough to shoot

(a) In this movement the regiment secured two or three Confederates in a house to the right of the cross-road which leads to the Peach Orchard.

(b) One of these men was Charles Marshall Wentworth, of company I — after the war, General Wentworth,—of Jackson, N. H.

the horses, so as to prevent their use by the enemy in running off a gun and two limbers which were near by. Finding by further investigation that the Confederates had retreated from that spot, Colonel Edwards ordered a detail from his regiment to run the gun and limbers back to our lines. The gun and other property proved to belong to Bigelow's 9th Mass. battery, left on the field the day before.

July 4th the regiment advanced with two other regiments, one of the latter belonging to Ayres' division of the Fifth corps, to look for wounded lying on the field, also to advance and locate the enemy's line. On the 5th it moved with the corps in pursuit of Lee. No casualties were reported in the regiment while on the field of Gettysburg. There were several men slightly wounded, on the reconnaissance, in the morning of July 4th, whose names we cannot fix; the files in the Adjutant-General's office at Augusta show that Private Franklin Bean of company I was killed July 2d, although this death occurred, a few days later, at Funkstown, Md.

PARTICIPANTS.

FIELD, STAFF AND NON-COMMISSIONED STAFF.

Colonel, Clark S. Edwards, Bethel.
Lieutenant-Colonel, Henry R. Millett, Palmyra.
Major, Aaron S. Daggett, Greene.
Acting Adjutant, Second Lieut. George A. Chandler, Lewiston, company A.
Quartermaster, William B. Fenderson, Biddeford.
Surgeon, Francis G. Warren, Biddeford.
Assistant Surgeon, Melville H. Manson, Limington.
Chaplain, John R. Adams, Gorham.

Quartermaster-Sergeant, Lucius M. Clark, Biddeford.
Commissary-Sergeant, James L. Dresser, Portland.
Hospital Steward, Orrin Q. Pratt, Hebron.

COMPANY A.

(Present for duty, including 1 present sick.)

Captain, Samuel H. Pillsbury, Biddeford.
First Lieutenant, Charles B. Dexter, Biddeford.
Second Lieutenant, George A. Chandler, acting as Adjt. (see Field and Staff).

SERGEANTS.

Charles H. Patrick, Gorham,　　　John L. Haskell, Gorham,
Richmond Edwards, Gorham.

CORPORALS.

Charles M. Ward, Gorham,   Charles M. Edwards, Gorham,
Morris Bumpus, Hebron,   David S. Crockett, Westbrook,
Theodore Shackford, Gorham.

PRIVATES.

Auld, James R., Boothbay,   Bangs, Leeman J., Farmington,
Brady, Patrick, St. John, N. B.,   Brooks, Abram S., Rome,
Cilley, Oliver, Gorham,   Darling, George L., Gorham,
Duffey, Peter, Gorham,   Elder, Alonzo S., Gorham,
Farwell, Walter H., Gorham,   Foss, Alonzo E., Limington,
Gilbert, Albert, Gorham,   Hall, Levi, Gorham,
Henley, Francis E., Westbrook,   Johnson, Charles W., Portland,
Lowell, Alfred O., Portland,   Nunan, William H., Kennebunkport,
Stackpole, Augustus J., Gorham,   Staples, Moses M., Baldwin.

MUSICIANS.

William H. Boyd, Gorham,   Alvin V. Tufts, Cornish.

ON SPECIAL DUTY OR DETACHED SERVICE: Sergeant William C. Phinney, Westbrook, brig. blacksmith. Wagoner Charles H. Stewart, Standish, teamster. Privates: James F. Harmon, Gorham, brig. com. dept.; Cyrus S. Libby, Gorham, teamster; Edward B. Phinney, Gorham, amb. train; Chauncy C. Shaw, Gorham, hosp. attendant; James G. Spaulding, Buckfield, brig. mail carrier.

COMPANY B.

(Including 2 present sick.)

Second Lieutenant, John S. French, Albion.

SERGEANTS.

First Sergeant, Walter Foss, Biddeford,
Samuel B. Brackett, Biddeford,   John Linscott, Biddeford.

CORPORALS.

Billings Hodgdon, Biddeford,   Junius W. Littlefield, Dexter,
Timothy Elliot, Biddeford.

PRIVATES.

Adams, Jesse W., Kennebunkport,   Bacon, George W., Biddeford,
Berry, Robert, Biddeford,   Brackett, Peter, Biddeford,
Chadbourne, Horace K., Biddeford,   Dearborn, Henry A., Biddeford,
Dickinson, Sewell, Augusta,   Elliot, Joseph, Biddeford,
Friend, Dennis W., Biddeford,   Hadlock, Benjamin P., Saco,
Hanson, Moses W., Biddeford,   Harper, John, Dexter,
Heney, Thomas, Biddeford,   Jeffrey, Jesse, Kennebunkport,
Knox, Thomas T., Biddeford,   Larrabee, Charles F., Biddeford,
Libby, Charles O., Biddeford,   Moore, Elliot, Buxton,
Moran, John E., Biddeford,   Nesbitt, John F., Biddeford,
Willey, Jacob O., Biddeford.

ON SPECIAL DUTY OR DETACHED SERVICE: Capt. Robert M. Stevens, Biddeford, ordnance officer div. h'dqrs. Privates: Cyrus P. Berry, Biddeford, clerk div. h'dqrs; Thomas W. Applebee, Acton, regt'l q'rm'r dept.; Charles H. Brown, Biddeford, cook corps. h'dqrs; Aaron H. Bean, Biddeford, Sumner L. Goodwin, Biddeford, and Horace P. Smith, Biddeford, amb. train; Jeremiah Kelley, Kennebunkport, hosp. att'd't; Samuel E. Scribner, Biddeford, teamster.

COMPANY C.
(Including 1 present sick.)

Captain, Edward M. Robinson, Anson.
Second Lieutenant, J. Augustine Grenier, Portland.

SERGEANTS.

David L. Farnham, Boothbay,   Benjamin F. Leavitt, Saco,
Martin Hughes, Portland,   Leonard Welch, Saco.

CORPORALS.

Charles H. P. Stevens, Saco,   John E. Wayland, Saco,
William H. Huntoon, Bangor.

PRIVATES.

Andrews, George H., Saco,   Atkinson, William H., Saco,
Avery, Dexter, Saco,   Baker, Albert B., Biddeford,
Bell, Joseph, Saco,   Brown, William, Greenville, Ct.,
Cadarett, Euzeb, Saco,   Chorters, James, Ireland,
Emery, Ira, Limerick,   Kimball, Luther G., Saco,
King, Milton J., Stafford, Vt.,   McCarthy, Andrew, Saco,
Morgan, George E., Wolfboro, N. H., Ricker, Frank, Saco,
Senate, James, Biddeford,   Small, George E. B., Saco,
Swift, John M., Bethel,   Tyne, Michael, Saco,
Wentworth, Samuel, Saco,   Whaland, Clark, St. John, N. B.
Whitten, Benjamin F., Buxton,   Wilbur, Joseph, Saco,
Willard, John H., Great Falls, N. H., Wormell, Sylvester S., Saco.

MUSICIAN: James B. Deas, Saco.

ON SPECIAL DUTY OR DETACHED SERVICE: First Lieut. Charles A. Waterhouse, Portland, amb. train; Wagoner Eli Dennett, Saco, teamster. Privates: Joseph C. Dennett, Saco, amb. train; Solomon Gordon, Augusta, teamster.

COMPANY D.
(Including 1 present sick.)

Captain, Charles H. Small, Topsham.
First Lieutenant, John H. Stevens, Acton.
Second Lieutenant, Frank G. Patterson, Augusta.

SERGEANTS.

First Sergt., Alonzo Haley, Topsham, Lorenzo D. Fox, Rockport, Mass.,
George M. Littlefield, Greenwood,   James T. Croswell, Brunswick.

CORPORALS.

Henry W. Farrow, Woodstock,   Emery P. Blondel, Topsham,
Ai C. Harrington, Topsham,   Thomas F. Parsons, Rockport.

PRIVATES.

Alexander, Randall T., Topsham,   Barron, James T., Topsham,
Beard, Charles, Moscow,   Carey, Seth F., Topsham,
Colby, George L., Topsham,   Colby, John P., Brunswick,
Doughty, Isaac G., Brunswick,   Dunning, Orlando, Brunswick,
Eastman, Orlando H., Mexico,   Fabian, Anthony, Biddeford,
Few, Robert, Brunswick,   Fox, David M., Porter,
Fuller, Alonzo M., Brunswick,   Hamlin, William, Bowdoinham,
Hassett, Lawrence, Lewiston,   Howland, James E., Topsham,
Johnson, Samuel L., Brunswick,   Lasson, Oscar O., Portland,

Leary, Daniel, Boston, Mass.,
Perkins, Stephen A., Rockport,
Thompson, Collins B., Topsham,
Walker, William A., Durham,
Whitney, Dunham, Brunswick,
Lubec, William, Brunswick,
Smith, Sewall C., Rumford,
Vickery, Albert, Brunswick,
Welch, Morris, Biddeford,
Willis, John, Biddeford.

MUSICIAN: George L. Harmon, Brunswick.

ON SPECIAL DUTY OR DETACHED SERVICE: Sergeant William C. Moody, Brunswick, amb. train. Privates: Charles Manning, Lewiston, div. q'rm'r dept.; Charles B. Vickery, Brunswick, and Jere Warren, Biddeford, hosp. attendants.

COMPANY E.

Captain, Frank L. Lemont, Lewiston.
First Lieutenant, Joseph Wight, Gorham.
Second Lieutenant, John C. Summersides, Gorham.

SERGEANTS.

Cyrenus P. Stevens, Greene,
John B. Bailey, Auburn,
Norris Litchfield, Lewiston,
Francis Day, Durham.

CORPORALS.

John Casey, Rumford,
Daniel Sheehan, Lewiston,
Isaac A. Blethen, Durham,
William H. Morse, Minot.

PRIVATES.

Adley, Alonzo, Lisbon,
Carpenter, Harrison, Concord, N. H.,
Goodwin, Increase F., Clinton,
Hamilton, George H., Lewiston,
Jones, Charles E., Turner,
Larrabee, William H., Lewiston,
Morton, William E., Poland,
Robinson, W. Scott, Sumner,
Verrill, John L., Poland,
Yeaton, Isaac C., Farmington.
Atwood, Rodney B., Lisbon,
Getchell, Albion, Farmington,
Goss, Frank F., Danville,
Haskell, Nathaniel, Lewiston,
Jones, David H., Auburn,
Merrill, Davis N., New Gloucester,
Purrington, Isaiah G., Lisbon,
Taylor, Samuel W., Wales,
Ward, Thomas, Lewiston,

MUSICIANS.

Edward P. Harmon, New Gloucester, Clifton Jones, Canton.

ON SPECIAL DUTY OR DETACHED SERVICE: Wagoner Ephraim H. Litchfield, Lewiston, teamster corps h'dqrs. Privates: Henry P. Estes, Lewiston, and Lemont Manning, Lewiston, div. q'rm'r dept.; Horace E. Kimball, Lewiston, Luther Litchfield, Lewiston, and Lucius L. Lothrop Lewiston, teamsters; David Small, Danville, amb. train.

COMPANY F.

Captain, Frederick G. Sanborn, Hopkinton, N. H.
Second Lieutenant, Orrin B. Stevens, Westbrook.

SERGEANTS.

1st Sergt., John Goldthwait, Windsor,
Llewellyn Goodwin, Stockton,
Benjamin Norton, Portland,
Michael J. Murphy, Portland.

CORPORALS.

Benjamin A. Norton, Portland,
Abner H. Herrick, Greenwood,
Daniel Y. Gallison, Paris, color-guard,
William Hayes, Portland.

PRIVATES.

Bradin, John, Portland,
Driscoll, Daniel, Portland,
Cushman, Cornelius, Portland,
Fitzsimmons, James, Portland,

Godfrey, John, Portland,
Hicks, Barnard, Burke, Vt.,
Kelley, Peter, Portland,
Kerrigan, John, Portland,
McCullom, George, Portland,
McEnnany, Michael, Portland,
Morris, Otto, Portland,
Patrick, George W., Portland,
Ricker, Hiram H., Gardiner,

Gormley, Michael, Portland,
Kelley, John, Portland,
Kelley, Robert, Portland,
Loney, John, Lewiston,
McDonald, John, Portland,
Morgan, Charles F., Greenwood,
Nelson, Frederick, Portland,
Pray, Leroy, Portland,
Timmony, John, Portland.

MUSICIAN: Frank C. Kimball, Portland.

ON SPECIAL DUTY OR DETACHED SERVICE: Sergeant Joseph C. Paradis, Portland, clerk div. h'dqrs. Wagoner Lincoln Grover, Gardiner, teamster corps h'dqrs. Privates: Thomas Feeney, Taunton, Mass., div. h'dqrs; Edwin H. Robertson, Brownfield, Albert A. Trull, Greenwood, brig. h'dqrs.

COMPANY G.
(Including 1 present sick.)

Captain, Alburn P. Harris, Portland.
First Lieutenant, Daniel C. Clark, Portland.
Second Lieutenant, Sidney H. Hutchins, Saco.

SERGEANTS.

1st Sergt., Archibald Wilson, Portland, Charles G. Hall, Vienna,
Alonzo Mitchell, Freeport,   George B. Parsons, Conway, N. H.

CORPORALS.

Ambrose Anthoine, Windham,   Charles H. Brewer, Freeport,
Edward J. Dolan, Portland.

PRIVATES.

Blake, James, Fall River, Mass.,
Brown, James, Brownfield,
Clark, Edward L., Portland,
Dealing, Francis O., Sidney,
Drinkwater, Phillip F., Portland,
Frost, Albert, Denmark,
Hamlin, Elvin L., Brownfield,
Killeen, James, Portland,
Kenney, Edward J., Portland,
Latham, Seward M., Cumberland,
Libby, Henry C., Gray,
Reardon, Michael, Portland,
Shaw, John M., Portland,
Welch, William A. S., Portland,

Brown, Enoch M., Brownfield,
Chick, Charles H., Litchfield,
Covell, Edgar C., Portland,
Dean, Charles H., Buxton,
Dudley, Michael, Portland,
Gray, Melville, Fryeburg,
Irvin, William, Portland,
Kelly, Timothy, Portland,
Kenniston, Jeremiah C., Brownfield,
Leavitt, Joseph, Portland,
Meserve, Levi P., Denmark,
Richardson, William, Portland,
Wallace, Elisha W., Windham,
Wentworth, Benjamin N., Brownfield.

ON SPECIAL DUTY OR DETACHED SERVICE: Privates: Lorestin Danforth, Portland, div. wagon-master; Isaac N. Jackson, Bridgton, brig. com. dept.: Charles W. Jordan, Portland, teamster; Stillman H. Saunders, Falmouth, hosp. attendant; Francis M. Smith, Portland, amb. train; Charles T. Webster, Portland, clerk div. h'dqrs.

COMPANY H.

First Lieutenant, John D. Ladd, Biddeford, commanding company.

SERGEANTS.

1st Sergt., Charles H. Dow, Standish, James G. Sanborn, Milbridge,
Thomas E. Lawrence, Portland,   John W. Jordan, Cape Elizabeth.

CORPORALS.

Anthony B. Gould, Pownal,   George W. Tappan, Gloucester, Mass.,
John Conlin, Lewiston.

PRIVATES.

Chase, Thomas R., Pownal,   Conlin, James, Portland,
Feeny, Edward H., Bangor,   Goodness, William, Paris,
Hunter, Sidney, Eastport,   Kelley, John, Ireland,
Knowles, James, England,   Miller, Frederick, Machias,
Murphy, Dennis, Biddeford,   Newell, Lendall R., Portland,
Pratt, Horace, New Vineyard,   Pridham, James H., Portland,
Richardson, Darius, Cornish,   Sturgess, George B., Portland,
Tracy, William, Portland,   True, George F., Exeter,
True, William W., Yarmouth,   Wilder, Samuel, Portland.

MUSICIAN: Charles F. Moody, Portland.

ON SPECIAL DUTY OR DETACHED SERVICE: Corporal George W. Briggs, Pembroke, div. q'rm'r dept. Privates: George W. Holmes, Bridgton, brig. com. dept.; George N. Maxham, Waterville, and Otis H. Skillings, Portland, amb. train.

COMPANY I.

First Lieutenant Lewis H. Lunt, Brunswick.
Second Lieutenant, John A. A. Packard, Hallowell.

SERGEANTS.

First Sergeant, P. Jordan Mitchell, Greenwood,
Bethuel S. Sawyer, Bethel,   David A. Edwards, Bethel,
J. Spencer Peabody, Gilead,   Enoch Whittemore, Jr., Paris.

CORPORALS.

Audrew J. Bean, Albany,   Cyrus Thurlow, Woodstock,
Cyrus R. Lawrence, Sumner,   Alanson M. Whitman, Woodstock,
Levi Shedd, Greenwood.

PRIVATES.

Adams, Thomas, Stoneham,   Andrews, David E., Andover,
Bean, Franklin, Rumford,   Bean, John E., Bethel,
Brown, Orrin S., Bethel,   Daily, Dennis, Boston, Mass.,
Edwards, Bryce M., Otisfield,   Evans, James M., Gorham, N. H.,
Farren, Patrick, Portland,   Foley, Patrick, Portland,
Foye, Edgar, Wiscasset,   Harper, William R., Rumford,
Howard, Michael, Washington,   Howe, Robert, Greenwood,
Jordan, Asa D., Norway,   Lapham, Richmond M., Rumford,
Lemont, Daniel, Portland,   Littlefield, James A., Greenwood,
Martin, Jere W., Rumford,   Parker, Alonzo S., Baldwin,
Wentworth, Chas. M., Jackson, N. H., Wormell, John S., Bethel.

ON SPECIAL DUTY OR DETACHED SERVICE: Wagoner Willoughby R. York, Bethel, teamster. Privates: Horace K. Chase, Rumford, teamster; George Cook, Old Town, brig. h'dqrs; Charles W. Horn, Milan, N. H., brig. com. dept.; James Kelly, Lewiston, cook; Stillman N. Littlehale, Riley Plantation, amb. train; Lorenzo D. Russell, Bethel, hosp. attendant.

COMPANY K.

(Including 1 present sick.)

First Lieutenant, Andrew S. Lyon, Freeport, commanding company.
Seond Lieutenant, John McLellan, Casco.

SERGEANTS.

William A. Tubbs, Hebron,   Simon L. Johnson, Buckfield,
Charles E. Harris, Poland,   Augustus A. Dwinal, Minot.

CORPORALS.

Samuel D. S. Duran, Raymond,   Albert W. Hines, Turner,
Henry C. West, Minot.

PRIVATES.

Bancroft, John F., Poland,   Brown, Arthur M., Minot,
Chase, Joseph A., Pownal,   Clark, James, Frankfort,
Dwinel, Harrison J., Minot,   Fardy, John, Lewiston,
Frost, William, Peru,   Goodwin, Ezra M., Minot,
Hackett, Edward A., Oxford,   Hutchinson, Almon H., Minot,
Jordan, Levi F., Poland,   Lombard, John C., Oxford,
Meserve, John, Casco,   Perkins, Harrison G. O., Oxford,
Phillips, Marshall S., Auburn,   Ricker, Samuel F., Raymond,
St. Clair, Alanson W., Poland,   Stone, James M., Otisfield,
Thompson, James W., New Portland, Verrill, Horace A., Poland,
Whitman, George G., Hebron.

MUSICIANS.

William B. Adams, Raymond,   Joseph P. Harmon, Harrison.

ON SPECIAL DUTY OR DETACHED SERVICE: Privates: Richard Bailey,
Minot, and Levi S. Robinson, Raymond, hosp. attendants; Stephen M. Barrows, Hebron, and Talbot G. Stuart, Casco, orderlies at div. h'dqrs; Charles
F. McKenney, Minot, amb. train; Joshua S. Spiller, Casco, q'rm'r dept.
corps h'dqrs.

DEDICATION OF MONUMENT,

OCTOBER 3, 1889.

ADDRESS OF COLONEL CLARK S. EDWARDS,

BREVET BRIGADIER-GENERAL OF VOLUNTEERS.

Mr. President and Comrades of the Fifth Maine:—

It has fallen to my lot on this memorable occasion to give a
brief, descriptive account of the part taken by the Fifth Maine
in the great battle of Gettysburg, which occurred on this historic field twenty-six years ago.   Before speaking particularly
of what the regiment did on those early days of July, 1863, I
wish, in as brief a manner as possible, to outline the history of
the regiment, so far as the principal engagements are concerned
—in which it participated—and thus correct a few errors which
have gone forth to the world as history.   Lest I may be misunderstood by others, I will say here that I do not claim that
the Fifth was the best regiment sent to the field from the old

State of Maine, but I do assert that she sent no better one. We make no unwarranted claim in asserting that the services rendered and the results achieved by the Fifth justly entitle it to be classed among the fighting regiments of the war, notwithstanding the fact that other regiments lost more men. Any claim of the historian that only those regiments that met with the heaviest losses were fighting regiments, does an injustice to many of the best regiments in the service.

In more instances than one, severe losses have fallen upon regiments through the stupidity of the commanding officer, or by some mistake in placing troops in an exposed position where soldiers were shot down by the enemy without a shot being fired in return. For if the loss is the only claim that entitles a regiment to be classed among fighting regiments, then the brave Warren and his men at Bunker Hill have been accorded praise that they did not deserve. To base the fighting qualities of a regiment entirely upon its losses, without regard to its accomplishments, is wrong, as every soldier knows. The same may be said of General Jackson and his army at New Orleans, where the loss was slight, though the achievements were brilliant. For the Fifth Maine we should claim for all time, full and complete recognition of its services.

The regiment was organized in May, 1861, although several of the companies were formed and filled in April. It was mustered into the service June 23d and 24th, having one thousand men, and at once started for Washington. In New York the regiment was presented with a banner, from the steps of City Hall, by the residents of the city who were formerly citizens of the Pine Tree State. The regiment reached Washington on the evening of June 27th, and went into camp on Meridian Hill, where it remained until July 9th, when it crossed the Potomac, and went into camp near Fort Ellsworth, doing picket duty until July 12th, when it advanced as far as Claremont, a point about a mile, or a mile and a half, in advance of any troops at this time. Here the regiment remained until July 17th, when it was ordered to move forward against the enemy at Bull Run. In this, our first engagement, the loss was slight. The next battle of importance in which the Fifth was actively engaged was on the peninsula, at West Point on the Pamunkey, May 7, 1862. It was here that the regiment made its first bayonet charge, driving the enemy from its intrenched position. The firing was hot and heavy ; the loss of men was two killed and five wounded.

May 24th the regiment, now in Slocum's division of Franklin's (Sixth) corps, skirmished and fought in line of battle at the Chickahominy River, driving the enemy, and finally forcing him across the bridge.

June 27th found the regiment in action in the rear of the McGee house, charging up the hill and across the open field, in the battle of Gaines' Mill. The division had been held in reserve exposed to a galling artillery fire in the forenoon, and at 2 o'clock in the afternoon was ordered across the river to the help of General Porter. So hard pressed was he that our division was sent piecemeal to various points of the line. The Fifth was finally ordered to support a battery near the centre. At about 5 o'clock it was ordered to the charge over the crest of the hill which the enemy held ; the men advanced without wavering, under a storm of bullets, shot and shell, drove the rebels before them and gained possession of the hill, and held possession until about dark, when they were relieved by other troops. In this engagement the Fifth lost ten killed, sixty-nine wounded and sixteen missing ; Colonel Jackson was wounded, and Lieut.-Colonel Heath, who assumed command, while reconnoitering was shot through the head and died instantly. The command of the regiment then fell to myself, then captain of company I. The next day, June 28th, we were engaged with the enemy at Golding's Farm ; June 30th at Charles City Cross Roads, Glendale, or Frayser's Farm, as it is variously called. Here the regiment experienced a terrific cannonade. The air was full of solid shot and bursting shell. Such fearful din of the cannon's roar was only once again experienced by the Fifth and that was, on the spot where we now stand, on the afternoon of July 3, 1863.

On the afternoon and evening of July 1, 1862, the regiment was at Malvern Hill. The great assault of the enemy was repulsed with fearful slaughter, though our loss was com-

paratively slight.   At Harrison's Landing we went into camp,
remaining there until August 15th, when we were transferred
to Alexandria, arriving there August 26th, and encamping at
Fort Lyon until the 29th, when orders were received to advance.
The regiment marched to Annandale, where it camped for the
night within hearing of Pope's cannon.   The evening of August
30th found us on the south side of Cub Run, covering the
retreat of Pope's army.   The night was spent in picket duty,
and on the following morning, August 31st, we recrossed Cub
Run, destroying the bridge in our rear, — notwithstanding the
report made by General Pope, as appeared in the war articles
published in the *Century Magazine,* that the Sixth army corps
did not advance beyond Annandale.   After a tedious march into
Maryland, through dust and under a scorching sun, September
14th found the regiment, with the 16th N. Y. on the right,
charging the enemy at the point of the bayonet at Crampton's
Gap, in the South Mountain range, about fifteen miles southeast
of Sharpsburg, or Antietam battlefield.   Discovering the enemy
to be in force at this pass, General Slocum made dispositions to
give battle.   Our regiment, Colonel Jackson in command, and
the 16th N. Y., constituted the advance, and were ordered to
assault the enemy.   For nearly a mile we moved forward under
a severe artillery fire, over an open field in full view of the
enemy, through a cornfield, and climbing five rail fences in our
way until, approaching within five hundred yards of the enemy,
they opened on us with musketry.   This we returned, and contested with them for over an hour, when our cartridges gave
out, and we fell back a few yards to better protection while
waiting for ammunition.   Directly after, however, the order
came to charge the enemy.   With a shout the men sprang forward at the double-quick, with the rest of the division, and
charged with the bayonet ; after receiving a volley or two into
our ranks the firing ceased ; the Confederates retreating, we
took posssession of the heights.   The regiment in this engagement lost thirty-five in killed and wounded.   This victory was
of no small importance to the Union cause.   On September 17th,
— one of the bloodiest days America ever saw, — was fought
the battle of Antietam, in which the Fifth Maine took an active

part, Lieut.-Colonel Scamman commanding. In this battle one historian says that more lives were lost in the same length of time than on any other field during the civil war.

On December 12th, in the battle of Fredericksburg, the Fifth advanced across the open plain near the Bernard house, and on the following day occupied an important position near the centre of the line of battle.

May 3, 1863, the second battle of Fredericksburg was fought by a portion of the Sixth corps. The Fifth Maine assisted in driving the enemy from Marye's Heights at the city of Fredericksburg. It was in this battle that Adjutant Bicknell was severely wounded. On the same day was fought the battle of Salem Church. In these two engagements the regiment lost about 100, being more than one-third of its number engaged. On the evening of May 4th, after some skirmishing, we crossed to the north bank of the Rappahannock at Banks' Ford; after an hour's rest the regiment recrossed the river and was sent forward a mile to perform outpost duty and cover the retreat of the corps, who were crossing to the north side. About 3 o'clock on the morning of the 5th the whole corps had crossed, when the men of the Fifth, weary and almost worn out, fell back to the river, and were the last to cross. So ended the regiment's participation in the ill-fated second battle of Fredericksburg or Chancellorsville, which carried the Fifth into three separate battles. Our loss in officers was especially severe: Lieutenant Brann was killed and Lieutenants Brown and Bailey mortally wounded; Captains Robinson and Dearing, Lieutenants Bicknell, O. B. Stevens and J. H. Stevens, wounded; Lieutenants W. E. Stevens and F. G. Patterson, taken prisoners.

After this the regiment went into camp, where we remained until we started north, on the campaign which terminated on this field before us. Our march was over routes which we had in part traveled during the Maryland campaign of the preceding year, under "Little Mac." July 1st found the regiment resting quietly in camp near Manchester, Md. None were aware that the enemy had at this time been met at Gettysburg and that a great battle had begun. During our march through Maryland a most cordial reception was given the boys in blue by the loyal citizens, who could not do too much for the defenders of their homes and their country. Intense enthusiasm prevailed wherever the stars and stripes were seen. As we marched through the streets of Westminster and Manchester, thousands of flags and handkerchiefs were waved by the noble women and patriotic children. No sacrifices were too great for them to make.

While enjoying the rest afforded by the brief delay near Manchester, though the weather was hot and sultry, an order was received commanding the corps to move immediately towards Gettysburg, thirty-six miles distant, where our troops were now hastily gathering behind the defenses of Cemetery Ridge.

Like the good soldiers they were, the Sixth corps sprang forward with alacrity to obey, the Fifth Maine leading in that famous march, which began at 9 : 30 P. M. On the evening of July 1st information had been received that a great battle was in progress, and that upon its issue depended the fate of the country. Every one cheerfully obeyed orders. On, on, through the night we marched, each hour bringing us nearer this sacred field. No halt was made for breakfast. The services of the Sixth corps were at this critical time needed at the front. The hot rays of a July sun poured down upon us, but no one faltered. The distant roar of cannon told us that the battle was on once more. Eager for the fray, the footsteps were quickened. Hour after hour tramped the Sixth corps. The noon of July 2d found the regiment twelve miles away. No time was taken for dinner, but on we marched, reaching Rock Creek at about 5 o'clock in the afternoon. Here the canteens were filled and some preparations were made for satisfying the hunger that each one felt, having taken no food, except by snatches, since the march began on the previous evening; but before coffee could be made orders came for the troops to advance. The news of the arrival of the Sixth corps was greeted with cheer after cheer, as the word flew from division to division along the lines. The Fifth Maine, that evening of July 2d, moved to the front, as far as Plum Run, some thirty or forty rods in advance of the position indicated by this monument, in the direction of Devil's Den, though later in the evening it formed its line on the right of Little Round Top. On the following morning the stone-wall—which still remains much as we left it—was thrown up. A few prisoners were found in yonder house — or rather in one which occupied the site of the present buildings. The morning of July 3d found the Fifth in an important position, though little was required other than holding what had been secured. Throughout July 3d the regiment remained in the position taken. The forenoon wore away. At one o'clock the storm of battle broke. The air was filled with bursting shells and solid shot. For nearly two hours the terrible cannonading continued. Then came the famous charge of Pickett, which was against the centre of the Union line, while we were further to the left. On the evening of July 3d three companies of the regiment went forward towards the Emmitsburg road to reconnoitre, to look for men who had been wounded the day before and to bring them in ; several were found ; we also found near the Trostle buildings, as if abandoned, a cannon, two limbers and some other artillery property, which we hauled back that night. This belonged to the 9th Mass. battery, and had been lost during the fight of Sickles' corps on the 2d of July. The battle of Gettysburg had been fought and won. In the afternoon and night of July 4th the rain fell in torrents, and under cover of the storm Lee began his movements towards Virginia.

On July 5th the regiment, while in pursuit of Lee's army, had engagements at Fairfield, and later at Funkstown and Williamsport. The next battle of importance was at Rappahannock Station, November 7, 1863. It was here that the Fifth Maine and the 121st N. Y., the gallant " Onesters," charged upon the works of the enemy, capturing nearly three times as many prisoners as there were men in the two regiments. Our troops took up positions on the right of the railroad and formed line of battle. The enemy having been pressed back from the high ground in front, the regiment advanced, under a heavy artillery fire from their batteries, to within short range of their rifle-pits. Lieut.-Colonel Millett was wounded in this movement by a shell-fragment. About sunset an advance was ordered and the regiment moved forward, notwithstanding the terrific musketry fire poured into it. Soon after, a movement to the right was ordered, and when the regiment lined up again it was to charge. With a yell, and amid a shower of bullets, the Fifth rushed on unmindful of danger. The enemy was taken by surprise and the rifle-pits were carried at the point of the bayonet. Meanwhile the troops on the left having, after a heroic and sanguinary struggle, carried the redoubts and fortifications at that point, the enemy, to escape, were pressing to a pontoon bridge, their only means of crossing the river. The arrival of the Fifth among them, and the confusion which it created, enabled us to gather the fruits of victory in unstinted measure. The bridge was secured to us, and after a little resistance a capture of some twelve hundred prisoners, among whom were two brigade commanders and many field and staff officers, was effected. Four battle-flags of the regiments opposing us were captured also, Lieutenant Lyon, commanding company K, taking the colors of the 8th La., Corporal Blondel of D that of the 6th No. Car., Corporal Shackford of company A that of the 54th No. Car., James A. Littlefield of company I that of the 7th No. Car. The flags were subsequently presented to General Meade. At this battle the swords of Colonels Penn of Louisiana and Godwin and Murchison of North Carolina, the two first named being in command of brigades, also forty-six other swords, were surrendered to the colonel of the Fifth; and Lieutenant McLellan and others also got some. Major Daggett was detailed by Colonel Upton, who commanded the brigade, to command the battalion which escorted the captured flags and trophies of the charge to General Meade's headquarters. Our loss in killed was 7, including Lieutenant French and acting Lieut. Tubbs (the latter's commission as Lieutenant being then on its way), and 28 wounded, several of whom died of their wounds. We must not forget to mention the active part taken by the Sixth Maine in this glorious battle. That regiment charged the enemy's redoubt at our left and won its renowned victory.

The last week of November, 1863, found the regiment, on the brief campaign south of the Rapidan, at Locust Grove, facing the enemy once more, but in this engagement our loss was slight. Two days later found the Fifth skirmishing across Mine Run with but small loss. Returning to our camp at

Welford's Ford, on the Major plantation, we remained, pleas-
antly situated, during the winter. The regiment, instructed in
drills and discipline, grew still more proficient.

The regiment broke camp at Hazel River May 3, 1864,
marched and crossed the Rapidan at Germanna Ford. The
regiment had about 275 effective men in the ranks, with the
following officers: Colonel Edwards, Lieut.-Col. Millett,
Major Daggett, Adjutant Parsons, as field and staff; the line
officers being Captains: Robinson, Small, Harris, Sanborn,
Ladd, Clark and Lemont (Captains Stevens and Walker being
detached at division headquarters); First Lieutenants: W. E.
Stevens, Dexter, Wight, Lunt, O. B. Stevens, Summersides,
Mitchell and Lyon; Second Lieutenants: Grenier, Patterson,
Hutchings, McLellan, Goldthwaite and acting Lieut. Paradis.

On the 5th and 6th participated in the battle of the Wilderness. During the three following days it was under fire, and
on the 10th took part in one of the desperate charges of the
great battle of Spotsylvania. The Fifth Maine was one of the
twelve picked regiments selected for the charge on the right of
the centre of the enemy's line. The Fifth numbered about 200
men in the ranks, 40 others, with three officers, being absent
on picket duty. As the twelve regiments were formed in line
of battle, General Wright said to the commander of the Fifth:
"Colonel, I give you the place of honor in this charge. I give
you one of the best regiments in the whole service as a support.
If you get into their works, serve them as you did at Rappahannock Station." The regiment referred to by the General as
a support was the noble Sixth Maine. Behind this was the 5th
Wis. On the right of the Fifth Maine was the 121st N. Y. —
as brave a regiment as was ever mustered into the service. In
the grand charge that was made, 11 of the 17 line officers of
the Fifth who went in were killed or wounded, and one-half of
the men were shot down while crossing a field not more than
ten rods in width, and in less than two minutes of time. The
defenses of the enemy were reached and passed. A hand-to-
hand conflict ensued. Nearly two thousand prisoners were
captured by the column, but many of the prisoners escaped;

the Fifth captured two colors, one of these being taken by Lieutenant Paradis.

You have heard and seen various skeptical inquiries and remarks concerning bayonet conflicts and wounds. Some time since a friend of his inquired of General Upton, our brigade commander, as to the use of the bayonet, and I give you an extract from his reply which any one can find in Fox's Regimental Losses, page 78, foot note, as follows: " * * bayonet wounds and sabre cuts are very rare. But at Spotsylvania there were plenty of bayonet wounds, and no picture could give too exalted an idea of the gallantry of the 121st N. Y., 5th Maine, and 96th Penn., as they led the assaulting column of twelve picked regiments over the formidable intrenchments which confronted them." And need I ask you, soldiers of the Fifth Maine, whether anybody got hurt by the bayonet? Think of our lion-hearted Corporal, Cyrus Thurlow, our strong man, who, having carried our colors through the battle of the Wilderness, when he found that we were to charge the enemy's works, came and asked to exchange the colors for a musket, that he might do his share of work that afternoon of May 10th; and going forward with us in the foremost ranks, pressed on into the second line of works where the fierce hand-to-hand conflict took place, to the bitter end and overthrow of our opponents; and where Thurlow, too, gave up his life for the great cause that he fought for. His last act, seen by his companions, was when his special antagonists, in a bunch, refused to throw down their arms; he instantly, defending himself, with fierce thrusts disabled two of them with his bayonet; but there were too many for him. The incredulous are referred to the official report of General Upton, Rebellion Records, Vol. 36, part 1, page 668, in which he describes some of the gallant deeds of the Fifth Maine regiment in this battle.

On the morning of May 12th, as Hancock's corps stormed the "salient," or angle, the Fifth Maine was ordered to join in supporting the attack. Moving to the right of the angle, it was the first regiment to charge the enemy at this point. The enemy's fire on our right compelled the right to fall back, making an angle, the open flank being about fifty paces from their works. Throughout the day and late into the night the battle raged. · It was here that the Colonel, Lieutenant Wight (a), and some other officers of the regiment ran up, by pushing with shoulders against the wheels, two guns that had ceased firing for lack of cannoneers and, by infantry volunteers aiding the artillery-men, made use of them during the contest. The brigade was relieved about 6 P. M., after ten hours of fighting. In the eight days of the campaign we had lost of our officers Captain Lemont and Lieut. Lyon, killed; Captain Clark and Lieut. O. B. Stevens, mortally wounded; Captains Robinson, Harris and Ladd and Lieuts. Grenier, McLellan and Hutchings, wounded, beside two or three others slightly wounded.

The morning of the 13th found the regiment with less than sixty men ready for duty, and only one line officer. This number was subsequently increased by the return of men detailed in the past and of those who had been slightly wounded. The regiment crossed the North Anna May 23d, and helped to destroy the Virginia Central Railroad, as far as Hewlett's Station. There was considerable skirmishing until June 1st, when late in the afternoon a sharp fight occurred at Cold Harbor. This was the first and only time in the history of the regiment that it acted as a support to infantry in a charge, and the first time that the regiment during some portion of an action was not on the front line of battle. Until June 12th the regiment was daily under fire. Crossing the James River at Bermuda Hundreds the Fifth reached the vicinity of Petersburg June 17th, and on the following morning, at 2 : 30 o'clock, was ordered out to make a charge. The order was, however, soon countermanded, as it was ascertained that the enemy was too strongly intrenched to be driven from its position. A movement was then made around Petersburg to secure the Weldon Railroad, where the regiment had its last fight with the enemy.

The order relieving the men from further service, the time of enlistment having expired, found them on the 23d of June in the rifle-pits on the line of battle, with loaded muskets facing the enemy. On the evening of the 23d the regiment marched

(a) Evidence concerning this act can be found on the files of the Pension Office at Washington.

to City Point, and on the following morning boarded the steamer *John Brooks* for Washington. But it was not allowed to leave the army until General Upton had expressed his sentiments in a letter, prepared by himself, which was read to the regiment as we were about to embark. Perhaps if I again read it here it may quicken your blood : —

"HEADQUARTERS SECOND BRIGADE, June 23, 1864.

"*Colonel Edwards, Officers and Men of the Fifth Maine Regiment:*—

"At the expiration of your term of service, I feel it a great pleasure to signify to you my appreciation of the services you have rendered your country. Your gallantry, your constancy, your devotion to the flag of your country, your patient endurance of fatigue during the campaigns of three long years, entitle you to the lasting gratitude and esteem of your countrymen. Springing to arms at the first sound of danger, you have given proof of your valor and patriotism on every field, from the first Bull Run to the present time. Leaving your native state with over one thousand and forty men, and receiving a large number of recruits, you now return with but two hundred and sixteen.

"The long list of battles in which you have participated, including Bull Run, West Point, Gaines' Mill, Charles City Cross-roads, Crampton's Gap, Antietam, Fredericksburg, Salem Heights, Gettysburg, Rappahannock Station, eight days' battle in the wilderness and at Spotsylvania court-house, and Cold Harbor, will account for your losses.

"Repeatedly have the colors of the Fifth Maine been floated over the enemy's works. From behind their intrenchments you have captured the battle-flags of five of the proudest regiments in the Confederate service; and while inflicting a loss equal to your own, you have in addition captured more prisoners than you have borne names on your rolls. But while your former services have won for you the admiration and confidence of your commanding officers, your example and conduct during the present campaign forms the brightest page of your history.

"After three years' hard fighting, well knowing the risks of battle, not even the ardent desire or the immediate prospect of being restored to your friends could dampen your ardor or enthusiasm; but like brave and patriotic men you have fought nobly to the end of your term, adding with each day increased luster to your arms. With this brilliant record and the proud consciousness that you have stood by your country in the darkest hour of her peril, you now return to your homes where you will receive the homage due the services you have rendered.

"Bidding each and every one of you, in behalf of your old comrades in arms, a hearty God-speed, I have the honor to be your obedient servant,

"E. UPTON, *Brigadier-General, Commanding.*"

On reaching Washington the Fifth was ordered into camp in a pasture near the boat landing, a place selected by the authorities ; but not caring to obey this order, the regiment marched into the city and camped for the night on the grounds of the Smithsonian Institute, remaining here until paid off on the evening of the 26th, when it started for the north.

Before leaving the army at Petersburg an order was received from the General commanding the army for the regiment to take home the battle-flags captured on the line of battle. During its term of service six flags had been taken — four at Rappahannock Station and two at Spotsylvania — though the regiment is only credited with the capture of five. The flag not accounted for in records was taken in the charge at Spotsylvania, May 10, 1864. Doubtless the member of the Fifth to whom the flag was given was killed, and the flag fell into the hands of some other command that later passed over the same ground. The flags are now in the state and national capitols. The staves are in the Memorial Building on Peaks Island. The army records at Washington, at the time the regiment passed through the city on its way home, showed that no regiment had up to that time captured more flags than the Fifth. During its three years of service it had captured more than two thousand prisoners. The regiment was mustered out at Portland, July 27, 1864.

POEM.

READ BY MRS. HELEN S. PACKARD,

WIFE OF LIEUT. JOHN A. A. PACKARD.

Oh, native State, I sing of thee!
    Broad field of Freedom's loyal thought,
Thy scented pines are dear to me,
    Thy vales with tenderest memories fraught.

Each northern blast that sweeps along
    Thy cragged hills, or mountain tips,
Is dearer far than sweetest song
    That ever fell from artist lips.

Thy salt sea marshes freshly blown
    By winds that sweep the open sea,
Thy gray old rocks with moss o'ergrown
    Are sacred still to mine and me.

Oh, grand old State! land where I drew
    My earliest breath, whose fresh, strong breeze
Told murmuring tales of valor true,
    And whispered in the leafy trees.

I come to-day, with every nerve
    Quivering with love for native sod ;
With courage every end to serve,
    One flag, one country, and one God.

THE VOICE OF MAINE.

Along the outmost eastern line
    That marks our country's unlocked gate,
Crested with hill, and towering pine,
    Fair lies our noble Pine Tree State.

Thy landlocked bays, thy islands green,
    Thy purpling mountains flushed with light,
Thy broadening streams that lie between,
    Are sweet to soul and sense and sight.

The blue Atlantic laps thy coast
    In tender song and music wild,
Thy granite hills, our pride and boast,
    Are dear to every wandering child.

Oh, rock-bound State! Not long ago,
    O'er rugged hill and fertile plain
A clarion voice spoke, and lo!
    Thy sons sprang up, oh, loyal Maine.

That voice aroused the slumbering hills,
    It sounded down the lonely coast,
Along the mountain streams and rills
    It woke to life a mighty host.

O'er rocky farm, through village street,
    Across the meadows green and fair,
In bugle note, and drums' loud beat,
    It sounded through the slumbering air.

It touched the bench, the loom, the wheel,
    It echoed loud the anvil's ring,
And dreaming student woke to feel
    That Self was slave and Duty king.

Not long ago. But yet the chimes
    That tell the tireless round of years,
Have sounded eight and twenty times
    The signal of life's hopes and fears.

It is not long, we measure space
    Not by the span that binds us here,
But in the light of deeds we trace
    Their names in letters bright and clear.

And were ye lacking, sons of Maine,
    When duty's call rang in your ears?
Your 'scutcheons show no blot, no stain,
    Undimmed by aught save loving tears.

Where are they now? Go, ask the Past,
 That opens wide to-day her door,
And bid her tell of shadows cast
 O'er hearts and homes forevermore.

She tells of shattered dreams and hopes,
 Of fires long quenched, of other years,
Of sunken graves on sunny slopes
 Kept fresh by memory's loving tears.

With background dark of hill and wood,
 'Neath rugged rock and leafy tree
We stand to-day, where once they stood
 A firm and tried phalanstery.

And here with us in proud array
 Stands that old band of comrades true,
Who marched with us that far-off day,
 Brave, loyal hearts 'neath garb of blue.

In spite of strange, tumultuous thought,
 That teems and crowds our busy brain,
We welcome those who with us fought,
 Back to our presence once again.

Oh, loyal, great, true-hearted ones!
 The noble Empire State ne'er gave
More faithful, brave, devoted sons
 To do their part amid the brave.

Though furrowed brow and silvered hair
 Tell the old story on each face,
Though time has plowed deep lines of care
 Instead of old-time, boyish grace,

Yet still to-day we give you cheer
 With throbbing hearts of joy and pain;
With you we drop the silent tear
 For those who ne'er came back again.

With you, we here rejoice once more,
 That we may give the friendly grasp,
And once again live old times o'er,
 And feel again the old hand clasp.

Oh, comrades from the Empire State!
 'Twere worth the living o'er again,
Those deadly days of war and hate,
 Those weary hours of strife and pain;

'Twere worth the suffering and the fear,
 'Twere worth the heavy debt we paid,
To see thy bronzed faces here
 Amid this green and leafy shade.

Between our parted, sundered lives
 Old Time has plowed a chasm deep,

But all his manacles and gyves
Can never chain true comradeship.

And so, across a silver bridge,
We give the clasping hand to thee,
Our comrades true, on plain and ridge,
Our comrades for eternity.

Bound close by ties that death nor fate
Can e'er have power to change or part,
Though shadows fall — the hour late —
Yet still each heart shall answer heart.

Here raged the conflict; sinking low
The sun shone red where cannon pealed,
And in the west, with molten glow,
Shed sullen radiance o'er the field.

On blood-stained grass, once fresh and green,
He cast his dying rays of light,
And then o'er all the dreadful scene
Low fell the friendly shades of night.

No whistling bullets chill our blood,
No cries ring through the autumn air,
But soft winds fall in tender flood
And trees and flowers are passing fair.

We hear no tread of martial feet,
No hoof beats ring with clattering sound
Across the grass and clover sweet,
No cannons peal their deadly round.

We see no serried columns there,
No loud, commanding tones we hear,
No phantom presence haunts the air,
No step is heard by conscious ears.

But here beneath these tranquil skies
We stand to-day in solemn thought,
And grateful prayers like incense rise
To those who suffered, bled and fought.

Oh, heroes from the Pine Tree State!
You kept the bridge in manly part,
Not blood nor carnage, death nor fate,
Could turn one true or loyal heart.

Did Nature in that far-off time
When slow she moulded, day by day,
Divine the purpose, grand, sublime,
Which grew within the hardening clay?

Did she e'er dream in ages past,
What miracles should balance fate,
And that from out her storehouse vast
Her treasures should commemorate?

Her mines of wealth imprisoned deep,
    Should grow beneath the chisel's will,
To towering shaft and pillar steep
    In forms of grace by human skill?

In every tinted granite vein,
    In every block of native stone,
In lordly oak and stately pine,
    The blossom of your fame is blown.

The radiance of your star shall glow
    Brighter than stars that shine at night,
And God in righteous power will show
    The balance sheet of truth and right.

In future's grasp your fame still lies,
    An untouched book, its pages clear,
A tiny tree that yet shall rise
    And spread its branches far and near.

Our glorious dead! Oh, comrades gray,
    Uncover now your reverent heads,
They sweetly sleep, step softly, pray,
    Above their low and narrow beds.

Sleep well, oh Dead, for you too soon
    Were past all passions, hopes and fears.
Above your graves each year shall bloom
    The grasses watered by our tears.

Above these consecrated grounds,
    We pledge our faith and love anew.
Time's shadow on the sunken mounds
    Shall never dim our worship true.

Our living heroes, ye who come
    To render tribute here to-day,
Victors are you, 'neath this fair dome
    Crowned fresh with ivy, palm and bay.

Live as ye fought in war's dark night,
    With faces turned to meet the foe,
Fight to uphold the freeman's right
    And render justice for each blow.

By our dear dead, whose spirits drift
    Above the mounds that hold their dust,
Be watchful, vigilant and swift,
    To ever guard your living trust.

Theirs be sweet rest, of valor born,
    Yours be the living, glowing name,
In golden text inscribed upon
    The shadowy muster-roll of fame.

HISTORICAL SKETCH.

The Fifth Maine regiment was raised in the spring and early summer of 1861, almost without an effort, responding quickly to the governor's call to arms. The swelling tide of patriotism could not be restrained ; the limits set by the national authorities were speedily reached, to the full measure of the number of men it was willing to receive in the military service. The Fifth was made up of companies newly organized, one each at Gorham, Biddeford, Saco, Brunswick, Lewiston, Bethel and Minot, and three at Portland. The company locations indicate that the rank and file came from the counties of Cumberland, York, Androscoggin and Oxford. The rendezvous was at Portland, and at its muster into the U. S. service on the 24th of June, 1861, for three years, its organization was as follows : —

FIELD, STAFF AND NON-COMMISSIONED STAFF.

Colonel, Mark H. Dunnell, Portland.
Lieutenant-Colonel, Edwin Illsley, Lewiston.
Major, Samuel C. Hamilton, Biddeford.
Adjutant, Charles S. Whitman, Portland, Second Lieut. Co. E.
Quartermaster, John S. Merrill, Gorham, Second Lieut. Co. A.
Surgeon, Benjamin S. Buxton, Warren.
Assistant Surgeon, Francis G. Warren, Biddeford.
Chaplain, John N. Adams, Portland.

Sergeant-Major, Frederick Speed, Gorham.
Quartermaster-Sergeant, Adelbert B. Twitchell, Bethel.
Commissary-Sergeant, Benjamin Freeman, Bethel.
Hospital Steward, William S. Noyes, Saco.
Band Leader, Jonathan Cole, Portland.

COMPANY OFFICERS.

Co. A.　Captain, Josiah Heald, Gorham.
　　　　First Lieutenant, William Merrill, Gorham.
　　　　Second Lieutenant, John S. Merrill, Gorham.
Co. B.　Captain, Lewis B. Goodwin, Biddeford.
　　　　First Lieutenant, Robert M. Stevens, Biddeford.
　　　　Second Lieutenant, Samuel H. Pillsbury, Biddeford.
Co. C.　Captain, Isaac B. Noyes, Saco.
　　　　First Lieutenant, Frederick S. Gurney, Saco.
　　　　Second Lieutenant, David S. Barrows, Saco.
Co. D.　Captain, Edward W. Thompson, Brunswick.
　　　　First Lieutenant, George B. Kenniston, Boothbay.
　　　　Second Lieutenant, Charles H. Small, Topsham.

Co. E.   Captain, Emery W. Sawyer, Lisbon.
          First Lieutenant, Aaron S. Daggett, Greene.
          Second Lieutenant, Charles S. Whitman, Portland.
Co. F.   Captain, George P. Sherwood, Portland.
          First Lieutenant, Nathan Walker, Portland.
          Second Lieutenant, Charles E. Atwood, Gardiner.
Co. G.   Captain, Henry G. Thomas, Portland.
          First Lieutenant, George W. Martin, Portland.
          Second Lieutenant, Thomas J. Sawyer, Portland.
Co. H.   Captain, Edward A. Scamman, Portland.
          First Lieutenant, Ambrose S. Dyer, Yarmouth.
          Second Lieutenant, Samuel Munson, Portland.
Co. I.   Captain, Clark S. Edwards, Bethel.
          First Lieutenant, John B. Walker, Bethel.
          Second Lieutenant, Cyrus M. Wormell, Bethel.
Co. K.   Captain, William A. Tobie, Poland.
          First Lieutenant, Hamlin T. Bucknam, Minot.
          Second Lieutenant, Burbank Spiller, Raymond.

The regiment left Portland June 26, 1861, proceeded to Washington and remained in that vicinity until the battle of Bull Run. Previous to this battle, in which it took part, the Fifth was assigned to a brigade commanded by Colonel Howard of the Third Maine, in Heintzelman's division. In October it was transferred to Slocum's brigade (Seventh) of General Franklin's division, and went into camp near Alexandria, and doing picket duty near Mount Vernon, with frequent skirmishes. The regiment was not at the siege of Yorktown, in April and May, 1862, but with Franklin's division remained on transports on the rivers. Early in May the regiment engaged in the field operations of McClellan, and after that had a share in the various battles of the Peninsula campaign, terminating at Harrison's Landing on the James River. May 18, 1862, the Sixth corps was formed, with General Franklin in command, composed of two divisions, Slocum's and Smith's. The brigade to which the Fifth belonged became the Second brigade of the First division, and throughout its subsequent history the regiment retained its place in the same brigade of the same division of the Sixth corps.

Returning from the peninsula when the battle of Second Bull Run was in progress, the Fifth took only a slight part in that, but was actively engaged at Crampton's Gap and at

Antietam September 14 and 17, 1862. The subsequent history of the regiment is so clearly defined in the Address, given on the preceding pages, by the officer who so long commanded the regiment and finally brought it home for muster-out, that we omit the details of its general campaigns. The regiment received a warm reception, amounting to an ovation, upon its arrival at Portland, the last of June, 1864; its march through the streets was a triumphal procession; a public reception and a royal feast attested the high regard in which each hero of the Fifth was held at home. The final muster-out did not take place until July 27, 1864 (a).

The men present, mustered out with the organization, numbered 193, besides the officers; 116 of the regiment had re-enlisted about the first of January, 1864, and the survivors of these, 78 in number, with the later recruits and several officers, were assigned to the Seventh Maine regiment, shortly after merged into the First Maine Veterans a regiment organized in Virginia September 20, 1864, made up from the officers and men of the Fifth, Sixth and Seventh Maine regiments who were not discharged or mustered out with their original organizations. This new regiment was assigned to the Third brigade, Second division of the Sixth corps and, being thus composed of excellent elements, made a brilliant record for itself in the campaign of General Sheridan in the Shenandoah Valley, September and October, 1864, taking part in the battles of Charlestown, Winchester, Fisher's Hill and Cedar Creek.

Rejoining the army of the Potomac in December, 1864, it in the spring participated with great honor in the breaking of the Petersburg lines and the pursuit of Lee's army until its surrender; it was mustered out June 28, 1865, rounding out, for many of the men, a term of four years' service.

(a) The monument inscription erroneously reads, "mustered out June 27," precisely as furnished to the executive committee by a representative of the Fifth Maine. The regimental officers have applied to correct the inscription to "July 27."

ROSTER.

The following information relating to officers of the Fifth
Maine regiment is obtained from the Volunteer Army Register,
published by the War Department August 31, 1865, and other
reliable sources : —

OFFICERS AT MUSTER-OUT JULY 27, 1864.

COLONEL: Clark S. Edwards, Jan. 8, 1863, — brevet Brig.-Gen. Vols.,
Mar. 13, 1865.

LIEUTENANT-COLONEL: Henry R. Millett, Jan. 8, 1863.

MAJOR: Aaron S. Daggett, Apr. 14, 1863, — Lieut.-Col. 5th U. S. Vet.
Vols., Jan., 1865; brevet Col. and brevet Brig.-Gen. U. S. Vols., Mar. 13,
1865; Captain 16th Inf't'y U. S. A., July, 1866; brevet Major and Lieut.-Col.
U. S. A.; Lieut.-Col. 25th Inf't'y, U. S. A.

ADJUTANT: First Lieut. George B. Parsons. Apr. 4, 1864.

CAPTAINS: Charles H. Small, Oct. 7, 1861; Robert M. Stevens, Feb. 7,
1862; Alburn P. Harris, July 3, 1862; Edward M. Robinson, Apr. 13, 1863;
Frederick G. Sanborn, Apr. 13, 1863; John D. Ladd, Nov. 1, 1863; Nathan
Walker, Nov. 1, 1863.

FIRST LIEUTENANTS: William E. Stevens, Nov. 1, 1862; Charles B.
Dexter, Nov. 1, 1862; W. B. Fenderson, Quartermaster, Nov. 26, 1862;
Joseph Wight, May 1, 1863; Lewis H. Lunt, May 1, 1863; John H. Stevens,
May 25, 1863, paroled prisoner, discharged Mar. 16, 1865; John C. Summer-
sides, Nov. 1, 1863.

SECOND LIEUTENANTS: Frank G. Patterson, Apr. 20, 1863; George A.
Chandler, May 3, 1863, paroled prisoner, discharged Mar. 16, 1865; Sidney
H. Hutchings, June 19, 1863.

SURGEON: Francis G. Warren, Jan. 9, 1863.

ASSISTANT SURGEON: Melville H. Manson, May 4, 1863.

CHAPLAIN: John R. Adams, June 24, 1861.

(The dates given above refer to rank or commission; those hereafter
given refer to the date of event.)

DIED.

LIEUTENANT-COLONEL: William S. Heath, killed in action June 27, 1862.

CAPTAINS: Frank L. Lemont, killed in battle of Spotsylvania, May 12,
1864; Daniel C. Clark, May 16, 1864, from wounds received in action, — previously served in First Maine regiment; Joseph C. Paradis, commissioned
June 8, not mustered to this grade, died June 18, 1864, of wounds received
in action at Cold Harbor.

FIRST LIEUTENANTS: Ambrose S. Dyer, Sept. 22, 1861, at Yarmouth,
Me; Smith G. Bailey, May 30, 1863, of wounds received in action at Salem
Church; Andrew S. Lyon, in action May 10, 1864, at Spotsylvania, reported
missing; Orrin B. Stevens, May 15, 1864, of wounds received in action
May 10, 1864.

SECOND LIEUTENANTS: Cyrus W. Brann, killed in action at Salem
Heights, Va., May 3, 1863; John S. French, killed Nov. 7, 1863, at battle of
Rappahannock Station.

PROMOTED AND TRANSFERRED OUT OF REGIMENT.

Promoted: Colonel Nathaniel J. Jackson, Sept. 24, 1862, to Brigadier-General of Vols , — brevet Major-General of Vols., Mar. 13, 1865; First Lieut. Richard C. Shannon, Oct. 23, 1862, to Captain and A. A. G. U. S. Vols.; First Lieut. Stephen H. Manning, Nov. 26, 1862, to Captain and A. Q. M., — brevet Brig.-General U. S. Vols.; Second Lieut. Frederick Speed, Nov. 28, 1861, to First Lieutenant and Adjutant Thirteenth Maine Vols.; Second Lieut. Henry W. Stinson, Apr. 30, 1863, to Captain and A. D. C. U. S. Vols.

Transferred: Captain John C. Goldthwait, June 23, 1864, to Seventh Maine regiment, afterwards to First Maine Vet. Inf., died of wounds Apr. 18, 1865; First Lieut. George E. Atwood, Oct. 7, 1862, to Twenty-fourth Maine regiment; First Lieut. P. Jordan Mitchell, June 23, 1864, to Seventh Maine regiment, afterwards to First Maine Vet. Inf., — promoted to Captain not mustered, died of wounds Nov. 12, 1864; Second Lieut. John McLellan, June 23, 1864, to Seventh Maine regiment, afterwards to First Maine Vet. Inf., — promoted to Captain, discharged July 5, 1865; Second Lieut. J. Augustine Grenier, June 23, 1864, to Seventh Maine regiment, afterwards to First Maine Vet. Inf., — promoted to First Lieutenant and Adjutant; Walter Foss, Sergeant, commissioned Second Lieutenant and First Lieutenant, transferred to First Maine Vet., not mustered, wounded, discharged for disability.

DISCHARGED.

CAPTAINS: Josiah Heald, Aug. 9, 1861; William A. Tobie, Sept. 20, 1861; Lewis B. Goodwin, Sept. 20, 1861; Burbank Spiller, March 23, 1863; John B. Walker, June 17, 1863; Samuel H. Pillsbury, Aug. 12, 1863; Albert L. Dearing, Sept. 8, 1863. FIRST LIEUTENANTS: Adjutant Charles S. Whitman, Nov. 21, 1861; William Merrill, Dec. 10, 1861; Josiah R. Brady, Feb. 14, 1862; Abel C. T. Stevens, May 7, 1862; George B. Kenniston, May 25, 1863; John A. A. Packard, Nov. 25, 1863. pro. from Second Lieut., not mustered as First.

ASSISTANT SURGEON: William S. Noyes, Mar. 31, 1863. Acting Surgeon, George E. Brickett, not must'd, as no vacancy; relieved Aug., 1862.

RESIGNED.

COLONELS: Mark H. Dunnell, Sept. 2, 1861; Edward A. Scamman, Jan. 8, 1863. LIEUTENANT-COLONEL: Edward Illsley, Sept. 24, 1861. MAJOR: Samuel C. Hamilton, Sept. 25, 1861. CAPTAINS: Isaac B. Noyes, Aug. 1, 1861; Henry G. Thomas, Aug. 9, 1861, — Captain 11th U. S. Inf'try, Colonel 19th U. S. C. T., Brig.-General Vols., brevet Major-General Vols., Mar. 13, 1865; E. W. Sawyer, Aug. 16, 1861; Edward W. Thompson, Sept. 8, 1861; Thomas J. Sawyer, Dec. 3, 1861; David S. Barrows, Jan. 23, 1862; George W. Patch, June 17, 1862; George E. Brown, Oct. 19, 1862; George P. Sherwood, Jan. 19, 1863; Hamlin T. Bucknam, Sept. 29, 1863. FIRST LIEUTENANTS: Fred S. Gurney, Aug. 15, 1861; John S. Merrill, Quartermaster, Sept. 2, 1861; George W. Martin, Oct. 13, 1861; Charles K. Packard, June 13, 1862; George W. Graffam, Adjutant, Oct. 18, 1863; Geo. W. Bicknell, Adjutant, Mar. 8, 1864. SECOND LIEUTENANTS: Samuel Munson, Aug. 25, 1861; Robert J. McPherson, Dec. 11, 1861; William H. Shaw, Jan. 13, 1862; Cyrus M. Wormell, Feb. 22, 1862; Simeon W. Sanborn, Oct. 16, 1862. SURGEON: Benjamin F. Buxton, Jan. 9, 1863.

OTHERWISE LEFT THE SERVICE.

First Lieutenant, Charles A. Waterhouse, dis. Mar. 11, 1864.

MONUMENT.

The monument of the Sixth Maine Regiment is located to the east of Big Round Top on the north side of a narrow road which, coming down from the slope of Big Round Top, crosses the Taneytown road, and stands about two hundred yards east of the latter road. It is a tall shaft of alternate red and white Hallowell granite, surmounted by an intertwined double red cross of the Sixth corps.

ADMEASUREMENTS: Base, 5 feet 2 inches by 5 feet 2 inches by 2 feet 9 inches; plinth, 3 feet 8 inches by 3 feet 8 inches by 3 feet 7 inches; shaft, 2 feet 9 inches by 2 feet 9 inches by 13 feet 2 inches; cap, 2 feet by 2 feet by 2 feet. Total height, twenty-one feet six inches.

It bears these inscriptions:—

6TH MAINE

INFANTRY,

3d BRIGADE,

1ST DIV.

6TH CORPS,

HELD THIS POSITION

JULY 3, 1863.

IN AFTERNOON MOVED

TO SUPPORT OF CENTRE,

THEN TO BIG ROUND TOP.

SIXTH MAINE REGIMENT,

THIRD BRIGADE, FIRST DIVISION, SIXTH ARMY CORPS,

AT THE BATTLE OF GETTYSBURG.

IN Russell's brigade, of the same division to which the Fifth Maine was attached, was the Sixth Maine, which had recently been one of the regiments of Burnham's famous Light Division. Like the Fifth it was a veteran regiment, and one of the most famous that carried the flag of Maine. Officers and men, the regiment numbered at Gettysburg about three hundred and fifty, its ranks still showing the losses at Fredericksburg, where it had greatly distinguished itself in the bloody charge on Marye's Heights. Col. Hiram Burnham, afterwards promoted for conspicuous services, was in command. Moving in the same division with the Fifth Maine, the Sixth suffered all the hardships of the forced march from Manchester to Gettysburg. Arriving at Gettysburg, Russell's brigade was held in reserve in the rear of the line formed by the Third division and by Bartlett's brigade. With ominous meaning the wild sounds of battle smote on their ears, and the flashings of the artillery discharges on the smoke of the evening conflict, like lightning in the storm cloud, aroused their fagged-out spirits like a command to charge ; but the Sixth were not called to enter the arena of strife.

This position in reserve was held during the night of July 2d, and on the morning of the 3d the Sixth Maine with the brigade were moved to the left, to a position on the Taneytown road just east of Big Round Top. There they formed part of a force intended to frustrate any attempt of the Confederates to get into the rear of the Union army. In this position, where the regiment remained nearly all day July 3d, the monument has been placed. The Confederates did not make the anticipated attack and there was no fighting.

On July 4th Russell's brigade being placed on the left of the Fifth corps line, the Sixth Maine found itself in line in the hollow between the Round Tops. The only recorded casualty in the regiment, at Gettysburg, is that of Phineas F. Bean, Private company I, wounded July 4th. On July 5th the regiment moved in pursuit of Lee.

The following letter, written by Adjutant Clark of this famous regiment, and dated at Cedar Rapids, Ia., October 25, 1891, and addressed to Gen. B. F. Harris, formerly the Lieutenant-Colonel, is subjoined, as it contains extracts from a diary which the Adjutant kept : —

My Dear Friend: —

I received your line this morning and return the enclosed memoranda of the Sixth Maine at Gettysburg. I have examined my pocket-diary written at the time on the field, as we lay there, and this memoranda corresponds with the diary as to our location. I wrote on July 2d, " Arrived on battlefield of Gettysburg at 4 P. M. Since that time a most terrific battle has been going on just in front of us, we being held in reserve. The rebels attacked our left and centre with great fury and overwhelming numbers, and for a while they were successful and our lines were pressed back, but they were finally repulsed with great slaughter. Everything promises victory to-morrow. We are in position on the left of our lines." The fight in our front was evidently the attack on Sickles at the Peach Orchard and Emmitsburg road, and the final repulse of the rebels was at Little Round Top.

On the 3d of July I wrote of our position : " Our brigade was not engaged with infantry, being posted on the extreme left, where the enemy did not attack us." This was evidently on the Taneytown road, as that was the left of our lines.

My diary does not show our position on the 4th, but speaks of our men gathering up the wounded and burying the dead, and my recollection is that it was between the Round Tops. That is the day you and I rode out to the Peach Orchard and drew the fire of the rebel picket line. Do you remember what a magnificent retreat we made?

On the 5th of July my diary shows that we were ordered out early for a reconnaissance of our front, from which we were recalled and sent in pursuit of the enemy. " Just at dark " (so the diary reads) "we came upon the enemy's rear at a pass in the mountains near Fairfield. The day was so far spent that we had not time to attack them, else we might have whipped Early handsomely, — for it was his division we came upon. We shelled him severely, and our skirmishers had quite a hot brush with his outposts." I have no recollection, however, that our own regiment was engaged. On the morning of the 6th he was gone. We stayed about Fairfield the 6th. Marched that night from 9 o'clock to 3 A. M. to and beyond Emmitsburg. On the 7th marched at 9 A. M.; went to and through Lewistown, and that night marched up the mountains in the rain and camped on the top at 2 A. M. in a potato field, where Colonel Burnham gave the order, "stick arms." Faithfully yours,

CHARLES A. CLARK.

PARTICIPANTS.

FIELD, STAFF AND NON-COMMISSIONED STAFF.
Colonel, Hiram Burnham, Cherryfield.
Lieutenant-Colonel, Benjamin F. Harris, Machias.
Major, George Fuller, Corinth.
Adjutant, First Lieutenant Charles A. Clark, Sangerville.
Quartermaster, First Lieutenant Addison P. Buck, Foxcroft.
Assistant Surgeon, William Buck, Harmony.
Chaplain, Moses J. Kelley, Montville.
Sergeant-Major, William H. West, Machias.
Quartermaster-Sergeant, William H. H. Bates, Eastport.
Commissary-Sergeant, George H. Snowman, Bucksport.
Hospital Steward, George T. Holmes, Foxcroft.
Fife-major, James L. Holmes, Foxcroft.

COMPANY A.
(Including 1 present sick.)
Captain, Alexander B. Sumner, Lubec.
First Lieutenant, Lyman H. Wilkins, Brownville.
Second Lieutenant, Horace S. Hobbs, Milo.

SERGEANTS.
First Sergt., Ira P. Wing, Brownville, John J. Fogg, Bangor.

CORPORALS.
William H. Blood, Sebec,   John B. Bates, Jr., Dover,
Edward P. Prescott, Williamsburg, Loumus Berry, Brownville.

PRIVATES.
Ames, Francis M., Dover,   Atwood, Charles E., Kenduskeag,
Bagley, Levi, Milo,   Berry, Charles H., Brownville,
Blanchard, Newton, Foxcroft,   Brawn, William H., Lubec,

Chase, Rufus G., Foxcroft,
Davis, Ozro W., Bangor,
Edes, Charles E., Foxcroft,
Gould, Isaiah S., Brownville,
Harris, Benjamin, Brownville,
Kimball, Alfred, Harmony,
Morong, Frederick W., Lubec,
Neagle, James B., Lubec,
Pratt, Fernando G., Foxcroft,
Stowell, Joseph N., Brownville,
White, Henry K., Sangerville.

Crockett, Seth B., Guilford,
Dawes, George W., Foxcroft,
Farrington, Henry H., Foxcroft,
Greenleaf, William A., Abbot,
Holden, George F., Bangor,
Lurchin, Hillman P., Lubec,
Morrill, Shepard, Brownville,
Plummer, Fred E., Foxcroft,
Sewall, William G., Foxcroft,
Titcomb, Frank W., Corinna,

ON SPECIALDUTY OR DETACHED SERVICE: Privates: Albert L. Bragg, Dover, and Andrew J. Robinson, Dover, at brig. h'dqrs; John E. Larrabee, Parkman, q'rm'r dept. div. h'dqrs; Clarence W. P. Osgood, Dover, in 3d N. Y. battery.

COMPANY B.
(Including 2 present sick.)
Captain, Levi L. L. Bassford, Calais.
First Lieutenant, Albert M. Murch, Ellsworth.
Second Lieutenant, John C. Honey, Amherst.

SERGEANTS.
First Sergeant, Charles M. Flint, Calais,
George E. Thomas, Ellsworth,
George W. Bowden, Ellsworth,
Albert L. Jones, Holden,
Cyrus L. Murch, Ellsworth.

CORPORALS.
Jophanus M. Withee, Hancock,
Jonathan K. Phillips, Dedham,
Lorenzo D. Cousins, Ellsworth.
George F. Peaks, Dedham,
Oliver H. Goodwin, Ellsworth,

PRIVATES.
Bennett, John W., Ellsworth,
Buker, Cyrus, Jr., Ellsworth,
Chase, Asa D., Calais,
Eldridge, Martin V., Newburg,
Fields, Alexander E., Ellsworth,
George, Herman S., Holden,
Hamilton, William, Ellsworth,
Jewell, Joseph R., Ellsworth,
Kitching, Robinson, Fred'ick'n, N. B.,
McKeen, James H., Ellsworth,
Moor, Isaac F., Mariaville,
Peaks, Henry, Dedham,
Royal, Benjamin B., Ellsworth,
Sweeney, William H., Ellsworth,
Thistlewood, Robert K., Alexander.

Billington, Charles L., Dedham,
Carrigan, Thomas, Milford,
Chick, Thomas W., Clifton,
Farrell, Albert F. H., Trenton,
Foster, Bartlett, Cherryfield,
Green, Allen V., Blissville, N. B.,
Hines, Jesse, Ellsworth,
Joy, Joseph A., Ellsworth,
McGary, Noah S., Calais,
Maddox, Edwin P., Hancock,
Murphy, Samuel, Calais,
Potter, Allen A., Ellsworth,
Scribner, Benjamin F., Bangor,
Sumner, Elliot L., Amherst,

WAGONER: David Clark, Ellsworth.

ON SPECIAL DUTY OR DETACHED SERVICE: Privates: Sylvanus S. Boynton, Ellsworth, William George, Ellsworth, William D. Thompson, Ellsworth, and David A. West, Ellsworth, 3d N. Y. battery; Apollos Hunt, Ellsworth, and Roscoe G. Taylor, Amherst, amb. train; Melvin S. Jellison,

Clifton, and Theodore J. Lyman, Ellsworth, inv. det'ment; Bartlett Lynch, Ellsworth, wagon train; Augustus J. Trueworthy, Dedham, hosp. dept.

COMPANY C.

First Lieutenant, Frederick A. Hill, Machias, commanding company.
Second Lieutenant, John L. Pierce, Machias.

SERGEANTS.

First Sergeant, Bayles A. Campbell, Pembroke,
Albion H. Campbell, Bowdoin,   Benjamin R. J. Thaxter, Machias,
Theodore Hill, Jr., Machias.

CORPORALS.

William H. Schoppee, Machias,   Samuel O. Bryant, Machias,
William R. Blackman, East Machias, James S. Libby, Cape Elizabeth,
William K. Stiles, Columbia.

PRIVATES.

Allen, George H., Machias,   Balch, Horatio G., Lubec,
Bradbury, James T., Machias,   Calkins, Frank A., Trescott,
Chandler, Hersey B., Jonesport,   Conniff, Thomas, Machias,
Crane, James E., Machias,   Dagnin, Patrick, Trescott,
Deary, James, Machias,   Falkner, John R., Machias,
Foss, George E., Machias,   Foss, James A., Machias,
George, John, Machias,   Hennessy, Jeremiah, Whitneyville,
Hitchings, Ellis L., Cooper,   Lamson, William H., Baring,
May, Thomas, Boston, Mass.,   McCann, Alexander, Baring,
McGrill, Thomas, Machias,   O'Regan, Michael, Portland,
Perry, John, Machias,   St. Germaine, Joseph, Marshfield,
Tower, William H., Sackville, N. S., Triffet, George W., Wesley,
Whitman, Stillman H., Baring,   Wilder, Caleb B., Machias.
MUSICIAN: Henry H. Bowles, Columbia Falls.

ON SPECIAL DUTY OR DETACHED SERVICE: Captain Charles F. Stone, Machias, signal service. Corporals William Allen, Machias, and Charles W. Perkins, Wesley, invalid det'ment. Privates: James Black, Whiting, brig. h'dqrs; Gilbert L. Edgecomb, Topsham, and David Millay, East Machias, q'rm'r dept. brig. h'dqrs; Harrison N. Elliott, Machias, div. h'dqrs; William H Getchell, Marshfield, 3d N. Y. battery; Silas Smith, Machias, q'rm'r dept.

COMPANY D.

(Including 4 present sick.)
Captain, Reuel W. Furlong, Calais.
First Lieutenant, Henry H. Waite, Calais.
Second Lieutenant, Edward Williams, Calais.

SERGEANTS.

1st Sergt. George P. Blanchard, Calais, Warren Fraser, Calais,
Frank A. Barnard, Calais,   James A. Chamberlain, Calais.

CORPORALS.

Sumner Anderson, Robbinston,   Hosea Q. Morton, Lee,
John Chamberlain, Calais,   William W. Weeks, Calais.

PRIVATES.

Allen, William, Calais,   Bacon, James M., Calais,
Clayborne, Richard, Calais,   Condon, Michael, St. Stephen, N. B.,
Coy, William W., Calais,   Doyle, Joseph, Calais,

Doyle, William, Calais,
Foss, Charles H., Calais,
Glover, John, Bangor,
Hunter, Albert, Princeton,
McEver, Hugh, Calais,
Moore, James, Calais,
Roach, Alexander, Calais,
Scott, Charles A., Machias,
Smith, Alonzo, Calais,
Swarbrick, Henry, Calais,
Yates, John, Bangor.

Fogg, Hugh M., Calais,
Glidden, Amaziah, Calais,
Hanson, Alexander, Calais,
Mahoney, Thomas, Calais,
McLellan, George W., Baileyville,
Pardue, James, Calais,
Ross, Thomas, New York City,
Scullen, Thomas, Calais,
Stables, John, Calais,
Tibbetts, Thomas, Calais,

MUSICIAN: John Nichols, Calais.

ON SPECIAL DUTY OR DETACHED SERVICE: Privates: William Coyle, Jr., Machias, teamster; James McCurdy, Princeton, and Thomas Mackey, Halifax, N. S., 3d N. Y. battery; Elias Smith, St. Stephen, N. B., amb. corps; Horace C. Wilson, Calais, Stewart's battery.

COMPANY E.

(Including 2 present sick.)

First Lieutenant, James B. McKinley, Bucksport, commanding company.
Second Lieutenant, Fred B. Ginn, Orland.

SERGEANTS.

First Sergeant, Henry Tapley, Bucksport,
Waldo S. Richards, Prospect,
Charles P. Dorr, Bucksport,

Moses S. Wardwell, Orland,
Greenleaf A. Goodale, Bucksport.

CORPORALS.

James Stubbs, Jr., Bucksport,
Samuel J. Clark, Jr., Veazie,

Alfred Treat, Bucksport,
Stephen B. Wescott, Bluehill.

PRIVATES.

Archibald, James, Calais,
Blaisdell, Austin D., Orland,
Carroll, John, Bucksport,
Clay, George W., Bluehill,
Doak, Charles H., Bucksport,
Foss, Nathaniel, St. Albans,
Harriman, Charles M., Orland,
Hunnewell, Calvin, Alexander,
King, Joseph, Calais,
Leavitt, John, Calais,
McDonald, Archibald, Calais,
Morton, Robert A., Pittston,
Ripley, Thomas, Waite,
Trundy, Austin H., Dover,
Webb, John, Bucksport.

Arnold, Byron P., Orland,
Brennan, Michael, Bangor,
Carter, Albina H., Bluehill,
Colson, Edward L., Bucksport,
Dudley, Francis J., Bangor,
Foss, Thomas B., St. Albans,
Heywood, Sewall L., Bucksport,
Keefe, John, Ireland,
Lampher, Edward D., Bucksport,
Lurvey, Francis G., Tremont,
McGlaughlin, Ira, Calais,
Richardson, William A., Orland,
Smart, Charles, Bucksport,
Verrill, Moses S., Bucksport,

ON SPECIAL DUTY OR DETACHED SERVICE: Privates: John Kennedy, Bucksport, and Greenleaf G. Webster, Bucksport, nurses in regtl. hosp. John M. Rice, Hampden, adjt. clerk; Lewis P. Abbott, Bucksport, art'y brig. Charles L. Davis, Bucksport, Albert N. Eaton, Oldtown, Jerome Hyde, Corinth, and Arthur I. Saunders, Orland, detached as teamsters; John Karnes, Houlton, saddler art'y brigade.

COMPANY F.

Captain, Theodore Lincoln, Jr., Dennysville.
First Lieutenant, Simon Pottle, 2d, Perry.
Second Lieutenant, Isaac C. Campbell, Pembroke.

SERGEANTS.

William Shehan, Dennysville,
Josiah Sears, Pembroke,

James R. Hayward, Dennysville,
Thomas Matheson, Dennysville.

CORPORALS.

Reuben N. Maker, Cutler,
Charles C. Leighton, Pembroke,
Josiah C. Fish, Perry.

Joseph Gilmore, Pembroke,
Michael Donnelly, Pembroke,

PRIVATES.

Averill, Stephen W., Cooper,
Benner, Amos C., Edmunds,
Blanchard, William M., Charlotte,
Cameron, John H., Pembroke,
Collins, Patrick H., Calais,
Finney, Ira J., Pembroke,
Gilman, Warren, Meddybemps,
Hersey, Azor H., Pembroke,
Lawton, John A., Dennysville,
McCarty, William, Perry,
Morrison, Reuben H., Pembroke,
Owens, Geo. H., Pembroke,
Rice, Lyman F., Hampden,
Sawtelle, Albert, Cutler,
Vickery, William H., Crawford,
Welch, Thomas, Pembroke,
Wood, Matthew, Meddybemps.

Babcock, Charles C., Pembroke,
Benner, Washington, Dennysville,
Bridges, Almon H., Charlotte,
Campbell, Adna H. R., Pembroke,
Dudley, Freeman F., Dennysville,
Gardner, Willard E., Meddybemps,
Henry, William O., Eastport,
Larrey, James, Lubec,
Lincoln, Otis, Jr., Perry,
Merry, James E., Robbinston,
Nutter, George F., Crawford,
Redman, John, Meddybemps,
Robb, Hugh, Jr., Cooper,
Sweeney, John, Portland,
Ward, Amos, Pembroke,
White, Thomas, Pembroke,

MUSICIAN: Robert B. Teed, Pembroke.

ON SPECIAL DUTY OR DETACHED SERVICE: Privates: Isaac Gardner, Dennysville, amb. corps; James F. Mitchell, Boston, Mass., 3d N. Y. batt'y; Bela R. Reynolds, Dennysville, signal corps; John W. Reynolds, Pembroke, and John Stoddard, Pembroke, art'y brig.

COMPANY G.

(Including 1 present sick.)

Captain, George W. Burnham, Cherryfield.
First Lieutenant, Lindroff W. Smith, Steuben.

SERGEANTS.

1st Sergt., George A. Dyer, Franklin,
William Shaw, Cherryfield,

John McGregor, Eastport,
Horace G. Jacobs, Cherryfield.

CORPORALS.

Fonze G. Leighton, Columbia,
George H. Peva, Cherryfield,
Hillman L. Tibbetts, Addison,
Joseph Robinette, Portland.

Charles Frye, Machiasport,
Samuel C. Chase, Cherryfield,
Nelson C. Wallace, Milbridge,

PRIVATES.

Andrews, Malcolm, Harrington,
Bean, John, Robbinston,
Boyden, Samuel, Robbinston,

Andrews, Samuel, Cutler,
Bennett, Henry, Harrington,
Conners, Horatio B., Cherryfield,

Davis, William F., Steuben,
Dixon, Robert, Cherryfield,
Granger, James, Calais,
Hunter, Mitchell, Cherryfield,
Leighton, William, Steuben,
Marshall, William, Eastport,
Mills, George W., Kenduskeag,
Pillsbury, Thomas L., Sebec,
Small, Joseph, Steuben,
Smith, Ansel E., Ellsworth,
Taylor, Charles E., Robbinston,
Whalen, John F., Portland,
Willey, Alonzo C., Cherryfield,

Dean, Israel, Robbinston,
Fuller, Alfred, Brunswick,
Griffin, John, Eastport,
Laughlin, Lawrence O., Cherryfield,
Maddan, Rufus, Cherryfield,
McGregor, Charles W., Eastport,
Mills, Harry F., Kenduskeag,
Scott, Charles, Calais,
Small, Thomas J., Cherryfield,
Stewart, John E., Columbia,
Walton, George F., Calais,
Willett, Louis A., Bradley,
Wilson, George I. G., Cherryfield.

WAGONER: Robert Bailey, Portland.

ON SPECIAL DUTY OR DETACHED SERVICE: Privates: Nahum H. Davis, Cherryfield, and Patrick Flynn, Boston, Mass., 3d N. Y. batt'y; Stephen S. Leighton, Columbia, musician; Charles Lynch, Cherryfield, and Gilbert McKinnon, Portsmouth, amb. corps; John Taylor, Robbinston, nurse regtl. hosp.

COMPANY H.

(Including 1 present sick.)

Captain, Joseph G. Roberts, Corinth.
First Lieutenant, Solomon J. Morton, Providence, R. I.

SERGEANTS.

First Sergeant, William H. Coan, Dexter,
Israel Hodsdon, Corinth,
Elisha Eddy, Jr., Corinth,

Otis O. Roberts, Dexter,
Albert T. Severance, Dexter.

CORPORALS.

James L. Mitchell, Sangerville,
Hiram F. Safford, Dexter,
Henry G. Lane, Bucksport.

Ferdinand W. Merrill, Williamsburg,
John W. Pettengill, Corinna,

PRIVATES.

Babkirk, Wallace D., Baring,
Batchelder, Alonzo, Garland,
Bean, John H., Dexter,
Bulger, Joseph, Bangor,
Cooley, George H., St. Albans,
Frost, George F., Crawford,
Gilpatrick, Thomas W., Baring,
Herrick, William H., Corinth,
Lovell, Asa B., Abbot,
McKusick, Howard M., Foxcroft,
Moore, William H., Bangor,
Osgood, Wesley A., Garland,
Quimby, Jacob, Jr., ———
Senter, William H. H., Bangor,
Smith, Edward, Charleston,
Stafford, Frederick C., St. Albans,
Vickery, Charles B., Bangor,
Weaver, Charles S., Parkman,

Banks, Alexander, Pembroke,
Beale, George E., Hudson,
Bradshaw, Robert, Calais,
Chapman, Orville D., Sebec,
Fitzgerald, Charles, Dexter,
Fuller, Oliver J., Dexter,
Hammond, Joseph S., Parkman,
Lovejoy, Jonas P., Dexter,
McKusick, Charles F., Parkman,
Moore, Alonzo W., Bangor,
O'Keefe, Patrick, Calais,
Page, Erasmus E., Charleston,
Roundy, James H., Bangor,
Short, Edward, Bangor,
Smith, Upton T., Bangor,
Sutherland, James W., Bangor,
Walsh, Joseph, Calais,
Whittier, Lendall H., Kenduskeag.

MUSICIANS.

Joseph F. Getchell, Bangor,   Charles F. Tibbetts, Charleston.

WAGONER: Ivory Webber, Bangor.

ON SPECIAL DUTY OR DETACHED SERVICE: Privates: Charles Chase, St. Albans, cook; Charles Dyer, Dexter, Gilman W. Frost, St. Albans, and Charles L. Ray, Augusta, teamsters; George T. Gould, Dexter, and Alfred McDonald, Charleston, quarterm'r dept.; Harrison T. Norton, Dexter, butcher brig. h'dqrs; Sylvanus B. Steward, Monson, inv. dept.; Edward J. Sturtevant, Dexter, amb. corps; William H. Tinker, Trenton, signal corps; Andrew R. Wheaton, Crawford, 3d N. Y. batt'y.

COMPANY I.

(Including 3 present sick.)

Captain, Lycurgus Smith, Freedom.

First Lieutenant, James M. Norris, Milford.

Second Lieutenant, Henry H. Chamberlain, Presque Isle.

SERGEANTS.

First Sergeant, Calvin T. Livermore, Sebec,

Walter B. Jenness, Hermon,   Isaac Pratt, Oldtown,

James S. Knowlton, Liberty,   Thomas Templeton, Milford.

CORPORALS.

Alvin B. Hudson, Bangor,   Sylvester F. Lyon, Lincoln,

James M. Murphy, Calais,   Franklin J. Elliott, Sebec,

David C. Whitney, Lincoln,   Samuel Emery, Jr., Veazie.

PRIVATES.

Bean, Phineas F., Oldtown,   Blackman, Joseph C., Oldtown,
Buzzell, Justus J., Oldtown,   Clark, Clement M., Bangor,
Estabrook, Joseph W., Bangor,   Eye, James, Calais,
Gardiner, George, Sebec,   Glidden, Andrew, Barnard Pl.,
Goodwin, Benjamin F., Stetson,   Hinkley, Oscar E. W., Oldtown,
House, George W., Lee,   Johnston, Charles W., Oldtown,
Keen, William A., Chester,   Ladd, Edmund, Barnard Pl.,
Lane, James A., Bangor,   Leddy, John, Jr., Calais,
Lisherness, Benjamin C., Oldtown,   Reed, Joseph L., Cooper,
Robbins, Asa, Baileyville,   Sibley, William T., Oldtown,
Sleeper, Geo. W., Haverhill, Mass.,   Spencer, Green C., Milford,
Stanchfield, Chauncy, Milo,   Stinson, Leander C., Oldtown,
Tibbetts, Andrew J., Carmel,   Tibbetts, Ira B., Exeter,
Webster, William M., Lincoln,   White, William J., Bangor,
Wiggin, Asa G., Stetson.

MUSICIAN: John W. Davis, Portland.

ON SPECIAL DUTY OR DETACHED SERVICE: Wagoner William H. Brown, Milo, det'd wagoner. Privates: Alonzo Cilley, Bangor, and Edmund Leard, Oldtown, div. h'dqrs; Hezekiah B. Harris, Oldtown, and Hezekiah F. Harris, Oldtown, brig. h'dqrs.

COMPANY K.

(Including 2 present in arrest.)

First Lieutenant, Charles T. Witherell, Eastport, commanding company.

Second Lieutenant, Percival Knowles, Bangor.

SERGEANTS.

Thatcher Vose, Robbinston, George M. Corbett, Eastport,
John Homer Coy, Calais, John A. Gray, Eastport, color-sergeant.

CORPORALS.

Joseph Whelpley, Eastport, Levi Flood, Alexander,
Joseph H. Dermott, Eastport, Thomas Sharkey, Eastport,
Frank E. Johnson, Robbinston.

PRIVATES.

Bagley, Daniel W., East Machias, Brisley, Thomas D., Cooper,
Brooks, Thomas, Lubec, Brown, George, Centerville,
Black, George W., Jr., Cooper, Chester, Peter, Robbinston,
Connell, John, Halifax, N. S., Cunningham, Allan, Edmunds,
Daus, Frederick, Moncton, N. B., Denbo, Henry C., Lubec,
Drew, Calef N., Whitneyville, Dugan, Patrick, Eastport,
Dyer, George M., Brunswick, Foster, Alonzo F., Marion,
Hammond, Charles, Eastport, Hannemann, Emil, Eastport,
Hayman, Madison B., Robbinston, Jones, Thomas, Alexander,
Lander, James C., Corinna, Lesure, Ira, Calais,
Logan, David, Calais, McDonald, Peter, Pictou, N. S.,
McGoren, John, Saco, Morrill, George, Calais,
Myer, Henri, Moncton, N. B., Nelson, Charles, Calais,
O'Brien, William G., Lubec, Pike, Jeremiah K., Portland,
Potter, Fergus, Eastport, Sadler, Thomas J., Alexander,
Seeley, George W., Edmunds, Seeley, Solomon W., Edmunds,
Smith, Cyrus N., Charlotte, Warton, William, Buffalo, N. Y.

MUSICIANS.

Stephen Canfield, New York City, Frederick Tucker, Eastport.

ON SPECIAL DUTY OR DETACHED SERVICE: Privates: Daniel Apt, Jr., Eastport, regtl. quarterm'r dept.; Edmund Davy, Charlotte, and George McAllister, Robbinston, regtl. hosp.; Jacob S. Hinckley, Eastport, amb. corps; Andrew J. Potter, Eastport, officer's servant; Robert R. P. Potter, Eastport, butcher brig. h'dqrs; William Stinson, Portland, Mott's batt'y; George F. Simmons, Calais, div. h'dqrs; Stephen A. Winchell, Calais, with Lieut. McIntee, art'y brigade.

HISTORICAL SKETCH.

COMPILED BY CHARLES HAMLIN,

FROM OFFICIAL REPORTS AND OTHER DATA FURNISHED BY SURVIVORS
OF THE REGIMENT.

This regiment was composed of the troops largely from eastern Maine, and was organized as early as the month of June, 1861. The Brownville Rifles was the only old organized and drilled militia company that joined the regiment. This became company A. The other companies were newly formed. It rendezvoused at Portland, and was mustered into the United

States service July 15, 1861, with the following original
organization : —

FIELD, STAFF, AND NON-COMMISSIONED STAFF.

Colonel, Abner Knowles, Bangor.
Lieutenant-Colonel, Hiram Burnham, Cherryfield.
Major, Frank Pierce, Bucksport.
Adjutant, John D. McFarland, Ellsworth.
Quartermaster, Isaac Strickland, Bangor.
Surgeon, Eugene F. Sanger, Bangor.
Assistant Surgeon, John Baker, East Machias.
Chaplain, Zenas Thompson, Portland.

Sergeant-Major, Percival Knowles, Bangor.
Quartermaster-Sergeant, Thomas W. Porter, Bangor.
Commissary-Sergeant, J. W. Snowman, Bucksport.
Hospital Steward, Charles A. McQuesten, Bangor.
Drum-major, Z. Buzzell, Bucksport.
Fife-major, John Washburn, Foxcroft.

COMPANY OFFICERS.

Co. A.   Captain, Moses W. Brown, Brownville.
        First Lieutenant, Charles H. Chandler, Foxcroft.
        Second Lieutenant, Addison P. Buck, Foxcroft.
Co. B.   Captain, Isaac Frazier, Ellsworth.
        First Lieutenant, Otis W. Kent, Ellsworth.
        Second Lieutenant, Albert M. Murch, Ellsworth.
Co. C.   Captain, Benjamin F. Harris, Machias.
        First Lieutenant, John H. Ballinger, Machias.
        Second Lieutenant, Charles F. Stone, Machias.
Co. D.   Captain, Joel A. Haycock, Calais.
        First Lieutenant, Reuel W. Furlong, Calais.
        Second Lieutenant, Henry H. Waite, Calais.
Co. E.   Captain, Joseph Snowman, Bucksport.
        First Lieutenant, Benjamin J. Buck, Bucksport.
        Second Lieutenant, Virgil P. Wardwell, Bucksport.
Co. F.   Captain, William N. Lysett, Pembroke.
        First Lieutenant, John M. Lincoln, Pembroke.
        Second Lieutenant, Simon Pottle, 2d, Perry.
Co. G.   Captain, Ralph W. Young, Rockland.
        First Lieutenant, Frank C. Pierce, Augusta.
        Second Lieutenant, Hiram B. Sproul, Cherryfield.
Co. H.   Captain, Cyrus Brown, Corinth.
        First Lieutenant, Joseph G. Roberts, Corinth.
        Second Lieutenant, George Fuller, Corinth.
Co. I.   Captain, Albert G. Burton, Oldtown.
        First Lieutenant Henry Soper, Oldtown.
        Second Lieutenant, William H. Stanchfield, Milo.
Co. K.   Captain, Theodore Carey, Eastport.
        First Lieutenant, Thomas P. Roach, Eastport.
        Second Lieutenant, Charles Day, Eastport.

It will be remembered that when the troops were called from Maine upon the breaking out of the civil war and were being organized into regiments, they were allowed, until 1862, to elect all their officers themselves. When the Sixth regiment was organized it was permitted to elect its own officers. Their first choice for Colonel was Major Henry Prince, Paymaster U. S. A., but he declined, feeling that he would be obliged to give up his commission in the regular army. The next choice was Abner Knowles, Esq., of Bangor, a distinguished lawyer.

The regiment left Portland July 17th and arrived at Washington on the 19th, where it was stationed at Chain Bridge, on the Potomac, and where it was engaged in building "Battery Vermont" and a small earthwork. September 3d the regiment crossed the Potomac into Virginia and was engaged several weeks in fatigue and picket duty, and in building roads and bridges, digging pits and erecting forts. The strength and skill of these trained woodsmen were the admiration of the officers and men of other regiments. Later in the fall the regiment was pushed forward to Lewinsville, occupying Fort Griffin through the fall and winter. In March the regiment was assigned to Hancock's brigade of Smith's division, and joined in the advance on Manassas. After remaining in camp several days at Fairfax Court House, the regiment proceeded to Alexandria and joined the movement against Richmond by way of the peninsula. It arrived at Fortress Monroe March 25th, and encamped near Hampton.

PENINSULA CAMPAIGN.—The army having been organized into corps, Smith's division was assigned to the Fourth corps, under Gen. E. D. Keyes. April 4th the regiment broke camp and joined the advance of the army towards Yorktown, where they arrived in front of the enemy's works on Warwick Creek at 3 o'clock in the afternoon, and went into camp. In December, 1861, Colonel Knowles having resigned, Lieut.-Col. Burnham was promoted Colonel, Captain Chandler to Lieut.-Colonel, and Captain Harris to Major.

At an early hour on the morning of April 5, 1862, the Sixth regiment left their camp at Warwick Creek and proceeded to reconnoitre the enemy's works in that vicinity. Four prisoners were captured, when the rebels commenced shelling the skirmish line of the Sixth, during which several men were wounded. The regiment, however, held their position until the reconnaissance was completed by General Hancock, with Lieutenant Comstock of General McClellan's staff. A second reconnaissance immediately followed, in the direction of Lee's Mills, and was attended with similar success. Another reconnaissance on the 7th proved a creditable affair to the Sixth, and which elicited from General McClellan his thanks.

At the battle of Lee's Mills on the 16th the Sixth supported our artillery, and was exposed to a heavy fire. On the 24th another successful reconnaissance was performed by the Sixth to Warwick Creek, which was followed by another on the 28th to the same place, a brisk skirmish occurring on each occasion.

At the battle of Williamsburg, May 5th, the Sixth supported Kennedy's battery from 1 to 5 o'clock P. M., under a heavy fire from the enemy's artillery, until by order of General Hancock the four right companies of the regiment were placed in an earthwork in the centre of our lines, while the other companies were formed immediately on the left. Thus disposed, the regiment received the hottest of the enemy's fire, but not a man wavered; and the enemy was repulsed with great slaughter by the fire of the regiment.

A charge was made by the Union forces and successfully executed. Two days after the battle General McClellan made a complimentary address to the Sixth for its services on this occasion, as he did to all the other regiments which General Hancock commanded.

The battle at Garnett's Farm took place June 27, 1862. At an early hour in the morning of that day the Sixth regiment, which formed a portion of the First brigade, under the command of General Hancock, was ordered to the front, where a working party were engaged in throwing up an intrenchment. On their arrival Colonel Burnham took a position a short distance in the rear of the earthwork, on the right, near a piece of woods, with orders to hold it at all hazards. In front of this earthwork was a large, level field, at the upper portion of which were planted the enemy's batteries, while in General Hancock's rear, at a short distance, was a deep ravine, on the opposite side of which we had a masked battery of siege guns. About 9 o'clock A. M. the enemy appeared in force on the left, as if preparing for an attack. Upon this, the working party with the force which supported it withdrew across the ravine.

At 10 o'clock the enemy opened with his artillery, directing his fire, principally, at the woods where lay the Sixth, and at our own battery, which had been unmasked, and which after an hour's rapid firing silenced the enemy's guns, forcing the rebels to retire out of range. During this duel the Sixth had two men killed and one wounded. At sunset the enemy again opened his batteries, but as before he was shortly compelled to desist firing and retired. When it was quite dark in the woods a few shots from the enemy, instantly followed by a volley along our whole line, brought every man to his feet. The attack, though sudden, was not unexpected, and immediately the enemy's fire was returned, and with effect, as was afterwards ascertained, when he advanced a short distance from the woods, and after nearly an hour's rapid exchange of fire silently withdrew. This was a singular combat in many respects, as no enemy could be seen, and his presence was manifested only by the flash and crack of his guns, and by the whistling of his bullets over the heads of our men. During the engagements the Sixth expended over fifty rounds of ammunition on an average. Many muskets were rendered useless by fouling the bores, in consequence of which, as well as from the want of ammunition, they with the remainder of the brigade were relieved by another brigade, and Colonel Burnham was ordered to withdraw quietly with his regiment and return to camp where he arrived at a little past 1 o'clock. During the engagement the casualties were one man killed and 23 wounded; three of the latter died shortly afterwards.

Next morning at 4 o'clock Colonel Burnham received orders for an immediate move. Breakfast was hastily eaten, and the work of getting in readiness promptly commenced. It was evident that a movement towards James River was contemplated. Colonel Burnham was ordered to report the whole of his command to General Smith for fatigue duty, when the men were furnished with axes and ordered to cut down the skirt of the forest in which was located their camp, in order to afford a range for our artillery in case the enemy made an attack. This being accomplished, the regiment was ordered to the left of the felled trees, with the rest of the First brigade, when, as the order was being obeyed, a rebel battery opened a furious fire, which was, however, shortly silenced by one of our own batteries. The Sixth, however, succeeded in getting into position with the loss of one man who was seriously wounded. Another brief engagement shortly followed, ending in the repulse of the rebels with great slaughter, and no further fighting took place in that vicinity that day. Meanwhile the Sixth kept their original position, while the greater part of our forces made their retreat. During the night they were bivouacked in line of battle, every man with his rifle at his side, ready to spring to his feet and give battle in case of an attack. At last only the division remained to which the Sixth belonged, and their position was evidently a critical one, for, notwithstanding troops were within supporting distance, it was plain that, in case of an attack, they would bear the brunt of the battle. But the enemy did not choose to attack.

On the following Monday (29th) the division began to fall back, leaving a proper force of cavalry and artillery behind as the rear guard of the corps. Falling back about three miles, they came to a large field containing a strong force of our troops and an immense number of baggage wagons. Positions were taken in line of battle, while a halt of about three hours was made, during which the retreat went on. Resuming the line of march, the division moved along leisurely until they reached a field a short distance from Savage Station. There another halt was made ; the division was deployed in line of battle and stationed in the edge of a piece of woods, in which position they remained until about 2 o'clock, when, keeping up the line of battle, they passed through the woods to Savage Station and halted a little way beyond. On resuming the march, they proceeded about a mile, when a rattling fire of musketry in their rear showed that the enemy had attacked our forces at Savage Station. Forthwith the division was marched rapidly to the scene of action, and when they arrived the battle was raging furiously. The Second brigade (General Brooks') was hurled into the thickest of the fight, while the remainder of the division was stationed as a support. By order of General Hancock, the Sixth was marched half a mile through a piece of woods and took a position on the right, in order to prevent the enemy from outflanking. The position was an honorable as well as a dangerous one. Colonel Burnham at once established communication with the rest of the brigade, and awaited an attack on his right flank, which he doubted not would be made as the enemy subsequently threatened. After a sharp and bloody engagement the rebels were repulsed. The Sixth did not actively engage in the battle, although they were under a heavy fire and shared many of its perils.

At 9 o'clock the division was again put in motion, leaving Heintzelman's forces to hold, for a time, the hard-earned field. The Sixth was placed in advance; and as it was anticipated that the rebel cavalry might make a dash upon the road and attempt to cut them off, to lead the advance was certainly an honorable position. The four right companies of the Sixth were detached and thrown some distance ahead as an advance guard. Two squads, under non-commissioned officers, were thrown still farther ahead, to feel the way. In this order they marched until 3 o'clock on the morning of the 30th, when they crossed White Oak Bridge and took position on the heights beyond. Here a halt was ordered by General Hancock, and the men, totally exhausted by the severe labors of the past twenty-four hours, threw themselves on the ground and were almost instantly asleep. At 10 o'clock the following morning White Oak Bridge was blown up, and our troops were deployed in line of battle upon the heights, where they could meet the enemy advantageously in case he made his approach. By order of General Hancock, Colonel Burnham posted his regiment on the extreme right of the line, near a creek, where it was thought the rebels would attempt to cross and turn our flank. He threw out pickets and let his men rest in line of battle. The day was exceedingly hot and oppressive. The long hours passed slowly away, and up to noon there was nothing which indicated the enemy's approach. Suddenly, without the slightest premonition, the enemy opened a spirited fire with twenty pieces of artillery from the opposite side of the creek. For a while the cannonading was terrific, an unceasing shower of shell raining upon a portion of our lines. In obedience to orders, the Sixth was marched from the right to the centre of our lines, taking a position in the rear of the batteries within supporting distance. This position was maintained throughout the fight, which raged for three hours with great fury, and during which the Sixth had two men seriously wounded. At 4 o'clock the enemy's guns were silenced and he withdrew.

At 11 o'clock the division was again put in motion, the Sixth still keeping the advance. Colonel Burnham was instructed by General Hancock to use the utmost vigilance, as it was confidently anticipated that the enemy would make an attack with the intention of cutting him off. He therefore detached the four left companies of his regiment, and put them under the command of Major Harris. The night was spent in rapid marching, and the fortitude of the men, worn out as they were by the severe labors of the preceding three days, was taxed almost beyond endurance. It was exceedingly warm, and the men suffered terribly from a scarcity of water; but with ranks well closed the brave fellows kept pushing steadily on. Twice during the night General Hancock sent orders for the advance guard to move with the utmost watchfulness and care, and be at all times prepared for the attack which was apprehended.

At length, on the morning of July 1st, at a few minutes past 4 o'clock, they emerged from the swamps of the Chickahominy, in sight of the James River, at Turkey Bend. Here they remained until 11 o'clock, when the brigade was put in motion, while they were stationed to guard a road where it was thought the rebel cavalry might make its appearance. In this position they remained until 3 o'clock the following morning, when Colonel Burnham was ordered to move with the rest of the division down the river. Through a violent rain-storm they marched until 2 o'clock in the afternoon, when they arrived at Harrison's Landing and encamped in a large wheat-field, where they remained until the next morning, when they were again put in motion and marched about three miles from the James River, where they halted.

THE ANTIETAM CAMPAIGN. — On September 11th the Sixth formed the advance of our column, and in a skirmish with the enemy at the foot of Sugar Loaf Mountain drove him back without loss.

At the battle of Crampton's Gap, on the 14th, the Sixth participated, though they were not actively engaged. On the 15th Colonel Burnham took possession of a pass in South Mountain after a sharp skirmish, during which he captured four prisoners. The position was held until nightfall, when his command returned to their brigade.

At the battle of Antietam, on the 17th, the Sixth arrived on the field at 10 o'clock in the forenoon, and took position towards the right of our lines, where our forces had just fallen back after a most desperate charge. The enemy opened fire on them, but he was driven back.

FREDERICKSBURG. — The Sixth participated in the battle at Fredericksburg. On the morning of December 12th they crossed the Rappahannock at the lower bridge. At 10 o'clock they moved up and took position under the intrenched batteries of the enemy, who shelled them severely during the day. The Sixth was in the centre of our line of battle, and their position was an exposed one, as the rebel batteries on their right enfiladed them with ease and accuracy. This position was maintained three days, during which time the men all acquitted themselves creditably. On January 3d the regiment was encamped near Belle Plaine, Va.

MUD MARCH. — Early on the morning of January 20, 1863, the Sixth left camp near Belle Plaine, and proceeded to Banks' Ford, where General Burnside intended to cross the river and give battle to the enemy; but the mud being so deep, on account of a two days' rain, the movement was abandoned and the regiment returned to its former camp, arriving on the 23d.

February 2d the regiment proceeded to Potomac Creek and went into winter quarters, having been assigned to the Light Division, composed of five regiments and a battery, and commanded by Colonel Burnham after General Pratt had resigned.

In March Lieut.-Colonel Chandler resigned ; Major Harris was promoted to Lieut.-Colonel, and Captain Haycock to Major.

CHANCELLORSVILLE CAMPAIGN. — On the forenoon of April 28th the regiment under the command of Lieut.-Colonel Harris marched towards the Rappahannock, and that night was engaged in transporting and launching pontoons preparatory to crossing the river.   April 30th the regiment proceeded to Falmouth, and on the afternoon of May 1st proceeded across the river and took position in the front line of battle.   May 2d an advance of the entire line was ordered, and the regiment went forward in line of battle, the skirmishers driving the enemy before them, until darkness put a stop to the advance.   During the night the regiment was ordered to proceed to Fredericksburg, and soon after daylight on May 3d it formed in line of battle in front of the heights of Marye ; and in a few moments after 10 A. M. the order to charge was given, and the regiment advanced on the double-quick.

MARYE'S HEIGHTS AND BROOKS FORD.*— In the charge on Marye's Heights, May 3, 1863, the Sixth Maine regiment was a part of the Light Division, an organization of picked regiments belonging to Sedgwick's Sixth army corps.   The Light Division on this historic occasion was commanded by Colonel Hiram Burnham of the Sixth Maine.   The regiment was commanded by Lieut.-Col. Benjamin F. Harris.   The charge was upon the very heights where Burnside had been repulsed with such dreadful slaughter in December, 1862.

The regiment was drawn up in front of the formidable position to be carried, and just in the rear of a slight rise in the ground which protected it from the enemy's fire until the forward movement was made.   In its front was a portion of the 5th Wis. deployed as skirmishers.   The rebel works were held by troops under the Confederate General Early, whom the Sixth Maine had met and wounded in its celebrated charge under Hancock at Williamsburg.   The works were well manned, swarming with rebel infantry, and in the redoubts at the top of

* [The editors are indebted to Brevet Colonel Charles A. Clark, Adjutant of the Sixth Maine, for the particulars of the charge at Marye's Heights, and also that at Rappahannock Station.—C. H.]

the heights was posted the famous Washington Artillery from New Orleans. Against such a position, which many thousands of troops in solid column had failed to carry under Burnside, it seemed incredible that this little regiment of less than four hundred men at the time of the charge, hurled as a single line of battle, should ever meet with success.

But no man in the regiment was dismayed. Lieut.-Colonel Harris required every gun to be uncapped, and gave strict orders against firing a musket until the works at the top of the heights were reached. The men carried their muskets at " arms port." The command for the attack was given at about eleven o'clock A. M. The men dashed forward with unflinching will. As the line swept over the roll of ground in its front it faced and at once came upon the " slaughter pen" of Burnside's calamitous battle. At once the stone-wall at the foot of the heights, the rifle-pits higher up, and the artillery in the earthworks at the top blazed forth death in every form. Major Haycock, a brave and gallant officer, fell at the first fire. Many of the men were struck down at this point. The regiment swept across the " slaughter pen" and attacked and carried the old stone-wall at the point of the bayonet. Without firing a shot, the men pushed on to the rifle-pits further up, and there the most desperate and bloody part of the engagement occurred. The rebels, driven from the stone-wall, made a determined stand with their other forces at the rifle-pits. They were driven out after hot resistance, and a shout of victory went up from the assailing line.

It has been asserted that the bayonet was not used in actual contact with the enemy during the war. The Sixth Maine in this charge, both at the stone-wall and the rifle-pits, used the bayonet and nothing else. Decimated by bullets, pierced through and through by canister and case shot from the enemy's artillery, it wasted no time in firing so much as a volley, but using bayonets or clubbed muskets, fought its way on to the redoubts. More than 25 of the enemy were killed at these points by the bayonet alone, and many were wounded. Private George Brown of company K bayonetted two of the enemy in succession, and then as the resistance was obstinate, he brained a third with the butt of his musket. Captains Young, Gray and Ballinger fell at these points, cheering on their men and fighting like the brave and true men that they were.

As the enemy's line gave way at the rifle-pits, the regiment swept forward, following the retreating foe so closely that they never rallied, and rushing on, scaled the earthworks at the top of the hill, capturing many prisoners and seven guns from the Washington Artillery. In five minutes from the time when the regiment started on its charge, its colors waved over the enemy's strongest work and the victory was won. The loss was 128 men and officers killed and wounded, out of less than 400 who were present for duty. There were many instances of individual gallantry which it is impossible to mention. Official reports record that Color-Sergeant John A. Gray, who afterwards fell at Rappahannock Station, was the first man of the Union forces to enter the enemy's works, and that he planted his colors there while the rebel artillery-men were still at their guns and the infantry making a stubborn resistance.

To identify the ground over which this magnificent charge was made, it may be stated that, facing the heights, it was just at the right of where the National Cemetery is now located. The left of the regiment passed over a portion of the ground now made sacred as the last resting place of those who fell for their country, and the line of the regiment extended to the right across the little ravine which now separates the old Marye brick mansion from the present residence of Colonel Charles W. Richardson, who was then of the Confederate artillery, and who met the regiment with the remainder of the Sixth corps later in the day at Salem Church. The residence of Colonel Richardson stands upon the very ground where the principal Confederate redoubt was stormed and carried by the Sixth Maine, and where the guns of the Washington Artillery were captured.

At Salem Church, on the evening of the same day, the Sixth Maine met Longstreet's forces, which had been detached from Chancellorsville by General Lee to check the forward movement of Sedgwick's corps. But the regiment was not very actively engaged.

The following night of May 4th, at Brooks' Ford, the Sixth

Maine was the extreme right of Sedgwick's corps and held a position which commanded Sedgwick's pontoons at Banks' Ford further down the river, over which the corps was withdrawn that night. It was a position of honor but extreme danger. The regiment, as at Marye's Heights, was the forlorn hope of the corps. Its safety and its successful withdrawal depended much upon the Sixth Maine.

As the rest of the corps was gradually retired, the regiment became detached from all of the other Union forces, and at 11 o'clock was entirely surrounded by the swarming Confederates. It was attacked by overwhelming numbers in the belt of timber where it was posted, and repulsed the attack handsomely. Then as the rebels were re-forming for the capture of the regiment which had successfully assailed its strongest position the day before, the Sixth Maine was at the last moment successfully withdrawn over a precipitous bluff in its rear, and made its way along the water's edge down to the pontoons, where it recrossed in safety, being the rear guard of the corps. Before it made its appearance at the pontoons it was believed to have been annihilated and captured at Brooks' Ford, where it had been posted as a probable sacrifice to insure the safety of the remainder of the corps. Adjutant Charles A. Clark was awarded a special Congressional Medal of Honor for his bravery, gallantry and coolness in handling and extricating his regiment from its perilous situation, and in saving it from annihilation and capture in the absence of his superior officers who were disabled and separated from the regiment at that time.

On the 11th of May the Light Division was broken up and the regiments composing it assigned to different brigades, in consequence of the discharge from the service of two years' and nine months' troops. The Sixth was assigned to the Third brigade, First division, Sixth corps.

GETTYSBURG CAMPAIGN. — On June 9th the regiment, in conjunction with two other regiments of infantry under the command of General Russell, arriving at Kelly's Ford, dashed across the river, surprising and routing the enemy. The pursuit was hotly continued until reaching Brandy Station, where it joined General Ames' force of infantry and cavalry, and the command retired to the north bank of the river, having accomplished the object of the expedition, which was the gaining of correct information about the movements of the enemy.

The regiment participated in the long and fatiguing marches of the Pennsylvania campaign and arrived at Gettysburg, having marched thirty-six miles in twenty hours. The Sixth was not actively engaged in that memorable battle, but it occupied a responsible position upon the extreme left flank of the Union army until the last desperate charge of the enemy upon our left centre, when it was ordered to act as a reserve. In the close pursuit of the enemy, July 5th, the Sixth regiment was in the front, skirmishing not infrequently with the enemy's rear, and kept this exposed but honorable position until Lee succeeded in crossing into Virginia. July 12th, the regiment being in line of battle near Funkstown, Md., supporting the skirmish line of the division, Captain Furlong, with his company (D), numbering only 25, went beyond the skirmishers and succeeded in surprising a portion of the enemy's pickets, killing and wounding about 30, and capturing 32 prisoners without losing a man. July 19th the regiment crossed the Potomac on its way into the interior of Virginia. The day following Colonel Burnham was ordered to Maine on duty connected with the draft, and the command devolved upon Lieut.-Colonel Harris.

The following is from the official report of Brig.-General Russell, commanding brigade, dated August 20, 1863 : —

"On June 28th this command broke camp near Edwards Ferry, Md., at 4 P. M. With the exception of much heavy marching and the share taken by it in the battle of Gettysburg, of which a report was forwarded from these headquarters on the 3d inst., nothing of moment occurred until Sunday, July 12th, on the morning of which last-mentioned day we were encamped within about two miles of Funkstown, Md.

"At 4 : 30 o'clock on the morning of July 12th we broke camp and marched out about half a mile beyond Funkstown, where we halted and formed line of battle.

"The Sixth Maine Volunteers was placed on the left of the road (its right resting on the road) leading from Funkstown to Williamsport ; the 5th regiment Wis. Vols. in the rear of the

Sixth Maine ; the 119th regiment Penn. Vols. on the right of the road, its left resting on the road, while the 49th regiment Penn. Vols. was stationed by the general commanding the division about a third of a mile to the right of the road, to support a battery in position at that point. A strong line of skirmishers was thrown out in front of the Sixth Maine, and the skirmish line was advanced a little during the morning and some brisk firing ensued therein.

"About 2 P. M. Capt. R. W. Furlong, commanding company D, Sixth Maine, with his company, in a highly daring and gallant manner, broke through the skirmish line, and, without losing a man, surrounded and captured 33 enlisted men, a captain and a lieutenant, — an entire company."

The regiment was encamped near Warrenton, Va., during the month of August, until the first part of September, when it proceeded to Culpeper Court House, and was engaged in repairing the roads between Culpeper and Hazel River. After rendering the roads and ford passable, the regiment returned to Culpeper and remained there till October 5th, when with the corps it proceeded to the Rapidan, relieving the Second corps.

October 10th the regiment started on the return march with the army and arrived at a certain point near Centreville and Chantilly, where a line of battle was formed, and the army remained there a number of days awaiting the enemy's attack. While there about fifty men of the Sixth, being on picket, were attacked by about five hundred of Stuart's cavalry, but they handsomely repulsed them after a very spirited skirmish.

October 19th the regiment advanced to Warrenton, and on the 7th of November, 1863, the Sixth Maine marched with the remainder of the Sixth army corps from Warrenton to Rappahannock Station.

RAPPAHANNOCK STATION. — The regiment was commanded by Lieut.-Col. Benjamin F. Harris ; the brigade by Gen. David A. Russell. The right wing of the regiment was thrown out as a line of skirmishers to cover the advance as soon as the works of the enemy were approached, at about 1 o'clock P. M. Over an open plain, broken and undulating, the enemy were pressed back vigorously for three-quarters of a mile, until within close proximity to the works. The other battalion of the regiment was then deployed and advanced as skirmishers, making a double line of skirmishers with the men about six feet apart. There were present for duty about 250 men and 21 officers. The Confederate works were held by two brigades of infantry and a battery of artillery. The position was commanded by the old adversary of the regiment, Gen. Jubal A. Early.

At about dusk General Russell gave the command for the regiment, deployed as a double line of skirmishers as already stated, to assault the works of the enemy in front, and he joined in the charge himself. The regiment was joined in the assault by about eighty men of the Twentieth Maine, under Captain Walter G. Morrill of that regiment. Captain Morrill had formerly been a member of the Sixth Maine, and when he saw his old comrades making the perilous charge, he ordered his own skirmishers forward upon his own responsibility and entered the rebel works with the Sixth Maine upon its right; and was by his almost unexampled courage and gallantry of the greatest assistance in the achievement which followed.

As at Marye's Heights, the Sixth Maine uncapped their muskets and advanced at double-quick, entering the works of the enemy without firing a shot. There a fierce hand-to-hand conflict ensued, in which bayonet and sword thrusts were delivered and received, and in spite of the terrific fire which the regiment had faced in its advance, and the brave and determined resistance which it encountered upon entering the works, this little band was none the less successful; and there, in the face of overwhelming and astounding superiority of numbers sheltered behind rifle-pits and redoubts, it captured the enemy's guns, his redoubts and works, and holding the position which it had gained, nothing was left but for other forces to come up and receive the surrender of the defeated and disorganized enemy.

The regiment paid dearly for its gallantry. It lost in killed and wounded 16 officers out of 21 engaged, and 124 enlisted men, or very nearly fifty per cent of all the men who went into the engagement, and more than seventy-six per cent of the officers who led the assault. General Russell was also slightly wounded, and Captain Russell of his staff seriously wounded.

This brilliant charge of the Sixth Maine received the immediate support of its twin regiment, the 5th Wis., which entered the works at the right of the Sixth Maine skirmishers, shortly after they were carried by the skirmish line, and gallantly aided in repulsing the attempts of the enemy to recapture their works.

Further to the right Colonel Emory Upton, commanding the First brigade, promptly put into the fight another heroic Maine regiment, the Fifth infantry, commanded by Col. Clark S. Edwards, and also the 121st N. Y. These regiments carried at the point of the bayonet, the works in their front into which the rebel forces had swarmed from the rifle-pits and redoubts to the left; and great numbers of prisoners surrendered to the Fifth Maine. This movement completed the discomfiture of the enemy and resulted in the surrender of his entire forces. The official reports of this engagement are given in Volume 29, Part 1, of Rebellion Records.

Colonel Upton, page 592 of this volume, reports that about dusk he was ordered to bring two of his regiments rapidly to the front to help hold the redoubts already captured by the Third (Russell's) brigade, and he says: "The Fifth Maine and 121st N. Y., being in the front line, were immediately ordered forward. The Third brigade still holding possession of the works they had captured, General Russell directed me to dislodge the enemy from a rifle-pit to our right of the redoubt, and from which he maintained an enfilading fire. Everything being ready, the line advanced at quick time to within thirty yards of the works, when the order to 'charge' was given. The works were carried at the point of the bayonet, and without firing a shot. The enemy fought stubbornly over their colors, but being overpowered soon surrendered. The Fifth Maine in this charge captured two colors." [The Fifth Maine captured four colors as shown by Colonel Edwards' report.]

The report of Col. Clark S. Edwards, page 594 of the same volume, shows that his regiment, the Fifth Maine, lost in this engagement 7 killed and 28 wounded. The 121st N. Y. is shown by the same reports to have lost 25 officers and men, killed and wounded, out of 314 present. The losses of the 5th Wis. were 59 in killed and wounded. The detachment from the Twentieth Maine who volunteered to join in the charge under Captain Morrill, lost 7 in killed and wounded.

The Sixth Maine lost more than all of the other regiments engaged in this fierce encounter. Its losses, as already stated, were 16 officers killed and wounded out of 21 engaged, and 124 enlisted men killed and wounded out of about 250 engaged.

The official reports in the volume above referred to give full credit to all of these regiments. Gen. John Sedgwick, commanding the Sixth corps, says in his report, page 575 : "The officers and troops engaged in the assault, particularly Brig.-General Russell, Colonels Upton and Ellmaker, and the 5th Wis. and the Sixth Maine Volunteers, deserve the highest praise that can be bestowed upon a soldier."

General Sedgwick also issued a congratulatory order in which he said : "The assault of the storming party under General Russell, conducted over rough ground, in the full fire of the works, could not be surpassed in steadiness and gallantry. The brigades of Colonel Ellmaker and Colonel Upton and the troops of the Fifth corps which participated in the assault have nobly earned the admiration and credit of their comrades and commanders."

"The Sixth Maine and 5th Wis. volunteers, for carrying the redoubt; the 121st N. Y. and Fifth Maine, for taking the line of rifle-pits with the bayonet and seizing the enemy's bridge, deserve a special honor."

General Meade also issued an order of thanks to the forces engaged, page 576 of volume referred to.

General Wright, division commander, said in his report, page 586 : "To the 5th Wis. and Sixth Maine, comprising the storming party, belong the honor of carrying the enemy's works; while the Fifth Maine and 121st N. Y. subsequently carried the rifle-pits on the right most gallantly, taking large numbers of prisoners. I must not omit to mention about fifty men from the Twentieth Maine, belonging to the Fifth corps, under Captain Morrill, who joined the storming party, and by their dash and gallantry rendered efficient service in the assault."

As already stated, the assault was made under the immediate

command and supervision of Gen. David A. Russell, who personally knew what transpired. He was himself in the thick of the fight and was wounded. His report, pages 587 to 590 of the volume above mentioned, contains the statements not only of a commanding officer, but of an eye-witness. He says that five companies of the Sixth Maine were deployed as skirmishers until the command reached the immediate vicinity of the fortifications, which were assaulted, and he adds : "Here the order was given to deploy the remaining five companies of the Sixth Maine, to double the skirmish line, and, with that formation and the 5th Wis. as a support, to make a charge upon the enemy's works. Upon the command 'Forward, double-quick,' the skirmish line with their support dashed on in a style never surpassed by any troops. The ground was of a nature well calculated to check the impetuosity of a charge. Across the way as they advanced the storming column encountered a formidable ditch twelve or fourteen feet wide, some six feet deep, and filled with mud and water to an average depth of three feet. Across this they came to a plain, broken with stumps and underbrush, while before the skirmish line in the advance could be reached a dry moat or ditch had to be crossed, nearly as formidable as the obstacles already passed. But over every hindrance, in the face of a heavy fire of musketry and artillery, the storming party pressed on with bayonets fixed, and never pausing to fire a shot. The left wing of the skirmish line entered the smaller redoubt upon the enemy's right almost at the same time that the right of the skirmish line leaped into the larger redoubt and the rifle-pit extending from its left. The 5th Wis. were directed upon the stronger work, and the right of the skirmish line wheeled down to aid their left in the smaller work. A desperate hand-to-hand struggle ensued. The foe was overpowered and the works were ours. Staff officers were sent to Col. Emory Upton, commanding the Second brigade of this division, with orders to him to bring up speedily two regiments of his command, and the 121st N. Y. and Fifth Maine, under Colonel Upton, were led to the assault upon the rifle-pits with commendable coolness, steadiness and bravery. They overcame the enemy everywhere at the point of the bayonet, and resistance was speedily over."

General Russell, referring to the heroic men of the Twentieth Maine, says : "Much praise is due to Captain Morrill of the Twentieth regiment, Maine volunteers, who commanded a skirmish detail of 75 men from the Fifth corps. His men joined the left of the Sixth Maine, and on learning the works in their front were to be stormed, he called for volunteers to aid their sister regiment. Some 50 men responded to the call, and by their valor and dash rendered most efficient aid."

The flags captured from the enemy in this desperate engagement were, by General Meade, forwarded to the Secretary of War, in charge of General Russell, accompanied by an escort of men from the above-mentioned regiments who were engaged in the contest. The communication from Secretary Stanton acknowledging the receipt of the flags said : "The Secretary desires me to convey his thanks to the officers and men engaged in those operations of the army which reflect such high credit upon the skill which planned and the bravery which successfully executed them."

Thus the unexampled bravery of the men who achieved this brilliant success, and the importance of the engagement at that particular period in the war, were acknowledged and applauded by the highest Union authorities and the most renowned Union generals. This elation in the Union army was not without its corresponding depression in the ranks of the enemy. General Early and even General Lee made elaborate reports attempting to explain the defeat sustained by the Confederates.

The losses of the Sixth Maine were very severe. According to that great historical work, "Fox's Regimental Losses in the Civil War," the losses of the Light Brigade in its famous charge at Balaklava were much smaller than those of the Sixth Maine at Rappahannock Station in proportion to the numbers engaged. He says : "The Light Brigade took 673 officers and men into that charge ; they lost 113 killed and 134 wounded ; total, 247 or 36 7-10 per cent."

Now compare this with the loss of the Sixth Maine at Rappahannock Station. It lost more than 43 per cent of the entire forces which it took into action, while among the officers of that regiment engaged, the loss in killed and wounded was

more than 76 per cent, which, in battle, among officers, has
few if any parallels in modern warfare.

In the same volume Fox gives the following account of the
Sixth Maine at Rappahannock Station and Marye's Heights;
on page 77 he says :—

"In this affair (Rappahannock Station) there was another
display of that dash and gallantry which was so eminently charac-
teristic of the Sixth corps. At Rappahannock Station, Captain
Furlong of the Sixth Maine leaped over the enemy's works,
and after emptying his revolver fought with a clubbed musket,
swinging it round his head until he fell dead. After the battle
his body was found among a pile of dead, several of whom had
been killed by the blows of a musket stock. The Sixth Maine
and 5th Wis. distinguished themselves particularly in this
action, leading the storming party and carrying the works with
the bayonet only. It was a brilliant success, resulting not only
in a victory, but in the capture of a large number of prisoners,
small arms, artillery and battle-flags."

On page 128 of the same work it is said : "There was no
more brilliant action in the war than the affair at Rappahannock Station, Va., November 7, 1863. The Sixth Maine was
the most prominent in that successful fight, although gallantly
assisted by the other regiments of the brigade. The enemy,
about 2,000 strong, occupied an intrenched position ; the Sixth
Maine, with uncapped muskets, supported by the 5th Wis.,
stormed their works and, springing over them, were engaged
in a desperate struggle, some of the fighting being hand to
hand ; bayonets were freely used, and in one case an officer
thrust his sabre through an antagonist. Good fighting was also
done at other points of the line, the total result being a brilliant
victory, with large captures of men and material. But the
brunt of the fight fell on the Sixth. It lost 38 killed and 101
wounded, out of the 321 present in action ; and of 21 officers
engaged, 16 were killed or wounded. This was not the first
time that the Sixth had leaped the enemy's breastworks against
the blazing muzzles of a line of rifles. In the successful assault
on Marye's Heights, May 3, 1863, the flag of the Sixth was the
first to wave over the enemy's works. The regiment was in

the famous 'Light Division' of the Sixth corps and did not fire a shot during the charge, but carried the works with the bayonet; and mention is made of one man in the Sixth who bayoneted two adversaries, and then brained a third with the butt of a musket. The loss of the regiment in that battle was 23 killed, 111 wounded and 35 missing. Major Haycock and four captains were among the killed."

The above reference to the officer of the Sixth Maine "who thrust his sabre through an antagonist" at Rappahannock Station is thus mentioned in the official report of Major George Fuller: "Adjutant Charles A. Clark was also severely wounded while in the works bravely doing his duty, but not before he had driven his sword into his adversary." Major Fuller remained in command of the regiment after Lieutenant-Colonel Harris was frightfully wounded. For his special gallantry in this battle Sergeant Otis O. Roberts of company H received a medal of honor.

On page 128 of Fox's book it appears that the total enrollment of the Sixth Maine was 1,213, and its total number of killed and wounded during its term of service was 519, or certainly more than 50 per cent of the actual combatants of the regiment. The Sixth Maine is one of Fox's "Three Hundred Fighting Regiments."

At Spotsylvania Court House, in May, 1864, the regiment lost, as shown on page 446 of Fox's work, 135 men and officers on that bloody field.

Locust Grove and Mine Run. — The Sixth went on the 27th of November to the support of the Third corps, then engaged with the enemy at Locust Grove. The prompt arrival of the command turned the fortunes of the day, and the enemy quickly retired. The regiment returned with the army and marched back to its former camp near Wilber Ford, where it remained on January 1, 1864.

From the report to the Adjutant General of Maine we glean an outline of the subsequent history of the regiment: —

Grant's Campaign. — The regiment remained in camp at Brandy Station, Va., from January 1, 1864, until the opening of General Grant's campaign, May 4th. Two days after this date they, forming a part of the Sixth corps, were engaged in the battle of the Wilderness, but not in that portion of the lines that suffered a heavy attack. At the battle of Spotsylvania, on the 8th, they were engaged and lost a few men by the enemy's sharpshooters; also participated on the 10th in the attack and capture of the enemy's works, and being compelled to retreat suffered a loss of 125 men. On the 12th the regiment, numbering only 70 men, was under fire eight hours, supporting General Hancock's forces, and losing 16 men and officers, killed and wounded. The regiment was engaged in several skirmishes, experiencing no casualties until arriving at Cold Harbor, where for twelve days the men were employed in building fortifications, skirmishing and picketing, losing in all about 15 of their number. On the 14th of June the regiment started up the James River, reaching General Butler's headquarters on the 17th and Petersburg on the 20th, where it remained until the 10th of July, when, its term of service expiring the 15th, they were ordered to Washington, arriving on the 12th. Here they volunteered to remain thirty days in defense of the city, and were marched to Fort Stevens. However, on the 13th they were relieved, and on the 17th left for Portland, about 165 in number, where they arrived on the 22d, and were mustered out on the 15th of August. About 238 re-enlisted men and recruits, whose term of service had not expired, were temporarily organized into a battalion, afterwards assigned to the First regiment Maine Veteran Volunteers, which was made up from the same class of men with part of the officers of the Fifth, Sixth and Seventh Maine regiments, organized by Special Order 311, par. 47, War Dept., A. G. O., September 20, 1864. An account of the brilliant history of this veteran regiment is given in the last portion of the historical sketch of the Seventh Maine, appearing on another page, and is omitted here for that reason.

ROSTER.

The following information relating to officers of the Sixth Maine regiment is obtained from the Volunteer Army Register, published by the War Department August 31, 1865, and other reliable sources : —

OFFICERS AT MUSTER-OUT, AUGUST 15, 1864.

CAPTAINS: Theodore Lincoln, Jr., Aug. 2, 1862, — commissioned Major, not mustered; Levi L. L. Bassford, Aug. 25, 1862, — discharged Apr. 25, 1864, recommissioned June 4, 1864; Joseph G. Roberts, May 28, 1863; Lycurgus Smith, June 20, 1863; Frederick A. Hill, Dec. 22, 1863; Frederick B. Ginn, Jan. 1, 1864.

FIRST LIEUTENANTS: Addison P. Buck, Quartermaster, Sept. 20, 1861; Solomon J. Morton, May 28, 1863; Percival Knowles, Aug. 15, 1863; Horace S. Hobbs, Dec. 22, 1863; John L. Pierce, Dec. 22, 1863; Frank H. Burnham, Apr. 30, 1864; Charles P. Dorr, May 3, 1864; John C. Honey, May 3, 1864.

SURGEONS: William Buck, Aug. 15, 1863. Assistant Surgeon, Samuel B. Straw, Oct. 24, 1863.

CHAPLAIN: Moses J. Kelley, Aug. 14, 1862.

(Dates given above refer to rank or commission, those given hereafter refer to date of the event.)

DIED.

MAJOR: Joel A. Haycock, killed in action at Fredericksburg, Va., May 3, 1863.

CAPTAINS: Sewall C. Gray, killed in action at Fredericksburg, Va., May 3, 1863; John H. Ballinger, killed in action at Fredericksburg, Va., May 3, 1863; Ralph W. Young, killed in action at Fredericksburg, Va., May 3, 1863; Thomas P. Roach, May 28, 1863, of wounds received at Fredericksburg, Va.; Reuel W. Furlong, killed in action at Rappahannock Station, Va., Nov. 7, 1863.

FIRST LIEUTENANTS: John D. McFarland, Adjutant, Aug. 12, 1862, of disease; Lyman H. Wilkins, killed in action at Rappahannock Station, Va., Nov. 7, 1863; James B. McKinley, killed in action at Rappahannock Station, Va., Nov. 7, 1863; Henry H. Waite, Nov. 13, 1863, of wounds received in action at Rappahannock Station, Va.; Lindroff W. Smith, killed in action at Spotsylvania, Va., May 12, 1864; James M. Norris, killed in action at Spotsylvania, Va., May 12, 1864; George P. Blanchard, died Aug. 6, 1864, of wounds received May 10.

SECOND LIEUTENANT: Isaac C. Campbell, killed in action at Spotsylvania, Va., May 10, 1864.

SURGEON: Freeland S. Holmes, June 23, 1863, of disease.

PROMOTED AND TRANSFERRED OUT OF REGIMENT.

Colonel Hiram Burnham, Apr. 1, 1864, to Brigadier-General of Vols.; killed in action Sept. 28, 1864.

TRANSFERRED: Captains: Edward Williams, July 14, 1864, to Seventh Maine, and to First Veteran regiment, discharged for disability; Charles T. Witherell, July 14, 1864, to Seventh Maine, and Sept. 20, 1864, to First Veteran regiment, commissioned Major, not mustered;—brevet Major, Oct. 19, 1864, muster-out June 28, 1865; Alexander B. Sumner, July 14, 1864, to Seventh Maine, and Sept. 20, 1864, to First Veterans, pro. Major;—brevet Lieutenant-Colonel Apr. 2, 1865, discharged June 16, 1865.

First Lieutenant: Adjutant William H. Coan, July 14, 1864, to Seventh

Maine, and after to First Maine Veteran regiment, discharged for disability Oct. 29, 1864.

Second Lieutenants: Ira P. Wing, July 20, 1864, to Seventh Maine, and after to First Veterans, pro. to First Lieutenant, muster-out June 28, 1865; John B. Waid, July, 1864, to Seventh Maine, and after to First Maine Veterans, pro. to First Lieutenant and comm'd Captain, muster-out June 28, 1865.

DISCHARGED.

LIEUTENANT-COLONEL: Benjamin F. Harris, July 19, 1864, for disability, comm'd Colonel, not mustered,—Major Fourth regiment Vet. Reserve corps, brevet Brigadier-General Vols., Mar. 13, 1865.

MAJOR: George Fuller, July 28, 1864, for disability from wounds, commissioned Lieutenant-Colonel, not mustered.

ADJUTANT: First Lieutenant Charles A. Clark, Feb. 11, 1864, for disability from wounds, appointed Captain and A. A. G. of Vols., assigned to staff of Gen. Hiram Burnham, discharged U. S. service Oct. 26, 1864;—brevet Lieutenant-Colonel U. S. Vols., recipient of medal of honor.

CAPTAINS: Albert G. Burton, Sept. 10, 1861; Benjamin J. Buck, Nov. 6, 1863; George W. Burnham, May 20, 1864.

FIRST LIEUTENANT: Simon Pottle, 2d, by reason of wounds, Feb. 13, 1864.

SECOND LIEUTENANTS: Henry H. Chamberlain, by reason of wounds, Mar. 25, 1864; Horace G. Jacobs, by reason of wounds, May 28, 1864.

ASSISTANT SURGEON: John Baker, Oct. 26, 1861.

RESIGNED.

Colonel: Abner Knowles, Dec. 11, 1861.

Lieutenant-Colonel: Charles H. Chandler, Mar. 9, 1863.

Captains: Moses W. Brown, Sept. 16, 1861; Joseph Snowman, Jan. 15, 1862; William N. Lysett, July 13, 1862; Isaac Frazier, July 19, 1862; Theodore Cary, Feb. 12, 1863; William H. Stanchfield, Apr. 6, 1863; Charles F. Stone, Nov. 5, 1863.

First Lieutenants: Isaac Strickland, Quartermaster, Sept. 20, 1861; Otis W. Kent, Nov. 5, 1861; Henry R. Soper, Jan. 4, 1862; Virgil P. Wardwell, May 30, 1862; John M. Lincoln, Aug. 8, 1862; Frank C. Pierce, Sept. 26, 1862; Isaac Morrill, Dec. 10, 1862; Benjamin M. Flint, Mar. 24, 1863; Albert M. Murch, Mar. 29, 1864.

Second Lieutenants: Daniel W. Freeze, Jan. 12, 1862; Charles Day, Feb. 26, 1862; Milton Frazier, July 19, 1862; Hiram B. Sproul, July 20, 1862; George H. Norton, Aug. 2, 1862; George Roberts, Oct. 7, 1862.

Surgeon: Eugene F. Sanger, Mar. 19, 1862,—promoted Brigade Surgeon, brevetted Lieut.-Colonel U. S. Vols. Assistant Surgeons: George W. Martin, July 16, 1862; Alden Blossom, Apr. 16, 1863.

Chaplain: Zenas Thompson, July 15, 1862.

OTHERWISE LEFT THE SERVICE.

Major Frank Pierce, dis. Feb. 25, 1862.

MONUMENT

OF

SEVENTH MAINE REGIMENT.

The monument of the Seventh Maine regiment, designed by General Selden Connor, stands upon a high point east of Rock Creek and marks the position held by the infantry on the extreme right of the Union army. It consists of a large, rough granite bowlder upon which is carved, as if resting against it, the shield of the National coat-of-arms, its thirteen stars and stripes sculptured in relief, bearing in its centre the Greek cross of the Sixth corps.

ADMEASUREMENTS: Base, 6 feet 6 inches by 3 feet 3 inches by 2 feet; tablet, 5 feet 6 inches by 2 feet 3 inches by 7 feet. Total height, 9 feet.

Upon the cross and base are the following inscriptions:—

7TH

MAINE INFANTRY

3RD BRIG. 2ND DIV.

6TH

CORPS

JULY 3D, 1863.

SEVENTH MAINE REGIMENT,

THIRD BRIGADE, SECOND DIVISION, SIXTH ARMY CORPS,

AT THE BATTLE OF GETTYSBURG.

THE Seventh Maine Infantry was attached to the Second division, commanded by Gen. A. P. Howe, in Neill's brigade. It had been mustered-in August 22, 1861, and bore upon its flag the names of many of the greatest battles of the war. After Williamsburg, General McClellan had thanked it personally; after Antietam he had sent it home to recruit with a personal letter expressing admiration for its gallant charge on that field. After recruiting the regiment was consolidated into five companies, and by command of the War Department sent to the front under command of Lieut.-Col. Selden Connor, an accomplished officer. At the second battle of Fredericksburg the regiment lost heavily in the charge on Marye's Heights. Upon arriving at Gettysburg it numbered about two hundred officers and men. Lieut.-Colonel Connor was the only field officer with the regiment at this time (a). Major T. W. Hyde was serving on the staff of General Sedgwick, commander of the Sixth corps, as Provost Marshal General. He accompanied General Neill and Colonel Connor when they rode forward to reconnoitre the ground which the Seventh occupied.

July 1st the regiment was at Manchester with the Sixth corps. It began the march to Gettysburg about midnight, several hours later than the Fifth and Sixth Maine. The shoes of the men were badly worn by the marches through Virginia and Maryland, and this lack of proper equipment added greatly to the hardships of this, the longest and most memorable of its forced marches.

Marching the remainder of the night and all day July 2d until about 5 o'clock in the afternoon, the soldiers of Howe's

(a) Colonel Mason and companies A, E, G and H were at Portland, Me., at this time on recruiting service. The other six companies were at Gettysburg.

division at last arrived on the field. In spite of their hunger and weariness, at the sound of the battle they moved forward with a "dashing readiness" which excited the admiration of their superiors (a). Neill's brigade was stationed in line on Power's Hill, considerably in the rear of the Union centre. They were hardly in line before disheartened stragglers from the front began to arrive, with dismal prophecies of the fate of the army. But on the right was the reassuring spectacle of the fresh columns of the Twelfth corps moving into the battle, while the Sixth corps was already in position to stay the Confederate advance should it extend so far. The scene on the field at this hour was terrible. A great cloud of smoke hung over the brow of a slight eminence in front of the Seventh's line. Upon the black linings of this cloud continually played the flashings of a battery which was thundering at the enemy from the summit of the knoll.

How the Confederate advance was stopped before it reached the Sixth corps lines has been told already. That night the Seventh Maine had very little rest, being moved about from one threatened point to another. In the morning of July 3d, when the Twelfth corps returned to recover the works which they had left vacant the evening before to go to Sickles' assistance, Lieut.-Colonel Connor was sent with the Seventh Maine and 43d N. Y. to extend the line on the Twelfth corps' right, east of Rock Creek, in order to prevent a Confederate advance to the Baltimore Pike. This brought the two regiments on the extreme right of the Union line, connecting with the cavalry which was watching the country beyond.

After the two regiments had crossed Rock Creek and moved up to the Baltimore Pike, General Neill with his staff and orderlies and Lieut.-Colonel Connor rode up to the brow of a slight elevation in the front. From this point a small house was visible on an eminence beyond. General Neill suggested that it would be well to occupy the house. But immediately the party received a sharp volley from Confederate skirmishers in and around the house. At this General Neill said, "Exercise your discretion, Colonel Connor; I will bring up the rest of the

(a) Report of General Howe, 1863.

brigade." Colonel Connor saw a stone-wall lying about a hundred yards down a slight declivity in front. Telling his men that they would do well to make the distance as quickly as possible, he gave the command to advance to the wall. It was in this advance and in a sharp skirmish to the left that the Seventh met its loss at Gettysburg. Two men were killed or mortally wounded, and five wounded.

The orders to the regiment were to hold the line thus taken but not to force the fighting, as General Meade intended only to hold the line in this place. The Seventh remained there all day, sustaining a skirmish fire. It is at this position that the monument of the regiment stands.

On the morning of July 5th the regiment followed the direct line of Lee's retreat through Monterey Springs Gap to Waynesboro.

PARTICIPANTS.

FIELD, STAFF AND NON-COMMISSIONED STAFF.

Lieutenant-Colonel, Selden Connor, Fairfield, in the field commanding.
Adjutant, First Lieutenant Charles H. Hasey, Houlton.
Quartermaster, First Lieutenant Charles B. Whittemore, Augusta.
Assistant Surgeon, Ai Waterhouse, Gorham.
Chaplain, Collamore Purrington, Presque Isle.
Sergeant-Major, Perry Greenleaf, Mercer.
Commissary-Sergeant, Ferdinand S. Richards, Hallowell.
Acting Hospital Steward, Thomas B. Powers, Private Co. D.
ON SPECIAL DUTY OR DETACHED SERVICE: Major Thomas W. Hyde, Bath, as Provost Marshal of Sixth corps, staff of General Sedgwick; Colonel Mason and Surgeon Eveleth, also Quartermaster-Sergeant Hooper and Hospital Steward Sanborn, were on recruiting service at Portland, Me.

COMPANY A.

First Lieutenant Timothy Swan, Houlton, on duty with company C.
Second Lieutenant Church E. Gates, Calais, detached, acting A. D. C. on staff of General Howe, commanding division.
The company, as an organization, was at Portland, Me., on recruiting service.

COMPANY B.
(Including 2 present sick.)

Captain, James P. Jones, China.
First Lieutenant, Eli H. Webber, China.

SERGEANTS.

First Sergeant, John C. McKenney, Phippsburg,
Xantheus A. Withee, Norridgewock, John F. Doe, Berwick.

CORPORALS.

Crossman Timmins, Bath,
Eben Dinsmore, Newport,
George H. True, Sangerville.

Thomas Lowell, Cornville,
Michael H. Smith, Lincoln, color g'd,

PRIVATES.

Atkinson, Leroy, Hartland,
Bragdon, Francis M., Poland,
Butterfield, George W., Presque Isle,
Clouquet, Lewis, Skowhegan,
Davis, Addison R., Appleton,
Greenlaw, Eben, Calais,
Hunter, John J., Biddeford,
Linnell, John, Skowhegan,
Mahoney, John, Augusta,
McAlister, George, Tremont,
Morton, Abraham, Palmyra,
Parker, William B., Skowhegan,
Rowell, Silas R., Eddington,
Thompson, Frederick G., Hermon,
Wakefield, Alonzo B., Gardiner.

Austin, Charles L., Vassalboro,
Burkett, Miles, Appleton,
Clark, Timothy, Boothbay,
Crabtree, Samuel, Jr., Appleton,
Givins, Thomas, Portland,
Hawes, Charles B., Union,
Leavitt, Calvin, Oldtown,
Littlefield, George H., Skowhegan,
Malone, John, Houlton,
McAntee, Hugh, Tremont,
Noyes, David, Pownal,
Rogers, Thomas, Bath,
Stephens, Joseph G., Athens,
Thompson, John, Hermon,

WAGONER: Seward Merrill, West Gardiner.

ON SPECIAL DUTY OR DETACHED SERVICE: Privates: Timothy T. Merrow, Vassalboro, Cowan's 1st N. Y. batt'y; John C. Elders, Belfast, regt'l pioneer; Silas Hamilton, Phippsburg, hosp. nurse; Ira W. Hatch, Presque Isle, hosp. cook; Robert Jackson, Portland, div. provo. g'd; William McDonald, Tremont, teamster div. h'dqrs; Alanson H. Smith, Harmony, teamster supply train; Isaac T. Wills, No. 2, R. 2, amb. corps.

COMPANY C.

(Including 1 present sick.)

Captain, Henry F. Hill, Presque Isle.

[First Lieutenant, Timothy Swan of company A, temporarily with company B.]

Second Lieutenant, Charles Lowell, Oldtown.

SERGEANTS.

First Sergeant, Warren T. Ring, Oldtown,
Eli McLaughlin, Oldtown,

Ira F. Stinchfield, Lincoln.

CORPORALS.

Moses W. McKay, Oldtown,
Nyron B. Roberts, Lincoln,
Alvin E. True, Lincoln.

Francis Laing, Lincoln,
Calvin R. Gullifer, Oldtown,

PRIVATES.

Barker, Josiah H., Bangor,
Bicknell, Benjamin F., Bangor,
Carney, James, Oldtown,
Dutton, Folsom, Oldtown,
Hanscomb, Frank O., Milo,
Jacobs, Wayland F., Oldtown,
Littlefield, Joel, Winterport,
Neddo, Joseph, Oldtown,
Stetson, George A., Bangor,
Weymouth, Jacob, Oldtown,

Betters, Felix, Oldtown,
Burton, Hiram L., Bucksport,
Colson, Anson, Winterport,
Flemming, John, Lincoln,
Hull, Oliver, Oldtown,
Licum, Thomas, Deer Isle,
Neddo, John, Oldtown,
Oakes, Benjamin, Oldtown,
Turner, Adrian E., Lincoln,
Wooster, Daniel M., Glenburn.

ON SPECIAL DUTY OR DETACHED SERVICE: Privates: Thos. Doughty, Oldtown, William McKenney, Oldtown, and William W. Pomroy, Cornville, teamsters div. h'dqrs; Thomas Fish, Oldtown, and William W. Harris, Oldtown, teamsters at brig. h'dqrs; Madison C. Rowe, Oldtown, amb. corps.

COMPANY D.

Captain, Joseph E. Walker, Portland.
Second Lieutenant, George H. Buker, Bangor.

SERGEANTS.

Eben True, Westbrook,   Edward Sisk, Martinsburg, N. Y.

CORPORALS.

Joseph F. Call, Richmond,   Benjamin F. Gay, Bath,
William H. Dunbrach, Halifax, N. S., on color-guard.

PRIVATES.

Batchelder, Albert J., W. Gardiner,   Brown, Josiah S., Linneus,
Call, Fred, Calais,   Cameron, Joseph, Hallowell,
Coolbroth, George F., Portland,   Cooledge, Roscoe, Dixfield,
Coolen, James, Southport,   Crowell, James, Bath,
Dillman, Jeremiah, Ireland,   Foote, John B., So. Berwick,
Foster, James E., Portland,   Gammon, William A., Presque Isle,
Grover, Abraham, Oldtown,   Hannaford, Joseph, Presque Isle,
Hodsdon, William B., Brunswick,   Jackson, Randall W., Bridgewater,
Kenniston, Horace, Conway, N. H.,   Kimball, Andrew J., Patten,
King, Richard, Portland,   Lombard, Thomas C., Litchfield,
McLaughlin, Amos K., Dennysville,   Marr, Jared, Georgetown,
Meader, George, Litchfield,   Palmer, Moses, Jr., Patten,
Peavey, Jasper W., York,   Pembroke,Charles P.,Gageboro, N. S.
Piper, George W., Hallowell,   Ridlon, Charles E., Saco,
Ridlon, Nathaniel, Saco,   Rounds, Charles H., Portland,
Rush, William B., Lewiston,   Syphers, Albion, Littleton,
Wadsworth, Frank, Houlton,   Wayland, James, Saco,
Williams, James D., Houlton.

ON SPECIAL DUTY OR DETACHED SERVICE: Wagoner William Barrows, Blanchard, at corps h'dqrs. Privates: Joseph E. Babb, West Gardiner, and James Nugent, Portland, regtl. orderlies; William A. Brown, Brunswick, and Scott Sally, Saco, musicians; Charles Bennett, Bath, corps h'dqrs; George R. Coney, Oldtown, regtl. mail carrier; Latimas C. Dillingham, Biddeford, brig. joiner; Robert Dingley, Hallowell, company cook; Benjamin F. Flanders, Gardiner, Conway's battery; George W. Haskell, Weston, mule driver; Thomas King, Bath, amb. corps; Simeon Knights, Portland, and John Powers, teamsters div. supply train; George L. Larkey, Calais, John Shields, Linneus, and Edward C. Snell, Houlton, regtl. hosp. nurses; Dennis Mahoney, Boston, Mass., regtl. tailor; Harvey Mitchell, Biddeford, regtl. marker; John Mullen, Houlton, teamster brig. h'dqrs; Thomas B. Powers, Presque Isle, acting hosp. steward.

COMPANY E.

Second Lieutenant Augustus F. Emery, Fairfield, on duty with company K. The company as an organization was at Portland, Me., on recruiting service.

COMPANY F.
(Including 3 present sick.)
Captain, Stephen C. Fletcher, Skowhegan.
First Lieutenant, George McGinley, Houlton.

SERGEANTS.
First Sergeant, Marcellus Vining, Windsor,

Henry Welch, Madison,
Jeremiah H. Moore, Kennebunk,

Romandel Fuller, New Vineyard,
Robert T. Crommett, Canaan.

CORPORALS.
Lot Sturtevant, Monmouth,
Chas. H. Waterhouse, Cape Elizabeth, John Oakes, Cape Elizabeth,
Charles W. Jones, Portland,
John Hart, Portland,

Woodbury D. Hatch, Cape Elizabeth,
Horatio P. Fernald, Albion,
John N. Messer, Waterville.

PRIVATES.
Adams, David, Westbrook,
Bluefield, Simon, Portland,
Brown, John H., Bangor,
Carey, Martin, Lancashire, Eng.,
Clark, Zebulon, Haynesville,
Cook, John A., Embden,
Cripps, Amos C., Portland,
Eames, Danville, Madison,
Ezekiel, Henry I., Portland,
Foster, Israel A., Portland,
Frazier, Peter, Solon,
Granville, Henry, Boston, Mass.,
Gustens, John R. B., Ireland,
Holmes, Alonzo S., Bath,
Jones, William, Rockland,
Leeman, George B., Abbot,
Mabury, Grinfield B., Casco,
Messer, Orrin R., Athens,
Palmer, Albion D., Thomaston,
Prince, Henry L., Bath,
Shorey, Franklin D., Palermo,
Smith, James W., Fayette,
Stevens, Charles B., Portland,
Sullivan, James, St. John, N. B.,
Trundy, William T., Portland,
Young, Samuel, New Portland.

Adams, William, Cape Elizabeth,
Brown, Henry J., Bath,
Buswell, George L., Dexter,
Clark, Frederick, London, Eng.,
Coffee, Dennis, Portland,
Cowen, Henry, Bangor,
Daggett, Wilson D., Hodgdon,
Ellis, William, Sidney,
Field, Eben M., Windham,
Franks, Henry D., Rockingham,
Graham, John, Ireland,
Green, George A., Portland,
Hayes, John, Portland,
Humes, Alexander, Eastport,
Lee, John T., Cape Elizabeth,
Lent, James, Richmond,
Maxwell, John B., Canaan,
Morrill, DeWitt C., Bangor,
Pocket, John, Bath,
Reynolds, Simeon O., Presque Isle,
Smellay, Alphonzo B., Portland,
Spaulding, Alonzo, Carratunk pl.,
Stevens, Edward L., Belfast,
Thompson, Elbridge G. C., Presque I.,
Washburn, Charles E., China,

MUSICIAN: Oramandel Robinson, China.

ON SPECIAL DUTY OR DETACHED SERVICE: Privates: Isaiah Allen, Lincoln, q'rm'r dept.; John R. Begg, Portland, regtl. teamster; George Henderson, Hartland, comp'y cook; Berthur Lyons, Hodgdon, regtl. pioneer.

COMPANY G.
This company as an organization was at Portland, Me., on recruiting service.

COMPANY H.
This company as an organization was at Portland, Me., on recruiting service.

COMPANY I.
(Including 3 present sick.)

Captain, John B. Cook, Lewiston.
First Lieutenant, Franklin Glazier, Jr., Hallowell.
Second Lieutenant, Hiram Church, Presque Isle.

SERGEANTS.
First Sergeant, John E. Bailey, Frederickton, N. B.,
Henry F. Daggett, Foxcroft, Charles H. Church, Presque Isle,
Henry M. Eaton, Presque Isle, Loran B. Wade, Presque I., color-sergt.

CORPORALS.
Thomas B. Rose, Presque Isle, Willis T. Jordan, Presque Isle,
James Phair, Presque Isle, Albion Hardy, Hampden,
Josiah Smith, Garland.

PRIVATES.
Briggs, Duncan, Buxton, Chandler, Julius C., Mapleton,
Clark, Robert, St. John, N. B., Condon, Sumner H., Bangor,
Conlen, Edward, Worcester, Davis, Richard, Bangor,
Drew, George, Jr., Portland, Eddy, Charles H., Clifton,
Gilchrist, David, King's Clear, Gilman, Henry H., Presque Isle,
Hardy, William B., Abbot, Hodgkins, George W., Stetson,
Lander, Charles, Monticello, Leeman, Hibbard S., Dexter,
Littlefield, Thomas D., Winterport, McCollor, James, Madison,
McIntire, George, Hodgdon, McNeal, Stephen A., Presque Isle,
Morrison, Samuel R., Bath, Mower, Benjamin F., Greene,
Plaisted, William S., Presque Isle, Reed, Oscar W., Oldtown,
Snow, Charles, Hampden, Staples, Greenlief B., Glenburn,
Stevens, Rufus K., Hudson, Stinson, Warren B., Albion,
Walker, James, Woodstock, Worcester, Charles S., Glenburn.

MUSICIANS.
Jeremiah Getchell, Presque Isle, Reuel D. Worcester, Hermon.

ON SPECIAL DUTY OR DETACHED SERVICE: Corporal Lewis E. Hardy, Hampden, div. provo. guard. Privates: Hiram Baker, Presque Isle, corps h'dqrs; Edward F. Garland, Winslow, amb. corps; Shepley C. Gerow, Hodgdon, regtl. pioneer; John Isham, Bangor, div. train master; Benjamin F. Mann, Providence, and Adelbert G. Webster, Bucksport, regtl. hospital nurses; Harrison Wescott, Ashland, company cook.

COMPANY K.
(Including 1 present sick.)

First Lieutenant, Andrew M. Benson, Oldtown, commanding company.
[Second Lieut. Augustus F. Emery of company E on duty with K.]

SERGEANTS.
Silas E. Hinckley, Monmouth, James W. Libby, Leeds,
Charles H. Hinckley, Monmouth, Charles C. Ellis, Monmouth.

CORPORALS.
James W. Estey, Calais, color guard, Richard Sculley, Castleton, N. B.,
Charles E. Plummer, Monmouth, Edward Cobb, Yarmouth,
Dennis Harris, Greene, Allison C. Crockett, Abbot.

PRIVATES.

Broad, Augustus, Unity,
Clements, Charles, Portland,
Dunning, Robert A., Brunswick,
Farrar, Warren, Wellington,
Ingalls, George B., Bridgton,
Luce, Albert A., Burnham,
Murray, William, Portland,
Plissey, Wesley, Fort Fairfield,
Smith, William H., Edmunds,
Sullivan, James, Houlton,

Carr, Samuel M., Liberty,
Conners, George W., Littleton,
Fargo, Elisha S., Augusta,
Howard, Bradford T., Litchfield,
Johnson, Capen W., Houlton,
Morgan, George, Lewiston,
Myrick, Edward, Unity,
Savage, William H., Solon,
Stone, Joseph H., Chelsea,
Thibadeau, Albert B., Houlton.

ON SPECIAL DUTY OR DETACHED SERVICE: Captain John W. Channing, Fairfield, corps h'dqrs. Second Lieut. Henry W. Farrar, Bangor, General Sedgwick's staff. Privates: Howard A. P. Reynolds, Burnham, Cowan's battery; Melville Marshall, Bradford, pack mule driver; Hiram S. Pollard, Fairfield, amb. corps; Thomas P. Smith, Oldtown, regtl. hosp. nurse.

REVISED REPORT OF CASUALTIES.

COMPANY B.

Private Thomas O'Neal, wounded July 3.

COMPANY C.

Private Folsom Dutton, missing July 2.

COMPANY F.

Private Martin Carey, wounded July 3.
Private Charles H. Waterhouse, wounded July 3.

COMPANY I.

Corporal Willis T. Jordan, wounded July 3.

COMPANY K.

Corporal Richard Sculley, wounded July 3; died of wounds July 4, 1863.
Private Wesley Plissey, wounded July 3.
Private William H. Smith, wounded July 3; died of wounds Sept. 1, 1863.

HISTORICAL SKETCH.

BY BRIGADIER-GENERAL SELDEN CONNOR.

The Seventh Maine regiment of infantry was mustered into the service of the United States at Augusta, August 21, 1861. The companies composing it represented many sections of the state: two were from Aroostook county, two from Kennebec, two from Penobscot, and one from each of the counties of York, Cumberland, Sagadahoc and Somerset. Other counties contributed largely to their rolls.

The following was the original organization : —

FIELD, STAFF AND NON-COMMISSIONED STAFF.

Colonel, Edwin C. Mason, Portland.
Lieutenant-Colonel, Selden Connor, Fairfield.
Major, Thomas W. Hyde, Bath.
Adjutant, Elijah D. Johnson, Lewiston.
Quartermaster, John K. Russell, Skowhegan.
Surgeon, Thomas C. Barker, Deer Isle.
Assistant Surgeon, Francis M. Eveleth, Presque Isle.
Chaplain, James A. Varney, China.

Sergeant-Major, Andrew W. Fuller, Winslow.
Quartermaster-Sergeant, Charles B. Whittemore, Augusta.
Commissary-Sergeant, Franklin Glazier, Jr., Hallowell.
Hospital Steward, Albert L. Frye, Lewiston.
Drum-major, Alonzo Guinam, Houlton.
Fife-major, George M. Bodge, Naples.

COMPANY OFFICERS.

Co. A. Captain, John W. Freese, Houlton.
First Lieutenant, Timothy Swan, Houlton.
Second Lieutenant, Joseph G. Butler, Presque Isle.

Co. B. Captain, James P. Jones, China.
First Lieutenant, William L. Haskell, Poland.
Second Lieutenant, Eli H. Webber, China.

Co. C. Captain, Charles D. Gilmore, Bangor.
First Lieutenant, John A. Bachelder, Oldtown.
Second Lieutenant, Albert P. Titcomb, Lincoln.

Co. D. Captain, Henry A. Dalton, Readfield.
First Lieutenant, Henry S. Hagar, Richmond.
Second Lieutenant, George E. Morse, Bath.

Co. E. Captain, John W. Channing, Fairfield.
First Lieutenant, Albert A. Nickerson, Fairfield.
Second Lieutenant, Augustus F. Emery, Fairfield.

Co. F. Captain, William M. Cushman, Portland.
First Lieutenant, James M. Andrews, Biddeford.
Second Lieutenant, Joseph E. Walker, Portland.

Co. G. Captain, Charles H. Gilman, Portland.
First Lieutenant, George B. Knight, Portland.
Second Lieutenant, Simeon Walton, Cape Elizabeth.

Co. H. Captain, Edward H. Cass, Bangor.
First Lieutenant, Thomas S. Cates, Bangor.
Second Lieutenant, Henry C. Snow, Hampden.

Co. I. Captain, Henry Rolfe, Maysville.
First Lieutenant, Hovey Austin, Presque Isle.
Second Lieutenant, Charles H. Hasey, Houlton.

Co. K. Captain, Greenleaf K. Norris, Monmouth.
First Lieutenant, Granville P. Cochrane, Monmouth.
Second Lieutenant, John B. Cook, Lewiston.

Colonel Mason was a Captain in the 17th U. S. infantry, stationed at Fort Preble. Lieut.-Colonel Connor had seen service in the 1st Vermont Volunteers.

The Seventh left Augusta on the 23d of August, under command of Major Hyde, Colonel Mason not having received authority from the War Department to accept a commission in the volunteer service, and the Lieutenant-Colonel having received leave of absence for a fortnight. On the way orders were received to stop in Baltimore, where it encamped at Rullman's beer garden and then at Patterson Park.

On the 5th of September Lieut.-Col. Thomas H. Marshall, Fourth Maine, was commissioned Colonel of the Seventh, and within a few days thereafter assumed command. September 16 the Seventh was ordered to Murray Hill, where it threw up the earthwork called Fort Marshall after its Colonel. Colonel Marshall was taken ill with fever soon after joining the regiment, and died on the 25th of October. He was an energetic and able man, and the soldierly aptitudes he showed in the short time he was in command of the regiment indicated that he would have distinguished himself if his life had been spared.

On the day of Colonel Marshall's death the regiment broke camp and changed its station to Washington. At Washington the Seventh was encamped at Kalorama and was in General Casey's provisional brigade. On the 7th of November the regiment marched into Virginia and joined the Third brigade of Gen. W. F. ("Baldy") Smith's division, near Lewinsville.

Colonel Mason assumed command on the 10th of November, under his commission of November 5, which he had been authorized to accept. During the month or more between the beginning of the illness of Colonel Marshall and Colonel Mason's assumption of command, the regiment was under the command of Lieut.-Colonel Connor.

Through the autumn and following winter the regiment, in common with its fellows of the army of the Potomac, was constantly employed in drill, guard, picket and fatigue duty. Officers and men were animated by the highest *esprit de corps*, and the regiment soon took rank among the first in point of discipline and drill. It suffered severely during that period from that great scourge of new levies — measles. The disease broke out at Baltimore, and continued its ravages to such an extent that the "Dead March" was heard through the camp with painful frequency.

A "reconnaissance in force" by the division soon after the affair which the Penn. "Bucktails" had at Drainesville greatly elated the regiment with the prospect of meeting the rebels, and caused it to turn out with unwontedly full ranks. Heroic aspirations were turned to disgust when, after a march of a few miles, a halt was made and a drill was ordered by the brigade commander to keep the men from straying.

A new company, nearly a hundred strong, Stephen C. Fletcher of Skowhegan, Captain, Lyman M. Shorey of Skowhegan and L. Byron Crosby of Albion, Lieutenants, joined the regiment the first day of February and became company F in place of the old F, disbanded.

On the 9th of March the army of the Potomac was set in motion. The Seventh marched out from its winter home, "Camp Griffin," and bivouacked with its new *tentes d'abri* near Fairfax Court House until the 14th, when it marched to the outskirts of Alexandria. On the 23d Smith's division embarked on transports at Alexandria for Fort Monroe, where it arrived and disembarked the next morning. Several reconnaissances served to furnish the troops practice for the serious work now imminent.

The advance of the army began April 4. The left column bivouacked that night at Young's Mills, "relieving" a force of the enemy who kindly left their camp-fires for the use of their successors. The next day the Seventh had the honor to form the skirmish line for the column. The country was thickly wooded for the most part, and the regiment justly won great credit for the skill with which their difficult duty was performed. Whenever an open space was reached the line was found to be perfect. Lieutenant Swan and Musician Brown on the extreme right lost touch with the line in passing some obstruction and fell into the hands of an outlying force of the enemy. The line was brought to a halt on the edge of a field by shells from the rebels' works a few hundred yards distant, on the opposite side of Warwick Creek. Joseph Pepper, a private, was cut in two by a shell — the first of the many brave fellows destined to fall in the Peninsula campaign. The Seventh occupied their line in skirmish order, and as a close support to the regiment that relieved them, for more than two days, exposed to the shells and canister with which the enemy raked their ground from time to time. It was the expectation of the troops in the front line that an assault would be made as soon as the army could be formed for that purpose ; but none was attempted. Siege operations were begun and weeks of wearing fatigue duty followed. Reconnaissances by our forces and the enemy's were frequent occurrences. On one occasion the enemy's skirmishers took advantage of a slashing, that had been made by " superior authority " through the woods in front of our picket-line for the protection of the camp, to make a near approach to the line and shoot down several of the Seventh who were on picket. Lieutenant Morse pursued with the support, took one prisoner and drove the enemy back.

Sunday, May 4, Captain Ayres fired his usual morning gun from his advanced works without eliciting the usual response. He crossed the creek and found the rebel camp deserted. The Third brigade was at once ordered to cross and ascertain, if possible, the whereabouts of our troublesome neighbors. Nothing was found in the camp but many defiant messages, written on boards and stuck up conspicuously. On entering the rebel camp the horse of Colonel McKean, 77th N. Y., stepped on something that made a sharp crack which on investigation proved to have been caused by the primer of a shell. Fortunately the shell was not ignited. The Lieutenant-Colonel of the Seventh was sent with two companies to reconnoitre along the road taken by the retreating enemy. The detachment found a dozen or more torpedoes buried in the ruts of the road and near bridges ; one was so arranged that pressure against a pole across the path leading to a spring would have exploded it. The work of detecting and unearthing these dangerous contrivances was so thoroughly done that no one was injured by them.

The division broke camp and started out on the road taken by the enemy as soon as willing hands could make the necessary preparations. The close of the day's march at near nightfall found it on the field of Williamsburg, where Stoneman had already begun fighting. Orders were given to prepare for a moonlight assault; but the evening was dark and rainy, and there was no moonlight and no assault. The following day, the 5th, the Seventh and the 33d N. Y. were detached from the Third brigade, the commander of which, Gen. J. W. Davidson, was then temporarily absent, and attached to the First brigade, Gen. W. S. Hancock. With these two regiments and the Sixth Maine, 5th Wis. and 49th Penn. of his own brigade, and Wheeler's and Kennedy's batteries, the latter commanded by Lieutenant Cowan, Hancock made a detour to the right until the York River was almost reached, and then turned to the left and soon came to a stream where a broad dam of earth had made a considerable pond. At the opposite end of the dam and close to it, an earthwork on a commanding hillock made a formidable looking *tete du pont*. If that were manned by even a small force it would be a very difficult matter to make a crossing. Evidently it was not known whether it was occupied or not, because the brigade was halted until scouts signaled that it was deserted. As soon as the field on the opposite bank was reached, the brigade was formed in a square with the artillery in the centre, and in this formation advanced until halted on an elevation crowned with an earthwork, from which the rebel work, Fort Magruder, was in plain sight at the distance of less than a mile. The brigade was on the flank of the enemy and within sight and sound of the raging battle. But Hancock's force was too small to undertake a flank attack on a force of the enemy strong enough to withstand the attacks that had been made upon it by Hooker's and Kearny's divisions of our troops, reinforced by others. He availed himself, however, to the utmost of his advantageous position by sending the batteries supported by the Sixth Maine, 5th Wis. and 49th Penn., to an advanced position whence they made it very uncomfortable for the enemy within and about the fort. Presently the skirmishers became engaged with those of the enemy. The Seventh was to the right of the redoubt with skirmishers out to protect the flank, and a part of the 33d N. Y. was in the redoubt on its left in line. For some hours the regiment had nothing to do but watch the batteries and skirmishers. All at once the scene changed. Two gray lines of infantry broke by the flank out of the woods in front of our batteries and on their right, crossed the field at double-quick and bore down on our front line. The two batteries and three infantry regiments of the advanced line kept their position and maintained their fire until the enemy was close upon them, and then fell back in order and slowly, firing in retreat as if on drill. When near the line held by the Seventh and the 33d N. Y. they halted, collected their skirmishers and took position to the left of the redoubt. The line was withdrawn a few paces by General Hancock in order that the men might be protected by the crest from the flying bullets. When the advanced line of the enemy, a good deal broken by the vicissitudes of their advance, was but a few yards distant, Hancock gave the order to charge. The eager line sprang forward with a yell, and the crest was at once crowned with a hedge of gleaming bayonets. By Hancock's order it came to a halt and opened a fire which speedily turned the on-coming enemy and strewed the plain with his dead. The skirmishers and flankers of the Seventh and 33d N. Y. in the woods on the right intercepted a large number of the retreating rebels and took them prisoners. The enemy's loss was over 500. The 5th No. Car. was practically annihilated. Its colonel reported that it was " so reduced as to be inefficient."

When the Seventh was at dress-parade the evening of the 6th, General McClellan with his large and brilliant staff appeared before it and took position in front of the colors. Arms were presented, and the General, after acknowledging the salute, addressed the regiment as follows : —

Soldiers:—

I have come to thank you for your bravery and gallant conduct in the recent battle. On this little plain you and your comrades yesterday saved the army from a disgraceful defeat. You would have deserved credit had you been forced to retire before the overwhelming odds that were brought against you. Your steadiness and the boldness of your attack were brilliant in the extreme. You have done honor to your country and your state, and in their gratitude they will accord to you the praise so justly your due. Continue to exhibit the same courage and the same soldierly qualities, and the triumph of our cause will surely and speedily arrive. In recognition of your merit you shall hereafter bear the inscription "Williamsburg" on your banners. Soldiers, my words are feeble, but from the bottom of my heart I thank you.

The address was "reported" immediately after dress-parade by the collaboration of Lieut.-Colonel Connor and Major Hyde.

The comradeship of the Seventh and the 33d N. Y. in this action caused a strong feeling of mutual regard to spring up between the two regiments. Thenceforth to the end they were "twin regiments." When the 33d was mustered out at the expiration of its two-years' term of service the three-years' men remaining petitioned to be assigned to the Seventh. Greatly to the regret of the Seventh the assignment to a regiment from another state was not deemed expedient. The men of the 33d, recruited mainly along the Erie Canal, were, like Sir William of Deloraine, "good at need."

The Seventh participated in a lively affair at Mechanicsville on the 24th of May, in which the brigade drove the enemy from the town and took possession of it. It was under fire in support of a battery, but was not actively engaged.

Smith's division crossed the Chickahominy after the battle of Fair Oaks and occupied a position on the right, next to that stream. The camp of the Seventh was on the hill, overlooking the swamp through which the Chickahominy runs and the slopes beyond it. Here the Seventh remained for more than three weeks doing picket duty, making earthworks, bridges and roads, and suffering severely from the diseases consequent upon camping and doing soldiers' duties in a highly malarious district and living on an unsuitable diet. The indications were that the army of the Potomac was considered to be "in a bad box." The bands were not allowed to play, and every care was taken that quiet should be observed throughout the camps. The prospect of a vigorous advance was the least of all. Altogether it was a gloomy and dispiriting period which was happily broken on the 26th of June by McCall's repulse of the sudden attack made on him at Mechanicsville on the north bank of the Chickahominy, by the Confederates under Gen. A. P. Hill.

The next day the battle of Gaines' Mill was fought by Porter and McCall against the bulk of Lee's army.

Towards evening the Third brigade was ordered to cross the river and reinforce Porter. As soon as the brigade was in line the rebels created a diversion by opening a heavy artillery fire on it and attacking the front then held by Hancock's First brigade. The only success they won was the countermanding of the order to reinforce Porter. The Seventh was ordered to the earthwork to support a battery. The next forenoon it lay in line on a wooded slope a few yards behind the picket line which confronted the enemy's pickets across a field, half a gunshot distant. Although the pickets stood out boldly, not a shot was fired on either side. An attack was expected at any moment and the Seventh eagerly waited for it, every man with his thumb on the hammer of his rifle. None was made during its tour of duty; but scarcely had it been relieved by other regiments of the brigade than a determined onslaught was made upon the line. It was bravely met and the enemy was turned back with great loss. The 33d N. Y. bore the brunt of the assault. In this affair the Seventh again supported the battery at the main line. Several of its men were wounded by bullets from the attack on the advanced line. While the brigade was at the front on the morning of the 28th their camp was riddled and plowed by a cross-fire of artillery from the front and from Gaines' Hill on the flank, across the Chickahominy. At an early hour on the 29th the retreat began. The scene at Savage Station was enough to demoralize a less stout-hearted army; commissary, quartermaster's and ordnance stores were being destroyed by wholesale to prevent their being of use to the enemy. The crackling of the flames and the explosion of shells sounded as if a battle were in progress. Troops were thronging into the field from the abandoned front, and uncertainty as to the proximity of the enemy or the quarter from which he might be coming seemed to prevail. In the midst of this confusion the order and discipline of the troops were not shaken in the least. Sumner's corps and Smith's division of Franklin's corps formed line by division at half distance in the edge of the field upon which the enemy was expected to appear in pursuit.

General Davidson, commanding the Third brigade, and Colonel Mason of the Seventh both succumbed to the terrific heat and were taken to the rear in ambulances.   Colonel Mason did not recover from the 'effects of this stroke and return to the regiment until after the battle of Antietam.   As no enemy came in sight after hours had passed and the rest of the army were well on their rearward march, Smith's division was ordered to resume the march.   The Seventh had marched a mile or more when sharp firing from the field it had just left indicated that the left of the line was engaged.   The Seventh was detached from the brigade and ordered back as a reinforcement.   Arriving on the field it met General Brooks, to whom it had been ordered to report, at the head of his Vermont brigade, resuming the march after repelling the attack of a superior force, and was by him directed to turn back and take up its march again.

After a long and fatiguing night-march along a narrow and rough road, the bridge at White Oak Swamp was crossed and destroyed in the early morning, and as each regiment was assigned its position, officers and men, overcome with fatigue and want of sleep, fell to the ground without looking for " soft spots " and instantly became oblivious of all war's alarms.

At noon, while the regiments of the brigade were resting on the wooded hillside where they had bivouacked, the enemy suddenly opened with thirty-one guns, firing " salvos by battery." Fortunately none of the Seventh were injured.   The enemy had given no sign of his presence, and this sudden and fierce cannonading found the division without formation to meet an attack from that quarter ; but dispositions were soon made.   The Seventh was placed in line in the edge of the woods and remained there until midnight, when it again took up the march towards the James.   While waiting here for the attack which was momentarily expected, but did not come because the enemy could not cross the swamp without bridges and in face of the artillery and skirmish fire which met them whenever they made an attempt, the battle of Glendale was raging to the left.   The thick woods shut the combatants from sight, but the sounds that arose from the field told clearly how the fight was going.   First the " rebel yell " indicated a charge ; then came the rattle of musketry as the foemen clashed; and next a brief silence, followed by three ringing Saxon cheers, which conveyed to their distant comrades as distinctly as a despatch from headquarters that Kearny and Hooker had met the enemy and rolled him back.

Another night march — wearied men and horses sleeping as they moved mechanically along the dusty road — and Smith's division, which had brought up the rear, broke from the forest into the lush clover of a broad field on the James at 5 o'clock in the morning. Again every man dropped down where he halted for the two hours of sleep which was all that could be permitted, many waking with heads aching from exposure to the broiling sun. The division moved out across Turkey Creek, and went into position on a small plantation in the midst of the woods, and there remained guarding the right of the line and unmolested, while the battle of Malvern Hill was fought by the left of the line, aided by the gunboats in the James. The division withdrew that night, the Third brigade bringing up the rear and destroying the bridges, and the next morning marched to Harrison's Landing.

The encampment at Harrison's Landing was not a pleasing period in any sense. The army of the Potomac had no consciousness of having been whipped, and yet it had been withdrawn from its objective point and placed on the defensive. All the loss of life, the toil and suffering of the campaign seemed to have been without compensating result. The Seventh had 500 men at Williamsburg and on the 12th of August only half as many for duty.

Under date of August 7, 1862, the commanding officer wrote in a personal letter: "The other day I was officer of the day for the division, and I left the command of the regiment with the only captain for duty." And under date of August 12: "The army has sent away all its sick. My regiment has barely 250 since our sick left us. I have but two captains present for duty — Cook and Fletcher — and nine lieutenants." The loss was caused principally by disease consequent upon the hardships of the campaign and the malaria of the swamps. Many officers were granted leave of absence, thus entailing double duty on those remaining with the regiment. There was much picket, guard and fatigue duty. Earthworks were thrown up and heavy guns mounted. All the regiments of the brigade had been compelled to leave their camps and camp equipage at Golding's Farm. The Seventh took away but two camp kettles, so that the men had to make their coffee in tin cups and fry their meat in tin plates.

The order to break camp and prepare for the march was a welcome one. The Sixth corps moved out August 16, and after two days of rapid and toilsome marching through heat and dust crossed the Chickahominy by a pontoon bridge two thousand feet in length in the evening of the 17th; thence it continued the march by way of Williamsburg and Yorktown and arrived at Fort Monroe the 21st, and took transports which anchored off Alexandria the evening of the 23d. The following morning the troops disembarked and went into camp a short distance from the city, and there remained until the 29th, when the corps marched to the assistance of Pope. The horses of the Seventh not having arrived from Fort Monroe, Lieut.-Colonel Connor, who was not well enough to march on foot, turned over the command to Major Hyde, who had joined at Fort Monroe, and went to the hospital at Alexandria. The march of the Second division of the Sixth corps to the relief of hard-pressed comrades was tardily begun and deliberately made. The division met the defeated army at Centreville and returned to the vicinity of Alexandria with it.

On the 6th of September the Sixth corps crossed the Potomac by Long Bridge and began the march through Maryland. It sauntered through a delightful country at a beautiful season and on the 14th encountered the enemy at Crampton's Gap. The Sixth corps climbed the mountain and drove the enemy from his strong position. In this affair the Third brigade supported the Second, and was not actively engaged though it had its share of the artillery fire that met the attack. It encamped at the head of the pass, and on the 17th marched to the field of Antietam, a distance of ten miles, the roar of the battle growing louder and grander as the field was approached. It had no sooner arrived than it was sent forward on the right of the line, where some of the fiercest fighting of the day had already taken place. The brigade advanced successfully, the principal loss falling on the 33d N. Y. and the 77th N. Y. on the right of the line. The Seventh lost a few men while driving a force from a building on the left. The brigade held its advanced position, some regiments suffering from an artillery fire. The Seventh was partially protected by bowlders and lost but few men ; but its turn for sacrifice was close at hand.

Between 4 and 5 o'clock in the afternoon Col. William H. Irwin of the 49th Penn., commanding the brigade, ordered Major Hyde, commanding the Seventh, to take his regiment and drive away the enemy's sharpshooters who, from the vicinity of Piper's barns near the Hagerstown pike, were annoying a battery in front of the line of the Third brigade. The proposed point of attack was evidently the rebel centre, a strong position held by a large force. The order seemed so rash that Major Hyde required it to be repeated in the hearing of the regiment before obeying it. The regiment went forward, crossing the Sunken Road filled with the enemy's dead, and charged at double-quick down a valley leading to Piper's barns. The valley proved to be a veritable *cul-de-sac*. The rebels from behind stone-walls on the right and front poured a heavy fire upon the devoted little band, and as it still went on, obliquing to the left, Major Hyde, riding in front of his line, saw a superior force waiting at the " ready," whereupon he moved the regiment by the left flank back past Piper's barns from which the rebels had fled, and thence, seeing a large force at the double-quick aiming to cut him off, he fell back through the orchard, where the enemy poured several volleys into the Seventh and then charged. Here the heaviest loss was met. From the fence in rear of the orchard the stricken regiment checked their pursuers with a terrible fire, and enabled Major Hyde, with the aid of Sergeant, afterwards Captain, Hill and his sabre bayonet, to make way for his horse through the tall picket fence. The survivors had no ammunition left. The enemy's dead proved that it had been expended with good effect. General Hyde, in his "Following the Greek Cross," from whose account the foregoing is taken, says : " I then formed the regiment on the colors, sixty-five men and three officers, and slowly we marched back towards our place in line. The batteries by Dunker Church opened on us at first, but I guess they thought we had pounding enough, for they stopped after a few shots. But our main line rose up and waved their hats, and when we came in front of our dear comrades the Vermonters, their cheers made the welkin ring. General Brooks had told their colonels when they begged to follow our charge : 'You will never see that regiment again.'" General Hyde says that he had fifteen officers and two hundred and twenty-five men in the morning, and he came out of the charge with three officers and sixty-five men.

Colonel Irwin, who would not probably have given the order but for the warping of his judgment by his drinking habits, was relieved of the command after the battle. The remnant of the Seventh was assigned to easy duty as guard at headquarters until ordered to Maine to recruit, in pursuance of orders referred to in the following communication :

HEADQUARTERS ARMY OF POTOMAC,
CAMP NEAR SHARPSBURG, MD., October 4, 1862.
To His Excellency, the Governor of the State of Maine:—
SIR:— In view of the reduced and shattered condition of the Seventh regiment of Maine volunteers, the result of arduous service and exposure during the campaigns on the Peninsula and in Maryland, I made on the 2d inst. a special application to the War Department that the regiment should be sent to report to you in Maine, that it might be recruited and reorganized under your personal supervision. I yesterday received the necessary authority, as you will observe by the copy of Special Order No. 271 from these headquarters, enclosed herein. I send the regiment to you for the purpose indicated. I beg that when this purpose shall have been accomplished, that the regiment may be ordered to report to me with all practicable despatch.
In returning this gallant remnant of a noble body of men, whose bravery has been exhibited on every field almost in the campaigns cited, to the State whose pride it is to have sent them forth, I feel happy that it has been in my power to signify, even in this insufficient manner, my appreciation of their services and of their value to this army, and I will venture on the latter account to ask your Excellency's best endeavors to fill at once their diminished ranks, that I may again see their standard in the army of the Potomac.
I am, with much respect, your obedient servant,
GEO. B. MCCLELLAN, *Major-General, U. S. A.*

The regiment had a warm reception as it passed through New York City and Boston. On the Sunday it remained in Boston a dinner was given to the officers at "Parker's" by the city government and the men were entertained at the Hancock House. It was enthusiastically welcomed on its arrival in Portland. The 17th Regulars, the Twenty-third, Twenty-fifth and Twenty-seventh Maine regiments under General Francis Fessenden, and many civic organizations escorted the veterans to the City Hall, and they were there addressed in glowing terms by Governor Washburn in the presence of the city government and as many citizens as the hall could contain.

Headquarters were established at Camp Lincoln, near Portland, and recruiting parties were sent to different parts of the state. Recruiting for old regiments was not easy at that period of the war; even the urgent request in McClellan's letter to the governor, for "His Excellency's best endeavors to fill at once the diminished ranks" of the Seventh, did not seem to effect the desired result. On the 21st of January, 1863, Colonel Mason received an order from the War Department to consolidate the men of the Seventh into a battalion of four or five companies of the maximum strength and send it to the front under command of the lieutenant-colonel. Companies B, C, D, I and K were strengthened by the transfer to them of all the men available, and the battalion so constituted, and numbering two hundred and thirty men, left Portland the 25th and after some delay in Washington waiting for transportation took a steamer for Belle Plaine. The little battalion was most heartily welcomed by all the regiments of "the old brigade" and was treated with special consideration by the new brigade commander, Gen. Thomas H. Neill, and by Gen. A. P. Howe, the successor of "Baldy" Smith as division commander.

The usual routine of camp life in winter quarters ensued. Major Hyde was detached from the battalion and assigned to duty on the staff of General Franklin, commanding the left grand division of the army of the Potomac, as acting Inspector-General, and later, when that division organization had been discontinued, he was appointed Provost Marshal General on the staff of General Sedgwick commanding the Sixth corps. The battalion was in splendid condition, and frequently received the commendation of the brigade and division commanders and the inspecting officers.

The spring campaign of the army of the Potomac opened the 28th of April. The Sixth corps broke camp that day and moved to the banks of the Rappahannock, the men carrying eight days' rations. Early the following morning Russell's brigade of the First division crossed the river in pontoons at Franklin's Crossing, surprised the enemy's pickets and held the south bank of the river while the engineer corps laid pontoon bridges at their leisure. On the evening of the 2d of May the Sixth corps crossed the river, and at an early hour the following morning advanced up the river to the vicinity of the city of Fredericksburg, and halted on the plain fronting Marye's Heights, Cemetery Hill to the right nearer the city. Skirmishers contested the advance towards Marye's Heights, and artillery on the heights directed its fire upon every exposed line and group. The Light Division was about to move out from the town against the works on Cemetery Hill. General Howe ordered General Neill and his regimental commanders to assemble around him that he might give them personal instructions for the advance he was about to order. This assemblage of mounted officers made a conspicuous group, and the gunners of the Washington Artillery at once made a target of it; shells fell all around in uncomfortable proximity; an orderly's horse was killed, and the practice was improving at every shot; under these conditions the final orders were very hastily given, and accepted without much inquiry as to details.

The first line of the division was composed of the Seventh Maine, 33d N. Y. and 21st N. J., preceded by the 77th N. Y. as skirmishers. The formation was rapidly made and the line went forward on the run, the guns on Marye's Heights doing their best to check their advance. The Seventh was on the right of the line. When near Cemetery Hill, — to the right of the advancing line, — the Adjutant-General of the brigade ordered the commanding officer of the Seventh to make that his objective point, presumably in order to assist by a flank attack the Light Division which was then assailing the front of the works towards Fredericksburg. Wheeling to the right, the Seventh went down a steep bank and crossed a morass which was swept by canister from the guns on Marye's Heights. Here

Adjutant Butler was killed, and many others fell, killed or wounded by the deadly enfilading fire. Halting a moment to dress the line, somewhat broken by the losses and the struggle through the deep mud, the regiment climbed the hill and found the works on its top deserted, and its recent occupants being pushed across the fields beyond by the victorious Light Division. Not a moment was lost in going to the aid of the other regiments of the Third brigade which had kept on towards Marye's Heights. The Seventh marched down the hill in a road running in the direction of the heights, crossed another at the foot of the hill which was swept by the fire of the guns that had just caused it to suffer so severely, formed line at the foot of the heights and pushed on towards the sound of musketry. Half way up the hill Col. L. A. Grant, commanding the Vermont brigade in the Second division, was met, eagerly looking for reinforcements. "I am glad to see you, Colonel," was his salutation to Lieut.-Colonel Connor, "we are having a hard time to hold our ground." In his report Colonel Grant says: "The 33d N. Y., Colonel Taylor, also came up about the same time and went into the engagement. The Seventh Maine, Lieut.-Colonel Connor, soon followed, and the enemy were entirely driven from that part of the hill. * * * I desire to bear testimony to the gallant manner in which Colonel Taylor and Lieut.-Colonel Connor came to our aid." The Vermont brigade was on the left of the Third brigade and may have struck the enemy before the 33d N. Y. became engaged. The Seventh went forward as rapidly as possible through the brush, passed a brass piece which had been captured, and came out on the left of the 33d N. Y., which was exchanging fire with the enemy across an open space. The effectives of the 33d seemed few in comparison with the dead and wounded with which the ground was strewn. The twin regiments cheered and the *Windsors* of the Seventh soon relieved the 33d from the pressure upon its thinned ranks and tired men.

The Third brigade after the capture of the heights moved towards Salem Church, and was placed on the left of the line to guard the flank, but did not actively engage in the bloody contest there, in which the rebels checked the advance of the

Sixth corps towards Chancellorsville. The next morning, as the Seventh was marching to a more advanced position, the infantry of the enemy in large force could be seen on the hills in front marching from the direction of Chancellorsville, and one of his batteries went into position and began shelling the regiment, wounding one of the color-guard. The Third brigade was placed along a crest in an open field in support of Rigby's battery, making the toe of the horseshoe which Sedgwick formed to cover Banks' Ford. At about 10 o'clock in the morning a rebel brigade formed in the open field behind some buildings and then advanced in line, with the evident intention of taking possession of a wooded hill which was occupied by two companies of the 49th N. Y. and company B of the Seventh Maine as an outpost. The attacking force was routed by these three companies, and more prisoners than they themselves numbered and the colors of the 58th Virginia were taken by them. Their success in the face of such overwhelming odds was due in part to their position on the hillside, where rocks and trees afforded protection, but chiefly to the water-proof cartridges with which company B was supplied. It is not known whether the two companies of the 49th had those cartridges or not. It was the first issue of the kind that had ever been made to the regiment and it proved to have been very timely. The paper was prepared in such a way as to be ignitable by the fulminate of the cap so that it did not require "tearing," and it was so thin that the cartridge slipped down the barrel of the Windsor rifle without the use of a ramrod. This cartridge made the muzzle-loader almost equal to a breech-loader in rapidity of firing.

Between 5 and 6 o'clock in the afternoon a sharp fire ran suddenly all along the picket line, and the valley was all at once filled with a gray-clad host in orderly and imposing array; skirmishers and a line of battle advancing, and behind them masses moving "division front" towards the left. The Seventh went down the slope in front of the battery far enough to allow the battery to fire over their heads, and hotly engaged the enemy. The 20th N. Y. — a German regiment — formed the left of the line, placed diagonally to protect the flank. It gave way before the assault upon it, leaving the flank exposed and

compelling the brigade to fall back.   The brigade withdrew in
an orderly manner to the position assigned it in the new line at
the head of the ravine through which the great force that was
seen moving around the left of the advanced line was making
its way, and there awaited the onset.   But the artillery fire created such havoc among the on-coming masses that the services
of the infantry were not required.   Late in the evening the regiment marched to a hillside near Banks' Ford.   All through the
night the mortar shells of the rebels were directed upon the ford
and the adjacent banks of the river, but fortunately with little
effect.   Early on the morning of the 5th the brigade recrossed
the Rappahannock, and after a few days re-established itself in
pleasant camping grounds near those it had occupied through
the winter.   Captain Fletcher with his company, F, from the
recruiting station at Portland, joined on the 23d, bringing the
battalion up to six companies.

The Second division broke camp the 5th of June and moved
to Franklin's Crossing.   It crossed the Rappahannock the next
day, capturing a Florida regiment in rifle-pits along the bank,
and occupied the plain.   It was relieved by the First division
on the 8th and returned to the north side of the river, and on
the 13th it marched to Potomac Creek, the first stage of the
long march to Gettysburg.   On the 20th it was at Germantown
and was sent to Bristoe Station as a corps of observation on the
flank of the army of the Potomac.   It marched thence to Centreville the 25th; to Dranesville the 26th; to Poolesville, Md.,
via Edwards Ferry, the 27th; to Hyattstown the 28th; to New
Windsor, via New Market and Ridgeville, the 29th; to Manchester the 30th.   At 9 o'clock in the evening, July 1, the
order came to fall in, and was promptly obeyed; but the corps
did not fairly start upon the march till near midnight.   It came
upon the field of Gettysburg at 5 o'clock the afternoon of the
2d of July, after a day's march variously estimated at from
thirty to thirty-five miles.

The Second division filed out of the Baltimore pike into a field
near Rock Creek, and after a few minutes' rest the Third
brigade crossed the creek and formed line in support of
a battery on Powers' Hill.   The brigade was moved several

times that night and with great care and circumspection. It must have occupied at one time a position in very close proximity to the rebels who had occupied the temporarily abandoned rifle-pits of that portion of the Twelfth corps which went to the aid of the Third, and had extended around them so that they were in rear of the Union line. The following morning General Slocum requested General Neill to stop the rebel advance on the south side of Rock Creek, which was annoying his right and threatening to cut off the Baltimore pike, the main line of communication. General Neill sent Lieut.-Colonel Connor, with the Seventh and the 43d N. Y. under his command, to protect the menaced point. The two regiments crossed the creek, and after moving a short distance on the Baltimore pike the whistle of bullets indicated the whereabouts of the enemy. Skirmishers were thrown out in the woods on the left by the Seventh Maine, and in the woods on the right by the 43d N. Y., and the line of the two regiments advanced in the opening at a run, and established itself in a favorable position behind a stone-wall. Several men were wounded by sharpshooters in crossing the field, and the skirmishers on both flanks had a sharp encounter before they succeeded in driving back the rebel skirmishers to a respectful distance. In this affair the 43d N. Y. lost one officer and one enlisted man killed, two enlisted men wounded and one captured or missing. The Seventh had seven men wounded, two of them mortally; these were Richard Sculley, who died the 4th of July, and William H. Smith, September 1st; both are buried in the National Cemetery at Gettysburg. Folsom Dutton, company C, was reported as missing at Gettysburg July 2, and was so borne upon the muster-out rolls of the company.

General Neill brought up the other regiments of the brigade as soon as possible, and prolonged and strengthened the line established by the Seventh and the 43d N. Y. Thus the Third brigade constituted the extreme right of the infantry. It was ordered to hold the position and not to undertake any enterprises likely to bring on an engagement in that quarter; so that through the day there was only an occasional shot, whenever the sharpshooters on either side saw the slightest opportunity to make one.

The brigade moved to the left on the morning of the 5th, passing through "Devil's Den," and marched to Fairfield over the road along which the principal part of Lee's army had retreated.   Here General Neill was given an independent command, consisting of his own brigade, Colonel McIntosh's brigade of cavalry and Martin's battery, and ordered to follow up the enemy on the road to Waynesboro.   At the entrance to Monterey Springs Gap the skirmishers of the rear guard made a stubborn stand, but did not linger long enough to meet the chances of the attack on their flank and rear which was in preparation.   They again checked the advance of their pursuers by burning the bridge over the Antietam near Waynesboro.   The brigade remained at Waynesboro several days and was very hospitably treated by the people of the town.   The brigade left Waynesboro the 11th and arrived at Funkstown, Md., the 12th.   Here Colonel Mason joined and resumed command of the Seventh.

Still following the retreating army, whose rear guard had made a brief stand at Funkstown behind strong earthworks, the Sixth corps crossed the Potomac at Berlin, Md., the 19th of July.   The itinerary of the Seventh shows that the subsequent period, until it went into winter quarters the 3d of December, was almost equally divided between marching and camping.   Its principal encampments were at Warrenton Springs, Stonehouse Mountain and Brandy Station.   The Seventh skirmished with the enemy October 12 at Brandy Station, and on the 19th, in connection with the 6th Vt., checked and drove back the rebel cavalry following up Buford ; on the 20th skirmished in advance of the corps and drove the enemy's skirmishers beyond Warrenton.   It was in the engagement at Rappahannock Station November 7, exposed to artillery but not actively engaged, and on the 27th it supported the Third corps at Locust Grove.

The 28th of November it advanced to Mine Run where, during the three succeeding days, the Seventh was in front and constantly skirmishing with the rebel outposts.   It recrossed the Rapidan the second of December, and on the third returned to Brandy Station and went into winter quarters.

In the campaigns of 1863 the Seventh marched, according to Colonel Mason's estimate, more than five hundred and sixty miles, and it took part in engagements in Virginia, Pennsylvania, and Maryland.

In December Lieut.-Col. Connor was commissioned Colonel of the Nineteenth Maine, and Major Hyde was promoted Lieutenant-Colonel, and Captain Jones of company B Major, of the Seventh. In the same month an order was issued by the War Department offering to enlisted men who had served two years a large bounty, release from the remainder of their current term of enlistment and thirty-five days' furlough, as inducements to re-enlist for three years. Under that order one hundred and sixty-one of the original members of the Seventh re-enlisted.

The only incident to break the routine of life in winter quarters was the movement in support of General Custer in his advance on Charlottesville with a division of cavalry. The Sixth corps moved from camp February 27, 1864, marched as far as Robertson's River and returned to camp the 2d of March.

The army of the Potomac broke camp and began the eventful campaign of 1864 on the 4th of May. The Seventh crossed the Rapidan at Germanna Ford at daylight on the 4th. The next morning the brigade was deployed on a road leading from Robertson's Tavern to the Germanna plank road. General Bidwell, Colonel of the 49th N. Y., who had succeeded to the command of the brigade, Neill having assumed command of the division in place of General Getty, wounded, in his report says: "We drove the enemy for about two miles, when we came on an intrenched line supported by artillery. Shortly after we had arrived at this point the enemy advanced a brigade, charging our extreme right regiment, but they were repulsed by the 49th N. Y. Vols. and Seventh Maine, we taking a number of prisoners and cutting off one of their regiments, which was captured by the 5th Wis. Vols." Dr. George T. Stevens, Surgeon of the 77th N. Y., in his "Three Years in the Sixth Corps," thus refers to this contest: "In these encounters the Seventh Maine and 61st Penn. regiments, who were on the right flank, received the heaviest onsets and suffered the most severely. At one time the Maine regiment found itself flanked by a brigade of rebels; changing front the gallant regiment charged to the rear and scattered its opponents in confusion."

At daylight of the 6th the brigade advanced to the attack, but after a vigorous assault, finding the enemy so protected by natural obstacles and the works with which they had strengthened their position, withdrew. Two hours later another unsuccessful assault was made and then the brigade intrenched where they were. Just before dark the enemy attacked. General Bidwell reports the affair as follows: "About half an hour before dark the enemy made a desperate attack on the right of the general line held by a brigade of each of the First and Third divisions. The Third division breaking caused the brigade of the First division also to break, and all fell back on our line. This, with a heavy attack by the enemy in our front, came near sweeping away the brigade, and, but for the unflinching bravery of the officers and men, would have done so. Our second line, changing front to rear, protected our flank, and the front line repulsed several attacks." General Hyde, who, as Lieutenant-Colonel, was still on the corps staff, in "Following the Greek Cross" says of this action, after referring to the information given him by a demoralized officer that the Seventh Maine "were wiped out," that he went to the front and found "the Seventh Maine holding its extreme right, refused. To my joy I found the regiment had changed front to rear on the tenth company and with the 43d N. Y. had stopped the rout, but at great cost; about half were killed, and the colonel, lieutenant-colonel and major of the 43d had been killed near our colors."

At dusk, the evening of the 8th, the brigade took up the march to Spotsylvania Court House, where it arrived the next evening and participated in an advance in which the enemy's line was broken; but there being no connecting troops on either flank the brigade was ordered to retire and intrench. This day, the 9th of May, was made sorrowful to the Sixth corps by the death of its beloved commander, Gen. John Sedgwick, instantly killed by a sharpshooter. The Seventh was selected as one of the twelve picked regiments to make an assault on the enemy's fieldworks the evening of the 10th. General Hyde, in "Following the Greek Cross," says that the regiment had already "lost so cruelly" that he "coaxed McMahon, chief of staff, to substitute another."

The Seventh had its full share in the hard fighting and cruel carnage at "The Angle" on the 12th. General Bidwell's report says: "The 43d N. Y., 61st Penn. Vols. and Seventh Maine were deployed on the right of this position, supporting General Upton's brigade. The first line losing heavily and closing to the left caused a vacancy which these regiments moved into and where they remained two hours, delivering a musketry fire, and were relieved and moved to the left to the support of a brigade of the Second corps. * * * After dark the whole line was withdrawn about 300 yards and went into bivouac for the night. Our loss in officers and men was very heavy in this engagement."

After occupying several other positions the brigade returned to The Angle and on the 18th was in the assault made at that point which resulted in a heavy loss to the brigade from artillery fire.

Spotsylvania was a "dark and bloody ground" to the Seventh. In this, the final campaign of the regiment, beginning with the Wilderness, and ending August 21, the expiration of its term of service, the loss of the Seventh as given in the report of the Adjutant General of the State of Maine for 1864–5, was officers killed, 8 ; wounded, 12 ; missing, 1 ; enlisted men killed, 68 ; wounded, 216 ; missing, 31. A large proportion of these casualties befell in these days of persistent efforts to break Lee's strongly intrenched lines at Spotsylvania Court House.

The Third brigade was not engaged at the North Anna. At Cold Harbor it shared in the futile assaults made on the strong position of the enemy,—a struggle so hopeless and useless that the army of the Potomac recalled it as a hideous nightmare.

The Sixth corps withdrew from Cold Harbor the 12th of June and crossed the James River the 16th. The Second division marched all night and at sunset on the 17th arrived in front of Petersburg. The Seventh was in the expedition to the Weldon Railroad made by the Second and Sixth corps on the 22d of June, and on the 30th marched to Reams' Station in the expectation of meeting the cavalry of Kautz and Wilson returning from their raid.

The First and Second divisions of the Sixth corps at nine o'clock in the evening of July 9 received orders to march to City Point, fourteen miles distant. They arrived at daylight and the two divisions embarked on transports before noon, on what duty they did not know until they learned on their arrival in Washington that Early was at the gates of the capital and that its only defenders were a few artillery-men, some detachments of the Invalid corps and improvised organizations of clerks and laborers in the department. The sight of the Greek Cross, fluttering at the head of the bronzed and war-worn veterans of the Sixth corps, gave welcome assurance to the anxious officers of the government and loyal citizens of the safety of the city. At 5 o'clock in the afternoon of July 12, the day after disembarking, an attack was made on Early, whose principal force was in front of Fort Stevens. General Wheaton, temporarily commanding the division, reports that he ordered Colonel Bidwell, commanding the Third brigade, "to select three of his very best regiments to assault and carry two strong, wooded hills in front," and that Colonel Bidwell chose the Seventh Maine and the 43d and 49th N. Y.; that the three assaulting regiments "dashed forward, surprising and hotly engaging the enemy, who was found to be much stronger than was supposed," so that it became necessary to deploy the other regiments of the brigade, and the important points were captured and held. General Wheaton reports: "The whole attack was as gallant as it was successful, and the troops never evinced more energy and determination. The losses were very severe, the brave Colonel Bidwell losing many of his most valuable regimental commanders." Every regimental commander in the brigade was either killed or wounded. Major James P. Jones, commanding the Seventh, was one of the three killed. Lieut. John E. Bailey of the Seventh was killed and Lieut. George H. Buker, wounded. President Lincoln was among those who witnessed the action from Fort Stevens.

After the fall of Major Jones, Lieut.-Colonel Hyde was relieved at his own request from staff duty and assumed command of the Seventh. No time was lost in following Early. The Sixth corps and two divisions of the Nineteenth, under

General Wright, set out July 13, and the almost unbroken series of marches that followed, in the hottest period of summer, nearly wore out the Sixth corps, which had been fighting and marching since the first of May. Not until its arrival at Halltown, on the 7th of August, did it halt long enough for a recuperating rest, and then it had but a few days' respite from toiling along dusty roads under a fervid sun. At Halltown, Va., the Sixth corps was assigned to Sheridan's army. On the 10th of August Sheridan began his advance up the Shenandoah. Having reason to apprehend an attack in rear, he withdrew to Charlestown and his lines there were assaulted by Early the 21st of August. The term of service of the Seventh expired that day, and those of its members who had not re-enlisted were about to take the cars for home when the attack began. They remained to take part in the action which resulted in the repulse of the enemy. They were mustered out at Augusta the 5th of September—eight officers and sixty-nine men.

Fox, in his "Regimental Losses in the Civil War," includes the Seventh Maine in his list of "Three Hundred Fighting Regiments" and gives statistics as follows : Total enrollment, 1,165. Officers killed and died of wounds, 15 ; enlisted men killed and died of wounds, 113. Total killed and died of wounds, 128,— 10.9 per cent of enrollment. Total killed and wounded, 555. Died of disease, accidents, in prison, etc., 3 officers, 209 men ; of this number 19 died in Confederate prisons.

Although the term of the Seventh had expired and its surviving members had been mustered out, its flag was still flying in the army of the Potomac over five companies of re-enlisted men and recruits to which had been joined two companies of the Fifth Maine and three of the Sixth Maine similarly composed, the regiment retaining the designation of Seventh Maine. Maj. S. C. Fletcher of the Seventh was its commanding officer. This regiment took part the 19th of September in the action at Opequon Creek, otherwise known as the battle of Winchester, in which the Sixth corps drove the enemy out of Winchester, and lost one officer, Lieut. B. F. Bicknell, killed, and 17 men wounded. It also did effective service at Fisher's Hill, on the 22d of the same month, losing two men killed and three wounded.

By a special order from the headquarters of the Sixth corps, dated October 2, the designation of the regiment was changed from "Seventh Maine" to First Maine Veterans. Major Hyde was commissioned its Colonel October 6, and on the 29th Major Fletcher was promoted Lieutenant-Colonel, and Capt. Alexander B. Sumner, formerly of the Sixth Maine, Major.

At the great victory of Cedar Creek, the 19th of October, when the Union army was surprised and put to rout by an attack in the obscurity of a misty morning, Sheridan, "riding down from Winchester," found the Second division of the Sixth corps the only infantry force opposing the enemy. In his report he says : "At Cedar Creek Getty's division of the Sixth corps and Merritt's and Custer's divisions of cavalry, under Torbert, confronted the enemy from the first attack in the morning until the battle was decided." The First Maine Veterans had 8 men killed, 2 officers and 58 men wounded in this battle.

Colonel Hyde, arriving a few days after the battle, found himself by virtue of his rank the successor in the command of the Third brigade, General Bidwell having been killed at Cedar Creek. He retained that command until the end of the war. The brigade left the Shenandoah the 9th of December and returned by rail to Washington, thence by transports to the front at Petersburg.

On the 25th of March the Third brigade took part in the advance which resulted in capturing the enemy's intrenched rifle-pits. The First Vets. was exposed to an artillery fire from front and rear and was enfiladed from the left by it. When the First brigade came up on the right the First Vets. was ordered to join it. Colonel Warner, commanding that brigade, reports : "The behavior of the troops was admirable. The pits and a crest about 300 yards beyond were carried, capturing many prisoners." He mentions Lieut.-Col. Fletcher among the officers who "displayed great personal gallantry."

In the attack which broke the rebel lines on the 2d of April the Third brigade formed the point of the wedge-like order in which the division charged. The assault was successfully made just before dawn, and the victorious division pierced the works and swept all before it as far as Hatcher's Run. Captain

Merrill of the First Vets. crossed the stream on fallen trees, and with fourteen men captured and brought back 79 prisoners. Returning to the camps it had captured, the division halted for coffee, and then advanced in line towards Petersburg, the First Vets. on the extreme left, in echelon to protect the flank. Owing to the position of the regiment and the work of the flanking party sent out from it by Colonel Hyde's order, it was largely instrumental in capturing a battery which was making the last stand of the day under the personal supervision of General Lee. The division advanced until it encountered the skirmishers of Longstreet's corps. Then the brigade was relieved, and the men, worn out with their "nineteen hours of continuous marching and fighting," went supperless to bed on the ground at their feet, to learn on waking in the morning that Petersburg had surrendered to the pickets, and to feel that the end of the war was at hand.

The Second division was not called upon for active work at Sailor's Creek, where the crippling blow was dealt by the other divisions of the corps. The losses of the First Maine Veterans from March 29 to April 9, 1865, were one officer, Lieutenant Messer, and two men killed, two officers and 26 men wounded.

Immediately after the surrender of Lee the brigade was ordered to move to the south "to assist in the capture of Gen. J. E. Johnston's army." It marched April 23, and on arriving at Danville, Va., the 27th, the news was received that Johnston had surrendered the day before to Sherman. Colonel Hyde was made military governor of Danville and the adjacent counties, and his brigade occupied the town until the 16th of May, when it went by rail to Richmond and thence marched to Ball's Cross Roads, near Washington, and encamped. The Sixth corps was not in time for "The Grand Review," and therefore had a separate review by the President, after which, on the 28th of June, 1865, the First Maine Veterans was mustered out at its camp.

ROSTER.

The following information relating to officers of the Seventh Maine regiment is obtained from the Volunteer Army Register, published by the War Department August 31, 1865, and other reliable sources : —

MUSTERED OUT, TERM EXPIRED, SEPT. 5, 1864.

COLONEL: Edwin C. Mason (R. A.), Nov. 5, 1861.

LIEUTENANT-COLONEL: Thomas W. Hyde, Dec. 1, 1863;—commissioned Colonel First Maine Vet. Vols., Oct. 6, 1864.

CAPTAINS: John W. Channing, Aug. 22, 1861,—brevet Major and Lieut.-Col., Mar. 13, 1865; William Crosby, June 23, 1864.

FIRST LIEUTENANTS: John A. Bachelder, Aug. 21, 1861; Franklin Glazier, Jr., May 22, 1863,—commis'd Quartermaster First Vets., Oct. 12, 1864; Augustus F. Emery, June 23, 1863, muster-out Sept. 5, 1864; Samuel S. Mann, Jan. 23, 1864.

MUSTERED OUT WITH FIRST MAINE VETERAN REGT. JUNE 28, 1865.

COLONEL: Thomas W. Hyde, commissioned Oct. 6, 1864; commanded 3d brig., 2d div., 6th corps from Oct. 20, 1864, to muster-out;—brevet Brig.-Gen. Vols., Apr. 2, 1865.

LIEUT.-COLONEL: Stephen C. Fletcher, Major Seventh, July 30, 1864, tr. to 1st Vets., pro. Lieut.-Col., Oct. 29, 1864,—brevet Colonel, Apr. 2, 1865.

CAPTAINS: Charles T. Witherell, Aug. 15, 1863, tr. from 6th Maine, tr. to 1st Vets., pro. Major, not must'd,—brevet Major, Oct. 19, 1864; George McGinley, Mar. 15, 1864; George H. Buker, June 23, 1864; Eli H. Webber, 1st Lieut. Seventh, Oct. 1, 1862, tr. to 1st Vets., pro. Captain, Nov. 16, 1864; William Crosby, Capt. Seventh, recommissioned in 1st Vets, Nov. 25, 1864; Augustus Merrill, 1st Lieut. Seventh, pro. Captain 1st Vets., Dec. 31, 1864,—brevet Major, Apr. 2, 1865; Warren T. Ring, 2d Lieut. Seventh, pro. 1st Lieut., and Captain 1st Vets., Feb. 13, 1865; Walter B. Jenness, Sergt. Sixth, re-enlisted, pro. to Captain 1st Vets., Mar. 25, 1865; John B. Waid, tr. from 6th Maine, 2d Lieut., pro. 1st Lieut., and Captain 1st Vets., Mar. 25, 1865; John McLellan, 2d Lieut. 5th Maine, pro. Captain 1st Vets., May 15, 1865.

FIRST LIEUTENANTS: Franklin Glazier, 1st Lieut. Seventh, recommissioned Quartermaster in 1st Vets., Oct. 12, 1864; J. Augustine Grenier, 2d Lieut. 5th Maine, pro. Adjt. 1st Vets., Nov. 17, 1864; William H. Savage, 2d Lieut. Seventh, tr. to 1st Vets., pro. 1st Lieut., Nov. 17, 1864,—brevet Captain, Apr. 2, 1865; Ira P. Wing, tr. from 6th Maine, 2d Lieut., pro. 1st Lieut. 1st Vets., Nov. 17, 1864; William C. Phinney, Sergeant Fifth, re-enlisted, pro. 1st Lieut. 1st Vets, Dec. 31, 1864; Perry Greenleaf, 2d Lieut. Seventh, pro. 1st Lieut. 1st Vets., Jan. 21, 1865; Warren P. Frazier, Sergeant Sixth, re-enlisted, pro. 1st Lieut. 1st Vets., Feb. 13, 1865; George W. Fogg, Sergeant Seventh, pro. 1st Lieut. 1st Vets., Mar. 13, 1865; Edward J. Dolan, Corporal Fifth, re-enlisted, pro. 1st Lieut. 1st Vets., Apr. 4, 1865; Daniel F. Goodrich, Sergt.-Major Seventh, pro. 1st Lieut. 1st Vets., Apr. 4, 1865;

William H. Blood, Sergeant Sixth, re-enlisted, pro. 1st Lieut. 1st Vets., May 15, 1865.

SECOND LIEUTENANTS: James Phair, Sergeant Seventh, re-enlisted, pro. 2d Lieut. 1st Vets., Feb. 13, 1865, commisioned 1st Lieut. June 23, not mustered; Silas Smith, Commis'y-Sergeant Sixth, pro. 2d Lieut. 1st Vets., Feb. 13, 1865; George M. Littlefield, Sergeant Fifth, re-enlisted, pro. 2d Lieut. 1st Vets., Mar. 13, 1865; Robert T. Crommett, 1st Sergeant Seventh, re-enlisted, pro. 2d Lieut. 1st Vets., Mar. 25, 1865; Josiah S. Brown, Sergeant Seventh, pro. 2d Lieut. 1st Vets., Mar. 25, 1865; Wainwright Cushing, Corporal Sixth, re-enlisted, pro. 2d Lieut. 1st Vets., Apr. 4, 1865; Frederick Benn, Sergeant Seventh, re-enlisted, pro. 2d Lieut. 1st Vets., Apr. 4, 1865; John W. Pettengill, Sergeant Sixth, re-enlisted, pro. 2d Lieut. 1st Vets., Apr. 26, 1865; Winfield S. Robinson, Corporal Fifth, re-enlisted, pro. 2d Lieut. 1st Vets., May 15, 1865.

SURGEON: Francis M. Eveleth, Feb. 13, 1863. ASSISTANT SURGEONS: Stillman P. Getchell, tr. to 1st Maine Vet. Vols.; Alpheus Packard, Jr., original commission in 1st Vets., Oct. 8, 1864.

(The dates given above refer to rank or commission; those hereafter given refer to the date of event.)

DIED.

COLONEL: Thomas H. Marshall, Oct. 25, 1861, of disease.

LIEUTENANT-COLONEL: James P. Jones, killed in action July 12, 1864.

CAPTAINS: Henry F. Hill, killed in action May 12, 1864; Joseph E. Walker, May 17, 1864, of wounds received at Spotsylvania; Henry Warren, killed in action May 18, 1864; John Goldthwait, tr. from 5th Maine and to 1st Vets., died Apr. 18, 1865, from wounds received in action Mar. 25th.

FIRST LIEUTENANTS: William L. Haskell, Oct. 18, 1862, of wounds received at Antietam,—pro. Captain, not mustered; Joseph G. Butler, killed in action at Fredericksburg, May 3, 1863; Adjutant Charles H. Hasey, May 15, 1864, of wounds received May 12th, battle of Spotsylvania; Alvin S. Hall, May 17, 1864, of wounds received in action; Marcellus Vining, May 19, 1864, of wounds received May 12th; John E. Bailey, July 31, 1864, of wounds received in battle; Benjamin F. Bicknell, killed in action Sept. 19 1864; P. Jordan Mitchell, tr. from 5th Maine, tr. to 1st Vets., pro. Captain, not mustered, died from wounds Nov. 12, 1864.

SECOND LIEUTENANTS: Ara C. Brooks, Sept. 26, 1862, at Point Lookout, Md.; Harlan P. Brown, killed at head of his Co. at Antietam, Sept. 17, 1862; Charles A. Goodwin, killed in battle of Antietam, Sept. 17, 1862; Luther C. Fairfield, Nov. 18, 1862; William H. Hooper, May 17, 1864, of wounds received in battle; Joseph Whelpley, killed in action Mar. 25, 1865,—Sergeant Sixth, re-enlisted, pro. 2d Lieut. 1st Vets,, Nov. 17, 1864, commis'd 1st Lieut., not mustered; Benjamin F. Hunter, mortally wounded Mar. 25, 1865,—Sergeant Seventh, re-enlisted, pro. 2d Lieut. 1st Vets., Nov. 17, 1864; Alvin A. Messer, killed in action Apr. 2, 1865,—Corporal Seventh, re-enlisted, pro. 2d Lieut. 1st Vets., Jan. 31, 1865.

PROMOTED AND TRANSFERRED OUT OF REGIMENT.

Promoted: LIEUTENANT-COLONEL: Selden Connor, Jan. 11, 1864, to Colonel 19th Maine Vols.; commissioned June 11, 1864, Brig.-Gen. U. S. Vols.

CAPTAINS: Charles D. Gilmore, Aug. 29, 1862, to Major 20th Maine Vols.;

John B. Cook, Jan. 1. 1864, to Major 22d U. S. C. T.; John W. Freese, Feb. 17, 1864, to 1st D. C. Cavalry, under President's commission, afterwards to 1st Maine Cavalry.

FIRST LIEUTENANTS: Quartermaster John K. Russell, May 6, 1862, to Captain and A. Q. M.; Quartermaster Charles B. Whittemore to Captain and A. Q. M., 1864; Adjutant Elijah D. Johnson, Oct. 13, 1862, to Colonel 21st Maine Vols.; Andrew M. Benson, Feb. 15, 1864, to Captain 1st D. C. Cavalry; H. Warren Farrar, June 7, 1864, to Captain and A. D. C.

ASSISTANT SURGEON: Ai Waterhouse, Mar. 16, 1864, to Surgeon 43d U. S. C. T.

Transferred: Second Lieut. Eugene Palmer, not mustered, to Inv. corps.

DISCHARGED.

MAJOR: Alexander B. Sumner, Captain 6th Maine, tr. to 1st Vets., pro. Major, Oct. 29, 1864, — brevet Lieutenant-Colonel, Apr. 2, 1865, disch'd by order June 16, 1865.

CAPTAINS: Edward Williams, tr. from 6th Maine, tr. to 1st Vets., disch'd Nov. 2, 1864; Granville P. Cochrane, Dec. 15, 1864, for disability; Timothy Swan, tr. to 1st Vets., disch'd Mar. 18, 1865, term expired; Albert A. Nickerson, tr. to 1st Vets.,—brevet Major, Oct. 19, 1864, disch'd Mar. 23, 1865, term expired.

FIRST LIEUTENANTS: Adjutant William H. Coan, tr. from 6th Maine, tr. to 1st Vets., disch'd Oct. 29, 1864, for disability; James A. Everett, tr. to 1st Vets., disch'd Feb. 15, 1865, for disability; William H. Larrabee, tr. to 1st Vets., pro. Captain, not mustered, disch'd Mar. 12, 1865, term expired; George R. Cony, 2d Lieut. Seventh, tr. to 1st Vets., pro. 1st Lieut. Nov. 17, 1864, disch'd Jan. 25, 1865; Walter Foss, commissioned 1st Lieut. Fifth, not mustered, tr. to 1st Vets., disch'd for disability from wounds Mar. 13, 1865.

SECOND LIEUTENANTS: Hiram Church, Nov. 23, 1863; Charles Lowell, Oct. 3, 1864, on account of wounds; Lemuel C. Small, tr. to 1st Vets., term expired Feb. 10, 1865; Augustus A. Dwinal, May 15, 1865, for disability from wounds,—Sergeant Fifth, re-enlisted, pro. 2d Lieut. 1st Vets., Jan. 31, 1865.

CHAPLAINS: James A. Varney, July 13, 1862; Collamore Purrington, tr. to 1st Vets., disch'd June 16, 1865, by order.

RESIGNED.

CAPTAINS: Henry Rolfe, Dec. 13, 1861; Greenleaf K. Norris, Nov. 28, 1861; William H. Cushman, Dec. 18, 1861; Hiram A. Dalton, Dec. 21, 1861; Charles H. Gilman, July 8, 1862; Edward H. Cass, Aug. 7, 1862; George E. Morse, Oct. 4, 1862; Henry C. Snow, Feb. 19, 1863.

FIRST LIEUTENANTS: James M. Andrews, Dec. 1, 1861; Thomas S. Cates, Jan. 21, 1862; Adjutant Henry S. Hagar, Mar. 6, 1862; George B. Knight, May 17, 1862; John H. Fogg, Aug. 5, 1862; Lyman M. Shorey, Dec. 21, 1862; Church E. Gates, Mar. 28, 1864.

SECOND LIEUTENANTS: Simeon Walton, Dec. 9, 1861; Hovey Austin, Dec. 24, 1861; L. Byron Crosby, June 26, 1862; Albert P. Titcomb, July 16, 1862; Henry M. Folsom, July 16, 1862; William G. Hall, July 23, 1862.

SURGEONS: Thomas C. Barker, Dec. 14, 1861; Samuel B. Hunter, Feb. 13, 1863.

MONUMENT.

The monument of this regiment stands on the north side of the Hanover road that leaves Gettysburg on the east, and near its junction with the Low Dutch road, crossing the former at nearly right angles. The front of the monument looks to the south and faces the Hanover road. It bears upon the face a design of a trooper in the act of mounting, sculptured in relief.

ADMEASUREMENTS: Base, 7 feet 6 inches by 3 feet by 2 feet; tablet, 6 feet 6 inches by 2 feet by 8 feet. Total height, 10 feet.

The following inscription is upon the face of the monument:—

THIS MONUMENT COMMEMORATES THE SERVICES OF THE FIRST MAINE CAVALRY ON THIS BATTLE-FIELD, JULY 3, 1863. COL. C. H. SMITH, COMMANDING.

3RD BRIGADE, 2ND DIVISION, CAVALRY CORPS.

The reverse of the monument contains the following inscriptions:

MIDDLETOWN	WINCHESTER
CEDAR MOUNTAIN	SECOND BULL RUN
SOUTH MOUNTAIN	ANTIETAM
FREDERICKSBURG	RAPPAHANNOCK ST'N
BRANDY STATION	ALDIE
MIDDLEBURG	UPPERVILLE
GETTYSBURG	SHEPARDSTOWN
SULPHUR SPRINGS	MINE RUN
FORTIFICATIONS	OLD CHURCH
OF RICHMOND	GROUND SQUIRREL
TODD'S TAVERN	CHURCH
HAWES' SHOP	COLD HARBOR
TREVILLIAN STATION	ST. MARY'S CHURCH
DEEP BOTTOM	REAMS' STATION
WYATT'S FARM	BOYDTON ROAD
BELLEFIELD	HATCHER'S RUN
DINWIDDIE C. H.	SAILORS' CREEK
HIGH BRIDGE	FARMVILLE

APPOMATTOX C. H.

NUMBER ENROLLED 3226

KILLED IN ACTION 101.   DIED OF WOUNDS 53.
DIED OF DISEASE 171.   DIED IN PRISON 165.

FIRST MAINE CAVALRY,

THIRD BRIGADE, SECOND DIVISION, CAVALRY CORPS,

AT THE BATTLE OF GETTYSBURG.

IN the concentration upon Gettysburg, General Gregg, with the First and Third brigades of his division, left Hanover at daybreak on July 2d, and about noon, after a tedious and exhausting march, took position on the Hanover road, near its intersection with the Low Dutch road, about three and a half miles east of the town. The brigade of Gen. J. Irvin Gregg was on the left, and in this brigade was the First Maine Cavalry, having, according to the morning report of June 30, 1863, present for duty 23 officers and 396 men. Many of its officers and men, as will be seen from the statistics given later on, were on detached service at corps, division, brigade and regimental headquarters. During the afternoon of July 2d there was some skirmish firing between the opposing lines, in which some of Irvin Gregg's men participated. About 10 o'clock in the evening our line was withdrawn, and the two brigades moved over to the Baltimore turnpike, near our reserve artillery, and there went into bivouac. On the morning of July 3d General Gregg resumed his position on the right of our infantry line, where the division, together with Gen. Custer's Mich. brigade of Kilpatrick's division, opposed the advance of General J. E. B. Stuart in the afternoon. The First Maine was not called into active service during the cavalry battle this afternoon until near its close, when it was ordered forward at the termination of the fight. Speaking of this cavalry engagement, Gen. D. McM. Gregg says: "On July 3, 1863, we stood on this field, armed men, to resist the advance of an enemy with whom we had made trials of strength ofttimes before and of late at Brandy Station, Aldie, Middleburg and Upperville. Our gaze was directed to the northward as we watched the approach of the columns of the enemy; right gallantly did they come sweeping on, with such well-aligned fronts and with such tremendous pace that it seemed as though nothing could stand against them. There was a meeting of the blue and gray, and for a time the issue was held in the balance.

"The struggle was ended by the retirement of the enemy to his starting point, discomfited by failure, with ours in hot pursuit. Severe as was the engagement, it could not be asserted that the Union forces that participated were never in a severer; these fought too many battles in that long war for such a comparison, but all will agree they never fought on a fairer field. Neither party asked nor expected aid from the main armies beyond. Our enemy had the advantage in numbers and position; we had the moral advantage of fighting on our own heath. It can safely be said that on no other field did Union cavalry whether on foot or in the saddle do more effective and brilliant fighting than on this. Had it fought less well here, the victory would have been with the enemy rather than with us" (a).

July 4th the regiment reconnoitered the position on the right of our lines, and advanced on the following day through Gettysburg to Cashtown, pursuing the retreating forces of Lee, and captured a large number of stragglers from the enemy, besides two or three thousand of his wounded. The next day the regiment advanced to Chambersburg, where it captured many more of the enemy's stragglers. From thence until July 15th every day but one was spent in marching to the Potomac, where it crossed the river at Harper's Ferry on the morning of the 15th of July.

PARTICIPANTS.

FIELD, STAFF AND NON-COMMISSIONED STAFF.

Lieutenant-Colonel, Charles H. Smith, Eastport.
Major, Stephen Boothby, Portland.
Adjutant, First Lieutenant Addison P. Russell, Houlton.
Quartermaster, First Lieutenant Clarence D. Ulmer, Rockland.
Assistant Surgeon, Alexander M. Parker, Westbrook.
Assistant Surgeon, Horace Stevens, Skowhegan.

(a) A shaft twenty-nine feet in height, erected by the survivors of Gen. Gregg's division and dedicated Oct. 15, 1884, marks the ground where the hand-to-hand sabre fight took place. This shaft and the greater part of the cavalry battlefield can be distinctly seen from East Cemetery Hill. Custer's Mich. brigade is also honored by a grand monument having bronze panels upon which, in bas-relief, are scenes illustrating the combat.

Sergeant-Major, Elisha A. Clifford, Lincoln.
Quartermaster-Sergeant, Orrin S. Haskell, Levant.
Commissary-Sergeant, Martin T. V. Bowman, Waterville.
Hospital Steward, Emery T. Gatchell, Brunswick.
Saddler-Sergeant, Henry W. Norwood, Bangor.
Chief Trumpeter, Isaac C. Brick, Augusta.

ON SPECIAL DUTY OR DETACHED SERVICE: Major Jonathan P. Cilley,
Thomaston, Judge Advocate on staff of Gen. Martindale; Surgeon George
W. Colby, at 2d brig. 2d div. Cav. corps h'dqrs; Com. of Sub. First Lieu-
tenant Eustace C. Bigelow, Portland, at 2d brig. 2d div. Cav. corps h'dqrs;
Hospital Steward Samuel C. Lovejoy, Rockland, at 2d div. hosp.

COMPANY A.
(Including 4 present sick.)
Captain, Sidney W. Thaxter, Bangor; commissioned Major, not mustered.
Second-Lieutenant, Horace S. Cole, Hampden.

SERGEANTS.

Miles Colbath, Exeter,	Joseph W. Phipps, Hampden,
Prentiss M. Clark, Levant,	Sidney W. Clark, Levant.

CORPORALS.

Milton C. Chapman, Newburg,	Alonzo J. Sawyer, Bangor,
Ansel Drew, Orono,	Charles H. McLaughlin, Oldtown,
Clifford N. Mayo, Hampden.	

SADDLER: John P. Cram, Bangor.
FARRIER: Frederick A. Harriman, Bangor.
WAGONER: John M. Mower, Vassalboro.

PRIVATES.

Bowen, John C., Hermon,	Davis, Thomas, Bangor,
Douggons, William M., Bangor,	Drew, Hiram T., Exeter,
Edgecomb, Albert, Exeter,	Foss, Benjamin R., Lee,
Lake, Enoch H., Levant,	Lewis, Frank, Orono,
Luce, William H., Burnham,	Lufkin, Otis E., Bangor,
Mansell, George F., Bangor,	Merrill, Orrin L., Alton,
Parks, James, Oldtown,	Peavey, Hiram, Exeter,
Ricker, Almon N., Oldtown,	Severance, Walter F., Greenbush,
Stevens, Asa M., Exeter,	Stevens, Charles H., Exeter,
Stevens, Edwin F., Corinth,	Sylvester, Joseph W., Etna,
Tolman, John F., Bangor,	Worcester, Edward P., Carmel.

ON SPECIAL DUTY OR DETACHED SERVICE: First Lieutenant Llewellyn
G. Estes, Oldtown, on Gen. Kilpatrick's staff.   Sergeant Elisha B. Cleave-
land, Lee, pioneer corps.   Privates: Charles E. Gardiner, Palermo, William
H. Severance, Greenbush, and Samuel A. Thompson, Lee, pioneer corps;
George M. Gray, Oldtown, hosp. dept.; Darius Peavey, Exeter, and John R.
Thurston, Bangor, q'rm'r dept.; Martin P. Colbath, Exeter, Charles D. Fur-
bish, Bangor, Ephraim B. Humphrey, Hampden, Augustus Lord, Jr., Levant,
James B. Peaks, Oldtown, and Harris G. Webber, Bangor, with the com-
pany; William S. Smith, Madison, teamster amm'n train; James M. Doe,
Orono, Luther J. Mack, Sidney, Lewis W. Soule, Frankfort, Benjamin F.
Young, Brewer, William Young, Exeter.

COMPANY B.
(Including 2 present sick.)
First Lieutenant, William P. Coleman, Lincolnville, commanding company.
SERGEANTS.
Orderly Sergeant, Jacob B. Loring, Thomaston,
Quartermaster Sergeant, James W. Poor, Belfast,
Commissary Sergeant, Elbridge Burton, Thomaston,
Aurelius Parker, St. George,   Austin McCobb, Lincolnville,
Alfred C. Strout, Thomaston.
CORPORAL: John Thompson, Searsmont.
BUGLERS.
Eben F. Brier, Belfast,   Henri J. Haskell, Palmyra.
SADDLER: John W. Leighton, Belfast.
FARRIER: Samuel M. Holden, Casco.
PRIVATES.

Barrows, Roscoe J., Lincolnville,	Bowler, Marquis, Palermo,
Brown, Charles S., Freedom,	Carr, Martin, Thomaston,
Cartin, Alvin A., Hope,	Clark, Edward H., Biddeford,
Guptill, Lemuel H., Belfast,	Hawes, Henry A., Union,
Jones, Eugene F., Union,	McAllister, Joseph, Rockland,
McGuire, Alfred D., Howland,	McIntyre, Charles A., Warren,
Phenix, Charles B., Union,	Robbins, John R., Swanville,
Shorey, Samuel, Belfast.	

ON SPECIAL DUTY OR DETACHED SERVICE: Captain Benjamin F. Tucker, U. S. Army, and Second Lieut. Frank M. Cutter, Union, on Gen. Gregg's staff. Corporal Samuel Burrows, Friendship, and Wagoner Rodney Sparrow, Union, q'rm'r dept. Privates: McKendree Davis, Friendship, Willard H. Lucas, Union, John Morse, Brunswick, Burnham C. Sleeper, Rockland, Orra P. Spear, Warren, Abiezer Veazie, Jr., Camden, and Ezekiel Winslow, Rockland, q'rm'r dept.; William W. Barlow, Union, and Eri A. Johnson, Camden, with Col. Phelps; Alonzo Beckwith, Belfast, Orderly for Gen. Pleasanton; Alfred Crocker, Bangor, Joshua Dow, Warren, and George W. Eaton, Waldo, div. amb. corps; Benson Gowen, Bangor, hosp. dept.; Surmandel Richards, Belfast, div. ammunition train.

COMPANY C.
(Including 1 present sick.)
SERGEANTS.
Ord.Sergt.,Horatio S.Libby,Gardiner, Henry F. Lyons, Manchester,
Francisco Colburn, Windsor,   Edward W. McClure, Bowdoinham,
Quartermaster Sergeant, William A. Winter, Farmingdale,
Commissary Sergeant, Charles H. Merrill, Gardiner.
CORPORALS.

Lorenzo Chamberlain, Hallowell,	Thomas J. Neal, Southport,
George E. Nason, Hallowell,	Samuel R. McCurdy, China,
William Dockendorff, Windsor.	

BUGLER: Alonzo D. Harper, Worcester, Mass.
SADDLER: William Trimble, Calais.
FARRIERS.
Moses S. Pinkham, Plymouth,   Michael Whalen, Whitefield.

PRIVATES.

Abbott, J. Holman, Winslow,
Arnold, Perry, Sidney,
Chadwick, David, Palermo,
Mariner, Ambrose, Augusta,
Peva, Freeman C., Windsor,
Ridley, Luther, Gardiner,
Snell, Charles, Sidney,
Tozier, Emelus, Monmouth,
Andrews, Eben, Gardiner,
Burns, John, Embden,
Hildreth, Charles A., Gardiner,
McCauslin, Franklin, Detroit,
Ridley, Jerome, Jr., Richmond,
Sanborn, Charles H., Dixmont,
Stevens, David M., Gardiner,
Weiler, William, Vassalboro,
Whitehouse, Charles H., Vassalboro, Wood, Benjamin S., Gardiner.

ON SPECIAL DUTY OR DETACHED SERVICE: Privates: Joseph A. Clark, Sidney, William B. Dunham, Vassalboro, and Parker G. Lunt, Gardiner, Orderlies for Gen. Gregg; William Elliott, Vassalboro, Edward Gilley, Augusta, William M. Goodspeed, China, John M. Mosher, Augusta, Albion P. Webb, Fairfield, Charles Whitten, Detroit.

COMPANY D.

(Including 1 present sick.)

Second Lieutenant, Andrew H. Bibber, Eastport, commanding company.
Acting Second Lieutenant, George E. Bugbee, Perry, comm'd, not mustered.

SERGEANTS.

Quartermaster Sergeant, John Gilley, Mt. Desert,

William B. Baker, Orrington,
Augustus R. Devereux, Penobscot,
John H. Daggett, Orland,
Nathaniel Bowden, 2d, Penobscot.

CORPORALS.

Joseph H. Lawrence, Orland,
Lyman P. Leighton, Addison,
Joseph N. Harrington, Penobscot,
William B. Grant, Penobscot.

FARRIERS.

Andrew B. Stetson, Eastport,
William P. Sennett, Calais.

PRIVATES.

Andrews, George P., Eastport,
Batchelder, Theodore J., Bucksport,
Carle, Lauriston W., Lyman,
Doe, Erastus A., Lubec,
Huston, Albert N., Bucksport,
Johnson, Albert R., Perry,
Moore, Moses D., Biddeford,
Preston, Robert, Machias,
Towle, Francis E., Indian River Pl.,
Williams, James T., Eastport.
Annas, Alonzo, Charlotte,
Bell, Charles H., Jr., Eastport,
Crane, Elbridge C., Kenduskeag,
Foss, William L., Machias,
Hutchins, Newell S., Verona,
Lane, Leander, Biddeford,
Moore, Wilson J., Unity,
Sawyer, Edwin H., Orland,
Vose, Elisha, Robbinston,

ON SPECIAL DUTY OR DETACHED SERVICE: Sergeant Phineas Foster, Jr., East Machias. Corporals: Eben L. Shackford, Eastport, Silas Leach, Penobscot, and Willard R. Merrill, Calais, teamsters q'rm'r dept. Saddler Elijah C. Wilder, Eastport, brig. h'dqrs. Privates: William H. Ayers, Charlotte, hosp. dept.; Loring W. Bell, Eastport, Orderly for Gen. Reynolds; Eleazer Eddy, Eddington, Silas P. Pendleton, Meddybemps, and Joseph W. Tatten, Calais, Orderlies for Gen. Gregg; Charles Gilpatrick, Orland, Orderly for Gen. Kilpatrick; Gilbert N. Harris, Eastport; George D. S. Robinson, Machias, Orderly for Gen. Tower; Charles Hutchins, Calais, mail agt. div. h'dqrs; Jonathan P. Moulton, Biddeford, Lewis Prescott, Phillips, and Isaiah

O. Richardson, Orland, pioneer corps; John Sennett, Meddybemps, with company; W. Frank Smith, Biddeford, regt'l h'dqrs; Mark P. Bulmer, Perry, Thomas Day, Mt. Desert, Peter N. Kane, Eastport, Lemuel R. Lurvey, Mt. Desert, Edward F. Morrill, Jay, James E. Stayner, Eastport, Alpheus H. Ward, Meddybemps.

COMPANY E.
(Including 1 present sick.)
Captain, Osco A. Ellis, Lincoln.
Second Lieutenant, George W. Hussey, Houlton.

SERGEANTS.
Orderly Sergeant, Winfield S. Collins, Houlton,
Quartermaster Sergeant, Charles M. Bailey, Chelsea,
John A. Heald, Lincoln,   Daniel W. Haines, Fort Fairfield,
James J. Gray, Houlton.

CORPORALS.
Lyman Vose, Houlton,   Edward W. Shields, Linneus,
Christopher C. Dunn, Houlton,   George Kitchen, Houlton,
John McCurdy, Princeton,   Bohan Field, Lee.
SADDLER: Benjamin A. Osborne, Lincoln.
FARRIER: Charles W. Lyons, Houlton.

PRIVATES.
Beatham, Robert, Enfield,   Burgess, Hiram E., Matinicus Isle,
Conners, Peter, Houlton,   Daggett, Monroe, Cary Pl.,
Daggett, Washington, Hodgdon,   Decker, Edward E., Fort Fairfield,
Decker, John C., Fort Fairfield,   Donnelly, James, Presque Isle,
Fellows, Samuel, Biddeford,   Forrest, Thomas, Houlton,
Gardiner, Albert, Fort Fairfield,   Greeley, Warren J., Haynesville,
Hunter, John M., Houlton,   Knapp, John P., New York City,
Luce, Hezekiah, Monticello,   Morrill, William, Biddeford,
Nodstrom, Charles E., Perry,   O'Brien, William, Houlton,
Sanborn, Benjamin F., Houlton,   Scannel, Timothy, Bridgewater,
Small, Albert, Belfast,   Small, William, Belfast,
Smith, James, London, Eng.,   Snow, William R., Woodstock, N. B.,
Stevens, Wilbur J., Athens.

ON SPECIAL DUTY OR DETACHED SERVICE: Sergeant Ansel Smith, Maysville. Corporals: Elijah E. Hall, Enfield, Oscar Richardson, Portland, Christopher C. Dunn, Houlton. Privates: Elbridge G. Chandler, Foxcroft, Patrick Cleary, Houlton, Albert E. Knights, Saco, Henry A. Ramsdell, Lincoln; Roscoe G. Beals, Leeds, hosp. dept.; Francis Ingraham, Ludlow, James K. Mann, Hudson, and James E. Siprell, Monticello, pioneer corps; Michael Mangan, Bangor, Gustavus L. Mills, Lincoln, William A. Osborn, Lincoln, Charles H. Scammon, Lincoln, and Charles E. Shields, Linneus, quartermaster department.

COMPANY F.
(Including 1 present sick.)
First Lieutenant, William Harris, Machias.
Second Lieutenant, William L. Boyd, Amherst.

SERGEANTS.
Orderly Sergeant, Joel Wilson, Gorham,
Quartermaster Sergeant, John E. Lougee, Parsonsfield,

Commissary Sergeant, Harrison J. Jack, Westbrook,
Lorenzo White, Paris.

CORPORALS.

Harmon T. Henley, Cape Elizabeth, John T. Lord, Limington,
Charles W. Skillings, Portland,   Waldo C. Beals, Patten,
Lewis Merrill, Oxford,   Levi Toothaker, Brunswick.

BUGLERS.

Charles F. Dam, Portland,   Albert C. Skillings, Portland.

FARRIERS.

Samuel J. Knowlton, Boothbay,   Frederick L. Chick, Limington.

PRIVATES.

Blackington, George E., Warren,   Cummings, Fred A., Paris,
Cutting, George D., Waterboro,   Evans, John G., Guilford,
Friend, Tyler B., Alfred,   Gore, Charles H., Westbrook,
Hamilton, Dimon, Waterboro,   Hamilton, Ivory W., Waterboro,
Hawks, Nathaniel S., Alfred,   Lougee, Enoch W., Parsonsfield,
Lougee, William H., Parsonsfield, Murch, Alfred B., Baldwin,
Perkins, Isaac T., Biddeford,   Pierce, Alfred, Baldwin,
Pitts, Isaac S., Waterboro,   Ring, James A., Dover,
Royal, George S., Pownal,   Sampson, Enoch, Augusta,
Shepherd, Albert D., Belfast,   Soule, Horatio B., Yarmouth,
Tukesbury, George D., Portland,   Whitcomb, Ripley C., Waldo,
Wyman, Charles W., Cumberland.

WAGONER: Samuel H. Jackson, Portland.

ON SPECIAL DUTY OR DETACHED SERVICE: Captain Walstein Phillips, Portland, on Gen. Gregg's staff.

Sergeants: Elisha DeWolf Harris, Portland, George H. Chase, Yarmouth, James A. Chase, Freeport. Privates: Alvin M. Brackett, Yarmouth, Peter C. Conner, Paris, Joseph T. Darling, Cape Elizabeth, Nathaniel S. Edwards, Parsonsfield, Harrison S. Evans, Greenbush, Melvin W. Eveleth, Portland, Henry F. Hallowell, Portland, Isaac S. Harris, Warren, Jonas W. Mason, Portland, Frank Pacott, Rockland, James Smith, New Gloucester, Charles H. Sylvester, Portland, Stephen Twombly, Yarmouth.

COMPANY G.

(Including 2 present sick.)

Captain, Isaac G. Virgin, Dixfield.
First Lieutenant, George E. Hunton, East Livermore.
Second Lieutenant, Samuel B. M. Lovejoy, East Livermore.

SERGEANTS.

Henry Little, Auburn,   Boynton Grover, Bowdoin,
Cyrus T. Reed, East Livermore.

BUGLER: William Maloon, Jr., Bowdoin.

SADDLER: Ira I. McFarland, Palmyra.

FARRIERS.

William Foy, Canton,   Albert Smith, Canton.

PRIVATES.

Baker, Frederick M., Lewiston,   Coffin, Joseph H., Webster,
Collamore, Elijah, Lewiston,   Doble, William, Livermore,
Forsyth, Nelson S., Lewiston,   Fuller, William F., Wilton,

Kelsey, John B., Canton,
Mower, Thomas H., Greene,
Robinson, Lucius M., Hartford,
Woodbury, Collins, Bangor.

Mitchell, John, Jay,
Northrop, George, Hanover, N. H.,
Rose, Seth G., Leeds,

WAGONER: Orren R. Stetson, Canton.

ON SPECIAL DUTY OR DETACHED SERVICE: Sergeant John B. Drake, East Livermore, and Privates, Benjamin M. Corliss, Hartford, James D. Foster, Gray, Carlton T. Gleason, Dixfield, Israel M. Hatch, Lewiston, Alonzo P. Russell, Livermore, and George W. White, Dixfield, Orderlies for Gen. Patrick, Provost Marshal, A. of P.; Charles R. Delano, Turner, George M. Delano, Turner, and George E. Reed, East Livermore, Orderlies for Gen. Paul; Charles W. Jordan, Lewiston, and William S. McClanning, Yarmouth, Orderlies at 1st brig. h'dqrs; Levi W. Wheeler, Leeds, teamster div. h'dqrs; Russell S. Bradbury, Greene, and Eben J. Pulsifer, Poland, hosp. dept.; Dennis Carty, East Livermore, John Coffin, Webster, and Leonard L. Rose, Leeds, q'rm'r dept.; Edmund C. Bowker, Sumner, and Hanson S. Field, Hartford, with co.; Henry A. Child, Paris, William H. Farnum, Rumford, Orlando A. Hayford, Peru, Riley L. Jones, Lewiston.

COMPANY H.

First Lieutenant, Henry C. Hall, Starks.

SERGEANTS.

First Sergeant, Nathan V. Cook, Solon,
John H. Wyman, Skowhegan,

George E. Goodwin, Skowhegan.

CORPORALS.

Robert A. Heal, Lincolnville,
John F. Robinson, Palmyra,
Daniel M. Foster, Skowhegan,

Philander S. Herrin, Skowhegan,
Benjamin C. Mosher, Starks,
David H. Whittier, Harmony.

SADDLER: George W. Smith, Skowhegan.

FARRIERS.

Benjamin J. Springer, Richmond,

William Hinkley, Richmond.

PRIVATES.

Buzzell, Samuel L., St. Albans,
Cyphers, Martin C., Ripley,
Douglass, George F., Hartland,
Emerson, Elisha D., St, Albans,
Harlow, James H., Embden,
Lewis, William N., Dennysville,
Merrill, Charles C., Harmony,
Murphy, Dennis, Skowhegan,
Russell, Cyrus M., Madison,
Tibbetts, Silas F., Concord,
Webster, Daniel, Exeter,
Young, William A., Wayne.

Corson, Charles A., Starks,
Doane, Edward H., Palmyra,
Dykes, William R., Dennysville,
Foster, William E., Skowhegan,
Heal, Luther L., Lincolnville,
Marshall, Benjamin F., Skowhegan,
Moore, William H., St. Albans,
Perkins, Thomas H., Fairfield,
Smith, Charles, Skowhegan,
Varney, Henry J., Skowhegan,
Willey, Llewellyn L., Corinna,

ON SPECIAL DUTY OR DETACHED SERVICE: Second Lieut. William F. Stone, Portland, q'rm'r dept. Sergeants: Willard H. Phelps, Hartland, Charles H. Foster, Skowhegan. Wagoner Calvin H. Brown, Palmyra, hosp. dept. Privates: Franklin B. Foss, Bingham, and Joseph Pomlow, Solon, q'rm'r dept.; Moses H. Fogg, Wales, and Llewellyn W. Fogg, Lewiston, hosp. dept.; John A. Hutchins, Brighton, and Charles E. Roberts, Solon,

Orderlies for Gen. Gregg; Aaron F. Bickford, Madison, John H. Garnett, Dennysville, Augustus W. Kimball, Harmony, John B. Leathers, St. Albans, Charles H. Marsh, No. 2, Aroostook Co., George H. Mayberry, Solon, George H. Rich, Bangor, Phineas P. Steward, Skowhegan.

COMPANY I.

Captain, Paul Chadbourne, Waterboro.
First Lieutenant, Frank W. Pray, Shapleigh.
Second Lieutenant, John R. Andrews, Biddeford.

SERGEANTS.

Orderly Sergeant, Samuel C. Smith, Alfred,

Collins M. Chadbourne, Waterboro,	George M. Emery, Buxton,
George W. York, Lyman,	John F. Hill, Berwick,
Charles C. Goodwin, Wells,	John C. Roberts, Newfield.

CORPORALS.

Leonard Webber, Newfield,	Simon Garvin, Shapleigh,
George D. Harvey, North Berwick,	Fred C. Drew, Biddeford.

FARRIER: Danville Newbegin, Newfield.

PRIVATES.

Allen, Ivory R., Waterboro,	Allen, Walter, Wells,
Cleaves, Horatio M., Dayton,	Cornell, Edward, Thomaston,
Doxey, John, Alfred,	Eaton, Albert J., Wells,
Fowler, Samuel H., Waterboro,	Goodrich, John H., Alfred,
Gurney, Isaac P., Biddeford,	Hill, Jeremiah, Waterboro,
Hodsdon, Moses M., Hollis,	Huntress, Henry O., York,
Hurd, Robert F., Berwick,	Hutchinson, Joseph, Biddeford,
Johnson, John B., Biddeford,	Littlefield, Charles F., North Berwick,
Littlefield, Oliver B., Wells,	Mann, George W., New Sharon,
Merrick, Stephen W., Sanford,	Merryfield, Jacob, Waterboro,
Perkins, Daniel, Biddeford,	Perkins, George E., Newfield,
Shehan, James R., Biddeford,	Spear, Edward, Saco,
Stoddard, Augustine O., Appleton,	Waterhouse, Eli S., Biddeford.

ON SPECIAL DUTY OR DETACHED SERVICE: Corporal Henry A. Willis, Thomaston, Ord'ly for the Colonel. Buglers: Benjamin F. Libby, Newfield, brig. band; Alvah M. Libby, Limerick. Privates: Thomas P. Coombs, Biddeford, dism't'd camp; Joseph R. Curtis, Belfast, with Gen. Kilpatrick; Moses Bedell, North Berwick, William Bond, Newfield, Albert M. Cole, Waterboro, Leland F. Davis, Berwick, Daniel H. Elliott, Winslow, Andrew J. Goodale, Wells, William H. Hall, Waterboro, Elbridge G. Johnson, Biddeford, Simeon M. Knight, Waterboro, Daniel J. Meeds, Biddeford, Delmont Moor, North Berwick, Samuel H. Murphy, Buxton, Russell Murry, Newfield, Edward Taylor, Kennebunkport, Freedom Warren, Waterboro, James V. Wood, Newfield, John P. Wood, Newfield.

COMPANY K.

(Including 1 present sick.)

First Lieut., Charles W. Ford, Bristol, com'g Co. from June 17 to Sept. 17, '63.

SERGEANTS.

Commissary Sergeant, Albert W. Hanson, Bath,

Ruel B. Stinson, Bath,	William M. Herbert, Bristol,

Thomas J. Sanford, Bowdoinham, promoted for bravery.

CORPORALS.

Charles A. Stevens, Littleton,   Silas C. Trafton, Georgetown.
BUGLER: William H. Drew, Richmond.
FARRIER: Levi Crowell, Rockland.

PRIVATES.

Ambrose, Charles, Bath,   Carpenter, Alpheus, Bath,
Como, Peter, Bath,   Cox, George H., Bath,
Gallagher, John, Fort Fairfield,   Grant, John P., South Berwick,
Looney, Michael, Clare, Ire.,   Sheahan, John P., Dennysville,
Spencer, William, Plymouth,   Staples, William, Eaton Grant,
Wall, Andrew, St. George,   Welch, Charles, York,
Witham, William, Bath.

ON SPECIAL DUTY OR DETACHED SERVICE: Corporals: Winsor B. Smith, Portland, Orderly for Gen. Wadsworth; Louira K. Broad, Houlton, pioneer corps. Privates: Charles E. Hamilton, Portland, Orderly for Gen. Wadsworth; Solomon Poole, Rockport, Mass., and Albert R. Walker, Berwick, Orderlies for Gen. Reynolds; Cornelius V. Baker, Houlton, q'rm'r dept.; James W. Chamberlain, Bath, and Zebard F. Hysom, Bristol, with the co.; Josiah Gatchell, Brunswick, hosp. dept.; Albert G. Merrill, Brunswick, div. hosp. dept.; Edwin C. Teague, Newcastle. Bugler James Edgar, Houlton, brig. h'dqrs. Wagoner Melville C. Crooker, Bath, teamster 2d cav. div. h'dqrs.

COMPANY L.

(At First Army Corps Headquarters.)

Captain, Constantine Taylor, U. S. Army.
First Lieutenant, Zenas Vaughan, Freeman, at regiment headquarters.
Second Lieutenant, John P. Carson, Mt. Vernon.

SERGEANTS.

Ord. Sergt., Hiram M. Stevens, Starks, Charles O. Gordon, Phillips,
Justus Webster, Farmington,   Levi H. Daggett, New Sharon,
Allen H. Washburn, Madison,   William J. Crooker, Alton.

CORPORALS.

Freeland N. Holman, Temple,   Isaac S. Starbird, Freeman,
Austin L. Jones, Weld,   Walter S. Snell, Madison.
BUGLER: Rufus G. Ellsworth, Freeman.
WAGONER: Charles Heald, Sherman.
FARRIER: Sherman H. Rogers, Anson.
SADDLER: Christopher McDonald, Portage Lake Pl.

PRIVATES.

Bangs, Roscoe R., Strong,   Barnard, Otis M., Chesterville,
Brooks, Alanson V., Farmington,   Brown, Orin H., Patten,
Bump, Hosea P., Dead River Pl.,   Clarkson, Charles B., Rockland,
Currie, David, Portage Lake Pl.,   Daley, James B., Patten,
Douglass, Abner L., Bradford,   Dunsmoor, Rufus M., Temple,
Earle, Henry D., Litchfield,   Emery, Carlton P., Industry,
Fish, Austin A., Lexington,   Frazer, Alexander, Masardis,
Gould, Asa S., New Sharon,   Harris, Albert H., Littleton,
Harris, Jason F., New Sharon,   Hovey, Silas G., Farmington,
Mace, Edward A., Farmington,   Odell, Solomon H., Farmington,
Ordway, Augustus, Island Falls,   Painter, James W., Masardis,
Perkins, John H., New Sharon,   Pinkham, James, Industry,

Pinkham, Samuel, Industry,
Pratt, Beniah W., New Vineyard,
Ricker, Milton F., Livermore,
Thompson, Albert, Farmington,
Wright, Alonzo T., Weld.

Pratt, Alonzo M., New Sharon,
Reed, Charles M., Clinton Gore,
Thomas, John B., Brownville,
Thompson, Benjamin F., Jay,

ON SPECIAL DUTY OR DETACHED SERVICE (These were not with the company, but may have been with the regiment if not otherwise specified): Sergeant Ebenezer S. Johnson, New Sharon, with Gen. Robinson. Corporal Edmund B. Clayton, Farmington. Bugler Henry A. Folsom, Fayette. Privates: Augustus D. Brown, Chesterville, Orderly for Col. Roy Stone, com'g brig.; Edward Cunningham, Patten, Orderly for Gen. Doubleday; William S. Bean, New Sharon, Webster Bell, N. Y. City, Collamore I. Clayton, Farmington, Rufus M. Clayton, Freeman, Levi W. Gould, New Sharon, Ezra H. McKeen, Farmington, George A., Shay, Argyle, Orrin Shepley, Bangor, Cyrus L. Stevens, Freeman, Henry A. Thompson, Dead River Pl., Reuben Vinal, Vinalhaven, Edmund W. Whitney, Farmington, Thomas P. Williams, New Portland.

COMPANY M.

Captain, George M. Brown, Bangor.

SERGEANTS.

Charles K. Johnson, Carmel,
John G. Fassett, Abbot,
Asa F. Hanson, Atkinson.

William H. Bradman, Parkman,
Erving Curtis, Abbot,

CORPORALS.

John W. Rogers, Hallowell,
Franklin Prescott, Newburg,

Edward Jordan, Bangor,
George A. Bartlett, Bangor.

FARRIERS.

Horace B. Emery, New Sharon,   John F. Wharff, Guilford.

PRIVATES.

Bartlett, Aaron, Dover,
Bray, George H., Monson,
Corliss, Marcellus, Carmel,
Cushman, George H., Monson,
Files, Joseph P., Detroit,
Green, Hermon R., Monson,
Hall, Sullivan T., Abbc.,
Huntington, Daniel B., Atkinson,
Leeman, Roscoe G., Abbot,
Miner, John L., Glenburn,
Porter, Ruel K., Plymouth,
Robinson, Preston, Fairfield,
Southard, Beldin, Alton,
Thomas, Robert T., Monson,
Varney, Joseph, Newburg,

Boyd, William M., Amherst,
Chamberlain, Isaac, Lincoln,
Cross, Eben G., Hudson,
Fassett, George L., Abbot,
Flint, Thomas, Abbot,
Greene, Oscar F. A., Troy,
Harvey, John F., Carmel,
Ingalls, Emery G., Detroit,
Lowell, Charles H., Abbot,
Phillips, George P., Chester,
Roberts, Seth, Monson,
Rogers, George, Bradford,
Stewart, Moses, Monson,
Tibbetts, George, Monson,
West, Llewellyn J., Franklin.

ON SPECIAL DUTY OR DETACHED SERVICE: Sergeant Zebina B. Hair, Sebec. Corporal Ebenezer P. Davis, Monson, with First corps. Privates: John F. Ford, Greenville, and Charles Gould, Veazie, with First corps; John S. French, Franklin, and Isaac Oakman, Whitefield, brig. train; George G. Herrin, Guilford, Orderly for Gen. Reynolds; Frank Gates, Monson, Orderly; Cyrus M. Geary, Dover, Augustus A. Graves, Guilford, Alexander L. Walker, Atkinson.

REVISED REPORT OF CASUALTIES.

COMPANY B.
Orderly Sergeant Jacob B. Loring, wounded.

COMPANY G.◀
Private Charles R. Delano, Orderly for Gen. Paul, wounded July 1.

COMPANY K.
Private Chas. E. Hamilton, Orderly for Gen. Wadsworth, w'd and pris. July 3.

COMPANY L.
Sergeant Ebenezer S. Johnson (a), Orderly for Gen. Robinson, w'd July 1.
Private Orin H. Brown, wounded July 3.
Private Edward Cunningham, Orderly for Gen. Doubleday, killed July 3.
Private Henry A. Thompson, wounded July 3.

(a) "It affords me pleasure to call special attention to the gallant conduct of one of my orderlies, Sergt. Ebenezer S. Johnson, First Maine Cavalry, whose chevrons should be exchanged for the epaulette. When we make officers of such men, the soldier receives his true reward and the service great benefit."—From Report of General Robinson, Second div., First corps. Rebellion Records, serial No. 43, page 291.

DEDICATION OF MONUMENT,

OCTOBER 3, 1889.

ADDRESS OF BREVET MAJ.-GEN. C. H. SMITH, U. S. ARMY,

FORMERLY COLONEL FIRST MAINE CAVALRY.

Comrades and Fellow Citizens: —

Gettysburg claims historically only a quarter of a century of the past, but all future generations will make pilgrimages to it and pay it homage. Because twenty-six years ago on this field great questions of human freedom, civil rights, the integrity of the domain of our unequaled country, and the preservation and maintenance of our unrivaled representative government were practically decided, settled and established. No more important questions affecting human freedom and popular government were ever determined on any battlefield. Gettysburg, therefore, the crisis of our greatest war, the Saratoga of the rebellion, has become the theme of orators, and is and will be the text of historians. History was made here in a day, but it may take years to correctly write it. The historian must have material assistance as well as mental qualifications and attainments; and these monuments, their emblems and legends, that mournfully decorate this great battlefield from front to rear, from flank to flank, will become his interpreters and assistants.

Yon distant front, where the First corps fought and the gifted Reynolds fell, is appropriately marked. The Peach Orchard and the Wheatfield have their monumental metes and bounds. The array of marble, granite and bronze on Cemetery Ridge is typical of the unfaltering men who defended it. Yonder Round Tops, where Chamberlain and his devoted followers, God bless them, did heroic work, are monuments themselves — yea, monumented monuments — immortal in history. Yonder shaft marks where Gregg, remote from support and charged with responsibility that seldom falls upon a subordinate in battle, defended this Thermopylæ of the battlefield. Every monument is a revelation.

It may now be properly asked, what does this monument to the First Maine Cavalry reveal? The answer, if confined to its operations upon this battlefield, would be rather unheroic and uneventful, and in substance about as follows : The regiment, greatly reduced in numbers by the casualties of battles and unusually hard service, arrived here July 2d, and bivouacked that night somewhere in yonder fields (toward Cemetery Ridge). July 3d it remained inactive for the most part, until the deafening roar of contending artillery began to shake the earth. It was then summoned in haste to this locality, and it came quickly. The cavalry battle yonder was at its height; the field was all astir with contending forces and the artillery was in full play. The division commander, General Gregg, who was evidently expecting its arrival, met the regiment near this place. He hastily pointed to a force of the enemy in the distance moving to our right, and directed the regiment to proceed on yonder (Low Dutch) road and "take care of it," adding at the same time that he would send another regiment to report to its commander.

The regiment started at once, but before it reached the enemy or got any chance to do the work assigned to it, the crisis of the battle was passed and the enemy began to retire. The regiment was then recalled from its advanced position on our extreme right and assigned to a position further to our left, where it had a sharp skirmish with the enemy, and was exposed to artillery fire for a time. Those unheroic events constitute in the main the active part taken by the regiment in that great battle.

But the Gettysburg of the First Maine Cavalry was not limited to this battlefield, but really began at Brandy Station, June 9th, and ended at Shepardstown, July 16th, a month and seven days, during which it was engaged in seven battles. Brandy Station was the opening battle of the Gettysburg campaign, and Shepardstown was the last one of the series, and the First Maine Cavalry took part in them all. Inasmuch, therefore, as its opportunities for distinction on this field were so limited, I shall take the liberty of referring briefly to its services on other fields during that campaign.

At Brandy Station Wyndham's brigade had the advance and was first to attack the enemy, and after a gallant fight was defeated at every point, and some of his guns were captured. Kilpatrick's brigade followed Wyndham's. The 10th and 2d N. Y. cavalry, in the order named, preceded the First Maine and were successively beaten and driven back. The First Maine was in the rear in column of fours, making its way along a narrow road. It came out of the timber, as it neared the battlefield, into an open plain at a trot. It then formed companies at a gallop, drawing sabres at the same time, and crossed that plain with well-preserved ranks, amidst the confusion of defeated troops and in the face of artillery well posted and vigorously served. It reached and crossed the railroad with undiminished speed, and struck and dispersed in its course a mounted column of the enemy. In less time than I can tell it the regiment encountered and destroyed mounted forces, dismounted forces and artillery. It drove the mounted forces helter-skelter, it rode over and left the dismounted forces in rear, it enveloped or rode over the guns of the artillery and left them silent, and thus destroyed the last organized force of the enemy on that part of the field. That charge, considering the size of the force that made it, the surrounding circumstances, the distance covered, the resistance encountered and overcome and the results achieved, has seldom been excelled by other cavalry charges in the history of the world.

June 17th Kilpatrick's brigade (no longer containing the First Maine Cavalry) met the enemy at Aldie, and after a hotly contested battle was beaten and routed. His guns were in imminent danger of being captured. The First Maine Cavalry, by its timely arrival, was able to charge the enemy and save the guns from capture. It also broke, turned and routed the enemy, as it did at Brandy Station. It charged on with great effect and great sacrifices, too, nearly a mile beyond the guns it had rescued, drove the enemy from the field and saved the battle at Aldie.

June 19th, at Middleburg, the regiment bore the brunt of the battle and by hard fighting and heavy losses defeated a larger force of the enemy and again won the day.

June 21st our cavalry advanced from Middleburg to Upperville, and easily drove the enemy to that place. At Upperville, however, the enemy made a bold stand and successfully resisted two attempts on the part of some of our cavalry to drive him further. The First Maine Cavalry was then singled out to charge the enemy. It promptly formed for the task, and at the same time received the following orders : "Charge into the town, drive out the enemy and get beyond it if possible." As the regiment, compact, swift and irresistible, and enveloped in cannons' smoke, disappeared in the village, Kilpatrick in his enthusiasm exclaimed: "Those Maine men would charge straight into hell if ordered to."

After Upperville, the regiment participated in forced marches through Maryland and this great state of Pennsylvania, and arrived here July 2d. The modest part it took in the great battle here has already been explained. After the battle the regiment joined in the pursuit, but did not get a chance to engage the enemy until it arrived at Halltown, south of the Potomac, July 15th, where it had an important skirmish while protecting the flank of our column. The next day, however, July 16th, at Shepardstown, it made up in full measure for its lack of opportunity here, by fighting the enemy from midday until dark, in one of the hardest-contested battles it was ever engaged in. That fight terminated the Gettysburg campaign, and it is not necessary here to pursue the history of the regiment any further, in detail.

But in connection with the foregoing, and apropos of this occasion, it is just and important, as a part of its record, to add that by the highest official decision, rendered March 7, 1865, the First Maine Cavalry was engaged in more battles during the war than any other military organization in the great and glorious army of the Potomac at that time; a fact in itself that sheds glory enough.

It is also equally just and important to note, that, from statistics recently compiled, it is now known that the First Maine Cavalry sustained greater losses in battle than any other mounted regiment in the war. In those important particulars the First Maine Cavalry had no equal, and its record of battles and sacrifices stands without a parallel.

The question, therefore, What does this monument commemorate and reveal? is answered in some measure, at least, and it appears most fitting that the patriotic State of Maine, our own beloved State, proud of the brilliant record she made in the war, and recognizing and appreciating the valor and devotion of her soldiers, should establish this monument of appropriate design, modest but enduring as the imperishable granite of which it is, here at this famed historic centre, to commemorate the great services, heroic sacrifices and unrivaled record of the First Maine Cavalry.

Brandy Station, Aldie, Middleburg, Upperville and Shepardstown are among the laurels that most appropriately adorn it.

If anything more is desired to complete it, let me suggest the roll of honor, the names of the fallen, of Douty, Summat, Kimball, Taylor and Neville; of Boothby, Ellis, Phillips, Harris, Bartlett, Russell, Heald, Collins, Comins and Stayner; of scores of rank and file who fell in battle, as the cypress with which to tenderly entwine it.

POEM.

BY LIEUT. EDWARD P. TOBIE.

This sculptured soldier here,
In readiness to mount and ride
Where duty's call or country's need
Shall point the way, whate'er betide,
With faith unbounded in his steed,
And knowing naught of fear,

With spirit that will face
Privations such as few endure
And danger dire to life and limb,
Face death, for love of country pure,
And calmly meet his summons grim,
Face aught except disgrace;—

This sculptured soldier here
Is type of thousands, good and true,
Who, six and twenty years ago,
Stood on this field, brave boys in blue,
Stood firm against th' invading foe—
And some lie buried near;

Not only here they stood,
But on a hundred fields of strife
They stood 'mid storm of shot and shell
And offered life for nation's life;
They did their duty grandly well,—
They did all soldier could.

This sculptured soldier here
Embodies all the service grand,
The days of suffering and pain,
The hardships met on every hand,
By nigh three thousand men from Maine,—
The State which we revere,—

And all the weary hours
Of picket duty day and night,
The campaigns 'neath a southern sun,
The march, the skirmish and the fight,
The battles fought, the victories won,
By these brave boys of ours,

And all the throb and ache
Of wounds received from fellow-men
And illness nothing could appease,
The dreary life in prison pen,
The death by battle and disease,—
All this for country's sake.

This sculptured soldier here
Will tell their story through all time;
And more than that, will teach to all
Who look on him, that 'tis sublime
To promptly answer duty's call;
And duty make so clear,

That in the coming years
The spirit of these gallant men
Throughout the land will e'er abide,
And should our country call again,
As many more will mount and ride
With neither doubts nor fears.

HISTORICAL SKETCH.

BY LIEUT. EDWARD P. TOBIE.

The First Maine Cavalry has the proud record of having been allowed the names of more battles on its flag than any other regiment in the grand old army of the Potomac, and of having lost more men killed in action and died from wounds than any other cavalry regiment in the service. Twenty-nine battles were borne upon its flag by general orders from the headquarters of the army of the Potomac, issued March 7, 1865, and six were added during the last grand campaign in the spring of 1865, which ended with the surrender of General Lee and the whole rebel army. These were engagements worthy of the name of battle, but beside these the regiment, or some portion of it, was in many a skirmish in which it met with casualties, and many in which it escaped harm. More than one hundred times were men of this regiment under fire where the bullets of the enemy did execution.

Organizing with 49 officers and 1,109 men, the regiment, by recruiting, by promotion, by re-enlistment and by transfer from the First District of Columbia cavalry, reached a total of 149 officers and 3,077 men, a total of 3,226 members. Of these, 11 officers and 101 enlisted men were killed in action, 3 officers and 53 men died of wounds received in action, one officer and 171 men died of disease, one officer and 165 men died in southern prisons, and one officer and 5 men were killed by accident; 447 were wounded, 72 were wounded and taken prisoners, and 539 were taken prisoners, 246 of whom were from the First District of Columbia cavalry before its transfer but their names were borne on the rolls of the regiment. This is in brief the history of this regiment, and it tells its own story.

The regiment was organized in the fall of 1861, the majority of the companies being mustered into the United States service in October of that year. John Goddard was appointed Colonel, Thomas Hight, of the United States Army, Lieutenant-Colonel, and Samuel H. Allen, David P. Stowell and Calvin S. Douty, Majors, and there was a full complement of field and staff officers, with line officers for twelve full companies.

The following is the original organization :—

FIELD, STAFF, AND NON-COMMISSIONED STAFF.

Colonel, John Goddard, Cape Elizabeth.
Lieutenant-Colonel, Thomas Hight, U. S. Army.
Major, Samuel H. Allen, Thomaston.
Major, David P. Stowell, Canton.
Major, Calvin S. Douty, Dover.
Adjutant, First Lieutenant Benjamin F. Tucker, U. S. Army.
Quartermaster, First Lieutenant Edward M. Patten, Portland.
Surgeon, George W. Colby, Richmond.
Assistant Surgeon, George W. Haley, Eastport.
Chaplain, Benjamin F. Tefft, Bangor.

Sergeant-Major, Addison P. Russell, Houlton.
Quartermaster-Sergeant, Eustace C. Bigelow, Portland.
Commissary-Sergeant, Charles S. Crosby, Bangor.
Hospital Steward, Samuel C. Lovejoy, Rockland.
Principal Musician, Artemas D. Bickford, Houlton.
Principal Musician, William L. Boyd, Houlton.
Band-leader, Alexander S. Davis, Houlton.

COMPANY OFFICERS.

Co. A. Captain, Warren L. Whitney, Newburg.
First Lieutenant, Sidney W. Thaxter, Bangor.
Second Lieutenant, Joseph C. Hill, Kennebunk.
Co. B. Captain, Jonathan P. Cilley, Thomaston.
First Lieutenant, William P. Coleman, Lincolnville.
Second Lieutenant, Frank M. Cutler, Union.
Co. C. Captain, Robert F. Dyer, Augusta.
First Lieutenant, Dudley L. Haines, Readfield.
Second Lieutenant, George S. Kimball, Gardiner.
Co. D. Captain, Charles H. Smith, Eastport.
First Lieutenant, Andrew B. Spurling, Orland.
Second Lieutenant, William Montgomery, Orland.

Co. E.   Captain, Black Hawk Putnam, Houlton.
        First Lieutenant, John H. Goddard, Portland.
        Second Lieutenant, Osco A. Ellis, Lincoln.
Co. F.   Captain, Nathan Mayhew, Portland.
        First Lieutenant, Stephen Boothby, Portland.
        Second Lieutenant, Jarvis C. Stevens, Portland.
Co. G.   Captain, Augustus J. Burbank, Lewiston.
        First Lieutenant, Zebulon B. Blethen, Lewiston.
        Second Lieutenant, Isaac G. Virgin, Dixfield.
Co. H.   Captain, George J. Summat, U. S. Army.
        First Lieutenant, Charles H. Baker, Skowhegan.
        Second Lieutenant, John R. Webb, St. Albans.
Co. I.   Captain, Louis O. Cowan, Biddeford.
        First Lieutenant, Paul Chadbourne, Waterboro.
        Second Lieutenant, Frank W. Pray, Shapleigh.
Co. K.   Captain, George Prince, Bath.
        First Lieutenant, George Cary, Houlton.
        Second Lieutenant, John D. Myrick, Augusta.
Co. L.   Captain, Reuben B. Jennings, Farmington.
        First Lieutenant, Constantine Taylor, U. S. Army.
        Second Lieutenant, George Weston, Oldtown.
Co. M.   Captain, George M. Brown, Bangor.
        First Lieutenant, John C. C. Bowen, Boston, Mass.
        Second Lieutenant, Evans S. Pillsbury, Guilford.

This was peculiarly a state regiment, the companies being apportioned among the different counties, the larger counties being allowed a company, while of the smaller counties two were allotted to a company. The regiment went into camp on the State Fair grounds at Augusta, the camp being named "Camp Penobscot." This camp was destined to be the home of the regiment all through that long, cold and dreary winter. In Sibley tents, banked up well with snow, and with a little stove hung upon a hollow iron pole which served at once for tent pole and for stove pipe, the boys lived that winter — that is, the majority of them did — and received their first taste of the hardships of a soldier's life. Many died in that camp, owing to the cold and the insufficient protection.

During the winter Colonel Goddard resigned, and Major Allen became Colonel, and Captain Whitney, of company A, Major. Lieut.-Colonel Hight also resigned, but the vacancy was not filled at that time. In March the regiment went to Washington, camping on Capitol Hill for a few days, and then began active campaigning.

MIDDLETOWN. — On the 30th of March five companies, under command of Major Douty, were sent to Harper's Ferry and the Shenandoah Valley, where they remained till the following July, when they rejoined the regiment. Scouting and guarding the railroad were the chief duties here till the 9th of May, when the command was attached to General Hatch's cavalry brigade and joined General Banks' force. There was skirmishing with the enemy on the 20th and 22d, and on the 24th this battalion held in check General Ashby's force of 3,000 cavalry and a battery, near Middletown, for hours, allowing General Banks to secure the better position and, according to General Ashby, "saving Banks' army." Later in the day the battalion made a gallant charge, in which it lost one killed, 10 wounded of whom one died, 13 wounded and taken prisoners of whom one died, and 49 taken prisoners of whom 6 died. Captain Cilley, of company B, was wounded severely and left on the field,—the first man wounded in the regiment, as he was the first to enlist in it. Assistant Surgeon Haley remained with Captain Cilley and was taken prisoner.

ALONG THE RAPPAHANNOCK. — The remaining seven companies left Washington on the 5th of April and marched into Virginia under command of Major Stowell, Colonel Allen having been left sick in New York. The history of that summer's campaign is a record of scouting, reconnoitering, — this regiment being the first Union force to go as far south as Culpeper Court House, — picketing, marching, orderly duty and some fighting, though at that period of the war the cavalry was not thought to be of much account, and was scattered among the different brigades and divisions of infantry, instead of acting together.

In June Major Whitney, with companies C and D, was sent out by General McDowell to communicate with General Banks, then at Williamsport. The little command dashed through Winchester, which was held by the enemy, in the early morning, creating great consternation among soldiers and citizens, and reaching General Banks delivered the orders and received new ones, returning the next day.

The regiment took part in the battle of Cedar Mountain, August 9th, being under fire though not actively engaged ; had a lively skirmish with the enemy at Brandy Station August 20th; endured all the hardships of General Pope's retreat, serving for a few days at General Pope's headquarters; and took part in the second battle of Bull Run, where, on the last day, it was under fire in different positions on the field all day long, and was employed at one time to prevent the infantry from straggling from the field. Upon the arrival of the army at Frederick City, Md., Colonel Allen was detailed military governor of the city, Capt. Charles H. Smith, provost marshal, and the major portion of the regiment was on duty in the city for a while, but company G took part in the battle of South Mountain, and company H was at Antietam. At Fredericksburg, also, the regiment bore an honorable part, being under fire all the time, though it was not actively engaged.

The losses during the year were 2 killed, 27 wounded of whom 3 died, 13 wounded and prisoners of whom one died, and 63 prisoners of whom 6 died.

During the winter of 1862-3 the cavalry of the army of the Potomac was organized into brigades, divisions and a corps, and from that time the cavalry-men had a different story to tell, and for the first time in its history the First Maine Cavalry was serving all together. This regiment was placed in the First brigade, Colonel Judson Kilpatrick commanding, Third division, Gen. David McM. Gregg commanding. The winter was spent in picketing, scouting, fatigue duty and drill.

During the year some changes had been made in the regimental officers. Colonel Allen resigned while at Frederick, and Lieut.-Colonel Douty, who had been promoted from Major some time before, was commissioned Colonel. Captain Smith, of company D, had been commissioned Major and then Lieutenant-Colonel. Captain Cilley, of company B, had been commissioned Major before he was wounded, but was serving with his company at that time. Captain Boothby, of company F, had been commissioned Major. Major Whitney had resigned, but this vacancy was not filled at once.

STONEMAN'S RAID. — The spring campaign opened with "Stoneman's Raid," in which this regiment took part. On this expedition there was some fighting, plenty of hard marching, a loss of sleep and a want of rations which tested the physical endurance of the men more severely, perhaps, than any other service during the whole four years of the regiment's history. During this raid companies B and I, while scouting near Louisa Court House, made a charge in which two were killed, one wounded, two wounded and prisoners, and 28 prisoners, including Lieutenant Andrews, company I. Lieut.-Colonel Smith, with one hundred men from each the First Maine and the 10th N. Y. regiments, was sent on an expedition to destroy a bridge over the South Anna River, ten miles from Richmond. The bridge was not destroyed, owing to the presence of a large force of the enemy, and Lieut.-Colonel Smith's orders being not to bring on a fight in any case; but the railroad was torn up, the station burned, and other damage done to the enemy.

BRANDY STATION. — The Gettysburg campaign commenced with the cavalry fight at Brandy Station, which place General Lee's cavalry had reached in the advance of his army on the way to Maryland and Pennsylvania. This fight occurred June 9th. General Buford's brigade of cavalry crossed the Rappahannock at Beverly Ford on the right, while General Gregg's division crossed at Kelly's Ford, at the left. Col. Percy Wyndham's brigade had the advance of this division, and attacked the enemy in the rear, nearly capturing General Stuart the rebel cavalry leader, but after a gallant fight was driven back, with three brigades in full pursuit. At this time Colonel Kilpatrick arrived upon the field, and sent in the two advance regiments of his brigade, the Harris Light and 10th N. Y., to the relief of Wyndham, but they were met by two heavy columns and driven back. At this juncture, when the day seemed to be lost, the First Maine arrived on the field, and forming squadrons at a gallop, drew sabre and charged the enemy, driving back the force which had just driven the remainder of the brigade and had turned its attention to the First Maine, driving the enemy from the cannon which had been pouring shot and shell upon the charging column, driving the enemy a mile or more. This, the first charge of the First Maine, was perfectly irresistible; there was no withstanding it. With the force of its own momentum the regiment went on and on, driving everything before it, and stopped only when it was impossible to go further. Upon halting, the companies were re-formed and counted off, and some of the men dismounted and opened fire with their carbines. Lieut.-Colonel Smith assumed command, Colonel Douty being in another part of the field, and discovered that the enemy was in his rear, having returned and manned the battery from which the gunners had been driven, while he had a small command and was alone. He quickly wheeled the regiment and started back over the same ground, and by suddenly changing direction to the right, as he saw the guns were about to be discharged, got out of range, and the shot and shell passed harmlessly by.

This charge of the First Maine Cavalry, General Kilpatrick many times stated publicly was "one of the best charges ever made," and "saved not only the brigade but the whole division in this action"; and he always claimed that "to the First Maine Cavalry he owed the silver star he won that day upon the field of battle." More than this, the Union success in this the first real cavalry fight of the war on a large scale, so much of which was due to this regiment, was a severe blow to the south, wresting from it, as the southern army and the southern press admitted it did, the boasted claim of the superiority of the southern cavalry.

The loss to the regiment in this engagement was one killed, 2 wounded, 7 wounded and taken prisoners, and 28 taken prisoners.

The Second and Third divisions of the Cavalry corps were now consolidated into one division, named the Second, and the brigades were reorganized, General Kilpatrick having command of the First, while the First Maine was placed in the Third brigade, under command of Col. J. Irvin Gregg.

ALDIE.—June 17th the regiment, after a march of twenty miles, arrived at Aldie, where a severe cavalry fight was in progress. The regiment was at once ordered to report to General Kilpatrick, whose troops had been engaged and were driven back in confusion. When Colonel Douty reached the top of a rather steep hill on the pike he was met by General Kilpatrick who appealed to him to save him as the regiment had done at Brandy Station. As soon as two companies — D and H — got up the hill they charged, led by Colonel Douty and Captain Summat, driving the enemy from a strong position behind a stone-wall. Major Boothby followed with several companies and took position at the wall, routing the enemy and holding the position until the arrival of Lieut.-Colonel Smith, who had been sent on detached duty with four companies, when Lieut.-Colonel Smith took command of the regiment. Colonel Douty was killed in the very advance, his body being found beyond the stone-wall. Captain Summat was also killed in the advance.

Beside the loss of Colonel Douty and Captain Summat, Captain Montgomery of company D was wounded, and the total loss in the regiment was 5 killed, 18 wounded of whom one died, and 4 taken prisoners. Upon the death of Colonel Douty, Lieut.-Colonel Smith was commissioned Colonel, and Major Boothby, Lieutenant-Colonel.

MIDDLEBURG.—Two days later, June 19th, the regiment fought here its most desperate and effective battle up to that date. There were no long-distance charges because the regiment was face to face with the enemy at the start and advanced in four columns. Lieutenant Ford, with company K, charged gallantly on the right of the pike, this company sustaining the heaviest loss in enlisted men of any company in the regiment. Captain Kimball, with company C, charged on the pike into the face and midst of the enemy and was driven back with loss, Captain Kimball being killed after he had nearly gained the rear of the enemy. Major Brown, commissioned from Captain company M June 4th, with companies E and M, charged obliquely to the left through a belt of open timber and encountered the extreme right of the enemy, a large detachment of whom were dismounted and behind stone-walls and commanded by a major. By dash and persistence Major Brown's detachment captured nearly the whole force, turned the enemy's right and greatly demoralized him. In this charge Lieutenants Neville, company E, and Taylor, company M, were killed. The balance of the regiment, under Colonel Smith, moved directly to the front and engaged the enemy wherever found, at short range. Colonel

Smith's horse was shot by a pistol ball at only a few paces. All who had pistols used them. In the meantime the 10th N. Y. cavalry, a small regiment, came to the support of this regiment. The enemy greatly outnumbered our force, and many of his men did not get into the fight at all. Still he retired after having resisted this fierce assault.

Beside the casualties already mentioned, Lieutenants Brooks, company C, and Vaughan, company L, were wounded, the entire loss being 10 killed, 19 wounded, 4 wounded and taken prisoners and 2 taken prisoners.

UPPERVILLE.—June 21st the regiment again met the enemy, the third time within a week. Two regiments of General Kilpatrick's command had been sent in to take the town of Upperville and hold it, and had been successively driven back. General Kilpatrick asked for the First Maine, saying, "They will go through," and the First Maine was ordered to report to him. Colonel Smith was ordered, with the regiment, to "charge through the town, drive out the enemy, and get beyond it if possible." As the regiment started to obey this order, General Kilpatrick said: "That First Maine would charge straight into hell if it were ordered to." On entering the town the regiment was met by a discharge of grape from a gun posted to oppose it, which gun was immediately captured. The enemy was dispersed and driven beyond the town, whither the regiment pursued and engaged him, killing and wounding many and capturing 75. The loss in the regiment in this fight was Captain Spurling, company D, and 5 men wounded, and one man taken prisoner.

The regiment, with the division, was busy for several days keeping watch of the enemy. The services of the cavalry from Brandy Station to Gettysburg, the fighting, the marching and the scouting, had the effect of keeping the enemy's cavalry all the time employed, thus preventing him from obtaining any knowledge of the movements of our army and keeping General Lee in the dark, and allowing the Union army to move as it chose, making the glorious victory at Gettysburg possible.

The following is the nominal list of casualties in the regiment in this campaign up to the battle of Gettysburg : —

Brandy Station, June 9, 1863.

Co. A.   Private Thomas E. Whitney, w'd and pris'r; Sergeant Scott S. Ellis, Corporals Horace H. Lowell, William H. Cleaveland, James B. Farnham, and Privates Simeon M. Dawson, Madison M. Grant, Anson O. Libby and Nathan L. Ricker, pris'rs.

Co. C.   Sergeant Reuben S. Neal and Privates Joshua H. Crane and Joseph Lunt, pris'rs.

Co. D.   Private Jerry E. Arnold, pris'r.

Co. E.   Privates Joseph Ayatt and Frederick Smart, w'd; Frank W. Leavitt, w'd and pris'r; Bugler Antoine Schouton, Privates Albert Haines and Benjamin C. Hicks, pris'rs.

Co. G.   Corporal John Dealy, Jr., killed; Corporal Edward P. Tobie, Jr., and Private George L. Duston, w'd and pris'rs; Sergeants Calvin B. Benson, Henry F. Blanchard, George E. Jumper, Corporals Daniel B. Doyen, Hannibal Bisbee, Jr., Privates Seth B. Goodwin and William H. Wyman, pris'rs.

Co. I.   Sergeant Charles W. Coffin, pris'r.

Co. K.   Sergeant William M. Loud, Corporal Alonzo Colby and Private John Dogea, w'd and pris'rs; Sergeants George F. Jewett, Edward B. Herbert, Corporal Edwin D. Bailey, and Private Francis Hart, pris'rs.

Co. M.   Corporal Waterman T. Lewis, pris'r.

Aldie, June 17, 1863.

Field and Staff: Colonel Calvin S. Douty, killed.

Co. D.   Private George W. Simpson, killed; Captain William Montgomery, Corporal John C. Ward, Privates Edward Dunbar and Samuel E. Griffin, w'd; Sergeant Nathan B. Webb, Corporal William Ricker, Privates Thompson M. Brown and Thomas B. Pulsifer, pris'rs.

Co. E.   Bugler Evander L. French, w'd.

Co. G.   Corporal Homer Child, Privates William O. Howes and Fernando F. Mason, w'd.

Co. H.   Captain George J. Summat, Privates Charles B. Decker and James A. Hurd, killed; Sergeants Daniel W. Hall (died), Henry W. Boston, Corporals Abner C. Emery, Lewis Andrews, Privates Hiram W. Allen, Llewellyn Goodwin, Sumner A. Holway, Peter Honan, Isaiah C. Mosher, and David W. Rhodes, w'd; Sergeant Washington I. Hurd (died), and Private James Canwell, w'd and pris'rs.

Middleburg, June 19, 1863.

Co. A.   Private Hiram T. Drew, w'd.

Co. C.   Captain George S. Kimball and Corporal John W. Neal, killed; Lieutenant Jonathan K. Brooks, Sergeant Charles G. Thwing, and Privates Charles J. Higgins, Alvin M. Johnson, W. Franklin Swift, Arnold F. Worthing, Henry Young, w'd.

Co. D.   Private Frank H. Hinckley, w'd; Sergeant Benjamin P. Knowles, pris'r.

Co. E.   First Lieutenant Mark Neville and Sergeant Charles C. Putnam, killed; Corporal George A. Russell and Private Batiste Le Sault, w'd.

Co. F.   Sergeant Benjamin G. Hawks and Private John T. Trefethen, killed; Sergeant Horace P. Holyoke and Privates Ambrose Reed, Howard M. Thompson, w'd.

Co. H.   Sergeant Willard H. Phelps, pris'r.

Co. K.   Sergeants, David Bryant, Jr., Justin L. Swett, and Corporal Charles R. Johnson, killed; Private Joseph B. Peaks, w'd; Sergeants William D. Elliott, David Tozier, Corporal Walter F. Haines and Private John Hogan, w'd and pris'rs.

Co. L.   First Lieutenant Zenas Vaughan, w'd.

Co. M.   Second Lieutenant Ephraim H. Taylor, killed; Sergeants Alanson M. Warren, John J. Thomas, and Wagoner Samuel Ingalls, w'd.

Upperville, June 21, 1863.

Co. D.   Captain Andrew B. Spurling and Corp. Simeon A. Holden, w'd.

Co. F.   Private Charles Eastman, w'd; Corporal John H. Merrill, pris'r.

Co. G.   Corporal Volney H. Foss, w'd.

Co. I.   Privates John P. Abbott and Walter Allen, pris'rs near Aldie, June 22.

Co. K.   Corporal Charles Burgess, w'd.

Co. M.   Private Reuel W. Porter, w'd.

GETTYSBURG.—July 3d the regiment took part in the severe cavalry fight on the right of the Union lines at Gettysburg, where the Union cavalry frustrated the enemy's attempt to turn the right flank and gain the rear at the time of General Pickett's famous charge in the centre. The regiment supported a battery in the forenoon, and in the afternoon was sent out with another regiment, both under command of Colonel Smith, to meet an advancing column of the enemy in the attack on the right flank. One battalion was dismounted and advanced into an orchard without difficulty, the advancing enemy halting and turning back upon meeting this force; and the remainder of this command was arranged for battle and held this part of the line during this engagement, the brigade occupying the gap of nearly two miles between the left of the forces engaged with the enemy's cavalry and the right of the Union infantry. The loss in this day's engagement was small. Sergeant Loring, company B, was wounded, one man was killed, 3 were wounded, and one was wounded and missing.

The regiment then joined the army in pursuit of the retreating enemy, marching and scouting continuously, and crossing the Potomac on the 14th. On the 15th the regiment was sent toward Charlestown from Halltown to take care of the enemy while the rest of the division moved in the direction of Shepardstown. On this expedition the regiment had a smart little skirmish, driving the enemy's cavalry and artillery a mile or more, and losing Assistant Surgeon Parker and 3 men, who were taken prisoners.

SHEPARDSTOWN.—On the 16th the regiment started out after forage near Shepardstown, but nearing the picket line met the pickets coming in, followed by the enemy. As the enemy reached the crest of a hill, Colonel Smith ordered Lieutenants Cole and Coleman, with companies A and B, to charge up the hill, and such was the impetuosity of this charge that the enemy was driven from the crest. Colonel Smith advanced the remainder of the regiment and held the crest for more than an hour, when the enemy massed in such numbers as to force him back some two hundred yards to a more favorable position. Here the 4th Penn. cavalry joined the First Maine, and by stubborn fighting the enemy—cavalry and artillery—was held until this force was relieved by the 16th Penn. regiment. Later in the afternoon the 16th Penn. was in peril, when the First Maine went to their support and again became actively engaged.

The heavy loss in this engagement tells how severe was the fighting. Lieut.-Colonel Boothby, Lieutenant Hunton, company G, and Lieutenant Bradman, company M, were wounded, and the total loss was 4 killed, 22 wounded of whom 4 died, 2 wounded and taken prisoners, and 7 prisoners.

This engagement was the end of the Gettysburg campaign, which began with the fight at Brandy Station, June 9th.

Soon after this the division was reorganized and made into two brigades, when Colonel Gregg's brigade, containing the First Maine, became the Second, and this regiment remained in that brigade for more than a year.

SULPHUR SPRINGS.—In October a reconnaissance was made by the regiment to Little Washington and Sperryville. The men had been in the saddle and on the march two full days,—10th and 11th,—a movement by the rebel army to turn the right flank of the Union army having been discovered, when on the morning of the 12th Colonel Smith was ordered to proceed with the regiment to Sperryville to observe any movement the enemy might make in that direction, and to report promptly whatever of the enemy he might discover. On this expedition the regiment was absent from the division four days, marching all day and night on the 12th, being twice cut off by the enemy, marching all day the 13th, moving all day and night the 14th, and marching and fighting all the 15th, making six days and two nights of constant marching and fighting. The regiment was officially reported as captured. The reconnaissance was in every way successful, General Meade speaking very emphatically to Colonel Smith concerning the value of the information obtained, which was forwarded to General Meade by Major Brown before the regiment got back to the army.

The loss on this expedition was Lieutenant Coleman, company B, and two men wounded of whom one died, one wounded and taken prisoner who died, and 22 prisoners one of whom died.

MINE RUN. — The regiment took part in the Mine Run expedition, the latter part of November, during which it did some skirmishing, reconnoitering and picketing in extreme cold weather, and served as rear guard for the whole army on the return from the expedition, December 2d, holding the pursuing enemy in check until the entire force had crossed the Rapidan.

The latter part of December the regiment, with three others, under command of Colonel Smith, the regiment being under command of Lieut.-Colonel Boothby, made a successful expedition through Thornton's Gap, in the Blue Ridge, to Luray, during which a large manufactory of Confederate government cavalry and artillery equipments, with contents, and several tanneries, were destroyed. There was a skirmish in front of Luray, and several prisoners were captured, and a charge was made at Little Washington in which one rebel was killed. Colonel Smith received from General Pleasanton a letter of commendation for the able manner in which he conducted the hazardous trip.

The losses in the regiment during this year were 24 killed, 80 wounded of whom 6 died, 20 wounded and taken prisoners of whom 2 died, and 110 taken prisoners of whom one died.

January 1, 1864, the regiment went with the division on an expedition to Front Royal and vicinity to reconnoiter. This was a hard, cold march, with the roads in bad condition, during which the men suffered more from cold than before in the service. While on this expedition Captain Taylor, company L, with four companies of this regiment and detachments from the other regiments, was sent to army headquarters to carry despatches. On their way they met a force of Mosby's men near Salem Church, when a spirited engagement took place, the enemy being driven by a charge by company H, under command of Captain Hall, and 25 prisoners were captured. On the return march a severe snow-storm made the roads and the marching even worse, and the regiment camped that night near Warrenton in six inches of snow, without tents, and with little to make them comfortable.

The regiment went into winter quarters near Warrenton, and there was a season of picketing, scouting, etc., 9 men being taken prisoners while scouting that winter, of whom 4 died. The last of February a strong detail of the regiment joined in the raid to Richmond, commonly called the "Dahlgren Raid," under General Kilpatrick, during which the regiment lost 7 killed, 4 wounded of whom 2 died, 3 wounded and prisoners, and 36 prisoners of whom 18 died.

In the spring of 1864 General Sheridan was placed in command of the cavalry corps of the army of the Potomac. The Second division remained in command of General Gregg, and the First Maine was still in the Second brigade, Colonel Smith commanding the regiment. But there had been some changes among the field officers. Lieut.-Colonel Boothby and Major Cilley remained; Captain Thaxter, company A, had been commissioned Major June 4, 1863, and Captain Taylor, company L, as Major February 18, 1864; Major Brown had resigned on account of disability incurred in the service.

TODD'S TAVERN. — The regiment crossed the Rapidan with the division on the morning of May 4th, and for three or four days was employed in scouting and skirmishing on the left of the army, then in the Wilderness, being under fire several times with little loss. On the afternoon of the 7th the regiment, with the brigade, was formed, dismounted, across the Catharpin road, near Todd's Tavern. A line of rail breastworks was hastily thrown up, and there was a lively little fight, or severe skirmish, that afternoon and the next forenoon, when the brigade was relieved by infantry. During this fight a portion of this regiment, under Lieut.-Colonel Boothby, with other regiments, the whole under command of Colonel Smith, joined in a charge against the enemy's infantry,—the carbine against the bayonet,— and the dismounted cavalry routed the rebel infantry. The loss in this engagement was 7 wounded of whom one died, the small loss showing the benefit of breastworks even though they be built in a hurry.

BEAVER DAM STATION.—On the 9th the whole cavalry force broke loose from the army and started on a raid in the enemy's rear, commonly known as "Sheridan's Raid to Richmond," which General Grant said "had the effect of drawing off the whole of the enemy's cavalry force and making it comparatively easy to guard our trains." On the morning of the 10th the column started with the First Maine in the advance, company G heading the regiment. Scarcely had the column passed headquarters, when the advance ran into the enemy's pickets and a running fight ensued for a mile or more, when the enemy was found in a strong line across a field beyond a creek. A brief skirmish, a charge by a portion of the regiment, and the enemy was brushed away, no more to hinder the march that day. In this little fight, known as Beaver Dam Station, Lieut.-Colonel Boothby received a wound which caused his death, and one man was killed and three wounded.

GROUND SQUIRREL CHURCH BRIDGE. — On the 11th, in the regular order of marching, it became the duty of the regiment to take the rear. The regiment was waiting quietly by the side of the road for the remainder of the division to pass, when it was ordered to go to the support of the pickets, which had been attacked. Riding a short distance, the men hastily dismounted, rushed into the woods, joined the pickets near Ground Squirrel Bridge and commenced firing. In a few moments the men were ordered to return to the horses as quickly as possible. They had barely got mounted when the enemy came down upon them, charging in three columns, and a fight ensued in which two men were killed, Lieutenants Libby, company C, and Johnson, company M, and 8 men were wounded; 12 were wounded and taken prisoners of whom 7 died, and Captain Vaughan, company M, and 18 men were taken prisoners of whom 7 men died. The enemy lost their famous cavalry general, J. E. B. Stuart, and one of the Generals Gordon. The regiment held the rear all the day, skirmishing frequently and making but little progress on the road.

Colonel Smith and Major Thaxter each had horses shot under them, and Colonel Smith was at one time entirely surrounded by the enemy but escaped recognition and managed to ride from among them.

FORTIFICATIONS OF RICHMOND.—By daylight on the morning of the 12th, having marched all night, the regiment followed the remainder of the column inside the outer fortifications of Richmond, and was given the important duty of protecting the rear of the whole force, which it did successfully with comparatively small loss. In the morning it supported a battery during a heavy thunder storm, when the sounds of the human artillery were well-nigh drowned by those of the artillery of heaven, and later had a lively skirmish with a force sent out from Richmond to harass the rear of the raiding force. In this engagement one man was killed, Major Thaxter, Sergeant Loring of company B, and 2 men were wounded, and 3 were taken prisoners of whom one died. The position of the cavalry on this day was in the "trap" which had been prepared to capture the whole force, but General Sheridan was general enough to get out of the trap, the First Maine holding the rear while he was opening the door in front.

Then came the return march to the Union lines, which were reached on the 25th, at the North Anna River instead of in the Wilderness. During this march there was the usual amount of picketing and scouting. On the afternoon of the 16th the regiment, with the pioneers of the whole division, under command of Colonel Smith, were sent ahead to repair Jones' bridge over the Chickahominy and put it in condition for the command to cross. While doing this the regiment stood guard by picketing all around. The force arrived on the morning of the 18th, when it was found necessary to build another bridge to facilitate the crossing, which was achieved in one hour and forty-five minutes, the quickest bridge-building on record up to that time.

HAWES' SHOP. — On the 26th General Grant was ready for another flank movement around the right of the enemy, and the cavalry had the advance, crossing the Pamunkey on pontoons early the next morning. On the 28th the regiment took part in the severe cavalry engagement at Hawes' Shop, which General Grant pronounced "the most severe cavalry fight of the war up to that time." The regiment supported a battery during this engagement, and the loss was small, one man being killed, but the strain on the men during that long afternoon was terrible.

COLD HARBOR. — June 2d the regiment met the enemy at Barker's Mills, the beginning of the battle of Cold Harbor, where a portion of the regiment skirmished through the woods mounted, and the remainder made a gallant mounted charge upon the rebel batteries, gained a good position on the hill and held it all day, in spite of two desperate attempts to drive it away. In the first of the engagement Chaplain Bartlett was killed and 4 men were wounded, of whom one died. The regiment remained on the skirmish line in this vicinity till the morning of the 5th.

TREVILLIAN STATION. — On the 7th the cavalry started on General Sheridan's raid towards Gordonsville, and the First Maine went with the division. There was the usual amount of hard marching, picketing and scouting, but little fighting until the 11th, when occurred the fight at Trevillian Station. Here the regiment had another day of supporting a battery, following it all day and taking up various positions; towards night the enemy's battery was driven from the position which it had occupied all through the fight, and our battery was placed on some rising ground with this regiment in its rear. In a short time the enemy's battery opened with canister, and threw the shells into our battery with wonderful accuracy, while the bullets flew all around the regiment. Colonel Smith took in the situation at once and moved the regiment to the left, where it was comparatively safe, the enemy's many missiles passing harmlessly by on the right. By this prompt action the regiment was saved from heavy loss, there being only 4 wounded.

There was a skirmish at Louisa Court House the next day

and then a week of tiresome marching on the back track, in
hot weather and over dusty roads. On the 21st there was an
engagement near White House Landing, in which the enemy
was pushed back to Black Run, where he made a stand, and
later in the day advanced in line of battle, but was repulsed
after a sharp fight. The First Maine had the right of the line,
fighting mounted in the forenoon and dismounted in the afternoon, and lost one killed and 4 wounded.

St. Mary's Church. — During the absence of the cavalry
on this expedition the army of the Potomac had crossed the
James River and was settling down before Petersburg, having
left a large wagon train at White House Landing. It now
became the duty of the cavalry to take this baggage train to
the army, and the march commenced on the 23d. The first day
this regiment had nothing to do but keep its place in the column. The next day, the 24th, fearing an attempt by the enemy
to capture the train, the division was sent early in the morning
on a road leading to Richmond to prevent any attack upon the
train from that direction. The First Maine had the advance
and company G had the advance of the regiment. After
marching a few miles the column was halted by the enemy's
pickets in the road at the edge of some woods, some two miles
from St. Mary's Church. A company of the regiment was
dismounted and sent into the woods, which drove the pickets to
the church, where the enemy made a stand. The remainder
of the regiment and the greater part of the division were soon
in line behind hastily-constructed breastworks, and a severe
fight occurred, in which Captain Ellis of E and Captain Phillips
of F were killed; Colonel Smith, Lieut.-Colonel Cilley, Major
Tucker (commissioned Major from Captain of B July 12th),
Captain Montgomery and Lieutenant Johnson of D and Lieutenant Hussey of E were wounded; Captain Carson and Lieutenant
Gordon of L and Lieutenant Johnson of M were taken prisoners; and Captain Myrick of K and Lieutenant Benson of G
were overcome by the heat; the total loss being 13 killed, 23
wounded of whom two died, three wounded and taken prisoners
and 19 taken prisoners of whom eight died. Colonel Smith
remained on the field till the close of the day, having two horses

shot under him after he was wounded, and the First Maine was one of the last two regiments to leave the field. This engagement was a severe one, the enemy fighting stubbornly and making a powerful effort to get at the train, and our troops fighting as stubbornly. At one time the enemy advanced even to the battery of the division, some of his men placing their hands upon the guns, but were driven back. The train was saved, and the division was not captured or destroyed. Nor did the enemy care to follow this division when it left the field, at dark.

Major Thaxter was now in command of the regiment, which went into camp July 4th for a few days' rest, having been actively campaigning for two months, during which time it had passed two nights in the same place but twice. July 26th a movement was made on the right of the army, across the James River, "with a view of cutting the enemy's railroad from near Richmond to the Anna rivers, and to take advantage of his necessary withdrawal of troops from Petersburg to explode the mine and make an assault." The First Maine, with the division, joined in this movement, during which one battalion had a sharp fight on the old Malvern Hill battle ground, capturing a number of the enemy and losing four men wounded, on the 28th; and the whole regiment had a skirmish on the picket line, on the same ground, during which two men were wounded, on the 29th.

DEEP BOTTOM. — August 13th commenced another movement across the James, which resulted in drawing so many of the enemy's troops from Petersburg as to make it possible for General Grant to take possession of the Weldon Railroad, which was done on the 18th. The First Maine, with the division, also joined in this movement. The regiment was on the skirmish line all day the 15th, one man being wounded, and on the 16th took part in the fight at Deep Bottom, where 4 men were killed, Captain Virgin, company G, and 21 men were wounded, and one was taken prisoner who died. In this engagement the 16th Penn. cavalry had the advance, the First Maine following. The advance found the enemy and had a running fight for a mile or two, when the Confederates made a stand. A brigade of the Second corps was brought up to assist the dismounted men in the woods. There was a lull in the skirmishing and the greater portion of the infantry had been sent to some other part of the line, when the enemy made a fierce attack, driving in the skirmishers. The First Maine was rushed to the front and had to stand the brunt of the attack, and being alone in the field and mounted, it was forced to retire to the further side of White Oak Swamp, where it made a stand and held the enemy at bay. There was more skirmishing on the 17th and 18th, during which 2 men were killed and 2 wounded one of whom died.

On the 19th Colonel Smith returned to duty, having sufficiently recovered from the wound received at St. Mary's Church, and took command of the brigade, Col. J. Irvin Gregg having been wounded at Deep Bottom.

REAMS' STATION.—On the 23d of August the division was sent to the Weldon Railroad, near Reams' Station, to help hold the railroad, which the enemy was strenuously endeavoring to recapture. The First Maine had a pretty little skirmish in the afternoon and evening while the rest of the brigade had a very hard fight, Colonel Smith commanding the brigade, losing 4 of his 5 regimental commanders, and being himself wounded, though he would not leave his command. On the 24th the regiment was on the skirmish line all day, but was not disturbed. On the 25th the fight was continued. The regiment was on the left and was not actively engaged, but was marched from position to position all day long, building two stout lines of breastworks which were occupied by the infantry, as the regiment was ordered further to the front, and being under artillery and musketry fire most of the time. Along towards night a shell fired by the enemy aimed at the right of the line came over to the left, so much had the line become doubled up, killing two men in G and wounding two in E. The loss in these three days of fighting was 3 killed, Colonel Smith and 5 men wounded and one taken prisoner.

For a month the regiment was engaged in scouting and picketing—always busy. On the 2d of September the regiment, in advance of the brigade, made a brilliant dash beyond the Weldon

Railroad and across the Peebles' farm, being the first Union troops to reach the Boydton Plank Road. The purpose of this expedition was the capture or destruction of the enemy's supply train, which had been parked on the Poplar Springs Road, about two miles from our infantry outposts. Sergeant Dodge of company I, and 12 men, had the advance and charged the enemy gallantly, drove him away from his barricades and pursued him about half a mile. Lieutenant Andrews with H charged another body and drove it more than a mile, but the train had been moved out at daylight, and the expedition was fruitless.

On the 16th of September the regiment, with the division, made a reconnaissance to Stony Creek, in pursuit of General Hampton's cavalry after its successful raid at Sycamore Church, in which two men were wounded.

On the 24th of September 8 companies of the First District of Columbia cavalry, which were recruited in Maine, were formally transferred to this regiment, and so many as were at the time serving with the former regiment and were in condition for service arrived and were assigned to the different companies. A very large number, however, were absent, in hospital, in rebel prisons, at dismounted camp waiting for horses, and on detached duty. The First District of Columbia cavalry took the field early in 1864. The total loss in the regiment previous to the transfer was 11 killed, 34 wounded of whom 2 died, 18 wounded and prisoners of whom 6 died, and 246 taken prisoners of whom 113 died.

WYATT'S FARM. — September 26th Lieut.-Colonel Cilley, promoted from Major July 11th, having recovered from wounds received at St. Mary's Church, arrived and took command of the regiment, relieving Major Thaxter, who had been in command since June 24th. Captain Tucker of B was promoted Major, to succeed Major Cilley. On the 29th the brigade was sent out to the Wyatt Farm. A portion of the brigade became engaged, but the fire of the enemy was so hot the troops would not stand, and Colonel Smith sent to Lieut.-Colonel Cilley for the First Maine to fill the gap. Captain Hall, with the Third battalion, reported to Colonel Smith and was ordered to take position across the pike and hold it at all hazards. Captain

Hall moved forward to a little cover and pushed up to the front with two companies on each side of the road, and held the position; the firing soon ceased. After dark the enemy charged upon the line but was driven back. The enemy captured a large portion of the right of the line, but Lieutenant Andrews charged and released all of them. Captain Hall was wounded, one man was killed, one taken prisoner. The brigade had both flanks turned and captured, but held firm. The first Maine was in the centre and held this position, thus insuring the success of the Union troops in this engagement. The loss in the brigade was about sixty.

BOYDTON ROAD. — On the 18th of October a new brigade was formed, the command of which was given to Colonel Smith, which he retained until the close of the war, having been in command of the Second brigade since the wounding of Colonel Gregg. The new brigade was called the Third, and was composed of the First Maine, 21st Penn. and 2d N. Y. Mounted Rifles. A few days later the 6th Ohio joined the brigade.

On the 27th the brigade had the advance in a movement on the left of the army, and found the enemy early in the morning behind breastworks at Rowanty Creek, on the Vaughan Road. The 6th Ohio and Captain Freese's battalion of the First Maine drove the enemy out, capturing the signal station, flags and six wagons. The brigade kept on the march to Gravelly Run, where the enemy made a stand, being well supported by works and artillery in the woods. The First Maine dismounted, carried the bridge under a heavy artillery fire and formed with the brigade across the road. The brigade then charged, routing the enemy and capturing some prisoners. The brigade followed to the Boydton Plank Road and was put across the road to meet General Hampton's force, which was trying to attain the rear of the whole Union force of cavalry and infantry. The Union forces stood back to back. The First Maine, under heavy fire by superior numbers and flanked so that it was between two fires, stood firm and held its ground, saving the brigade and thus saving the whole position. It was here that Major Thaxter, whose commission had expired, yet remained with his command which he led with special gallantry, for which he has been accorded a Congressional medal of honor.   Thus the regiment took part in three distinct engagements in one day.   This was known to the men of the regiment as the "Bull Pen," but is borne on the battle flag as Boydton Road.   Lieutenant Collins of E and ten men were killed, Captain Chadbourne of I, Lieutenant Jackson of G, Lieutenant Lee of H, and 58 men were wounded of whom 5 died, and 10 were taken prisoners of whom one died.

BELLEFIELD. — From December 7th to the 12th the regiment with the brigade took part in the cavalry and infantry raid to Bellefield, an errand of destruction to the Weldon Railroad from Stony Creek Station to Bellefield, a distance of fifteen miles, to obstruct the transportation of supplies to the rebel army.   The regiment burned the bridge, station buildings and barracks, destroyed the railroad for three-fourths of a mile at Stony Creek Station on the Nottoway River, and destroyed the railroad nearly to the rebel works at Bellefield.   The regiment served as rear guard on the return march, fighting almost continuously.   The weather was very cold with a storm of rain and sleet, and the men suffered severely.   Two men were wounded of whom one died.   This expedition was successful, the railroad being destroyed the entire distance.

During the year, while on detached duty, Captain Russell of C received wounds from which he died ; Lieutenant Cutler of B was wounded ; Lieutenant Harris of F was killed by accident.

The total loss in the regiment during 1864 was 54 killed ; 189 wounded of whom 17 died ; 18 wounded and taken prisoners of whom 7 died ; and 112 taken prisoners of whom 41 died.

HATCHER'S RUN.—Then came picketing and scouting for nearly two months.   February 5, 1865, the regiment, with the division and an infantry force, started on an expedition which resulted in extending the Union lines two or three miles on the left, to Hatcher's Run.   On this expedition the regiment was on the skirmish line and under fire, in different positions, all day with small loss.

DINWIDDIE COURT HOUSE.—At the opening of the spring campaign, 1865, Lieut.-Colonel Cilley was in command of the regiment ; Major Taylor was serving on the division staff,

Major Tucker was in command of the cavalry depot at City Point and Major Chadbourne, promoted from Captain of I Dec. 12, 1864, was in command of the 2d N. Y. Mounted Rifles in the absence of its colonel. Gen. D. McM. Gregg had resigned, and the 'ivision was in command of Gen. George Crook.

March 29th the regiment started with the whole cavalry force, under command of General Sheridan, on what proved to be the last grand campaign of the army of the Potomac. On the 31st about the middle of the forenoon the regiment, then in bivouac near Dinwiddie Court House, was ordered to go to the aid of the pickets at once. The remainder of the brigade was posted along the bank of a creek (Great Cat Tail or Chamberlain's Bed), to protect the ford and prevent the enemy from crossing. Arriving in the vicinity of the creek, Captain Myrick's battalion was ordered to cross and reconnoiter the woods and adjacent country, while the remainder of the regiment was dismounted and prepared to fight on foot in a field behind a rising ground. About one o'clock heavy firing indicating that Captain Myrick's battalion was being driven in, the remainder of the regiment was advanced to the top of the hill in line of skirmishers. Arriving there they found Captain Myrick's battalion fighting manfully in the road, while beyond this battalion was a force of the enemy's cavalry charging up the road, and in the field, coming out of the woods that skirted the creek, a long line of dismounted men. The boys opened fire and with a cheer started for the enemy. The rebel cavalry in the road fought bravely, but the First Maine repeaters were too much for them and they were forced to retire, the dismounted line in the field going with them. The First Maine followed quickly and took position in the thicket on the bank of the creek, and prepared to hold it. A scattering fire was kept up till between four and five o'clock, when the enemy made a gallant charge and forced the regiment and the whole brigade back slowly, the men fighting for every inch of ground and being pressed back by mere force of numbers. At last the regiment reached a line of breastworks behind which was a Union force, and the fight was over. In this engagement the whole division took part, though this regiment bore the brunt of the fighting, being in the road and at the ford, and losing more than all the remainder of the division, and the stubborn fighting of this regiment enabled General Sheridan to place his troops in a position of his own choosing, thus contributing to the glorious victory at Five Forks the next day. So this engagement was really part of the battle of Five Forks, though borne on the battle flag as " Dinwiddie Court House."

The loss in the regiment was Lieutenant Stayner of D and 15 men, killed; Major Chadbourne, Lieutenant Comins of A (who died), Lieutenant Fuller of B, Captain Howe of D, and 71 men wounded, of whom 9 died; and 7 taken prisoners, of whom 2 were wounded.

The day after the engagement at Dinwiddie Court House, April 1st, the brigade, having suffered the most severely, was allowed a partial rest, and this regiment was sent on picket in the rear, to guard the train. The evening of the next day the march was taken up, the regiment being rear guard for the train.

By the 3d Petersburg had been captured, Richmond evacuated, and the rebel army was in full retreat with General Sheridan in close pursuit, and this regiment joined in the pursuit. On the 5th the brigade was hurriedly sent to the support of the First and Second brigades, which had attacked Lee's retreating army successfully, capturing five pieces of artillery, wagons and prisoners, but had been surrounded by rebel infantry. These brigades being relieved brought in their captures, and though this regiment had some severe skirmishing, having the rear on the return and being at one time nearly surrounded, the loss was small, one wounded and one taken prisoner.

DEATONSVILLE.—The morning of the 6th the cavalry was early in motion, marching on a road nearly parallel with the road on which Lee's army was retreating, the wagon trains of the enemy being in sight on the hills in the distance. Between eleven and twelve o'clock the brigade turned to the right, marched a short distance in the direction of the rebel trains and then charged upon the trains, this regiment being on the right of the road. There was a scramble through a swamp in the woods, and before half the regiment had got through this, with a cheer the boys sprang up a hill, halted till the rest of the regiment had arrived, then started on the charge in another direction. This charge was not successful in reaching the train, and after remaining in the vicinity an hour or two the regiment retired, having lost Captain Heald of E and 4 men, killed; Adjutant Little, Captain Freese and 8 men wounded, of whom 2 died, and one wounded and taken prisoner.

SAILOR'S CREEK. — The regiment then followed after the column, which continued on its way, the corps commanders sending brigades or divisions to charge upon the enemy's retreating train at every cross-road. Along in the afternoon the division was ordered to take position on Sailor's Creek, at the left of General Custer's division, which was having a severe engagement. Here the regiment charged dismounted upon the enemy posted behind breastworks and drove him away, reaching and passing the enemy's train, which the rebels had fired when they saw capture was inevitable. At the same time the other troops, the cavalry and the infantry of the Sixth corps, charged all along the line, with the result that a large portion of the enemy's train was destroyed and seven general officers and thousands of prisoners were captured. The loss to the regiment in this engagement, so fraught with important results, was 2 killed; Lieutenant Poor of B, who was detailed to act as Adjutant when Adjutant Little was wounded, and 3 men wounded of whom 2 died.

FARMVILLE. — Early on the morning of the 7th the column was in motion. The regiment had a skirmish at Briery Creek, where one man was killed and one wounded, then charged and drove the enemy, then followed the brigade to Farmville, where a lively fight was in progress in which the artillery took part. The enemy had been driven out of the town, it was thought, and the regiment was ordered to charge into the town and capture all the prisoners possible, and it started promptly upon what proved to be its last mounted charge. Adown the hill the boys went, in face of an artillery fire from the enemy, into the town on three roads, and through the town, where they met with a heavy volley of musketry right in their faces. Then there was a remarkably lively skirmish for a few minutes, and finally the enemy was driven away from the town; the regiment advanced to the top of the hill beyond, where there was skirmishing, and the fighting ended there, although the Second brigade was having it hot a little further to the right. In this engagement the regiment lost 1 killed, 3 wounded, and 1 taken prisoner.

APPOMATTOX COURT HOUSE.—The next day's march brought the brigade to Appomattox Station at dusk. The orders were to unsaddle and go into camp, and were cheerfully obeyed, for there had been little rest and sleep since the campaign opened. But the men had not fairly eaten supper and spread their blankets before the order came to "saddle, pack, and be ready to move out immediately." The brigade with two pieces of artillery was sent out to hold the Lynchburg road through which General Sheridan believed General Lee, being in a tight place, would try to escape during the night. The brigade marched through burning wagons, burning stores, and all the debris of a demoralized retreating army, until the enemy was found about midnight, and then formed a line of battle near the top of Clover Hill, this regiment being dismounted and posted across the road, while the remainder of the brigade was on the right of the road with the guns in rear. Firing commenced with dawn the 9th of April. For a while it was a skirmish fire which grew quite hot at times, and finally a strong force of rebel infantry was seen coming around the left. This force approached slowly, the First Maine boys, swinging around with the road to meet them, poured into them a heavy fire. But the enemy's force was too strong, outnumbering the Union cavalry ten to one, and slowly pressed back the little brigade, the boys fighting stubbornly until the woods in rear of the field were reached, when the brigade was relieved and it withdrew from the field; it was relieved by the colored infantry of the Twenty-fifth corps, then serving with the Twenty-fourth corps. The infantry charged across the field and the war was ended. The loss to the regiment in this the last engagement of the army of the Potomac, in which it held a post of honor, was 2 killed; Lieutenant Coburn of A and 17 men wounded of whom four died; and one taken prisoner.

The total loss to the regiment in this brief and brilliant campaign was 27 killed, 117 wounded of whom 18 died, 3 wounded and taken prisoners, and 8 taken prisoners.

After more marching the brigade settled down at Ettricks, near Petersburg, this regiment being sent into different counties to do the work for the freedmen which the Freedmen's Bureau was later created to perform. While here Perry Chandler of company G and Melvin Preble of company K organized and taught a free school in the village, and did excellent service in that line for about two months, until the regiment was mustered out, August, 1865, its work being done, and gloriously done.

ROSTER.

The following information relating to officers of the First Maine Cavalry regiment is obtained from the Volunteer Army Register, published by the War Department August 31, 1865, and other reliable sources.

OFFICERS AT FINAL MUSTER-OUT, AUGUST 1, 1865.

COLONEL: Charles H. Smith, June 18, 1863,—brevet Brig.-Gen. Vols., Aug. 1, 1864; brevet Maj.-Gen. Vols., Mar. 13, 1865; commiss'ed Col. 28th U. S. Inf., July 28, 1866, tr. to 19th Inf.;—brevet Brig.- and Maj.-Gen. U. S. A., Mar. 2, 1867; retired Nov. 1, 1891.

LIEUTENANT-COLONEL: Jonathan P. Cilley, Sept. 2, 1864,—brevet Col. Vols., Mar. 13, 1865; brevet Brig.-Gen. Vols , June 2, 1865.

MAJORS: Constantine Taylor, Feb. 24, 1864,—brevet Lieut.-Col., Mar. 13, 1865; Benjamin F. Tucker, Sept. 3, 1864, — brevet Lieut.-Col.; Paul Chadbourne, Feb. 21, 1865.

ADJUTANT: First Lieutenant Thaddeus Little, Mar. 25, 1865.

CAPTAINS: John D. Myrick, July 1, 1863,—brevet Major U. S. Vols. and U. S. A., commiss'd First Lieut. 10th U. S. Cav., 1867, resigned May, 1872; Henry C. Hall, July 30, 1863,—brevet Major, 1865; Andrew M. Benson, Feb. 16, 1864,—tr. from 1st D. C. Cav., previously Lieut. 7th Maine Inf.; John W. Freese, Feb. 18, 1864, brevet Major, 1865,—tr. from 1st D. C. Cav. and 7th Maine Inf.; William S. Howe, Mar. 15, 1864,—tr. from 1st D. C. Cav.; Jacob B. Loring, Sept. 5, 1864; William L. Boyd, Mar. 25, 1865; Levi H. Daggett, Apr. 14, 1865; George W. Hussey, May 1, 1865; Joel Wilson, May 16, 1865.

FIRST LIEUTENANTS: James Maguire, Feb. 8, 1864,—tr. from 1st D. C. Cav.; Commissary M. T. V. Bowman, Feb. 13, 1864; James H. Russell, Feb. 19, 1864,—tr. from 1st D. C. Cav.; Edward P. Merrill, Mar. 4, 1864,—tr. from 1st D. C. Cav.; Orrin S. Haskell, Oct. 1, 1864; George F. Jewett, Nov. 25, 1864; J. Kidder Brooks, Dec. 3, 1864; James W. Poor, Dec. 12, 1864; Henry A. Willis, Apr. 14, 1865; Benjamin A. Osborne, May 1, 1865; John E. Lougee, May 16, 1865.

SECOND LIEUTENANTS: Joseph W. Lee, Feb. 24, 1864,—tr. from 1st D. C. Cav.; William S. Farwell, Feb. 26, 1864, — tr. from 1st D. C. Cav.; Henry D. Fuller, Mar. 24, 1864,—tr. from 1st D. C. Cav.; Edward Jordan,

Dec. 12, 1864; William J. Crooker, Dec. 16, 1864; George E. Jumper, Apr. 14, 1865; Edward P. Tobie, Jr., May 3, 1865; Albert R. Johnson, May 4, 1865; Charles A. Stevens, May 4, 1865; Jefferson L. Coburn, May 4, 1865.

SURGEON: Horace Stevens, Dec. 3, 1864. ASSISTANT SURGEONS: George J. Northrop, Apr. 2, 1864,—tr. from 1st D. C. Cav.; Frank Bodfish, May 3, 1865.

CHAPLAIN: Samuel H. Merrill, Mar. 4, 1864,—tr. from 1st D. C. Cav.

MUSTERED OUT WITH THE ORIGINAL MEN, NOVEMBER 25, 1864,

BY REASON OF EXPIRATION OF TERM OF SERVICE.

MAJOR: Sidney W. Thaxter, July 24, 1863;—recipient of Congressional medal of honor.

CAPTAINS: Horace S. Cole, Dec. 1, 1863; Isaac G. Virgin, Dec. 31, 1862. FIRST LIEUTENANTS: William P. Coleman, Jan. 22, 1862; Horatio S. Libby, July 24, 1863; Phineas Foster, Jr., Feb. 9, 1864; Calvin B. Benson, Feb. 9, 1864; John R. Andrews, July 24, 1863; Frank W. Pray, Dec. 23, 1863. SECOND LIEUTENANTS: Frank M. Cutler, Jan. 22, 1862; William F. Stone, Oct. 23, 1862, muster-out Dec. 6, 1864; Samuel C. Smith, Aug. 20, 1863. SURGEON: George W. Colby, Oct. 31, 1861.

(Dates given above refer to rank or commission, those given hereafter refer to date of the event.)

DIED.

COLONEL: Calvin S. Douty, killed in action at Aldie, Va., June 17, 1863. LIEUTENANT-COLONEL: Stephen Boothby, June 6, 1864, of wounds in action of May 10.

CAPTAINS: George J. Summat, killed in battle of Aldie, June 17, 1863; Osco A. Ellis, killed in battle of St. Mary's Church, June 24, 1864; Walstein Phillips, killed in battle of St. Mary's Church, on staff of Gen. Gregg, June 24, 1864; Addison P. Russell, Sept. 20, 1864, of wounds received in action; John A. Heald, killed in action Apr. 6, 1865.

FIRST LIEUTENANTS: William Harris, killed accidentally at Jones' Bridge, Va., May 17, 1864; Charles K. Johnson, in southern prison, May 27, 1865.

SECOND LIEUTENANTS: George S. Kimball, pro. Captain, not must'd, killed in battle of Middleburg, Va., June 19, 1863; Ephraim H. Taylor, killed in battle of Middleburg, June 19, 1863; Mark Neville, killed in battle of Middleburg, June 19, 1863; William H. Bradman, July 30, 1864, of disease; Winfield S. Collins, killed in battle of Boydton Road, Oct. 27, 1864; James E. Stayner, killed in battle of Dinwiddie C. H., Va., Mar. 31, 1865; Leander M. Comins,—tr. from 1st D. C. Cav., Apr. 8, 1865, of wounds received at battle of Dinwiddie C. H.

CHAPLAIN: George W. Bartlett, killed in action, June 2, 1864, at Barker's Mills, Va.

PROMOTED AND TRANSFERRED OUT OF REGIMENT.

CAPTAINS: Llewellyn G. Estes, Dec. 8, 1863, to Captain and Major, A. A. G., — brevet Brig.-Gen. U. S. Vols., Mar. 13, 1865; Andrew B. Spurling, Jan. 12, 1864, to Major, afterwards Lieut.-Col., 2d Maine Cav.,—brevet Brig.-General U. S. Vols., Mar. 26, 1865; Andrew H. Bibber, Apr. 22, 1865, to Captain and A. A. G.; First Lieut. Charles W. Ford, Jan. 21, 1865. to Captain and A. Q. M.; Asst. Surgeon Sumner A. Patten, to Surgeon, Board of Enrollment, Apr., 1863.

DISCHARGED.

MAJOR: David P. Stowell, Feb. 15, 1863.

CAPTAINS: William Montgomery, Oct. 8, 1864, for disability; Edward T. Sanford, Dec. 8, 1864, for disability,—tr. from 1st D. C. Cav.; Thomas C. Webber, Feb. 2, 1865, for disability,—tr. from 1st D. C. Cav.; Charles C. Chase, May 20, 1865,—tr. from 1st D. C. Cav.

FIRST LIEUTENANT: Commissary Eustace C. Bigelow, Dec. 30, 1863, for disability.

SECOND LIEUTENANTS: Marcus A. Vose, Jan. 10, 1863; Henry S. McIntyre, Feb. 1, 1863; George E. Bugbee, Dec. 4, 1864, for disability; Sylvanus R. Jackson, Mar. 6, 1865, for disability,—tr. from 1st D. C. Cav.; Henry F. Blanchard, Mar. 18, 1865; John F. McKusick, Apr. 10, 1865,—tr. from 1st D. C. Cav.

ASSISTANT SURGEON: Alexander M. Parker, Sept. 1, 1864, for disability.

After expiration of term of service: Captains: Zenas Vaughan, July 24, 1863, pris. of war May 11, 1864, disch'd May 29, 1865; John P. Carson, Mar. 30, 1864, pris. of war June 24, 1864, disch'd Feb. 24, 1865. First Lieutenant Charles O. Gordon, Mar. 30, 1864, pris. of war June 24, 1864; disch'd May 6, 1865. Second Lieutenant Lorenzo White, May 20, 1865.

RESIGNED.

COLONELS: John Goddard, Feb. 12, 1862; Samuel H. Allen, Dec. 12, 1862.

LIEUTENANT-COLONEL: Thomas Hight, W. P. R. A., Mar. 14, 1862.

MAJORS: Warren L. Whitney, May 13, 1863; George M. Brown, Feb. 11, 1864; Daniel S. Curtis, Jan. 18, 1865,—tr. from 1st D. C. Cav.; Joel W. Cloudman, Feb. 20, 1865, for disability,—tr. from 1st D. C. Cav.

ADJUTANT: First Lieutenant Jarvis C. Stevens, Dec. 26, 1862.

CAPTAINS: Nathan Mayhew, May 20, 1862; Augustus J. Burbank, Aug. 14, 1862; Zebulon B. Blethen, Dec. 1, 1862,—recommissioned First Lieut. in and tr. from 1st D. C. Cav., muster-in revoked; Louis O. Cowan, Dec. 2, 1862; George Prince, Dec. 9, 1862; George Cary, Jan. 4, 1863; Reuben B. Jennings, Jan. 15, 1863; Black H. Putnam, Feb. 19, 1863; Robert F. Dyer, June 4, 1863,—recommissioned in and tr. from 1st D. C. Cav., resigned Nov. 21, 1864.

FIRST LIEUTENANTS: Charles S. Crosby, Oct. 31, 1861; John C. C. Bowen, Feb. 18, 1862; Charles H. Baker, June 13, 1862; George Weston, Oct. 10, 1862; John R. Webb, Oct. 14, 1862; John H. Goddard, Feb. 23, 1863, for disability; Evans S. Pillsbury, Mar. 5, 1863, for disability; Dudley L. Haines, Mar. 12, 1863; George E. Hunton, Oct. 1, 1863.

SECOND LIEUTENANTS: Joseph C. Hill, Oct. 24, 1862; Samuel B. M. Lovejoy, Apr. 16, 1864.

QUARTERMASTERS: First Lieutenants Edward M. Patten, May 8, 1862; Andrew Griffin, Mar. 9, 1863; Clarence D. Ulmer, May 26, 1865.

CHAPLAINS: Benjamin F. Tefft, Dec. 24, 1862; Samuel Fuller, May. 5, 1863.

OTHERWISE LEFT THE SERVICE.

Asst. Surgeon George W. Haley, dis. Nov. 15, 1862; First Lieutenant Miles Colbath, dis. Sept. 3, 1864.

MONUMENT.

This monument, of Hallowell granite, stands on the north side of Baltimore Pike about 1,200 yards towards the town from Rock Creek where it crosses the pike, and about 600 yards in an air-line north from the summit of Powers' Hill. It marks the place where the battalion stood on the evening of July 2d. It has an equal-sided shaft with a pyramidal apex, the junction with the base accented by a double projecting fillet and scotia beneath molded in from the upper edge of the plinth, being a part of the same block; it rests upon a broad sub-base showing a beveled water table.

ADMEASUREMENTS: Base, four feet six inches by four feet six inches by one foot three inches; plinth, three feet two inches by three feet two inches by two feet three inches; shaft, two feet three inches by two feet three inches by six feet six inches. Total height, ten feet.

Upon one side of the shaft appears, in relief, the five-pointed star of the Twelfth Army Corps, and below the star the following inscriptions:

10TH MAINE

BATTALION.

PROVOST GUARD.

12TH CORPS HD. QRS.

MAJ. GENL. SLOCUM.

TENTH MAINE BATTALION,

HEADQUARTERS' GUARD, TWELFTH ARMY CORPS,

AT THE BATTLE OF GETTYSBURG.

COMPILATION BY MAJOR JOHN M. GOULD.

AS historian of the 1–10–29th Maine regiment it has fallen to my lot to narrate the part taken by the Tenth Maine battalion in the battle of Gettysburg. It is not possible for me to make the familiar quotation, — "all of which I saw, and part of which I was,"—therefore I have been compelled to learn the facts from the actors.

Of the 205 members of the battalion who were "present for duty" in the battle, 88 have been visited or reached by mail. From these I have got the narrative which follows. Memories are very treacherous after so long a time, but every statement made here seems to be well vouched. A copy of the monthly return for June 30th, which was really made July 1st while Reynolds was fighting, is the basis of the rolls of the members present; the return names the "absent"; I have learned the "present" by help of the survivors.

On April 26, 1863, when the Tenth Maine regiment was ordered home for muster-out, 244 three-years' men, of whom many were absent wounded, were retained "in the field." These were organized into three companies, styled the Tenth Maine battalion. The men were very efficient in guard and kindred duties. At the great inspection of Hooker's army in February, 1863, when only eleven regiments were named as having "earned high commendation," the Tenth was one. It was natural, therefore, that Gen. Slocum should detach the battalion from the brigade (Knipe's, formerly Crawford's) for the provost guard of his army corps, the Twelfth.

Captain John Q. Adams as senior officer of the battalion took command, but when Gen. Slocum learned that an old wound made marching difficult for the captain, he detached him to be provost marshal of the corps. Captain Beardsley thereupon took command of the battalion and was in charge during the Gettysburg campaign.

A large number of men were at once detailed for guard duty around corps headquarters, also as wagoners or mechanics under the corps quartermaster, and for clerks or orderlies of the various staff officers, consequently the number actually in line armed with muskets at the time of battle was considerably less than the number present for rations. A cattle-guard of sixteen men was detailed from the battalion a short time before starting on the Gettysburg campaign; they had the care of about two hundred beeves, and when upon the march they followed the hospital supply train, which moved immediately behind the troops. A detail into this guard would ordinarily be considered desirable by a soldier in search of adventure and a free and easy life. Their part at Gettysburg was to march to the front, as usual, with the corps on July 1st, then when it was discovered that they were too near the enemy they were sent back to Westminster, Md., marching all night of the 1st and part of the 2d day and once more going to the front during the night of July 3d–4th, and then moving with the army in pursuit of Lee. There was a plenty of free and easy adventure but only a little sleep in all this.

The pitching and striking of the headquarters' tents was also done by the battalion, Sergeant Maurice Hayes being especially charged with this duty. He had twelve men under him, and they were also expected to put the headquarters' grounds in the best and neatest possible condition.

The itinerary of the Twelfth army corps will be found in Vol. XXVII, Part 1 (Serial 43) of the Official Records, page 140. The battalion usually marched in the rear of the corps and camped near to Gen. Slocum, always ready for any emergency and able to answer promptly any call of the general or his staff.

Colonel Beardsley writes : "We came up by way of Frederick, Md., crossed the Pennsylvania line and camped near Littlestown, Pa., the night of June 30th. Some Union cavalry came in during the night and turned over to me a number of Confederate prisoners (a) which they had captured near York, Pa. ; one of these was a Lieut.-Col. from North Carolina who was wounded. Dr. Howard was awakened and attended to him and the other wounded ones. In the morning we took all of the officers to the hotel and gave them a breakfast."

The morning of July 1st, therefore, found the battalion lying quietly in bivouac at Littlestown, ten miles from the battlefield. At 8 A. M. they marched toward Two Taverns, where a halt was made. About noon the regular monthly inspection and muster (postponed from the day before) was in preparation when the news was brought that the First corps was fighting at Gettysburg and that Gen. Reynolds had been killed. Gen. Slocum immediately galloped to the front, while Gen. Williams took command of the Twelfth corps and promptly followed after. On arriving at the field, Gen. Slocum's headquarters were established on Powers' Hill, but the main body of the battalion was at once put to the task of arresting the stream of stragglers and skulks which is always flowing out in rear of the fighting line. Here let it be stated that there was less skulking at Gettysburg than at any other of the great battles of the army of the Potomac. This line was across the Baltimore Pike, the stone bridge over McAllister's Run being in the centre of it, the left extending toward but not reaching the Taneytown road. The line was shortened or drawn in altogether during the night, only a small guard being left on duty. The battalion remained in this vicinity during the other two days. In the afternoon of the second day, when the attack was made upon Greene's brigade on Culp's Hill, the battalion was for a few hours on the northeast side of the Baltimore Pike, near the point where Gen. Williams' headquarters are designated on the official maps and where the battalion monument now stands. But numerous details had reduced the command by this time to a score or two of private soldiers with a disproportionate number of officers and non-commissioned officers.

As soon as the battalion arrived near the battlefield a call was made for guards to go here and there to do all the various

(a) Col. King's diary gives the number as fifty and names Lieut.-Col. Paine as one.

duties needful. Few of these can now be accurately defined, but it is well remembered that a field hospital of the Twelfth corps was at once established near Powers' Hill, where Slocum's tents were pitched, and among others a detail of six men was sent for Dr. McNulty, medical director of the Twelfth corps, additional to those who helped at first to establish the field hospital; five men were sent to the Signal officer to assist him to get to work; they found enough to do, under his direction, for the whole three days. A number of women and children who had left their homes when the First and Eleventh corps fell back were put under the care of the battalion and sent farther to the rear. On the second day corporals Coy of D and Jones of B with six men each were sent to guard springs near the centre of the field, that the water might be used exclusively for the wounded. When the attack was made on Sickles they were relieved.

A party of Confederate prisoners was turned over to the battalion during the evening of the first day, and a detail of thirty men under Lieut. Libby was made to escort them to the rear. Stillman Emerson describes this as "an all-night march" with an immediate return to the front again on the 2d, where they all arrived on the early morning of July 3d "never so tired, hungry, cross and sleepy." Lieut. Libby's remembrance of this event is, that there were twenty-seven prisoners and that they were sent eighteen miles to the rear and there turned over to troops belonging to Gen. Patrick, Provost Marshal-General of the army.

From many correspondents comes a pleasing word given as evidence of good feeling between the battalion and Gen. Slocum. They say that when supper time came, July 1st, the general did not hesitate to ask Corporal Thad. Cross, who chanced to be near, if he had anything to spare in his haversack. Cross without flinching promptly produced a hardtack and a slice of raw salt pork, and they say this was all that the commander of the right wing had for "tea" that night.

A little before noon of the second day Gen. Slocum called for "six volunteers for a dangerous duty," men to go without arms, but with their canteens and haversacks. The private soldiers of the battalion were nearly all off on various details at that moment. It thus happened that so many who went were non-commissioned officers. The general instructed them to go out on the right (east or northeast) till they found the enemy. They were to make note in a book furnished them of all the houses and springs they saw, and to get the names of all the tenants of the houses. If captured they were to pretend that they were hunting for food and water. As well as can now be determined, they passed along the main line of the Twelfth corps on Culp's Hill to the right, then out through the line of the 2d Mass. regt., past the Union pickets, and through the rough woods till they found the enemy's pickets. First Sergeant Tarr writes that the four men of A, (Cole, Fletcher, himself and one now forgotten) went and returned together, and that the scouting party was sent out to learn the significance of the movement that had been observed of Confederate troops and wagons toward the Union right. The scouts went through the woods, climbing trees occasionally for observation, till they came to an opening where were a house and outbuildings. On reaching the house Tarr saw enemy's soldiers in the outbuildings watching them. He feigned not to see the enemy, but quietly explained to the others that they would have to run, and at a signal from him they all made a dash back to the woods. The confeds fired at them but no one was hurt. They all reported to Gen. Slocum and had received his thanks before 2 P. M.

Henry F. Cole writes that he and Sydney W. Fletcher, both of company A, "went over the mountain" (Wolf Hill) and through woods all of the way. About a mile out they met a man and his daughter who told them that the Union picket line was half a mile farther, but the scouts knew it must be the Confederate line, and advanced cautiously till they came to an opening. Here they found the enemy's picket line stationed near a barn. They drank from a spring near by, where the enemy's pickets also filled their canteens, and a little before 2 P. M. got back to Gen. Slocum, who thanked them well for their promptness and the information they had brought.

First Sergt. Kallock and Sergt. Anderson of D appear to

have gone to the same house that Sergt. Tarr had visited earlier (probably the one marked E. Deordorff on the maps). Anderson while drinking at the spring-house saw a man, who appeared to be the farmer, standing in the door of the barn up the hill. As the man turned he showed his cartridge box, whereupon Anderson ran behind the spring-house and told Kallock, who made sport of this and started alone for the barn; but Anderson seeing a squad of soldiers approaching sang out to Kallock, and both ran for the woods. The Confederates fired at them, but they got away safely and passed farther to the right (east) till they were sure that the enemy's line was stationary, i. e., not a line of skirmishers advancing. They did not get back to General Slocum until late in the afternoon; he thanked them also very heartily and remarked that he had feared they were captured.

The main object of these scouts was to learn if the enemy was attempting to flank the right of Meade's army, but Gen. Slocum also used the information they brought in concerning the position of the houses, springs, etc., to construct his map of the field.

Colonel Beardsley thus describes an incident which must have occurred late in the afternoon of the second day : —

" * * * I was considerably impressed by seeing the very large park of artillery and wagons without a guard or any body of men excepting our little battalion. You will understand of course, although I did not then know it, that we were near the head of the valley behind Cemetery Hill, and that the pike which continued up the hill in front of us led into the town of Gettysburg, from which we were distant, as I think from subsequent observation, about half a mile. As I afterwards found out we were about 300 yards from the line of battle occupied by our corps upon Culp's Hill on the extreme right of the army of the Potomac, being well up inside of the line.

" This line of the Twelfth corps was on considerably higher ground than we were, but between us and it there was a thick growth of underbrush of considerable height which prevented us from seeing or having any knowledge of it at the time. We had learned, however, very shortly after our arrival there that our corps was in line of battle outside of us in that direction, and that they had thrown up a rough breastwork along the ridge. * * *

"We began to hear skirmish firing in front of us but considerable distance away; this firing gradually approached us, but it was not heavy. I presently noticed that a good many men came straggling out of the underbrush and crossed the pike below us.

"As the skirmish firing came nearer the number of these stragglers increased very largely. They were going back without any order or formation. I walked down towards where they were and presently saw an officer whom I knew as belonging to our corps. I was surprised to see him there, and I asked him where he was going. He replied: 'I am looking for the Twelfth army corps.' Pointing to the front where we heard the firing I said: 'If you will go out in that direction you will probably find the Twelfth corps.' I never saw one get more angry than he did in an instant. He said: 'I have been in the breastworks of the Twelfth corps within a few minutes, and if you have the nerve to go with me I will go back there; the Confederate troops are in possession of them.' After he got cooled a little he told me in substance that he had been put upon picket in front of the corps; that during the day he had been pushed back by a line of Confederates heavier than his own; that he had gradually fallen back upon the breastworks expecting to find the corps in the works; that the Confederates were now in possession of the works, which he advised me were not more than 300 yards from where we were; and that there was no force except our battalion between the enemy and the reserve artillery, ammunition and baggage of the army of the Potomac.

"I found a stray cavalry-man, took his horse away from him and sent one of my command forward with instructions to find Gen. Slocum if possible, or otherwise Gen. Meade, and report to him the situation; and if he could find neither Slocum nor Meade to try to inform some other corps commander. I formed the battalion in line and kept them there for some hours. The night became very dark. After a time we heard the tread of marching columns coming down the pike from the front. They proved to be our own Twelfth army corps. After going some distance beyond us they halted and fronted, which brought their backs to us. I heard the command given, "Forward in line," and they went up the hill through the underbrush. In less than five minutes firing began. It was sharp and for a few minutes really heavy, and then died out. In the gray of the early morning following (July 3d), the firing broke out again and was very heavy perhaps for ten minutes. Then Confederate prisoners began to come down through the underbrush with escorts and were turned over to me. A good many of them were sent in, both officers and men. I was curious to know the facts in regard to the occupation of the breastworks, and I conversed with several of the Confederate officers who talked very freely. Their statement was substantially that two brigades of Ewell's corps, covering the advance of his whole force, had struck our picket line out some miles, that they had driven them in front of them until they came to the breastworks, and had driven them through the breastworks which were then unoccupied. The Confederate officers stated that upon occupying the breastworks their command came to a halt ; that then the two brigade commanders conferred ; one insisted upon pushing down the hill and attacking whatever they found, but the other refused to do so, saying that they were now in the lines of the army of the Potomac and in a position which they ought to hold ; that if they went down the hill they would fall upon a force which would probably annihilate them in a few minutes. This view prevailed ; they sent couriers back to Ewell to advise him of the situation and waited for his arrival. They said that in the night our people attacked them and there was some fighting, but not much because it was so dark they could not see each other and they were all mixed up, but in the morning the Twelfth army corps cleaned them out in a few minutes. Some of the Confederate officers told me that they were so mixed up in the melee the night before that when they woke up in the morning they found themselves lying amongst our soldiers. They also told me that while lying in the breastworks they could hear our teams going up and down the pike and the drivers talking to their horses and cracking their whips.

They said that an apparent indifference to their presence in the breastworks convinced them that there was a very strong force there to take care of them."

Sergeant Edward P. M. Bragdon gives the following account of the part taken by a hospital detail after the battle was over :—

"On the morning of July 4th I reported with thirty-eight men, all glad for a change, at the field hospital of the Twelfth corps, Surgeon H. Ernest Goodman, 28th Penn., in charge. He referred us to Maj. (name forgotten) who showed us where to pitch our tents, ordered roll-call twice a day, and a daily report in writing. Dr. Goodman's quarters were in a stone house(a). Tents had been pitched for the wounded, and the big barn was also crowded. Even the basement of the barn was packed with Confederate wounded. In the field adjoining many stragglers had pitched their tents. We were ordered to visit all of these, get their names, company and regiment, have them strike tents, and pitch them again on a line parallel with ours, and to be under my orders. There were 38 of these stragglers, mostly westerners; they were sent to their regiments before a fortnight. At Dr. Goodman's suggestion we fenced in a plat for a cemetery in the field east of the house; one-half was for the Blue, and the other for the Gray. I divided our men into squads: one for burying the dead, another to guard the wagons, cattle and quarters, a third to provide head-boards and to letter them. Josiah Smith and Eph-raim C. Benson were especially apt in cutting the names of the dead upon wooden head-boards improvised from cracker boxes.

"In about ten days I got a chance to stroll around the field in the direc-tion of Round Top. In going there I visited a small barn (b) where a hos-pital flag was flying. In the barn lay two dead Confederates. I heard the cry of 'Water!' 'Water!' 'Give us water!' 'Hurry! we are dying for water!' I looked around, and crouching in corners, leaning against the posts of the barn, or lying in the ground-mow were Confederate soldiers, all wounded, and the most of them had lost a leg or arm. I found a canteen and hurried to the spring. How those poor fellows did bless me! There were thirteen living men. In another part, in the calf pen, was a darkey whose leg was gone nearly to the body. He had plainly suffered a great deal and his skin was changed to "old gold" color, but he was game to the last and was full of gratitude to me.

"After thus 'standing the drinks for the crowd' I inquired how they came there. They said that they were wounded and taken prisoners the second day, and were brought to this barn where their wounds had been dressed. They could not tell what command had captured them, but sug-gested that whoever they were they were ordered away in a hurry, and the prisoners had thus been left to no one in particular. They said that the woman of the house had brought them bread every two or three days, and that one of their own comrades had at first been able to get to the spring for them, but for a number of days the woman had not been seen and their com-rade had failed to get water for them, so that they were all near the ragged edge of despair when I found them. I made them as comfortable as I could

(a) Marked Geo. Bushman on the U. S. Engineer's map.
(b) Apparently the house marked J. Eckenrode on the maps.

and returned immediately to Dr. Goodman with the news.   It was at length arranged that I should detail a party of my men to bury the dead, and that the living should be brought over to our hospital in our ambulances.   We had it all done before we slept, and all of us who engaged in the task felt glad that we had done it.   Several of the worst cases died during the night or the next day, and I do not know if any lived to be exchanged.   *   *   *

"After this the weather grew even more hot and oppressive.   Deaths among the severely wounded increased in numbers and we were kept busy day and night.   In the course of time the great general hospital was ready northeast of the town, and we put aboard the ambulances all who could be thus removed.   Then came the tug — or rather the lug — of war.   The wounded who could not bear the jolting in the ambulances had to be carried upon stretchers to the general hospital nearly three miles away.   Nearly all of our detail were put to this task.   Two round trips daily was all that any one could make, and even this was exceedingly trying work.   In spite of all our efforts we could not help making a jar or jolt or a stumble occasionally, and then the poor wounded fellows would cry out with pain.

"One day a party from another field-hospital passed near our camp, the stretcher bearers so 'blown' that they dropped their burden to rest. We went up to them and found it was Adjutant Roberts of the Seventeenth Maine, who had the summer before been promoted from company B of our old Tenth Maine; he asked if I could detail a relief to assist his weary men, but before I could answer a squad of us volunteered and picked up and went off with the Adjutant.

"In about four weeks all our work was done and the Twelfth corps hospital was no more.   Dr. Goodman praised us highly for our good behavior and for doing all our duties so well, and told us that he should send us to 'the front' in two days.   *   *   *

"*   *   *   We broke camp and went by rail to Baltimore, Washington, and Rappahannock Station, and marched to Kelly's Ford."

It should be noted in closing that though nearly all of the battalion were at times under artillery fire none were injured ; and the answers to the question whether any one fired a musket during the battle make it sure they did not.   Furthermore, as they had no colors there has never arisen the question whether "Gettysburg" should be inscribed upon them.   Finally, it is only fair to "the battalion" boys for me, as one of "the regiment," who was discharged and served again with them in the Twenty-ninth Maine, to say that they never claimed more than they performed at Gettysburg or anywhere else.   They simply did what they were ordered to do, and did it so promptly and well that Gen. Slocum gave them a most hearty and flattering "good-bye" when the time came for him to take final leave of them.

PARTICIPANTS.

FIELD, STAFF AND NON-COMMISSIONED STAFF.

Acting Field Officer, Captain John D. Beardsley of company D.
Acting Quartermaster, First Lieutenant Charles F. King, company D.
Assistant Surgeon, Horatio N. Howard, Abbot.
Sergeant-Major, Samuel Hanson, Biddeford.
Quartermaster-Sergeant, Thomas S. Bugbee, Washburn.
Hospital Steward, John McLaren, English army.

COMPANY A.

Captain, John Q. Adams, Saco, Provost Marshal of corps.
First Lieutenant, Edwin W. Fowler, Saco, commanding company.
Second Lieutenant, Charles E. Pierce, Saco.

SERGEANTS.

First Sergeant, James F. Tarr, Biddeford,
Horace C. Berry, Woodstock,   George P. Fernald, Saco,
Edward P. M. Bragdon, Biddeford,   John Reardon, Biddeford.

CORPORALS.

Stephen H. Dyer, Biddeford,   Thaddeus Cross, Saco,
William Hopping, Biddeford,   John Collum, Jr., Saco,
James Jennings, Biddeford.

PRIVATES.

Bailey, George H., Bridgton,   Benson, Ephraim C., Peru,
Berwin, Joseph, Eastport,   Burnell, Frank (28th N. Y.), Lockport,
Chappell, Joseph H., Saco,   Cobb, Edwin A., Bridgton,
Coburn, Charles F., Weld,   Cole, Edwin, Saco,
Cole, Henry F., Woodstock,   Donihue, George L., Freeport,
Fletcher, Sydney W., Biddeford,   Gaffeny, John (28th N. Y.), Lockport,
Gould, Joseph, Saco,   Guiney, James, Lewiston,
Hodsdon, Isaac W., Byron,   Irving, Robert (28th N. Y.), Lockport,
Jepson, Leonard, Lewiston,   Jones, Albert N., Weld,
Jones, Gustavus W., Weld,   Keighley, William, Biddeford,
Kenney, Dennis, Biddeford,   Larrabee, Emery E., Lewiston,
Lee, Edward, Magaguadavic, N. B.,   Leighton, Ivan, Biddeford,
Leighton, Moses, Saco,   Littlehale, Alanson M., Newry,
McDougall, Archibald, Prince Edw. Is.,   McIntire, George E., Dayton,
McLaughlin, Tyler H., Weld,   Moore, Moses T., Biddeford,
Rawson, Charles C., Whitneyville,   Roberts, Charles F., Biddeford,
Rowe, Daniel M., Saco,   Staples, James, Jr., Biddeford,
Taylor, Leonard B. (28th N. Y.)—N.Y.   Thurston, James H., Danville,
Towle, Samuel T., Rockland,   Young, Oliver B. (28th N.Y.), Lockport.

ON SPECIAL DUTY OR DETACHED SERVICE: Musician Patrick Hickey, Jr., Biddeford, Drummer. Wagoner Henry H. Shapleigh, Lebanon, wagon train. Corporal Joseph Littlefield, Kennebunk, and Privates William S. Davis, Biddeford, William T. Dodge, Westbrook, Daniel Hanson, Saco, George W. Hatch, Kennebunk, and Emery A. Holman, New Gloucester, cattle guard. Privates: Elbridge G. Berry, Carthage, James A. Russell, Weld, and Willard M. Russell, Weld, amb. train ; Edward Gillis, Miramichi, N. B., orderly for Gen. Williams ; David B. Smith, Weld, batt'y F, 4th U.

S. ; Stephen E. Welch, Sanford, corps blacksmith ; Phineas C. Witham, Weld, orderly and assis't of Surg. Howard ; Jeremiah Donovan, Biddeford, in arrest.

COMPANY B.

Second Lieutenant Charles H. Haskell, Pownal, commanding company.

SERGEANTS.

First Sergeant, Wilbur W. McKenney, Saco,

Oliver B. Jones, Portland,	Jeremiah P. W. Roach, Windham,
Albert P. Smith, New Gloucester,	Edward A. Burnell, Portland.

CORPORALS.

John F. Wells, Portland,	Stillman Wilson, Freeport,
Thomas Foster, Bristol,	Albert F. Colley, Gray,
Charles Allen, Biddeford,	Willard W. Judkins, Carthage.

MUSICIANS.

Charles A. Hersey, South Paris,	Henry A. Hersey, South Paris.

PRIVATES.

Andrews, William Wallace, Otisfield,	Ballard, Samuel F., Fryeburg,
Bodge, William, Windham,	Brett, John F., Portland,
Charles, Daniel E., Lovell,	Emerson, Stillman H., Biddeford,
Flanders, Daniel, Portland,	Floyd, Osgood F., Porter,
Foss, David C., Portland,	Fox, George H., Dexter,
Goodridge, Lewis E., Naples,	Greenleaf, Solomon, Norway,
Hall, Alanson A. (28th N. Y.), Lockport,	Howard, Simeon, Westbrook,
Irish, Benjamin R., Sumner,	Judkins, Eastman, Carthage,
Judkins, Orville, Weld,	Kidder, Wm. (28th N. Y.), Lockport,
Marriner, Greenleaf T., Westbrook,	Mitchell, Arthur S., Carthage,
Moulton, Mathias, Portland,	Neal, Ansel, Portland,
Nutting, James, Bethel,	O'Hara, William, Portland,
Paine, Frank O., Windham,	Plant, Charles F., New Gloucester,
Putnam, John A., Franklin Plantation,	Ripley, George K., Paris,
Sanborn, Dudley F., Lewiston,	Sargent, George W., Oxford,
Smith, Louville, New Gloucester,	Snow, Israel T., Jackson,
Stanley, William S., Porter,	Stinchfield, Samuel E., New Glo'ster,
Taber, George W., Vassalboro,	Thurston, George H., Portland,
Usher, Joshua L., Sebago,	Verrill, Edward P., Raymond,
Vickery, Isaiah H., Danville,	Wetherby, William, Naples,
Wilkinson, John W., Portland,	Wing, Samuel F., Rumford.

ON SPECIAL DUTY OR DETACHED SERVICE: Privates: Nathaniel Cash, Naples, Ezekiel H. Hanson, Portland, George H. Hoit, Portland, Storer S. Knight, Westbrook, and Edward H. Sawyer, Portland, cattle guard; George W. Smith, Scarborough, wagon train.

NOTE. According to the monthly return of June 30th there should be only sixty-one names present in Co. B, but I am unable after a great deal of study and correspondence with the survivors to learn which man, if any of the above, was absent. J. M. G.

COMPANY D.

Captain, John D. Beardsley, Grand Falls, N. B., commanding battalion.
First Lieutenant, Charles F. King, Portland, acting Quartermaster.
Second Lieutenant, Chandler A. Libby, Limestone Pl., commanding company.

SERGEANTS.

1st Serg., Henry H. Kallock, Ashland, George MacDonald, Ashland,
James Gillespie, Fort Kent,   Charles H. Anderson, Smyrna.

CORPORALS.

Maurice Hayes, Houlton,   Charles H. Corson, Bangor,
Oliver B. Coy, Welchville,   Howard Taggart, Portage Lake,
Edward L. Prindall, Portland.
    WAGONER: Charles B. Canney, Bangor.

PRIVATES.

Boody, Leonard G., Portland,   Brady, Wm. H. (28th N. Y.), Batavia,
Buck, Daniel F., Harrison,   Bucknam, Amos, Portland,
Caman, Aug. W. (28th N. Y.) —, N. Y. Casey, William, Castle Hill,
Day, Vinal J., Ashland,   Doody, John H., Portland,
Dow, Alexander, Ashland,   Duran, Benjamin, Westbrook,
Ferrell, William E., Portland,   Giberson, Simon, Sarsfield Plantation,
Green, Charles A., Portland,   Johnson, Freeman W., Limestone Pl.,
Libby, Elias T., Ashland,   Manderville, Marcus A. (28th N. Y.),
McGoverin, Dennis, Portland,   Newfane, N. Y.
McGowan, Michael, Portland,   McKenney, Daniel B., Lincoln,
McNeil, Nelson, Fort Fairfield,   Miller, John, Fort Kent,
Milligan, Wallace, Castle Hill,   Moore, Edward K., Portland,
Montreuil, Firman, Ashland,   Nearst, Augustus (28th N.Y.) Lockport,
O'Connor, John W., Fort Kent,   Randall, James L., Castle Hill,
Read, John, (28th N. Y.), ——, N. Y. Roche, Wm. (28th N.Y.) Lockport, N.Y.
Sears, Hiram, Fort Kent,   Sheridan, James, Portland,
Shorey, Joshua R., Enfield,   Simpson, Josiah, Portland,
Smith, Jefferson, Ashland,   Souci, Jerry, Canada East,
Spring, William G. J., Portland,   Stannorth, John A., Portland,
Stinson, James, English army,   Turner, John F., Portland,
Twist, James, Mapleton,   Wait, Thomas, Fort Kent,
Wallace, William, Ashland,   Ward, David, Fort Kent,
Wescott, John, Masardis,   White, John, Fort Kent.

    ON SPECIAL DUTY OR DETACHED SERVICE: Sergeant Joseph G. Brown, Portage Lake, in charge of cattle guard. Privates: Amos Kelley, Lyndon, William T. Keyes, Portland, Joseph W. Small, Upton, and Josiah H. Smith, Biddeford, cattle guard; Adin Ballou, Portland, and Leonard G. Jordan, Portland, clerks corps h'dqrs; Joseph T. Chapman, Bethel, drummer; Martin Gaitley, Portland, and Daniel W. Stackpole, Portland, wagoners; Charles Kehoe, Portland, orderly of Gen. Slocum; Peter Michaud, Can. East, batt'y F, 4th U. S.; Alonzo Nutter, Freeport, and Joseph Smith, Fort Kent, batt'y M, 1st N. Y. Artillery.

    NOTE. The battalion had no field officers. The men with "28th N. Y." against their names were transferred to the Tenth batt'n from the 28th N. Y. regiment, which had been brigaded with the Tenth Maine and was mustered out a few weeks after the latter.

HISTORICAL SKETCH.

BY MAJOR JOHN MEAD GOULD

LATE OF 1-10-29th MAINE REGIMENT.

The Tenth Maine regiment was the reorganization of the First Maine, a three-months' regiment. It was mustered into U. S. service October 4 and 5, 1861, to serve the remainder of two years' service due from the First Maine members, i. e., till May 3, 1863.

The First Maine was formed from militia companies of which eight existed previous to the civil war, namely : Portland Light Infantry, Mechanic Blues, Light Guard, Rifle Corps and Rifle Guard, Lewiston Light Infantry, Norway Light Infantry, and Auburn Artillery. The two other companies were raised at Portland and Lewiston.

The Tenth regiment was composed largely of members of these companies with recruits from the western part of the state, nearly all from the counties of Cumberland, Androscoggin, York and Oxford, excepting company D, which originally was from Aroostook County.

The following was the original organization of the Tenth Maine : —

FIELD, STAFF AND NON-COMMISSIONED STAFF.

Colonel, George L. Beal, Norway.
Lieutenant-Colonel, James S. Fillebrown, Auburn.
Major, Charles Walker, Portland.
Adjutant, First Lieutenant Elijah M. Shaw, Lewiston.
Quartermaster, First Lieutenant William S. Dodge, Westbrook.
Surgeon, Daniel O. Perry, Portland.
Assistant Surgeon, Josiah F. Day, Jr., Portland.
Chaplain, George Knox, Brunswick.
Sergeant-Major, John M. Gould, Portland.
Quartermaster-Sergeant, Charles F. King, Portland.
Commissary-Sergeant, Charles Thompson, Norway.
Drum-Major, William Allen, Gray.
Fife-Major, Alpheus L. Greene, Portland.
Hospital Steward, George J. Northrop, Portland.
Regimental Band Leader, Daniel H. Chandler, Portland.

COMPANY OFFICERS.

Co. A.　Captain, John Q. Adams, Saco.
First Lieutenant, Ephraim M. Littlefield, Saco.
Second Lieutenant, Charles E. Pierce, Saco.

Co. B.   Captain, James M. Black, Portland.
          First Lieutenant, Charles W. Roberts, Portland.
          Second Lieutenant, Alfred L. Turner, Portland.
Co. C.   Captain, William P. Jordan, Portland.
          First Lieutenant, Benjamin M. Redlon, Portland.
          Second Lieutenant, Benjamin F. Whitney, Windham.
Co. D.   Captain, George W. West, Somerville, Mass.
          First Lieutenant, John D. Beardsley, Grand Falls, N. B.
          Second Lieutenant, Henry M. Binney, Somerville, Mass.
Co. E.   Captain, Albert H. Estes, Portland.
          First Lieutenant, Cyrus Latham, Portland.
          Second Lieutenant, Andrew C. Cloudman, Portland.
Co. F.   Captain, William Knowlton, Lewiston.
          First Lieutenant, Edward S. Butler, Lewiston.
          Second Lieutenant, Abel G. Rankin, Lewiston.
Co. G.   Captain, Henry Rust, Jr., Norway.
          First Lieutenant, Jonathan Blake, Norway.
          Second Lieutenant, William W. Whitmarsh, Norway.
Co. H.   Captain, Charles S. Emerson, Auburn.
          First Lieutenant, James C. Folsom, Auburn.
          Second Lieutenant, Phineas W. Dill, Auburn.
Co. I.   Captain, Nehemiah T. Furbish, Portland.
          First Lieutenant, Hebron Mayhew, Westbrook.
          Second Lieutenant, John T. Simpson, Portland.
Co. K.   Captain, George H. Nye, Lewiston.
          First Lieutenant, John F. Witherell, Monmouth.
          Second Lieutenant, Fayette Bicknell, Oxford.

Seven months were spent in a continuous round of guard-duty, drill, parade, and attention to the nicer details of discipline. For a number of months the companies changed station every fortnight, shifting to and from various points on the B. & O. Railroad, between Baltimore and Harper's Ferry and Martinsburg, Va., and along the Washington branch of that road. Late in March, 1862, the regimental headquarters were at Harper's Ferry and the companies all in Virginia. Early in May headquarters were in Winchester, Va., when Stonewall Jackson made his famous descent upon the remnants of Gen. Banks' corps and drove all out of the Shenandoah Valley. This first experience of the regiment in battle, May 25, 1862, was made more unpleasant from the failure of Gen. Banks to get orders to Col. Beal, who was left with his regiment standing in the streets of Winchester while the enemy nearly surrounded the city. The regiment got out with but small loss in killed and wounded; but many of the sentries and the sick were cut off and made prisoners. The evening previous companies C and I, under Capt. Wm. P. Jordan, had successfully persuaded the Confederate General Ewell, who was advancing upon Winchester, that it was time to halt for the night. This evening and night service was really a battle on a small scale. It is reckoned in the regiment as one of its best services.

The march of company B (Portland Mechanic Blues), on the 24th and 25th, is also noteworthy in that they covered 55 to 57 miles in 24 hours or less. The regiment lost in the two days 3 killed, 12 wounded, and 65 others taken prisoners.

In June the regiment, now a part of Crawford's brigade, returned to Virginia with Banks' corps, and after several reconnaissances in various parts of the valley was sent to Culpeper C. H. Gen. John Pope was now given command of the army, and attempted to check the advance of Lee.

At Cedar Mountain, eight miles south of Culpeper C. H., August 9th, 1862, the Tenth had its first severe battle. Here Gen. Banks reversed the error of May by sending the Tenth to combat single-handed a large part of the army under Stonewall Jackson. After a short and murderous action the regiment was compelled to retreat, having lost 39 killed or mortally wounded, and 134 severely wounded, or 37.5 per cent of the number engaged.

Then followed Pope's retreat and the Second Bull Run, during which, however, Banks' corps was not engaged though the Tenth lost ten of its number by capture, mostly the sick in Culpeper hospital.

The Maryland campaign followed; the Tenth having received about a hundred recruits took a prominent part in the battle of Antietam, September 17, 1862, checking the advance of Hood's veterans in the famous East Woods. Here also at considerable disadvantage of position the Tenth had a bloody and stubborn fight in which 31 were killed and mortally wounded, and forty were seriously wounded, or one-fourth the number engaged. The ratio between the killed and wounded in this engagement is remarkable.

The important ford over the Potomac at Berlin, Md., was guarded by the regiment for the next three months, with companies stationed also at other fords and important contiguous points. The Twelfth corps did not follow McClellan into Virginia, but was kept in Maryland until December, when positions were taken near Fairfax Station; from thence, at the time of the "mud march" (Jan. 19–23, 1863), the corps moved forward to Stafford C. H., where the Tenth Maine remained till their term expired, and April 27th they were ordered home.

The friends of the regiment claim that the men were of a superior grade of intelligence; and that they attained an excellence in drill and knowledge of guard-duty far above the average of volunteer regiments.

At the time of muster-out it had lost more men killed and died of wounds (73) than any other Maine regiment; while the deaths by disease, etc., had been fewer than is usual (52, including 6 starved to death in rebel prisons and 4 accidental).

So far as is known the Tenth Maine drum corps was the largest and best drilled of all in the army of the Potomac.

But the officers and men of the Tenth, mustered-out in May, began efforts for reorganizing under special authority in July, enlisting as "Beal's Veterans." Four companies reporting in September, were mustered November 13th; others followed, and the last company was mustered-in December 17, 1863, for three years, the regiment becoming the 29th Maine, Colonel Beal in command. Leaving Maine in February, 1864, they took the field in Louisiana, were assigned to the Nineteenth corps, and went on the Red River expedition, meeting the enemy at Sabine Cross Roads, Pleasant Hill and Cane River Crossing, the loss aggregating 27 wounded (3 mortally).

The Tenth battalion companies joined the regiment in May. The corps was brought to Virginia and was in Sheridan's Shenandoah Valley campaign of 1864. Colonel Beal had the brigade after April 19th, and Major Knowlton commanded the regiment at Opequon Creek, where he was mortally wounded, when the command passed to Captain Turner, senior officer present. Fisher's Hill and Cedar Creek followed. In the last battle Major Nye commanded the regiment in the morning, until wounded, succeeded by Captain Whitmarsh, and later in the day by Captain Turner. The loss here was 127 killed and wounded, — 34 per cent of those engaged.

The Twenty-ninth was mustered-out June 21, 1866.

ROSTER.

The following information relating to officers of the Tenth Maine regiment is obtained from the Volunteer Army Register, published by the War Department August 31, 1865, and other reliable sources : —

OFFICERS AT MUSTER-OUT MAY 7–8, 1863.

COLONEL: George L. Beal, Oct. 3, 1861; Col. 29th Maine, Dec. 17, 1863,— brevet Brig.-Gen. Vols., Aug. 22, 1864; Brig.-Gen. Vols. Nov. 13, 1864; brevet Maj.-Gen. Vols., Mar. 13, 1865.

LIEUTENANT-COLONEL: James S. Fillebrown, Oct. 4, 1861.

MAJOR: Charles S. Emerson, Mar. 17, 1863; Lieut.-Col. 29th Maine, Nov. 30, 1863.

QUARTERMASTER: 1st Lieut. Charles Thompson, Sept. 12, 1862; Q. M. 29th Maine, Sept. 16, 1863.

CAPTAINS: John Q. Adams, Oct. 4, 1861, tr. to 10th batt'n and 29th Maine; Alfred L. Turner, Oct. 25, 1862,—Captain 29th Maine; William P. Jordan, Oct. 5, 1861,—Captain 29th Maine, brevet Major, Mar. 13, 1865; John D. Beardsley, Oct. 15, 1862, tr. to 10th batt'n and 29th Maine,—Major and Lieut.-Col. 109th U. S. C. T., Sept., 1864; Herbert R. Sargent, Aug. 9, 1862, —Capt. 32d Maine, Mar. 23, 1864, tr. to 31st Maine, Dec. 12, 1864; William Knowlton, Oct. 4, 1861,—Capt. and Maj. 29th Maine, killed at Opequon, Sept. 20, 1864; Jonathan Blake, Oct. 21, 1861; Elijah M. Shaw, Mar. 26, 1863; Hebron Mayhew, Sept. 17, 1862; George H. Nye, Oct. 4, 1861,—Capt., Maj. and Col. 29th Maine, brevet Brig.-Gen. Vols., Oct. 28, 1865, brevet Maj.-Gen. Vols., Mar. 13, 1865.

FIRST LIEUTENANTS: Edwin W. Fowler, May 27, 1862, tr. to 10th batt'n and 29th Maine; Benjamin F. Whitney, Oct. 25, 1862; Benjamin M. Redlon, Oct. 5, 1861,—Capt. 29th Maine, brevet Major Vols., Mar. 13, 1865; Charles F. King, Jan. 10, 1863,—tr. to 10th batt'n and 29th Maine, Capt. Maine Coast Guards, Jan. 6, 1865; John M. Gould, Aug. 9, 1862, acting Adjt.,—Adjt. 29th Maine, and Major Dec. 20, 1864; Edward S. Butler, Oct. 4, 1861,—Capt. 29th Maine, Sept. 16, 1864; William W. Whitmarsh, Oct. 21, 1861, — Capt. 29th Maine; Granville Blake, Sept. 26, 1862,—Capt. 29th Maine, brevet Maj. Vols., Mar. 13, 1865; Albert H. Johnson, Sept. 17, 1862; Fayette Bicknell, July 5, 1862.

SECOND LIEUTENANTS: Charles E. Pierce, Oct. 4, 1861,—tr. to 10th batt'n and 29th Maine; Marcus Delano, Mar. 2, 1863; Chandler A. Libby, Mar. 2, 1863, tr. to 10th batt'n, resigned July 17, 1863; Henry F. Smith, Dec. 18, 1862; Charles H. Haskell, Apr. 27, 1863,—tr. to 10th batt'n and to 29th Maine; Henry R. Millett, Oct. 21, 1861,—Capt., Nov. 6, 1864, 29th Maine; Horace Wright, Oct. 26, 1862; Charles C. Graham, Sept. 17, 1862,—1st Lieut. 29th Maine, brevet Captain Vols., Mar. 13, 1865; Albert E. Kingsley, June 26, 1862,—Capt., Oct. 18, 1864, 29th Maine.

SURGEON: Josiah F. Day, Jr., Oct. 22, 1862,—Surgeon 29th Maine with same rank, brevet Lieut.-Col. Vols., Mar. 13, 1865. ASSISTANT SURGEON: Horatio N. Howard, Sept. 5, 1862,—tr. to 10th batt'n and 29th Maine, Surgeon 30th Maine, May 16, 1865.

CHAPLAIN: George Knox, Oct. 4, 1861,—Chaplain 29th Maine, Oct. 18, 1864, accidentally killed at Cedar Creek, Oct. 31, 1864.

(The dates given above refer to rank or commission; those hereafter given refer to the date of event.)

DIED.

CAPTAINS: Andrew C. Cloudman, killed at battle of Cedar Mountain, Aug. 9, 1862; Nehemiah T. Furbish, killed at battle of Antietam, Sept. 17, 1862.

FIRST LIEUTENANTS: James C. Folsom, killed at battle of Cedar Mountain, Aug. 9, 1862; George W. True, Sept. 20, 1862, mortally w'd at Antietam.

SECOND LIEUTENANTS: Albert W. Freeman, Aug. 25, 1862, mortally w'd at Cedar Mountain; William Wade, killed at battle of Antietam, Sept. 17, 1862; Edward Brackett, Sept. 18, 1862, mortally w'd at Antietam; Charles H. Colley, Sept. 20, 1862, mortally w'd at Cedar Mountain; Joseph H. Perley, Jr., Dec. 18, 1862, of consumption.

SURGEON: Daniel S. Tracy (not mustered for want of opportunity), died from overwork and exposure, about Oct., 1862; name not on regimental rolls.

PROMOTED AND TRANSFERRED OUT OF REGIMENT.

(Additional to those entering 10th battalion.)

CAPTAINS: Henry Rust, Jr., to Lieut.-Col. 13th Maine, Oct. 14, 1861, Col. 13th Maine, May 18, 1862, brevet Brig.-Gen. Vols., Mar. 13, 1865; George W. West, to Major 17th Maine, Aug. 18, 1862, Col. Oct. 22, 1863, brevet Brig.-Gen. Vols., Dec. 2, 1864.

FIRST LIEUTENANT: Charles W. Roberts, to Adjt. 17th Maine, Aug. 18, 1862.

QUARTERMASTER: 1st Lieut. William S. Dodge to Captain and A. C. S. of Vols., Nov. 22, 1862, brevet Major Vols., July 14, 1865.

DISCHARGED.

SECOND LIEUTENANT: Reuben Alexander, Dec. 8, 1862 (and soon after died), dis. from wounds at Cedar Mountain; Band-master Daniel H. Chandler, Sept. 8, 1862.

RESIGNED.

MAJOR: Charles Walker, Jan. 26, 1863.

CAPTAINS: Albert H. Estes, Jan. 16, 1862; Cyrus Latham, Mar. 28, 1862; James M. Black, Oct. 25, 1862.

FIRST LIEUTENANTS: Ephraim M. Littlefield, May 26, 1862; Abel G. Rankin, Apr. 4, 1863, for ill health,—Captain 29th Maine, brevet Major Vols., June 25, 1866; John F. Witherell, June 26, 1862, for ill health.

SECOND LIEUTENANTS: Benjamin M. Bradbury, June 26, 1862; Phineas W. Dill, Jan. 10, 1862; John T. Simpson, July 10, 1862.

SURGEON: Daniel O. Perry, Oct. 21, 1862. ASSISTANT SURGEON: James Sawyer, Jan. 30, 1863.

OTHERWISE LEFT THE SERVICE.

Second Lieutenant Henry Martin Binney, dis. Dec. 30, 1862,—afterward 1st Lieut. and Captain 28th Mass.

HIGH WATER MARK MONUMENT.

This monumental structure is located at the "copse of trees," and at the point in the Union line where the Confederate assault on July 3d fell with greatest weight and was pushed to the last extremity by desperate but unsuccessful gallantry. It stands on the west side of the macadamized, battlefield road, named Hancock Avenue, on the southern slope of Cemetery Hill, about the centre of the whole Union line of battle. Upon a bronze tablet inserted on the front of the plinth of the monument is the following legend:—

COMMANDS HONORED.

IN RECOGNITION OF THE PATRIOTISM AND GALLANTRY DISPLAYED
BY THEIR RESPECTIVE TROOPS WHO MET OR ASSISTED TO REPULSE

LONGSTREET'S ASSAULT

THE FOLLOWING STATES HAVE CONTRIBUTED TO ERECT THIS TABLET.
MAINE, NEW HAMPSHIRE, VERMONT, MASSACHUSETTS, RHODE ISLAND,
CONNECTICUT, NEW YORK, NEW JERSEY, DELAWARE, PENNSYLVANIA,
WEST VIRGINIA, OHIO, MICHIGAN AND MINNESOTA.

Upon the bronze pages of the book that surmounts the plinth are set forth the divisions, brigades, and batteries that contended in this assault, among them being Harrow's brigade of Gibbon's division of the Second corps, of which the Nineteenth Maine regiment was a part, and among the Union forces enumerated as assisting in the repulse appears Dow's Battery of McGilvery's Artillery brigade. Upon a bronze tablet on the north side of the monument enumerating organizations that met the assaulting column is found the Nineteenth Maine regiment, also company D, 2d U. S. Sharpshooters.

In general terms the monument consists of the following elements: A massive open bronze book rests at an incline, propped by two pyramids of cannon balls, upon the plinth of polished Fox Island, Maine, granite; the plinth upon a polished Quincy granite base seven feet four inches wide by nine feet in length and sixteen inches high; the whole planted upon a rough-faced sub-base or water table of Gettysburg granite.

Outside the base is an esplanade constructed of granolithic cement, with curb of hammered granite, approached by two granite steps in front, affording a walk about five feet in width, separated from the water table by a raised dais, also curbed. At the north and south extensions the esplanade ends in quarter-circle wings, upon each of which stands a field piece.

The monument with stone approaches covers a space eighteen feet six inches by forty-eight feet six inches.

The legend upon the open pages of the bronze book (without preserving the lines) reads as follows:—

HIGH WATER MARK

OF THE REBELLION.

THIS COPSE OF TREES WAS THE LANDMARK towards which Longstreet's assault was directed JULY 3, 1863.

THE ASSAULTING COLUMN was composed of Kemper's, Garnett's and Armistead's Brigades of PICKETT'S DIVISION, Archer's, Davis', Pettigrew's and Brockenbrough's Brigades of HETH'S DIVISION and Scales' and Lane's Brigades of PENDER'S DIVISION.

Supported on the right by Wilcox's and Perry's Brigades of ANDERSON'S DIVISION; on the left by Thomas' and McGowan's Brigades of PENDER'S DIVISION; and in rear by Wright's, Posey's and Mahone's Brigades of ANDERSON'S DIVISION, and assisted by the following artillery:

CABELL'S BATTALION, consisting of Manly's, Fraser's, McCarthy's, and Carlton's, Batteries. ALEXANDER'S BATTALION, Woolfolk's, Jordan's, Gilbert's, Moody's, Parker's and Taylor's Batteries. ESHLEMAN'S BATTALION, Squires', Richardson's, Miller's and Norcom's Batteries. DEARING'S BATTALION, Stribling's, Caskie's, Macon's and Blount's Batteries. CUTTS' BATTALION, Ross', Patterson's and Wingfield's Batteries. POAGUE'S BATTALION, Wyatt's, Graham's, Ward's and Brooke's Batteries. PEGRAM'S BATTALION, McGraw's, Zimmerman's, Brander's, Marye's and Crenshaw Batteries. McINTOSH'S BATTALION, Rice's, Hurt's, Wallace's and Johnson's Batteries. CARTER'S BATTALION, Reese's, Carter's, Page's and Fry's Batteries. BROWN'S BATTALION, Watson's, Smith's, Cunningham's and Griffin's Batteries.

REPULSE OF

LONGSTREET'S ASSAULT.

Longstreet's Assault was repulsed by Webb's, Hall's and Harrow's Brigades of GIBBON'S DIVISION SECOND ARMY CORPS; Smyth's and Willard's Brigades and portions of Carroll's Brigade of HAYS' DIVISION SECOND ARMY CORPS; and the First Massachusett's Sharpshooters (unattached), portions of Rowley's and Stannard's Brigades of DOUBLEDAY'S DIVISION FIRST ARMY CORPS; HAZARD'S SECOND CORPS ARTILLERY BRIGADE, consisting of Woodruff's, Arnold's, Cushing's, Brown's and Rorty's Batteries.

Assisted on the right by Hill's, Edgell's, Eakin's, Bancroft's, Dilger's and Taft's Batteries on CEMETERY HILL; and on the left by Cowan's, Fitzhugh's, Parsons', Wheeler's, Thomas', Daniels' and Sterling's Batteries and McGILVERY'S ARTILLERY BRIGADE, consisting of Thompson's, Phillips', Hart's, Cooper's, Dow's and Ames' Batteries, and by Hazlett's Battery on Little Round Top.

And supported by DOUDLEDAY'S DIVISION OF THE FIRST ARMY CORPS, which was in position on the immediate left of the troops assaulted.

THE THIRD ARMY CORPS moved up to within supporting distance on the left, and ROBINSON'S DIVISION OF THE FIRST ARMY CORPS moved into position to support the right.

The State of Maine cheerfully contributed the sum of five hundred dollars to assist in erecting this monument, which was the full amount asked for in that enterprise by the Gettysburg Battlefield Memorial Association.

As has been already stated, the Nineteenth Maine regiment, whose monument stands a short distance southerly of this position, was moved at the crisis of " Longstreet's Assault " to this place, when with Harrow's brigade, Gibbon's division, Second corps, it engaged the enemy. It was also towards this part of the line that the Third and Fourth Maine regiments were rapidly moved, under heavy artillery fire from the Confederates, to support the Second corps line, near the close of the desperate struggle. Tablets furnished by the State of Maine have been recently located by the Gettysburg National Park Commissioners marking the positions of the Third and Fourth regiments.

This monument was dedicated June 2, 1892, by appropriate services. Maine was represented on this occasion by a number of officials and prominent citizens. The Maine Gettysburg Commissioners were represented by their chairman General Hamlin, General Heath, Major Thaxter and Major Stevens, members of their Executive Committee. General Heath was formerly colonel of the Nineteenth Maine, commanding that regiment in the battle of Gettysburg.

ADDITIONAL PARTICIPATING OFFICERS.

The following is a list of general, staff, and other officers either resident or native of the State of Maine who served in the army of the Potomac at the battle of Gettysburg, and not belonging to any of the Maine organizations : —

OLIVER O. HOWARD, Major-General U. S. Vols., commanding 11th corps. — Major-General U. S. A.

ALBION P. HOWE, Brigadier-General U. S. Vols., commanding 2d division, 6th corps. — Brevet Major-General U. S. Vols. ; Colonel 4th Art'y U. S. A.

RUFUS INGALLS, Brigadier-General U. S. Vols., Quartermaster army of the Potomac. — Brigadier and brevet Major-General U. S. A.

SETH WILLIAMS, Brigadier-General U. S. Vols., Adjutant General army of Potomac.—Brigadier and brevet Major-General U. S. A.

ADELBERT AMES, Brigadier-General U. S. Vols., commanding 2d brigade, 1st division, also commanding 1st division, 11th army corps. — Captain 5th U. S. Art'y ; brevet Major-General U. S. A.

ROMEYN B. AYRES, Brigadier-General U. S. Vols., commanding 2d division, 5th corps. — Captain 5th U. S. Art'y ; brevet Major-General U. S. A.

JOHN C. CALDWELL, Brigadier-General U. S. Vols., commanding 1st division, 2d corps. — Brevet Major-General U. S. Vols.

JOSEPH S. SMITH, Lieut.-Colonel U. S. Vols., Asst. Commissary of Subsistence, Chief Commissary of 2d corps, staff of Major-General Hancock. — Brevet Colonel and Brigadier-General U. S. Vols. ; recipient of Congressional medal of honor.

WILLIAM H. OWEN, Lieut.-Colonel U. S. Vols., A. Q. M., Chief Quartermaster of 5th corps. — Colonel and Inspector Q. M. Dept.

CHARLES HAMLIN, Major and Assistant Adjutant General U. S. Vols., Adjutant General 2d division, 3d corps. Mentioned in official report of Gen. Humphreys, commanding the division at Gettysburg, who expressed his "sense of the obligations he was under for the valuable services rendered him on the field by Major Hamlin."—Brevet Colonel and Brigadier-General U. S. Vols.; Asst. Inspector of Art'y.

FREEMAN McGILVERY, Major Maine Light Artillery, commanding 1st Vol. brigade, Reserve Artillery. Mentioned in official report of Gen. Tyler, commanding Artillery Reserve at Gettysburg, calling attention to "the intrepid conduct and excellent judgment displayed by Major McGilvery."— Lieut.-Colonel Maine Light Artillery.

CHARLES H. HOWARD, Major U. S. Vols., Aide-de-Camp on staff of Major-General Howard, 11th corps. — Colonel 128th U. S. Col. Inf.; brevet Brigadier-General U. S. Vols.

JOHN MARSHALL BROWN, Captain and Assistant Adjutant General U. S. Vols., staff of Brigadier-General Ames, 2d brigade, 1st division, 11th corps. Mentioned in official report of Gen. Ames as having "rendered most valuable services during the three days' fighting. With great coolness and energy he ably seconded my [Ames'] efforts in repelling the assault made by the enemy on the evening of the 2d." — Lieut.-Colonel 32d Maine regiment; brevet Colonel for gallant and meritorious conduct at the battle of Gettysburg; brevet Brigadier-General U. S. Vols., March 13, 1865.

EDWARD B. KNOX, Major 44th N. Y. Vols. — Brevet Lieut.-Colonel U. S. A.

JOHN A. DOUGLASS, Surgeon 11th Mass. Vols.

CHARLES H. FLAGG, Captain 142d Penn. Vols., acting Inspector-General 3d division, 1st corps. Killed July 3d. Mentioned for gallant conduct in official report of Gen. Rowley.

STEPHEN H. MANNING, Captain and A. Q. M. U. S. Vols., Chief Quartermaster 1st division, 6th corps. — Brevet Brigadier-General U. S. Vols.

WILLIAM H. MILLS, First Lieutenant 14th U. S. Inf. — Brevet Major U. S. A.

EDWARD A. ELLSWORTH, First Lieutenant 11th U. S. Inf.

LEWIS H. SANGER, First Lieutenant 17th U. S. Inf. — Brevet Major U. S. A.

WILLIAM H. CHAMBERLIN, First Lieutenant 17th U. S. Inf. Killed at Gettysburg.

WILLIAM HARMON, First Lieutenant 1st Minn. Inf.

WILLIAM STONE, First Lieutenant 19th Mass. — Brevet Major.

IRA W. TRASK, First Lieutenant U. S. Vols., regiment not ascertained. — First Lieutenant 9th U. S. Cav. ; brevet Captain U. S. A. for gallantry at Gettysburg.

SAMUEL ADAMS, Assistant Surgeon 8th U. S. Inf. at army headquarters.

MICHAEL C. BOYCE, Second Lieutenant 10th U. S. Inf. Mortally wounded at Gettysburg.

HARRY L. HASKELL, Second Lieutenant, Acting Adjutant, 125th N. Y., of Willard's brigade.

GETTYSBURG SUMMARIES.

MAINE PARTICIPANTS AND CASUALTIES REVISED.

Total of Maine under Meade, 330 officers, 5,012 men.

These may be classed as follows :—

Commands and detachments fully engaged, 185 officers, 2,658 men.

Commands only slightly engaged, or in reserve, 96 officers, 1,420 men.

Non-combatants, including those detailed, 49 officers, 934 men.

Casualties among the fully engaged class :—

Killed and died of wounds, 18 officers, 205 men. Wounded, 35 officers, 486 men. Missing and prisoners, 13 officers, 209 men. Aggregate loss of this class, 966, which is more than one-third of those engaged. The number of killed and wounded was 744,—26 per cent of those engaged.

Besides the above casualties there were 2 killed, 7 wounded and 1 missing, from the commands only slightly engaged.

PART 2

DEDICATION OF MONUMENTS

ERECTED BY THE STATE OF MAINE ON THE BATTLEFIELD OF
GETTYSBURG.

OCTOBER 3, 1889

ORDER OF THE DAY.

National Salute, to be fired at 9 o'clock A. M., from Cemetery Hill. Minute guns.

Inspection of the Maine Monuments by the Governor of Maine, the Maine Gettysburg Commissioners, accompanied by Hon. Hannibal Hamlin and other members of the Maine party. Regimental reunions and dedicatory exercises at the different Monuments on the visit of the carriage party.

Dedication of the Maine Monuments, at the County Court House, commencing at 8 o'clock P. M.

Gen. Joshua L. Chamberlain, President of the day. Brevet Brig.-Gen. Francis E. Heath, Marshal of the day.

Executive Committee Maine Gettysburg Commission:
Charles Hamlin, Bangor; Francis E. Heath, Waterville; Charles B. Merrill, Portland; Sidney W. Thaxter, Portland; Greenlief T. Stevens, Augusta.

ORDER OF EXERCISES.

ADDRESS. — Gen. Joshua L. Chamberlain, Ex-Governor of Maine and Colonel of the Twentieth Maine Regiment, on taking the chair.

PRAYER. — Rev. Theodore Gerrish of the Twentieth Maine Regiment.

ADDRESS. — Presentation of the Maine Monuments to the Governor of Maine, by Gen. Charles Hamlin, chairman of the Executive Committee, Maine Gettysburg Commission, and Assistant Adjutant-General Second division, Third corps and Inspector of Artillery.

RESPONSE. — Presentation of the Monuments to the Gettysburg Battle-field Memorial Association, by Hon. Edwin C. Burleigh, Governor of Maine.

RESPONSE. — In behalf of the Association, Hon. James A. Beaver, Governor of Pennsylvania, or his representative.

ORATION. — Gen. Selden Connor, Ex-Governor of Maine and Lieut.-Colonel of the Seventh Maine Regiment.

PRAYER AND BENEDICTION. — Rev. G. R. Palmer, Nineteenth Maine Regiment.

The day, one of the most beautiful of October, was used for the regimental reunions and for visiting places of interest upon the field. It was the rare pleasure of the company to hear the stories of many exciting scenes of the battle from the lips of narrators, who had also been actors in those scenes.

In the evening the general dedicatory exercises occurred in the Gettysburg Court House before a large audience. The programme was carried out as arranged. Major Greenlief T. Stevens, secretary of the executive committee, called the assembly to order and in a brief and fitting manner introduced General Joshua L. Chamberlain as president of the day who, on taking the chair, made the following address : —

GENERAL CHAMBERLAIN'S ADDRESS.

The State of Maine stands here to-day for the first time in her own name. In other days she was here indeed — here in power — here in majesty — here in glory; but as elsewhere and often in the centuries before, with that humility which is perhaps the necessary law of human exaltation, her worth merged in a name mightier than her own, so here, content to be part of that greater being that she held dearer than self, but which was made more worthy of honor by her belonging to it — the United States of America. For which great end, in every heroic struggle from the beginning of our history until now, — a space of more than two hundred years, — she has given her best of heart and brain and poured out her most precious blood.

To-day she stands here, in a service of mingled recognitions; humbly submitting to that mysterious law of sacrifice and suffering for the deliverance from evil; bending sorrowfully above the dust to which have returned again the priceless jewels offered from her bosom; proud that it was her part and lot that what was best in her giving and what was immortal in her loss should be builded into the nation's weal; and stretching out her hand, of justice and of grace, to raise along these silent lines of battle monuments eloquent of her costly devotion and of the great reward. She stands here — not ashamed when the roll of honor is called, to speak her own name, and answer, Here !

The organization of the army of the Union was a counterpart of that of the Union itself. In its ultimate elements and separate units of organization, the personal force and political authority of each State were present; but they were merged and mingled in another order, which took another and higher name when exercised jointly, in a single aim, for the common weal. For reasons various but valid, the regiments and batteries of the several States were, for the most part, separated in assignment, distributed to different brigades, divisions, corps, armies. Some sad suggestions there were among these reasons; for one, the care that in some great disaster the loss might not fall too heavily on the families of one neighborhood. But there was a greater reason. Our thoughts were not then of States as States, but of the States united, — of that union and oneness in which the People of the United States lived and moved and had their being. Our hearts beat to that one high thought; our eyes saw but the old flag; and our souls saw it, glorious with the symbols of power and peace and blessing in the forward march of man.

But now that this victory is won, this cause vindicated, and the great fact of the being and authority of the People of the United States has been thus solemnly attested, — the moral forces summoning, and as it were consecrating the physical as token and instrument of their convictions, — now, the several States that stood as one in that high cause come here in their own name, — in the noblest sphere of their State rights, — to ratify and confirm this action of their delegates; to set these monuments as seals to their own great deeds, and new testament of life.

To-day we stand on an awful arena, where character which was the growth of centuries was tested and determined by the issues of a single day. We are compassed about by a cloud of witnesses; not alone the shadowy ranks of those who wrestled here, but the greater parties of the action — they for whom these things were done. Forms of thought rise before us, as in an amphitheatre, circle beyond circle, rank above rank; The State, The Union, The People. And these are One. Let us — from the arena, — contemplate them, the spiritual spectators.

There is an aspect in which the question at issue might seem to be of forms, and not of substance. It was, on its face, a question of government. There was a boastful pretense that

each State held in its hands the death-warrant of the Nation;
that any State had a right, without show of justification outside
of its own caprice, to violate the covenants of the constitution,
to break away from the Union, and set up its own little sovereignty as sufficient for all human purposes and ends; thus
leaving it to the mere will or whim of any member of our
political system to destroy the body and dissolve the soul of
the Great People. This was the political question submitted
to the arbitrament of arms. But the victory was of great
politics over small. It was the right reason, the moral consciousness and solemn resolve of the people rectifying its
wavering exterior lines according to the life-lines of its
organic being.

There is a phrase abroad which obscures the legal and the
moral questions involved in the issue, — indeed, which distorts
and falsifies history : " The War between the States." There
are here no States outside of the Union. Resolving themselves
out of it does not release them. Even were they successful in
intrenching themselves in this attitude, they would only relapse
into territories of the United States. Indeed, several of the
States so resolving were never in their own right either States
or Colonies ; but their territories were purchased by the common
treasury of the Union, and were admitted as States out of its
grace and generosity. Underneath this phrase and title, —
" The War between the States," — lies the false assumption that
our Union is but a compact of States. Were it so, neither party
to it could renounce it at his own mere will or caprice. Even
on this theory the States remaining true to the terms of their
treaty, and loyal to its intent, would have the right to resist
force by force, to take up the gage of battle thrown down by
the rebellious States, and compel them to return to their duty
and their allegiance. The Law of Nations would have accorded
the loyal States this right and remedy.

But this was not our theory, nor our justification. The
flag we bore into the field was not that of particular States, no
matter how many nor how loyal, arrayed against other States.
It was the flag of the Union, the flag of the people, vindicating
the right and charged with the duty of preventing any factions,

no matter how many nor under what pretense, from breaking up this common Country.

It was the country of the South as well as of the North. The men who sought to dismember it, belonged to it. Its life was a larger life, aloof from the dominance of self-surroundings ; but in it their truest interests were interwoven. They suffered themselves to be drawn down from the spiritual ideal by influences of the physical world. There is in man that peril of the double nature. " But I see another law," says St. Paul, " I see another law in my members, warring against the law of my mind."

There is here, I admit, an intrinsic confusion, one arising out of the very nature of the case ; for both sides claimed to be fighting for the same things : " self-government," " freedom,"— if that means liberty to act one's own will, — and even " constitutional rights." But the simple fact is, — and a most momentous one, — that the same human life runs in many spheres ; and here people were feeling and thinking and seeing and acting in one sphere and capacity on one side, and in another on the other side. Temperament, education, habit, have place sometimes in mighty consequences. Here, one party limited their interests by the bounds of States ; the other by the bounds of Country comprehending the rights of Man. The truth is, our political life and being are in two capacities, — people of the States, and people of the United States. Every man and woman of us lives in both at once. In the ruling sentiments of a complex people the likenesses may be very great, yet some small differences become the starting-points for great issues of right and wrong, — pivots on which mighty movements swung.

No, not a war between the States ; but a war between the Spheres !

No one of us would disregard the manly qualities and earnest motives among those who permitted themselves to strike at the life of the Union we held so vital and so dear, and thus made themselves our foes. Truly has it been said that the best of virtues may be enlisted in the worst of causes.

Had the question of breaking up this Union been submitted to the people of the South as American citizens, I do not believe it possible that such a resolution could have been taken. But the leaders in that false step knew how to take advantage of instincts deeply planted in every American heart; and by perverting their State Governments, and making their conspiracy seem to be the act and intent of the States, sprung an appeal to the sentiment of loyalty to the principle of local self-government; and the thrilling reveille of cannon swept the heart-strings of a chivalrous and impressionable people. There are times when it is more natural to act than to reason, and easier to fight than to be right. But the men that followed that signal made a terrible mistake. Misled by fictions; mistaught as to fact and doctrine by their masters of political history and public law; falsely fired by misdirected sentiment; mazed in the strange contradiction that they were at once the champions of democracy and the exponents of aristocratic superiority, they heeded not the calm, true life rolling on deep within, — the mightier solution of differences, — the great coherence of affinity, stronger by counterpoise of attractions and interfusion of unlikenesses, than any mere aggregation of sameness of elements. They did not recognize the providential facts of history, beyond the wilfulness of man, — that interior constitution, formative and directive of all others, — that deeper organic law, — that divinely pressing ideal, by which a Nation grows.

There was no war between the States. It was a war in the name of certain States to destroy the political existence of the United States, in membership of which alone, on any just theory of the government, their own sovereignty as States inhered, and could make itself effectual. To this absurd pass did that false theory come, — a war of States against the people; and if successful, the suicide of States.

Our enemies, it is true, by their choice of field, secured the opportunity to say they were resisting an invader; that they were fighting for their native soil and birthright; for their homes and all that men hold dear in them. We understand the power of sentiments like these, even when abused and played upon by indirection.

The State is dear to all of us. It is the guardian of what

we may call home rights ; the almoner of home-born charities ; the circle within which likeness of material, identity of interests and sympathy of sentiment make a crystal unity. Were our own State attacked in its high place and rightful function, we should defend it as valiantly as our brethren of the South were made to think they were defending theirs. But no such assault was made. We fought against no State ; but for its deliverance. We fought the enemies of our common Country, to overthrow the engines and symbols of its destruction wherever found upon its soil. We fought no better, perhaps, than they. We exhibited, perhaps, no higher individual qualities. But the cause for which we fought was higher ; our thought was wider. We too were fighting for birthright and native soil ; for homes and all the sanctities of life, wide over the land, and far forward through the years to come. For all this belongs to us, and we to it. That thought was our power. We took rank by its height, and not of our individual selves.

It is something great and greatening to cherish an ideal ; to act in the light of the truth that is far-away and far above ; to set aside the near advantage, the momentary pleasure ; the snatching of seeming good to self, and to act for remoter ends, for higher good, and for interests other than our own.

To us this people in its life on earth was a moral personality, having a character and a commission ; hence responsibility ; hence duty ; hence right, and its authority. The Union was the body of a spiritual Unity. Of this we were part, — responsible to it and for it, — and our sacrifice was its service.

Our personality exists in two identities, — the sphere of self, and the sphere of soul. One is circumscribed ; the other moving out on boundless trajectories ; one is near, and therefore dear ; the other far and high, and therefore great. We live in both, but most in the greatest. Men reach their completest development, not in isolation nor working within narrow bounds, but through membership and participation in life of largest scope and fullness. To work out all the worth of manhood ; to gain free range and play for all specific differences, to find a theatre and occasion for exercise of the highest virtues, we need the widest organization of the human forces consistent with the laws of cohesion and self-direction. It is only by these radiating and reflected influences that the perfection of the individual and of the race can be achieved.

A great and free country is not merely defense and protection. For every earnest spirit, it is opportunity and inspiration. In its rich content and manifold resources, its bracing atmosphere of broad fellowship and friendly rivalry, impulse is given to every latent aptitude and special faculty. Meantime enlarged humanity reflects itself in every participant. The best of each being given to all, the best of all returns to each. So the greatness as well as the power of a country broadens every life and blesses every home. Hence it is that in questions of rank, of rights, and duties, Country must stand supreme.

The thought goes deeper. There is a mysterious law of our nature that, in this sense of membership and participation, the spirit rises to a magnitude commensurate with that of which it is part. The greatness of the whole passes into the consciousness of each; the power of the whole seems to become the power of each, and the character of the whole is impressed upon each. The inspiration of a noble cause involving human interests wide and far, enables men to do things they did not dream themselves capable of before, and which they were not capable of alone. The consciousness of belonging, vitally, to something beyond individuality; of being part of a personality that reaches we know not where, in space and in time, greatens the heart to the limits of the soul's ideal, and builds out the supreme of character.

It was something like this, I think, which marked our motive; which made us strong to fight the bitter fight to the victorious end, and made us unrevengeful and magnanimous in that victory.

We rose in soul above the things which even the Declaration of Independence pronounces the inalienable rights of human nature, for the securing of which governments are instituted among men. Happiness, liberty, life, we laid on the altar of offering, or committed to the furies of destruction, while our minds were lifted up to a great thought and our hearts swelled to its measure. We were beckoned on by the vision of destiny; we saw our Country moving forward, charged with the sacred trusts of man. We believed in its glorious career; the power of high aims and of strong purpose; the continuity of great endeavor; the onward, upward path of history, to God. Every man felt that he gave himself to, and belonged to, something beyond time and above place, — something which could not die.

These are the reasons, not fixed in the form of things, but formative of things, reasons of the soul, why we fought for the Union. And this is the spirit in which having overcome the dark powers of denial and disintegration, having restored the people of the South to their place and privilege in the Union, and set on high the old flag telling of one life and one body, one free- dom and one law, over all the people and all the land between the four great waters, we now come, as it were, home; we look into each other's eyes; we speak in softer tones; we gather under the atmosphere of these sacred thoughts and memories, — like the high, pure air that shines down upon us to-day, flooding these fields where cloud and flash and thunder-roll of battle enshrouded us and them in that great three days' burial, — to celebrate this resurrection; to rear on these far-away fields memorials of familiar names, and to honor the State whose honor it was to rear such manhood, and keep such faith, that she might have part in far-away things.

But there are other reasons, more determinate and tangible, reasons embodied in positive forms, which are matters of knowl- edge and understanding. I have said that the issue brought upon us was a question of politics. Every one knows that I do not mean that this was a party question, as to what partic- ular set of persons or policies should have control of the Gov- ernment. And when I say that it was a political question, this is not saying that it was not also a moral question. For I do not think that politics and morals are so utterly alien and exclu- sive, one from the other, as some find it necessary to maintain. It is true that on one side politics is concerned with forms, methods, measures; and herein acts chiefly upon economic and tactical considerations. Still, all these must be conformable, or at least not alien, to the great constructive principle which holds to the motive and to the final cause of action.

Politics, I believe, is the organization of the human elements and powers for the promotion of right living, and to secure the noblest ends of living attainable in human character. It is, then, a domain which on its higher side takes cognizance not alone of rights, but of rightness, and of human worth, and of a nobleness which has a moral and divine ideal. The sphere of politics, therefore, is the highest range of thought and action, and the widest field of practical ethics set before the mind of man for its earthly career.

The issue before us, while having its ultimate ground in reason and great ethics, and the perfectibility of man, was practically one of positive, public law. It was an issue, as we believed, to enforce the performance of constitutional obligations undertaken deliberately and freely and under solemn pledges, as the expression of the deepest convictions of the mind and conscience of the people. If we were right, then there was such a being and power on this earth as the People of the United States of America. If we were wrong, then there was no such People, but a chaos of jarring elements and antagonizing interests. The forces ranged themselves across this line. It became the test of what we call Loyalty. This was a positive, practical question. The test was sharp. The answer must be final.

That question has been answered; at the cost of toil and treasure, of blood and tears. The people have made themselves the expounders of their Constitution. The decision has been accepted by clear, constitutional and legal enactment; confirmed by the supreme judicial tribunals of the land; and, we fervently trust, sealed by the benediction of the Most High. We are one People; and the law of its spirit is supreme over the law of its members.

But grave responsibilities come with great victory. The danger is not so much, I think, from renewed attacks of those who lost, as from the tendencies of power on the part of those who won. It should be distinctly borne in mind that we were not antagonizing the principle of local self-government. Our triumph was for all the people, and in full recognition of the value in our political system of recognizing local centres of influence

and of government.   The "lost cause" is not lost liberty and
right of self-government.   What is lost is slavery of men
and supremacy of States.

It was necessary for us to save the Union.   In the stress
and sharpness of the conflict we were forced to strain to the
utmost all the central powers of the Government, and leave it
to the after-wisdom of the People to restore the equilibrium of
powers, to see to it that the abnormal necessities of war should
not be made precedents for the law of life and growth.   Necessity is a dangerous plea for the privilege of power; especially
when the sole judge of it is the power pretending it.   In times
of peace, when the free faculties of the people are proceeding
by natural and spiritual laws of growth, the powers of government should be jealously guarded, and its agents held close to
the thought and purpose of the people.   The national authority
we have vindicated by the war, means in the last analysis that
Congress is the sole judge of its own powers, and sole executor
of its own will.   This is a tremendous trust.   God grant that
it be ever exercised, not in willfulness of power nor by force of
chance majorities, nor to favor particular or partisan interests,
but with the large and long look, and with the deep sense of
constitutional obligation and of supreme trusts, for the common
well-being.

To this end the place of the State in our political system is
one of vital importance.   The inter-action of local and national
capacities is a peculiarity in our system, without parallel and
but little understood in other lands, and liable to be too little
regarded in our own.   We make much account of checks and
balances in the separation of the three Departments of the
Government — Legislative, Executive and Judicial.   A similar
theory does not hold England from pressing steadily towards
a concentration of power in the hands of her House of Com-
mons, now practically absolute.   We rely justly on the lines
of division between State and National powers, a wisdom to
which England has not yet attained, but of which the skillful
recognition makes the strength of the German Empire of
to-day, while the lack of it has held back the French Republic
for a hundred years.

Local self-government alone could not have constructed this People ; but without local self-government as an instrumentality in our representative system, neither Government nor people could hold together. The generative and formative forces are in the local centres. These vortexes of living energy, touching and interfusing, are rounded into oneness and bound together by the deep, central consciousness of mutual service and a common destiny. In the course of history, which we call the orderings of Providence, local traditions, sentiments, needs and aspirations have made up the strong composite character of this country. So long as the people of each decided local type and centre feel that in the institutions, laws and policies of the great People shaping the larger life, their own freedom is secured, their own thoughts and interests are represented, they will feel bound together by the central attraction of a vital force, and no lesser influence nor lower impulse can tempt away their loyalty, patriotism and pride of partnership.

But it is not enough that the State is supreme in its sphere, and that departments of government shall not encroach upon each other. Our strongest safeguard is in personal participation in the direction and destiny of the Nation. It is not the separation of spheres and offices in the administrative order, but the interpenetration of State and National capacities in the organic order. The political unit of organization is neither the individual nor the State ; but the people of each State, — each man acting, not in his personal capacity, but in his political capacity ; exercising not his isolated, "natural rights" in the commonly conceived, fictitious, impossible sense, but the powers and franchises recognized in him or conferred upon him in the Constitution of his State, which is the appointed order of the common life. Our "self-government" is not the aggregate will of so many Ishmaelites, but the political people of the several States in their responsible character and mature convictions, regulating the civil order in their own State, and reaching out to their larger interests, administering the great trusts of the Nation. Just as in the sphere and function of the States is the surest safeguard of liberty, — as those who are to make and execute the laws which affect the daily life and dearest interests are chosen from among citizens whom the people know, and can trust and can vouch for, — so it is within the power of the same people, acting yet through their State organizations, to see to it that in the election of Representatives, Senators and Presidents only such men are chosen as well understand the delicate articulations by which liberty is kept alive, who are brave to reverse the false maxim that the law cares not for the least but only for the great, and who represent not the mere will of a momentary majority, but the heart and conscience of the manifold people which make their vote the voice of God.

When the martyr President, standing on this hallowed ground at the consecration of this cemetery, uttered that noble climax of his immortal speech, " We here highly resolve that the government of the people, by the people, and for the people, shall not perish from the earth," he meant such a people as I have described. Surely he did not mean in this sublime utterance to justify the rule of mob majority, nor to furnish a watchword for revolutionists like those who a century ago in France knew not how to overthrow tyranny without overturning also the foundations of society human and divine, nor a pretext for the anarchists and dynamiters of to-day who in the name of the people would let loose a riot of discordant and irresponsible individualism — a carnival of savage greed and frenzied passion.

He meant government ; he meant a people holding its liberty under law ; exercising its sovereignty by deliberation and delegation ; respecting its minorities ; checking its own caprice and facility of change ; relegating great questions to its sober second thought ; its consciousness alive in every part, but guided ever by great commanding convictions, and pressing forward as one for the goal of a common good.

Part and parcel of this political being of the people is this State of ours. As such she stood on these hills and slopes a generation ago, of the foremost of the people's defenders. Whether on the first, the second, or the third day's battle ; whether on the right, caught and cut to pieces by the great shears-blades of two suddenly enclosing hostile columns ; on the left, rolled back by a cyclone of unappeasable assault; or on the centre, dashed upon in an agony of desperation, terrible, sublime; wherever there was a front, the guns of Maine thundered and her colors stood. And when the long, dense, surging fight was over, and the men who made and marked the line of honor were buried where they fell, the name of Maine ran along these crests and banks, from the Cavalry Fields, Wolf's Hill, Culp's Hill, and the Seminary Ridge, down through the Cemetery, the Peach Orchard, the Wheat Field to the Devil's Den and the Round Top Crags — a blazonry of ennobled blood!

Now you have gathered these bodies here. You mark their names with head-stones, and compass them about with the cordon of the State's proud sorrow. You station them here, on the ground they held. Here they will remain, not buried but transfigured forms, — part of the earth they glorified, — part also of the glory that is to be.

No chemistry of frost or rain, no overlaying mould of the season's recurrent life and death, can ever separate from the soil of these consecrated fields the life-blood so deeply commingled and incorporate here. Ever henceforth under the rolling suns, when these hills are touched to splendor with the morning light, or smile a farewell to the lingering day, the flush that broods upon them shall be rich with a strange and crimson tone, — not of the earth, nor yet of the sky, but mediator and hostage between the two.

But these monuments are not to commemorate the dead alone. Death was but the divine acceptance of life freely offered by every one. Service was the central fact. That fact, and that truth, these monuments commemorate. They mark the centres around which stood the manhood of Maine, steadfast in noble service,—to the uttermost, to the uppermost! Those who fell here — those who have fallen before or since — those who linger, yet a little longer, soon to follow; all are mustered in one great company on the shining heights of life, with that star of Maine's armorial ensign upon their foreheads forever — like the ranks of the galaxy.

In great deeds something abides. On great fields something

stays.   Forms change and pass ; bodies disappear ; but spirits linger, to consecrate ground for the vision-place of souls.   And reverent men and women from afar, and generations that know us not and that we know not of, heart-drawn to see where and by whom great things were suffered and done for them, shall come to this deathless field, to ponder and dream ; and lo ! the shadow of a mighty presence shall wrap them in its bosom, and the power of the vision pass into their souls.

This is the great reward of service.   To live, far out and on, in the life of others ; this is the mystery of the Christ, — to give life's best for such high sake that it shall be found again unto life eternal.

PRAYER OF REV. THEODORE GERRISH.

O Lord, thou hast been our dwelling-place in all generations.   We thank thee for the favorable circumstances under which we are permitted to meet; that in visiting this historic field where once rolled and tossed the flames of war we now look upon slopes and plains which are robed in garments of peaceful prosperity.   We have come to fulfill a mission for our distant State, to dedicate sixteen monuments which she has cut from her own granite hills to commemorate the places where her brave sons fought for liberty and union in this terrific conflict.   We have thanked thee, O Lord, this day as we have visited these monuments that the sons of Maine during those bloody days were true to the principles which they had sworn to defend; that the banner which bore the word " Dirigo " was ever in the forefront of battle; and that each regiment, battery and squadron by deeds of heroic valor honored the State from which they came, in all portions of the field, — where great Reynolds fell, where Custer's mad squadrons charged, in the Wheatfield, the Peach Orchard, Round Top and Cemetery Ridge.   They did their duty well, and together stormed the heights of military glory and renown.   We thank thee that our State has not forgotten her brave sons, but has sent her chief executive officer and other honored citizens to grace this occasion with their presence.   Grant that these monuments during the years to come may teach lessons of patriotism to the coming generations and thus perpetuate the principles for which we fought.   Bless our State with great prosperity, and grant that it may ever have gallant sons to defend its honor and integrity.   Bless our governor; grant that he may have wisdom to discharge the vast responsibilites which rest upon him. We pray to thee to bless the State upon whose soil we are assembled, the goodly State of Pennsylvania.   We remember in the days of peril when the federal arch tottered over the belching volcano of treason, that the keystone of the arch remained firm.   Grant that its future may be as prosperous as the past; that it may increase in prosperity, intelligence, patriotism and all that constitutes greatness and power.   Bless our country.   We thank thee for its unparalleled growth and development. May thy care be over every section from sea to sea, until its resources shall be developed, and it become the centre of the nations of the earth, lifting them all God-ward with its arms of religious power. And now be pleased to pour thy richest blessings upon the old comrades, the survivors of the Civil War. They are scattered now; some are poor, others sick, maimed and discouraged. Too frequently they are forgotten and misunderstood. But thou, Lord, knowest all about them. And although some may be wayward and wicked, be pleased to remember that they were loyal to the principles of Christ, and offered themselves as a sacrifice upon the altar of their country. Grant that the great Christ may pour his spirit upon their hearts and that through his blood they make the necessary preparations to meet him in the heavens. Bless all the exercises of the hour. Lead us through life and gather us in heaven for the Redeemer's sake. Amen.

ADDRESS OF GENERAL CHARLES HAMLIN

PRESENTING THE MONUMENTS TO THE GOVERNOR OF MAINE.

It was a beautiful and solemn thought to dedicate the October fullness of this day to the memory of our fallen comrades. The rich fruitage of the harvest month is suggestive of the unequaled blessings we enjoy through a united government, in whose defense they gave their lives, — a supreme sacrifice.

The place, too, reminds us that in repelling the invader of northern homes from the soil of the Keystone State, it was fitting that the soldier from the farthest east, — the Pine Tree State, — should be found here, in the trembling and perilous balance of the historic and decisive battle of Gettysburg, defending Liberty and Union.

We do not claim a monopoly of the glory won on this field ; but it is with justifiable pride, as we scan the line occupied by the living arch throughout the long three days' contest, we note the pivotal points made memorable by the presence and conspicuous valor of Maine soldiers. From right to left, in front and centre, the land is enriched by their blood. Seminary Heights, Emmitsburg road, Peach Orchard, Wheatfield, Devil's Den, the Round Tops, Cemetery Ridge, Ziegler's Grove, Stevens' Knoll, Hanover and Low Dutch roads, if they could speak, all would attest their bravery.

A patriotic and generous people have caused these monuments, made from the enduring granite of our own hills, to be erected to the memory of their sons who fell here. The liberality of the appropriations by the State is a decorous response to the desires of its surviving veterans and citizens, that the deeds of their valiant dead shall be suitably perpetuated on this, the greatest monumental battlefield of the world.

In behalf of the commission to whom this work has been confided, and their grateful comrades, I return our thanks to the State for its appreciative bounty. In their behalf I now request our chief executive, the Governor, to accept the monuments from us, that he may, in turn, deliver them to the Association in whose faithful care they will finally rest.

ADDRESS OF HON. EDWIN C. BURLEIGH

GOVERNOR OF MAINE

PRESENTING THE MONUMENTS

TO THE GETTYSBURG BATTLEFIELD MEMORIAL ASSOCIATION.

Gentlemen of the Gettysburg Battlefield Memorial Association:
The monuments which we this day dedicate are in honor of the soldiers of Maine, who fell here in the bloody struggle for the Union of the States and for constitutional liberty. These memorials will perpetuate not only the glory of individuals but also the just fame of the brave organizations to which they belonged. In a still larger sense they will commemorate the fame of the State which tenderly cherishes the memory of her sons, who, in the sacred cause of country, made the last great sacrifice which men can make — they gave their lives!

By the world's common agreement the victory won on this battlefield was the crisis in the war which was waged for the integrity of the Union. We come to it now, — as millions will come in the future generations of the Republic, — to pay our tribute to the patriotic endurance, to the lofty courage, to the matchless heroism which forever consecrated the ground upon which we stand.

God grant that if danger shall ever again menace our beloved country, the example of the brave men who lie here will inspire the hearts and nerve the arms of our descendants who shall inherit and enjoy the greatness and the grandeur of the inseparable Union of the States.

Gentlemen, it gives me great pleasure, in behalf of the State of Maine, to intrust these memorials to the care and custody of your worthy and patriotic organization.

ADDRESS OF MAJOR JOHN M. KRAUTH

FOR THE BATTLEFIELD MEMORIAL ASSOCIATION

REPRESENTING GOVERNOR BEAVER OF PENNSYLVANIA.

Governor Burleigh and Veteran Soldiers of the State of Maine:

It is a cause of deep regret, both on your account and mine, that the honored President of the Gettysburg Battlefield Memorial Association, the Governor of this Commonwealth, is unable to be present with you on this impressive and interesting occasion. But other engagements have detained him much to his regret. But, gentlemen, the Battlefield Memorial Association bid you a hearty and cordial welcome here to-day. Permit me to specially welcome your illustrious and honored guest, the venerable ex-Governor, Senator and Vice-President, the honorable Hannibal Hamlin, a gentleman in whom all recognize a noble and constant friend of the armies of the Union as well as the confidential associate, co-laborer and co-patriot of the immortal Lincoln, and one whom every patriot respects, reveres and loves for his great public services extended over more than a half-century of our Nation's life.

We welcome you because you have made this sacred pilgrimage from your distant home to perpetuate the memory of your comrades who fell for the holiest of human causes, and to commemorate the services which you shared with them in maintaining the integrity of the Union and the establishment of impartial liberty throughout our whole land. We welcome you because you are worthy sons of an honored State which sent over 72,000 brave men to battle for the Union, whose services were conspicuous and illustrious on every battlefield of the

Republic. We welcome you because we are not unmindful of the patriotic ardor which inspired your Legislature and your Excellency to grant generous appropriations to carry out and consummate the object of the Battlefield Association, and we express our profound gratitude and sincere thanks for the encouragement and aid which your unselfish zeal has given to our work.

But Maine did more here, for which we and every patriot should be grateful, than even this. We have not forgotten that here at Gettysburg, where treason and slavery threw down the gage of battle on the soil of the free North, the men of Maine were omnipresent. On that fateful first day of July, when the divisions of Heth and Pender and Rodes, in overpowering numbers, bore down upon the gallant men of the First army corps, Maine men were there; on the second day, when Longstreet threw his veteran legions upon Sickles' thin line, Maine men were there; in the thickest of the conflict, where the fighting was fiercest and most deadly in the Wheatfield, on Round Top, on the Union right, on the cavalry field, Maine men were there; and upon yonder plain, where rebellion reached "high water mark," when the dauntless columns of Pickett and Pettigrew,

"Whom you faced with deathless valor on so many Southern fields,"

with fiendish desperation delivered their terrible, almost irresistible, blow, Maine was grandly represented. Men of your sister states stood with you, but you were of that grand and honored corps which broke, scattered and destroyed that proud, defiant, assaulting column, and proclaimed to the hosts of rebellion, "Hitherto shalt thou come and no further, and here shall thy proud waves be stayed."

We cordially congratulate you upon the completion of these chaste and beautiful monuments. Their tasteful and finished forms, their simple but suggestive inscriptions, modestly tell the story of the patriotic self-devotion and unflinching loyalty to duty of fifteen organizations of the Grand Army of the Union. These monuments tell of bravery and valor, but they tell of more than these, for they tell of duty and patriotism, and they summon all who look upon them hereafter to answer

their call.   The Memorial Association, in accepting these
enduring memorials, appreciate the fact that their act is no
unmeaning ceremony, but that we are assuming a sacred trust,
and one which you rightly expect us to faithfully and conscien-
tiously execute.   I can assure you that this Association accepts
these monuments in this spirit, and that we will zealously guard
and protect them, and after the work of the present organization
shall be done, we will transmit them to the custody of a board
of directors who believe, with us, that the principles for which
your sons died were right, and those against which they fought
were deeply wrong ; that if the cause for which they gave " the
last full measure of devotion" was worth dying for, it is equally
worthy of eternal commemoration.

May these classic monuments stand a perpetual memorial
to the heroism, courage, sacrifice and patriotism of the noble
and gallant sons of Maine, is the earnest wish of all the members of the Association whose representative I am to-day.

ORATION BY GENERAL SELDEN CONNOR.

Governor Burleigh, Mr. President, Comrades and Friends: —

It is holy ground we tread to-day.   As I stand before you,
Maine soldiers of the Union and of Gettysburg, honored in
being your spokesman, I should not be true to my duty if I
did not first of all give some expression to the emotion these
scenes and this service awaken in your hearts, filling them to
overflowing, — the consciousness that we are here pressing with
our footsteps soil hallowed by the life-blood of thousands of our
comrades.   A few short years and Gettysburg will be but a
cold abstraction, void of that warm human interest which has
moved us to our pilgrimage hither ; though memorable and
glorious this historic field is destined to remain as long as men
prize liberty, a conspicuous landmark in the grand route of
human progress, a commanding monument in the nation's
pathway.

Here was the culmination and turning point of the gigantic
conflict which, by common consent, was to determine the fate
of free popular government.   For three days the life of a nation,

the triumph of progress or reaction, the destiny of a continent hung balanced upon this spot of earth as on a pivot. When the battle clouds that palled these vales and slopes had rolled away, and the silence and peace of nature had returned to these violated fields and their guardian hills, the balance had firmly settled to the side of truth, justice, country, humanity. The arena of so august an arbitrament will be memorable forever. The fame of a victory so rich in blessings to all men for all time will remain bright with a fadeless glory. When the struggle of the giants was ended and the victory won, the lifeless forms of three thousand of your comrades lay upon the field, and of the fourteen thousand wounded many were so sorely stricken that their remnant of life was but a painful lingering for a few hours or days. Their felt, yet unseen presence, comrades, is the strongest and uppermost consciousness within us to-day. It seems as if they had been left on guard all these years and were lying in solemn, hushed bivouac along these slopes, faithful to their trust as in the days gone by. Treasured and ineffaceable memories of comradeship, pride in the heroism here displayed, regret at the precious sacrifice here demanded, lend to this spot of earth where our comrades fell and we now walk in peace, a peculiar consecration which will last so long as a comrade remains to press this sacred turf. Gallant, eager spirits, flushed with the purple light of youth and inspired by its hopes and dreams, how truly may we apply to them the tribute paid to youthful heroes two thousand years ago! "They have perished from the city as the spring from the year."

The soil soaked with their blood is holy ground, and over it like a mighty presence glory and gratitude brood proudly and lovingly. For them there are

> "Laurels of light and tears of love forever more.
> *   *   *   *   *   *   *   *   *
> Laurels of light moist with the precious dew
> Of the inmost heart of the nation's loving heart,
> And laurels of light and tears of truth
> And the mantle of immortality;
> And the flowers of love and immortal youth,
> And the tender heart-tokens of all true ruth

And the everlasting victory!
And the breath and bliss of liberty;
And the loving kiss of liberty;
And the welcoming light of heavenly eyes,
And the over-calm of God's canopy."

On the 30th of June Gen. Meade, who had been in command of the army of the Potomac but two days, promulgated his order notifying his army of the expected battle, and in a few words adverting to the importance of the issues it involved. None knew better than he that his words were not needed to convey information to the men of his army or to impress upon them the responsibilities of the hour. He knew that the spirit of his order pervaded the whole army from colonels to drummer boys; for it was the army of the Potomac he addressed, — the protector of the capital, the breastplate that covered the nation's heart. Many and deep were the wounds it had already received at that proud post of honor. In the two years of its existence by what arduous and terrible processes had it been forged into the thunderbolt of war that here displayed its power! by what experiences had the boys of '61 been moulded and hardened into veterans, obedient, patient, self-reliant, brave with the high courage that does not shrink from known danger! and the army of the Potomac been wrought into a perfect organism as sensitive to the will of its head as the trained charger to his master's hand. "I am a Roman citizen" was once a sufficient claim to distinction. An illustrious Greek took pride in the thought that it was "no mean city" to which he owed allegiance. If association can give honor — if the glory of the whole is reflected upon the parts, how great honor and glory are his who can say, "I belonged to the army of the Potomac." Of more worth than any measure of consideration that may be meted out to him is that precious possession of the soldier of the army of the Potomac, — the love and pride that swell his breast at the thought of the grand old army — a thought which will be to him a joy, a triumph and a consolation to his dying day.

The battle to which Meade's order sounded the call is the best known of all the battles of the war. Many causes have combined to make it such. It was the turning point of the war and its greatest battle. It was the battle that came nearest home to the country. The enemy was putting some of the richest portions of our territory under contribution, and his presence and boldness were carrying alarm to great cities that had never entertained the thought of being included in the theatre of war, and arousing apprehension throughout the whole country. From a military point of view the battle has been an exceptionally interesting and instructive study to the soldier and the student of the art of war, and many valuable treatises upon it have resulted from their labors. It was designedly and deliberately fought by both armies. The scene of the duel was the open country and the events of the tragic drama were so separated and correlated as to be readily followed and understood.

If aught else were wanting to set an imperial and imperishable seal of fame upon Gettysburg, the consummate act was performed by that wise ruler, that great and true-hearted man, the noblest product of our time, Abraham Lincoln. There was a dramatic fitness in his presence here in honor of those who filled the measure of the service to which he had called them by a soldier's death upon the field. Though it was not his privilege to range his armies in order of battle, to launch them against his people's enemies and, under the stress of duty, to woo amid the wild turmoil of the conflict a glorious release from the never-ending labors, the infinite anxieties and sore heartaches of the great task that was set for him, he was none the less the commander-in-chief, giving to the functions of that high office as close and unremitting care as if he had been an officer of the guard in the near presence of the enemy. Sometimes during the war there were murmurs of dissatisfaction at the restraints exercised at Washington upon the movements of the armies, and subsequent criticism has been severe upon the administration for its interference in military affairs. But whatever opinions may be held as to the wisdom or unwisdom of the specific exercises of his authority, none can gainsay the loyalty to duty of Abraham Lincoln. Amid a multitude of conflicting counsels from advisers skilled in an art he did not profess, he was ever mindful of the responsibility he could not delegate, and decided upon the course that his sagacious mind deemed the most prudent.

The words he uttered here, with a studied reticence doubly impressive in so great a master of speech, are as a monumental inscription to be read to remote generations. They breathe the lofty genius of the battle in which the existence of free government was at stake. As the vision of the embattled hosts, the intermingled contestants in deadly strife, of crags and plains gloomed with the infernal incense of battle and lurid with the flashing of war's dreadful enginery, of trampled fields strewn with the dead and dying, — rises before us, the loud and confused sounds of the strife seem the accompaniment of a mighty voice declaring, like the chorus of the ancient stage, the meaning of the tragedy, and proclaiming " the government of the people, by the people, and for the people shall not perish from the earth."

The story of Gettysburg has been so well told that it would be idle to attempt to here rehearse it. Let us but glance at its various features and phases in order to indicate the part that Maine soldiers bore in the action. " Indicate " is the word, because within the limits imposed by this occasion no adequate account of the services of Maine regiments and batteries could be given. Their deeds, if recited with the Homeric minuteness and fidelity which Kinglake has bestowed upon the exploits of his English heroes in the Crimean war, would fill a bulky volume with shining pages. No one man can tell the whole story which we and coming generations would know. The battle already has its Napiers, Jominis and Bancrofts. We are not waiting for *the* historian to arise, but we may fear that the casualties of time are daily taking from us many a man who leaves untold the heroic saga of his personal share in those eventful July days,—a tale that may seem simple and void of interest to him, but which would be of precious worth to his countrymen to all time.

What men will want most to know of Gettysburg is how it seemed to the thinking brains and throbbing hearts that made up the soulless mechanism of war whose volition was the will of the commanding officer ; to the man who, grasping sword or musket, awaited the coming onset with swiftly flashing, agonizing thoughts of home and friends and sweet, familiar haunts of peace, and of the dread possibilities of the minutes close upon him, nerving his being to do and dare as country, honor and duty called; and who met the foe with a fierce hatred, a sickening fear that they might prevail in spite of all that he and his comrades could do to overmaster them, and a wild longing to command some fell destruction to sweep them from the face of the earth. Let this occasion, comrades, inspire you with the purpose to give enduring form to your recollections of your army life that posterity may have fuller knowledge of the splendid army to which you belonged, of the character and spirit of the men who composed it and of their deeds and sacrifices. Such testimony, giving as it must an insight to the toils and sufferings of the individual soldier, will show how dreadful a thing is war and enforce the lesson that it can be glorious only when it serves a cause so high and noble as to countervail the extreme of human misery. Many notable instances will occur to you of comrades who have done their duty well with tongue and pen as once with sword or musket. They should be many times multiplied in the few years of life and memory that remain to the army of the Potomac.

On the morning of July 1st General Buford with his cavalry command encountered the advance of Hill's corps of Lee's army. He gallantly held them in check and sent back for aid to Reynolds, who was promptly on the field with Wadsworth's division to which was attached Hall's Second Maine Battery. There was work at hand for the new-comers and at once. The Second Maine Battery was placed by Reynolds in person in a position from which a battery of the cavalry division had just been withdrawn, and there for half an hour Hall held his ground with his six guns, returning the fire of seventeen pieces which the enemy brought to bear upon him and, in default of infantry support on his right, defending himself against the enemy's infantry with double-shotted canister. The contest became too unequal to continue. Rained upon by artillery and musketry Hall withdrew all his guns, the enemy so close upon him that six horses of the rear piece were bayoneted and the gun would have been lost but for the timely advance of infantry. Eighteen men wounded, thirty-eight horses killed, the commander's own horse shot under him, and three pieces disabled, prove more eloquently than any words how well they held their post in the forefront of the desperate fight on that brave day when the gallant Reynolds met a soldier's death and the First corps stubbornly held the field against overwhelming numbers, confident that their comrades of the army of the Potomac were pressing forward to aid them.

The Sixteenth Maine was on the extreme right of the line of the First corps. Such a position is sufficiently trying under ordinary circumstances, subject as it is to being overlapped by the enemy and thus to be exposed to a fire in flank and reverse. The Sixteenth not only had this danger to encounter from Hill's forces in front, but when Ewell came on the field from the north his forces bore down directly upon its flank with the fire of thirty pieces of artillery supporting his attack. The Eleventh corps, formed at a right angle to the line of the First, left a gap between its left and the right of the First and through it Ewell's men poured in. The devoted regiment, thrust like a lance head into the very midst of the enemy swarming from the west and the north, remained steadfast at its post. Tilden and his men were surrounded and swept away to undergo the horrors of Southern prisons. Retreat, when practicable, would have been dishonor. Who will deny to them a generous share in the final victory over an enemy thinned by their volleys and taught discretion by their firmness?

When the shattered battalions of the First and Eleventh corps were driven back through the town, Hall's battery delivered a Parthian fire from time to time as it retired through the streets, and kept the pursuers at a respectful distance. At the same time Stevens' Fifth Maine battery, which had been posted near the Seminary, found the opportunity it had been waiting for and wrought fearful execution upon the lines of the advancing enemy, saving precious time for the formation of the new line on Cemetery Heights, though at a great cost to itself.

The Fifth battery withdrew through the town and ascending Cemetery Hill was met by Hancock, who called out for "the captain of this brass battery" and ordered him to plant his guns where he could stop the enemy from coming up the ravine.

His six Napoleons were not long in opening fire and they maintained it so diligently and effectively as to check the advance of the enemy in that quarter. Colonel Bachelder has properly recognized the great service done by this battery on the first and second days by bestowing the name of its commander on the ground it occupied — the spot now known as " Stevens' Knoll."

On the second day the long-expected blow fell heavily on Birney's division of Sickles' corps, comprising the brigades of Graham, Ward and de Trobriand. Maine was nobly represented in that fighting line though our State had but a single regiment in each brigade. Lakeman with his Kennebeckers, the Third Maine, the regiment which Howard took to the front and Heath was promoted from to meet, as Lieutenant-Colonel of the Fifth, an early and lamented death at Gaines' Mill, was temporarily detached from comradeship with the Fourth in Ward's brigade and assigned to Graham. With him they held the Peach Orchard, the famous angle of Sickles' much-criticised line, until crushed by converging and cross fires, "wrapped in a vortex of fire," says the Comte de Paris, outflanked and overwhelmed, the remnant of the defenders of an untenable position was driven back, scattered and confused, to recover the touch of elbows on the true line of battle. The centre of Birney's line was held by de Trobriand, with whom was the Seventeenth under Merrill; and Ward's brigade completed the line to the foot of Round Top, the Fourth Maine, commanded by Colonel Walker, constituting the extreme left. No intelligent follower of the events of the battle can fail to concede to these two brigades the high praise accorded to them with unanimous voice by every historian of the fight. If Longstreet had succeeded at his onset in breaking Birney's line, the way was open to him to a lodgment in the centre of Meade's position. But he had to do with Kearny's men, and the wearers of the red lozenge were not accustomed to break at the touch of the enemy. It was their line and they proposed to stay by it, though there was not a regiment in reserve to which they might look for help. The confident onslaught of Hood's brigades was as confidently met. Not until the rebel reserves were brought forward did those staunch brigades give way, and then only as they were compelled by sheer weight of outnumbering assailants, who were made to pay dearly for every inch of ground gained. So stubborn was their resistance that Meade, who had not looked for the attack to fall upon his left and therefore had made no provision to meet it, was afforded time to bring up reinforcements. Our two regiments did their full share of the good work of their brigades. In the annals of the Seventeenth the Wheatfield which it held until relieved, though taken in flank and grievously torn, has a conspicuous place. The regiment which had been trained by Berry, that capable soldier whose merits had gained him high command and would have advanced him to greater distinction had not Chancellorsville numbered him among its victims, the Fourth Maine, formed the left of the line and wrought havoc with their blazing rifles among the gray-clad swarms that sought to dislodge them from the weird rocks and hollows of Devil's Den.

There are sometimes in the affairs of men occurrences which so tend to favor some end of supreme moment as to forbid the thought that they are merely accidental, and to cause them to seem the direct offspring of a superhuman intelligence, a signal manifestation of a divine purpose, and are therefore styled "providential." In this high sense of the word the series of happenings on Little Round Top on that eventful second of July was providential. Human foresight and promptness of action, soldierly ardor and bravery, and patriotic devotion were indeed grandly displayed on that eminence which offered itself that day as the prize of valor; but all these would not have availed if the peculiar prosperity attending them had failed or been marred in any respect. Fortunate for our arms was it that timely succor saved Vincent's right. Fortunate was it too that his left was guarded by so sturdy a regiment as the Twentieth Maine, under a commander so gallant and able as Chamberlain! "Fortunate" do I say? Is it not easier to believe that the interposition of so many happy chances at a juncture so pregnant with grave results was heaven-directed rather than fortuitously bestowed by blind fate? The Twentieth finds that besides the numerous and persistent foes that press upon it in front others are continually arriving on its flank, so that the left has to be refused more and more in order to oppose a front to them. There is something malignant in this ever-encircling attack, — something far more dreadful than the annihilation or capture of the little band defending the height; it is the deadly clutch it seeks to fasten upon the throat of the army of the Potomac, and thus upon the life of the nation. The sons of Maine feel that the sternest command of duty is laid upon them. The defense of their comrades, the welfare of their country, rests with them. Nobly do they respond to the call. The Pine swings against the Palm. At Chamberlain's command they leap forward, tiger-like, to the charge, and Little Round Top is saved.

When the disaster which the character of Sickles' line invited had befallen it, and the angle at the Peach Orchard was broken in, making an opening for the advance of Longstreet's brigades, some of which fell upon the flank of Birney's division and the divisions of the Fifth and Second corps which had come to his assistance, while Barksdale moved directly forward upon the centre of Meade's position; when Humphreys, threatened in the reverse by Longstreet's forces, and attacked upon his right by a division of Hill's corps, was forced back, there was no continuous Union line in position to relieve the broken line falling back and receive its oncoming pursuers. The situation was a critical one. Meade and Hancock were making the most strenuous efforts to bring troops from the right to complete a new line. In this emergency the artillery is energetically and effectively at work to disconcert the attack. McGilvery has placed the remnants of his batteries brought off from the vicinity of the Peach Orchard in an advantageous position, and, in the words of Gen. Hunt, "with these and Dow's Sixth Maine battery, fresh from the reserve, the pursuit was checked."

The Sixth battery was not the only Maine organization that took part in the repulse of this dangerous attack. The Nineteenth Maine, Col. Heath, had been placed by Hancock in advance of his main line as soon as he perceived that Sickles' line was beginning to give way. The rearward movement of

Humphreys' division carried a portion of his line over the men of the Nineteenth who were lying down until their turn should come. As soon as these hard-pressed men had passed, the Nineteenth was on its feet barring with solid and undaunted front the way of the rebel line. Scarce fifty paces from them is it when the Nineteenth, with a fire by battalion, brings it to a halt. A deadly interchange of firing ensues in the midst of which Heath's attention is called to a rebel regiment on his left, and only a score of yards from it, deploying from double column. A part of Captain Starbird's left company is thrown back and opens an enfilading fire before which the surprised column melts away. The Nineteenth falls back a short distance upon the false report that its right is being turned; learning its mistake it goes forward beyond its former position, captures many prisoners, recovers several guns, and occupies an advanced position through the night.

Change now the scene to the right. The Fifth Maine battery is posted at the head of the ravine separating Cemetery Hill from Culp's Hill. Ewell's attack on these positions was intended to be simultaneous with that on our left and centre, but that on Cemetery Hill falls later, when but little daylight is left. Col. Alexander, Longstreet's Chief of Artillery, writing of the charge of his batteries after the crushing of our line at the Peach Orchard, says: "An artillerist's heaven is, after a tough resistance, to follow the routed enemy and throw shells and canister into their disorganized and fleeing masses." I fancy Stevens could rejoin that there is a sterner joy in raking with canister, at short range, hostile battalions exposing their flanks as they make their slow way up a steep acclivity, climbing to the attack; for then the artillerist feels that the insulting enemy is delivered into his hands, and that, as the ranks go down under his fire, he is not merely destroying the foe, but defending his menaced comrades. Such an opportunity had the Fifth battery when the brigades of Hoke and Avery assaulted Cemetery Hill, and well was it improved.*

---

* Captain Stevens was severely wounded in the afternoon of the 2d. Lieut. Edward N. Whittier commanded the battery when it aided so effectively in the repulse of Hoke and Avery.

As the evening gloom crept over the field and the fragments of the baffled regiments of assault, having done all that brave men could do, had fallen back from their attempts against our right, left, and centre, the rebel commanders scanned the ridge they had vainly sought to gain, to find encouragement for a renewed attack. The sight was not inviting to them. From Round Top to Culp's Hill dark lines and masses of men and rows of grim batteries betokened a composure and readiness they did not deem it advisable to disturb or challenge. The full significance of that array they did not know. Sedgwick was there, and the Greek cross was aligned with the disk, the trefoil, the diamond, the cross of Malta, the crescent and the star.

The Sixth corps, summoned at midnight, had marched through the night and steadily on through the long, hot summer day and formed upon the field, thirty miles from their bivouac, just in time to aid in repelling the attack had there been need. Its presence gave cheer and renewed courage to the whole army. The Fifth, Sixth and Seventh Maine regiments were proud to own the badge of that corps.

With the dawn of the third and last day of the battle the struggle is renewed by Slocum and his Twelfth corps. The enemy had taken advantage of the opportunity to establish themselves in that portion of the position which the Twelfth had left to go to the support of the centre. After four hours of musketry as incessant as the rolling of a drum the Twelfth re-occupied its works. In the meantime Slocum requested Neill, whose brigade of the Sixth corps was on Powers' Hill, to send troops to protect his right and the Baltimore Pike south of Rock Creek, from the enemy moving in that direction. Neill entrusted that service to the 43d N. Y. and the Seventh Maine, under the commanding officer of the Seventh. Those regiments met with some loss from the brisk fire of skirmishers as they advanced at a run over the crest and down the slope of an open field to a stone-wall which afforded an advantageous position; and here, forming the extreme right of the infantry line of the army, they remained throughout the day, under orders to hold the position but not to bring on fighting, their skirmishers exchanging an occasional shot with those of the enemy.

The Nineteenth was the only Maine regiment which had an opportunity to participate in the magnificent repulse given Pickett's magnificent charge. As his imposing array came on in such numbers and with such audacity and air of power as to cause the boldest to hold his breath, it struck the Second corps at an angle which enabled the Nineteenth to pour an almost flanking fire upon it. The weight of the charge falls upon Webb's brigade with a crushing force. With one accord the regiments on Webb's left, the Nineteenth among them, rush, regardless of order, to his assistance — a mob, but a fighting mob, against which Pickett's onset expends its fury in vain. Col. Hall, who commanded an adjoining brigade, in his report names the Nineteenth among those regiments that assisted in the repulse.

The First Maine Cavalry was in the splendid cavalry action on the right in which Custer bore so brilliant a part. Though not actively engaged, it aided by its presence in thwarting the doubly futile purpose of the rebel cavalry to reach the Baltimore Pike, and there work their will on the mob of broken troops that were expected to crowd that avenue of retreat, fleeing before Pickett's irresistible charge. In the campaign preliminary to the battle the First cavalry rendered distinguished service ; notably in the great cavalry battle at Brandy Station which won for our horsemen a lasting prestige, and in the fight at Aldie, — a name suggestive of glory and sorrow, of the chivalrous charge that rescued comrades from imminent peril, and of the fall of the valiant Douty. The Fifth and Sixth, as trusty and war-tried regiments as any that fought that field, rendered a like service at Gettysburg, standing in readiness to leap to any call, however desperate the duty. Edwards led the Fifth, and the Sixth was under Burnham, that grim old warrior, beloved by his men and honored by all who knew his soldierly worth ; his death in the last campaign of the war, following close upon his well-earned promotion, added a shining name to Maine's list of patriot martyrs, and his memory remains dear and undimmed in the hearts of his men and brother-soldiers. The Tenth Maine was represented by a detachment at the headquarters of the Twelfth corps.

Such, in meagre outline, was the part of Maine in the greatest battle of the war. In proportion to the number of her troops in the action, no one of the eighteen states whose regiments flew the stars and stripes on this hard-fought field contributed more than Maine to the victory. It is somewhat remarkable that seven of her nine infantry regiments in the army, and all three batteries, were in the front line and that the service of so many of them was of a unique character, having an important bearing upon the grand result. At whatever point the battle raged, sons of the Pine Tree State were in the melee. The sad measure of their services is the loss they suffered. In military parlance the word conventionally used to express severity of loss is "decimated." When one-tenth of a battalion is struck down it implies bloody work. Colonel Fox, in his valuable work on Regimental Losses, gives the percentage of loss in killed and mortally wounded at Gettysburg of the Sixteenth and Twentieth Maine as ten per cent each ; of the Fourth, thirteen per cent ; of the Third, fourteen per cent, and of the Nineteenth, fifteen per cent. The corresponding percentage of loss of the Seventeenth, derived from other sources, was twelve per cent. The entire loss to Maine was one thousand and twenty-three. Of this number three hundred and two were reported captured or missing and of these all but nineteen were reported by the Third, Fourth and Sixteenth ; and their loss under this head testifies to the good conduct of those regiments and proves how tenaciously they clung to their difficult and exposed posts ; the Sixteenth, as we have seen, was sacrificed almost to a man while holding the right of the line on the first day ; the Third was at the Peach Orchard angle where, says Fox, "the tenacity with which the Third Maine held the skirmish line is worthy of note " ; the Fourth was for a time in an isolated position, occupying the ravine between Devil's Den and Little Round Top, and was the left of the line until the Twentieth stood on Little Round Top. The Maine regiment which suffered most in killed and wounded was, as might be expected from its share in meeting the attacks on the centre on the second and third days, the Nineteenth. Of the four hundred and forty taken into engagement it lost one hundred and ninety-nine, only seven of which number were reported as captured or missing. The percentage of entire loss was forty-four. To show by comparison the severity of such losses as this Colonel Fox cites the Light Brigade, whose loss in its famous charge at Balaklava was but thirty-six per cent. The brigade to which the Nineteenth belonged suffered the severest loss in this battle that any brigade of the Union armies incurred in any one action of the war. The percentage of loss was sixty-one. The highest percentage of loss of any German regiment in the Franco-Prussian war was forty-nine.

Maine's contribution to the army of the Potomac at Gettysburg in general officers was a notable one. Gen. Seth Williams, Adjutant-General, and Rufus Ingalls, Quartermaster-General, were so identified with that army, while commanding officers came and went, as to seem inseparable from it. Howard, an officer of the regular army, at the outbreak of the war went to the front from his native State as Colonel of the Third Maine. The duty that here devolved upon him was an extremely trying one. At the moment of his arrival he found himself in command at the height of a serious engagement with a constantly increasing force of the enemy. Whatever claims may be urged for credit in selecting Cemetery Hill as the main position of the army, the fact remains that Howard took possession of the hill with a division of his corps and made such preparations for defending it that the First and Eleventh corps found it a secure rallying point, so formidable as to cause the victorious enemy to pause even in the full flush of their advantage. This height, the head and front of the Union position, Howard bravely and skilfully kept throughout the battle. Caldwell, first Colonel of the Eleventh Maine, commanded the first division of the Second corps. The assistance his four brigades gave the left when Birney had been driven back was among the most prominent events of the battle. A. P. Howe, of the regular service, and Adelbert Ames, first Colonel of the Twentieth Maine, commanded divisions. Colonel McGilvery handled his artillery brigade in a conspicuously brilliant and effective manner. Major Charles Hamlin, A. A. G. of Humphreys' division of the Third corps, and Capt. John Marshall Brown, A. A.G. of

Ames' brigade in the Eleventh corps, received the commendation of their commanding officers for their services and conduct throughout the battle. Major Thomas W. Hyde was Provost Marshal on the staff of Gen. Sedgwick, and Lieut.-Col. Joseph S. Smith was Commissary of Hancock's corps. All these staff officers were general officers by brevet at the close of the war. Gen. Lysander Cutler, whose brigade of the First corps fought so long on the first day, passed so many years of his life in active business in our State as to give her strong claim to him. If Maine could appropriate to her own honor the soldiers of Gettysburg who had their birth and breeding on her soil, and were schooled at her homes in the hardy virtues that glorify American manhood; if she could call to her own standard her stalwart sons who went from the dark forests of the Penobscot, the Kennebec and the Androscoggin to the pineries of Pennsylvania, Michigan, Wisconsin and Minnesota; and from her rugged hillside farms to the prairies of the West; and those who had sought to better their fortunes in the cities and towns of her sister states of New England — all who were enrolled in the organizations of their adopted states and fought under the same broad banner of the Union, how long her line would stretch and what increased splendor of achievement and sacrifice would flash from her scutcheon!

Cut from the granite of our native hills, we bring hither memorials of valor and patriotism and implant them on the soil — thank God! — of our common country. Each marks a spot where sons of Maine stood shoulder to shoulder facing the enemy, their misguided countrymen, ranged in arms to destroy the country won by the blood of their fathers, and proved by the test of well-nigh a hundred years to be the best hope of mankind. Pillar and shaft and block, so long as time shall spare them they will bear mute but impressive witness of the glorious fall of those who died the thrice-blessed death of the patriot, before the faces of their fathers and under the walls of their country's capital. Inwrought with legends and with the knightly emblems that were proudly worn by the soldiers of the army of the Potomac and graced the fluttering pennons of its great leaders, they are instinct forevermore with honor to the brave and tribute to the chivalrous spirit of the grandest army that ever marched to battle. But they will fail to breathe the spirit of our higher intent if they stand merely as the chroniclers of a battle won; of heroes slain; of a noble armament; of a country saved. We dedicate them to the past in the fervid hope that the memories they evoke may have immortal power to keep alive and strengthen whatever tends to maintain this precious, blood-bought country one, free, strong and pure. With joy and thankfulness we hail these peaceful, prosperous, happy days. Reunited in a stronger bond by the memories of a common suffering and heroism, the late foemen now face the same way and move forward together for the glory of a common country. Everywhere throughout the land there is growth, development, energy, promise and hopefulness. But perfect harmony, untroubled ease, progress without check, can never rule in a great country with widespread millions of people, among complex interests and various and constantly varying conditions. At each remove of a free people's onward course new dangers, hardships and difficulties stimulate to renewed effort and deeper thought, test the quality of the manhood and citizenship of each generation, and thus lead on to higher states and nobler ideals. O, troubled Patriot, if, in the years to come, fears and forebodings oppress your spirit, and the burden is heavy and the way is dark, and dangers threaten, come to this field and stand among these silent monitors and learn that resolved hearts, fired by a deathless purpose, can make a way through the heaviest gloom to the fair sunlight beyond.

PRAYER AND BENEDICTION, BY REV. G. R. PALMER.

Our Father who art in heaven, we acknowledge thee as the God "by whom kings reign and princes decree justice." With reverence, contrition and joy we approach thee. "Hear thou in heaven, thy dwelling-place, and when thou hearest forgive." We thank thee for our country's unusual destiny, her eventful history, for the men who feared God, stood for the right, sought freedom to worship God, and on the shores of this land drew their first full breath of liberty.

We rejoice that our country still lives and enjoys peace, prosperity and freedom; that when this young republic was tested in fire and blood, brave and true men with an outburst of loyalty sprang to the defense of our country and gave it a new birth of liberty, that this government established to secure the equal rights of all might help to a higher liberty all the nations of the earth.

Through divine protection these veterans of our army are permitted to meet on this field where was fought a critical battle and achieved a decisive victory for the Union ; and here we acknowledge thee alike in our joys and our sorrows, and standing on this hallowed ground in the midst of the thousands slain, we give praise unto thee as in the moments of our supreme delight. Be pleased to accept this offering we bring to thee, these monuments made with hands and by this service declared sacred, that we may honor thee, that we may enshrine anew in our hearts the comrades who died for our country, that we may teach the lesson of self-sacrifice to our children and our children's children.

May the thought of the sufferings of our soldiers rebuke our impatience in trial, and our desire for self-gratification. May these monuments and this national burying place ever awaken holy emotions and lofty aspirations in the hearts of our countrymen. As we dedicate these memorials in honor of loyal men who saved liberty on this field, and many of whom laid down their lives, help us to consecrate ourselves to thee and to the accomplishment of their unfinished work, that as they broke the fetters of the slave, we may unloose the chains that bind the soul, that Christian civilization may bring the peoples of all nations and religions in this land we love to undying allegiance to this benign government of ours.

And thou who hast said that "whatsoever is done to thy weakest and thy humblest one is even done to thee," appear in behalf of the poor and oppressed and wretched of our world. May thy continued favor bless this land where our fathers died. Let freedom's holy light shine upon our way, and everything that hath breath praise the Lord, and rocks and hills their silence break to shout thy glory forth, and unto thee, O God, will we give the praise, through Christ, our Lord.

"The peace of God, which passeth all understanding, keep your hearts and minds in the knowledge and love of God, and of his son, Jesus Christ, our Lord ; and the blessing of God Almighty, the Father, the Son, and the Holy Spirit, be among you and remain with you always. Amen."

SOLDIERS NATIONAL CEMETERY.

BY G. W. VERRILL.

As a frontispiece in this volume the likeness of the monument in the Soldiers' National Cemetery at Gettysburg is shown. Maine took part in establishing this cemetery and erecting this noble monument, appropriating for the purpose the sum of forty-three hundred dollars. A brief recital of some of the facts, which may have been forgotten, will not be inappropriate here.

The movement was initiated soon after the battle, to secure a common burial place for those Union soldiers who fell upon that battlefield, whose remains had not been taken away by their relatives or friends. The various states that had participating troops, through their governors, selected commissioners one from each state to represent those states in deciding upon the details, the main features of which were to secure and lay out suitable grounds, remove the dead to this final resting place, erect a common memorial monument and provide for the management and care of the grounds.

Maine was represented by Benj. W. Norris as her commissioner. The beautiful site of Cemetery Hill was selected and about seventeen acres, adjoining the local cemetery and extending from Baltimore pike to the Taneytown road, were purchased. The plan of interment was in concentric rows as around a centre, the distance of a semi-circle. The separate sections or lots appropriated to each state made segments of the semi-circle. At the centre of the semi-circle a worthy monument was to stand.

The work of disinterment, identifying, coffining and removal began October 27, 1863. The whole number then re-buried was 3,512.

In this hallowed ground 104 bodies identified as belonging to Maine were placed. In addition she has her share of the 970 that could secure no further recognition than the fact of being Union soldiers who freely gave their lives to the cause;

these also are carefully placed here with honors equal to the others. The names of 1,699 of those buried here are unknown, but nearly half of these were traced to the states to which they belonged and many to their proper regiments. Without doubt the names of not a few were inaccurately established. Lines of granite headstones, of a uniform pattern and about a foot in height, mark the heads of the graves in the circular rows, which are broken by aisles radiating from the centre. Upon these headstones are inscribed the names and enrollments so far as known. The following is the list of Maine men, with some corrections of headstone inscriptions, and notes of errors impossible to correct : —

THIRD REGIMENT.

Captain John C. Keen, Sergeant-Major Henry S. Small, Orderly Sergeant Eben S. Allen, Sergeant Nelson W. Jones, Corporals: Amos H. Cole, Eben Farrington, John L. Little. Privates: Calvin H. Burden, John W. Jones, Alsbury Luce, Joseph A. Roach, Allen H. Sprague. One, name unknown.

FOURTH REGIMENT.

Second Lieutenant George M. Bragg. Privates: Crosby R. Brookings, Isaiah V. Eaton, John S. Gray, George F. Johnson, Michael Rariden, John F. Shuman.

SEVENTH REGIMENT.

Corporal Richard Sculley, Private William H. Smith.

SIXTEENTH REGIMENT.

Corporals: Frank Devereux, George D. Marston. Privates: E. Bishop, Frank Fairbrother, William H. Huntington, Albion B. Mills, Harrison Pullen. Two, names unknown.

SEVENTEENTH REGIMENT.

Corporals: Samuel C. Davis, Austin Hanson, Bernard Hogan, George W. Jones. Privates: William H. Day, Samuel L. Dwelley, Moses D. Emery, Samuel O. Hatch, Ira L. Martin, Fessenden M. Mills, Monroe Quint, Royal Rand. In section F a grave marked " R. Finch, E, 17th Inf." cannot be ascribed to any member of this regiment.

NINETEENTH REGIMENT.

Captain George D. Smith, 1st Sergeant Thomas T. Rideout, Sergeants: William E. Barrows, Jesse A. Dorman, Enoch C. Dow, Alexander W. Lord, Chandler F. Perry. Corporals: Hollis F. Arnold, Samuel C. Brookings, John Merriam, Robert T. Newell, Alfred P. Waterman, George H. Willey. Privates: John F. Carey, Charles J. Carroll, Frank Coffin, Charles W. Collins, Abijah Crosby, Charles E. Harriman, George E. Hodgdon, Louira A. Kelley, William H. Low, James T. Neal (Heal?), Reuel Nickerson, Loring C. Oliver, James Robbins, Samuel B. Shea, Hushai C. Thomas. Two, names unknown.

TWENTIETH REGIMENT.

Second Lieutenant Warren L. Kendall. 1st Sergeants: Isaac N. Lathrop, George S. Noyes, Charles W. Steele. Sergeant William S. Jordan.

Corporals: Melville C. Day, William S. Hodgdon, Joseph D. Simpson. Privates: Frank B. Curtis, Moses Davis, Elfin J. Foss, Benjamin W. Grant, Goodwin S. Ireland, Orrin Walker. Eleven, names unknown. In section F a grave marked "Corp. W. K——, 20th Inf." cannot be ascribed with certainty to any member of this regiment.

FIFTH BATTERY.

Private Sullivan Luce.

FIRST CAVALRY.

Private Edward Cunningham.

In section G a grave marked "J. Bartlett," and another in section C marked "——— —ickels, G," cannot be ascribed to any Maine troops engaged.

The dedication of the cemetery took place Nov. 19, 1863, which was prior to the erection of the monument. The ceremonies were appropriate and impressive. On that occasion the lamented Abraham Lincoln, President of the United States, standing upon the spot indicated for the monument, delivered his immortal dedicatory address. An oration by Edward Everett was a part in the exercises. There were present many representatives from the army and navy, cabinet officials, members of Congress, Ministers of France and Italy, a French admiral and other distinguished foreigners; also the governors and their staffs of many of the states interested, and a concourse of citizens from all over the North.

As one enters the gateway to-day from the Baltimore pike he notices the pillars on either side surmounted by eagles, and beneath them the inscriptions of the names of those states whose soldiers are buried within. Just inside is a life-size statue of General Reynolds. Turning to the left and following the driveway under the bending arches of foliage a short distance, the noble monument springs into view. The superstructure is sixty feet in height, of white marble. It consists of a massive pedestal, twenty-five feet square at the base, bearing aloft a colossal statue to represent the Genius of Liberty. She stands upon a three-quarter globe, holding in her right hand the victor's laurel wreath, and on her left arm carries our national flag shown in careless folds.

Projecting from the angles of the base of the pedestal are four buttresses, each supporting one of the four allegorical statues representing War, History, Peace and Plenty. There are panels between the four statues for suitable inscriptions.

The main die of the pedestal is octagonal in form, panelled upon each face. The cornice and plinth above are heavily moulded; upon this plinth rests an octagonal, moulded base bearing upon its face, in high relief, the national arms. The upper die and cap are circular in form, the die being encircled by stars equal in number with those states whose sons contributed their lives as the price of victory won at Gettysburg. On one of the panels the visitor will find the words of Lincoln's address : —

" Four score and seven years ago our fathers brought forth on this continent, a new nation, conceived in Liberty, and dedicated to the proposition that all men are created equal.

" Now we are engaged in a great civil war, testing whether that nation, or any nation so conceived and so dedicated, can long endure. We are met on a great battlefield of that war. We have come to dedicate a portion of that field, as a final resting place for those who here gave their lives that that nation might live. It is altogether fitting and proper that we should do this.

" But, in a larger sense, we can not dedicate — we can not consecrate — we can not hallow this ground. The brave men, living and dead, who struggled here have consecrated it, far above our poor power to add or detract. The world will little note, nor long remember what we say here, but it can never forget what they did here. It is for us the living, rather, to be dedicated here to the unfinished work which they who fought here have thus far so nobly advanced. It is rather for us to be here dedicated to the great task remaining before us, — that from these honored dead we take increased devotion to that cause for which they gave the last full measure of devotion — that we here highly resolve that these dead shall not have died in vain — that this nation, under God, shall have a new birth of freedom — and that government of the people, by the people, for the people, shall not perish from the earth."

THE MAINE GETTYSBURG COMMISSION AND ITS WORK.

BY CHARLES HAMLIN,

CHAIRMAN OF EXECUTIVE COMMITTEE.

Very soon after the battle of Gettysburg prominent citizens of the burgh, realizing the great historical value it would occupy in the war of the Rebellion, organized themselves under the name of the Gettysburg Battlefield Memorial Association, and procured a charter from the State of Pennsylvania under which they purchased lands, built roads, and took such measures as were necessary to preserve in their original condition the grounds occupied by the forces of both armies on each day of the battle. Another important object of the Association was to erect monuments upon the field to mark the positions held or occupied by our troops. The State of Pennsylvania having a special interest began with commendable zeal to carry out these purposes, and with generous appropriations of upwards of $150,-000 constructed and erected about 120 monuments in 1887–8. Massachusetts also was awake and erected monuments among the first. And the survivors of the 20th Maine erected a fine monument on Little Round Top in 1886.

Agitation of the project of having monuments to Maine regiments began in Maine at regimental reunions and in Grand Army posts in the summer of 1886, and steps were taken to bring the matter before the next legislature. The first active movement with a well-matured plan was initiated by the writer, who procured the introduction of a memorial into the legislature, at its session in 1887. Others followed. A public hearing before the Committee on Military Affairs was given January 27, 1887, to the mover of the memorial and the other petitioners in the hall of the House of Representatives, at which

hearing he urged a liberal appropriation, assisted by Major G.
T. Stevens, Gen. Selden Connor, Gen. C. W. Tilden, Gen.
C. P. Mattocks, Gen. Geo. L. Beal, Col. C. B. Merrill, Col.
Edward Moore, Col. H. R. Millett, Major H. S. Melcher,
Major A. R. Small, Major W. H. Green, Lieut. H. N. Fairbanks, Capt. P. M. Fogler, Capt. J. M. Webb and others.
The committee made a favorable report, and a Resolve, c. 29,
approved February 25, 1887, granted $2,500 for the purchase
of land and $12,500 for the erection of monuments. The
Resolve provided that the appropriation should be expended
under the direction of a Commission of sixteen members,
including the Governor and also one member of each regiment, battery, battalion, company or staff officer, who were
present at the battle, to be appointed by the Governor. The
expenses of the Commission were fixed at $1,000, and the
monuments were to be completed and erected on or before
November 1, 1890. Col. Edward Moore and Major W. H.
Green of the 17th regiment, also Hon. J. W. Wakefield,
Quartermaster of the 19th regiment, who were members of the
legislature at that and subsequent sessions, gave their personal
attention and influence in procuring the necessary appropriations. Their timely and forcible speeches were efficient with
the legislature.

The Commissioners appointed, and their successors, are as
follows : —

LIST OF MAINE GETTYSBURG COMMISSIONERS.

The Governor of Maine (*ex officio*).
Brevet Brig.-Gen. Charles Hamlin, Vol. Staff.
Brevet Brig.-Gen. James A. Hall, 2d Battery (deceased).
Brevet Brig.-Gen. Charles W. Tilden, 16th Regiment.
Brevet Major Greenlief T. Stevens, 5th Battery.
Col. Moses B. Lakeman, 3d Regiment.
Col. Elijah Walker, 4th Regiment.
Lieut.-Col. Charles B. Merrill, 17th Regiment (deceased).
Capt. Geo. W. Verrill (to succeed Col. Merrill), 17th Regt.
Brevet Major-Gen. Joshua L. Chamberlain, 20th Regiment.
Brevet Brig.-Gen. Francis E. Heath, 19th Regt. (deceased).
Capt. Charles E. Nash (to succeed Gen. Heath) 19th Regt.

Brevet Major Edwin B. Dow, 6th Battery.

Brevet Brig.-Gen. Clark S. Edwards, 5th Regiment.

Brevet Brig.-Gen. Benjamin F. Harris, 6th Regt.(resigned).

Lt.-Col. Alexander B. Sumner (to succeed Gen. Harris) 6th Regiment.

Brig.-Gen. Selden Connor, 7th Regiment (resigned).

Brevet Brig.-Gen. Thomas W. Hyde (to succeed Gen. Connor), 7th Regiment.

Brevet Major-Gen. Charles H. Smith 1st Cavalry (resigned).

Maj. Sidney W. Thaxter (to succeed Gen. Smith),1st Cav'y.

Col. Jacob McClure, Company D, 2d U. S. S. S. (deceased).

Lt.-Col. John D. Beardsley, 10th Battalion.

In May, 1887, the Commission, excepting Colonel McClure, 2d U. S. Sharpshooters, and Colonel Beardsley, 10th Maine Battalion, met at Gettysburg and organized by the choice of Gov. J. R. Bodwell as president and Gen. B. F. Harris, secretary. An Executive Committee, consisting of Messrs. Hamlin, Stevens, Heath, Merrill and Smith, was also appointed at the same meeting, whose duties were to supervise the work of the Commission, receive designs, etc., for the monuments, contract for their construction and erection, arrange for their dedication, publish a report of their proceedings, and, in general, to have charge of all such matters pertaining to the Commission as may be done by an Executive Committee.

The Commission then proceeded, with a representative of the Gettysburg Battlefield Memorial Association, to designate upon the field and agree upon the location of monuments. The Executive Committee were further instructed to take charge of the location of the monuments of such commands as were not represented upon the field by their Commissioners, viz. : 10th Maine Battalion and Co. D, 2d U. S. Sharpshooters.

The Executive Committee was organized at a meeting held June 18, 1887, at the Senate Chamber of the State Capitol, by the selection of Messrs. Hamlin and Stevens as chairman and secretary respectively. Subsequently Major Stevens was also elected treasurer and has acted as such. Gen. C. H. Smith not being able to attend the meetings of the Committee, he being Colonel of the 19th Infantry U. S. A. and absent from the state, sent in his resignation. This vacancy was filled by the appointment of Maj. Sidney W. Thaxter, who has since served with the Committee. The secretary was directed to issue a circular to each regiment, battalion and battery association, and to Co. D, 2d U. S. Sharpshooters to furnish the Committee with designs for monuments. These designs were ordered to be sent to the chairman, who deposited them for safe keeping with Gen. B. F. Harris, custodian of public buildings, at the State House. The designs of the monuments of the 10th Battalion and Co. D, 2d U. S. Sharpshooters, were under the personal supervision of the chairman of the Executive Committee, assisted by General Tilden of the Hallowell Granite Works. During this and the following year the Committee were engaged in supervising the designs and specifications of monuments; procuring the approval of the legends, inscriptions, etc., by the Memorial Association; procuring designs and specifications for monuments where none were furnished or were insufficient and incomplete; and contracting for their construction and erection.

At its meeting February 22, 1888, at the Council Chamber in the State House, Augusta, the contract for the construction, transportation and erection of the monuments was awarded to the Hallowell Granite Works. And the chairman was directed to prepare a suitable petition to the next session of the legislature for an increase of appropriation necessary to complete the contract, defray the expenses of dedication, also furnish uniform flanking tablets or markers for such commands as might request them.

Application was accordingly made to the legislature at its session in 1889 by the chairman of the Committee, assisted by Major Stevens, secretary, and an additional appropriation of $10,000 was granted by a Resolve, c. 136, approved February 12, 1889.

During its sessions April 23, 1889, at the Council Chamber in the State House, the Committee voted to appropriate $200 in aid of the construction of the High Water Mark Monument, so that the 19th Maine regiment should have a suitable inscription thereon.

The chairman was empowered to appoint committees to arrange for the dedication exercises at Gettysburg. The following appointments were made : Committee on Transportation, Major Thaxter and General Heath; Order of Exercises, Major Stevens and Colonel Merrill; Invitations, Governor Burleigh and General Hamlin.

The sum of $240 was appropriated for tablets for the 2d Maine Battery, and the 3d, 16th and 20th regiments. The secretary and Gen. C. W. Tilden, treasurer of the Hallowell Granite Works, were appointed a committee on unfinished legends.

It was voted that the time for the dedication of the monuments be fixed on October 3, 1889. (See exercises of dedication, page 545 *ante.*) General J. L. Chamberlain was selected to preside as President of the day. Gen. Selden Connor was invited to accompany the Commission and deliver an oration at the dedication exercises. The chairman and secretary, at the session of the Committee, September 21, 1889, were requested to prepare a report of the Commission, and to incorporate in it photographs of the monuments and such other views as should be found desirable. In 1890 the Committee held a session July 26th, at the Falmouth Hotel, Portland, to hear and consider requests of different officers relating to inscriptions on the monuments and other matters they desired to have appear in the report of the Committee, viz. : Col. Edward Moore, Col. H. R. Millett; Capts. G. E. Brown and G. W. Verrill; Lieutenants Hunt and Whittier.

Voted to draw an order of $212 to pay for a bronze tablet on the monument of the 17th Maine regiment.

At the session of the legislature in 1891 the following account of appropriations and expenditures was made by the chairman and secretary of the committee : —

ACCOUNT OF APPROPRIATIONS AND EXPENDITURES.

APPROPRIATIONS.

1887.	Resolves making provisions for monuments, purchasing land and improving the same on the battlefield of Gettysburg,	$15,000.00	
1889.	Maine Gettysburg Commission,	10,000.00	$25,000.00

1887.	EXPENDITURES.	
October 7.	Treasurer Gettysburg Battlefield Memorial Association, as the State's donation for land,	$2,500.00
1888.		
December 29.	Hallowell Granite Works,	4,000.00
December 29.	J. R. Bodwell, for expenses of Commission to Gettysburg and return, May, 1887,	1,000.00
1889.		
April 29.	Hallowell Granite Works,	6,000.00
September 28.	Hallowell Granite Works,	5,000.00
September 2.	Charles Hamlin, Chairman of Executive Committee, for expenses of Commission and invited guests to dedicate monuments, October 3, 1889,	2,000.00
1890.		
January 2.	Hallowell Granite Works,	2,000.00
March 26.	Hallowell Granite Works,	500.00
1889.		
May 24.	Traveling expenses of Messrs. Hamlin, Stevens, Thaxter, Heath and Merrill, Executive Committee, to date,	126.94
1890.		
October 6.	Tablet for 17th Regiment, as approved by the Gettysburg Association,	212.50
October 6.	Paid for clerk hire,	50.00
December 31.	Amount not drawn, and reverted into treasury,	1,610.54 $25,000.00

At this session of the legislature in 1891, by a Resolve, c. 125, approved April 3d, the sum of $5,000 was granted for the following purposes : —

$200.00   19th Maine Regiment (High Water Mark Monument).
  25.00   Change of flanking stones of 5th Battery, Seminary Heights.
 150.00   Change location and legend of monument of 5th Maine Regiment.
 203.00   Balance due Hallowell Granite Works.
 300.00   17th Maine Regiment tablet or monument for July 3d, etc.
 150.00   Accrued expenses of Executive Committee.
  64.00   Photo. negatives of monuments.
3,600.00   Printing and binding reports.
 308.00   Prospective incidental expenses of Executive Committee.

The death of Col. Charles B. Merrill, April 5, 1891, created a vacancy in the Commission and Committee, and it was filled May 12, 1891, by the appointment of Capt. George W. Verrill, who has since served with the Committee.

At the session of the Committee September 4, 1891, among

other business it was voted to draw a warrant of $300 to pay for the tablet of the 17th Maine regiment, a design for the same to mark its position on the third day having been submitted and approved. Each member of the Maine Gettysburg Commission was requested to furnish the Committee on or before December 1, 1891, a report of what they desired relating to their own regiment, battery, etc., to appear in the Committee's report. The secretary was directed to send to each member of the Commission a copy of the material relating to his command then in possession of the secretary prepared by Asher C. Hinds of the *Portland Press*.

The secretary furnished the materials above called for, but much time elapsed in procuring responses from the regimental and battery associations. The chairman of the Committee made repeated calls upon those interested to furnish the desired information, but failed to procure it. From several Commissioners he failed to elicit a reply. This fact will account for the reason why several of the chapters and articles in Part I. of this volume have been prepared by persons who were not members of the regiment or battery in question; and the delay in part in finishing the report of the Committee. Other Commissioners, however, have earnestly assisted in the work. In the meantime it became apparent that the material on hand was not sufficient to make a book of desirable size and worthy of publication as a suitable report. After some further delay and discussion it was decided to incorporate two new features in the book that, it is believed, will make it of value and interest to all the survivors of the battle of Gettysburg, as well as the families and friends of all who fell upon that field. These new features are, first, a list of men and officers who participated in the battle, with a list of casualties; and second, a historical sketch of each regiment, battalion, battery or other Maine organization that served in the Gettysburg campaign.

The committee are indebted to Capt. C. E. Nash for suggesting some of these new features. He has since been appointed a member of the Commission in place of Genl. F. E. Heath, whose death occurred December 20, 1897.

The lists of participants and casualties, excepting those of the 4th, 16th and 17th regiments, were prepared primarily by Maj. Charles J. House, of Augusta. The data from which these lists were made are in the office of the Adjutant-General of Maine, the best records available after all access to the rolls and records of the War Department, at Washington, was found on application to be beyond our power. While some errors will doubtless be found in these lists of names, it is believed they are as accurate as research and personal inquiry, after the lapse of so many years, can make them. Any one discovering errors in these lists, which are liable to occur, especially in initials, owing to disparities in the records, is requested to notify the Executive Committee at once. Some use has been made of the Volunteer Army Register issued August 31, 1865, by the War Department, in preparing the rosters at the close of the historical sketches. But that compilation has been found to be unreliable, and the editors of this volume have endeavored to verify and correct from other sources whatever errors they have found in it.

In 1893, at the session of the legislature for that year, by a Resolve, c. 217, approved March 28, $200 was granted to Dow's 6th Maine battery, and $150 to Co. D, 2d U. S. Sharpshooters, that they might have a proper place and suitable inscription on the High Water Mark Monument. The description of that monument given on page 537 *ante* shows how the appropriations have been applied.

In 1894 the Committee began to arrange some of the details of publication of its report, including the half-tone illustrations of the monuments. In expectation of receiving the materials from the Commissioners, already alluded to, the chairman was authorized to arrange the material for publication and to employ necessary assistance. Major Stevens and Captain Verrill were appointed a committee on illustrations, binding, etc.

In 1895 no further application for money was made to the legislature, and the Committee held only two sessions. At the meeting held August 14, 1895, at the office of Captain Verrill in Portland, Major Stevens submitted his report as treasurer. Captain Verrill was authorized to procure plate and proofs of a design for maps. The chairman reported upon the progress made in procuring lists of participants and casualties. At a later meeting held at the Bangor House, December 4, 1895, further progress was made relative to the map of the first day by Captain Verrill; particularly as to showing the locations of the 16th Maine regiment.

In 1896 the Committee held two meetings at which the maps as prepared by Captain Verrill, being the first, second and third days of the battle and in colors, also one of the cavalry battle, and diagrams showing the positions of the 3d, 4th, 17th and 20th regiments on the second day of the battle were approved and adopted. Historical sketches of 1st cavalry, by Lieutenant Tobie, and 5th Maine battery, by Major Stevens, were read and adopted, to be printed subject to the supervision of the Committee. Captain Verrill was also appointed co-editor with the chairman, and he was authorized to negotiate and make a contract with The Lakeside Press for printing and binding.

In 1897 the Committee held three sessions at the Court House in Augusta, and devoted their time to reading and examining the various papers submitted by the Commissioners of regiments, batteries, battalions, etc. After such changes, corrections, etc., as were needful, the papers were deposited with the chairman to be edited by him and his associate, Captain Verrill.

The chairman was requested to apply to the Commissioners of the Gettysburg National Park, successors to the Memorial Association, for authority to erect tablets to mark the positions of the 3d and 4th Maine regiments in support of the 2d corps during Longstreet's assault, July 3d. Also to apply to the legislature for an appropriation for the same and any other money needed for the purposes of the Commission. Designs by Colonels Lakeman and Walker for these tablets were submitted by the Hallowell Granite Works and approved. A contract for their construction and erection was awarded that company after an appropriation had been granted as stated below and authority for the location obtained from the Park Commissioners.

The legislature at its session in 1897, on the application of the chairman and secretary, granted an appropriation of $200 each for tablets for the 3d and 4th Maine, as requested. See c. 139 and c. 140, Resolves of 1897.

And on their application, by Resolve, c. 232, approved March 25, 1897, a further appropriation of $750 was granted for completing the work of the Commission, $400 being for incidental expenses incurred by the Committee, and $350 towards an additional 1,000 copies of the report.

It should be stated here that the estimate in 1897 of the cost of an edition of 3,000 volumes, proposed to be published, was based upon a book containing about 500 pages. The two appropriations granted accordingly would have been sufficient, it is believed, for the purpose; but the volume will contain over 600 pages besides two additional illustrations, — the tablets of the 3d and 4th regiments. Hence, by reason of the increased cost of the volume, the funds available are not sufficient to bind the entire edition of 3,000 copies in leather as contemplated. A portion of the edition has therefore been placed in paper covers, part of which going to the Commissioners and part to the State Library.

The appropriations for expenses of the Commission being exhausted, the transportation of the books falls upon those receiving them.

In September, 1897, the Executive Committee met the Commissioners of the National Park and agreed upon the location of the tablets of the 3d and 4th Maine regiments. A hearing was granted upon request of Colonel Walker of the 4th Maine to change the location of the flanking stones of that regiment. These stones have since been relocated as requested by Colonel Walker. They also made an inspection of all the Maine monuments and found them in good condition except the 4th Maine, which standing in a depression on a large bowlder at Devil's Den was endangered by snow and water lodging under the base of the shaft. This has been corrected by cutting a channel in the top of the bowlder that permits the water to escape. The diamond badges in the sides of the shaft of this monument were found to have been fastened with gypsum and had become loose and were in danger of falling out. They have been reset and fastened with cement.

The only matter remaining undisposed of by the U. S. Park Commissioners is an application made by the 17th Maine Association through this committee for a change in the course of Sickles' Avenue, or a branch of the same, in the Wheatfield to delineate the line of battle held by this regiment; if favorably acted upon, this will probably be followed by a request for the placing of a suitable marker to show an important position held by the 17th on that ground.

In closing this report it is proper to state that no member of the Commission or of the Executive Committee has received any pecuniary compensation for the labor and time spent in the work of the Commission. After the monuments were erected and dedicated the principal duties of the Commissioners were accomplished; but those of the Executive Committee, as will be seen, have remained unfinished. The collecting of the data necessary to a full report made in the manner adopted has required more time than was anticipated, but the result justifies, it is believed, the delay and expense. Each legislature that has appropriated money in aid of the Commission has approved the method adopted in bringing together the materials of the report; and the plan of the book has had the commendation of the Military Committees.

The chairman of the Executive Committee desires to express the high sense of obligation he is under to his associates, especially to Maj. G. T. Stevens, the secretary and treasurer; also to the assistant editor, Capt. G. W. Verrill, for preparing the four maps in colors, diagrams to show the changes in location of regiments during the three days of the battle, revising lists of men and officers present, the casualties and the officers' rosters, besides editing, arranging and preparing papers for the Committee and the printer, and in connection with proof-reading and other work. In reproducing an account of the battle on the second day along the front of the 1st division (Birney) of the 3d corps, his intimate knowledge and study of the movements of both armies have added to its historic value.

INDEX.

ADDRESSES AND ORATIONS.
Burleigh, Edwin C.—Dedication 561
Chamberlain, Joshua L.—16th Maine 63—, Dedication 546
Connor, Selden,—Oration, Dedication 564
Edwards, Clark S.—Regimental dedication 373
Hamlin, Charles—Dedication 560
Hobson, William,—Oration, regimental dedication 217
Krauth, John M.—Receiving Maine monuments 562
Lincoln, Abraham,—Dedication of Soldiers Cemetery 585
Moore, Edward,—Regimental dedication 211
Smith, Charles H.—Regimental dedication 481
Walker, Elijah,—Regimental dedication 176
APPROPRIATIONS BY MAINE.
For monuments, markers, etc., at Gettysburg 587, 589-591, 593-595
For Soldiers National Cemetery and Monument at Gettysburg 582
AUTHORS, AUTHORITIES. See CONTRIBUTORS.
Table of Contents VII

BADGES, distinguishing troops 151
BATTLE OF GETTYSBURG—(Also see GETTYSBURG) 1
BATTLES, LISTS OF—See the organizations under GETTYSBURG.
BATTERIES, Hall's, Stevens', and Dow's—(See GETTYSBURG) 14, 80, 325
Fourth Maine mentioned 241, 336
Seventh Maine mentioned 125

CASUALTIES—See Maine organizations under GETTYSBURG.
At Gettysburg, Summary of Maine 542
CAVALRY FIELD 470
CEMETERY, Soldiers National at Gettysburg 582
CEMETERY HILL 7, 89
CHAMBERSBURG PIKE 16
COMMISSIONERS, MAINE GETTYSBURG III, 587
History and work of 586
COMMITTEE, EXECUTIVE, MAINE GETTYSBURG COMMISSION III, 588
Summary of its work 586
CONTENTS, table of VII
CONTRACTS, for monuments and markers 589, 594
For printing and binding Report 594
CONTRIBUTORS—Original matter for this publication
See also table of CONTENTS VII
Beardsley, John D. 519, 523
Belcher, S. Clifford 41
Bragdon, Edward P. M. 526
Chamberlain, Joshua L. 63, 260
Clark, Charles A. 397, 414
Cole, Henry F. 522
Connor, Selden 438
Edwards, Clark S. 373
Gould, John M. 518, 531
Hall, James A. 15-23
Hamlin, Charles 1, 26, 334, 405, 586
Hinds, Asher C. 592
House, Charles J. 593

598

Hunt, Charles O.	114
Johnson, Hannibal A.	128
Lakeman, Moses B.	128–135
Miller, Samuel L.—quotation	259
Pratt, Gustavus C.—foot-note	197
Prince, Howard L.—quotation, foot-note	258
Small, Abner R.	46
Stevens, Greenlief T.	82–92, 103
Tarr, James F.	522
Tilden, Charles W.	42
Tilden, C. K.	45
Tobie, Edward P.	487
Twitchell, Adelbert B.	29
Verrill, George W.	193, 194, 197, 223, 582
Walker, Elijah	164, 176, 186
Whitmore George L.	292
Whittier, Edward N.	92
Wiggin, Francis	66
COPSE OF TREES	313, 538
CULP'S HILL	7, 89
DEDICATION OF MAINE MONUMENTS.	
(See regimental dedications under GETTYSBURG.)	
Order of the day and exercises	545
Address by Gen. J. L. Chamberlain	546
Prayer by Rev. Theodore Gerrish	559
Address by Gen. Charles Hamlin	560
Address by Governor Edwin C. Burleigh	561
Address by Major J. M. Krauth	562
Oration by Gen. Selden Connor	564
Prayer and Benediction by Rev. G. R. Palmer	580
DEVIL'S DEN	160, 194, 251
DOW'S BATTERY—Also see GETTYSBURG	325
EDITORS	594
EXECUTIVE COMMITTEE OF MAINE COMMISSIONERS	III, 588
EXPENDITURES	591, 595
GENERALS, MAINE	540
GETTYSBURG.	
Battle of	1
Maine artillery, infantry and cavalry in battle of, in numerical order:	

Second (Hall's) Battery

Monument and marker	14, 21
Engagement, Participants and Casualties lists	15–25
Historical Sketch	26
Roster of Officers	35
Mentioned	4, 6, 13, 82, 104, 151, 590

Battles and skirmishes 27: *Cross Keys* 27, *Cedar Mountain* 28, *Rappahannock*, *Thoroughfare Gap* 28, *Second Bull Run*, *Chantilly* 29, *Fredericksburg* 30, *Chancellorsville* 32, *Gettysburg* 15, 32, *Wilderness, Spotsylvania* 33, *North Anna* 27, *Bethesda Church, Cold Harbor* 34, *Petersburg* 34.

Fifth (Stevens') Battery

Monument and marker	80, 86, 95
Engagement, Participants and Casualties lists	82–103
Historical Sketch	103
Roster of Officers	124
Mentioned	4, 7, 11, 13, 29, 65, 290, 570, 574

Battles and skirmishes: *Rappahannock* 103, *Thoroughfare Gap* 104, *Second Bull Run* 29, 104, *Fredericksburg* 105, *Chancellorsville* 107, *Gettysburg* 82, *Wilderness, Spotsylvania, North Anna* 111, *Cold Harbor* 112, *Petersburg* 114, *Opequan* 117, *Fisher's Hill* 120, *Cedar Creek* 121.

Sixth (Dow's) Battery
Monument   325, 334
Engagement, Participants and Casualties lists   326-334
Historical Sketch   334
Roster of Officers   346
Mentioned   5, 10, 13, 290, 573, 593
Battles and skirmishes: *Cedar Mountain* 336, *Rappahannock Station, Sulphur
Springs, Blackburn's Ford* 336, *Second Bull Run* 336, *Chantilly* 337, *Antietam* 338,
Gettysburg 326, 340, *Mine Run* 341, *Wilderness* 342, *Spotsylvania* 343, *North Anna,
Cold Harbor* 344, *Petersburg* 344, 346, *Deep Bottom* 345.

Third (Lakeman's) Regiment
Monument and marker   126, 129, 132
Diagram showing position   197
Engagement, Participants and Casualties lists   127-145
Itinerary, Gettysburg campaign   135
Historical Sketch   145
Roster of Officers   156
Mentioned   4, 9, 10, 13, 167, 178, 194, 197, 236, 238, 290, 571, 590, 594
Battles and skirmishes: *Bull Run* 147, *Yorktown* 148, *Williamsburg, Fair Oaks,
Seven Pines* 148, *White Oak Swamp, Charles City Cross Roads, Malvern Hill* 149,
Second Bull Run 149, *Chantilly* 150, *Mouth of Monocacy* 150, *Fredericksburg* 151,
Cedars, Chancellorsville 152, *Gettysburg* 127, 153, *Wapping Heights* 153, *Auburn,
Kelly's Ford, Locust (or Orange) Grove, Mine Run* 154, *Wilderness* 154, *Spotsyl-
vania, Fredericksburg Road, North Anna, Totopotomy, Cold Harbor* 155.

Fourth (Walker's) Regiment
Monument and marker   158, 167, 176
Diagrams showing positions   194, 251
Engagement, Participants and Casualties lists   159-176
Dedication of monument, address of Colonel Walker   176
Historical Sketch   176, 186
Roster of Officers   188
Mentioned   4, 9, 10, 13, 127, 147, 148, 153, 218, 232, 234, 235, 252, 290, 351, 571, 593, 594, 595
Battles and skirmishes: *Bull Run* 177, *Yorktown* 177, *Williamsburg, Seven Pines,
Fair Oaks, White Oak Swamp, Glendale* 177, *Malvern Hill* 178, *Second Bull Run,
Chantilly* 178, *Mouth of Monocacy* 178, *Fredericksburg* 179, *Cedars, Chancellors-
ville* 179, *Gettysburg* 159, 179, *Wapping Heights* 153, 183, *Auburn, Kelly's Ford,
Locust (or Orange) Grove, Mine Run* 183, *Wilderness, Po River* 183, *Spotsylvania*
185, *Fredericksburg Road* 237, *North Anna, Totopotomy, Cold Harbor* 185.

Fifth (Edwards') Regiment
Monument   364
Engagement, Participants list   365-373
Dedication of monument   373
Address of Brevet Brig.-Gen. Edwards   373
Poem of Helen S. Packard   385
Historical Sketch   373, 390
Roster of Officers   393
Mentioned   4, 12, 13, 112, 236, 421, 463, 576
Battles and skirmishes: *Bull Run* 374, *West Point* 375, *Chickahominy* 375, *Gaines'
Mill, Golding's Farm, Charles City Cross Roads, Malvern Hill* 375, *Crampton's
Gap, Antietam* 376, *Fredericksburg, Second Fredericksburg, Salem Church or
Chancellorsville* 377, *Gettysburg* 365, 378, *Funkstown, Williamsport* 379, *Rappahan-
nock Station* 379, *Locust Grove, Mine Run* 380, *Wilderness,* 381, *Spotsylvania*
381-383, *North Anna, Cold Harbor* 383, *Petersburg* 383.

Sixth (Burnham's) Regiment
Monument   395
Engagement, Participants list   396-405
Historical Sketch   405
Roster of Officers   427

Mentioned   4, 13, 231, 236, 380, 381, 443, 463, 576
Battles and skirmishes: *Yorktown, Lee's Mills* 408, *Williamsburg* 408, *Garnett's Farm* 408, *Savage Station* 410, *White Oak Bridge* 411, *Crampton's Gap, Antietam* 413, *Fredericksburg* 413, *Marye's Heights* 414, *Salem Church, Brooks' Ford* 416, *Gettysburg* 396, 418, *Funkstown, Williamsport* 418, *Rappahannock Station* 419, *Locust Grove, Mine Run* 426, *Wilderness, Spotsylvania* 427, *Cold Harbor* 427, *Petersburg* 427.

Seventh (Connor's) Regiment

Monument	430
Engagement, Participants and Casualties lists	431–438
Historical Sketch	438
Roster of Officers	466
Mentioned	4, 10, 13, 236, 575

Battles and skirmishes: *Yorktown* 442, *Williamsburg* 443, *Mechanicsville* 445, *Gaines' Mill* 446, *White Oak Swamp* 447, *Crampton's Pass, Antietam* 449, *Second Fredericksburg or Marye's Heights* 453, *Banks' Ford* 455, *Gettysburg* 431, 456, *Brandy Station* 458, *Locust Grove, Mine Run* 458, *Wilderness* 459, *Spotsylvania* 460, *Cold Harbor* 461, *Petersburg* 461, *Fort Stevens* 462, *Opequon Creek* 463, *Fisher's Hill* 463. First Veteran battles: *Cedar Creek* 464, *Petersburg* 464, *Appomattox* 465.

Tenth Maine (Beardsley's) Battalion

Monument	517
Engagement, Participants list	518–530
Historical Sketch (including 1st, 10th, 29th regts.)	531
Roster of Officers of 10th regiment	535
Mentioned	4, 13, 589

Battles and skirmishes (includes 1st, 10th, 29th regts.): *Winchester* 532, *Cedar Mountain* 533, *Antietam* 533, *Sabine Cross Roads, Pleasant Hill, Cane River Crossing* 534, *Opequon Creek, Fisher's Hill, Cedar Creek* 534.

Sixteenth (Tilden's) Regiment

Monument and marker	37, 42, 44
Diagram of positions	45
Engagement, Participants and Casualties lists	38–62
Historical Sketch	66
Roster of Officers	76
Address of Gen. Chamberlain	63
Mentioned	4, 6, 13, 15, 82, 236, 285, 570, 590, 593

Battles and skirmishes: *Fredericksburg* 69, *Chancellorsville* 71, *Gettysburg* 38, 71, *Mine Run* 72, *Wilderness, Spotsylvania, North Anna* 73, *Totopotomy, Bethesda Church* 73, *Petersburg, Weldon Railroad,* 73, 74, *Hatcher's Run* 74, *White Oak Road, Five Forks* 74, *Appomattox* 75.

Seventeenth (Merrill's) Regiment

Monument and marker	190, 191, 193, 200
Diagrams of positions	194, 197
Engagement, Participants and Casualties lists	192–210
Dedication of monument	210
Prayer of Rev. C. G. Holyoke	210
Address of Brevet Lieut.-Col. Moore	211
Poem of Captain Verrill	215
Oration of Brevet Brig.-Gen. Hobson	217
Historical Sketch	223
Roster of Officers	246
Mentioned	4, 9, 13, 162, 176, 184, 290, 362, 571, 590, 592, 596

Battles and skirmishes: *Fredericksburg* 227, *The Cedars, Chancellorsville* 228, *Gettysburg* 192, 229, *Wapping Heights, Auburn* 230, *Kelly's Ford, Locust Grove, Mine Run* 231, *Wilderness* 233, *Po River, Spotsylvania, "Salient"* 235, *Fredericksburg Road, North Anna, Totopotomy* 237, *Cold Harbor* 238, *Petersburg Assaults* 238, *Jerusalem Road* 239, *Deep Bottom* 240, *Peebles' Farm, Fort Hell* 241, *Boydton Road* 241, *Infantry Raid* 242, *Hatcher's Run* 242, *Fall of Petersburg* 244, *Deatonsville, Sailor Creek* 244, *Farmville, Appomattox* 245.

Nineteenth (Heath's) Regiment

Monument 289, 295
Engagement, Participants and Casualties lists 290–310
Historical Sketch 310
Roster of Officers 322
Mentioned 4, 12, 13, 185, 236, 330, 573, 576, 589
Battles and skirmishes 321: *Fredericksburg* 312, *Chancellorsville* 313, *Gettysburg* 290, 313, *Bristoe Station* 314, *Mine Run* 315, *Wilderness* 315, *Spotsylvania* 315, *North Anna, Totopotomy* 315, *Cold Harbor* 316, *Petersburg, Deep Bottom, Strawberry Plains* 316, *Reams' Station* 318, *Boydton Road* 319, *Hatcher's Run* 320, *Fall of Petersburg, High Bridge* 321, *Farmville, Appomattox* 322.

Twentieth (Chamberlain's) Regiment

Monuments 249, 250
Diagram of positions 251
Engagement, Participants and Casualties lists 252–272
Historical Sketch 273
The Last Act 286
Roster of Officers 287
Mentioned 4, 10, 13, 164, 246, 290, 420, 422, 572, 590
Battles and skirmishes: *Antietam* 274, *Shepherdstown Ford* 275, *Fredericksburg* 275, *Chancellorsville, Middleburg* 276, *Gettysburg* 252, 276, *Sharpsburg Pike* 278, *Rappahannock Station* 278, *Mine Run* 279, *Wilderness* 279, *Spotsylvania* 280, *North Anna, Bethesda Church, Cold Harbor* 281, *Petersburg, Jerusalem Road, Weldon Railroad, Peebles' Farm* 281, *Infantry Raid, Hatcher's Run, Quaker Road, Gravelly Run, Five Forks* 282, *Appomattox Court House* 283.

First (Smith's) Cavalry Regiment

Monument 469, 481
Engagement, Participants and Casualties lists 470–481
Dedication of monument 481
Address of Brevet Maj.-Gen. Smith 481
Poem of Lieut. Tobie 486
Historical Sketch 487
Roster of Officers 514
Mentioned 4, 13, 576
Battles and skirmishes: *Middletown, Winchester, Cedar Mountain* 490, *Second Bull Run, South Mountain, Antietam, Fredericksburg* 491, *Stoneman's Raid* 491, *Rappahannock Station, Brandy Station, Aldie, Middleburg, Upperville* 492-497, *Gettysburg* 470, 497, *Shepardstown, Sulphur Springs* 498, *Mine Run* 499, *Dahlgren Raid, Old Church, Todd's Tavern, Beaver Dam, Ground Squirrel Church Bridge* 501, *Fortifications of Richmond* 502, *Hawes' Shop, Cold Harbor, Trevillian Station* 503, *St. Mary's Church* 504, *Deep Bottom* 505, *Reams' Station* 506, *Wyatt's Farm* 507, *Boydton Road* 508, *Bellefield, Hatcher's Run, Dinwiddie Court House* 509, *Deatonsville* 511, *Sailor's Creek, High Bridge, Farmville* 512, *Appomattox Court House* 513.

Company D, Second U. S. Sharpshooters

Monument 348
Engagement, Participants and Casualties lists 349–353
Historical Sketch 354
Roster of Officers 362
Mentioned 10, 13, 160, 162, 255, 258, 589, 593
Battles and skirmishes: *Rappahannock Station* 356, *Sulphur Springs, Gainesville or Groveton* 357, *Second Bull Run, South Mountain, Antietam* 358, *Fredericksburg* 359, *The Cedars, Chancellorsville* 359, *Gettysburg* 349, 360, *Wapping Heights, Auburn, Kelly's Ford, Locust Grove, Mine Run, Wilderness, Po River, Spotsylvania, Fredericksburg Pike, North Anna, Totopotomy, Cold Harbor, Petersburg, Jerusalem Road, Deep Bottom, Peebles' Farm, Boydton Road, Hatcher's Run* 361,

Maine Generals, Staff and other additional Officers, at battle 540
Summaries of Maine Participants and Casualties 542
Dedication of Maine monuments by Maine 545

602

HALL'S BATTERY—Also see GETTYSBURG   14
HIGH WATER MARK MONUMENT   537

ILLUSTRATIONS—See MAPS, also MONUMENTS

LINCOLN'S ADDRESS   585
LOSSES AT GETTYSBURG, Maine troops   542

MAINE DEAD, buried at Gettysburg   583
MAINE GETTYSBURG COMMISSION   III, 587
   Its History and Work   586
MAINE TROOPS, at Gettysburg
   (See REGIMENTS and BATTERIES under GETTYSBURG)
   Additional participating Officers   540
   Summaries of Participants and Casualties   542
MAPS OF THE BATTLE   6, 8, 11, 12, 45, 194, 197, 251
MILITIA COMPANIES mentioned   145, 354, 531, 533
MONUMENTS AND MARKERS.
   (See the Maine organizations given under GETTYSBURG)
   High Water Mark Monument   537
   National Cemetery Monument   Frontispiece
   General dedication by Maine, and transfer ceremonies   545

OFFICERS, Maine, additional to Maine organizations   540
ORATIONS—See ADDRESSES and

PARTICIPANTS—See Maine organizations under GETTYSBURG
   Additional participating Officers   540
   Summary of Maine   542
PEACH ORCHARD   131
PICKETT'S CHARGE   295, 538
PLUM RUN   160
POEMS AT DEDICATIONS.
   Packard, Helen S.   385
   Tobie, Edward P.   486
   Verrill, George W.   215
POWERS' HILL   456, 520, 575
PRAYERS AT DEDICATIONS.
   Gerrish, Theodore   559
   Holyoke, Charles G.   210
   Palmer, G. R.   580
PREFACE   V

REGIMENTS—See GETTYSBURG for those at that battle
   1st Maine Heavy Artillery mentioned   237, 239, 240, 246, 362
   1st Maine Sharpshooters battalion mentioned   285, 286, 363
   1st Maine Veterans mentioned   392, 427, 464, 466
   1st D. C. Cavalry Maine companies mentioned   488, 507
   2d Maine (infantry) mentioned   252
   10th Maine mentioned   224
   11th Maine mentioned   354
   31st Maine mentioned   236
   32d Maine mentioned   236, 241, 541
ROCK CREEK   575
ROUND TOPS, LITTLE AND BIG   251, 254, 259

SEMINARY HEIGHTS   45, 83
STAFF OFFICERS   540
STEVENS' KNOLL   571
STEVENS' BATTERY—Also see GETTYSBURG   80
SUMMARIES OF PARTICIPANTS AND CASUALTIES   542

"VALLEY OF DEATH"   182

WHEATFIELD   192, 194, 197, 251

Suggested reading list:

"Bayonet! Forward": My Civil War Reminiscences by General Joshua Lawrence Chamberlain

The Passing of the Armies: The Last Campaign of the Armies by Joshua Lawrence Chamberlain

Lee: A Biography by Clifford Dowdey

Crisis at the Crossroads: The First Day at Gettysburg by Warren Hassler

The Great Invasion of 1863 or General Lee in Pennsylvania by Jacob Hoke

Gettysburg to the Rapidan by General Andrew A. Humphreys

A Diary of Battle: The Personal Journals of Colonel Charles S. Wainwright 1861-1865 edited by Allan Nevins

The Attack and Defense of Little Round Top, Gettysburg, July 2, 1863 by Oliver W. Norton

Sickles the Incredible: A Biography of General Daniel Edgar Sickles by W. A. Swanberg

Soul of the Lion: A Biography of General Joshua Lawrence Chamberlain by Willard Wallace

Through Blood and Fire at Gettysburg: My Experiences with the 20th Maine Regiment on Little Round Top by Joshua Lawrence Chamberlain

The Killer Angels: A Novel About the Four Days of Gettysburg by Michael Shaara

At Gettysburg or What a Girl Saw and Heard of the Battle by Tillie (Pierce) Alleman

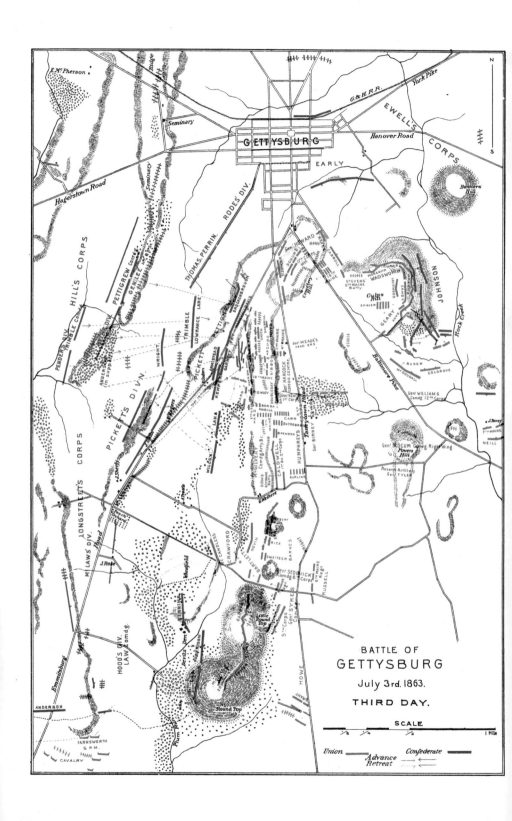

BATTLE OF
GETTYSBURG
July 3rd. 1863.
THIRD DAY.

SCALE

⅛ ¼   ½   1 Mile

Union ——————   Confederate ——————
              Advance ——→ ←——
              Retreat ·····→ ←·····